For

Michael Baker

Contents

Acknowledgements ix
List of Illustrations x
Notes on Contributors xiii
Introduction xvii

Dic Edwards

Theatre for the Evicted 3
Dic Edwards
The Letters of Edward Bond to Dic Edwards 17
edited by Hazel Walford Davies
The Charisma of Non-Sense: The Plays of Dic Edwards 65
Charmian Savill
Looking for the World Through the Word: The Social Imagination of Dic Edwards's Drama 74
Anna-Marie Taylor
A Dereliction of Duty 82
Hazel Walford Davies interviews Dic Edwards
Reviews: Dic Edwards 88
Chronology: Dic Edwards 110

Edward Thomas

'Not much of a dream then is it?' 115
Edward Thomas interviewed by Hazel Walford Davies in Gallipolis, Ohio, July 1997
Caught in the Act: On the Theatricality of Identity and Politics in the Dramatic Works of Edward Thomas 131
Heike Roms
Edward Thomas: Negotiating a Way Through Culture 145
David Adams
Edward Thomas: Geography, Intertexuality, and the Lost Mother 159
Katie Gramich
Tryweryn of the Soul: Edward Thomas's 'Flowers of the Dead Red Sea' 174
David Ian Rabey
Edward Thomas: A Profile 186
Heike Roms
Reviews: Edward Thomas 192
Chronology: Edward Thomas 246

CONTENTS

Charles Way

Dead Man's Hat 251
Charles Way

Charles Way's Professional Journey 263
David Adams

The Creative Process of a Theatre Writer 278
Graham Laker interviews Charles Way

Reviews: Charles Way 288

Chronology: Charles Way 313

Greg Cullen

I Paint Me In The World And The World In Me 319
Greg Cullen

Greg Cullen's Drama: Spiritual Realism and Chaotic Necessity 327
David Ian Rabey

Inner Need and External Demand: The Plays of Greg Cullen 347
David Adams

Love, Anger and Money 362
Greg Cullen in conversation with David Ian Rabey

Reviews: Greg Cullen 369

Chronology: Greg Cullen 401

General Essays

State of Flux: Metaphors of Society and Nation in the Work of Charles Way, Dic Edwards and Edward Thomas 405
Roger Owen

America and the Theatre of Small Nations 416
Gill Ogden

Further Acknowledgements 428

Index 429

Acknowledgments

I should like to thank Edward Bond for his generosity in allowing me to include his unpublished letters to Dic Edwards. (Full acknowledgements of the Edward Bond material are listed on p. 428.) I also wish to thank the editors of the newspapers and periodicals noted in the four review sections for agreeing to the inclusion in this volume of reviews of productions of various plays by the four dramatists. (Detailed newspaper acknowledgements are given on p. 428.) In the search for archive material and photographs I was given every assistance by the theatre companies associated with the four dramatists, and I am grateful to Kevin Low for the trouble he took to track down the cover photograph.

I acknowledge an award from the David Hughes Parry fund of the University of Wales, Aberystwyth for typing assistance in preparing the volume for the press. My thanks are due to Douglas Houston for copy-editing and William Howells for the preparation of the Index. Dyfed Elis-Gruffydd of Gwasg Gomer saw the volume through the press with minimum fuss and maximum efficiency. I am also indebted to Michael Baker of the Arts Council of Wales and to Robin Reeves, editor of the *New Welsh Review* for supporting and encouraging my interest in the work of dramatists writing out of Wales.

I am particularly grateful to the contributors for meeting deadlines so efficiently and, in several instances, for their readiness to postpone other projects in order to give priority to their essays in this volume. My main thanks go to the dramatists whose work the book is designed to celebrate – Greg Cullen, Dic Edwards, Edward Thomas and Charles Way – who so readily and cheerfully answered all my queries and enquiries.

List of Illustrations

DIC EDWARDS (between pages 6/7)

Dic Edwards, Photo: Simon Chapman
Looking for the World (1986)
Low People (1989), Photo: Malcolm Andrew
Regan (1991), Photo: Keith Morris
Regan (1991), Photo: Keith Morris
Casanova Undone (1992), Photo: James Graham
Wittgenstein's Daughter (1993), Photo: Kevin Low
Wittgenstein's Daughter (1993), Photo: Kevin Low
Dic Edwards: *Utah Blue* workshop, Theatr y Werin, Aberystwyth (1997), Photo: Keith Morris

EDWARD THOMAS (between pages 118/119)

Edward Thomas
The cast of *House of America* (1988), Photo: Tony Standley
House of America (1988), Photo: Tony Standley
House of America (1998), Photo: Tony Standley
House of America (1992), Photo: Tony Standley
House of America (1992), Photo: Tony Standley
House of America (1992), Photo: Tony Standley
House of America (1992), Publicity photo: Linton Lowe
House of America (1997), Photo: Brian Tarr
House of America (1997), Photo: Brian Tarr
Edward Thomas with a model of the 1997 set of *House of America,* Photo: Nick Treharne
Tŷ'r Amerig (1997) A performance of the first translation into Welsh of *House of America*, The Cabin, Aberystwyth (1997), Photo: Lowri Huws
Adar Heb Adenydd (1989), Photo: Brian Tarr
Adar Heb Adenydd (1989), Photo: Brian Tarr
The Myth of Michael Roderick (1990), Photo: Tony Standley
Flowers of the Dead Red Sea (1991), Photo: Tony Standley
Flowers of the Dead Red Sea (1992), Photo: Linton Lowe
Flowers of the Dead Red Sea (1992), Photo: Tony Standley
East from the Gantry (1992), Photo: Kevin Low
Hiraeth: Strangers in Conversation (1993), Photo: Tony Standley
Envy (1993), Photo: Brian Tarr
Song from a Forgotten City (1995), Photo: Brian Tarr
Song from a Forgotten City (1995), Photo: Brian Tarr
Song from a Forgotten City (1995), Photo: Brian Tarr
Song from a Forgotten City (1996), Photo: Brian Tarr
Song from a Forgotten City (1996), Photo: Brian Tarr

Edward Thomas and Russell Gomer: *Flowers of the Dead Red Sea* workshop, Theatr y Werin, Aberystwyth (1997), Photo: A. Parry-Jones
Gas Station Angel (1998), Photo: Pau Ros

CHARLES WAY (between pages 262/263)

Charles Way, Photo: Simon Chapman
On the Black Hill (1986)
On the Black Hill (1986), Photo: Phil Cutts
On the Black Hill (1986), Photo: Phil Cutts
Paradise Drive (1989), Photo: Keith Morris
Paradise Drive (1989), Photo: Keith Morris
In the Bleak Midwinter (1990), Photo: Brian Tarr
In the Bleak Midwinter (1990), Photo: Brian Tarr
Dead Man's Hat (1997), Photo: Brampton Studios
Dead Man's Hat (1997), Photo: Brampton Studios
Dead Man's Hat (1997), Photo: Brampton Studios
Eye of the Storm (1995), Photo: Brampton Studios
The Search for Odysseus (1993), Photo: Brian Tarr
The Search for Odysseus (1993), Photo: Brian Tarr
The Search for Odysseus (1993), Photo: Brian Tarr
Ill Met by Moonlight (1994), Photo: Brian Tarr
Ill Met by Moonlight (1994), Photo: Brian Tarr
The Dove Maiden (1996), Photo: Brian Tarr
Charles Way: *Dead Man's Hat* workshop, Theatr y Werin, Aberystwyth (1997)

GREG CULLEN (between pages 326/327)

Greg Cullen
The Snow Queen (1983)
Past Caring (1984)
The Bride of Baron Duprav (1984)
Taken Out (1985)
Tarzanne (1987), Photo: Charlie Baker
Frida and Diego (1993)
Frida and Diego (1993)
Frida and Diego (1994)
Frida and Diego (1998), Student production, Aberystwyth
Silas Marner (1996), Photo: Phil Cutts
Silas Marner (1996), Photo: Phil Cutts
Bridbrain (1996), Photo: Sgrîn/BBC
Whispers in the Woods (1997)
Greg Cullen: *Mary Morgan* workshop: Theatr y Werin, Aberystwyth (1997) Photo: Keith Morris
Greg Cullen: *Tarzanne* workshop, Theatr y Werin, Aberystwyth (1997), Photo: Keith Morris

Notes on Contributors

DAVID ADAMS has been *The Guardian* arts correspondent for Wales since 1980 and is theatre correspondent for *The Western Mail.* He is Honorary Visiting Fellow at University College, Worcester and lectures on theatre at the Universitiy of Glamorgan and at Cheltenham and Gloucester College. He has been advisor to the Arts Council of Wales, South Wales Arts, Yorkshire Arts and Merseyside Arts. He is the author of *Stage Welsh* (Gomer, 1995) and is currently working on a history of theatre in Wales for Seren Books.

EDWARD BOND is an influential British socialist playwright. Amongst his plays are *The Pope's Wedding* (1962), *Saved* (1965), *Early Morning* (1968), *Lear* (1971), *Bongo* (1973), *The Woman* (1978), *Restoration* (1981), *War Plays* (1985), *September* (1990), and *In the Company of Men* (1996).

GREG CULLEN, damatist, is Artistic Director of Mid Powys Youth Theatre and lectures on the 'English-medium Theatre in Wales' course for the Department of Theatre, Film and Television, the University of Wales, Aberystwyth. In 1997 his film 'Birdbrain' won the BBC/Wales Film Council PICS competition. His essay 'The Graveyard of Ambition?' appeared in *Staging Wales: Welsh Theatre 1979-1997*, ed. Anna-Marie Taylor (University of Wales Press, 1997). His volume *Three Plays* will be published by Seren Books during 1998. For details of performances and publications, see pp. 401-2.

HAZEL WALFORD DAVIES is Senior Lecturer in Theatre Studies in the University of Wales, Aberystwyth. She lectures widely on theatre and cultural studies at American universities and has been Kilby Visiting Professor in Drama at Wheaton College, Illinois. Her volume *Saunders Lewis a Theatr Garthewin* (Gomer Press) won an Arts Council Book of the Year Award in 1996. She publishes regularly in the theatre section of *The New Welsh Review* and is currently completing *Now You're Talking*, a volume of interviews with twelve dramatists working out of Wales.

DIC EDWARDS, dramatist, is Fellow in Creative Writing in the University of Wales, Lampeter. He also contributes to courses on creative writing and theatre in the University of Wales, Aberystwyth. His volume of three plays, *The Shakespeare Factory, Moon River: The Deal, David* was recently published by Seren Books. For details of performances and publications, see pp. 110-11.

KATIE GRAMICH is Head of the English department at Trinity College, Carmarthen. She has published an edition of Allen Raine's *Queen of the Rushes* (Honno Classics, 1998) and has co-edited *Dangerous Diversity: The Changing Faces of Wales* (University of Wales Press, 1998). She is the editor of the English-language section of *Book News from Wales*.

GRAHAM LAKER is Lecturer in Theatre Studies in the University of Wales, Aberystwyth. He was previously Artistic Director of Cwmni Theatr Gwynedd, where he directed over twenty productions, including a dozen new plays. He has published extensively on theatre in Wales.

GILL OGDEN is a community theatre worker in Ceredigion and also teaches Continuing Education courses for the University of Wales, Aberystwyth. She has worked as director and writer for Welsh-language theatre companies and has been policy officer for Arts and Young People for the Arts Council of Wales. Her essay 'A History of Theatre in Education in Wales' appeared in *Staging Wales: Welsh Theatre 1979-1997*, ed. Anna-Marie Taylor (University of Wales Press, 1997).

ROGER OWEN is Lecturer in Theatre Studies in the University of Wales, Aberystwyth. He has worked as a professional actor with Brith Gof, Moving Being and the Jesus and Tracy performance group. He has published reviews and articles on modern drama in *New Welsh Review*, *Planet* and *Barn*.

DAVID IAN RABEY is Senior Lecturer in Theatre Studies in the University of Wales, Aberystwyth. His critical writings include *British and Irish Political Drama in the Twentieth Century* (Macmillan, 1986), *Howard Barker: Politics and Desire* (Macmillan, 1989) and *David Rudkin: Sacred Disobedience* (Harwood, 1997). He is Artistic Director of Lurking Truth/Gwir Sy'n Llechu Theatre Company, for which he has written *The Back of Beyond* (1990), *Bite or Suck* (1997) and *The Battle of the Crows* (1998).

HEIKE ROMS studied theatre, musicology and philosophy at Hamburg and spent a number of years in theatre administration. She was Assistant Director of the Internationales Sommertheater Festival, Hamburg, and is currently a columnist for *Planet*. She is a contributing editor of *Performance Research* (Routledge).

CHARMIAN SAVILL has contributed articles on theatre in Wales to *Euromaske*, *Planet*, *The New Welsh Review*, and *Barn*. She has published essays in *Small is Beautiful: Small Countries Theatre*, ed. Claude Schumaker and Derek Fogg (Theatre Publications, Glasgow, 1991) and in *Staging Wales: Welsh Theatre 1979-1997*, ed. Anna-Marie Taylor

(University of Wales Press, 1997). Her play *The Consecrator* was performed by Made in Wales in Theatr Clwyd and the Sherman Theatre, Cardiff in 1988. She is currently preparing a one-woman show of her collection of prose poems, *Chimera*.

ANNA-MARIE TAYLOR is Lecturer in the Department of Continuing Education in the University of Wales, Swansea. She has published widely on European drama and is a theatre columnist for *Planet*. She is editor of *Staging Wales: Welsh Theatre 1979-1997* (University of Wales Press, 1997).

EDWARD THOMAS, dramatist, is Artistic Director of Fiction Factory and also a television script writer and director. He contributes to theatre courses at various colleges in Wales and lectures on the 'English-medium Theatre in Wales' course in the Department of Theatre, Film and Television, the University of Wales, Aberystwyth. The award-winning film version of his play *House of America* appeared in 1997 and his latest play *Gas Station Angel*, commissioned by the Royal Court, was published by Methuen in 1998. For details of perfomances and publications, see pp. 246-47.

CHARLES WAY, dramatist, is currently writer in residence at the Sherman Theatre, Cardiff. His play *The Search for Odysseus* received two productions in Germany during 1998, and the award-winning *A Spell of Hard Weather* was performed in French in Canada. His play *Playing from the Heart*, written for Polka Theatre, London, opens in September 1998. He is also on commission with BBC TV Wales, writing a three-part drama, *The Circumference of Love*. He lectures on the 'English-medium Theatre in Wales' course for Departemnt of Theatre, Film and Television, the University of Wales, Aberystwyth. For details of performances and publications, see pp. 313-15.

Introduction

Hazel Walford Davies

This volume of essays responds to a demand from theatre practitioners, critics, academics, students and members of the public alike for critical perspectives on the work of playwrights working out of Wales at this time. The American usage, 'working out of ' has several advantages over 'working in' or 'from' Wales. It connotes, not only simple location, but a sense of the wider sources and resources, both cultural and structural, that shape the work, whether directly or indirectly, in this still most public of art forms. Relatively few of the plays by the four dramatists celebrated in this volume have, realistically, a Welsh setting, though all four dramatists stress the relevance of their writing to Wales. The very word 'standpoints' comes from where you stand. 'Working out of' therefore covers the different degrees to which a Welsh dramatist *uses* the location of Wales; it covers even cases where Wales itself is not relevant at all. And the Americanism seems particularly appropriate at a time when plays written in Wales so often find America itself to be a defining theme – in Edward Thomas's *House of America*, for example, or Dic Edwards's *Utah Blue* or Charles Way's *Dead Man's Hat*. In this way, the American poet Ed Dorn, author of the poem 'From Idaho Out', addressing his poetic mentor Charles Olson in Olson's home town of Gloucester, Massachusetts, also makes the phrase 'out of Gloucester' extend itself into 'from Gloucester out':

> and to him
> are presented at night
> the whispers of the most flung shores
> from Gloucester out.

The aim of drama, as of all literature, is to create alternative worlds, whether moved towards or moved out of, whether reached or missed or abandoned. The fact that the characters of the American Eugene O'Neill's *Bound East for Cardiff* in 1916 don't actually arrive in Cardiff isn't the point.

And yet this volume had a most particular geographical inception, a very local habitation and a name. During 1997 I invited Greg Cullen, Dic Edwards, Edward Thomas and Charles Way to lead a series of public workshops at Theatr y Werin, Aberystwyth, aided by a grant from the Arts Council of Wales. In the group discussions that followed these highly successful events, the participants urged the need for initiating a debate, now, on theatre writing in Wales. It seemed logical to begin such a debate by concentrating on the work of the four playwrights themselves. Many of the contributors to this volume of essays had also participated in those same workshops and had worked closely alongside the four dramatists in the enactment of the texts on the stage. So the idea for the volume grew naturally out of the critical moment of each workshop. There are of course other fine English-language dramatists of Wales whose plays deserve serious attention, and it is to be hoped that this will be the first of many critical volumes on the plays, and on the performance of plays, by dramatists contributing to theatre in Wales and beyond. The advantage of this particular volume's source in the Aberystwyth workshops is marked also by the role played in those workshops by the dramatists themselves. Wordsworth famously said that it is one of the duties of the poet 'to create the taste by which he is to be enjoyed'. He did so, as also did T.S. Eliot, by writing critically outside – but at crucial tangents to – the work itself. The Aberystwyth workshops were revealing in the way in which they widened our view of the contexts of these plays by having the dramatists themselves there talking, and contributing informally, without being required to become published commentators on their own work. This is a model for the widening debate about the arts that higher education must continue to have in Wales. An informed discussion and analysis of the work of such playwrights, and the welcome publication of playtexts by Seren Books and Parthian, indicate that theatre writing, too, is at the forefront of what the Welsh and the world now describe proudly as 'Welsh writing in English'.

State of Play has many voices – Like T.S. Eliot's Maine seaboard, 'many gods and many voices' – and therefore a variety of perspectives. Dic Edwards, who was born in Cardiff and who has lived in Wales all his life, starts the volume on a challenging note by arguing that, even within Wales, he is an evictee, a man cast out from language, culture and nation. He protests that he cannot be a Welshman 'because for me, there is nothing I can identify this nation with.' Neither, he argues, can he be described as a Welsh writer, 'because I do not write in the language the English language calls Welsh and the other sense of being a Welsh writer doesn't, for me, exist.' That touch whereby the fact of the 1500-year-old literary language of Welsh can be described coolly as a 'language the English language calls Welsh' is not only a nice philosophical roundabout; it reveals the distance that lies between three out of the four dramatists celebrated here and that *other* language that stands behind English writing in Wales. Of the four, only Edward Thomas is Welsh-speaking. In Shakespeare's phrase, 'the isle is full of noises'. Dic Edwards sees his theatre as 'theatre for the evicted' and the themes around which his plays revolve are 'stupidity and the self-obsession and the myopia that cause it'. In his discussion of the plays he analyses the function and effect of language and the issues central to his dramatic preoccupations. He sees theatre as a forum, essentially a moral place, whose aesthetic concerns should, ideally, be led by the playwright, not the director.

Edwards acknowledges a 'mentor' – in Edward Bond, and Bond's letters provide an invaluable insight into the nature and development of Edwards's dramatic writing. In the letter of 8 November 1997 Bond comments on Dic Edwards's essay for this volume: 'You are kind enough to say that I have been your mentor. If that is so, then I am a Mentor who has learnt from Telemachus – whom you remember he sent out on his own journey'. The Bond letters can focus on Edwards's work all the more powerfully, of course, because they are, further back, a reflection of Bond's own view of theatre and theatre-writing in the British scene as a whole, and of the nature and reception of Bond's own work. They illustrate Edwards's writing process and the revisions, the drafting and redrafting, that go into the final version. Charmian Savill, too, highlights this multi-version feature of the work in plays such as *Wittgenstein's Daughter* and *The Idiots*. Her reading of *Utah Blue* leads into a telling analysis of other plays by Edwards and of the theatrical experience offered by his challenging dramatic strategies and structures. Thus, although in an Edwards play 'a consistent morality is expressed throughout,' the dramatist also 'takes care to subvert expectations and avoid predictability . . . through the unexpected actions and surprising journeys towards which he leads his characters'.

The 'disturbing' nature of Edwards's dramatic worlds – in the sense of the regular unsettling of audience expectations – is a feature pin-pointed also by Anna-Marie Taylor. Her main concentration, however, is on the relationship between the word and the world,' since 'Edwards's plays are singular in the use they make in putting acute emphasis on the word, often in the form of long "oratorical" speeches, to express the imagination of social life'. She explores the recurring structural pattern of the plays, the 'autobiographical awareness' of the characters, and highlights the major concerns within a typical Edwards play. She also argues convincingly that 'Edwards's quest for finding ways of representing the contemporary world, and in particular its manifestation in and through the social imagining of the late twentieth century, has many links with commentators such as Appadurai and Giddens on the nature of the individual within late modernity'.

In my own interview with Edwards, the dramatist again emphasises the fact that he sees theatre as a forum for debate on the nature of society anywhere. To ignore the serious societal purpose of theatre, he claims, is a 'dereliction of duty'. Whereas cinema and television are primarily entertainment-led, theatre should 'enable us to look at our lives and our society in a new way and a way that helps us progess'. He emphasises the importance of using dramatic language in a way that 'gives us the idea of truth'. (One is reminded of a Johnsonian phrase of Raymond Chandler's – that the critic's language, too, like that of the writer, should be one that 'builds a house for the truth'.) From this standpoint Edwards also looks critically at the 'so-called Welsh theatre' scene and concludes by echoing the theme of his opening essay and claiming 'refugee status, a kind of temporary citizenship'.

Edward Thomas, a Welsh speaker, does not reject Welshness. In fact, his plays set out to offer a redefinition of Wales in terms of cultural and political identity. In the interview with me that opens the section of essays on Thomas, he describes himself as 'a Welsh writer with international aspirations'. He strikes an optimistic, post-devolution note in his claim that his plays explore ways in which it is possible 'to reclaim and reconstruct the past and make it your own' and 'to create an attitude and a confidence'. Indeed, the two words 'attitude' and 'confidence,' put the other way round, would be fair milestones on the road to the new view of Wales from the inside that has come about over the last three decades or so. With this attitude, Edward Thomas can gather around him the confidence that enables him to cast a cold eye, not only on the state of theatre in Wales in the 1990s – where, like Dic Edwards, he regrets a 'failure of the imagination' – but also on the seductive, usable concept of the American Dream.

In her essay Heike Roms takes up the question of the role played by Thomas's 'theatre of invention' in the creation of a new Welsh identity. Through an exploration of such theatrical notions as 'role-playing, visibility and memory' she discusses and illustrates the paradoxes inherent in Thomas's model for a 'theatre of invention'. In a fresh and theatre-based analysis of the plays that constitute *New Wales Trilogy* she shows how, while remaining within the representational framework of theatre, Edward Thomas 'subjects the theatrical conventions of play, perception and narrative to endless scrutiny'.

Fresh scrutiny is the dominant aim of each writer in this volume. David Adams, while stating that 'Edward Thomas is far more about Welshness than *Trainspotting* is about Scottishness or Friel about Irishness,' also argues that the work is not *simply* about Welshness. It is also about 'negotiating a way through culture' and the difficulty of 'making sense' of it in a postmodernist age. He sees Thomas as a 'cultural entrepreneur' and relevantly, therefore, places the work within the context of what he calls 'the Edward Thomas industry' and of Welsh theatre practice in the late twentieth century. In this wide-ranging essay Adams also draws on biographical detail in his discussion of Thomas's interweaving within his plays of fact and fiction, actuality and myth, the specific and the universal.

In a closely argued essay, Katie Gramich draws attention to the postmodernist ideology of Thomas's plays and to what she describes as 'the obsessive intertextuality which seems to enclose and re-enclose the text in a series of ever more stifling referential boxes.' In his interview with me Thomas confesses that within his plays he is 'pretty obsessed . . . with absent fathers.' Gramich on the other hand argues that Sid's identification with his absent father in *House of America* can be viewed 'as a cover-up for a continuing maternal obsession' and that in Thomas's plays the 'aspiring male character has a continuing attachment to the mother which is nothing short of obsessional'. Gramich explores the presentation of the received image of the Welsh Mam within the plays and the disquieting relationship between sons and mothers. In her analysis of gender she argues that while the female roles within an Edward Thomas play present a clichéd notion of female identity, yet, 'from a feminist point of view, Edward Thomas's habitual mockery of macho roles and behaviour and his parodying of clichéd icons such as the Welsh Mam effect a destabilisation which can only be threatening to the patriarchal status quo'. Gramich also discussess Thomas's rejection of naturalism in favour of the experimental, the significance and effect of his subversion of elements within a chosen genre, his employment of popular culture, and the role of American myth and identity within the plays.

David Ian Rabey focuses specifically on *Flowers of the Dead Red Sea.* Working from an analysis of Wales as a divided consciousness whose will to action is in thrall to an external power that internalises Wales's nationhood into a regionalism, he ironically folds into his own title – 'Tryweryn of the Soul' – that other 'dead sea', the still but still imaginatively potent Merionethshire valley drowned in the early 1960s to provide water for Liverpool. In Wales as elsewhere (three of his analogies – via Kennelly, Friel and Heaney – are with Ireland) Rabey sees theatre, with its energies of *perfomance*, *intensification* and *choice*, as the prime energising way out of paralysis. And in these terms, in *Flowers of the Dead Red Sea*, he recognises 'the most profoundly painful and angry of Thomas's plays, and perhaps thereby . . . his most emotionally accessible in terms of its depressive yet defiant extremity'. In this context, the play is about the need to save, out of a depressed past, a defiant future.

It is appropriate therefore that the item which follows Rabey's essay is Heike Roms's profile of Edward Thomas, written prior to the narrow 'Yes' vote for devolution. It reflects a fresh confidence, a belief in the world-wide currency of artists working out of Wales. For Edward Thomas, however, the success of such artists represents a 'despite culture,' entrepreneurial rather than establishment-based. And, further, according to Thomas this new eclectic culture revolves in the main around the music and film scene, 'leaving the theatre lagging behind'. The portrait casts a sharp light on the nature of Thomas's craft and his view of contemporary theatre in Wales: the profile shows Thomas – and this is an unstated corollary of Rabey's essay, too – looking towards Europe.

But there is also another, equally potent, land. In *Dead Man's Hat*, Charles Way, like Edward Thomas in *House of America* or Dic Edwards in

Utah Blue, travels for his myths, not south-south-east, but westwards. Although Way's play, as the dramatist explains, is based on Jack Shaefer's film *Shane*, the tone of the play, unlike that of the film, is 'cynical rather than elegiac' and questions and challenges the romanticism of the myth of the American West. Charles Way's own essay is an analysis of the play as narrative, the play as metaphor. Again in his discussion of *The Dove Maiden* Charles Way shows how he seeks to take the audience, through narrative, into an exploration of a moral world. While at ease with the form of the play, the audience is challenged by the content since in *The Dove Maiden* 'form and content are warring factions, not partners'. One might extricate from that carefully chosen cliché, 'warring factions,' a term that has come to describe one of the really new international literary forms of the late twentieth century – the form called 'faction', that border country between fact and fiction. It is a useful reflection at this stage since it reminds us how drama in such a strongly political situation as that of Wales in the twentieth century has had to find its imaginative forms in either *retreat from* or *allegiance to* an actual situation that will not go away – Wales's still powerfully bilingual situation, for example. Or, if not in *retreat* or *allegiance*, in that border country of both retreat *and* allegiance, the border country of *new arrival*.

David Adams traces Charles Way's journey as a dramatist 'from issue plays to the more philosophical spiritual work of the nineties'. He places Way's work in the tradition of popular theatre, with its roots in medieval drama, and while seeing Way as 'the product of community theatre' he also sees him transcending the necessary impermanence of that kind of theatre. Adams points out that more people in Wales have seen a Charles Way stage play than one by any other writer working out of Wales and that he 'has also been produced in the rest of Britain more than any other living Wales-based playwright.'

Charles Way is essentially a Border person, in particular of the Monmouthshire/ Hereford border – if 'particular' is at all a possible word regarding a border. John Powell Ward, editor of the excellent 'Border Lines' series of monographs on 'border' authors published by Seren Books, has written, 'How wide is the border? Two, five or fifteen miles each side of the boundary; it depends on your perspective, on the placing of the nearest towns, on the terrain itself, and on history . . . Most significant perhaps is the difference to the two peoples on either side. From England, the border meant the enticement of emptiness, a strange unpopulated land, going up and up into the hills. From Wales, the border meant the road to London, to the university, or to employment, whether by droving sheep, or later to the industries of Birmingham and Liverpool. It also meant the enemy, since borders and boundaries are necessarily political. Much is shared, yet different languages are spoken, in more than one sense.' Either way (literally), it is the natural borderer in Charles Way who sees the 'frontier' possibilities in *Dead Man's Hat*, an American extension of the notion of border country that has a particular resonance in Wales itself. While the concern to be accessible (another 'border' consideration) is crucial to Way, his work, like that of all the other dramatists represented here, is full of 'innovative stagecraft techniques that exploit the necessities of form' beyond the exigencies of place, even while not forgetting them.

In the interview with Graham Laker, Way draws a comparison between contemporary theatre in Wales and the one that existed in 1980 when he first moved to Wales. In 1980, because of adequate funding for small theatre companies it was possible for a dramatist to develop a long-standing relationship with particular companies. Now, with the contraction of funding, companies can no longer develop that close relationship with a writer. Consequently, to make a living, the dramatist has to diversify. Way began his professional career by writing for TIE companies, children and young people's theatre, and community theatre. The essentially collaborative nature of those excellent forms extended naturally into his work for television. The dramatist himself defines a Charles Way play as one where the manner in which a story is told is recognizable, in 'short scenes which fold into one another, or the use of song, or perhaps a thread of poetry or magic which runs through quite a number of them'. He discusses the process of his theatre writing, and says that 'To know something about the process of acting and directing, of how plays work on stage visually as well as aurally, makes you a theatre writer rather than any other sort of writer'. He considers the way in which preliminary workshops with companies can aid the writing process even though ultimately, in his case, the script has to be the province of the playwright. In a wider context, he urges the importance, in a televisual age, of actively nurturing a relationship between the theatre company and its community, he broaches the possible role of a National Theatre for Wales, and sees the need to encourage theatre writing in which dramatists are given the opportunity to be part of the entire production process itself.

Greg Cullen's voice emerges clearly in his reflections on the kind of theatre he seeks to achieve through the form and associative powers of his plays. He explains that he has aimed 'to make the stage as theatrical as possible' and to give the audience 'a roller-coaster ride'. He also traces his professional journey from his beginnings with a tradition where theatre had to have a direct political purpose through the 'poetic constructs' of plays such as *The Whistleblower* or *Tower* to the more recent *Cherubs* which reflects Cullen's wish to 'bring beauty into the world alongside my rage and disgust'. He also reflects interestingly on the influence on his work of his working-class beginnings and the Irish Catholic culture of his childhood.

Dovetailing with these considerations as seen by the dramatist himself is

David Ian Rabey's approach to Cullen's work from the perspective of what Gwyneth Lewis has termed 'spiritual realism'. Rabey argues that this is a dimension of Cullen's plays that 'suggests and demonstrates the importance of imaginative awareness to augment basely material considerations and evaluations of people, places and events'. In readings of several of the stage and radio plays Rabey demonstrates Cullen's dramatic method through an enlightening analysis of form, theatre language, staging and audience response. His essay also analyses Cullen's chief concerns within the plays. In the discussion of the poetic drama *Cherubs*, for example, Rabey claims that the play 'invites a national psyche to confront its own potential for adulthood and grow up accordingly'. Rabey's view that the play offers 'a salutary challenge to the incestuous tendencies of the Welsh imagination, theatrical or otherwise' is obviously itself challenging. In his own essay Cullen draws attention to the fact that within any play of his 'there is an inflamed desire to act for justice'. Rabey also identifies this aspect and suggests, for example, that Cullen is 'Wales's equivalent to Peter Flannery and Jimmy McGovern who also identify moments when being a (wo)man and playing by the rules don't work anymore, necessitating significant explosion within a corrupt and cowardly world'. But, Rabey argues, Cullen is also a 'theatre poet creating resonant social myths and artful fantasies which are too shrewd, worldly and generous to forget the playfulness which is essential to life and theatre'.

David Adams places Cullen's work within the specific cultural contexts of the company for which he works and the geographical area out of which he writes – and the audience that these provide for *what* he writes. These pressures Adams sees as the 'external demand' made upon a dramatist who has also particularly strong inner creative needs. Adams thinks of Cullen's artistic journey as a move away from 'agitprop and issue-led work to non-prescriptive drama'. He underlines the dualism that manifests itself throughout Cullen's work, 'that constant artistic dilemma, the resolution of the potential conflict between "inner need" and "external demand" whether to write from inside or respond to outside forces, the balance of artistic integrity and social responsibility'. He traces the journey of the playwwright from his theatre involvement in London in the late seventies and early eighties to his move to Theatr Powys in 1983 where Cullen's work developed and changed, and where his theatre became 'a debate with the audience'. Adams, like Rabey, points to the lyrical and mythical (the 'poetic'?) in Cullen's work and, again like Rabey, sees *Cherubs*, a play 'that reads almost like an extended, spontaneous poem,' as Cullen's most powerful work to date.

In his interview with David Rabey, Cullen confirms, in his discussion of *Tarzanne*, Adams's claim that as a dramatist he has become more aware of the 'symbiotic relationship between play and audience'. He himself isolates

Taken Out, as Adams does, as 'the first play in which I could recognize my own case and the personal way in which I had argued it'. It is uncanny how the development of all important literary careers depends on the author recognising at some stage or other his or her own authentic voice. It is also uncanny how universal the writer's language is when he or she acknowledges that fact. W. B. Yeats described one of his poems as 'the first lyric with anything in its rhythm of my own music': 'The first play,' says Cullen, 'in which I could recognize my own case'. It is against this experience of his own craft that Cullen, too, discusses the issues that activate his work. This involves mainly his views on the limitations of what Edward Bond's plays seem to suggest, that 'all contradictions can or should ultimately be resolved by rationality'. Cullen believes that human beings will never behave completely rationally and must therefore rejoice in the idea of 'chaotic necessity'. His essay also embraces the role of memory in his plays and the central shaping part played by Mid Powys Youth Theatre in his professional life.

It is in the nature of all really original creative work, that there should be obviously much that marks any four dramatists off from one another. Roger Owen nevertheless offers 'a notion of Welshness' that can embrace and accommodate them. Focusing on Dic Edwards, Edward Thomas and Charles Way, he analyses the very different theatrical worlds, staging techniques and social vision of the three dramatists, bringing out the 'disputes and divisions' within the plays. For Owen, these disputes and divisions can be seen as '*the* signifiers for Welsh identity in the nineties' and that by this token Welsh identity is defined, 'not as a prescription, and certainly not as a liturgy, but a lively and ongoing debate, one which binds together virtually incompatible visions of the nation and the people'. In this way, these four dramatists present us with a vision of a nation 'tenuously, but tenaciously, held together by conflict'. Cleanth Brooks once argued that paradox is at the very heart of all serious literary endeavour, but that the writer's aim is always a sense of unity. There seems no reason why paradox (Roger Owen's 'tenuous' yet 'tenacious' and 'held together' by 'conflict') shouldn't also inhere in the claim that these four quite different dramatists are, quite equally, and very fully, writing out of Wales.

And, of course, what most often unifies (because it *transcends*) the differences and divisions in modernist and postmodernist creative writing is the role of myth. As was mentioned at the outset, the myth that seems most often to beckon the dramatist writing out of Wales is that of America. Gill Ogden examines the role of the American Dream in the theatre of Wales, Ireland and Scotland. In an anlysis of the theatrical representation of the search for national emblems and identities she explores the uses made of 'the mythical America as an alternative location or frontier for contesting versions of identity'. Useful here is her discussion of two postmodern performances that 'exploit the frontier myth in order to pose an alternative resistance to hegemonic discourse, not appositional but inclusive'.

It seems appropriate that an Introduction that started off with the notion of 'writing out of' a particular national situation should end with mythic inclusiveness. It highlights the imaginative advantage that a small nation like Wales can take of what is, at the end of this millenium at least, the increasingly dominant world-presence of America. But it is an advantage that is all the more advantageous in being taken not wide-eyed but circumspectly. This is a volume about four important writers in that most naturally self-effacing of all literary forms, drama, the form which, while powerfully reinforcing our beliefs, also frees us through the suspension of disbelief. And a natural appropriateness also inheres in ending with an American poet on that very subject. In his poem 'Children Selecting Books in a Library,' Randall Jarrell movingly reminds us that

> we live
> By trading another's sorrow for our own, another's
> Impossibilities, still unbelieved in, for our own . . .
> 'I am myself still'? For a little while, forget:
> The world's selves cure that short disease, myself.

Dic Edwards

Theatre for the Evicted

Dic Edwards

Eviction

Everything whole and good is a reconciliation of the opposites within it. This is the basic human, social, dramatic paradigm. It is the dialectical paradigm. (Thesis, antithesis, synthesis.) The failure of this reconciliation in people produces schizophrenia. Its failure in societal terms produces revolution. Its failure culturally produces what I call *the evicted.* My journey as a writer begins with this reality.

A culture reflects a unity. Without a unity there is no culture. Wales is not a unity and so there is nothing that can be called Welsh culture. It may even be the case that the thing *Wales* does not exist in any really meaningful sense. *Cymru* exists while *Wales*, as the word suggests, describes a strangeness. Those who live in this strangeness are like people without a true home. People on the street. Evictees. People who live in this strangeness don't have the cultural experiences of a people who belong (to a nation, say), they have the experiences of the evicted. These are the people I write my plays about and for.

I cannot be a Welshman. This is because, for me, there is nothing I can identify this notion with. In other words, I don't believe in *Wales.* On the other hand, though I do not belong there, either, I can believe in *Cymru* because it is a place that has a unity and an identity around a language. (Where it is is wherever people's first language is Cymraeg.) In *Wales* there is a division of language. The consequence of this is that I am not a *Welsh* writer because I do not write in the language the English language calls Welsh and the other sense of being a Welsh writer doesn't, for me, exist.

My background is urban working-class and so I have a natural cultural identity with working-class people in other nations, but within my own 'nation' (this thing called *Wales*) that identity is with the working-class people of Cardiff, where I was born. I am, like them, an evictee. This is because Cardiff is the capital of *Wales* – which doesn't exist in any meaningful sense, while to say that Cardiff is the capital of *Cymru* is certainly a cultural nonsense if not a serious infringement of the rights of the people who live in *Cymru.* It means that Cardiff is the capital of nowhere and must be itself, like people who live *with nowhere to live*, evicted.

It may be the case that members of the working-class of many nations are in some sense evicted but then they would have their own culture. Even this is denied the people of *Wales*. It is, quite simply, because there is a supposed all-inclusive Welsh Culture! This is the paradox. The supposition causes us to be always talking about it as though it existed; we're always talking about it because it isn't there. Most modern nations are, anyway, multi-cultural.

Of people who live in this *Wales* – especially writers – the epithet *Anglo-Welsh* is often used. The sub-conscious refutation of any multi-culturalism is here given a cruel and ironic twist. This epithet, while apparently recognising diversity, is in fact grotesquely insulting, conferring, as it does, a second-classness. It is, in a phrase, that non-reconciling of opposites that I've referred to, and proof of its badness. Just consider it. The word 'Welsh' is 'English', anyway. A reasonable translation of this phrase might be (speaking, say, of a writer) 'one who writes in English in that part of the world known as *Wales* because the language of the people who live there is English. In other words: those who write in English in an English speaking country.' To convey the sense it seems to be wanting to convey, the phrase would need to be *Anglo-Cymraeg*. This would be meaningless, of course, because *Cymraeg* could not be characterised as English! What it really suggests is that the writer is neither; has no real identity culturally and is, therefore, an *evictee.* This is because the truest description of, say, me, is that I am an *English* writer and yet I am not English, either. And so I must be existing as if on the street, shut out from any culture that I might expect to belong to.

In my dreams, Cardiff is the capital of a country which has close federation with Cymru. This country is called Gallia. It makes me a Gallic writer.

Bound out from Cardiff

I've gone into this business of identity to draw attention to where I'm coming from and why my plays are heading out to where they're going. In a *Kaleidoscope* interview for BBC Radio 4, which took place on the set of my play *Utah Blue* at The Point in Cardiff, it was suggested that my writing about Gary Gilmore, my writing about America, wasn't writing about *Wales*. But writing about Gary Gilmore was writing about my condition. And, anyway, as a playwright, where I began was a place where an American was bound east for Cardiff! One of the first plays I read, and therefore one of my earliest influences, was *Bound East For Cardiff* by Eugene O'Neill. O'Neill grew up in hotel rooms and on ships and carried the world in the scents and smells on his clothes, just as a world in all its diversity appeared in his diversifying theatre. This diversity is a sure sign of eviction. But, then, O'Neill knew all about not belonging.

People who live in ports look out to sea. Look out to the world. I look out just in this way to find my subjects. And though I've left Cardiff behind I carry the sense of it with me. The sense of it being a home of *evictees* and also a departure point for the world. In this sense, Casanova in my play

Casanova Undone (Citizens Theatre, Glasgow and The White Bear, London) is a Cardiffian. So is Alma, the woman known as Wittgenstein's Daughter in the play of that name (*Wittgenstein's Daughter* – Citizens Theatre, Glasgow and White Bear Theatre Club, London), and as is the timeless Regan in *Regan* (Welsh Tour by Theatr Powys) or The Prince in *The Idiots*. So is Gary Gilmore in *Utah Blue*, Gustavo in *the fourth world* (Theatr Clwyd), Kitty in *Long To Rain Over Us* (Leicester Haymarket) the family of Leo in *Low People* (Leicester Haymarket), and even Paddy in *Looking For The World* (Sherman Theatre Main Stage) – and to a lesser extent his wife Sylvia – who would blind himself to his condition. And then there is Lola in *Lola Brecht* (Casataway Theatre Co., National Tour) who suffers an eviction imposed by her husband. Finally, there is Doctor Corkfoot in *The Man Who Gave His Foot For Love* (Spectacle Theatre Company, Welsh Tour). All are Cardiffians.

In the only play I ever wrote about Cardiff – my first play, *At The End Of The Bay* (Sherman Theatre) – everyone is evicted: that theme that embodies my aesthetic philosophy . And in the Saturn Club (where, on the wall, a god eats his child), Spargo and Fuse play a pointless endgame (Fuse and Spark) while their world falls apart about them. And all this introduces a theme that sets me on my way: stupidity and the self-obsession and myopia that cause it.

Stupidity

Edward Bond has been my mentor. He struggles endlessly against the reaction in the theatre, almost like Sysiphus endlessly climbing his mountain with no perceptible success. When I set out, Bond advised me never to write for a particular audience. He is right. Audiences have become afraid and look to the theatre as places of comfort and safety. If writers write for audiences under these circumstances, they immediately take away one of its fundamental reasons for being, which is to challenge our safe assumptions and all assumptions of safety. I therefore don't write for audiences (unless I'm writing for children). I write about them.

I don't belong to the school of thought that argues that we are all living in some kind of existential impermanence. I believe that we exist in a condition of almost permanent stupidity that we must struggle always to rise above. We are the subjects of stupidity. In the immediate situation it is not our fault. There are masters of stupidity. Our politics are a mastering of stupidity. Our politicians are its disciplinarians. Some of these masters of stupidity have found their way into our theatres in controlling positions. This is doubly deplorable as theatre should be in the front line in the fight against this particular manifestation of the human condition.

Spargo and Fuse in *At The End Of The Bay* are subject to decisions made about their world, their Bay, by the disciplinarians of stupidity. Yet, in order to survive they make a go of their own stupidity with pluck, bound to scorn wise counsel because there is no one to say that *they* are not the wise. Regan in *Regan* is different. She wakes at night in a cold sweat. Her own ghost counsels her: why do people give up so much for so little? As *Regan* was being born, Desert Storm was raging in the Gulf. To save the unsaveable (Kuwait), so many died. Why was so much given up for so little? The world joined Sysiphus and Bond in climbing their mountains endlessly with no apparent success. There is no apparent success but there is Radical Meaning – the answer to the small, selfish gains which cost so much. Radical Meaning: Bond on his climb stops, waits for other climbers and, out of his and their related experiences, creates parables which seek to bring wisdom to bear on the condition.

If a man calls himself Nameless (in *Regan*), he is hiding something. If he comes bearing mottoes to save you in a language you don't understand – *nuntius magne societatis* (I am the messenger of the Great Society) – and calls himself Nameless, he relies on your stupidity and greed for the smallest possible gain with no care for the possible cost. Though he is obviously the embodiment of everything you should be wary of: he is saviour, con-man, evictor. John Rakestraw is subject to the slave within him (the *evictee*) and will embrace Nameless rather than solve his problems and confront his slavehood. He has given in to his condition of eviction. He will even abuse his daughter Regan to prove how cast out he is.

I called Regan Regan after King Lear's daughter. For me, Regan in Shakespeare's play is moral in the modern sense while, for example, Cordelia is moral in the classical sense. Cordelia is a tragic heroine. Her moral status is determined by this. She *does* nothing. She simply *is*. What happens to her happens because of tragic necessity. Regan on the other hand acts in a modern way. Her character *does*. And what it does is unexpected. This is because it is as if it is the product of a conscious, reasoning mind (no matter how unreasonable) and not because of anything deterministic. Regan in my play is trapped, almost, in a tragic drama where an inevitability is always threatening. But because she is not Cordelia, she can act against the trap. Regan (through her ghost) is modern. If I had made Regan Cordelia, my play's resolution – its synthesis – would have been pessimistic instead of optimistic as it is.

The first play I ever loved

The first play I ever loved was Shakespeare's *Measure For Measure*. It is a 'problem' play because it is so modern. It is about society. It is about justice. It is about socialism. It is almost a mirror image of the socialist creed! Every play I have ever written owes something to *Measure For Measure*. *Looking For The World* is a modern domestic comedy set within a Greek tragedy. The measures are the opposite. As I have said, everything whole and good is a reconciliation of the opposites within it. Everything that

Dic Edwards

(*photo*: Simon Chapman)

Looking for the World (1986)

Low People (1989)
(*photo*: Malcolm Andrew)

Regan (1991)
(*photo*: Keith Morris)

Casanova Undone (1992)
(*photo*: James Graham)

Wittgenstein's Daughter (1993)
(*photo*: Kevin Low)

Wittgenstein's Daughter (1993)
(*photo*: Kevin Low)

Dic Edwards: *Utah Blue* workshop, Theatr y Werin, Aberystwyth (1997)
(*photo*: Keith Morris)

exists subscribes to this dialectical paradigm. Moral activity derives from it. Even in Classical justice which is about retribution rather than finding a balance for the greatest good (which is why *Measure For Measure* is modern). Oedipus is the good king, and bad human being. Justice comes out of the resolution of this conflict. Ancient justice demands that Oedipus blind himself, so that he can no longer look into the eyes of his wife who is his mother. Paddy Milanne is the Trade-Unionist-of-Good-Intention and the man made bad by moral laziness and abominable fascist comfort. He is Cardiffian. Thebes is Cardiff. Oedipus is Cardiffian. Like Oedipus, Paddy passes on into darkness. His wife Sylvia must bleat in the silence. The silence left by his stupidity has evicted their language. His stupidity has helped determine the tragic outcome of the play.

Language: The Philosophical Barber

Tony Unsworth cuts hair. Tony Unsworth studied philosophy. One day in the mid-eighties he handed me a book, a biography of the linguistic philosopher Wittgenstein. The book was written by a William Bartley III. It argued (the simplest way to put it) that when Wittgenstein wrote 'whereof one cannot speak one must remain silent' – by which he was referring to matters of morality – he was dismissing, philosophically, what could be spoken about, his own private morality. Bartley pointed out that Wittgenstein was known to be a homosexual, that he had hidden the fact, and so, presumably, considered it immoral. Bartley's theme, in effect, was that Wittgenstein's philosophy was constructed to preserve a kind of bourgeois respectability for himself. I quickly felt that this argument could be used to paint a much larger picture.

I wanted to write about how language (in this case the English language) can be manipulated by the custodians of language, Oxbridge academics in the main, for ultimately political reasons, and I felt that the best way to show this in a postmodern environment was to draw a picture of a parallel, metaphorical conspiracy undertaken for sexual/moral reasons – in this case, the conspiracy surrounding the conception and birth of Alma, known as the daughter of Wittgenstein. This was of course my own fabrication.

Wittgenstein had written, in the *Tractatus Logico-Philosophicus*:

> the correct method in philosophy would really be the following: to say nothing except what can be said, i.e. the propositions of natural scence, i.e. something that has nothing to do with philosophy…[1]

That is, tautologies like 'A triangle has three sides', in which the sense of the sentence is already contained in its subject. Because, if you like, the sense of truth is not contained in the sense of language. Well this may be all right for the instigators (and manipulators) of ideas, but where does it leave ordinary people whose only authority may be found in the very nature of the language they speak? If they are not able to argue for truth, how are they to argue against the lies of the powerful? They are evicted. The issues of *Wittgenstein's Daughter* are central to my dramatic preoccupations.

Wittgenstein's philosophy is the foundation of postmodernism

In a note which appears in the published text of *Wittgenstein's Daughter* I write:

> Postmodernism with its uncertainty is like a mine field. In the play I quote from a newspaper article to show this: 'Every value is equal to every other value, nothing is real or natural or authoritative, everything is up for interpretation – goodness, God, literary meaning or merit, artistic or architectural standards, even gender.' Alma struggles through this minefield in which philosophical truth is caricatured as lie or in which simple lie masquerades as philosophical truth. Her journey is through a post-holocaust postmodern landscape in which history seems to mean nothing and values are manipulated by the dead as, perhaps, in a nightmare.

After the fascist propaganda of the thirties and the forties, came the new post-Wittgensteinian philosophy. It declares a function for language which isn't about seeking out truths. This language is only about itself. So all the dying done in the thirties and forties was worth, perhaps, only a tautological sentence: the dead are those who have perished. (Paul de Mann, a French historian, had been a fascist but it was meaningless to say it so he escaped justice in academia.) Derrida, the French philosopher, tore apart sentences to see if they contained words! Philosophers danced to the tune: this is the end of philosophy! Fukayama later said we were at *the end of history.*

Scenes at the end of history

In my play, Alma has come in search of who she is. She was conceived after the rape of her mother by the boxer Beckett, Wittgenstein's first lover, in order to have it look as though Wittgenstein had fathered the child and therefore, could not be a homosexual. (The stupidity of the situation is that Beckett himself is homosexual!) She discovers this about herself. But her searching has meant that Wittgenstein's Ghost cannot rest, cannot find that eternal silence. This is because he is the embodiment of unreconciled opposites and her arrival has acted as a catalyst to show this. The Ghost is the unreconciled philosopher and human-all-too-human man. My fabricated conspiracy is a metaphor for this non-reconciling of opposites and its manifestation: postmodernism and the effect of postmodernism on language itself.

Values

Alma has married a man (Celine) who has become a fascist. His reactionary credo is voiced in the simplistic language of cliché. What language does she have to gainsay him? All is cliché. Any sense of *value* is reduced to a postmodern cacophony. Should Alma have her baby? Is there a language she can give it to fight the devaluing language of its father?

She knows that the man said to be her father was a philosopher of language. And, surely, philosophers deal in values. We know what she discovers: betrayal born of the unreconciled: that the man, the philosopher, who may have given the world values and a means of fighting fascism by giving radical meaning to language, was not only not the father she thought he was but the destroyer of those very values, with his attack on language and radical meaning. Alma determines to have her baby and to give it the language of Radical Meaning. (One element of Radical Meaning: the *meaning* of our lives is contained in the promise of our children.) She gives birth over her mother's grave, after pushing Beckett aside. This is what she says:

> ALMA: I can speak to you mother. O, have I had my trials! You see it all began....Well I'm pregnant but my husband is a fascist! It made me think: it will come it will come again as sure as anything: the footsoldiers of the holocaust are on the march all over Europe. Well I was afraid to bring my child into such a world. I used to say things like: this is no world to bring a child in to. I was deeply moved by clichés. But now, well it's as if I've learned to speak again! It much to do with ...*Talk*! There's one cliché that I think is true: yo talk yourself into trouble! I've remained silent about this. fertilisation. I've had to. I haven't been able to face it! What have come to that we face the prospect of children with shame! That's what it is! But why am I ashamed? Only because I allowed myself to speak *their* words! So much so that I couldn't speak about the one thing I wanted to speak about! Silence is shame! That's the reality of silence! Could I bring my child into this world? A world in which the philosophy is all dead? A world in which ideas count for nothing? A woman needs ideas, mother! It's all she has to fight with! But now I'm angry! I'm angry with the philosophers! People are speaking to me as if I were an idiot! Everywhere I look there are faces looking at me out of screens saying things to me as though with authority *as though with wisdom*. Things that are lies! And what they've got on their side is that most of those looking back into the screens believe them! But children need to have a real language to be able to ask the way. Just in case they get lost in Disneyland! Well, I will be my baby's language and she will be my best idea![2]

In the face of fascism, language may be all we have to give us justice.

Appearance and reality

In the Notes on the Play (*Wittgenstein's Daughter*), arguing that dramatic form in the play comes out of the conflict between *real* and *apparent* language, I say that there is

> the apparent language of our speech which is purely descriptive [it is no less valid as a language for speaking a lie than for speaking a truth] and the underlying language of what it is to be human. The conflict between these two languages informs crucially the language of dramatic synthesis where, in terms of the play, meaning resides . . . There is a conflict between the real language of being human and the apparent language of everyday discourse. To a large extent it's that conflict on which my dramatic intention writhes. The outcome, I hope, is an expression of the human condition and even a search for the meaning of that. (Radical Meaning). [Apparent language is the language of bourgeois politics. Real language is the language of humanity tortured by the language of bourgeois politics]. For most of the play, the real language of being human is one Alma can't use. Because what she might want to talk about – the birth of her baby, she can't speak of. Not until she's gone through the minefield. The play goes from the cliché to *the world*, i.e. The synthesis achieved between Alma's quest [real language] and the history of Beckett and The Ghost related through an apparent language [cf. the language of biography]. The dramatic synthesis is achieved at the moment of her being able to speak about her child-to-be. The play is utterly simple but fraught.

Appearance versus reality is, perhaps, the most dramatic of opposites that need synthesising.

In *Casanova Undone*, Casanova seeks to keep alive his reputation in order to give the memoirs he's writing credibility. But this conflict between what appears to be happening (the 'servicing' of old aristocratic maids of the *ancien régime* who come to him for a last taste of what was) leads not only to his sad demise but to a new sexuality (between Sophie and Angelique) – a sexuality of liberation, investigation and justice, displacing Casanova's imprisoning, reactionary, selfish sexuality. This is the wholesome, good synthesis that comes out of this appearance/reality conflict.

The wise and the foolish

Nequidquam sapit qui sibi non sapit – 'His wisdom is vain who for himself is not wise' is Casanova's own account of the unresolved dialectic. Just as they tried impossibly and immorally to preserve Wittgenstein's reputation, so Casanova – evicted by the revolution (he as a prominent representative of the *ancien régime*, it could be argued, contributed to its causes) – struggles, in my play *Casanova Undone*, to preserve his. Of course, it is not Casanova who is wise, but Sophie, whom he uses in his grand scheme, selfishly. In fact, it is in Sophie that the opposites that need to be reconciled exist. Casanova may be only a catalyst, and an ironic one at that, because a manifestation of the reconciliation of the opposites produces Sophie's wisdom.

The opposites in Sophie are male and female. The resolution lies in her recognising her true sexuality. The dramatic irony here becomes acute because the whole purpose of Casanova's existence in the play is to have the reputation born of his sexuality preserved. In the outcome, while hers is revealed, his is revealed as a wasteful pointless sham. The point is that, even if his sexuality was what it was claimed to be, so what? It hasn't helped him become wise in his old age, but rather the reverse.

And so Casanova gives the appearance of having wisdom because, to begin with, he *seems* wise. He argues against Sophie who has had enough of servicing the old maids with dildoes as Costa:

> CAS.: Don't be so petty! You should subordinate your will to the fine service you give, just as I sublimate mine! Besides, you know it's a delightful idea that they go to bed with only an apparent Casanova but wake up with the real! It's not dishonest to experience by proxy the joy others would be experiencing if they weren't miserable, so why should this be dishonest? It serves a greater goal![3]

Unfortunately, he is not wise. His condition of eviction (The Revolution) has left him powerless but he is too arrogant to accept it and fails to heed his own wise counsel (above). He believes the lie and fools himself into thinking he can still *do* it. But he can't. He tries to do it with Angelique and can't, and has to face the terrible truth. His schemes – the product of someone who thinks he's wise but isn't – finally bring Sophie and Angelique together and Casanova, like all wise fools, loses everything.

Silence

The language dichotomy described in the notes from *Wittgenstein's Daughter* quoted above, that between apparent (bourgeois) language and the language of the struggle to be really human in the face of inhuman forces, is the focal dynamic in my play *Low People*.

Here, I should say what I mean by 'bourgeois'. Essentially, I'm talking about a system of values in which a thing is not valued by its intrinsic worth but by an extrinsic worth put upon it, in this case a worth derived from money-value. This money is the product of a market system which is motivated not by need, but by supply and demand, which can be manipulated. In other words you may say of *art* in a bourgeois system that it is not *needed*. It is there only if an 'audience' can be convinced that it wants it, and is attracted, for example, by effective marketing. What this situation produces is, on the one hand, elitist 'art' which is totally irrelevant to the main body of the people's lives and is, in fact, a commodity which has had a high price attached to it because someone rich has been convinced that they should pay a high price for it (and then, of course, it will *grow* in price, because of what happens to money, not to art) and on the other hand, easy or popular art, 'easy' because easily-marketed to a mass audience. The *real* art, the art we need in order to make *progress* as a society, the art on which in the end what we call civilisation is based, the art that comes out of our *needs* as a community, is in the main unmarketable in a bourgeois society. This is why it relies on various subsidies. This is why it is really only paid lip service to.

What happens with art in a bourgeois society is also what happens with language. Everything has to serve the system of evaluation. The system is not based on truth but on what you can get people to believe with your marketing. In bourgeois society, the extrinsic value put on a thing is considered the standard by which we make value judgments about *all* things. This perverse notion of value permeates everything, especially language, which finds itself in the service of money-making forces. In the end it becomes difficult to make judgments, and moral activity is seriously compromised. 'Bourgeois' is, of course, an unfashionable word. But it is the only word I know for an apparently democratic society that is, in fact, deeply *un*democratic, particularly in its capacity for undermining moral activity. Everything is about presentation, a triumph of form over content. Language loses meaning. It loses even its need to be spoken.

Nietzsche called this process *the transvaluation of values*. It leads, ultimately, to what he called *European nihilism*. For me, this is what happens when the primary needs of people in a society are abandoned to the needs of capitalism and, put crudely, to money-making. Interestingly, in one of his first works, *The Birth of Tragedy*, Nietzsche argued that Greek Attic Tragedy – the theatre of Sophocles and Aeschylus – came from the fusion of the *Apollonian* and the *Dionysian* – that is, from the forces of order and disorder. More complexly: the Apollonian may be associated with the beautiful, immovable, formal structures of Greek architecture like The Parthenon, while the Dionysian is associated with ancient ritual and dance, or what we would now call the expressive, the creative. So this fusion or reconciliation is between form and content, which is why it worked to produce immortal art as opposed to expensive trinkets.

In *Low People*, the language of Leo's family is utterly basic. It is used to describe their needs. It is utterly truthful. It is so truthful that the child Verity, who has the lowest status in a family already with little status, and consequently little language, is virtually silent. Leo's employer, Benthos, a seemingly reasonable man – liberal, plausible and thoroughly bourgeois – is withholding some of Leo's pay, money that Ursula is saving in order to buy some help for her child. Benthos and his wife Nadir speak volumes but say little of any truth. There is a money plot and Verity finally speaks when she sees Nadir stealing the little money her mother has saved. The opposite languages are resolved in her simple cry of 'Mummy!', and she is brought out of her eviction.

Imperialism and language imperialism

In *the fourth world*, Charles is the spurious, liberal-bourgeois *par excellence*. His language of plausible argument is an assault on his wife Helen's plain speaking. Hers is another form of silence and eviction. But it has wider implications in the presence of the fifteen-year-old Gustavo, who has come from the Third World, disabled by Charles from speaking about the truth of his society that he'd like to speak about. Helen's struggle to force Charles to see the truth about Colombia and the circumstances of Gustavo's life brings her out of this silence. In the end it is Charles who finally causes himself to be evicted by his stupidity – a stupidity derived from his absurdly pompous self-assurance and refusal to face the truth, which is such a threat to his comfortable life.

In *The Man Who Gave His Foot For Love*, Doctor Lewis, another kind of specious fellow – a quack and would-be shaman living in a South American village at a time of wide political unrest, – to ingratiate himself with the villagers tells them that he has a potion that will kill the pirhana in the river which eat the cattle as the men take them across. (This is based on a true story by a black friend of mine, Michael Burrows. He lived in Cardiff's dockland when it could still be called Tiger Bay with some credibility. He was half Arapaho Indian. He died falling out of a window in a police station in London.)

The play is about the stupidity that comes out of political repression – a stupidity often self-made in order to be able to live with the repression, rather than fight it. Lewis puts the potion in the river and then stupidly puts his foot in to show that the potion is working. His foot is promptly eaten. Suddenly, Lewis becomes a saviour. They put a cork on the end of his leg, call him Doctor Corkfoot, make him a shaman and worship him. They have conferred on him an authority that is unwarranted; an authority that their stupidity has instructed them to confer. He becomes, accordingly, cruel and fascistic and evicts them. Their only alternative is to learn from the revolutionaries and fight back. Of course, this is not a play about a real revolution. It is a play about – *theatre,* a play about the place theatre should have in our lives, that place where we may once again befriend our intelligence.

What is wrong with our theatre?

British Theatre is a director's theatre. It is led *aesthetically* by dire
This is at the heart of what is wrong. It should be lead, aesthetically, by writers – who know that theatre in practice is an *actor*'s medium. Theatre

just isn't a director's medium' even if film *is*. The idea of theatre as a director's medium derives mainly from the age of Victorian melodrama with those enormously powerful actor-managers. Of course, directors are needed for casting and blocking – someone needs to have an eye on what things look like *architecturally* – though there is sometimes a virtue in abandoning even this. Anyway, this is not a matter of blocking, or of architecture. If it was, there'd be no argument. It is a question of morality.

Theatre is a moral place

If we think of film as the director's medium and theatre as the actor's medium, as I argue, then we need to look at how an audience's relationship with a film differs from its relationship with a play. The basic relationship difference is that the experience an audience has with a film is a passive and *amoral* one; the experience it should have with a play is a creative and, therefore *moral* one.

Take Victorian melodrama. Here the writing (and many plays were written and produced in this form) would serve the impresario. What became important was the attempt to create greater realism – which meant more realistic sets, encouraged by the invention of photography. There is one famous case of a play in which the set involved a church (or temple) and the roof of the theatre was taken off in order to put the dome in place! Actors were required to act a *style.* The throwing of the voice became necessary as the proscenium arch stage distanced the audience (though not in the Brechtian sense!). As a consequence, the acting style became very unnatural – unnatural acting on realistic sets! It should be noted that the development of the proscenium arch has been utterly antipathetic to theatre's purpose. In this theatre, designer and director became the gods and the actors mere playthings (much as it is today). Out of proscenium-arch theatre came the cinema.

Victorian melodrama failed because it was a victory of form over content. It was Bernard Shaw who synthesized these elements with basically the same form and laid the foundation of modern theatre. (A famous declaration of his was that a play should finish not with a swordfight but with an argument.) And where Victorian melodrama failed, the new form, cinema, succeeded. This was because cinema is, basically, an entertainment. In a film you are taken on a ride, the more exciting the better. In theatre the audience needs to be taken on a *journey.* The audience's experience in the cinema is a passive one. The audience *expects* the director to take them on a ride and, after a hundred years, they have some idea of what to expect. Cinema is quintessentially a visual experience, which is why, for many, the golden age was that of the *silent* cinema.

This film/theatre dichotomy is a little like the Cordelia/Regan one I mentioned earlier. Film is like Cordelia: we know what to expect. Theatre is like Regan: we should never know what to expect – and what we actually get should test us morally. The creative experience the audience must have in theatre can only be achieved when the director knows his place and abandons the idea of giving the audience his own private vision. What should happen in a play is that the actors respond to the philosophical and moral arguments of the play (so it's important that a play should have those arguments!). All the greatest plays, from Sophocles through Shakespeare to Shaw and Bond, have been plays with complex moral and philosophical cores. What makes them so great is their ability to make these arguments accessible to the audience, an accessibility facilitated by the use of *moral moments*.

The actor must be allowed to use his own humanity, his own intellectual responses as a sentient being who is, nevertheless, in the grip of emotions which can be both an enablement and a hazard – and to use all this in order to relate to the moral and philosophical arguments of the play. He must be allowed to investigate as both human being and character, the depths of the argument and how they affect the relationships between the people *on the stage.* An actor should never switch off his mind and pretend he's not himself in order to play the character! This is so often the mistake. This is when we get *acting* instead of acting, the frightened actor hiding behind a mask to defend himself from the onslaught of the true human realities that the writer has presented him with. Of course, one hears that we all wear masks anyway, but this doesn't affect the principle of what I'm saying. If the play is the director's interpretation, then you're getting the director's view of the arguments. He may manipulate and direct the audience in the direction he wants to take them. This is an immoral activity because it takes away the audience's, and the actor's, right to be morally involved.

The Man Who Gave His Foot For Love, like all my plays, was written with this analysis of theatre's responsibility very much in mind. (It's no good expecting directors to behave properly and know their place, if writers don't write responsibly). It was written for Spectacle Theatre Company which is primarily a TIE Company. I've written extensively for them in recent years. Apart from this play, which is not a TIE play, I have written five plays for schools: *Moon River: The Deal*, *The Shakespeare Factory*, *David*, *Kid* and *Vertigo*. TIE Companies are currently in the forefront of producing real theatre and Spectacle, with the leadership of Steve Davis, is one of the best. He is very much a theatre director who's working for theatre, and not for himself. I've learned a lot from working with him. That learning has become a part of my understanding of theatre and influenced the mainstream play *The Man Who Gave His Foot For Love*. Yet, astonishingly when it was produced and presented at Chapter Arts Centre, a director from one of Cardiff's leading theatres (with, alarmingly, a brief for encouraging young people into theatre) advised people not to go and see the play. His reason wasn't clear. He did not know what his reason was! And the reason he didn't know is because he doesn't know what theatre is. He is a leading example of what's wrong with our theatre. He is a manipulator not a moralist. His position is a paradoxical one. How does he reconcile the two sides of the paradox? He evicts the audience from my play! From my theatre. In Cardiff. Which is where I began . . .

Notes

1 Ludwig Wittgenstein, *Tractatus Logico-Philosophicus*, ed., A. J. Ayer, trans., D. F. Pears and B. F. McGuiness (Routledge: London, 1961), p. 151.

2 Dic Edwards, *Wittgenstein's Daughter* (London: Oberon Books, 1993), pp. 61-2.

3 *Casanova Undone* in Dic Eswards, *Three Plays, Casanova Undone, Looking for the World, Long to Rain Over Us* (London: Oberon Books, 1992), p. 21.

The Letters of Edward Bond to Dic Edwards

edited by Hazel Walford Davies

In 1981 Dic Edwards attended a two-week theatre workshop at the University of Wales Conference Centre at Gregynog, Powys. There he met Tony Coult who, two years previously, had written a critical study of Edward Bond's work (*The Plays of Edward Bond: A Study,* London: Eyre Methuen, 1979).) After a highly successful exploration and performance by conference participants of a scene from a work-in-progress by Dic Edwards, which ultimately became *At the End of the Bay*, Tony Coult suggested to the dramatist that he should send a sample of his work to Edward Bond. In response to an initial letter, Edward Bond agreed to read his work, and Dic Edwards then sent him the one-act play *Late City Echo*. And so a correspondence was begun that has lasted for seventeen years.

According to Dic Edwards, 'the correspondence is a two-way interest. It's not so much that Edward Bond is an overwhelming influence on me; indeed I have sometimes been of help to him, as with the notes to *The War Plays*. I think that's why the correspondence has flourished. It's not been simply a case of Edward Bond telling me how to write. It's been an exchange of ideas. But I do also, of course, see him as a mentor.' The two dramatists have met only once, when, in November 1989, Dic Edwards attended a performance of Edward Bond's play *Jackets* at the Leicester Haymarket Studio.

In a generous response to a request for permission to publish the letters in this volume, Edward Bond in a letter to the editor of 14 February 1998 commented as follows:

> I was surprised to see that the letters go back seventeen years. Seventeen years ago must be when I first read one of his plays – but it remains vivid in my mind. He is not the only disgracefully neglected writer I know – but in some ways the neglect of his work is the most serious I know. Because I think he is a strikingly original and important dramatist – and a dramatist I have learnt from.
>
> The people who run theatres are, most of them, incompetent. They marginalise theatre by seeking a false popularity. They want to please with the anodyne and conventional. People will not go to the theatre unless it is urgent for them to go to it. In the past the greatest thinkers and creators often worked in theatre. Now it has to be trinket-sellers. But I think there is a particular problem about Dic Edwards. It goes without saying that a contemporary

playwright shouldn't understand Wittgenstein or have read Dostoevsky (who?) or Wittgenstein (how do you spell it?) – but apart from that, I think most Artistic Directors would think his work is cerebral. It is, but no more than Shakespeare's or Molière's or Brecht's or the Greeks. What is just as important about his plays is that they are also physical and passionate and dynamically theatrical. He is a real 'stage-maker' who understands the stage, directing and acting. It damages our theatre that his plays aren't more widely seen than they are.

12 November 1981

Dear Dick Edwards,

Thanks for your letter. I'm glad *Late City Echo*[1] went well – and that you were able to learn some things from it. Your observations on the audience were very good – I've sometimes found myself being in an audience and going through the same process.

The Saturn Tramp at the Bay's End[2] does seem a bit over the top – it's like two titles joined together. I always find titles difficult – I've now arrived at the point where I usually reduce them to one word, with an article before. This saves me a lot of bother!

Can I quarrel with something in your letter? 'I hope I don't let people down'. A very Welsh attitude, probably based on the idea of not disappointing the chapel? You have the usual obligations to yourself, your audience, and the truth – and following those three obligations, especially the last, you will often have to let people down. Which is the least one could ask of you! I'm sure that if anyone likes your work it's probably because they recognise its value – but not because they were the definitive arbiters or judges of what was good, and you certainly have no obligation to them!

I'd like to read, if you cared to let me, anything else you write. Good luck, anyway.

Yours sincerely
Edward Bond

29 November 1982

Dear Dick,

I thought I'd let you know I've had a letter from Rob Ritchie[3] explaining why they couldn't bring *At the End of the Bay* into the Court. Mainly a question of money (though I gather one of the cast wasn't available and they thought one of them was weak). But as the Cardiff company had no money the Court couldn't raise enough money for a transfer without cutting into their next show.

I gather that originally Rob and Danny[4] both wanted to produce the play Upstairs but were outvoted. Anyway Rob thinks there's a danger that if you don't get attached to a theatre soon your best qualities will become 'written out'. He doesn't mean that your abilities are limited! – merely that he recognized the frustration. I don't agree with this but don't see why we should disabuse Rob. It's better if he goes ahead and tries to fix something.

He was also impressed by the Made in Wales company. Anyway, I thought I'd let you know what he'd written. No doubt he's already told you all this – but I thought it might give you a post-production lift to know that there are people who recognise the quality of your work sufficiently to want to fight for it.

Hope things go well.

Best wishes
Edward

15 March 1983

Dear Dick,

Thanks for your last two letters and the play.[5] The play has been radically rewritten. It's difficult for me to read because I still have the strong impression in my mind of the earlier version. I said that in some ways I found that obscure. There might be a danger that the present play is over-explained. The use of the drawing goes to one of the centres of the play. But perhaps 'lessons' of this sort (I've used them myself) cannot be used to explain a centre? The play itself is about the centre. Lessons are about how the centre is disguised and can't be seen: the mechanisms of obfuscation rather than of reality (you see the difference). So there's a feeling that the characters are being reduced to the diagram. They also end up talking about another man and his wife who become very real. But we feel the lesson applies more to them, the other couple: what experience had Paddy and his wife had that makes them see *through* the lesson? Well, you will say, a very dramatic experience: but that experience has been reduced to the lesson, what we don't see is their learning experience. For this reason the play falls unproductively into two halves. The lesson doesn't really explain as much as it seems to do. There is so much in the play it can't contain. The procession of the dead (which is done brilliantly, the man running about in the noise), the strange relationship of the two prostitutes and their relationship to Babar. The line is a dramatic device that you may have picked up from workshops! How to be true to your own need to write? The experience that made you want to write the play – the questioning you felt – may not be contained in the rewrite. It's difficult for me to tell – because, as I say, I have the other play in my head.

You must go on. You must be ruthless and abandon work if necessary. In the end no one can help you over the top – they can only give you a leg up from below. That you have a good experience at the RSC workshop is fine.[6] But don't transfer all your creative struggle to such situations. You must grapple with your own voice. Playwriting can't be taught. This is because although there are techniques, the truth is that the creative problems are solved by the *creation* of techniques which are the answers to those problems (and these techniques then become part of other people's perceptions and practices). You have to invent new human behaviour by seeing human beings differently – in a way made necessary by their changed lives. They learn how to live their lives by living them: they are *born* in the deep end. They invent the bicycle by riding it. The privileged position of theatre (or other related arts) is that they can do this in controlled circumstances: it isn't life at the planning stage, because theatre is an element in life and although the actors' emotions are false the audiences' are not: it is life in active construction. What is a privilege is that the elements of the problem can be constructed in such a way as to force an immediate elucidation. I hope this makes some sense. I feel you could become a very competent writer – or something more. Learn inside the theatre – but more important, learn from the city where the theatre is. Beware of those who build bridges but have no river. Go on writing. Write what you want: not what others want of you by lunchtime. Does this sound arrogant? In the end you have more to give them – just as they have more to ask from you and give to you.

I'm sending you a programme from my interesting Essex nightmare[7] (in which I learned from the students but not the teachers – and this isn't a sentimental observation). The poem about Sisyphus might interest you.[8]

Best wishes
Edward

1 September 1983

Dear Dick,

I'm sorry I'm a bit late in responding to *Assumption*.[9] I've been away for a few weeks. But I've now been able to read it.

The subject is one you feel very deeply. It's almost as if you were talking about half your life. It has an air of total reality. The island and the people on it exist. This is remarkable because such enormous psychological and historical forces play on it. At times you handle the themes magnificently: the death of Paddy is an obvious example. But what you want to say still puzzles you. As you yourself know. You are unsure of your relation to your material. After all you are talking about half your life. But in all the versions I've read the end is, if I remember clearly – and certainly in the last two instances – the least convincing part. It's as if you wanted to wrap the play up. To impose some conclusion. But the conclusion seems projected from the play: not inherent in it. The solution is realistically logical but not dramatically logical. The two women say too much to each other on the last two or so pages. What they say is coherent and probably real to life. But why does Emmeline fight so strongly with or for Mary? There is a rapport between the two women but there is also a revolution and Emmeline would have other, major concerns. I can see that the characters stand for more than their birth certificates and home addresses – and so they can embody major arguments. But the characters are so real and elsewhere in the play the other dimensions are implied: Jesus/Jose/Babar/Paddy/Angels/Angelo – the larger dimensions are implied (I've of course only touched on some) but at the end implication (and the emphasis that gives) gives way to something more on the surface: the argument surfaces as if the method of the whole of the earlier part of the play had been insufficient for carrying the argument. There is a gear change. The death of Paddy is very good. The 'death' of Mary needs to be conveyed by some equivalent piece of theatre. Actually one feels it's already latently there, in the coffin, dress and so on. Perhaps Emmeline should just be very busy with her revolution – and doesn't want to waste time on this one death – adjusting the flag and so on?

I can't really help you because the play is so uniquely your own: I can only see when it doesn't work. Perhaps you should move on from 'half your life'. Perhaps the themes are as yet too incoherent for you. Perhaps you're trying to write all your plays in one – always a good sign, but frustrating for the writer. The Jose/Paddy theme has almost got lost: what effect does this theme have on Paddy? What streak in his character corresponds to Jose and how have you dramatised it? And how does Mary dramatise her relation to it?

The play is wealthy with material. Perhaps you should leave it for a while and come back to it later. This could mean you could write something else in the meantime. But don't lower your aim.

Drama is more like a juice than a scent. A juice is held in a shape: the apple, the orange. A scent pervades. But with a taste there is also a scent: so drama also pervades. But the shape is vital. With this play you are unsure about the shape. The experience pervades you like an atmosphere (this gives it its remarkable reality, for something so improbable!). But you must make it as concrete as the apple or orange: at the end one still hears the rustle of plans and the figeting of alternatives. I don't mean flippantly – the play can be as serious as chess, or as macabre as Paddy's death.

I think my advice at this stage is to write a story (my name for a play) about something that attracts and interests you – but isn't autobiographical in any immediate way: and to use all your craft on this. At the moment, it seems, that when you're not writing 'deeply' you're almost jobbing at someone else's wishes. Yet you can only develop the structural crafts you need to deploy what you (clearly) deeply need to say, by being creatively free to write in your own way an 'external' theme, a story about others. I don't know if this is clear? I don't mean that you should write trivially as opposed to deeply. I mean that you should take your deep understanding to a subject with which you can 'play' more: delight, like the surgeon, in the satisfaction of a skill. Look through a window at strangers. All this is in a way bad advice – but good for you at the moment.

I say all this because I want to see a play of yours produced under circumstances which you deserve. You have promise which was given under oath.

I shall shortly be able to send you a Methuen play script of my little play *Derek.*[10] It reads slightly but acts well. The book also includes Choruses from *After the Assassinations* – the product (or all of it I can bear to print) of my Essex University ordeal.

I'd like to see your daughter's notes about *Summer.*[11] But I don't see how you can have a fourteen year old daughter.

About Peggy's comments on *Assumption.*[12] She's over seventy and yet spends about three hours very early before dawn every morning sitting in bed and reading new typescripts. She probably has to use a magnifying glass: when she reads letters in her office she holds them an inch from her right eye, squints with it and closes her left. Its probably tough for her to read a script like yours. Frankly, your scripts are lazily produced. You should punch holes on the left and hold them together with one of those metal fasteners – I don't know what they're called. I'm glad she lectured you about your scripts! I make sure my own are better turned out: it is a courtesy. In your case I don't mind too much because they're worth reading – but imagine struggling through a badly presented script of a third rate play – which I'm sure Peggy often does. It must make her touchy on the subject. And now you can complain about my eccentric typing: I'm using a new machine and the salesman said it would make typing a hundred times easier.

Best wishes,
Edward

29 December 1984

Dear Dick,

I'm sorry to be so late in thanking you for sending me a copy of *Looking for the World.* Two of my early plays have been revived by the Royal Court.[13] I didn't want to get involved but it became necessary. I found that 'Royal Court directing' has been reduced wholly to naturalism (or perhaps in some of their works a readjustment but not a development of naturalism). This meant that they couldn't direct my plays. With *The Pope's Wedding* the problem wasn't so serious. The play is largely naturalistic – though towards the end other things happen. But *Saved* isn't naturalistic. To give an example of what I mean, the 'gang' were being dealt with as specimens of sociobiological group interaction, or power games. These exist in their scenes but the play doesn't consist of such things. When the play is reduced to these things the mechanics of the play, the dramaturgy, don't work – since they are tracking a different end. I wouldn't, for instance, be content with showing power struggles within a group: I would want to show why there are power stuggles. Naturalism asks: 'what?' realism shows what and asks: 'why?' And the 'why' obviously determines the way the 'what' is shown. So all the time I felt that my plays were being reduced and trivalised: observed rather than being interpreted: as if you look at say a cuneiform script and tried to understand how it was made (the calligraphy is derived from the stylus and the clay block) rather than what the text said. This is also *your* problem: because these directors decide what plays are staged. If they were running the theatre when I wrote *Saved* they would have insisted that I rewrite what are in fact its most revealing parts. Certainly they'd have *insisted* on dialogue in the last scene. I always had to fight for it to be kept silent in the first productions. In *The Pope's Wedding* Stafford-Clark wanted to cut the tins at the end and insisted that the solo-scene in which the boy looks at the cup and 'works' at the table, before returning to his corpse, won't work. One of the reasons why many writers who've begun their work since I started are unable to tackle the major themes which are really storming away inside their heads is that they have no chance to learn an appropriate theatrical craft. I don't mean that one should simply reproduce the skills of the past – but one must know what these are in order to develop them for one's own needs. The Court works on an approach to acting, on a human psychology, which is bourgeois, derived (no, stuck with) Ibsen: and since human psychology is to a considerable extent based on cultural-pattern – that is, humans imitate models – this can be made to work. Yet the psychology employed in acting can't be radically different to the psychology used in living. But in living, actual historical pressures cannot be avoided as they can be in the theatre: so the street-psychology is, now, more radical than the theatre-psychology. Yet my plays are based on the street psychology – they are 'art', only to the extent that they apply extended concepts to raw experience. They are not a higher experience being imposed on a mundane experience. Because of these misunderstandings – which became crucial in the case of *Saved* – I had to get involved in the productions – but always at the last moment, always in the sense of coming in and applying first aid to the body that was being operated on by the head surgeon . . . I can do this (just) because I now have some authority (the secret is, I discover, that I say what you are doing is very good but absolutely wrong and now I'm going to leave the theatre: they then ask me to stay: but that night they ring you and say don't come in tomorrow. You ask why? They say they are concerned with maintaining their own authority – their ego takes precedence over service to the actors.) But what can younger writers do? It seems to me you are prisoners of directors and funding boards. It isn't that the writer is a special sort of individual, or has a special sort of sensitivity: but he is an initiator, an immediate interpreter – and he has to learn the grammar which conveys dramatic information: he is also a creator because his work is part of the struggle by which people realise their ever-developing identity. The writer has to redefine the problem. That is his job, and when it's done others can do their job. At the moment writers are being stopped doing their job. They have to struggle with a form of directorial control (on stage and before) which is based on existing interpretations – not new ones. I see my plays being devoured by a corpse.

So you have to struggle largely unaided. I can only counsel you to be radical: to ruthlessly grasp and portray the truth: not to look to the theatre but to the city in which the theatre stands. This is difficult but the only saving discipline. Which brings me to *Looking for the World*. The play seems to have become almost a basic exercise with you: it's gone through many metamorphoses – and I've seen that you've changed as a writer in the course of them. You began with a profound social and personal concern (after all, history is experienced through psychology) and you've tried ways of making this public: in some of the ways you've been in danger of losing some of the concern – your need to communicate is so strong.

Only communicate? – but what? It seems to me that this final version is the best so far. Perhaps you have lost a little of the existential-shock of the first version I saw. You mustn't do this, you must protect your own senses: it's what Dante meant at the opening of *De Monarchia* about being fruit on the tree by the river, and not the all-devouring whirlpool. Yet you have to communicate – as he also made clear. It seems to me you've developed the skills to do this. You have handled your craft responsibly. Consider the use of the boat horn in *Looking for the World*: tourists and prisoners both coming on boats. Consider the use of the chain sounds. Or the use of noncommunication, with the audience understanding the two languages. The temple/hotel steps. And any director with sense would make the blinded man's final entry classical down the steps – like Oedipus going away with a passport. Directors will tell you that the play begins slow and that the end is melodramatic. Shit! I write in one of my introductions about the advantages of the dramatization of the analysis being melodramatic. The character of the wife has developed enormously: the man's character has been somewhat reduced, he's less complex and so presents less of our problems to us. He's now too close perhaps to that mad Greek maitre d'hotel.

I like the play very much. Even more, I admire the process of development you've gone through in the various writings. It seems to me, since our theatre directors are so limited in their vision – they're really involved in self-service – that you have a hard struggle to get produced. But you seem to be setting about this in a practical way. You are making necessary progress. I think some of the people you've worked for have been demanding that you diminish yourself. But if you are yourself *looking for the world* and do so with the existential shock at its stupidity and barbarity and that personal joy in its beauty and strength (both of which I know you have) then you are working in the only way possible for you: retaining Dante's fruitful tree and also taking your fruit to market. I'm sick of apologising to people for not having my own theatre. Perhaps you will have one before I do.

Good luck for 1985.

Best wishes
Edward

[1985]

Dear Dick,

It's been so long since I wrote to you! I've been unwell – my shoulder and arm suddenly, in the middle of last year, became very painful. It's due to sitting at a typewriter for hours on end and typing with two fingers. Learn to type properly!

I've had to use my arm as little as possible – although I've been putting together a collection of poems and songs I had lying around. I was inspired by the poem you sent me at Christmas![14]

I suppose the physical pain has been the real problem – but also the mental catatonia caused by the appalling state of the Theatre. The RSC, NT and Royal Court all headed by wasteful and irrelevant manipulators, and outside London, Theatres bleeding to death through the cuts. And because so many writers don't understand the nature of their own craft, they collapse culturally and intellectually: I've just read a newspaper article by Howard Barker (I don't know the date, I have a photocopy) in which he seems to ask for a theatre of tragedy for the élite and to praise the cultural value of pain. Perhaps I misunderstand or perhaps these ideas are only passing fancies. Otherwise he would remind me of Rilke in his castle praising the virtues of poetry.

A Young People's Theatre in Wales is doing *Human Cannon*[15] and the Youth Theatre in Cambridge are also doing it. So this has energised me again. I'm starting to think about a new play. I hope I sent you the two books of War Plays?[16]

You say you'd like to dedicate one of your plays to me.[17] That is more than kind of you. Normally I would ask anyone who wanted to do that not to – but I would be very happy if you did it. Your work has a special quality in my mind. I've read many plays by writers who want to get them performed, but yours have a visionary insight which most of the others don't. Your plays are very *basic*, when you're allowed to write what you want to.

I'm sending you a photocopy of one of my poems. It's adapted from an Indian scripture – The Dhammapada. The book has a chapter on living and working with fools!

Best wishes
Edward

30 December 1986

Dear Dick,

I hope you had a happy Christmas. I finished (more or less) writing a new play just before Christmas: so I felt pretty exhausted and just rested. Are you still working on the Wittgenstein play?[18] I've been reading a lot of and about him. After a while it becomes quite simple – this gazing into the crystal ball till you see the light.

The Casanova play[19] was something of a surprise. A side of you I hadn't before seen so clearly displayed. I found it – after having only read it once – a bit unfocused. I want to say as clearly as I can why, because its perhaps a general statement that could be made about your writing. Everything is intensely real and actual: when doors open you feel the wind – or to be more accurate (since doors are a special problem) when the glass is put down you hear the clink. And your people wear clothes. The reader feels them on them, and how the clothes touch their arms when they gesture – and as if sometimes they're too tight or too loose. This is an odd ability you have, to create the world – even when your title says you're looking for it – and I think I've mentioned it before. But there is something odd. I was going to say: sometimes the people inside these real clothes are ghosts. But that certainly isn't true: they are alive – but they have *been* dead – and brought back to life. Resuscitated by your creative energy: and this shouldn't actually happen, should it? You have a very strong power to dramatise: and this lets you get away with murder . . . In the Casanova play, what is the main plot? Is it the biography of Casanova (and perhaps Sade?). How does this relate precisely to the French Revolution (or any revolution?). I mean: precisely? Is the biography the best way of analysing the revolution – precisely? Does it happen that the life-story does this by chance? How is one involved in (wrapped up in and revealed by) the other? Precisely. And what is the relation to the rest of the plot theme about fame? How does that relate to the revolutionary theme? Each of these themes you dramatise very very well. But how do they evolve/involve from/in each other? That's what I mean by unfocused. Now (and I'm sure I've told you this before) if you can write as well as you can – you have to take responsibility for your writing. Someone who wrote less well wouldn't have this problem: at the right moment he'd produce a sentimental gesture and we'd be comfortably hurried along – but you will produce a sentence which suddenly stops one in one's tracks: and *then* one wants to know precisely where one is. Am I making sense?

If you think of the *World* play: how many hard-worked versions have there been? All work in some way, some better than others. But before you accepted responsibility for your characters you should have decided how each contained the other, how the stage-earth related to the proscenium sky. You would then have known how to use your doors! – real people would have come through them: of course they might be highly artificial, theatrical-devices – but they'd've had the reality of your stage. The prostitute in Prague speaks like one of your characters: this is fine – but how did you decide she should? Perhaps she shouldn't be able to engage Casanova in his particular stage-language – which seems designed for his own *real* life: what is the prostitute's real life? Perhaps running messages isn't such hard work – in comparison with some of her other jobs? But all the same, it's tiring: *I* feel her shoes, I'm not sure *she* does. I know *you* feel them, but that isn't the point. I'm not sure how you made your decisions at this moment: and I would know if you'd considered the problem properly, because the problem would then have been revealed in the solution (you know, the way a tired person can smile through their tiredness: it makes the smile stronger: so with good solutions one always senses that they are concrete because they carry the weight of the problem). Actually, you do what I'm asking very well – it's your sense of reality: but it still can co-exist with the arbitrary, actually it isn't that: it's more evasive. There is only one reason for this: you don't plan your plays carefully enough before you write them. You need to consider them more, design the scenes, put together the opportunities more tellingly, before you write them. Why does Casanova's description of the king's feast come when it does: why not at the start of the play – or the end: perhaps he should tell it to the woman in the street at the end? I don't know – I want to know if you'd *considered* such possibilities. I think the version of *World* is the best I've read: but it's lost something which it should also have had – the first bloom of death: fear – which fuelled the anger that made you want (need) to write the play. Instead there is terror – wonderfully articulated. The fear is in the night-chains – the terror is in the daytime 'bar room' talk between father and son. Each incidentally has a woman witness (this is your virtually innate dramatic sense). But the terror now over-balances the fear: or so I suspect – one would have to see/hear the chains scene acted. At the moment it doesn't seem a sufficient counter-weight to the talk scene. But I don't think you can now put it back in its pristine condition – from the first play – because you've gone on further with your understanding of the play. This seems as if I'm asking you to write out of ignorance. But of course I'm not at all. It's just that you need to retain the energy of your own need to solve the problem, your first need to approach these characters. You can combine the two things – and you ought to.

It is absurd that a play like *World* isn't produced. *Casanova* is more problematic, because I think it's unfocused for the reasons I've said: you haven't adequately designed the machine before you created it. *World* is now in a better state than it ever was before: but this version should've come earlier in your relationship with the play – and it could: the reality was always there, the real clothes – but you were afraid of the people. You were still looking at their faces, *trying* to look – it required a little 'staring-out'. A face-to-face confrontation with his characters isn't all right for the dramatist: he must also creep up behind, listen to gossip about them, see them as others see them – his own truthful state isn't enough, because he isn't a doctor diagnosing them and curing them: he is a dramatist using them. In the end the characters will speak for themselves – with the integrity they've managed to cling onto, or the experience of their own heroism, or the stupid comedy of their own self-deception.

There's a danger that I'm talking about my own way of working. You know I plan everything very carefully – but then I'm always taken by surprise by the spontaneity and willfulness of my characters – and I can give them their head, because I've carefully put the ground under their feet. Really, the more you plan the more they surprise you: the more you discover the more they have to reveal when the moment of writing comes. Being true to the characters means knowing exactly (precisely) what you want to use them for: then invite them to your play, and like guests at a good party they make their own entertainment. I'm sure that in general writers don't prepare enough: they're afraid of losing spontaneity or becoming thematic, and almost the opposite is true.

I hope you don't think these remarks too critical. You know I write them out of respect for you as a writer – and because your plays should be more widely produced. But I think I've put my finger on a truth about you when I say: there's a moment of death between you and your characters. If you saw a body in a morgue you might say: 'I can imagine just what they were when they lived'. That's how film makers work. A dramatist works in another way. He is a detective who sets out to commit a crime. I'm sure that in a sense a creative act is a crime against the routine and profane. It's rescuing something under glass or lock-and-key – smash and grab: but you must be prepared. At the moment you're a little like a master criminal astonishing himself with his ability as a pick-pocket.

You can cut out some odd sentences in the first three quarters of *World*. Not any particular patch – just odd phrases which get repeated unnecessarily: and also there are a few loose threads floating around from earlier drafts. And I'm not sure about the tape in the auditorium at the end. But that could easily be tried out: perhaps it does need it – certainly the blabbing would work well that way (you really are very clever). The play works magnificently and should be seen. I'm returning the typescript of *Casanova* but keeping *World* – for obvious reasons. If you send the play to any theatre remove my name – it would be a kiss of death.

28 September 1987

Dear Dick,

I've been away for a couple of months living on the river. I usually try to plan a new play there. But this year there was no sun and two lots of proofs to read. So I've come home to write.

I've read the *Wittgenstein*. You won't need me to tell you that it's an extraordinary play. All the characters are clever – with (oddly) perhaps the exceptions of the truly 'evil' ones, the Austrian klein-amtlinger. The central device of the two Wittgensteins works very well – dramatically useful and subjectively appropriate for a philosopher. You could probably develop this relationship further. I know they fight and W1 tries to strangle W2 – but what about the moments when they forgive each other, love each other? Are those moments possible? Or dramatically useful?

I thought the uses you make of Wittgenstein's philosophy to illuminate his position in life were very striking – in fact you make ideas which are often difficult, seem almost obvious. That's real theatrical philosophy (whereas *Jumpers* is theatrical exhibitionism). To understand someone in our society means to know what they're suffering from, to interpret their symptoms etc: but here you make it clear that in order to understand someone needs to know what they understand – and then theatre moves onto a completely new plane: after all, that's what *Hamlet* is about. (Try telling a social worker 'There are more things . . . etc:' it's not that I'm against social workers or the good they often do: but it's often a service, rather than a 'productivity'.)

The play is also a departure for you – but almost all your work is (the exceptions are when you submit to the group – rather than to the crowd and the society, which is what writers should submit to). So it's difficult to comment on usefully, because I suspect you'll be doing your own work on it. Really one is left only to admire and envy your ability. So I'll try and make some practical criticism. The net is very widely flung. Why does W feel guilt? Specifically, why does he relate to his homosexuality in the way he does? Would he feel guilty now? What evasions does guilt offer you in the way of salvation (Tolstoy's collection of short stories is very bad: they don't contain a philosophy to live by – although I admit the story of the two pilgrims to Jerusalem is very beautiful – but in the others there is a lot of wasting masochism and hysteria). How does Wittgenstein's guilt relate to the developing fascism in his society? That odd story about his brother being deserted by his men and then killing himself – is left dangling or leading into emptiness. How does it relate to the other brothers' suicides? This strange need for companionship, support, exchange? – Why didn't Wittgenstein kill himself – it's not clear he was even tempted. I should say: ever tempted).

These questions come from the excitement I get from reading the play. It's a bit like looking at a range of mountains. If you rewrite it, it may well come out very differently – I've had that experience of your plays already! I think it's vital for you to decide – to learn how to decide – what you want a play to do before you set out to write it. You don't have any problem about the 'doing' – the problem is in the definition of the task. Of course this can't always be decided absolutely – if it could there wouldn't be any need for plays or perhaps any form of art other than those which exercise the body and try to pack it inside the mind (which is ultimately what dance, for example, is trying to do). Art is the one undertaking in which one cannot succeed – or at any rate, success gets its great strength from its failures. (The Sistine Chapel is formally a lie – and change the technique very slightly and you'd have chocolate-box, yet it conveys ultimate human experiences, including their fragility.)

I don't know who you can send it to. I had a visit from a director of the RSC – he was telling me of his plans for Stratford next year. He seemed completely empty. He was talking about using the Other Place as an experimental venue (venue is an RSC word). But by experiment they mean tossing a coin to see if the images on the sides change while its spinning in space. Experiment needs to be based on definition, on purpose. But for them theatre is an accident which might lead to success – a 'hit'. The idea that theatre must be an understanding of society isn't open to them. They don't even have an 'RSC Shakespeare' – a company doctrine of what Shakespeare is, what is possible in his plays for us. They have all these resources and energies – and use them to toss the coin in the hope the face will change. There should be a company interpretation of what Shakespeare *is*, which naturally will develop and sometimes radically change. This means that the 'subject' of all their work would have a philosophy and a politics – and so an aesthetics and a dramatics. Instead they treat it like a consumerism – what will the fashion be this year? What colour, what noise, what new face?

The problem of theatre is that it combines cultural extremes. There is the *Oresteia* – but also the question of what shoes Orestes should wear. In this way drama reflects the practicality of society. But you can so easily forget that theatre is a 'purpose', just as you need never ask: what am I living for? And so they end up carrying out lung and heart transplants in corpses and boasting of their surgical brilliance.

If you have rewritten *Wittgenstein* I'd very much like to re-read it. I'd hoped to be able to send you a copy of my new poem book,[20] as a way of saying thanks for the play. But it hasn't yet come from the publishers.

Best wishes
Edward

[c. October 1987]

Dear Dick,

How are you? I'm sorry I haven't been in touch. I've been living on the river for seven weeks. Very chilly. But I did a lot of reading.

I'm sending you a copy of my newest play. It's just been rejected by the National. I didn't want to send it to them. There was no chance they'd do it. But my agent wanted to send it and . . . you have to go along with your agent. I'm afraid the new man at the National Theatre is a cypher. My wife thinks he's afraid – that will make him aggressive and timorous at the same time. It's these mixtures that are always destructive. Like naivety and cunning – or even worse, innocence and cunning – which is really destructive.

I begin to understand drama. Oedipus is driven through his fate in a story told by gods. At the end he is made a saint of the gods: and this sanctifies not merely his sin but also the pleasure he had in sinning – how else could he have got to Colonus? And so at the end we very much have a 'typical' family man: Oedipus fussed over by his dutiful daughters and attacked and exploited – and attacking and abusing – his troublesome sons. No wife – she's hung: presumably pleasure cannot be sanctified in women? And so the monstrous is domesticated and made habitual – the last scenes of *Oedipus at Colonus* seem to take place round a kitchen table. The general becomes particular, the dinner plates are washed up in the ocean. And Antigone goes out for her Sunday afternoon walk that will take her to her death in the stone room. I begin to understand that drama has always set out to make the monstrous acceptable and normal – because the stories are told by gods or demons – or other powers outside us – and not by men and women to each other. Truly epic drama would be the stories human beings tell to each other.

I'm also sending you some photocopies of bits I've written for the RSC's Restoration programme:[21] I haven't been to one of the rehearsals. I don't expect anything. If it's good it would be outside the run of RSC work – and why should it be? They will agitate the surface and call it a production – they will not re-produce, analyse, the play's deep structures. The metaphors of the play lie in its deep structures. A story tells you nothing. It's the telling of the story that tells you.

I think that in the past drama has always secretly justified evil – because it needed to legitimize opposition in some way, while appearing to repress it (plays after all aren't written by kings but by their poets and jesters) – just as the ruling lies always have to have a foundation or buttress of truth. You can convince people they have three hands – but only for seven or eight days; then they begin to accuse you of robbing them of their third hand – and so you have to reinvent the situation. I think evil no longer has an angelic role – as it does in Milton and Shakespeare.

I'm moved when the furies turn into guardians – in a curious way the Greeks were a time apart, because they were the first to turn stone into flesh and gods into people (not animals) – but by the time of Macbeth the furies have become their old selves. Now stories can no longer be told by gods or demons, because evil has now become too dangerous. They must be the stories we tell each other. We tell them on the authority of our humanness – which is fragile but approachable and corrigible.

Let me know how you are

Yours
Edward

7 March 1989

Dear Dick,

Sorry I haven't written for so long. Several things seemed to come up at once. I haven't written anything seriously since the middle of last December. BBC TV have filmed *Bingo* and I spent some time at the rehearsals. I found them disturbing. A TV film is seen by millions. But the work was banal and to a formula. Plays are about family rows (the Coronation Street model). If there are villains (Eastenders) they were wicked – gangsters. There is no social reason for crime. I tried to make them see that Shakespeare is concerned with the world he lived in and the relation of that world to his kitchen. No – the kitchen is his world. Direction was literally: say that line slower – raise an eye when you say that – have a good row – lean over her and shout . . . Why doesn't the banality get noticed? The camera does tricks and the editing does more tricks. There's a basic style – BBC classic Drama or Commercial-ad-video – and this is jazzed up in the direction and cutting room. Really TV is reviving the Victorian novel in its worst forms.

Then I saw the RSC *Restoration*. The same problem. Everything reduced to basic Stanislavsky (at least as he's understood to be) socio-biology. I was shocked by how little had been made of the second half of the play. The first half – set in the Restoration world – survived: but the second half, which analyses the ways people are deceived and how they help to produce their own repression and exploitation, was wasted. There was no aesthetic joy, no theatrical strength – because the director doesn't understand the world he's in. Ex-public school. He's very nice – though under pressure he tends to look for bolt holes (when one should lock the doors).

I really must try to write something cogent about aesthetics in the theatre.

The problem is still the method/treatment. The actor discovers the character in himself. Like finding an energised doll inside you. This will then animate you. You will understand why the character is an arsonist. Because he wants to be, is angry etc. This discovery will not only enable you to act the action of setting something on fire, but will also tell you how to set it on fire, how to watch it etc. But it seems to me there is a gap. Yes the character is the sort that will do the action written in the play. The actor understands this – he senses the motive inside him as if he's discovered an animal. But suppose the action is: lift the cup. It's understood why the character will do this – it's poisoned or he's thirsty etc. Then comes a further stage: how will he lift the cup, drink, set it down – in character? But it can't merely be that: because it has to be on a stage. This means that the actor must behave in a way the (real) character wouldn't – no one need see the (real) character drinking, but you must see the actor. This means that all acts are stage-acts and occur within the architecture and geography of the stage: the audience takes active part in them in a way they wouldn't with the real character. It's this social no-man's land that the actor has to occupy: the character can't occupy it – and even to say that actions are characteristic (and that this gives them their form) doesn't solve the social-stage-problem. It seems this social space puts its own pressures on the action: it's the social, shared space which shows the way things are done. But if you went to the bottom of the character wouldn't you find another social space – the pressures that went onto the character's psyche to make him what he is and act as he does? If so, then any action must reach back to the cause – the origin – of the motivation: and can't be stopped at the motivation. Literally can't – because the character can't go back into his own past – but the actor must: it's the only way he could relate to the character in the present, in the stage-space – which creates a sort of gesture which avoids the character. So in Greek drama kings behave god-like (and also man-like) because that's the origin of what they are – kingship is antecedent to their particular humanity. So the kingship is a social gestus: the space is filled with the gestus – the space between the actor and the character: which is also the space between the actor and the audience. In some ways this space is mapped out by the story. It says there will be a killing – and the story may include explanations of the killing which predate the psychological motive for the killing. But it can't do this completely – because these explain-actions themselves need to be acted – and can't avoid the space between character and actor. And probably the determinants in earlier scenes would not be the character which comes to possess the motive (to kill) but would represent the social authorities and institution-officers who convey the formative social pressures onto the character. And these pressures have to be understood in terms of external-pressures (which makes them social and political) and not in terms of psychological drives etc (they're the origin of these drives). So this means that to play a character the actor might well need to identify and use within himself an energy suitable to that of the character – but he must act gestures socially, and that means with his own energy (the two energies couldn't be split apart). To understand – have insight into – a character doesn't show you how to play it. The very social space of theatre – into which the actor must move – requires something else: because it's socially shared and signalled. It might be that there were historical times when the theatre wished to allow the character to fill the social-stage-space: either because individuality wasn't yet understood in an extended form and so the problem didn't so much as exist – and acting was then the state in which the actor was possessed by the god (or muse, or inspired). And for Shakespeare it's as if a new individuality wished to claim the space directly for itself – just as it had translated holy writ into common language. So Hamlet addresses the space as if he – and not the actor – were in it. But in our age that won't do: we couldn't base story-telling on that. We now see ourselves as objects of investigation. Analysts of all sorts, doctors, sociologists enter into our psyche – even if they find something recidivist or atavistic there – it's found by modern scrutiny: we modernly understand ancient behaviour. So do we discover the actable (and its truth) in the same way? But the space is the process of discovery (with its historical forms) and not what is discovered. So if we tried to fill the space with the discovery and not make it part of a process but merely exhibit a product – then it would be as if an ape did experiments to find the Freudian unconscious in human beings. Hardly art! The space between the actor and the character must contain the reason why people need theatre now. Why they're going to be entertained (you can't beg the question of what will entertain them, since they're entertained by the horrific and tragic as well as the droll and sentimental). The whole business of writing is to create characters and situations in which this space becomes most exposed and most in need of being entered. I think writing can't wholly designate what the characteristics of the performance should be – merely define their area and perhaps the slant of the land. We have to make the space useful and productive (I don't mean only the stage space, but the social space that exists between the psyches of the characters and the actor). But this means a new form of theatre – new theatre aesthetics.

What's happened to your Casanova play? As you asked me not to reread it I didn't. But I'm very curious to know. I think that since I started to write the theatre has never been so dead as it is now. When I was in the TV studios I looked up in the canteen – and suddenly saw Peter Hall staring at me with great intensity. And with a sort of sadness or misery or bewilderment I thought. But it may have been indigestion. I suppose he doesn't know how brutally he has behaved – I don't mean to me, but to culture!

To go back to that social-space: it's usually thought that it's good art when the writer most completely occupies the space with the character – as Beckett and Pinter wish to do. But real art is to keep it open but questioning – demanding truthful occupation. Beckett would occupy it with ironic-intensity – since the character must occupy it with the writer's energy – and Ionesco with (when you come down to it) whimsey – and whimsey always has great authority!

Let me know how you are and what you're doing.

Best wishes
Edward

30 May 1989

Dear Dick,

I'm sorry I couldn't come to Leicester on one of the two days you were there.[22] It was a holiday weekend and that was the only day I had free. In fact I almost didn't make it. The holiday traffic was so heavy that I didn't get to the Haymarket till 7.45. I thought the play began at 7.30 but I went on in hope! – and hoped they'd let me in even if it had started.

It's the first play of yours I've seen. I'm trying to imagine what I would have felt if I didn't know any other of your plays. Very surprised, I should think. As it was I *was* surprised. Basically by what a strong theatre man you are. I mean that the play takes to the stage as if it had been born on it. I shouldn't have been surprised by this, because I knew it: but to see things working on the stage is always a surprise (it always comes as a surprise – or sometimes a let down – to see how Hamlet is stabbed). The basic structure of the play is simple. The periodic return of the worker to his statement – which gets terser till its final refined form, the tersest of all. Also the simple melodramatic (in the right sense) theatrical confrontations: that the girl identifies the thief (did you deliberately not let the mother ask the girl to speak more – explain – try to give her words to repeat etc,. after she'd said 'Mummy'?) – the woman discovering that the working class woman is related to the workman etc. These are good strong moments of theatre – like Gertrude drinking the poison – and if you can't make them you're probably not really a dramatist. (I imagine that Goethe can't make them?) I think it might have been better not to have the sounds of the machines, traffic etc taped, but simply have used the hammering. I'm told that was your first idea. The rhetoric of machine noises belongs more to the SDP fascist than to the worker – perhaps the basic hammering would have been more his rhetoric? Of course the SDP fascist does own the machines – but who eventually owns their rhetoric, to whom do the machines speak? – the worker? The girl finds her language – her voice – beyond the rhetoric of tears: the language of ideas remains with the SDP fascist. Then there is the religious jargon (a sort of knocking your head against the wall) of the Mother. I'm not sure that these various types of rhetoric are finally brought together into a proper dramatic elucidation). The worker doesn't find his language – he stubbornly repeats his phrase: is this a passport to the future? – or does he read more? He presents the SDP fascist with a problem he can't solve – but that's a negative solution for the worker. The Mother's religious rhetoric is redundant, though it might enable her to make protective, money gestures to the child, still her love for the child often takes the form of an assault! The child speaks – but will she say what the worker can't: and that means will she say how to replace the SDP fascist? I had a very strong feeling of looking at an X-ray of the present time: but my image doesn't take us far enough because the doctor who looks at the X-ray *has* health-and-cure as his *competence*; as spectators we need to be able to see in the X-ray the patch which indicates disease, and the opposing patch which indicates aggressive health – cure. So I think I felt somewhat as I do at the end of *Good Person of Sezuan* – there must be another way. Actually I felt more than this, because the Good Person merely has a problem and a contrivance to solve it in an unsatisfactory way: your Worker has a problem and a stubborn force that will – ultimately – solve it. He asks for money. The money is like coins he wishes to put in the mouth of the living, that they (his daughter) may speak. I could go on because the play opens up whole strings of questions. It seems to represent our dilemma with great force.

The most unusual thing about the play is probably that it combines great emotional power with intellectual brilliance. No wonder you have something of a problem with present day theatre! – you're quite simply too good for it, and that's the top and bottom of it. I can't easily respond to the play because it makes unusual demands of a spectator, but they are very good demands. I admired what the cast had done. Of course they needed much longer to rehearse and a lot of what they did was necessarily snatching at things – I don't mean they did this destructively but merely in order to be helpful: and you know how those quick gestures with which people sometimes catch falling or toppling things can have their own elegance. So the acting was sometimes like that. But I wanted to know where they would take the play if they had more time to work on it. You need an original way of playing – not unique, because I think it's what's needed by any new, relevant theatre – it's the process started by Brecht which we have to take further. The cast should be congratulated on what they did – they served the play well. I understand they liked working with you and get a great deal of help from your involvement with them: it wasn't an author telling them how to do his play (which they wouldn't have liked) but interesting them in the problems of the play – and those are the common problems of our time and theatre.

I can't say anything more at the moment, but I'll probably return to the play. It'll certainly stay in my mind. I still think you haven't yet found a way or working that's right for what you do: you might be too speculative. Of course rewrites are necessary but sometimes I think yours are so drastic that you haven't absolutely committed yourself – that means, accepting responsibility for – what you do before you start to put it seriously down on to paper. Perhaps because you are excited and intrigued by the problems. Fair?

Nick Philippou[23] – whom you met – has spoken to me about the play. He was as fascinated by it as I was. He thought (if I understand him right) that the production might have made the play a little too expressionistic? – perhaps laying out its structures more than working through its dynamics. But that last comment is my gloss on his remark. In any case, the director should be congratulated as well as the cast – within two weeks his work was remarkable. He could easily have gone off in the wrong direction (and you don't need me to tell you that). The play leaves me with a feeling of human kindness and human desperation – and of danger. Perhaps in the end it makes the audience feel like the child? Are you shocked?

I understand they'll probably do your *Casanova* next. I'm not sure that the *Casanova* isn't too brilliant? – and whether or not you shouldn't return to the contemporary scene? God knows there are not many writers who deal with it as urgently as you can.

I've finished drafting the introduction to *War Plays*. It's some 45 pages long. I'll send it to you and I'd be grateful for any comments you could let me have. Be critical – tell me where it is obscure or redundant. I have a bit more time to work on it but want to finish with it soon.

Best wishes
Edward

10 June 1989

Dear Dick,

Thanks for writing again about *Low People*.[24] My reactions to the play were off the cuff and I haven't had a chance to read it. My copy is with a friend. Can you send me five more copies – and I'll pay for them and the postage. There's no reason why you should pay for that.

You say in its dynamic is its reason. I can understand that and it's an effect you have achieved. I certainly felt the dynamic shape. The worker's insistence became more like his hammering. I think you're probably right about having the recorded machine sounds – though I'm still tempted by the other idea. Perhaps the machine sounds should be made more abstract – somehow fusing in with the owner's political fantasizing.

I don't agree with what you say about the church language. Its power lies in its knowledge of its limitations? I think that religion is now a form of reaction and is absolute and has no sense of limitation. I can see that – although I don't think even *it* was aware of the limitations – the nonconformism of the 18th and 19th century might have been progressive: though I doubt it. But I think present day religion is wholly fascistic – a danger to the working class as much as any other right wing mythology. The idea of the modern proletariate reclaiming a language of faith which has been stolen from them isn't, I think, practical. If they had to relate only to the Bible it still would not be practical. But 'faith' is so effectively manipulated now by the media (think of the films which diabolise children) that it isn't an access of understanding but an increase of ignorance. You say what could the mother have to teach the child? And answer – that's for the future. But I think you make the audience ask these questions. It isn't simply for the future. If Leo is to win back his stolen life he will have to consider these things or – god help us – someone will start doing it for him. Anyway an audience may well want to know what you think. I absolutely accept that the play works on your level. But it does prompt more searching in the audience – indeed you say you want that, and so many of my responses to the play are of that sort. Someone said to me that the worker was put forward rather like a character in an early O'Neill play – an energy more than an articulation. I repeat that I can accept that and the play does work on that level. But when one sees a play by you one is very conscious of your mind, and one asks: why isn't he saying? – can't it be said? So one responds then by saying how can I – the audience – help the worker? This is also a good reaction. But where do we go? There should be some indication. I didn't feel the worker was inarticulate, in fact: I felt he was merely not telling us. But the more I think about the play the better I think it is. Remember we saw it after a very limited rehearsal period – and it really does need longer. As soon as I get a copy I'll reread it. Incidentally I'm probably wrong about saying it might be better to do another contemporary play and not the *Casanova*. Both would be best of all, of course. I'll write to you again about it.

I'm sending you the draft of the introduction to *War Plays*. I haven't re-read it since I last typed it. Please tell me what you think and give me any suggestions you feel would help. I've tried to make it polemical and wide-ranging – because I want to provoke theatre workers into thinking about what they do. All the teaching seems to be about a few secrets and tricks – it's as if young writers and actors were being shut up inside themselves instead of being allowed out.

The main thing is that I leave you with the excitement I felt when I saw *Low People*. I suspect that you write impetuously and without sufficient planning – this is because you have so much in you and it needs if not ordering then balancing. I think when I say 'accept responsibility' for what you do – for your characters and your audience – I may have touched a useful point for you? A creative worry?

Regards
Edward

6 April 1990

Dear Dick,

I'm sorry I haven't written sooner. I didn't read *the fourth world*[25] on the weekend I'd intended to. I caught flu. So I left it till I felt better. Your stuff isn't sickroom reading.

Like all new plays of yours, this was unexpected. My main reservation about it is the element of criticism of Highgate-socialism. All you say is true – but are Highgate-socialists worth your scrutiny? Couldn't that be left to Christopher Hampton? (No.) But what would happen if you put this argument in another setting? I also didn't quite understand Helen's background. Where did she come from? There wasn't sufficient indication in her manner of speaking. I don't mean account – I mean really heard her parents speaking in her – it's as if she was putting a glass shield between them and her, which is alright – but you need to see her fingers holding the glass. And why had Charles married her? Was he crossing a cultural barrier when he did? If so, doesn't she have (in this) something she can or must use against him in their disagreements. If she can't 'understand' Gustavo, *should* Charles have married her? I think her origins need to be more precise for the audience.

That's my two serious questions. Another is that some of the earlier scenes were a bit long – somewhere in scenes 2-4, up to 'The Lesson'. The reason for this is that the first scene is so dramatic, that it works when the play seems to move to a completely different world – and an audience enjoys the story-telling skill of this, but then it's as if they (I anyway) started to hanker to get back to it for elucidation. As *The Lesson* scene is very strong (on the page – and would be even stronger in performance) this then stands side by side with the first scene (as a dramatic foundation as the play continues) and so after that there isn't a problem.

I know I'm fantasising but the wallet stealing seems to say something about Helen's background (as if Charles would half suspect someone from her class to have once been a shoplifter: of course that wouldn't be part of his moral attitude towards her – it's just that in critical confrontations people strip themselves down to the most vulgar, naive generalisations – the 'bigot within'. But it probably wouldn't help you to go into this. It's just that one's mind goes searching for Helen's past.

Gustavo is very well drawn – very convincing. That he's an orphan seems a strange piece of absolute truth – a fact that stands, in the desert created by the meeting of cultures, like a pillar of salt. You also create his foster parents very well – though I've probably got a too rosy image of the woman. Mainly Helen describes only the man. I think the jacket should be on the hanger. It should be as if it had somehow got discarded when the man was drunk – and somewhere near the top of the scene Helen tidies it by putting it on the hanger. (Perhaps I'm being too naturalistic).

My chief feeling is (apart from the theatrical enjoyment) that of admiration for its subtlety and complexity. I've felt this complexity in your plays before. I feel that someone like Pinter creates fake complexity – if you unravelled it you'd say 'is that all? But what shall we ask of them?' I don't feel this about your complexity. Pinter uses style as a sort of camouflage. Your style is simply whatever is necessary to reach truth. The Pinter danger is that the style intrudes at the end. As the truth. This again isn't so with you. At the end everything is laid out. It's like watching people wandering round a minefield – but the field is of glass and we can see the mines. One's response is to want to go and help the people. I don't think you write many characters willingly who one wouldn't choose to want to help. (One would help Iago). I'm sure my recollection is wrong about this, but it's an impression you give. Perhaps you should create a monster? It's really good news that someone's going to publish a collection of your plays. I'd be pleased to try to write an introduction.[26] You and the publisher will have to indicate what form it should take – what areas it should cover. It's kind of you to put your Leicester Theatre poem in the back of the book.[27] I discover that one can be proud without arrogance. Think about the monster. As you have an amazing power of dealing with complexities with such lucidity – and not making them frustrating or mendacious perhaps you could handle a monster? But you must do what you choose to do: you are your own guide. In the end the most important influence on any important writer – such as you – is himself.

Best wishes
Edward

P.S. Having read the play you can imagine my wretched frustration at not having seen it. I'd like to know if the actors had any difficulty.

5 May 1990

Dear Dick,

Thanks for your letter. I have to answer it without having it by me – going on memory. You seem to think that there was a difference between my method in *Jackets* and yours in *the fourth world*. That somehow (if I state it correctly from memory) I show the processes in the characters by which they arrive at decisions – and that you don't, but somehow (in *the fourth world*) impose your own decisions. (I paraphrase.) But I don't agree with this. I had a strong sense from your play of people really struggling with their problems and trying to articulate them – making them clear not only to others but to themselves, so that they know how they should act. (It's a bit like someone committing, say, a crime – and giving a commentary as they do it – but I don't mean they are criminals, merely the unexpected sense of thought accompanying and interrogating action). I think this is true of all your characters. And then what happens is that someone (often) suddenly produces an incontrovertible truth from past experience which has been there all the time – like some rocky bed to a river – or as if, if you ran your hand along the knife blade long enough, you must eventually come to the point. I think those two things are absolutely part of your strength as a writer. I also think now that my earlier remarks about Helen may have been wrong or anyway overstated. I find she stays very much in my mind. Perhaps it was just asking something like what did Mona Lisa have for breakfast? So I've revised my reasoning: I would like to know more – but not for the reason I thought. It's as if there's a world beyond that. A world where she and Gustavo are both native-born, in the same world. In a sense she is Maria – I don't mean on any symbolic level, but more analytically. And Gustavo's replacement parents are her own parents too. Does this make sense? I mean that those relationships are the bed rock of a world – a sort of giant stone chess board on which they must manipulate their moves in order to hold onto their sanity: and as if there their identities are fixed and can only be altered when their frail autobiographical daily selves meet them. As if that's what makes the different continents real. It's almost as if in some way the characters were carved like bas-reliefs in the rocks of their continents – and that world of mutable necessity is what they judge everything by, when they sit around in their frail dress and trousers and talk about theory, which is like a minute text written on a flag! Does any of this make sense? I'm trying to tell you what the play does inside my mind.

I don't worry about the insults I get! Though I can't quite understand why people need to be so particularly insulting. It can't be to do with me personally (which is something of a relief) but to do with what I write – because I get insulted by total strangers. I think there's a lot of pretence – some people are happily bastards (they see it as their duty to civilization) but others think being nice and humane is easy – and I think I may challenge them on this too closely: that there is no difference between a god and a devil, for example – that deities solve some problems (and impose others) but they can't even begin to solve the problems of good and evil. And that you can't discount the psychological mind in politics – that materialism makes sense only because it has to be rendered in terms of other experiences which themselves create the facts of the material: that material things do not live a life of their own or have their *own* history. And so it comes down to a contrivance – or hopefully a negotiation – between necessity and free will. People are not prepared to question themselves radically enough because they want answers that solve the problems – and don't make them face the problems.

I've sent a copy of *the fourth world* to my friend Ian Stuart.[28] I hope this is okay. He liked *Low People* very much. I'll also give it to Nick Philippou. Incidentally I don't think we'll meet in the summer. I probably shan't be here.

Best wishes
Edward

5 October 1990

Dear Dick,

Here's the introduction to the book of your plays. Consider it as a draft. I can amend it or you can reject it. I thought I'd write something very general and then tie this in directly with your plays at the end. It seemed the best way I could bring out the importance they have for me at any rate. No doubt others will find other things in them.

I haven't heard from you about the meeting you had with NALGO[29] (is it?) some time ago. I presume the publication is going ahead. Though perhaps – as with my publishers – there will be several planned publishing dates before one is finally met.

I hope you're well. I've finished *Olly's Prison*[30] (the tv play) and I'll send you a copy shortly. I see from your letter that I didn't send you the Oedipus. I'll try to look it out and send it with *Olly's Prison*.

Your new stuff is very interesting. There are dangers in it. It *is* in some respects expressionistic – and expressionism must be used as a scalpel and not an engine. But I'm sure you're aware of that. I can understand why there has been a change in your writing. But your earliest plays (or at least those I read) have remained vividly in my mind because they had the force of expressionism without its windiness. You're certainly right to go ahead in the direction you are, but you must be very clear why you are going in that direction.

It doesn't strictly follow on from the last paragraph, but there were about three sentences in *The Great Society* which had bathos. I can't offhand recollect which sentences but your own discrimination in language will guide you. I'd very much like to see *The Great Society* or *Long to Rain Over Us*[31] staged. It would require a new approach by actors and director – a new access of power which couldn't be achieved at the cost of losing discipline. It would be interesting. It's such a pity that Leicester is now off the map –

the necessary experimental work could have been done there. The solutions wouldn't come immediately to the actors.

Best wishes
Edward

25 January 1991

Dear Dick,

I apologize for not responding to *Regan*[32] sooner. I have only just read it. I wanted to read it over the Christmas holiday but I had to put it off. I've rewritten the introduction to the War Plays, it's now called a Commentary . . . and I've now got the proofs of the main text (though not of the Commentary). As soon as I get the whole thing I'll send it to you.

It's difficult for me to write about *Regan* because I had the earlier version very much in my mind as I read the later version. So I have to make an effort to see the later version as others will see it. The first version was a surprise. It struck me as pre-Raphaelite. Did I tell you this? I might not, in case you might have misunderstood. The pre-Raphaelites used the iconography of the past not in order to retreat from the present – but in order to turn the present into a map, so that they could see it more clearly: and also because they felt that certain important parts of human experience (parts which had a formative effect) were so hidden in the present – under the fog of industrial smoke, you might say – that they could only find clear evidence of them in the past. There was something so mysterious about modern industry, to them, that it was almost an iron-and-steel mysticism – so they wanted to see the carpenter, the wheelwright, the potter to know what labour is. I had an impression, in your earlier version, of a search – and I found the outbursts of melodrama compelling: the pre-Raphaelites couldn't accommodate melodrama because they *did* use the past as a design of order. Industrialism was so clearly chaotic and disruptive but they couldn't see any gain in chaos, convulsion, change. It seemed that you needed to be more truthful. The impression was of a map with real people walking over it – or the design-drawings of a house with real people in them.

Some of this has gone from *Regan*. The melodrama has become simpler, the design more architectural – almost descriptive. I think that there is difficulty about your 'versions' – I must have told you this before. Each version is (usually) very different from the others – the changes aren't what are usually called improvements or elucidations. They are more fundamental – as if you needed to look at the problem from another angle. I think you can only be completely successful when you combine these various angles. Your strongest gift (or certainly one of them) is being able to create a dense and immediate sense of life – of total reality. Your people are always recognisable – they are real, solid, have nerves – but always, also, surprising – you can make them do the unexpected because they are, fundamentally, so real that the unexpected isn't the arbitrary or implausible. With a lot of writing (often modishly successful) one hears the words but when the characters are silent there is nothing: in your texts the characters go on breathing round the others even when they are not talking. You must be a good listener – but there are also times when you don't hear, but scheme. This is alright, provided the subject is appropriate. Although you create a great sense of the immediate and real I think that what lies behind your plays is a more cosmic sense. You put things in large contexts (it's why the sea was present in a lot of the early work of yours that I read). But you don't become abstract. With *Regan* and the subject of taxes an audience inevitably thinks of the poll tax – and the relationship between that and the vision of the great society would probably be worrying for it.

I can imagine an agitprop play that would look at taxation historically – going back to Tyler, looking at the American revolution from the angle of taxes, looking at taxes for nuclear weapons and so on. And the historical continuity of the problems would be the larger context. But your basic need as a writer is to go one stage further: not merely to induce action but to examine the truth of human action, the need to be human. This needs to be nailed down to an immediate, real situation, probably – the philosopher reads the newspaper. But if you 'allow' yourself 'versions' isn't it because you are more interested in the problem than in communicating it? What in the first version of *Regan* was so 'unimportant' that you could drop it from the second? And if it was droppable why was it in the first version? What was it communicating there? It might be that I misunderstand. Often when people write about my plays I know they haven't seen them – they have only read them. That's my case here. Seeing your play at Leicester was a revelation to me because, although I already liked your work, I didn't realise how good it was: its sheer force. And I know there's a lot in the new version of *Regan* that will work more powerfully on the stage than it can on a page. But perhaps it's wrong that it should work powerfully? – it might avoid questions that need to be asked. Why is Thomas Rakestraw an 'idiot'? And why are you closer to him than the other characters? Within the idiot's head there must be a great pool of nothing that the idiot doesn't know about: but you, clearly, don't have the privileges of idiocy. I feel you know about the place where the idiot, and the bored person, and the self-satisfied person, can't go. But I suppose another reason for not going is fear. And I wonder if your versions are not really the footprints of fear?

This is very impertinent of me – but I've known you long enough, not to have the right to be impertinent, but to take the risk. The problem you have in communicating is to do with your 'versions'. Why should an audience – or an actor – be open to a particular communication – when the next communication might be the important one? I'm repeating myself – you don't take your writing seriously enough. You are, in a good sense, one of the most serious writers I know – but you don't take yourself seriously enough as a writer. Fear is also fascination – and you are fascinated by your themes and people. Real fear has nothing frightening about it; and then to look at what's fearful isn't a compulsion – or a duty or a necessity, or not only these two things. It's something one owes the innocent. I shall stop or I shall begin to ramble. These are just the ideas *Regan* provokes in my head. I've only read it once and I'll read it again. Of course the play should be done – it needs great simplicity but strength, the actors must know what they're doing. And it needs time. I haven't said how good it is: the face at the window, the disguises, the sickness (mental and physical), the knots between love and hate, the sleepers who watch. But your way of avoiding writing is to write.

Let me know what you think.

Best wishes
Edward

13 February 1991

Dear Dick,

Thanks for your letter. My reply is a bit late (as usual). The snow must have looked beautiful in Wales. Snow needs hills.

I'm sorry if my last letter sounded angry. I didn't mean it to. I wouldn't have any right to be angry – even if I were I don't think I'd be impertinent enough to express it. Perhaps I sometimes write to you in a careless – but not thoughtless – way. If so it is because I think I have some feeling for your plays – they speak to me directly (though 'speak' is not the right word: they are very visual and physical). Really people need to see your plays not merely read them, and that goes for me too.

I might be wrong about your 'versions'. It's just an impression I get. I think you – when you write – may be handicapped by not having enough of your plays performed often enough – to see them in different versions by different actors and directors. I don't think either of the two 'versions' I have read of *Regan* are 'bad' in any way. Perhaps the second version clarifies certain of your intentions which were unclear in the first version. But it seems to have required a change of gear, a change of approach. The texture of the second version is different. It is more abstract (not in a bad sense). The first version seems to be more desperate – more a struggle with immediate danger. The second version is perhaps shrewder, subtler – with more theatrical authority. It's more controlled. And yet it's also more mysterious – because the struggle has been recollected in tranquillity (not the right word but it'll have to do).

But this creates a problem. You are not a writer whose talents work best when they are dealing with specific, circumscribed subjects. I think implicit in all you write are the very widest questions – though they are often seen in an immediate, domesticate 'occasion'. The holiday hotel might be in a Cook's catalogue – but the sea and its gangsters, before the balcony, is infinite – the bay is full of tigers. Wozzeck is based on a particular run-of-the-mill (to be impertinent) murder – and yet the play opens out onto the broadest of questions. It begins with doctors, military officers, experiments, men in killers' (army) uniforms who are not allowed to kill except to orders, an obsession with the dead which always indicates that the living are in trouble) and the sun and night. Your plays remind me of this. (Is my impression right that your plays tend to have doors, windows, balconies in them? – is there a ladder in Wittgenstein or has that just seeped into my recollection because of the metaphors?) Wozzeck tries to contain its expansiveness in romanticism – as if the world just needed setting to the right, melancholy tune. Of course that way of containing the experience isn't appropriate for you. Perhaps somewhere you want (either in order to communicate, or for yourself) to reduce the second world to the first? – the expansive to the immediate. But you couldn't just return to the first versions – the second stage is also needed. That would be true to real life, of course: we have to catch the train on time. It means that in a strange way you tend (and I don't mean more than tend) to reverse the proper order of your versions: the first versions tend to be the revised ones, the latter versions tend to be the drafts. I can't be more impertinent than that, can I! Does this make any sense? I really do write it in good will. You don't need my advice or opinion – you need productions. Our present theatre is too trivial to understand you – but audiences would.

Best wishes
Edward

11 April 1991

Dear Dick,

Thanks for your letter. I already owed you a letter. I haven't thanked you for your 'language' poem[33] – which, as you suggested, is about more than language, or in any case more than the differences between two specific languages. It's stuck in my mind in a curious way: like a cube with six sides of glass, physical but also non-physical. I'm deliberately not reading it at the moment – it seems to be taking on a life of its own in my mind. I'll reread it later.

Your new job sounds good.[34] Of course, the disadvantages will appear in their due time . . . This isn't pessimism. There are always drawbacks, and there have to be ways of turning these into advantages – or if they really *aren't* that, then knowing how to respect the wounds they make. I don't mean Nietzsche's idea of illness being in some way healthy – which I think in his case is just a tragic foretaste of madness – Nietzsche couldn't cope with the demands of being healthy. It's more like learning to live with one's own innocence.

I'm sending you a copy of *War Plays* with the revised Commentary. Your comments on the draft were a help and stimulus. I hope you find something useful in the new Commentary.

My news: I'm pretty sure BBC won't film *Olly's Prison* – I'll know definitely in a few weeks, but I've more or less already been told. ('We'll hang you IF we can find a rope . . . as the judge said.) But I've got a production of *Summer*[35] on in Paris (Nick Philippou saw it by chance and said it was good). An Italian company is going to do *The Woman*.[36] They're using a published translation, which is – I think – good. A relief, because translations are a nightmare. The main thing is that we both go on writing. 'Culture' is changing almost by the moment – the media, technology, the wars, the booms, the depressions . . . It's as if the processes of culture are themselves becoming empty and dehumanizing. A skeleton haunts the land looking for its flesh. The extraordinary media circus with the Kurds – their Exodus is a consequence of 'our victory'. The puppet-like Major and the hermaphrodite Thatcher. The old Black and White villains of Hitlers and Mussolinis and Churchills and Roosevelts have been replaced by an animated toy shop: our politicians are salesmen offering us cut price 'democracy'. I don't want to be a romantic, but more and more it's only when I talk to children that I'm confronted with the urgency and possibility of being human.

I'm also sending you a passage I found in Melville's *White-Jacket*. It's very striking. Melville was really a man without a country – for all his American classic status – and without a language: he sicks-up dead languages of the Bible and the Jacobeans. But when he is involved in the others' problems (and not his own, even if they are the means by which he becomes involved in the others') he writes with an astonishing directness.

Your new company is a *base, which all writers need*. Having found a base I advise you to dig downwards.

Best wishes
Edward

12 November 1991

Dear Dick,

I'm sorry there's been some sort of disagreement between you and the theatre you're working at.[37] I don't know anything about the disagreement but it would be very sad if people can't be reconciled. You need a continuing, reliable situation to develop your work. It's challenging but only because it meets the complexities of situations – it doesn't confuse or mystify them. I read a notice of *Regan* which made the point that it's the sort of play theatres should be doing for local communities. So often theatre patronises them and your work doesn't. I think actors and directors also need your sort of work – otherwise skills are lost in comforting and easy tricks. Audiences want more than that – the trouble is audiences don't trust the theatre anymore! If the audiences don't trust us we're wasting our lives working in it as well as wasting our audiences' time. It seems to me you're a writer worth trusting – it shines through your work and gives it its great force. I hope people can come to see this.

I'll let you have the poems I'm doing for the National Theatre as soon as I've made good copies. Keep well. Doing good things is never easy!

Best wishes
Edward

12 February 1992

Dear Dick,

It isn't the first time I've had to apologise for being late in writing. Things have been busy – with the stage, TV, life and a death. I didn't want to write till I'd had time to quietly read *Ecce Homo*.[38]

It is a very particular play. I don't know anyone who writes like you. Some time ago – about Wittgenstein, I believe – there was a strong new direction in your writing. This play combines sensuality and intellect in a very unusual way. In the end I suspect neither is the most important thing,or rather they are important in contributing to something else. I've only read it once. I saw that a very careful argument was being made out and pursued with responsible logic – in a way I felt there were two arguments (this isn't the erotic-and-intellect point) and that I needed to put them together: that was the 'audience work'. This will be much clearer in production. I shall have to read it again. But the argument is profoundly radical: this is the 'something else' I mentioned, it is a radical examination of our present social structure. And it does this through three people and one two-in-one room (apart from the very end). So there is a feeling of leisure (which I imagine there always *is* at the height of a revolution) and yet great urgency. This comes from the terror – and from death. There seems always to be a child on stage . . ? A barren woman and an impotent old man. But I think old age always wears short trousers and little dresses. It also swings between science – a laboratory table – and art: the music of Bach. There is a great stillness in the play which I haven't yet penetrated. It must be done very simply and strongly. Each thing must be clearly defined – each element – and keep within its boundaries: so that it can reflect the other worlds around it – as in the side of a globe you can see images of other globes. The play will tempt bad direction . . . and (though less easily) bad acting. Because it is, after all, also a farce – as well as being a tragedy. We might as well realise we are just rejects from the primeval sea, with the biological ambitions – and impedimenta – of ancient forms of life long since dead: and then we can find our simplicity and grace and accept the responsibility of being human. That's what I feel about *your very profound play*. I don't know what critics will make of it – I know that audiences would understand it, but they may have stopped going to the theatre – and who would blame them? I'll try and make a helpful suggestion: you could trim the, say, first third a little? Some of the argumentation between Casanova and Costa? Some of their witticisms seem a little strained – which is another point.

I'm sending you a few copy letters to keep you informed of what I'm doing – or rather what I have had done to me! *Company of Men*[39] is being done in Avignon this Summer – and *Bingo*[40] in Le Havre (I met the translator and he seems really intelligent). And there's stuff on in Germany. *Olly's Prison* has been filmed and is now being edited. It was an interesting, frustrating stupid time. I understood the problems of acting much better. There is *no* appropriate method of acting my plays – or I suspect yours – at the moment. It will have to be created.

I hope you are well. I don't know if I'll be able to get to Glasgow to see the play.[41] I'm going to write a play for BBC TV education service. And then I want desperately to write for the stage. *The Sea* at the National Theatre is rather dull[42] – the director drowned in the shallow end.

I haven't even asked how your problems with the Theatre worked out. I am a very remiss friend – you must forgive me.

I hope you and your family are well. *Ecce Homo* is very good.

Edward

27 December 1992

Dear Dic,

I read *Alma*[43] on Boxing Day, so it counted as a Christmas present. I can see the play was influenced by your 'vastation', if that's the word for it. The play seems to have a scrupulous exactness – and points to something behind itself, but not in a worrying way – it doesn't make the play feel incomplete, it gives it precision and definition. But the play is totally unclassifiable. Your use of farce in desperately serious situations reminds me of Wedekind in the original *Lulu* tragedy. I think in performance it will be more painful than it reads. It seems complete and entire in itself – and yet I think it is probably a transition play which marks a journey to somewhere else. In your plays there is usually a sense of dread – but not in this play. Which is odd – it gives it its sharp, crystal quality, as if any suffering can be borne because the farce will keep it at a little distance. You have replaced your more usual darkness with light. Of course writers can see in the dark . . .

The Court should do it, but they won't.

I used your strange experience[44] in my workshops at the RSC – as an example of the working of imagination, that it had its own dynamic and rational grammar beyond our socialised reason. It's as if your mind kept something back so that you could write *Alma*, in order for the writing of *Alma* to give you access to what had been held back. Does this make sense? I feel you have been given a new source of creativity, of knowledge. I think, also, that you have to return to the characters of your earlier plays – I don't mean exactly the same characters, of course, but to their reason for needing you? It's as if you can't go out through the doors any more but must climb out through the windows – into the vision of what you see, into the vertical maps (which is what windows are). Doesn't *Alma* at the end – grasping two dead bones – give birth, rebirth, to your need to be a writer? This play is so amazingly confident and accomplished, it can only be a new beginning?

Best wishes
Edward

[1993]

Dear Dic,[45]

Thanks for your letter about *Tuesday*.[46] There are a handful of people whose remarks on my plays I find useful and respect. You're one of them – and you have, in this context, the advantage of being a fellow writer. What you say is illuminating and stimulating. I'm sending you a poem as a thank-you! After I'd written it I heard a spokeswoman for the UN High Commission for refugees on the radio news explaining that relief convoys in former Yugoslavia are shot at by people of all the religions and nationalities involved. She said: 'People do not want the children of their enemies to be fed'.

I've revised *Tuesday*. I've made it clear why the soldier tells one story to the girl but another to the father: the first story is the soldier's and the girl's 'secret', they won't trust it to the father because he'd be scornful. I've also altered the order of the end. Now when the father goes the girl talks first about the incident with the gun and then about the child in the desert – so you have a sense of her mind broadening out to other people's problems as a consequence of her own problem (the incident with the gun). Now it goes from the particular to the general, before it closed in from the general to the particular and might suggest a looking obsession or narrowing. The BBC building is strange.[47] The windows are permanently sealed (except in executive suites). You enter by using an (issued to staff) electronic gadget which works the barriers. You can't control the level of heating.

All lights go off automatically at 8 p.m. – if you're higher management you have another electronic, remote-control gadget – you press it at the eight and hey-presto! All the (huge) floors are open-plan – people build little shelters for themselves with cupboards, files etc – like refugees from space and time and prying eyes. The centre of the 'complex' (which is the name for a building, but also for a state of mental distress) is a garden (quasi Japanese of course) under a glass roof. I call the garden 'the cemetery'. I'm sure in twenty years they'll be burying executives in it as a sign of special favour.

Yours
Edward

25 May 1993

Dear Dic,

I've finally finished *Tuesday*. It was an odd experience – struggling with an institution. It has a will of its own and the institutionees become its tools.The institution wills and does certain things and this becomes almost the institutionees' character. So when you ask for something different they say: No this is how it's done. And if you ask for it again they panic and almost go to pieces – they have become part of the institution by which they live and so you are threatening their actual being. Of course some of them can be enticed away from the institution's will and then they become creative and enthusiastic: they begin to understand what they're doing – and then they can teach you (the newcomer) many new things. But often the institution wins: after all, the skeleton is armed with its own bones. But I was able to get quite a lot of what I wanted. BBC Education are showing it in three separate parts over three weeks in June (4, 11, 18 – all at 12.00 to 12.30 in the morning). Please try to see it and let me know what you think.

I think you've written the libretto very well. I found myself wanting to sing it as I read it. You've constructed it with real artistry and skill. I hope the composer understands how to use it – it made me wish I could compose music. A couple of lines I didn't like: 'Peter is forever dead'! No he isn't – so I understand the irony but at the time it seems bathos. What about 'dead forever'? – or 'dead dead dead'? Probably neither are any good. 'Dead forever' would be better than 'forever dead'. It would bring home the shock of the word dead. Second: 'My blood is like a solution of hot spices'. Solution seems weak – its sub-meaning of solving the problem doeen't help. And solution as a state seems undescriptive. What about 'a boiling' or 'a seething'? as if the boy had been boiled in her blood? Finally I thought the wife is over-explicit when she talks of 'these mystical forces'. She interpretes the story too intellectually at that moment – the story itself is telling us more than her explanation of it or her commentary on it. If she could describe her feeling of being trapped more viscerally and less cerebrally. But these are just suggestions. I really enjoyed reading it – it's beautifully told. A guarantee of the rightness (legitimacy? – justification?) of the complexity of some of your adult plays is this simplicity which shines through them. It means that even your most cerebral plays could never be mere intellectuality in the way Tom Stoppard's are. The complexity is truly simplicity joined with depth.

I'm now free to start writing plays again . . ! All the *War Plays* are being done at Avignon next year: this year they're doing the first stage production of *Olly's Prison*. And we now seem to have good German translations of *Men* and *Olly* so things aren't too bad. I'm sorry it's been so long since I last wrote. The BBC was full time!

Regards
Edward

P.S. I did send you the printed version of *Olly*, didn't I? – and thanks for letting me read *Tree*.[48]

9 June 1993

Dear Dic,

I hope you're well. Actually you owe me a letter but I'm writing because of the enclosed slip. A composer Param Vir (? – I don't know him) wants a libretto. David Rudkin suggested me and it's tempting. But I know I must concentrate on some more stage plays – telly and a not-to-be-made film have taken up too much time. So I thought of you. I admired very much the *Tree* libretto you sent me – the situations and words seemed really crafted for music: not the stuff of some boring middle-class novelist indulging in the musical art . . . I think young people would get a lot of situation and excitement out of anything you wrote, so I'm writing to you on their behalf.

If you want to pursue it further let me know. I'll contact Tom Erhardt[49] and you and the composer should exchange texts and tapes to see if you'd like to work together. If the suggestion has no interest for you I won't give them your name.

This letter is brief – but at least to the point.

Regards
Edward

You should write about your strange experiences on the cliff – trying to relearn the forgotten music.

13 September 1994

Dear Dic,

I took *3 Deaths of an Idiot*[50] away with me on the boat. I got back yesterday. I'm sorry I haven't written sooner but it's difficult to write letters on the boat.

The play was unlike the play I had expected. Which doesn't surprise me. It also – I suspect – reads differently from how it will act. The language is mostly simple and lambent with an occasional Molotov cocktail thrown in. But the simplicity comes from discipline and a thorough understanding of what you are doing. But those who don't already know your work need to remember how passionate much of it is. Of course this is often very clear. But there is almost an hallucinatory effect in which extremes of emotion are being conveyed with great simplicity and things from the depth are shown almost matter-of-factly on the surface. Even when you hurt you do it with circumspection. Reading the text was like listening to the curtsy of a great soul.

And these remarks are true also of the plotting and of the story. All good plays are like maps unrolling. And the eye has to wander backwards and forwards to understand where one is and is going. You deal with a wide range of subjects but each development helps to bring the whole map into presence – the details reflect the whole. It is strange to realise that the play takes place in a night club and a few small rooms – but this spaciousness is in all your plays (and really comes from the range or your mind): I remember in the first of your plays I read that there seemed to be a sea outside the windows. And here the little rooms are surrounded by mountains.

The play must be unique to its own genre! – and I would very much like to see it staged. It would act very well – it's very graphic. The chairs work like much of your language: it's as if they under-cut, laconicize, the passion – but really all your objects are like fingers curled on triggers.

It's written with great skill and authority. I thought (I've thought this before about some of your plays) that, say, the opening third might be cut a little but I could very easily be wrong. Perhaps like the chairs it's necessary. I also felt – strangely – that perhaps I didn't need the final confessional scene, that it could end with Grace and Walker outside the chapel (p. 132). This is because I knew that the map – a white sheet with lines and hieroglyphics unrolled under a light – contained the sites of a disaster. All maps looked at as closely as that do. But it's like buried treasure – when you've located it on the map is there any point in digging it up? – that's what the characters do, not the author (if you see my point: you consciously manipulate storytelling and so we relate to the author as well as to the characters). It's almost a little grotty – as policemen congratulating themselves as they dig up bodies. No doubt I'm wrong about this and the bodies do have to be faced – perhaps the map does have to suddenly become dark. Usually you protect us by a vicious humour (it has to be vicious to be protective in the world you describe) and it can't be there in the dark scene. I know I have to trust you: and anyway it would all be clear in rehearsals what was needed. I have other news to tell you but I want to leave it to another letter. Now I just want to thank you for letting me read the play and tell you how much I admire it.

Best wishes
Edward

River Wissey
1 August 1995

Dear Dic,

I don't have to apologise for my long silence because you know the only reason for it would have been that I was dead or busy. On this occasion it was the second.

Thanks for sending me *Utah Blue*.[51] It's a strange, powerful play. You can't simply read the dialogue, you have to see it all the time – then its real power, its existential exploration, becomes obvious. It isn't about death, I think, but about living: because Gary Gilmore is 'dead' he's able to look at his life with objective passion – not abstractly – and this makes him everyman, everybody (unintended joke!). I would like to have seen it staged but it doesn't matter, I can run a good production in my head: not the ideal production because for that you need the idiosyncratic insight of actors – and I think the text would find something rivetting in any group of actors.

I hope the operas are an interesting experience. Henze[52] had a tantrum with me – he behaved like a prima donna – because of his mis-use of the last text I wrote for him (he turned my 60 minute skit into 3 hours of Wagner . . .) but I miss not working with musicians.

The RSC are doing *Bingo*. I'm told (by my wife and friends) that the production is bad – I shan't go to see it. The RSC have been really irresponsible in the way they've handled my stuff – they learn nothing. Noble is bland and trivial – he turns everything into wedding cakes and merely boasts about the number of tiers (?spelling). But I don't mind – things are going well abroad. *Tuesday* opens in Paris in October and there are interesting things coming up in Germany. And an Italian *Summer*. But most interesting is the number of amateur productions: this year *Sea, War Plays* (complete), *Cannon, The Woman, Saved*[53] and others. Nothing will repair the professional UK stage till writers are fully integrated back into theatre. Your text makes demands that Stanislavsky, Brecht, naturalism classicism, can't use – they could have a shot at aspects of it but they wouldn't be able to fully use it. The director of *Bingo* just didn't know how to use the text – and because he couldn't resort to RSC tricks there was nothing there. But when he does an RSC Shakespeare – or Arthur Miller – he's enormously successful though I'm told the productions are empty and futile. They all carry out first-class chiropody on wooden legs. I've written some odds and ends – for SCYPT,[54] various programmes, and some Notes on Imagination – when I get off the boat in September I'll send them to you. I'm enjoying myself thinking and reading and I've been adopted by two greylag geese as well as the usual swans. I hope you are well – have you remembered your 'visit/vast/ation'? Your writing has entered into a new orbit. I'm not bitter about our present theatre, but it's shameful that directors are so far behind you.

Forgive my brevity but boat-letters are brief.

Regards
Edward

By all means use my letter for the publication of *Regan*.

5 October 1995

Dear Dic,

I'll be interested to read your reworking of *3 Deaths of an Idiot*. I'm not at all sure my comments about the end were right – it would be different in the theatre to what it is when you read it. Perhaps the voices in darkness are needed.

Your reference to Brecht intrigued me. We're just back from the Berliner Ensemble. We went over the Brecht house, read from his books, stared at his typewriter, stood before his bed and walked to his grave. It's very beautiful. I feel I ought to write an interesting letter but we both had heavy colds when we got back and I'm still recovering – it's my first day up.

The Ensemble production of *Olly's Prison* was frustrating. I like and admire Palitzsch[55] and I respect his work; but he's applied Brecht formulae in places where I thought they didn't help. I ought to write about this more fully. If I can get round to it I'm going to write a sort of commentary on the play – not too long – and send it to my German agent to be given to the directors of the other productions (I think there are two planned). I want to make it general but start from the Berliner Ensemble production. I'd like it to be a general guide to handling my stuff – showing how it is put together. I'm sure our big probems – yours and mine – is that we don't have a theatre where we can show what we meet. Directors are either spiv-gangsters – or are well-intentioned but bewildered and then self-defensive. We can't show what modern theatre is – what modern playwriting requires. The world moves on and the theatre is left behind.

The RSC don't want to do *Coffee*.[56] I'm sending you a copy of a letter from Adrian Noble to my agent in which he tells him that the RSC don't want to do it. My wife said the letter was obscene – and Ian Stuart called it a 'vile letter'. It is, at any rate, a silly letter.

I'm also sending you a copy of Vol 1 of my letters[57] – together with the errata slip . . .

I don't have any good advice for your 'creative writing' course.[58] I suppose: work on their texts – ask them if X is exactly what they mean – and then how could they make it more X – and what happens if you do Y to it – so that they get a tactile feel of writing. The more difficult thing is to give them access to their imaginations – to help them to see that their imaginations must be provoked by what's seen in reality – and not fished in for its own sake. Imagination should be like a window that is broken by a stone thrown from reality – Imagination is then released. But don't search for it: search for the stone. Soon the Imagination will then search with you. A year seems a long time to wait for Theatr Clwyd to do *3 Deaths*[59] but it will pass too quickly. I'll write about Berlin when my temperature subsides. There were tanks outside the synagogues – painted the municipal green they used to put on the lower half of school corridor walls.

Best wishes
Edward

P.S. There is an annoying mistype on p 28 of your copy of *Coffee* – in the 5th speech from the bottom Gregory should say 'Aint that *coffee* ready yet?' And on page 40 – the second lot of directions should say, 'puts sugar in his *coffee*' (not tea!). I thought I'd add something to West's lines so that it records 'The nipper I shot first off'.

11 March 1996

Dear Dic,

I'm answering your letter to me of 1 Dec last year . . .

Things have been busy. I've spent time trying to help threatened TIE companies – the Coventry Belgrade and Big Brum. I did a one-off workshop for IDEA with Big Brum actors. I don't like doing one-offs, it's tempting to be clever or to give people a 'good time', just out of self-defence – difficult to do anything else in just three hours. And there've been proofs and letters – and work with translations – there's a new French translation of *Saved* (I have confidence in the translator) but a mess with the German translator of *Coffee* – in the end she gave it up after I'd said I'd lost faith! – she just didn't understand how play dialogue works and had got the dramaturge of a prestigious German theatre to say she was right and I was wrong. All very silly. German dramaturges are no better than their English cousins. Well, that's in the past (for the time being).

I've read *Lola Brecht*.[60] You say it's about war but I think you'd agree it's also about peace. The strange state of mesmeric sub-violence we live in. People find non-meaning in their lives, objects don't have a function anymore. It's like being in the middle of the Atlantic Ocean and trying to feel the bottom with your feet. The political leaders are zombies or puppets or clowns or sinister. And we're stranded in a strange hotel by a railway line. I feel the play gives the feeling of contemporary life (of the lives of a lot of contemporaries). History strangely confusing, the mystery of the present not even intriguing – Kafka would die of boredom. And people's own passions swimming around in them like sharks attacking them. And everything as decorous as a shop window. I think the play gets all this. And I don't accept what you say about the non-realism of the characters. In a sense that's so, and yet they are immediately recognisable and their presence has consequence, they're not arbitrary. You say they're the tools of discovering what's real – but aren't real people that anyway, doesn't reality charge them its fees every so often? It's – as usual coming from you – a strange play: it's like seeing an island of earth floating in the sky – I've felt something like that before when I've read one of your plays. As if the foundations of existence were exposed and as if the earth were trying to hide its exposed nakedness.

It ought to be a recognisable play to any theatre director. More writers are writing of your world. But look what's happened at the National Theatre – they've appointed the most useless of professionals – an aged whizz-kid.[61] I've agreed to direct *Company of Men* at the RSC Pit later this year – really because I felt sorry for my agent, who works hard and I usually say no . . . But I'm not looking forward to it, have no conviction about it. But I'll do it. It's worth contacting foreign agents. Their stock response is: Has it been done in the UK, if not why not . . .? But it's sometimes possible to break through. I think, if you like, it might help a little if I sent the scripts with a covering letter? I'd be happy to do this if you wouldn't think I was interfering. I suggest Rudolf Rach in Paris and Suhrkamp in Germany. Perhaps you could send them two scripts – you ought to choose these.[62] Does this sound a good plan? It's disgraceful that the UK theatre doesn't support you – and other – writers more. The problem is, even when they put plays on they don't know how to do them (at least not often). I haven't had a new play produced in the UK (stage) for 14 years – and I wish it was going to be longer: that is absolutely true. But of course I was lucky to make a break-through abroad before the UK theatre collapsed. I'll have copies of *At the Inland Sea* soon (it's my short TIE play) and I'll send you a copy.

Best wishes
Edward

River Wissey,
30 July 1996

Dear Dic,

You'll gather I'm away from home on the river. The new version of *Idiot* is waiting me at home. I shan't be able to read it till September. I understand that Suhrkamp haven't yet been able to place any of your plays. I've also heard from Brigitte Landes (who translates my plays into German) that the German theatre is in a running-down state. She says it reminds her, now, of the British theatre. I think Suhrkamp will go on trying – I'll encourage them to. I trust Hans-Jürgen Drescher[63] – he will do what he can.

The situation is frustrating for you. I have been fortunate because I was able to get a finger-hold on the cliff face while theatre was still energetic and enquiring. Now Peter Hall has been appointed to run the Old Vic – and Trevor Nunn complains about the state of West End theatre: he directed *Les Miserables, Starlight Express* – and I think *Cats* and other wall-paper. It is like a pimp complaining of prostitution. But isn't this just the truth of our times and *why* we write?

They don't burn our books. They don't put us in prisons. They don't send us into foreign exiles. It's true that I have some productions – but the number shouldn't be exaggerated. And I have a few very good and loyal friends who try to make my work known. But I can still sympathise with your situation: I remember the years when I was not performed. The neglect is a paradoxical sign that what we write is needed. I can only believe that in time people will make that need known.

If all good drama is the search for justice – is the confrontation of innocence with corruption – then our experience is our lesson. It must teach us to write better – to write more exactly and more passionately. We can complain of our lives – but the lives of the characters we invent are worse than ours: and we have a human need to record their lives, to give them language. To give language to the fictional sounds a bit like making rocks and rivers talk! Well if we have to, do we listen? It is not enough to write our characters, we must listen to what they tell us. Our first responsibility is to be their listeners. If we don't do this completely, when the time comes for other people to listen to them – we will have lamed our characters, they will not speak what is in their lives. Of course there are the nightmares: the hunched figure sitting in the drenching rain and writing the epitaph in ink on the stone. Well people will come and see the blotched marks or even, if they have to, look at the blank stone and think of pages. After all, we write so that others may learn to write. This isn't a consolation because there is no consolation. No one believes our books and so there won't be any stained-glass memorial windows. We just write – all this occurs to me because of spending a little time at the RSC – which is a house of idiots in which some decent people work among the half-dead. My life would be less if I didn't know your work. I am angry that the theatres don't use it as often as they should. I suppose they are the exiles and the prisoners – the idiots' house.

Best wishes
Edward

8 November 1997

Dear Dic,

I've been away in France and busy with other things. This is my excuse for my usual delay. There seems so little time and hardly *any* time to write!

You are on a long journey. Certainly as a writer – and that must mean as a person. The eighteenth and nineteenth century travellers – going into the darkness of Africa and the mists of Asia – explored what was already there. But they also discovered themselves, found themselves mirrored in an alien terrain and culture. They found out who they were – but were probably prisoners of the cultures they left. I think that when France rejected Rimbaud at home they mutilated him when he ran away to Africa: he died among nuns, which Bacon said was the worst way to die. But all this was already there, even for Rimbaud: he traced over an existing map.

This isn't possible in our time, we're too self-conscious. When I look back over your plays I feel that you are not exploring what is already there. If a dramatist – a writer – travels it isn't over land but in time. The land traveller walks over what's there – but I feel that time is behind you, struggling to catch up with you. Struggling because time is awkward and trying to balance bundles and loads from the past. I have a feeling that you have gone ahead into time and that means not discovering as the land traveller does but creating. And for you there can't be any turning back. A land traveller can turn back – even when he or she is wounded they can be taken by litter and boat and train back to their home, as Rimbaud was. But when you have gone ahead of time – as I'm sure you have you can't turn back because you cannot get back into the past: it is shut against you. This is so even if you are travelling under impressions of the past. Because the impressions are not memories – the impressions have projected you – like a projectile – ahead of time. Physically this isn't possible – it doesn't obey any laws, Newtonian, Einsteinian, quantum – but creatively it is so. Memory and chance are the only materials we have out of which to create what is new. Remembrance of Things Past – this is a false guide, like being asked to remember your death. But you as a writer exist beyond death, work beyond it. If anyone were to know everything they would immediately become limited – they would know the ultimate dimensions and thus knowledge would be their prison. There must be an element of this in creativity – I don't mean the retrospection which often passes for creativity – but that you know the prison but cannot escape from it – and do not seek to, it would be absurd – and so you then have to tell the truth. Truth isn't possible in churches and shrines and law courts or on altars or even graves – it can only be told in prisons. I am quite sure of this – and that prison makes everything else a grave and is itself the way to freedom. Prison is a broken wall. When the wall is unbroken, it's easier to be comfortable but not happier.

Perhaps this is why all creative (not negative performers) writers give the impression of dealing with light and, consequently, also with darkness. Or is this just my personal reaction? Prison travellers measure time not by clocks but by light. I still see in my head the light and darkness of your play, the first one I know, set in Tiger Bay (tigers are barred). The way light fell through windows and onto tables, the way shadows fell about people. It's because we travel into time when we read or see a play – but the writer is ahead of time. So all your plays are marked by light – whether it's the light on steps by the Mediterranean or the dingy light in a hovel – or the strange placards of light in *Idiots*, where light and darkness seem to be torn apart, wrenched apart, as if they'd been falsely glued together. In a way you can only enter the place that is ahead of time by dreaming – but it is not the dreaming of recollection – not memory, but consequence: *given* this I will make *that*.

Our theatres are often most buried in the past when they think they're being novel. The unravelling of experience and time – not the remembrance of things past but the creation of the past that hasn't yet 'clocked-in' (I can only describe what I mean in that feeble joke) – our theatre cannot understand this. How old-fashioned all those sci-fi futuristic films and novels are! – as if the future were an invention of Rudyard Kipling. Because you are in the future, you are to those who run theatres invisible. But you are at home.

Your introduction to the new book is very interesting about you as a writer.[64] I can understand what you mean about the evicted – evicted from nation, culture, language – but that isn't your core experience, I think. You can't be evicted from time when you are ahead of it – it's like being in the susurration that is ahead of a wave: to tell what has happened by what's going to happen; but that puts it negatively, and really chronology breaks down there. To serve time: that makes a creating writer.

Your journey is easily describable in the details of what you write. But the overall journey is what is important – to write on light: when you do that you make light concrete, and in comparison other objects are intangible – they have their strength, certainly, because they are a form of fate – but they are negative: they are darkness, which can never see itself. You are kind enough to say that I have been your mentor: if that is so, then I am a Mentor who has learnt from Telemachus – whom you remember he sent out on his own journey.

I could write a lot about all this, because I think the handling of time is at the very centre of drama – and of the psyche. Humans cannot mature in the way in which an acorn matures into a tree – the acorn vanishes. We're more like the strata of a land: layers of granite, chalk, igneous lava, sea-stone – one on the other. And socially, politically, culturally, we can find ourselves in situations which address particular layers – that's why people do unexpected, 'uncharacteristic' things – both brutal and benign, dreadful and self-denying (and often the latter two go together) – so we have to take responsibility for our various selves, not find ourself. And when we do that we can take responsiblity for the world (to use my grandiose phrase). This is what your journey of plays is about. But I must think more about these things.

France was interesting. *Company* is a success. *Jackets* has opened in Germany – also a success. And I saw a very good performance of *Vests* in Birmingham. And then on top of that, a really good performance of *Early Morning*[65] at the NT Studios! So I can't quite imagine how it's happened! And when I was in Paris I went to some rehearsals of *Saved* at a small sort of theatre-factory in a suburb called Alfortville – a young, dedicated director, but the direction was applied to the text not taken from it. I did a little re-rehearsing and discovered some interesting things – but I'll write about these another time. In the 'stoning scene' actors must not concern themselves with 'psychological motivations' – in the play all the 'motivations' are put into the objects, and this combines the psychological and the social – so the actor has to make 'TE use'[66] of the objects in the scene or there is nothing to act except a dead part. I'm sending you a copy of *Vests* and holding on to the things you sent me. I hope I may.

Best wishes
Edward

Notes

1 *Late City Echo* was produced at the Sherman Arena, Cardiff in 1981. The success of Dic Edwards's play was one of the factors that led to the founding of Made in Wales Stage Company.

2 *The Saturn Tramp at the Bay's End* was the working title of *At the End of the Bay*. This was the first of the 'New Era' plays set in Tiger Bay. It was produced by Made in Wales Stage Company at the Sherman Arena, Cardiff in 1982.

3 Rob Ritchie was Literary Manager at the Royal Court in 1982.

4 Rob Ritchie and the director Danny Boyle went to see the 1982 production of *At the End of the Bay* at the Sherman Arena, Cardiff.

5 *Looking for the World* – the play is published in Dic Edwards, *Three Plays* (London: Oberon Books, 1992).

6 In 1982 Dic Edwards was one of the six dramatists invited to attend the RSC 'One Year On' workshop run by Stephen Lowe at the Barbican.

7 During 1982 Edward Bond was writer-in-residence at the University of Essex, Colchester.

8 'The Stone' in Edward Bond, *Poems 1978-1985* (London: Methuen, 1981), p.163.

9 *Assumption* was the working title of *Looking for the World*.

10 Edward Bond, *Derek* with *Choruses from After the Assassination* (London: Methuen, 1983).

11 Dic Edwards's daughter, Amanda, had chosen to write a school assignment piece on Edward Bond's play, *Summer: A European Play* (London: Methuen and Chicago Publishing Company, 1982).

12 Dic Edwards had sent *Assumption* (*Looking for the World*) to his agent Peggy Ramsay, who was also Edward Bond's agent.

13 Max Stafford-Clark directed *The Pope's Wedding* at the Royal Court in 1985. It formed a double-bill with *Saved*, directed by Danny Boyle.

14 Dic Edwards and Edward Bond exchange poems at Christmas.

15 'Action Pie' produced *Human Cannon* in Cardiff.

16 *The War Plays*, Parts One and Two were first published as a Methuen Paperback original and Part Three was published as a separate volume in 1985 by Methuen. All three parts, *Red Black and Ignorant, The Tin Can People, Great Peace*, were published in a revised edition by Methuen in 1991.

17 Dic Edwards dedicated *Looking for the World* to Edward Bond.

18 Dic Edwards, *Wittgenstein's Daughter* (London: Oberon Books, 1992).

19 An early draft of *Casanova Undone*. The final version is published in Dic Edwards, *Three Plays* (London: Oberon Books, 1992).

20 Edward Bond, *Poems 1978-1985* (London: Methuen, 1987).

21 The RSC revival of Edward Bond's *Restoration* opened at the Swan Theatre, Stratford-upon-Avon on 13 September 1988. It was directed by Brian Michell. The play was published by Eyre Methuen in 1981.

22 Dic Edwards's *Low People* was produced at the Leicester Haymarket Studio in 1989. The director was David O'Shea.

23 Nick Philippou, director. He directed the production of *Jackets* which Dic Edwards saw on the occasion of his meeting with Edward Bond at the Leicester Haymarket Studio, 1989.

24 Dic Edwards, *Low People* (Lampeter: Bardprint, 1989).

25 Dic Edwards, *The fourth world* (Lampeter: Bardprint, 1990).

26 See Edward Bond's Introduction in Dic Edwards, *Three Plays* (Oberon Books, 1992), pp.6-8.

27 The following poem by Dic Edwards was published with the playtext *the fourth world* (Lampeter: Bardprint, 1990).

On meeting Edward Bond
at Leicester Haymarket Theatre, Nov, 1989

The wind torn from the well
the city torn from the wind
streets scorched velvetine
arms dislocated from arms against you
schooling tears
I went to Yenan

The flower of youth gathers by the Yellow River
beyond the horizon the universities of the enemy
they send 100 carts to steal our wheat
we sent the carts back with their dead
We put fire to the burners
learned well in Yenan

28 Ian Stuart is the editor of the four volume edition of Edward Bond's letters, published by Harwood Academic Publishers in 1994, 1995 and 1996. Volume 4 is forthcoming.
29 In 1990, at the time of the Poll Tax controversy, NALGO offered one thousand pounds to Moving Theatre in London to commission a play about unfair taxation. They offered the commission to Dic Edwards, and he wrote *In the Great Society*, an early draft of *Regan.*
30 Edward Bond, *Olly's Prison* (London: Methuen, 1993). *Olly's Prison* was filmed in 1991 and transmitted by the BBC, Spring 1993.
31 *Long to Rain Over Us* was produced at the Leicester Haymarket Studio in 1987.
32 Dic Edwards, *Regan* (The Press Gang, 1991).
33 The title of the poem was 'The Language Machine'.
34 For a period during 1991, Dic Edwards was writer-in-residence at Theatr Powys, Newtown.
35 *Summer* was first produced at the National Theatre in 1982.
36 Edward Bond, *The Woman: Scenes of War and Freedom* (London: Eyre Methuen, 1979). *The Woman* was first produced at the National Theatre in 1978.
37 In Dic Edwards's words, 'Within a couple of months of receiving Edward Bond's letter on 11 April 1991, Theatr Powys had sacked me for wanting to be a radical'.
38 *Ecce Homo* was the working title of *Casanova Undone.*
39 *In the Company of Men* is included in Edward Bond, *Two Post-Modern Plays* (London: Methuen, 1989).
40 Edward Bond, *Bingo* (London: Eyre Methuen, 1974).
41 *Casanova Undone* was produced at The Citizens Theatre, Glasgow in 1992.
42 Edward Bond's *The Sea* opened in the Lyttleton, Royal National Theatre, 12 December, 1991. It was directed by Sam Mendes.
43 *Alma* was the working title of *Wittgenstein's Daughter.*
44 At the end of 1992 Dic Edwards experienced what he has described as 'a bit of a breakdown':

> During a walk a sentence came to me which broke down all my certainties, and I found that the reassuring palpability of reality had gone. I described the experience in a letter to Edward Bond who referred to it as a 'vastation'.

45 In 1992 the dramatist dropped the 'k' from his Christian name and adopted the Welsh form 'Dic'.
46 Edward Bond, *Tuesday* (London: Methuen, 1993).
47 The BBC building, White City.

48 Dic Edwards's libretto, *The Juniper Tree*, was written for the Broomhill Opera Company. It was performed in the Summer of 1993 at the Broomhill International Opera Festival.
49 Tom Erhardt at Casarotto Ramsay became Edward Bond's agent after Margaret Ramsay's death.
50 Dic Edwards, *3 Deaths of an Idiot* (unpublished).
51 Dic Edwards, *Utah Blue* (Made in Wales, 1995).
52 Hans-Werner Henze, a modern German composer, well-known for his nonconformist musical style and his left-wing political commitment.
53 Edward Bond, *Saved* (London: Methuen, 1966), *The Woman* (National Theatre, 1978), *Human Cannon* (Quantum Theatre, Manchester, 1986).
54 Standing Conference of Young People's Theatre.
55 Peter Palitzch, a pupil of Brecht and a director at the Berliner Ensemble. In 1993 joined the management of the Ensemble.
56 Edward Bond, *Coffee* (London: Methuen, 1995).
57 Ian Stuart, ed., *Edward Bond, Letters 1* (London: Harwood Academic Publishers, 1994).
58 In 1995 Dic Edwards was invited to teach a Creative Writing course at the University College of Wales, Lampeter.
59 *3 Deaths of an Idiot* was scheduled for production at Theatr Clwyd, Mold, during Autumn 1995. The director was to be Helena Kaut-Howson, Theatr Clwyd's Artistic Director. However, in June 1995 Helena Kaut-Howson's three-year contract was not renewed, and *3 Deaths of an Idiot* was consequently shelved.
60 Castaway Theatre Company toured Dic Edwards's *Lola Brecht* in the U.K. in 1996.
61 Trevor Nunn.
62 Dic Edwards chose *Three Plays* (London, Oberon Books, 1992) and a play called *The Idiots* (unpublished). Edward Bond sent the plays to Rudolf Rach in Paris and to Suhrkamp Verlag in Frankfurt.
63 Hans Jürgen Drescher, Head of Theatre at Suhrkamp Verlag.
64 A reference to Dic Edwards's essay, 'Theatre of the Evicted', published in this volume.
65 A revised version of *Early Morning* is included in Edward Bond, *Plays One* (London: Eyre Methuen, 1977).
66 Theatre Events. Edward Bond has explained in a letter to Dic Edwards, 4 September, 1992, that 'the TE is not the text but what is done to the text: the use'. For an analysis and description of 'Theatre Events' see 'Commentary on the War Plays' in Edward Bond, *The War Plays* (London: Methuen, 1991), pp.298-340. See also various letters in Ian Stuart, ed., *Edward Bond, Letters 1* (London: Harwood Academic Publishers, 1994), pp. 41-76.

The Charisma of Non-Sense: The Plays of Dic Edwards

Charmian Savill

The dramatist David Rudkin has remarked in conversation that, from the writer's point of view, plays often fall into two categories: *blood* plays (those which gush out like blood from a wound, or grow with the insistence of the blood's pulse in the body) or *stone* plays (those which are hard to move, which demand the author work around them, painstakingly chipping out each moment). Dic Edwards's 1995 play *Utah Blue* announced itself to the writer very much as a 'blood play', involving some revision of the second half prior to performance but not the elaborate revisions and redraftings required by *Wittgenstein's Daughter* (1993) and *The Idiots* (1997), these two 'stone plays' being more characteristic of the way Edwards usually works. In the wake of eighteen years of British Conservatism, *Utah Blue* stands as an urgent distillation of the violence of its protagonist's attempt to speak out his will and desire despite a rising tide of fascism which has many resonances beyond the play's American setting. Indeed, many of Edwards's plays are about the pain of existence and the will to be heard or acknowledged in defiance of a fascistic environment. His characters' lives are blocked by huge boulders of cynicism and self-interest; those with faith chisel away and make some mark, others commit literal or metaphorical suicides. I will begin this essay with a reading of the 'blood play' *Utah Blue*, which explores the life and death of a man who demands that the state allow him to 'commit suicide'. The rest of the essay will identify other themes in the writing of Edwards, such as negligibility, fear of the imagination and the counteracting forces of language and action.

Part One of *Utah Blue* presents the life and death of Gary Gilmore, the American murderer who confessed to the killing of two men in 1976, and who insisted on the right to be executed by firing squad at Utah State Prison in January 1977. Aspects of the character are variously played by the living Gary and by his ghost. The audience is introduced to his lover Nicole, who recounts humorously their first sexual encounter. Both characters, Gary and Nicole, address the audience directly in Brechtian style, inviting the audience to reflect on the nature of the character's reality and of the audience's own reality. The audience is encouraged to maintain a critical scepticism towards all versions of the story, including the "official" one. Furthermore, to this end, Edwards prefaces each scene with a descriptive title which often takes the form of a provocative proposition, such as 'GARY IS A BLANK SHEET ON WHICH SOCIETY WRITES ITS HORROR STORY'. As the play progresses, linear history is shuffled like a pack of cards; time becomes less relevant than the foregrounded emotions which the characters express. The audience's attention is moved from Gary and Nicole's first encounter to a scene in which Gary's mother Bessie talks to the dead body of her son. Her memory of him is vivid, and provokes her to wonder what she might have done to prevent his death, and this initiates in her a further anxiety on behalf of his younger brother Mikal. In Scene Three ('WE LIVE IN A CULTURE OF MURDER'), Gary presents an argument which begins to act like a metaphor for the form and content of the play: 'The universe! Everything is in one thing . . . It's all one substance and we're just different bits of the substance'. He becomes more attractive in his demonic energy and searching intelligence, seeking to impress his individuality on an alternatingly indifferent and malevolent social environment. His playing out of his life and death partly represents a contradictory fury towards his inherited Mormonism, which he ultimately denounces for its inherent violence, though the play demonstrates that it also provides a deeply imprinted pattern which he finds difficulty in shedding. His social environment has dismissed his attempts at art (his paintings), drowning his aspirations and re-creating him as someone who seeks possible salvation through sexual fulfilment; with ironic significance, this only becomes possible for Gary when he is locked up. He determines to take a further step towards reading meaning into or out of his life, tempting those social forces ('the Meaners') who have always controlled his life to do something which he himself has decided upon: his own right to death. Nicole understands his need to claim his own execution for himself, and further ritualizes the event with the celebratory acts of stripping naked and singing outside a Mormon church, whilst at the same time levelling the formal accusation, 'Tell me, Church! Tell me, God! Tell my soul! Why do we kill people who kill people to show that killing is wrong?'. Edwards consistently demonstrates the contradictions in his characters, who themselves discover that meaning is a slippery piece of effluent that is washed out into the sea at the mercy of moon and tides. Bessie declares: 'Gary was alive in SPITE of himself! He was dead before he was born! He's only gone back!'.

After Bessie's death, Mikal announces his determination to be a writer and partly assimilates the ghost of his brother Gary; particularly, their twinned desires for Nicole effectively seem to make them different facets of the same man. As for Gary, Mikal's first attempts end in frustrated impotence, but Mikal's explanations of his reasons for continued existence in Part Two form a counterpoint to Gary's need to embrace death in Part One ('I sucked death's teat . . . I was death's artist'). Mikal's dream of suicide is a reflective incorporation of further aspects of Gary's history, and reveals other possible reasons for his journey to self-destruction. Gary's Body – an animation of his ghost – continually reminds the audience of his feelings as a human being (despite his appearance as an executed cadavre) and their expression in both actions and words. He watches Nicole's vehement refusal to submit to the persecution of 'the cops on the streets' with fear and rage, and tries to tell his mother 'Look at all the guys who've kicked the shit out of you, Ma!'. Trapped by his fixed history, he continues as a posthumous presence to repeat and project the patterns of his upbringing, insisting 'There's no way you can just amend things!'. Mikal, though more optimistic after having achieved sexual communion with Nicole, continues to search to pin down meaning and make it connect with him on his own terms. He forces Gary's Body to admit that the killing of the two men was 'meaningless', and that the state helped him to 'commit suicide'. Gary's Body's response refuses the structures of truth or meaning: he seems to tell Mikal what he wants to hear, and then asks 'Who gives a fuck?'. Mikal's silence and then laughter suggest that his own freedom from the ghost of his brother is possibly in sight. *Utah Blue* asks that the audience work to read the characters existentially, much as they do themselves, amidst Edwards's constant challenging and subverting of standard clichés of 'understanding a character'. Through this form of characterisation, *Utah Blue* offers a playful demonstration of the shifting points of sense and meaning, and a theatrical experience which is both unbalancing and exhilarating.

Just as Gary Gilmore peers into a mirror and sees a reflection of his historical, political and social environment – begging the questions, what does our reflection do to us? How do we act on what we 'are'? – the Concierge in Edwards's *Wittgenstein's Daughter* seeks to encapsulate into one word his own understanding of how history and politics have shaped his own existence: 'SARAJEVO . . . It's where the century – the real history of it – started in 1914, and it's where it's ending. And what's the result? They put it all up and they pulled it all down then they put it all up again and pulled it all down. Again. You can be certain about one thing: nothing is certain . . .'.

Wittgenstein's Daughter ploughs the furrows of many of Edwards's favourite themes: stupidity, obsession and non-communication. Many of his plays revolve around the stupid actions of people driven by fear: fear of the imagination, of others or of themselves. In *The Idiots*, documentary journalists repeatedly demonstrate their inveterate stupidity, patronising attitudes and inability to communicate with anyone despite their obsession with 'real news'. One television journalist proclaims: 'It's our duty to dig out the pain . . . If one was doing a documentary on the homeless, one would want to interview the thinnest, frailest subject living in the smallest cardboard box! One has to make things look as bad as possible. One has a duty . . . one raises the stakes to punch home the meaning! The more real the suffering, the better'. *The Idiots* shows how a televised interview with a refugee, described as the way to expand and develop humanity in other people, in fact involves humanity being stamped upon. Similarly, in *Utah Blue*, those in authority remain uncharacterised, except by Gary's term 'The Meaners', but represent an invisible wall of stupidity, more enshrined than personified. Edwards's plays reflect a deep sense of frustration aimed at those who should be capable of understanding because of their privileged positions in life, but who wilfully avoid such understanding; instead, they cram their own heads and hearts with personal gratification and disclaimers concerning their own responsibility. Hence the frenzied responses and impassioned attempts by the disempowered to feel alive in a world ruled by the stupid. *The Idiots* is a particularly extreme merry-go-round of characters who misjudge and mismatch at every turn, in a darkly satirical indication of a world gyrating into non-sense. One character comments: 'Have you ever blown bubbles . . .? . . . Some bubbles get too big and burst. Others live for a short while and make a pretty sight. That's the civilization you've come into. Those bubbles are ideas: aesthetic ideas, political ideas, ideas about . . . life. We've made ourselves negligible'.

However, though Edwards's plays are presided over by leaders who are patronising, fearful, greedy and myopic, his plays strive to reclaim meaning by providing scenarios almost devoid of humanity which are nevertheless inhabited at their margins by characters who fight to stay alive in the fullest sense, beyond the restrictions of mere existence. In their attempts to break free of fascistic structures and influences, many of the characters become bewildered or silenced. The naïvety and openness of their responses to the political darkness around them leaves the more informed or 'knowing' spectator on a knife-edge, watching with trepidation as these characters traverse the treacherous terrain around them. Occasionally, some characters aspire to a similarly 'knowing' stance and possibility of action, such as Nana in *Looking for the World*, who has assembled a sense of past and future which endows her with bravery in the face of the military rule in Greece. She recalls how 'People . . . believed in themselves. THEN I had a home. Now people are afraid. They will use me to get rid of their fear'. Indeed, she becomes the focus of all the shamefully accumulated bile of self-disgust that the Greek male characters feel: they abuse her verbally and physically and finally murder her. In *Utah Blue*, Gary refuses shame and thus breaks the 'Meaners'' monopoly on meaning and power, and so resists negligibility ('All my fucking life, what I mean's been decided by the Meaners . . . so now I'm deciding').

A more romantic dramatic strategy occurs in *Wittgenstein's Daughter*, where the birth of Alma's child heralds her triumph over fascism: salvation seems possible and imminent through the smashing of silence and the creation of new ideas and language. Thus, Edwards's plays often push characters into situations where innocence is lost and where the resulting bewilderment gives way to the initiation of a process of understanding. *Lola Brecht* (1996) and *The Idiots* are notable exceptions to this process, in that they plunge characters deeper into confusion, misunderstanding and stupidity, initiating in the spectator or reader a productive frustration and active irritation. In an interview with Hazel Walford Davies, Edwards refers to the 'fascism' of the Thatcher years and the prevailing mindset that constitutes its continued imprint: '. . . it's exactly this that has led to the fear of creativity and the fear of people responding to creativity. Culture has become afraid of art – it's a paradox'.[1]

Edwards's drama addresses this fear centrally and precisely, and identifies fascism as a fearful bid to eradicate the imaginations which give his characters their uniqueness, complexity and humanity. These are the very qualities which lead the characters to their refusals to conform to expectations, and to their discoveries of ways of operating on their own terms. Gary's self-will in *Utah Blue* infuriates those who do not understand him, but the reader or spectator is given access, dramatically, to more information, which affords a three-dimensional view of Gary's situation. Natasha, a singer and poet in *The Idiots*, demonstrates a creativity that both seduces and mystifies, confounding those around her because she fulfils no expectations. Nana in *Looking for the World* and Alma in *Wittgenstein's Daughter* both derive the courage to act from their imaginations; it is their respective views of how they want the world to be that propels them on their journeys.

Edwards also highlights how people do and do not talk to each other, and the ways they talk out the meanings of their actions and hopes, often in isolation. The ghosts in *Utah Blue* and *Wittgenstein's Daughter* symbolise in different ways the difficulty of communication and the sense that we are all essentially alone: the ghost of Gary has to speak out, even though no one knows (apart from the theatre audience) that he is there or will react; the ghost of Wittgenstein tells his living friend, Beckett, 'you are outside the limits of your language', by way of reminding him of his apartness and difference. Edwards's earlier plays *Low People* and *the fourth world* emphasise people's inability to talk and make others understand the meaning of their lives. *Low People* ends with the juxtaposition of the communication becoming possible and impossible. *the fourth world* ends with two of its characters in a tableau of the blissful aftermath of communication and understanding: sleep; the third character achieves a moment of realization ('*he suddenly relaxes as if relieved of a great tension*'). It is rare in Edwards's drama for conversation to generate communication, understanding or sympathy; more often, it involves complicated or blatant lies, maintenance of status, fear of the other, misplaced judgement in passion, bullying or taking advantage of another character's vulnerable status. The power of talk is constantly examined, as an index to both liberation and dispossession. Speech becomes a central and sensual thing to those who live on the edge, who are different in their resistance to pessimism, who are unafraid but not necessarily hopeful. Initially, characters such as Alma in *Wittgenstein's Daughter* wander in a wilderness of shame, outside what is generally designated or perceived as the flow of life, until their imaginative resistance impels them into speech. Curiosity, together with a need for full expression of the self, propels characters such as Gary and Alma into speech, in situations which emphasise the danger and courage involved in speaking out.

However, Edwards's play *The Idiots* demonstrates conversely or perversely that talking need not ultimately lead to anyone making any sense out of anything. Edwards's less heroic characters often speak in order to reveal mere constructions of their own self-interest, rejecting contact and maintaining the status quo which has been handed down to them. The world represented by this status quo may be alien to them, but they nevertheless strive to preserve and mummify it, because the possibility of change (which is associated with the other characters' bids for contact and understanding) involves the fear of loss of power, control and status. One character in *Looking for the World* has been trained in the Greek military as a soldier and a torturer by being beaten and tortured himself; he claims: 'We got used to it so we knew what to expect . . . Greek justice is and always will be the best justice that ever existed in human society'. The complexity of the human situation around him has been erased; the simplicity of fascism has enslaved him to its violence.

Indeed, many of Edwards's plays illuminate the situations of people who have bought into an ideology. In *Regan, Looking for the World, the fourth world* and *The Idiots,* characters demonstrate (knowingly and naïvely) the fabric of lies, levels of stupidity, fear, low self-esteem, vindictiveness and greed that are required to maintain and feed the over-simplification and prescriptiveness of most ideologies, into which Edwards plants characters like time-bombs, who are ticking steadily towards exploding into a fully-fledged sense of their own humanity, and thus knocking down the ideological walls that incarcerate them. Their journey is shown as complex, painful, frightening and always surprising. Edwards's characters seem to be in a state of perpetual drowning, but managing occasionally to gasp for air. Their gasps do not necessarily permit breakthroughs of understanding; indeed, they often represent a knowledge which plunges them into a further bout of indefinition. Indefinition, with its attendant qualities of instability and dislocation, replaces the concept of an exclusive truth, as when Alma confronts her own dislocation as part of her journey to find and understand her parents: 'I am lost. I don't mean on a street or a street corner or in a supermarket or on a beach. I am lost from somebody's heart. Lost from somebody's history. My own! . . . I've never before been able to speak about being lost. As though there were never enough words with enough ideas behind them to enable me to describe it!'.

Thus, in *Wittgenstein's Daughter*, Alma negotiates ideas – her own and others' – as to how to live and make sense of the world. Her fascist husband dismisses both her and her dead father. A more sympathetic figure, the Concierge, advises 'Get away. Only somewhere where things appear at least to have retained some dignity. Some value. Go somewhere cloistered . . . You need to sit down and reflect. Or you'll end up like me. Worn down by the cares of the century'. Alma's journey takes her to Cambridge, but affords little time to sit down and reflect. As if in order for her to progress beyond her state of negligibility, the play forces her into mysterious encounters: she meets the ghost of Wittgenstein, who is introduced to her as Carrington, bandaged to disguise his face; she thinks she finds the skeleton of her mother, but discovers something different. She encounters intricate webs of historical lies, which, to her credit, only renew and deepen her questioning activities: Why does parental identity matter? Does language matter more than history – or are they the same thing? Are history and philosophy merely fanciful imaginative or therapeutic constructs that enable people to survive their identities? Does truth exist in either history or philosophy, or is it a 'black hole' – an identification of nothingness which obliges people to prove some kind of value and worth in what has been written and thought? Edwards often leads his protagonists towards what promises to be a moment of reflection, revelation or confirmation, then confronts them with further bewilderment and challenge. Alma's inexorable journey, in particular, brings her to a keener sense of disconnectedness and isolation in the world, even as its rigours clarify her sense of purpose. The end of *Wittgenstein's Daughter* is romantic but unsentimental, like that of Wertenbaker's *The Grace of Mary Traverse*, emphasising the danger and hope associated with birth, in a notable final stage direction: '*She pulls her knickers off and opens her legs. The lights go down as she clutches two of Wittgenstein's bones and hits out with them to fight off the pain*'.

Indeed, the structures of Edwards's dramas often suggest and reflect the impulses of a cruel joker at play, as he evokes a powerful sense of expectation which is frequently subverted: for example, *Wittgenstein's Daughter* raises the hope that Wittgenstein's ghost will be made visible to Alma; instead, the ghost disappears permanently in an explosion, which makes Alma lose consciousness. Similarly, the premise of *The Idiots* is founded on a misunderstanding between Smerdyakov, a refugee, and Malcolm Walker, a television journalist: the gulf between them becomes such that the reader becomes desperate for any kind of connection, which is continually and ironically forestalled. The characters' strategies reveal stupidity and misunderstanding, without yielding to breakthrough, moral restitution, affirmation or hope for any kind of communion. In this respect, *The Idiots* resembles the structure of Edwards's earlier play *Lola Brecht*: the reader or audience member is led to hope for some kind of eventual catharsis, which the play ultimately refuses.

During a workshop in Aberystwyth in 1997, Edwards expressed his concern that his plays provoked argument and a questioning of moral values; in an interview with Hazel Walford Davies, he has publicly confirmed his conscious identity as 'a very political person, but in the Aristotelian sense. I don't exist without politics'.[2] The short episodic scenes and frameworks for political analysis in Edwards's drama, particularly in plays such as *Low People, the fourth world* and *Regan*, have strong stylistic affinities with the questioning thrust of the best examples of Theatre-in-Education. Edwards is a strong supporter of Theatre-in-Education, and much of his philosophy of writing has been informed by his work for TIE companies, such as Spectacle. His more recent plays, such as *Wittgenstein's Daughter* and *Utah Blue*, have become 'more abstract', as Edward Bond comments in his Introduction to Edwards's volume *Three Plays*[3]: they 'often erupt in a sort of poetic melodrama. The language and imagery have changed in order to be more precise'. A consistent morality is expressed throughout Edwards's drama, through the proposition that the most vulnerable members of society – young people, women and the poor – need to be listened to and included centrally in whatever patterns of living are designed by the powers that be. But Edwards also takes care to subvert expectations and avoid predictability in his stories, through the unexpected actions and surprising journeys towards which he leads his characters. For example, at the end of *Looking for the World*, Sylvia faces the possibility of having a husband who is a murderer; the stage directions specify a '*silence in which Sylvia's world is collapsing*', as she literally cannot speak the language of the land in which she finds herself. The reader or audience member is left to contemplate the extent of her catastrophe and isolation, and propelled into imagining and constructing what might be her immediate future.

The 'athletic tension' which Bond notes in Edwards's plays emanates from the characters' settled daily lives being thrown into contact with chaos. Edwards sets up a dialectic between the practical exigencies of their daily routines and the truly non-sensical aspects of life which they encounter. Frequently, a mundane action, such as eating fish and chips (in one scene of *Wittgenstein's Daughter*), becomes a bizarre and unsettling experience in which the familiar and the unusual become intertwined; the audience, like the characters, experience a sudden loss of *terra firma* regarding possibilities. In this way, Edwards's plays show life as a constant battle of wits. In defiance of the deception of exclusive truth, such as is represented by the 'Meaners' in *Utah Blue*, Edwards's writing encourages wilful, charismatic and various responses to the non-sense that surrounds us. The personal crises of protagonists such as Alma and Gary release them into catastrophic action, demanding that they

> act with purpose, not only to demonstrate the chaos both emotionally and intellectually we find ourselves in, but to start tearing down the curtain so that we can start to paint the world again for ourselves.[4]

Notes

1 Hazel Walford Davies, 'Theatre as Forum' [interview with Dic Edwards], *New Welsh Review* 31 (Winter 1995-6), p. 82.

2 Ibid., p. 80.

3 *Casanova Undone, Looking for the World, Long to Rain Over Us: Three Plays by Dic Edwards* (London: Oberon, 1992), p. 8.

4 Sleeve notes to the Style Council CD *Confessions of a Pop Group* (Polydor, 1988) attributed to 'The Capuccino Kid' (most probably Paul Weller).

Looking for the World Through the Word: The Social Imagination in Dic Edwards's Drama

Anna-Marie Taylor

The plays written by Wales's most prolific contemporary English-language dramatist Dic Edwards can make very uncomfortable reading and viewing. His extravagant and often unrelenting employment of dramatic dialogue can make aural demands on the audience that go well beyond what might be expected in the theatre. Similarly, the world that he wrestles with in his drama can prove highly disturbing, again capable of unsettling our expectations. What I should like to explore in this essay is the relationship between the *word* and the *world* in a number of Edwards's plays since the mid-1980s, an association which has got increasingly complex as his work has matured and as he has ventured to take on ever more demanding subject matter.

In a study of cultural identity in the globalized world *Modernity at Large*, Arjun Appadurai considers the difficulties faced by ethnographers in representing the role of the imagination in social life. Whilst 'until recently, whatever the force of social change, a case could be made that social life was largely inertial, that traditions provided a relatively finite set of possible lives . . . in the past decade, . . . deterritoralization of persons, images and ideas has taken on new force'.[1] For Appadurai, the challenge in anthropology is to construct what he terms 'genealogies of the present', that is, a dialogue between individual heritage and a wider history in which 'the terrain would be open for interpretations of the ways in which local historical trajectories flow into complicated transnational structures'.[2]

The cultural and imaginative terrain of those who no longer inhabit a 'relatively finite set of possible lives' is described by Appardurai as an *ethnoscape*, the restless repertoire of imaginative possibilities (and impossibilities) in a shifting world where 'the warp of . . . stabilities is everywhere shot through with the woof of human motion, as more persons and groups deal with the realities of having to move or the fantasies of wanting to move'.[3]

The problem of representing the transitoriness and complex hybridity of experience that constitutes late twentieth-century living is shifted to questions of individual agency within (post)modernity by cultural sociologists such as Peter Alheit, Anthony Giddens and Ulrich Beck.[4] Here the breakdown in agreed social and religious truths, domestic and economic structures, and in agreed life-courses, so symptomatic of late modernity – a possible sign of which is the lack of agreement as to what to call the age we are living through (is it late, high, post or even (post) modernity ?) – is seen as a major feature of a 'risk society' in which 'individualization' of life choices is paramount. For Giddens, in particular, such a shift away from traditional certainties is seen as resulting in much greater autobiographical awareness, with increasing onus on the individual to chart, design and be aware of their own life narratives, a both liberating and daunting perception of the self.

I have dwelt a while on discussions of the self in late modernity as it seems to me that Dic Edwards's plays, more than those of any other playwright in Wales, take on the challenge posed by Appadurai to find ways of representing today's lived imagination, as well as recognizing the individualization of life-choices in the contemporary world. Whilst experimental groups in Wales such as Alma Theatre, Brith Gof and Volcano Theatre have also dramatized such complex issues in their work, Edwards's plays are singular in the use they make in putting acute emphasis on the word, often in the form of long 'oratorical' speeches, to express the imagination in social life.

For the purposes of our discussion, it is appropriate to begin with the aptly titled *Looking for the World* (first performed in 1986 at Cardiff's Sherman Theatre). In this searing account of the social imagining that underpinned the Greek Junta, Edwards presents us with several individuals whose traditional certainties are shattered as their 'repertoire of imaginative possibilities' are rudely extended and jolted. Set in a dilapidated Greek hotel at the time of the Generals' rule, the play examines the growing realization of the underlying reality of the various characters' worlds. Sylvia and her husband, left-leaning Paddy, Cardiffians in their fifties, are holidaying on a Greek island which is no longer any cradle of civilization but is increasingly a prey to militaristic terror.

At first sight, the south Wales couple appear to be comic creations, innocent Brits abroad, set loose amongst curious foreigners. However, Edwards moves swiftly from caricature, and, above all in his developing use of intensely stated interior monologues in this play, conveys with skill the threatened security of all his characters. Eventually the drama culminates in a tragic, brutal undermining of Greek and Welsh cultural certainties. For the holiday-makers, the journey abroad becomes a flight not away from, but *into* the real world, as their parochial individual histories intersect with wider questions of militarism and masculine aggression.

Paddy, 'a socialist, . . . a democrat, . . . a trade unionist . . . a councillor' who is eager to escape mass tourist venues, and is enamoured of the idea that the Greeks 'have a natural kind of equality', maintaining 'that Greek justice is and always will be the best justice that ever existed in human society', undermines such equality and sullies all his egalitarian credentials by collaborating in the sordid murder of a female tramp. Sylvia, like many female characters in Edwards's plays, is allowed greater (and much more painful) insight, confronted as she is by the knowledge that the world she has looked for on holiday is no longer one she can fly away from, and 'when I'm home having my cup of tea with Rhona this will all seem like a film'. She is no longer an accidental tourist, a fleeting visitor to another social reality (an activity so emblematic of late modernity), but a participant in a human tragedy, perpetuated not just by the Greek hotel owner but the masculine self-assertion of her own husband as well. Belligerence has come into the living quarters.

The intrusion of the world of politics into domestic life is felt more dangerously by Melina, the wife of the hotel owner. For her, the cultural certainty that 'my family IS my world' is menaced from within rather than by outside forces. Her clan-like belief in the strength and autonomy of the family is severely challenged by the return of her son from military training, his humanity and fellow feeling twisted into hatred against his supposedly Communist enemies. He is now serving as a soldier on his home island which has been turned into a prison camp, 'the place of tribunal'. Along with the outsider figure Nana the tramp, Melina is allowed the greatest perception in the play, articulated in her impassioned statement of her inability to to '. . . understand . . . what's happened to . . . to people? People who give birth to babies and feed them . . . people who grow the food, make the clothes . . . socks . . . coats . . . people who look after the babies, the children . . . send them to hospital if they're sick . . . nurses, people who drive the ambulances; people who build the roads to drive the ambulances on.'[5]

Thus in *Looking for the World*, the cultural parameters of everybody's lives are cruelly distorted, as one form of social imagining based on the idyllic Greek island world, the heroic nature of masculinity and the civilizing influence of the united family, is replaced by its obverse; a nightmarish breakdown in compassionate involvement in the lives of others where a certain type of political imagining distorts domestic life with considerable cruelty. Above all, in a play which frequently uses highly distinctive internal monologues (often signalled as being incomprehensible to those on stage through being in another language) , Edwards's characters are depicted as trying to voice in desperation these huge shifts in the way they see the world. However, as is portrayed even more evidently in later plays, the word is not necessarily able to explain the brute realities of the world. There is a disjuncture between expression and raw experience, which cannot be easily translated into words, and on occasion is more readily translated into aggressive action.

In *Looking for the World* Edwards explores such a misalliance through employing the dramatic technique of interconnecting two random sets of individual lives, a literary device he returns to in later writings including the untransmitted television drama *The Emperor of Ice Cream* (1995) and stage plays such as *The Idiots* (1996), *Regan (In the Great Society)* (1992), and *Lola Brecht* (*scenes in the middle of history*) (1994). In the last play (performed Castaway Theatre, Aberystwyth, 1995), the geographical location is somewhere in Middle Europe, between Prague and Poland, the historical positioning post- Stalin, Havel and Honecker. In this tantalizing, often enigmatic piece, Edwards mixes farce, quasi-historical realism and grotesque semi-surrealistic episodes to create a play that reads and performs as if it were a seance with the dark side of twentieth-century Mittel Europa. Edwards takes on the conundrum tackled by German playwrights such as Heiner Muller and Peter Weiss in plays such as *Hamletmaschine* and the *Marat/Sade*, and found in Britain most notably in work by Howard Barker such as *The Europeans*, which is how to give dramatic expression to a social imagination which can encompass sadistic sexuality, blind belief, barbarous behaviours, and the almost gleeful extirpation of other individuals.

As in *Looking for the World*, Edwards focuses such an attempt to understand the workings of a savage mentality through and around the experiences of an ordinary woman, Lola Brecht, 'short and almost fat . . . a common woman' who 'has been born without destiny'. Accompanying her arrogant, pedantic husband, Lola journeys towards Prague, possibly on the trail of a charismatic demagogue, Bonnke, who has built up and marshalled a particular view of the world through having mastery over the word. Sexually brutalized as the play develops and constantly belittled by her husband, Lola gradually develops an awareness of her own historical positioning, and at the end of the drama when caught in crossfire, she grasps some sense of self-worth and claims her part in a wider history. She is no longer insignificant, a woman 'who has lived by her husband's sermons' and who has been 'sliding along in the slime of someone else's history'.

This trajectory from lack of worth and submission to self recognition and action is a structural pattern that recurs in several of Edwards's plays, above all in what he has termed the 'epic journeys of the interior', experienced more often than not by his female characters. In *Regan (In the Great Society)* (performed 1992 by Theatr Powys), one of Edwards's most accessible plays, this movement towards self-awareness is well utilized. In this study of the abuse of power over the weak and credulous, Edwards gives the main voice in the play to a dead hunchback girl. Although it was originally conceived as a response to the Thatcherite Poll Tax of the early 1990s, Edwards defamiliarized the immediate political campaign by setting the play in medieval times. The pitifully poor and wretched Rakestraw family is manipulated and abused by a millennial figure, John Nameless who promises them happiness and avoidance of tax through joining 'the Great Society'. However, it becomes clear that their currency of repayment to Nameless's quasi-utopian sect is submission to his will, particularly in the offering up of Regan to his sexual use. Narrated retrospectively by the ghost of Regan, the play ends on a note of triumph as she recalls the sexual humiliation of Nameless which changed the relationship of power between them:

> That was it! It was unbelievable! I was quite prepared for him to do it. Right in front of them Because then they would have become involved. Then they wouldn't have been able to hide any more. But I didn't expect that he wouldn't be able to do it! But that's what happened. He couldn't do it! No power. They took his power away . . . It was brilliant! It was the best day of our lives![6]

This autobiographical awareness, this movement from ignorance to being able to articulate and thus challenge the reality of the world, is repeated in Edwards' witty and confident play *Wittgenstein's Daughter* (performed Glasgow Citizens Theatre, 1993) . Edwards here tackles the whole question of social imagining through the word head on, as he states in the notes on the play:

> And Wittgenstein did say that if you can imagine a language you can imagine a world. He was not saying this to suggest that we can imagine a language but rather that we can't. And so we can't imagine a world. We only have the world we've got and that world, in the end, I believe, defines the language that we speak . . .[7]

Edwards's most direct statement on the relationship between the word and the world is dramatized forcibly in *Wittgenstein's Daughter*. Alma Wittgenstein, the putative daughter of the famous philosopher, embarks on a journey (again a key motif of Edwards's work) from Paris to Cambridge in order to discover her own origins. From the beginning of the drama, she is positioned in a distinct history, as she is pregnant by Celine, a French neo-fascist leader. In Cambridge, she encounters another set of historical circumstances and collection of values, but these are gradually revealed not to be the expected ones of '. . . the centre of the civilized world. Where history is made complete. By the virtue of thought that is; because thinking is made immoral in Cambridge.'

As in *Looking for the World*, such a vision of civilizing values, however, is seen to be a chimera, and rather its obverse is more pertinent, as Cambridge's values in Wittgenstein's day did not extend to public tolerance of sexual difference. Alma's birth and personal history are discovered to be founded upon lies and her origins are bound up with an attempt to disguise the eminent philosopher's homosexuality. The language of that particular

Cambridge world was predicated upon an official silencing of an important aspect of Wittgenstein's world.

Like his 'daughter' Alma, the free-thinking philosopher, who extended the whole debate on the nature and communicative ability of language, was also caught within an academic and political establishment that determined discourses of power within the university and the wider world. This determinedly anti-naturalistic play, in which, for example, the Austrian philosopher is depicted as a ghost kept in a cupboard by his centenarian, ex-boxer lover, dispenses with realistic detail. However, Edwards ends the play on what might be seen as an Ibsenite note, that is the self-enlightenment of Alma, who declares at the philosopher's graveside, echoing in part Wittgenstein's words:

> Well I'm pregnant but my husband is a fascist! It made me think: it will come it will come again as sure as anything: the footsoldiers of the holocaust are on the march all over Europe. Well I was afraid to bring my child into such a world. I used to say things like: this is no world to bring a child in to. I was deeply moved by clichés. But now, well, it's as if I've learned to speak again! It *is* so much to do with . . . *Talk!* . . . But why am I ashamed? Only because I allowed myself to speak *their* words! So much so that I couldn't speak about the one thing I wanted to speak about! Silence is shame! That's the reality of silence! . . . Everywhere I look there are faces looking at me out of screens saying things to me as though with authority *as though with wisdom* things are lies! . . . Well, I will be my baby's language and she will be my best idea![8]

This autobiographical awareness, the 'individualization' and realization of the self, is delineated more acutely and disturbingly in Edwards's study of the murderer Gary Gilmore in *Utah Blue* (performed The Point, Cardiff, 1995). Edwards investigates the role of the imagination in social life in these 'scenes in a culture of murder' to show how Gilmore's particular *ethnoscape* (to apply Appadurai's term) is created through his own death-haunted upbringing as a Mormon in confluence with wider North American imaginings of the violently active self as heroic. This cause célèbre of the 1970s which attracted much journalistic attention at the time is treated by Edwards, not in semi-documentary fashion, but in the style of *Regan* and *Wittgenstein's Daughter*, that is, in a partly grotesque, avowedly non-naturalistic fashion. The play here mainly takes place as a debate between the highly articulate, deceased Gilmore and his humane, uncomprehending brother Mikal.

Both brothers attempt to voice the world they inherited. However, the liberal standpoint presented by Mikal is eclipsed by the convictions of his brother who has turned a pathetic act of violence into powerful validation of his self. In Gary Gilmore's culture, death is the only certainty, and his wilful call for execution gives autobiographical significance to his life, for as we learn in one of Edwards's developed interior monologues and most accomplished passages of writing:

> . . . When I was a kid, death would whisper into my ear at night. That's how I got to sleep. And as I grew up, death would walk with me to school. Yeah! In school I learned with death; in the playground I played with death; when I played hookey, I played hookey with death. Death was in my school bag; in my lunchbox; in my pencil case; with my paint brushes. Death came down the chimney at Christmas and death lit up the Christmas tree . . . Death taught me love. Death taught me life. Death taught me to see just as death taught me to paint. I was death's artist.[9]

This persuasive, uncompromising speech, resulting in its character's self exegesis is characteristic of the way that Edwards has refined and crafted the word in his work. His frequent use of such a rhetorical device is a highly distinctive feature of his drama, the world of which – be it that of masculine self-assertion in *Looking for the World*, the psychic mentality of Middle Europe in *Lola Brecht*, the brutalization and submission of the poor in *Regan*, the inadequacies, lacunae and power discourses manifest in language in *Wittgenstein's Daughter* and the weddedness to a culture of death in *Utah Blue* – does not always readily translate into words. As I stated at the beginning of this essay, Edwards's quest for finding ways of representing the contemporary world, and in particular its manifestation in and through the social imagining of the late twentieth century, has many links with commentators such as Appadurai and Giddens on the nature of the individual within late modernity.

What is also perhaps apparent in Edwards's drama – and I do not wish to impute any particular 'Welshness' to his often idiosyncratic work – is the recognition of older, more established rhetorical forms in his use of extended and impassioned speeches. Edwards's expression of 'the epic journey within' through bold and vigorous monologues which try to summon up the often invisible and inexpressible reality of the individual in a complex world, shares features with the fervent Welsh religious sermon and the fiery political speech. Not only does the world they present disturb us, but the manner of its saying disturbs us too.

Notes

1 Arjun Appadurai, *Modernity at Large* (Minneapolis: University of Minnesota Press, 1996), p. 53.

2 Ibid., p. 65.

3 Ibid., pp. 33-4.

4 See, for example, Peter Alheit, 'Changing Basic Rules of Biographical Construction: Modern Biographies at the End of the Twentieth Century' (1993), a paper presented at the Third International Symposium, 'Biography and Society', Hamburg, 1992. See also Anthony Giddens, *Modernity and Self-Identity: Self and Society in the late Modern Age* (Cambridge: Pality Press, 1996).

5 *Looking for the World*, in Dic Edwards, *Three Plays, Casanova Undone, Looking for the World, Long to Rain Over Us* (London: Oberon Books, 1992), p. 131.

6 Dic Edwards, *Regan* (The Press gang, 1991), p. 45.

7 Dic Edwards, *Wittgenstein's Daughter* (London: Oberon Books, 1993), p. 6.

8 Ibid., pp. 61-2.

9 Dic Edwards, *Utah Blue* (Cardiff: Made in Wales, 1995), p. 18.

A Dereliction of Duty:

Hazel Walford Davies interviews Dic Edwards

HWD: *You've often said that you are a working-class Welshman. But your plays deal with middle-class subjects in a highly intellectual way. This is true especially of a play like* Wittgenstein's Daughter.

DE: The severe reality is that the vast majority of people who go to the theatre are middle-class people, because theatre is too expensive for the working-class to afford. Culturally of course it's more complex than that. My audience is a middle-class audience, and if I were to write a play for them about a working-class situation in an analytical way it would come over as something of a complaint, a harangue or just anger. It would be dismissible in dramatic terms. Working-class plays of course *are* written, and written mostly by middle-class people, but they tend to be what I'd call 'chocolate-box' plays which just paint a picture of working-class life. You can imagine a middle-class photographer from New York going to the dust-bowl in Oklahoma back in the thirties during the depression, and taking photographs of these startled, almost unbearably lost people there, and taking the photographs back for the middle-classes of New York and Washington to see. These middle classes would probably marvel at the quality of the photographs, but would do nothing to help the people who were starving out there in the dust-bowl. But the photographs would do a hell of a lot for the reputation of the photographer. In a sense that is what theatre for the working class is like in this country. The kitchen sink, slice-of-life stuff is, in my opinion, just sentimental nonsense. What I'm interested in is looking at the condition of the working-class in all its complexity, and trying to analyse the complexity. The lives of the working-class are largely shaped by the middle-classes. It's probably no coincidence that the same people run the theatres, too, and so they are perfectly happy with a middle-class portrayal of the working-class. If the middle-classes shape the lives of the working class, I want to know how responsible they are. I'm very critical of the people who govern us, namely the middle-classes, and that's why I write plays about them. But I'm a dramatist, not a politician or a propagandist. I think we live in a society, even under New Labour, where debate is marginalized once again. I've explained my views to you elsewhere about theatre as a forum for debate, the idea being that theatre can help us to progress as a society.[1] I think that in the overwhelming sea of creativity there is these days in film, television and literature, there is very little which deals with any kind of analysis of society. I think it's not too much to ask that there be a little island or a space in this ocean where people can debate the nature of society.

HWD: *In your Introduction to* Wittgenstein's Daughter *there's a note on 'real language' and 'apparent language'. Are these the languages of the two classes?*

DE: The 'apparent language' is the language of everyday discourse and the 'real language' is the language of being human. In the note, I qualify that by adding that the language of everyday discourse in our society is the language of the bourgeois classes, and the 'real language' is the language of the humanity tortured by the language of bourgeois politics. No, it's not exactly the language of the two classes. I find that the working-class speak a kind of language that derives from that of the middle-classes. The real language should really be the language of theatre – that's the point. In life, as in kitchen-sink drama, language isn't fulfilling its role properly. There is of course a fundamental difference between the language of the two classes. Working-class people say 'We can't do that; we're not allowed to', whereas the middle-class, collectively, would be more inclined to say, 'We must be able to do that, we must find a way of overcoming our inability to do it'. Language is so important. The literary arts don't just *use* language, they are actually *about* language. I take the famous line, 'A rose is a rose is a rose', to be a line about language because it implies that there is a constancy about language that in more fanciful moments we might like to call truth. To me the whole point about language is that it begs for truth, and it's only the practice of language that gives us the idea of truth. It's a bit like colour. Colour only exists because we can see, but in another sense it exists because of light. And language demands of us access to the light. If we don't want truth, why speak? To use language for a purpose other than to tell the truth is to waste language, it's anti-language. Some of our leading, most famous dramatists use language in the service of the ego, either to show what great representational painters they are or, in other cases, to show off their facility at the witty aside. They use language, and consequently theatre, falsely. Oscar Wilde was witty, but what makes a play like *The Importance of Being Earnest* so important is that the wit implies the serious, luminous core and the truth of the language he's using. It's not merely a superficial blessing as in the case of some of Wilde's imitators today who aren't even witty. Wit, to work, has to have an intellectual depth. I'm currently reading *Arcadia* by Tom Stoppard, and it's so superficial. You simply can't believe any of it. It's a dereliction of duty in some ways. It was the 'best play of the year' some years ago, but the stuff is empty. I do think that it's related to the proliferation of television and cinema writing. And I think it's going to get worse.

HWD: *I know you have strong views about the relationship between film and theatre. Could you talk about this relationship?*

DE: Well, there *isn't* a relationship. Two things couldn't be more different. I'm alarmed at the ease with which the plays of, say, someone like David Hare translate from stage to screen. I'm ashamed because he's regarded as a playwright. For an audience, cinema is essentially a passive experience, whereas theatre is an active and creative experience. Cinema and television are, of course, primarily entertainment. What a cinema audience sees is what comes through the camera, which is one way of seeing and which the director controls. So ultimately you're seeing what the director sees. This clearly precludes the notion of debate. In the theatre the situation is absolutely different, or should be. Of course, one of the failings of modern theatre in Britain is that it has become 'Director's Theatre', and the tendency now is to have the director's vision. This is appallingly reactionary. It's like living in a dictatorship where you do what the dictator wants you to do. In British theatre you see what the director wants you to see. The director looks at a text, chooses what he wants to see and then directs in a dictatorial, fascistic way. Under such circumstances real theatre can't happen. In theatre you have live people on stage and live people in the audience, and the gap between the audience and the stage is full and fraught. It's like the aura at a political meeting where everybody is putting forward a point of view. The gap that exists between the screen and the audience is a dead gap. Its only business is to carry as much light as is needed to see the film. This reality about theatre suggests a society, people in one place, and the society progresses, develops and advances out of debate. It seems to me to be a negation of society if all we're concerned with in theatre is being titillated in some way. If in any circumstances in history, a group of people in a society come together for the sole purpose of being titillated then you can say that this is a society in collapse. The obvious example is Roman society in decline. It may be argued, of course, that in a restaurant you can have a corporate body of people. But there's no debate going on there, because in a restaurant people are separate at their own tables. There's only an illusion of people being together. In a restaurant you're distracted by people coming and going, by the waiter, by the food. In theatre there's no such distraction. The experience in the theatre is focused and intense. To waste that on trivial joke-telling as in West End comedy is a dereliction of duty. Of course, some big theatres are designed to help you forget that you're in the theatre and make you believe you're in a cinema. Cinemas came out of, in many respects, Victorian melodrama which was really just entertainment with some heavily plotted story which used music very often – hence melodrama – to elicit emotive responses. And, of course, Victorian melodrama has been in many ways discredited. It's an aberration. Theatre should be looking back to find its roots. Also, I think there are some kinds of theatres where you can even have a meal while you're watching the play. What an outrage. It sounds as if all the people in that space, the actors and the audience, are two separate species. But there should be an interaction between the actor and the audience; in a sense it should be as if the actor had just stepped out of the audience. Edward Bond says that society sends the audience to the theatre. This makes so much sense. This means that in the theatre space we recognise an intensity of experience going on, which does what all art does, which is to enable us to look at our lives and our society in a new way and a way that helps us to progress.

HWD: *You've talked about your view of theatre. What about your view of yourself as a Welsh dramatist? You've recently declared that you're not a Welsh writer, indeed not even a Welshman.*

DE: No I'm not, and it's a pity. It's a conclusion I've arrived at from the application of logical thought. Is Normal Mailer an American or a Jew? If I were living in America and someone asked Is Dic Edwards an American or a Welshman, I would have to say 'I'm American.'

HWD: *Why couldn't you say that you're a Welsh American?*

DE: If anyone asked 'Is Dic Edwards Welsh or British?' I'd have to say 'I'm British', because there's something about being Welsh that's a little like being Jewish. There's an intensity about it that can be compared to the racial intensity of being Jewish. And, I suppose, historically, some of the experiences have been the same. I suppose I'm a bit like Bob Dylan who was once a Jew and became a Christian. Presumably he felt that he couldn't, with justification, call himself Jewish. I was once Welsh, and now am British, because I can't with justification call myself Welsh. I don't speak the language. I suppose I'm a bit of a purist. There's this anomaly that's taken place in Welsh culture. So much, by definition, of what is truly Welsh is predicated now on the language. During the last fifteen or twenty years so many people have come into Wales because they haven't been able to get work in England, and they've learnt the Welsh language, and taken positions in the media and the arts, and so on. These are basically middle-class English people who are filling cultural positions in Wales. So the major influence in Wales is that of middle-class English filtered through the Welsh language. There are serious implications here, devastating ones, because we are creating outside Welsh-speaking Wales – which will always have a cultural identity of its own – a cultural waste land. So you will understand that my argument about not being Welsh is an intellectual one and not an emotional one. If you want to see this anomaly on a grand scale look at the so-called Welsh Theatre – theatre outside Welsh-language Theatre. It's not Welsh at all. What's Welsh about the Torch Theatre in Milford Haven? It hasn't, I don't think, ever had a Welsh artistic director. Or take Theatr Clwyd. Has that theatre ever had a Welsh artistic director? It looks as if Theatr Clwyd, as I understand it, is to be regarded as the National Theatre of Wales. When I went up there, not so long ago, out of the repertoire of plays they were doing at the time, one was a sixties proto-gay play, which isn't a gay play anyway, and is in fact a supercilious commentary on the situation of gays before the legislation which freed them. I'm talking about *Entertaining Mr Sloane* which isn't funny any more because the joke has been blown anyway. The other play was *Equus* which is an entirely superficial play about someone who stabs horses. It has, I suppose, some interesting if not very original psychological notions. It's most notable for its superficial spectacle rather than for a true theatrical experience. And then there was *Abigail's Party* which isn't a play, but a television piece, which is one of those insulting pieces in terms of humanity, written by Mike Leigh, a master of insults. He hasn't anything remotely to do with Wales. Theatre like Theatr Clwyd, situated in Wales, won't produce plays by Welsh playwrights.

HWD: *So how should Welsh theatre proceed?*

DE: That's an interesting choice of word, 'proceed', because it is rather a procession rather than a progression of the kind of plays I've talked about. It's a procession of plays that are irrelevant even to their cultural origins, but which are, for some reason, felt to be appropriate in a Welsh context. I voted for the Welsh Assembly because I was hoping that, when it's instituted, the playwrights of Wales, within the Welsh Playwright's group, which we hope to enlarge, will be able to join a debate about theatre that ultimately could possibly lead to a theatre that is *about* debate in Wales. How can any theatre in Wales claim to be reflecting a Welsh culture when it refuses to use the playwrights of Wales? Many of those playwrights have had to work outside Wales. There's a whole list of writers living in Wales whose plays have been done throughout Britain, in London, Leicester, Glasgow, Northern Ireland, Europe and North America. There's no trace of them in mainstream Welsh theatre like Theatr Clwyd.

HWD: *You've just mentioned the 'Welsh Playwright's Group'. Are you a member?*

DE: I'm an honorary member. I claim refugee status, a kind of temporary citizenship. Yes, I'm a refugee in Wales. Incidentally I spell my name now with a 'k' instead of 'c', to mark the change that logic has brought to my status.

Note

1 See Hazel Walford Davies, 'Theatre as Forum' [interview with Dic Edwards], *New Welsh Review* 31 (Winter 1995-6), pp. 77-83.

Reviews

LONG TO RAIN OVER US

Long to Rain Over Us (Haymarket Studio, Leicester)
The Times, 17 November, 1987.

This thoughtful and sprightly play, commissioned from the Welsh poet and playwright Dick Edwards, is set on the periphery of an unguarded prisoner of war camp in Leicestershire. Geographically, this is the centre of England, and the exact nature of the true and honest Englishman is one of the topics aired in a tightly-packed 90 minutes.

'Why don't the Irish want to be English?' muses the wooden-legged colonel (Trevor Baxter) in charge of the camp, his tender scalp protected with a knotted hankie from the unseasonably fierce sun. Since he is voicing his words in the hearing of an eccentrically resolute Irish girl, Kitty (Kate Lonergan), he gets a crisp and Celtic reply.

The land is in need of rain and three of the four male characters stand in need of a woman, the odd man out being Lomax, a conscientious objector also detained in the camp. When Kitty dosses down with him in the hay he turns his back. Stephen Boxer gives him the preoccupied air and rapid speech of one whose thoughts are also rapid.

An Italian and a German complete the cast, a jackbooted pair who start off close to caricatures but who develop into a beguiling double act when scheming to grab the girl and expose Lomax, with the colonel's connivance, as a fraud and coward.

The comedy in this is fresh and surprising, and the accompanying dangers come across vividly in the performances of Nicholas Hewetson's restless Italian, wriggling as if troubled by olive pips in his pants, and Bill Leadbitter's Braun, a confused but confident admirer of both Hitler and Freud.

Though he allows the action to move too hastily to its climax, David O'Shea's direction draws the main story steadily into prominence above the author's firework display of other ideas. A fascinating evening.

Jeremy Kingston

LOW PEOPLE

Low People (Haymarket Studio, Leicester)
The Guardian, 23 May, 1989.

Dick Edwards' programme notes to *Low People* give an analysis of ten years of Thatcherism, or Benthosism for the purposes of this drama. I wish writers didn't feel this overwhelming urge to explain their work, the play is labelled a parable and it's surely in the nature of parables to have elements of wilful obscurity. Why spell it out?

Low People, the third play in the Haymarket's new writing season, is 'about faith, good faith and bad faith'. Leo and Ursula are the victims of bad faith, Leo having been underpaid by his employer, Benthos, for his work at the demolition firm of Slakers and Waters. They live in abject poverty, scraping money together to help their mute and distressed daughter Verity. Benthos and his wife Nadir have grown fat on the profits. He aspiring to the council; she doing good works for charity.

Leo doggedly fights for his right to compensation: Benthos, the opportunist, sees him as a blackmailer. The scenes switch between Leo's wretched hovel and Benthos's office as the moral argument proceeds. God, because of his insecurity, has taken refuge in the church and is not to be relied upon for sound judgement.

The starkness of Leo and Ursula's moral stance and the wretchedness of their situation come across in searing, no holds barred performances by Deborah Hurst and Michael Brogan. Jack Elliott and Denise Stephenson as Benthos and Nadir are allowed more frivolity, more wit, everything splendidly tongue in cheek: he's inclined to come out with revelations like 'Fascism is the fear of democratisation by the bourgeoisie – write that down, would you?'

David O'Shea directs a powerful but somehow unsatisfactory allegory.

Pat Ashworth

Low People (Haymarket Studio, Leicester)
The Stage, 15 June 1989.

Benthosism, playwright Dick Edwards would have us believe, is the theory that power is all and that the end justifies the means. This, he says, is the age of Benthosism. Now, through his play parable *Low People*, part of the Leicester Haymarket Studio season of new plays, he exposes Benthosism.

I'm not sure that I go along with his views and theory, but that didn't stop me from admiring the performance of this powerful work, very well presented. It has all the elements necessary for a cry against society. There's the callous employer, ripping off his workers, his gullible wife, the hardworking employee who does 80 hours work and gets 40 hours pay. In their hovel the worker's wife scrimps and saves to get the cash she is sure will cure their young daughter, who cannot speak.

How well Jack Elliot plays the nasty, who convinces himself that he is being plotted against. It is really through his mouthings that we are shown the evils of Benthosism, and how believable Jack Elliot makes the character. Denise Stephenson gives the right gloss to the wife not quite convinced that what her husband is doing is right, but a party to it just the same.

There was some nice interaction between her and Deborah Hurst, as the struggling wife, who combined a belief that everything would be all right in the end with her battle for survival. Michael Brogan caught all the hopelessness of the wronged worker for whom nothing ever seems to go right.

If you look beneath the surface, there's some very deep stuff in this play. As I said, you might not go all the road with the message, but if you like good, strong theatre you can't help but like this production.

Quentin Clark

THE FOURTH WORLD

the fourth world (Theatr Clwyd)
The Evening Leader, 23 February, 1990.

When the violence of Colombia confronts a comfortable middle class couple in their home the result is an explosive situation.

The Fourth World by Theatr Clwyd writer in residence Dick Edwards deals with what happens when a young Colombian student stays in the UK home of his English teacher.

The teacher, played by Nicholas Pritchard, knows the problems afflicting a third world country like Colombia but does not want to discuss them. His wife, played by Helen Gwyn, knows little of such things but is eager to discover more.

All the action takes place in the couple's sitting room as their student guest, played by Dominic Hingorani, and the memories he brings with him from Colombia drive a wedge between the couple.

The wife gets more and more involved with the student, though for a woman who constantly claims to be stupid and an English learner at one point they play a game of mental chess which would tax a grand master.

The Fourth World is a thoughtful play which challenges our attitudes to third world countries as we look at them from the apparent comfort and safety of the west.

Nicholas Pritchard gives a fine portrayal of the academic who knows a lot more than he is willing to say and Helen Gwyn puts in a great performance as his inquisitive wife.

The play is a joint production between the Made in Wales Stage Company and Theatr Clwyd, and with more joint work in the pipeline it bodes well for the future.

the fourth world (Theatr Clwyd)
The Independent, 27 February, 1990.

The Made in Wales Stage Company has been devoted to presenting new Anglo-Welsh work since 1982. Despite financial problems, a new initiative with Theatr Clwyd means that they are now actually increasing the number of their productions. But if Made in Wales means exactly that, it does not necessarily mean that the work is about Wales. They clearly do not collaborate with that condescension which expects 'national' or 'regional' writing to tell us a bit about its own patch before we turn back to the world at large.

Dick Edwards's play is about all three worlds, and posits a fourth, although the action is confined to the white-carpeted circle of a contemporary English sitting-room. The setting and play are entirely naturalistic, though the surrounding inky blackness of Gilly Adams's production does just suggest how islanded this place is. Also, between each scene four vertical shafts of light stand sentinel and the actors freeze momentarily before they re-enter, implying that they are caught in some more distant perspective.

Nevertheless, the basic circumstance of this domestic three-hander does strain against its subject somewhat. On one level it is a familiar marriage drama in which incompatibilities are discovered and the resulting strife intensified. Charles is a voluble teacher of English to foreign students who presented his liberal credentials to himself some time ago and has not seen fit to query them since. Helen, in her co-ordinated track clothes, is virtually his ornament, but begins to exercise her mind. The catalyst for this is Gustavo, a visiting Colombian student.

In its leakier moments the play seems bent on presenting the worst dreams of any foreign student 'staying with a family': uncomprehendingly bored by one partner and incomprehensibly seduced by the other. But Dick Edwards's intention is more serious and complex. In Charles's arrogant, and Helen's fumblingly earnest assumptions about Gustavo's life amid the murder and corruption of Latin America, we see First World misunderstandings about the Third World blunder into real pain.

The play does, however, need a stronger narrative line. At present there is too much diversion in word-play, especially Charles's love of paradox. Intelligent and plausible as Nicholas Pritchard's playing is, it was still not clear whether or not Charles is indelibly soaked in irony. Also, too much information is saved for the end, giving Dominic Hingorani, very good at Gustavo's gaucheness, too much to cope with. Helen Gwyn has a difficult task with Helen's immature and not always convincing changes but manages outstandingly. Her voice may lack some range, but her acting is economic and concentrated and should become better known. *the fourth world* matches her for concentration, but not economy.

Jeffrey Wainwright

the fourth world (Theatr Clwyd)
North Wales Weekly News, 1 March, 1990.

the fourth world is a powerful, compelling drama about the confron-tation between a young Colombian man and a middle-class British couple.

The play explicitly highlights the atrocities in Colombia, where murder is the main cause of death for men between the ages of 15 and 44.

Written by Welshman Dick Edwards, the writer in residence at Theatr Clwyd, the play is set in the home of a university lecturer, who teaches English to foreign students.

Nicholas Pritchard, better known for his role as the handsome hunk in the current Daily Mail television advert – in which he rescues a woman being pestered by louts – plays lecturer Charles.

He is married to Helen, played by Helen Gwyn. As a couple they share liberal views and think they know what goes on in the world, at least until the arrival of the young Colombian.

the fourth world (Theatr Clwyd)
The Chronicle, 9 March, 1990.

Take a Colombian student and a comfortable, worry-free, middle-class British family, put them together and what do you get? Mental angst, mistrust, psychological battlegrounds and general ill-feeling – that is the way playwright Dick Edwards sees it in *the fourth world* which was staged at Theatr Clwyd.

In his powerful drama a Colombian native tries to come to grips with the most laid back of British lifestyles while his hosts' channelled attitudes refuse to widen under growing cultural clashes.

Gustavo Jimenez, played with superb feeling by Dominic Hingorani, has by his sheer presence caused enormous ideological friction between Charles and Helen Waldegrave, portrayed by Helen Gwyn and Nicholas Pritchard – known to millions as 'Mr Cool in the Daily Mail advert'.

The play sets out to be a powerful indictment of the apathetic way many people think. It achieves that in no uncertain terms. But it frequently plunges into a quagmire of amateur philosophy and profound thought.

the fourth world was performed by Made in Wales in co-production with Theatr Clwyd Company.

Guy Holland

REGAN

Regan (Crickhowell)
The Guardian, 8 October 1991.

Is Cordelia being petty to be obstinate over nothing, and is Regan the more moral character in King Lear? Dick Edwards thinks so, which is why the principal character in his new play as writer-in-residence with Theatr Powys is so named.

Subtitled 'In The Great Society', it is a provocative, challenging work about the nature of morality, liberal democracy, and freedom.

It does not sound like the usual community theatre fare and it is not, and all the more welcome for that. It is set in 1381 and 1991 and our crookback heroine, Regan (bravely played by Catrin Epworth), stepping out of role to act as contemporary narrator, is the hapless one trying to find a moral thread among the cant and false prophets.

At the time of the Peasants' Revolt, it is the story of the myth of the Great Society created by the church and law makers, a dream that rebounds on the impoverished Rakestaff family when the poor priest they trust returns, in smart modern dress, as the tax collector.

In contemporary terms, it is an extended parable about the ludicrous and unfair poll tax, class consciousness, and the scam of bourgeois democracy.

It is strong, meaty stuff, more in the style of Barker and Hare than the usual easily accessible, direct, targeted theatre we expect from the community label, but it does mean that some of the cast clearly find problems in delivering the text.

With the exception of Reg Stewart, they are generally inexperienced and while there are some committed performances, such a complex play of ideas can slip away.

Nevertheless, in the Clarence Hall in Crickhowell there was a heartfelt applause that suggests that theatre in the community can deal with complex themes and succeed.

Guy Roderick's production sets the action close to the audience but sometimes lacks pace and does not always make the story clear. Meri Wells's impressive metal set looks good but I suspect distorts rather than explains the acting and the anachronistic setting.

In brief, the play is not always well served. But it is a stimulating piece of theatre that will improve as it tours Wales.

David Adams

Regan (Aberystwyth)
The Stage, 5 December, 1991.

Most of us have dreams of leaving the lives we inhabit at some time or other. However, hopes for a better existence, either on earth or in the hereafter, have often been exploited by politicians and religious leaders throughout human history.

Dick Edwards takes this sorry truth as the starting-point for his sombre and richly textured play. The Rakestraw family seeks escape from a dark age of fear, slavery and mysterious taxation laws through belonging to the millenial Great Society, presided over by the priest-figure, John Nameless. But the religious leader becomes a secular tyrant, and the family is subjected to brutal abuse by its perceived saviour.

Regan enquires disturbingly into the nature of power over others. The unsettling effect is enhanced by Meri Wells's set design, constructed as it is out of the detritus of modern life, that strikingly indicates the Rakestraws' life on the edge – a precariousness that is suggested also by the disconcerting use of lighting.

It is a pity then that this production by Theatr Powys does not seem to have complete faith in Edwards's commissioned play. The tone of the playing is pitched too stridently, too early on to allow his ideas enough clarity, and it is never certain whether the play is intended as a political allegory or not.

Having said that, all is not lost, and there are moments of strong acting and dramatic tension, when the disquieting poetic language comes to the fore.

In particular, Catrin Epworth demonstrates the complexity of human motivation skilfully, with her performance as the hunchback daughter Regan who is tortured by her need to be desired at odds with stubborn independence.

Marie Lewis

CASANOVA UNDONE

Casanova Undone (Citizens Theatre, Glasgow)
The Herald, 27 March, 1992.

Casanova is old, deaf, and past it. He sits in a room in Paris in the Terror, writing his memoirs to the sound of the mob and musketry – recording for posterity the reputation by which he will be remembered.

Ah, but what's reputation if it can't be sustained? To prove that he's Casanova yet he will host those ageing ladies who still yearn to put his reputation to the test.

It's a con, of course. The big C is impotent and the act must be performed with the aid of his companion, a female dressed as a male, and a stock of dildoes. Nice bits of teak they are, too. The trick is that we're all alike in the dark. It's the sensation that counts.

Playwright Dic Edwards has a gift for the telling phrase and an eye for the bizarre, though the wit wears thin and the incongruities become too much in the end. The brilliant opening scene is best of all. Alas, it comes in a rush and then the play flags inexorably.

Casanova Undone is rich with nicely turned lines and it revels in the byways of sexual obsession. It's also a philosophical tease. Nothing is quite what it seems.

The production by Robert David MacDonald at the Citizens Second Theatre presents this world premiere stylishly, and designer Kenny Miller finds elegance in a small space.

The cast of three are excellent: Roberta Taylor as the faithful, harassed Sophie (or Costa in trousers), Siobhan Stanley as a beautiful emissary from a former conquest of Casanova, and Tristram Jellinek as the vain old rake himself – not just good but even Gielgudish.

John Fowler

Casanova Undone (Citizens Theatre, Glasgow)
Scotland on Sunday, 29 March, 1992.

Casanova Undone is a beguiling play by Welsh playwright Dic Edwards which alternates off-the-cuff moral philosophy with deliciously dirty bits. The whole is a critique of sexuality and power which ultimately rejects the model of sex as a battle-ground where the combatants fight for the ultimate sensation, and seducers notch up conquests: proposing in its place a perhaps more frightening union where domination has no place and the individual gives up the selfish sense of self. Needless to say, the first model is male, the second female.

The playwright's lavish taste is language, and a hugely sympathetic performance from Tristram Jellinek as the decrepit Lothario ensures that in this Citizens production there is nothing dryly theoretical about the piece. The ending falls short of convincing, but the rest is as enjoyable as an ideologically-sound Restoration Comedy.

A parallel theme is explored in the First Theatre, where Wedekind's *Lulu* is updated to a world of monumentally bleak interior decor and black leggings. The director/designer here is Jon Pope, who spins out Lulu's resonant, almost ritualistic, tragedy with a lighthanded realism which can encompass shocking stage effects and a strong element of avant-garde fashion show.

Julie Saunders, as the earth spirit trapped and crushed by bourgeois erotophobia, looks gorgeous, and strongly, sometimes uncomfortably, evokes the infinite tractability of woman. She expresses her truest self rarely but upliftingly in a full-throated, face-splitting laugh at the whole seething mess of it.

Casanova Undone (Citizens Theatre, Glasgow)
The Scotsman, 30 March, 1992.

There is a large bed, with a decidedly crumpled, lived-in-look to it, standing with an inanimate leer in the centre of the room, and what else could be expected when the inhabitant of the apartment is the great lover, Casanova? But the title, *Casanova Undone*, of the play at the Second Theatre in the Citzs carries with it the promise of defeat and the threat of irony.

Nothing is what it seems. This is a Casanova (played with the refined grandeur of an ageing patrician by Tristram Jellinek) whose salad days are gone, who sits in a closed room in Paris, surrounded by his own self-preening illusions – that he was the first bourgeois, that he was the originator of all youth cultures and, almost incidentally, that he exercises a magnetic appeal for women – while around him the puritanical votaries of the Great Terror swear death for all hedonists and voluptuaries.

Author Dick Edwards is skilled at dismantling myths, and not merely in showing Casanova as conceited and impotent but in portraying structures of self-mythologising that leads these women to sleep with the image of Casanova rather than with the man.

It is a highly literate as well as witty play, with some acute aphorisms and sharply turned dialogue, quite splendidly acted by all three performers.

Joseph Farrell

Casanova Undone (Citizens Theatre, Glasgow)
The Observer, 5 April, 1992.

The fine, compacting translation [of *Lulu*] is by Robert David MacDonald, who has also directed *Casanova Undone* by the Welsh playwright Dic Edwards in the Citizens second auditorium.

This witty and compelling philosophical farce spotlights the degenerate rake, his potency on the wane, in Paris during the Reign of Terror. His erection, like the old order, is flagging, but his reputation is maintained by the ingenious ministrations of his transvestite servant, Costa, and a bedful of polished wooden dildos.

Taking three episodes from Casanova's memoirs, Edwards links an early seduction to the final appointment at the court of Count Waldstein in Bohemia through the Parisian intervention of the curious Angelique (Siobhan Stanley, exotic and svelte, with hair like Rapunzel's). The scenario is complicated by her fascination with Costa, whom Roberta Taylor presents as a delightfully mature, rough compound of Sganarelle, Cherubino and Hofmannsthal's Octavian.

MacDonald bathes his precise and sexy production (designed by Kenny Miller) in gorgeous secular and religious music, with not so much a nod as a bow towards Nino Rota's glass harp score for Fellini's more casually episodic *Casanova*.

In the film, Donald Sutherland played the legendary lecher as a comical old goat for whom the sexual act was an interlude in the permanent bliss of expectation. In Glasgow, Tristram Jellinek is a reminiscent roue of noble profile, scathing vanity and the glinting malevolence of second childhood. A lovely performance in a fine new play.

Michael Coveney

Casanova Undone (Citizens Theatre, Glasgow)
Plays and Players, May 1992.

It would be curious to know whether, now that they have three theatres under their control rather than the traditional one, the directors of the Glasgow Citizens are choosing works to be performed as one overall package, rather than as single plays. For the spectator, one of the more unexpected by-products of the new arrangements is that plays and what they say acquire a deeper resonance by being seen side by side rather than being simply consigned individually to some dark and dry area of the memory.

There are new faces among actors, writers and directors; the company has renewed itself and has in the process gained something of a co-operative feel. This is not to imply that Messrs Havergal, MacDonald and Prowse have suddenly relinquished control, but that the actors have the opportunity of moving from stage to stage, and of developing in a definite context. Julie Saunders who last month played the Andromache role in Craig Raine's *1953* in the smallish Second Theatre this month finds herself playing the title role of *Lulu* in the wide spaces of the main house itself . . .

Lulu can be interpreted in a thousand ways, but none of them benefits from naturalistic precision. Sex and the power and fragility that accompany it, sex and the uncertain identity it bestows, sex and violence, sex and the hold of an ambiguous father figure, even sex and fun are among the themes which emerge from Wedekind's sprawling masterpiece, and Mr Pope and his troupe craft swaggering or stuttering frameworks for each of them, without plucking one notion for favoured status.

The Welsh playwright Dic Edwards might be embarrassed to have his work bracketed with Wedekind, but he is a highly accomplished demolisher of myths, with an ear for polished dialogue and a mind for the aphorism. Just because we have to lower our standards doesn't mean we have to live by them', says Casanova, seen in *Casanova Undone* in his closing days in a Paris made fearsome for hedonists by the puritanical votaries of the Terror. The only woman of importance in his life is his faithful servant, Sophie, who dresses as a man to perform the foreplay rituals which are now beyond her master, but whose main task is to bolster his inadequate ego. Tristram Jellinek, with his fussy mannerisms and fastidious speech, is the reincarnation of those patrician figures who people Velazquez' later paintings, but in both Roberta Taylor and Siobhan Stanley he has excellent fellow performers.

Lulu and Casanova represent opposing myths, both given to using sexual power for self-assertion, both ending crushed, the one under the hammers of a perverted killer, the other under the weight of a perverted ego. Both are dependent on others, for identity more than for gratification, but each uses the power that sexual force gives in separate ways. Both productions are stimulating and provocative.

Joe Farrell

Casanova Undone (White Bear Theatre, London)
Time Out, 21-28 July, 1993.

Casanova's embellished memoirs pulsate with *de trop* eroticism. Welsh playwright Dic Edwards opens his sensational play with Casanova on his last legs, vainly scribbling down feats of hedonism for posterity in a seedy Parisian apartment during the French Revolution. 'That's it! That's the truth,' he exclaims. It is, of course, anything but.

He can't get it up. So, Casanova's female servant, armed with a dildo, fulfils the desires of 'that random drift of noble slags'. The introduction of a deliciously preposterous plot acts as a catalyst for abstract *pensées* about sex and sexuality, aesthetics, and 'the bourgeois blueprint: a bible of lies'. The writing is sanguine and sophisticated: 'The Terror of the Revolution. It's new. You're old. It's a metaphor for what happens to all of us.' Decadence is a wilful fear of the future.

A spirited production is marred by Jack Elliot's blustering lead performance. Casanova is deaf; we're not. The mistaken exchange 'Happiness is forsaken'/'A penis has a foreskin?' violates our eardrums unnecessarily in the tiny venue. But we listen hard, relishing the fun of the bursts of philosophical debate. Championed by Robert David MacDonald at the Glasgow Citizens (where this play received its première), Edwards's *oeuvre* is shamefully avoided by mainstream London venues. 'People don't want Truth; they want 'entertainment'' – which is what his intellectually zestful writing gives.

Simon Reade

THE JUNIPER TREE

The Juniper Tree (Broomhill)
The Guardian, 20 July, 1993.

Broomhill, in Southborough, just outside Tonbridge, was once the idyllic country residence of a mid-19th century Lord Mayor of London, Sir David Salomons.

Conceived more for the demonstration of scientific experiments than for artistic performances, the theatre has a warm, wood-panelled interior, high proscenium, deep stage and sizeable orchestra pit, and is thus quite a discovery for chamber opera companies.

Already it boasts an International Opera Course . . . and on the week-end it offered a semi-staged presentation of a specially commissioned opera by Andrew Toovey, entitled *The Juniper Tree* . . .

Dick Edwards's libretto for the opera, laid out in four scenes lasting in all about 45 minutes, carefully disentangled the many strands within the original Grimm's fairy tale. If some of Toovey's music – its bursts of shriekingly high clarinet writing and assertive, astringent harmonies – called to mind Birtwistle (a composer who might well have been attracted to the story), there the resemblance ended.

While Birtwistle would have excavated some ritualistic formal pattern from the plot, Toovey concentrated on achieving a fluent narration, moving in and out of actuality and dreamlike sequences with sureness and conviction. From the opening viola solo to the final song of the Bird, his score was rich in references to folk music. Maybe Toovey will enrich some passages where his invention wore thin: but overall, the opera was well made and striking – and certainly a good first for Broomhill.

Meirion Bowen

The Juniper Tree (Broomhill)
The Observer, 25 July, 1993.

Broomhill, a Victorian house between Tonbridge and Tunbridge Wells, was built by Decimus Burton for Sir David Salomons, Lord Mayor of London, and enlarged by his nephew. In its theatre, opera returns to Kent after the Arts Council assassination of Kent Opera. This season: *Dido, La serva padrona, The Beggar's Opera, Ariadne auf Naxos*, and, a Broomhill commission, Andrew Toovey's *The Juniper Tree*.

Toovey and his librettist, Dic Edwards, have given lively form to the Grimm tale about a stepmother who kills her stepson and stews him for dad's dinner, and the daughter who collects the bones. By placing them under the juniper tree beneath which the boy was conceived – evergreen, ever-renewing nature – his metempsychosis is achieved into a sweet-singing bird and his eventual resurrection. Nursery Grimm, in days before children's tales were politically corrected, prepared one as surely as Wagner for the perils of life.

Toovey's telling, pared for four singers and septet, is direct in its melodic contours, but subtle and strong in its working. The performance – directed by Stephen Langridge, conducted by Charles Hazlewood, with his EOS ensemble – was a workshop try-out, enacted score-in-hand, and it was vivid.

Anne-Margaret Cameron, the daughter, was fresh, steady, delighting. Nicholas Hariades, boy and bird, was a fleet, gleaming, unhooty male soprano. Mary King was a passionate, exact stepmother. (Toovey and Edwards, unlike Grimm, allow her to survive, with a redemption-through-love possibility.) *The Juniper Tree* has a future.

Andrew Porter

The Juniper Tree (Broomhill)
Opera Now, October 1995.

Comprehensibility was also at a minimum for the first half of Andrew Toovey's opera *The Juniper Tree*, first performed from scores at Broomhill in 1993, now given full staging (directed by Stephen Langridge).

As we took our seats, the *trittico* set was still on the stage, plus music stands. We were then treated to a selection of the latest Toovey *oeuvres* for voice and assorted instruments, some of a quite appalling awfulness. His setting of Rilke's sublime poem 'Herbst' (Autumn) calls out for repressive legislation. We were then allowed a short interval, presumably to recover, before being bundled into two large coaches and trundled through the Kent countryside to some unidentified location, where, in a huge workshed we were treated to a quite remarkably good performance of *The Juniper Tree*.

It is one of the grimmest tales in the Grimm brothers' collection, of a stepmother who cuts off her stepson's head, frames her own daughter, cooks the boy and serves him up to the father when he comes home from work. The wife is obsessed by the juniper tree, as her husband once told her his treasure was buried at its roots. (He finally tells her the treasure was his dead wife.) During a storm a Magic Bird appears who Tells All, and finally changes back into the boy. Happy End.

Several things were remarkable here. First, the music of rare lyrical intensity, plus very sensitive and rewarding writing for the voice. Second, the structure of the opera itself (libretto by Dick Edwards), which kept a very tight hold on tension and momentum, and skilfully presented the different approaches possible to this mind-boggling tale. My favourite was an absurdist element strongly reminiscent of the textbook dialogue of Ionesco's *The Bald Prima Donna*, where couples talk like elementary dialogue in an English language textbook. A third plus was a truly excellent cast, of Marcia Bellamy as the Mother, Richard Morris as the Husband, Jacqueline Homer (who had previously sung for us at Broomhill) as the Daughter, and Nick Hatlades as the Son and the Magic Bird – a young counter-tenor who will certainly go far.

Fourth plus was Stephen Langridge's near-perfect directing; fifth, excellent playing from the Musicians, led by Charles Peebles, and sixth – in spite of faffing around over half of Kent in the dark, we did get our train back to London.

Della Couling

THE BEGGAR'S NEW CLOTHES

The Beggar's New Clothes (Broomhill)
The Independent, 25 August, 1993.

If you are going to try a steamy reinvention of *The Beggar's Opera*, you might think twice before trying it in Tunbridge Wells – but then do it anyway. The Broomhill audience who had made it past the strong-language warning signs, and down the vertiginous steps to the lakeside garden where a big performance tent was set up, looked a little uneasy at the prospect. They sipped drinks at tables in the café-style space, wondering what to make of the 18-point manifesto in the programme, or the handful of musicians who wandered about intoning catchy ditties. Half an hour on, three of the less patient watchers, disgusted in Tunbridge Wells, made an exit that lost some of its dignity when the man was obliged to return for a handbag.

Broomhill, the house where the personal opera theatre of Sir David Salomons, Britain's first Jewish MP, is under restoration, has had an ambitious summer programme (still to come, Jonathan Miller directing *Ariadne auf Naxos*). Too ambitious, maybe, since it evidently found problems in attracting the sort of sharp young crowd that must have been in mind for *The Beggar's New Clothes*. Still, the show drew warm applause as well as bewilderment. So it should: the collaboration between 606 Theatre and the EOS ensemble is rude and raw, but Gordon Anderson's staging keeps up its flair and pace through a near 90-minute span, and holds on to its precarious balance between the bawdy and the barbed with some gusto.

This is that rare thing, political theatre that can make you laugh whatever side you are on. Dic Edwards has written a *Beggar's Opera* for John Major's England, keeping the characters and the general shape of the plot but planting them in a world of deviants, mainliners and Young Tories. It does get wordy, but it manages to wrap up its radical analysis in some alarmingly succinct speeches and then to deliver a stream of one-liners that puncture its pretentiousness as firmly as they lighten the grossness of the sexual encounters.

Warren Belshaw's music switches rapidly in and out, like the numbers in John Gay's original. Meant for actors rather than operatic voices, it goes for instant punch and fluency and achieves a couple of strong *Les Mis*-type tunes, some suggestive scoring for a pair of trombones, a song about Macheath that's too close for comfort to 'Mack the Knife', and a genuinely touching moment (duly reprised) for the hypocritical but trapped Mrs Peach. Between them, the authors go for get-rich-quick targets that range from Italian tenors with hankies to vacuous pop songs for kids, in a number about lollipop-sucking which means exactly what you think it might.

There is a dynamic Macheath from Danny Sapani, and strong singing from Anna Galvin as Polly Peach and Lucy Tregear as her mother. Charles Hazlewood directs six musicians – only five on Thursday, however, thanks to an absent clarinettist – who continue roaming around the tent, dressed as the beggars of the day, and rightly prefer energy to fastidiousness. All in all *The Beggar's New Clothes* could do with 10 minutes' worth of tightening up, but just as the steam threatens to run out it achieves a climax that tips from black farce to high pathos in a couple of seconds. Not quite Brecht and Weill, but certainly more fun.

Robert Maycock

The Beggar's New Clothes (Cockpit)
Evening Standard, 25 August, 1993.

The Beggar's Opera was produced in 1728 and its success was as immediate as it was inevitable. The joy of it came as much from John Gay's bawdy satire on contemporary politicians and stuffy Italian opera conventions, as from Pepusch's adroit arrangements of many of the most popular song-tunes of the day.

Exactly 200 years later Kurt Weill and Bertolt Brecht produced a German update with *The Threepenny Opera* and the success of this version was as easily attributable to its extraordinary tunefulness and pointed satire as it was in John Gay's 1728 original.

Both works succeeded because they preached a message of no-nonsense in a vernacular which was at once easy and pleasing. Brecht's later revisions to *The Threepenny Opera* put a Marxist slant on the play which was not there before. Perhaps it was this that prompted Hans Keller to describe it as 'the weightiest possible lowbrow opera for highbrows and the most full-blooded highbrow musical for lowbrows'.

In any event the latest updating, *The Beggar's New Clothes*, by Dic Edwards, makes a socio-political meal out of it all which looks set only to bamboozle lowbrows and bore the highbrows.

Words and phrases like Nietzsche, Kant, bourgeois, Man and societal values are bandied about with a nonchalant disrespect for the coolness of a modern British audience. In *The Beggar's New Clothes* everyone proselytises and nobody entertains. I realised quite near the beginning when Mr Peach says: 'If you want to see the future, look at my bum', that I was in for a fairly dull evening.

Where both Pepusch and Weill revelled in contemporary musical idioms, Dic Edwards has had to look backwards, not only for his ideas, but for the accompanying music as well. Snatches of the National Anthem and the Red Flag mingle ingloriously with music from Verdi to Weill but no point is being made. Scrabbling desperately through the programme booklet for a clue as to what on earth was going on, I wondered why all the cast spoke in middle-class accents. Doesn't that somehow miss the whole point of *The Beggar's Opera*?

Dic Edwards's programme notes explained it all in a blinding flash of nausea. Of course! it's all about theatre luvvies. 'Naturalistic theatre is not necessarily bad – the worst form of bourgeois theatre in the modern era is that which appears to have a conscience.' Pass the sickbag please!

Alexander Waugh

The Beggar's New Clothes (Cockpit)
The Times, 26 August, 1993.

Critics love to enthuse over a show. Discouraging readers from seeing something feeble may be our social duty, but urging you to share in some happy experience is what warms our altruistic hearts.

This updated version of *The Beggar's Opera* was pressing, till well into the second half, the enthusiasm button. Dic Edwards has spiked his new lyrics with acid, the dialogue is funny: performances tingle with energy and directorial ideas are adventurous. Furthermore, Tom Hadley's simple set looks so good. A few boxes of old clothes serve for chairs and a bed, and no other furniture is provided, but a cloud of bleached garments soars up the full height of the rear wall, like white witches taking off for *Walpurgisnacht*.

Peach (Mark Heal) is in the used-clothes business, Macheath (Danny Sapani) runs a protection racket, and the character representing corrupt authority is Nickum (Phil McDermott), tax inspector, every mention of whose name is followed by five warning notes on the double-bass, as if the *Close Encounters* theme was being played at very low speed.

The Beggar's Opera is a mould for all seasons. When a playwright wishes to attack rascality, hypocrisy and corruption in high places, he can always adapt John Gay's story, change the lyrics, add a few contemporary tunes (the original songs were the popular airs of the day) and presto! – society roasts in his satire. Or would do if Edwards's declared belief in the power of theatre were borne out by reality.

He prefaces the show with a brief criticism of mere entertainment, and tells us to listen to the words. Which we do. With relish. He can rhyme Schopenhauer with petit-bourgeois, which is pretty classy, and not only does he make Peach a quick-witted, silver-tongued cynic, but in Heal he has a comic actor of the agility and vocal inflections to exploit the character's rich potential.

Edwards replaces the hordes of beggars, flaunting their non-existent injuries, with hoards of fashionably distressed clothing. 'For the rich to wear used jeans is equivalent to buggering the poor without risk.' The fit of his updated version does not bear detailed examination, but the surrounding commentary can be sharp.

So what goes wrong in the second half? The stammering Filch is so comically pathetic as Dylan Brown plays him that we have been enticed into ignoring the adage that nice people do not laugh at the consonantly challenged. But suddenly he must posture as a Mafia man, the dapper Sapani is seen to be on heroin (for no good reason), and even the singing becomes muddy, cramming too many words to a note. Macheath offers to give Polly (Anna Galvin) his lollipop: I should like to have heard her reply.

Yet the memory of the good moments persists. Gordon Anderson's direction for 606 Theatre craftily integrates the six-piece chamber orchestra, EOS, into the action, so that when Mrs Peach (Lucy Tregear) is warned to be on her guard, the trombones close in and threaten her with their jabbing metal-work. 606 is a vigorous company, teeming with ideas, and I enjoyed their *Honest Whore* at the Boulevard last year. But they have not pulled off so unified a work this time, and it is perverse to have found no way to include 'Over the hills and far away', the original show's only famous tune.

Jeremy Kingston

The Beggar's New Clothes (Cockpit)
What's On, 1-8 September, 1993.

It's off the trodden trail but the Cockpit near Lisson Grove is rapidly raising up the 'must see' list of venues. And its latest offering, Dic Edwards's radical reworking of John Gay's classic satire *The Beggar's Opera*, is certainly a reason not to book yourself on the next Edinburgh shuttle. Apparently there were walk-outs in Tunbridge Wells – it's not *that* shocking, but the *The Beggar's New Clothes* does reflect the 'arse end' of social order which thrives on harpooning weak targets (foreigners, disabled people) with gleeful lack of taste and in this instance (gulp) crude charm.

'Bourgeois' is the bogey-word, but this too is bourgeois theatre. Nietzsche in practically the first number? Come ON. So if the didactic attempts to strip away the mystique of theatre and contextualise the production in real life don't leave indelible marks, that's no loss. 'So we live as we oughta?' and 'Whose play are we acting in?' are the main refrains, Edwards lamenting within his framework of disgruntlement the rise of multi-channel TV at the expense of domestic discussion and protest.

Edwards depicts a topsy-turvy society ruled by the depraved and the corrupt, where begging is taxed and tax inspector Nickum (in lederhosen no less) has a predilection for bestiality. The 'new clothes' peddled by Mr Peach take fashion trends a step further towards the ludicrous: jeans ingrained with body fluids which, in Tom Hadley's static design, swirl up to the rafters.

Edwards has something to say but it's Gordon Anderson's physical treatment which catapults us round the big dipper: Warren Belshaw's derivative music catches the ironic melodrama, the players (chamber orchestra Eos) melting into the action, while the humour stretches from right-off jibes to Peach's Basil Fawlty-style anatomical excesses (superb stuff from Mark Heal) to lines in the lyrics which deliberately refuse to scan or rhyme. And there are two show-stopping set-pieces in Dylan Brown's Thatcher/Hitleresque version of 'Mack the Knife' and in a secretly photographed sex-with-animals session.

Forget Olivier. Forget anyone else, in fact. This Macheath (Danny Sapani) is a black 'young Tory' extortionist with a cheeky smile, a drug habit and union-jack underwear, singing 'Watch out for the socialist'. The production lapses when trying too hard to be too clever and it offers no cure for the ills it identified but black humour, audacity and imagination steer it through. Drinks all round.

Caroline Rees

The Beggar's New Clothes (Cockpit)
Ham and High, 3 September, 1993.

The original *Beggar's Opera* was staged in Lincoln's Inn Fields. No-one else would have it. Dic Edwards's stunning reworking of John Gay's 200-year-old classic wouldn't have looked out of place there today, in spite of the fence.

Instead designer Tom Hadley has dragged streetlife 1993 indoors, literally plastering a chainlink fence with crud-stiffened clothing that even the crusties have discarded.

These are eagerly bundled up and sold on by Peach, the urban beachcomber who lives on the scum of the earth, last amoeba-but-one on the fashion foodchain which begins with Yohji Yamamoto and ends with Inspector Nickum, Peach's very own financial parasite.

In Dic Edwards's world the poor are as desperate as they are deserving and closer to the bestial for it. Nowhere has the world of dog eat dog been so graphically and shockingly illustrated.

Employing a chamber orchestra, Eos, 606 Theatre Company fluidly creates an intelligent, biting modern satire that has all the flamboyant ease of a band of ragamuffin strolling players.

Dylan Brown, as Peach's otherworldly sidekick Filch, and Danny Sapani as the razor-sharp Macheath, stand out from what is already an excellent cast.

Amanda Blinkhorn

The Beggar's New Clothes (Cockpit)
Morning Star, 10 September, 1993.

This play by Dic Edwards is a retelling of John Gay's 18th century satire *The Beggar's Opera*. The production is a collaboration between two very inventive and innovative young groups, 606 THEATRE and chamber orchestra EOS.

Entering the theatre there are three sides of seats looking onto a street scene with the musicians in scruffy uniform warming up. A violinist plays alone while a guitarist and double bass player smile at each other as they ham.

Behind them is a great squall of petrified clothes, clinging to wire netting as if carried by a enormous frozen wind. Suddenly two people come down the aisles right among the audience and the play begins.

This was theatre that had the audience enthralled.

Heavy philosophical discussion and political debate would suddenly take flight on the wings of music whose seemingly effortless production (as musicians casually strolled on to the scene) belied its ingenious construction.

The actors did not play roles, but used the rough masks of character to talk about theatre and its relationship to society.

Each one plots against the other: the lumpen bourgeois Mr and Mrs Peach against the bestial Nickum (who threatens to tax the profits of begging), Filch (first 'cripple' and then 'wop') against his rival MacHeath and Polly and Nancy against them all.

The question they keep on asking is who is in whose play?

Adam Goldstein

WITTGENSTEIN'S DAUGHTER

Wittgenstein's Daughter (Citizens Theatre, Glasgow)
The Scotsman, 10 September, 1993.

There is a bell which clangs and jangles discordantly at the opening of each scene, or round, in Dic Edwards's challenging and enigmatic new play which invites people with some of the great names of 20th-century European culture – Wittgenstein, Celine and Beckett – to clamber into the ring for the renewed tussle.

It is the discordance of the bell which counts, for nothing on stage is quite in harmony with what it seems. Wittgenstein's daughter is no offspring of the philosopher, Celine is not the French writer nor Beckett the Irish playwright, although Wittgenstein's ghost is the genuine article.

These people are coarser images of their past selves, this Celine a National Front thug, this Beckett a boxer, this Wittgenstein's daughter the product of a coerced coupling between a prostitute and an enamoured disciple who wanted to protect his master from the accusation of homosexuality.

Perhaps this coarseness of the later generation is the point of the whole thing. Edwards seems to suggest that philosophical thought and cultural activities can indeed deprave and corrupt, and that today's rampant nihilism and random vandalism flow from yesterday's draining of language of all ethical content.

Certainly not since Stanley Eveling used to write for the theatre have I seen a play so imbued with the ideas of philosophers. The ending of history, the communication of values, the intertwining of private conduct and public thought are among subjects touched on, even if the author has then a tendency to shy away from them.

The deepest discordance is between the style of play and the urgency of the ideas. Rather than a coherent plot, Edwards prefers a quirky, flexible framework which allows the production to change tone and colour as it goes. The daughter (Anne Marie Timoney) is in quest of her father, and perhaps an intellectual heritage, but she is also pregnant by the thuggish Celine and, after an encounter over fish and chips with the spectral Wittgenstein, will give birth in the philosopher's tomb.

It is heady and intriguing stuff, especially given the physical style of acting. Robert David Macdonald, who also directed, cuts a fine figure in string vest and Donald Duck boxing shorts as Celine.

Joseph Farrell

Wittgenstein's Daughter (Citizens Theatre, Glasgow)
The List, 23 September, 1993.

Better news over at Glasgow's Citizens Theatre where fine productions are running in the two studios. *Wittgenstein's Daughter* is a new play by Dic Edwards in which a woman who believes herself to be the daughter of the moral philosopher Ludwig Wittgenstein, discovers that she was actually brought in to the world by his colleagues as a cover for his homosexuality. Her hatred of cliché and quest for truth is compared to his hatred of pretence and desire to achieve linguistic perfection; and both are set against the deceit that has affected her whole life. As with *Casanova Undone*, Edwards's last play for the Citz, this new piece has the sheen of saying something more clever or profound than it actually does, but it also has a greater sense of purpose and forward drive and adds up to a more satisfying whole.

Directed by Robert David MacDonald, who appears both as a neo-Nazi in Mickey Mouse underwear and as Wittgenstein's ghost wrapped in bandages, the play is performed in a clean white boxing ring, the characters' costumes crisply colour-coded by designer Rebecca Loncraine. Anne Marie Timoney gives a compelling performance as Alma, the assumed daughter, trying to make sense of her end-of-millenium blues without malice or anger, just genuine spiritual curiosity. Her search is offset by Beckett, the boxer and companion to Wittgenstein, played in his younger years by a spikey, amoral Daniel Illsley and in his later years by a world-weary, more politically adroit Patrick Hannaway. Dic Edwards fires in unusual directions to try and hit what I imagine he sees as the moral vacuum in contemporary society. Thanks to an intelligent interpretation, here is a production that does justice to his theme.

Mark Fisher

Wittgenstein's Daughter (White Bear Theatre, London)
What's On, 9 February, 1994.

Dic Edwards's play *Wittgenstein's Daughter* is intellectual, accessible, funny and provocative. Alma, who has always believed she is Wittgenstein's child, is pregnant by her neo-fascist husband Celine. Driven to despair by his platitudes and lack of moral responsibility she confides her fears to a strange concierge in a Parisian hotel, who persuades her that she must confront the spectres of her past if she is to build a future for her child. After her husband attacks her in his underpants and socks she flees to Cambridge where she meets Beckett, a retired boxer and Wittgenstein's first lover. During the course of an extraordinary evening she eats fish and chips with the philosopher's ghost, his face bandaged so he will not be recognised, and discovers that history is not what has happened but what is said to have happened . . .

As Alma, Robyn Moore takes the first act to settle into the play, treating every line as if it were a thesis and killing her performance with a passionate weightiness. This may in part be an effort to counter the ridiculousness of Celine, whom James Snell plays with an incongruous accent borrowed from the worst excesses of *'Allo 'Allo*. (Indeed, reducing him to mere parody defuses the threat that his fascism and diminished morality presents.) However, Moore's performance in the remaining acts is motivated by a more genuine passion, and as a result we are treated to a sentient and humorous delivery.

Snell returns as Wittgenstein's ghost, beautifully sober as this distinguished and demanding phantom, while Roger Monk's Beckett is mesmerising. The character is supposed to be a hundred years old, and Monk physicalises this with sincerity and exaggeration. The muscles in his neck struggle to form each word: he is loveable, cantankerous and bitter. His performance alone makes the play worth seeing. Ronald Rees' direction is superb, allowing the absurd to ride in tandem with the mundane, and he skilfully captures the love that dare not speak its name between the philosopher and Beckett. (As Beckett bandages the ghost's head he pulls the bandage away from the ear to whisper: it is at once preposterous and tender.) At one point Alma remarks that the world has become a cartoon: 'The words are in bubbles and they never change the stories.' Theatrically at least, *Wittgenstein's Daughter* attempts to redress the balance.

Louise Stafford Charles

UTAH BLUE

Utah Blue (The Point, Cardiff)
South Wales Argus, 24 February, 1995.

Like so many murderers, the name Gary Gilmore still fascinates almost 20 years after the crime which led to his execution, spawning books, a film and even a punk rock record.

The Made in Wales Stage Company's first production in a new season at this atmospheric new venue – a former church in the heart of Cardiff's docklands – is a hard-hitting, uncompromising play about the life and death of the Texas-born killer.

Gilmore, portrayed here in a mesmerising, eerily convincing performance by Dorian Lough, was executed by firing squad at Utah State Prison in January 1977 – at his own request – for the apparently motiveless murders of two men.

Dic Edwards's play explores Gilmore's strict Mormon background, his troubled youth and relationships with his impressionable younger brother, Mikal (Andrew Howard) and morbid, melancholic mother, Bessie (Hilary Beckett), who lulls her sons to sleep with tales of the day her father took her to watch a public hanging.

It gives us an insight into Gilmore's destructive brand of philosophy and fatalism. And, perhaps most significantly, the production looks at his passionate, obsessive love affair with Nicola (Linda Quinn, impressive in a hugely demanding role).

Publicity for the play warns of graphic language, 'loud bangs' and nudity – and they're not kidding. Heartbeat it ain't, folks!

There are also simulated sex scenes, and all this adds up to a brutal, emotional, gut-wrenching, couple of hours – definitely not for the fainthearted.

Jeremy Johnson

Utah Blue (The Point, Cardiff)
The Independent, 1 March, 1995.

Coming to the point took on a new meaning in Cardiff last week, when the city's new arts space opened its doors for the first time. The Point, a handsome church now beautifully refurbished and rechristened, nestles at the heart of the docklands, a mile from the city centre and just minutes from the site of the city's much-debated opera house.

Formerly St Stephen's Church, it ceased functioning in the 1970s, but in its heyday at the beginning of the century it was prosperous and influential. It now seems surprisingly large, given its position, but, as Maggie Russell, the venue's artistic director, points out, it was originally at the heart of a rising industrial society.

'At the turn of the century, Cardiff was one of the busiest ports in the world because of the coal and steel it exported. Because it was a seafaring community, the church was very important – people would go to church before they went to sea. You can tell it was one of the most prosperous churches in Cardiff not just from the size, but from the huge stained glass windows. They saved up and commissioned a new window on a seafaring theme every five years. Two of them are by the William Morris company: they are insured for £75,000 each – they are actually worth more than the building.'

It seems appropriate that the church, once at the centre of the port's industrial life (it is only yards away from the mammoth Coal Exchange), should now be part of the regeneration of the area and its new lease of life as a cultural and business community. It flourished for a while in the Seventies as St Stephen's Space, the performance base for the dance company Moving Being, but since then has lain dormant.

Its current rebirth is thanks to a literal marriage between the arts and business. Maggie Russell's partner, Steve Allison, runs Design Stage, a graphic design company currently housed nearby. The company bought the building and, when its conversion is complete, will be based in it. This means that, while Cardiff Bay Development Corporation gave them a grant to do up the building (roughly equivalent to a quarter of the total refurbishment cost of £400,000), no public money is going into its running.

Russell is emphatically positive about this sort of relationship between the arts and business. She points to the fact that the building will constantly be in use, so there will be no need to give it an artificial life during the day, and that encourages a sense of stability. And by putting her instincts boldly into practice she feels that she is making a point about the vitality of the cultural life of Wales.

'Usually, business sponsorship of the arts amounts to giving some money and having your name on the bottom of the poster. I'm very interested in finding ways for the arts to develop their own autonomy. I think we're all clear now that the Arts Council doesn't have the money to really grow. So we have to come up with new strategies so that the arts can survive and flourish.'

Russell has tried to retain the character of the church in the restoration. 'I wanted to create a simple but very beautiful building for the arts, rather than consigning new theatre and music to a black box above a pub. We've tried to show respect for the building.'

Russell has programmed the space for the next six months with a combination of drama, music and performance art. She has chosen companies that have a following so that they face less box-office risk, and will also host business conferences to bump up the income. First in is Made in Wales, a lively and dedicated theatre company that has spent much of its 13-year-long existence touring new work around Wales. It is presenting a season of four new Welsh plays and for Gilly Adams, the company's artistic director, The Point is a godsend.

'It's a glorious opportunity, long-awaited. We badly needed a venue in Cardiff dedicated to new writing, but we had no money ourselves to run a venue. It has meant that we have been able to do a proper season of work for the first time – normally we only ever do one production at a time.'

The company launched its season with what could only be described as a baptism of fire – Dic Edwards's *Utah Blue*, a brooding, provocative play about the American murderer Gary Gilmore and his bizarre interior world. It is a dark, challenging piece, powerfully performed, and by no means the sort of obvious 'Welsh' play you might have expected. It will be followed next week by the Welsh premiere of Lucinda Coxon's *Waiting at the Water's Edge*, which was well-received in London, then a play be Peter Lloyd and an adaptation of Caradoc Evans's 1930s best-seller *Nothing to Pay*.

'We've chosen four very different plays that represent some of the best new writing in Wales,' Adams says.

Sarah Hemming

Utah Blue (The Point, Cardiff)
Gair Rhydd, 6 March, 1995.

'If there was a heaven, we'd have to go through hell to get there; most people settle for hell', so reads the legend on the flyer for tonight's performance. The Point Theatre is a converted church in the fast developing, devilishly controversial, Cardiff Bay Development. Oh, the irony. Utah Blue is the first in a series of new plays; and if described in music terminology it would be coined as New Wave of New Wave. It is a controversial, minimalist, realist dramatic production, and it works extremely well. The set and the setting, combined with the proximity of the audience, placed on three sides of the stage, intensify the action leaving you nervous and frightened, yet intrigued.

Utah Blue is based on the actions of Gary Gilmore (Dorian Lough) who shot dead two men in cold blood in Utah 1977. Nothing so incredible there, but his infamy springs from his subsequent demands for his own execution, following the state's life sentence.

Thankfully the play manages to avoid the obvious, and staid, route of a 'dramatic' unfolding of events (how long until Kevin Costner produces an epic version?) and concentrates on the elements of Gilmore's psyche which produced the man and his disposition. What emerges is a man confused by sexual desire married to impotence, Mormon values corrupted by carnal curiosity and a creative artist destroyed by reality. His gradual acceptance of fate and futility is in stark contrast to the moral qualms of his brother, Mikal.

The catalyst for the play's protagonists are the females: one femme fatale, one maternal, affecting both brothers. The girlfriend fucks them both, physically and mentally, in scenes that shock. The violence and overt sexuality remind you of the current trend for ultra-reality (i.e. sex and violence) à la Quentin Tarantino. The needless disposal of all her bodily drapes became the biggest half time talking point amongst the smokers who congregated outside the theatre. 'In the name of art' seems to cover just about every needless nude scene designed to pull in the punters.

Apart from this, the play seems to extol every aspect of the appeals of modern, homegrown talent. Okay, the set (two camp beds and a chair) seemed budget, but the performances certainly weren't. The powerful imagery leaves you drained, wallowing in Gary Gilmore's hell, not caring what his heaven might hold.

Hamish Nisbet

Utah Blue (The Point, Cardiff)
The Stage, 6 April, 1995.

The life of Gary Gilmore, his apparently motiveless murders of two innocent men and his execution at his own request by firing squad form the basis of this compelling yet repellent play.

Utah Blue, by Dic Edwards, launched the Made in Wales Stage Company's 1995 season at The Point. All four plays being staged span themes of gender, murder and physical abuse – and *Utah Blue* certainly qualified. Edwards's drama was uncompromising in its violence, brutality and sexual obsession. These were given full rein by director Michael McCarthy.

Whether this play provided any significant insights into the mind and motives of Gilmore, the so-called 'culture of murder' and the values of the society he grew up in is a matter for conjecture. Whatever, it made for a provocative and harrowing two hours.

The strength of the acting was unquestionable. As Gilmore, Dorian Lough gave a simply charismatic portrayal, with Andrew Howard dynamic as his brother Mikal. Linda Quinn, as Nicole, the sexually explicit catalyst of so much of the action, displayed notable skill, while Hilary Beckett, as Bessie, the mother of the two men, provided some most welcome quiet and moving moments.

John Holliday

Utah Blue (The Point, Cardiff)
New Welsh Review (Spring 1995).

Under the astute guidance of Gilly Adams the Made in Wales Stage Company has proved a champion of new writing in Wales for over ten years. Dic Edwards has been a writer associated with the company from the beginning.

In *Utah Blue* he has a story to tell. We all know it. But this does not prevent him from presenting strong images of the executed man that disturb and dominate the stage. In the second half, however, Gary Gilmore – for this is the tale of the murderer who demanded his own death – is reduced to a ghost haunting the players on stage in a way that reduces action and interest. Gilmore's speeches – great arias that Edwards has made a speciality of his own – have no place now in an action that sidelines him.

In Michael McCarthy's energetic production the stage is dominated by the chair. Not the electric chair. Gary Gilmore was executed by shooting. In the first half Gilmore sits in the chair, unstrapped, he languishes in it, almost plays in it, it is his familiar. He is shot and disposed of by the interval after forty five minutes of high-octane interaction between the four characters – Gary himself, his brother Mikal, his wife Nicole and his mother. The danger of bathos in a second act that has to follow this looms large and is not entirely overcome. Any sensationalism and melodrama is eliminated, but Gary's ghost is no substitute for the presence of Gary interacting with his relatives as in Act 1. He hangs around and witnesses his brother replicate his own approach, his own sex, his own failure with Nicole – and its comedy too. This interesting technical parallelism emphasizes the contrast between the two brothers and opens out a new subject for the second half: two contrasting versions of maleness. Unfortunately there is not all that much difference in the drawing of the male characters. Same upbringing – mixture of Mormon authoritarianism and blood-lust revenge, a household riven by parental violence and dissension. In real terms there's all the difference between the two. Mikal is still alive. He is free, alive, and apparently an artist – something Gary either failed to be or didn't want. What Gary did want is the love of the father. This is clear from Edwards's source – Mikal Gilmore's autobiographical writings. Gary wanted the love, and he wanted the out – the true independence he reckoned Mikal had found for himself from the family.

But the father is an absent character. So the focus on motive – why did Gary kill the two men who were the first humans he got hold of that night of the killings? – is blurred by this omission. But Edwards offers plenty of other suggestions ranging from the practical to the philosophic and existential. Indeed the brothers carry out long high-pitched discussions – making the play less of a completed action and more of an extended argument kept going by unflagging energy and eloquence. The tendency is towards speechifying but the mixture of direct audience address and interaction on stage is skilfully handled and results in a layered effect that successfully presents the painful complexity of human connections.

Along the way there are satiric speeches – ironic realizations of futility. These provide good examples of Edwards's gift for radical ridicule. They underpin the play's harsh comedy and are more clearly focused than some of the more tendentious attempts at philosophizing.

The connection with Wales? Edwards himself offers no excuses for writing of these American characters, but he does see in the events a warning of social breakdown that has its relevance in the neglect – amounting even to abandonment – of Wales in its post-industrial decline.

Graham Allen

The Man Who Gave His Foot for Love (Chapter Arts Centre Cardiff)
New Welsh Review (Winter 1995-6).

The best of the conventional plays was, to my mind, Dic Edwards's *The Man Who Gave His Foot for Love*. Edwards, who currently has two operas in production, depicts a comically murderous Latin American reality, shrouded in crass superstition and the kind of myth to which only we fallible mortals could possibly give credence. A visiting Welsh doctor, ostensibly rational and humane, is slowly sucked into the evil and corruption of the ramshackle hell-hole, led on by his lust for the beautiful Indian wife of a blind guitarist and his unscrupulous mother. The songs are harmonically intricate, with lyrics sometimes hauntingly poetic, or rousing in the manner of Weil or Eissler. The stagecraft, implicit in the structure, reveals the maturity of a writer who has synthesised plot, character, language and music to create an absurd universe in which black humour can flourish, weaving a disturbingly dark spell around the audience, even as they laugh.

Mark Jenkins

CHRONOLOGY

DIC EDWARDS – STAGE PLAYS

Late City Echo	The Sherman Theatre Company, Sherman Arena	1981
At The End Of The Bay	Made in Wales Stage Company, Sherman Arena	1982
Canned Goods	Made in Wales Stage Company, Sherman Arena	1983
Looking For The World	Sherman Theatre Company, Sherman Main Stage	1986
Long To Rain Over Us	Leicester Haymarket Company, Haymarket Studio	1987
Little Yankee	The Torch Theatre, Milford Haven	1987
Doctor of the Americans	The Central School of Speech and Drama, London	1988
Low People	Leicester Haymarket Company, Haymarket Studio	1989
the fourth world	Theatr Clwyd Company, Emlyn Williams Theatre	1990
Regan	Theatr Powys, Wales Tour	1991
Casanova Undone	Citizens Theatre Company, Citizens Theatre, Glasgow	1992
	London City Theatre Company, White Bear Theatre, London	1993
The Beggar's New Clothes	606 Theatre Company, Broomhill International Opera Festival, Kent and Cockpit Theatre, London	1993
The Juniper Tree	Opera libretto for Broomhill Opera Company performed by the Company	1993
	Broomhill International Opera Festival	1995
Wittgenstein's Daughter	Citizens Theatre Company, Citizens Theatre, Glasgow	1993
	London City Theatre Company, White Bear Theatre, London	1994
Utah Blue	Made In Wales Stage Company, The Point, Cardiff	1995
Lola Brecht	Castaway Theatre Company, UK Tour	1996
The Man Who Gave His Foot For Love	Spectacle Theatre Company, Chapter Arts Centre, Cardiff and Tour	1996

3 Deaths of an Idiot (1995), *The Idiots* (1996) and *Idiots!* (1997). These are three separate versions, based on Dostoevsky's *The Idiot*. Unpublished.

THEATRE IN EDUCATION PRODUCTIONS
(All for Spectacle Theatre Company)

Moon River/The Deal	Wales Tour	1992
The Shakespeare Factory	Wales Tour	1993
David	Wales Tour	1996
Kid	Wales and Northern Ireland Tour	1997
Vertigo	Wales Tour	1997

PUBLICATIONS

Dic Edwards, *Low People* (Lampeter: Bardprint, 1989).
Dic Edwards, *the fourth world* (Lampeter: Bardprint, 1990).
Dic Edwards, *Regan* (The Press Gang, 1991).
Dic Edwards, *Three Plays: Casanova Undone, Looking For The World, Long To Rain Over Us* (London: Oberon Books, 1992).
Dic Edwards, *Wittgenstein's Daughter* (London: Oberon Books, 1993).
Dic Edwards, *Utah Blue* (Cardiff: Made in Wales, 1995).
Dic Edwards, *The Shakespeare Factory, Moon River: The Deal*, *David* (Bridgend: Seren Books, 1998).

Edward Thomas

'Not much of a dream then is it?'

Edward Thomas interviewed by Hazel Walford Davies in Gallipolis, Ohio, July 1997.

HWD: *You and I drove last night from the airport in Columbus, to the University of Rio Grande, Ohio.*[1] *En route we passed houses that were mirror images of the one constructed for the film* House of America. *Today, however, here in Gallipolis, within a stone's throw of the spot where the Welsh immigrants from Ceredigion disembarked at the beginning of the last century, we see nothing that kindles the imagination or reinforces the myth of America as the land of the Dream. As Boyo says to Sid in* House of America, *'Not much of a dream then is it?'*

ET: Too right. This is my first visit to rural Ohio, and after our bizarre journey from Columbus down here, the line between fiction and reality is really blurred. We had a burger and French fries last night in a diner where the table-mats illustrated Jesus on the Cross and a tableaux of praying hands. Well after midnight, we arrived at Gallipolis to find that there was no room for you at the inn [The Holiday Inn, Gallipolis]. And then, this morning I went on a journey that made me think I was really existing in a dream-world. On the banks of the Ohio here in Gallipolis there's a notice indicating 'Beach Front'. That's a joke. In Europe, or indeed, even in Wales, such a magnificent riverfront would boast a pub, a restaurant, a viewing area, but all you see on this 'beach front' is a convoy of lorries delivering iron or steel bolts to large factories. Along the front, too, is a ribbon of cheap diners and dime stores. I despise the 'Happy Shopper' mentality of America. American functionalism is the exact opposite of my aesthetic concerning fiction and the imagination. Here in Gallipolis the banks of the Ohio are full of elongated trucks – penis extensions to the male machismo. They're functional. America itself has a functionalism, a concreteness that has a reality overload. Take this town. Gallipolis has a population of 30,000, but it hasn't a restaurant worth the name. All you have is a strip of fast-food shops, cheap mini-malls, a gun-store and economy motels. These Americans live in bulk. On my hotel television this morning the list of the ten American best-sellers were as follows: Pamper nappies, peptic indigestion tablets, Scotowels, acid tablets, another brand of nappies, acid tablets again, yet another brand of acid tablets, the fifth brand of acid tablets, nappies again, the sixth brand of acid tablets. Americans seem to be living on indigestion tablets, and it seems to me, from the television advertisements, that all their problems can be solved by acid tablets and nappies. But the way of life here has no hips, no romance, no imagination, no possibilities. It's functional and false. Language doesn't mean anything over here. I don't think people listen when others say, 'Have a nice day.' I just heard you say 'Thank you' to the woman who filled your coffee cup and told you to have a nice day. I myself felt like saying 'Fuck off' or 'Wash my socks'. But of course the answer would be 'Pardon sir? Have a *really* nice day'. Here in Wales we are far more impolite than the Americans, but when we are polite, we mean what we say.

HWD: *The Dream then is certainly dead and buried?*

ET: For me it's a fiction. But look around us. Everywhere in this town we see the American flag flying which means it's very much alive here. And the American Dream is still a hugely concrete exportable myth. But the idea of the Dream of freedom and equality is wrapped in crass commercialism. The Dream is still a global phenomenon and America is eminently successful at exporting crap all over the world – Mickey Mouse, Macdonald and KFC. I am both attracted and repelled by America. American dramatists are lucky in having an exportable mythology. Take Sam Shepard, for instance. He can go to a caravan in the mid-West and write what appears to be a pretty domestic play, but somehow its branches can reach out, and it becomes a dramatic counter-argument to the American Dream. A dramatist writing in Wales has no global myths although we do have myths and stories that sustain us at home. But, unlike Sam Shepard, we have no *exportable* myths. And so a dramatist who works from a country without global myths has to work with primary colours. Either you create a myth and export it, or you work in pastel shades which nobody can relate to or understand. What people want to buy are British myths. When we as a Company travel abroad, what our audiences expect is a British kind of theatre, but we seek to define our theatre as Welsh theatre.

HWD: *You're due to lecture tomorrow to a large group of Celtic scholars, some from Wales but most of them from America. No doubt you'll tell the audience that Wales has no exportable myths. Do you think they'll agree with you?*

ET: No. But you'd have the same problem with any group of exiles. The Conference is entitled 'Visions of Wales', and I'm aware before I give the lecture, that the American vision of Wales is a million miles away from what real Wales is like in the 1990's. I'm not interested in smashing their vision, but what I'd like to emphasise tomorrow is that the Wales of the future – and I hope Wales has a future – will be an eclectic, modern European society, where 'Britain' has become an anachronism. In the Wales of the future the coalmines will have disappeared, our ability to compete internationally on the Rugby field may or may not exist, the Eisteddfod may or may not exist, but I hope that the image of Wales that the Welsh Tourist Board currently exports will have disappeared for ever. Rivers, mountains, the Druids, the Mabinogion and the Gymanfa Ganu do not represent my Wales. I want a Wales at ease with itself and rejoicing in its natural eclecticism. I don't want to see a Wales locked in a debate about Welsh and English. I want a multicultural Wales with a myriad of sustainable myths. The old Wales is a country without an architecture, without a symbol like an opera house. The new Wales has to be fast, maverick and imaginative, and innovative and inventive in its aim to be a small, interesting country within an European context, a country where the albatross of Britain has finally fallen from its neck. It certainly has fallen from my neck. I like England, but not Britain.

But the important thing for me is to see a grown-up Wales, which is self-defined and not stereotypical. It's healthy to have self-defined myths. I find that our culture is sometimes very servile to stereotypes, and my argument is that we have to have the confidence to construct our own sense of who we are. Wales has never had a self-conscious modernist or postmodernist age which means that Welsh people can wear flowers, a red beach jumper, have spiky hair, listen to Margaret Williams and hymns and drop acid all at the same time without any contradictions. Wales is all inside-out, back-to-front and postmodern without even knowing it. Take this as an example. Richey James from Manic Street Preachers one day went whistling along Pontypool High Street and then his car was discovered abandoned on the Severn Bridge. Do you know that some people in America think that Richey James is a mythical figure? Pontypool High Street then becomes like Jim Morrison's grave in Paris or the Chelsea Hotel in New York where Dylan Thomas stayed. It's wonderful seeing Americans walking Pontypool High Street looking for the grave of Richey James. So you don't have to have your 'hero' in the Chelsea Hotel in New York any more. You can find him in Kwik Save in Ponty, asphyxiated auto-erotically!

HWD: *Early on in your career, however, you went to America for your mythology. In* House of America *Sid says, 'I wish I'd been born someone else, somewhere else.' For you, America was that 'somewhere else'.*

ET: I grew up wanting to be someone else and it seemed to me that there was a possibility of being that someone else in America. America was hip and Wales was the opposite of that. Most of the people I went to school with wanted to clear off out of Wales because Wales had no contemporary mythology. I became Jack Kerouac for a short period of time and I ran a fringe theatre in Fulham. I shared a flat and a girl-friend with an American. He was a bisexual and I was heterosexual and she was, well, disappointed. In our fiction he was Neil Cassidy because he didn't have an education, and I was Jack, because I had graduated from the University of Wales, Cardiff. We lived a fantasy life. He wrote sub-Neil Cassidy poems and I wrote sub-Jack Kerouac poems and Roger McGough liked them. During a read-out I realised I wasn't Jack Kerouac and I saw clearly that the poems were crap. I stopped playing the Kerouac game there and then. I realised also how false the larger mythology of the American Dream was. If Russia had been 'cool' at the time I wrote *House of America*, I could have written about the 'Russian Dream'. But in 1989 the concept of the American Dream was in the ascendant – baseball hats were being worn back-to-front, bowling alleys, Kentucky Fried Chicken, Macdonalds – all these were being peddled over here, and the multiplex cinemas, based on American models, gave us the impression that America wasn't over there but all around. The truth is that I have a love-hate relationship with America. My concern is that it exports a kind of monoglot culture, a dangerous simplicity, a facile world which, as an European, I find counterproductive. I was twenty-seven when I wrote *House of America*. Now I'm looking for a different kind of theatre.

HWD: *Can you describe your kind of theatre?*

ET: I've often said that I write dramas of possibilities, inasmuch as my plays don't begin from a certainty. To be Welsh at the end of the Twentieth Century you need to have imagination. The one thing you need on your birth certificate is the word 'imagination'. I call my plays 'dramas of possibilities' because I, as much as any other person, am searching for a path, for meaning. My job as fiction-maker is to make up fictions because good fictions tell good truths. Sometimes, to kick off a play, I have only a landscape, not a particular theme. But I'd probably argue that all my plays have the same theme, and I probably will have to put up with that theme for the rest of my career. However, I don't think that's necessarily a bad thing since variations on a particular theme can be interesting.

Edward Thomas

(*photo*: Simon Chapman)

The cast of *House of America* (1988)

(Photo: Tony Standley)

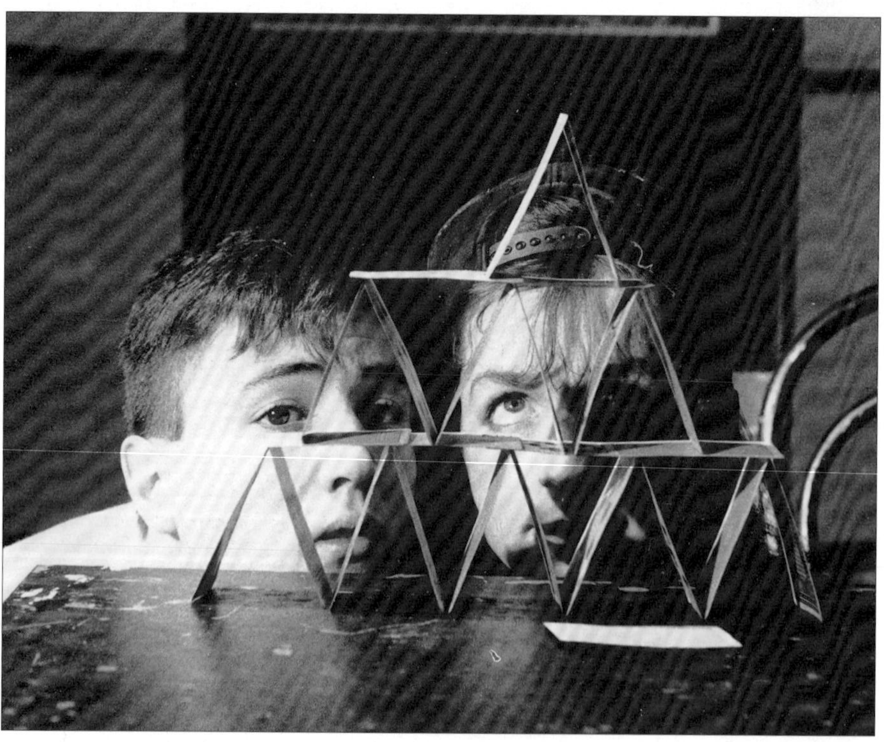

House of America (1988)

(Photo: Tony Standley)

House of America (1988)
(Photo: Tony Standley)

House of America (1992)
(Photo: Tony Standley)

House of America (1992)
(Photo: Tony Standley)

House of America (1992)
(Photo: Tony Standley)

House of America (1997)
(Photo: Brian Tarr)

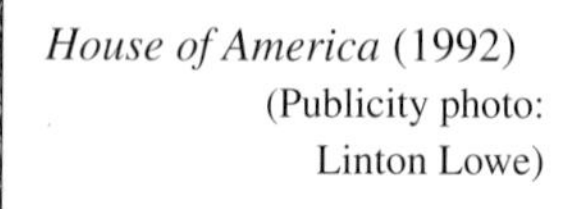

House of America (1992)
(Publicity photo:
Linton Lowe)

House of America (1997)
(Photo: Brian Tarr)

Edward Thomas with a model of the 1997 set of *House of America*
(Photo: Nick Treharne)

Tŷ'r Amerig (1997) A performance of the first translation into Welsh of *House of America*, The Cabin, Aberystwyth (1997)
(Photo: Lowri Huws)

Adar Heb Adenydd (1989)
(Photo: Brian Tarr)

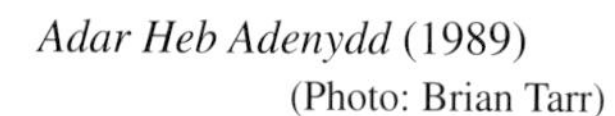

Adar Heb Adenydd (1989)
(Photo: Brian Tarr)

The Myth of Michael Roderick (1990)
(Photo: Tony Standley)

Flowers of the Dead Red Sea (1991)
(Photo: Tony Standley)

Flowers of the Dead Red Sea (1992)
(Photo: Linton Lowe)

Flowers of the Dead Red Sea (1992)
(Photo: Tony Standley)

East from the Gantry (1992)
(Photo: Kevin Low)

Hiraeth: Strangers in Conversation (1993)
(Photo: Tony Standley)

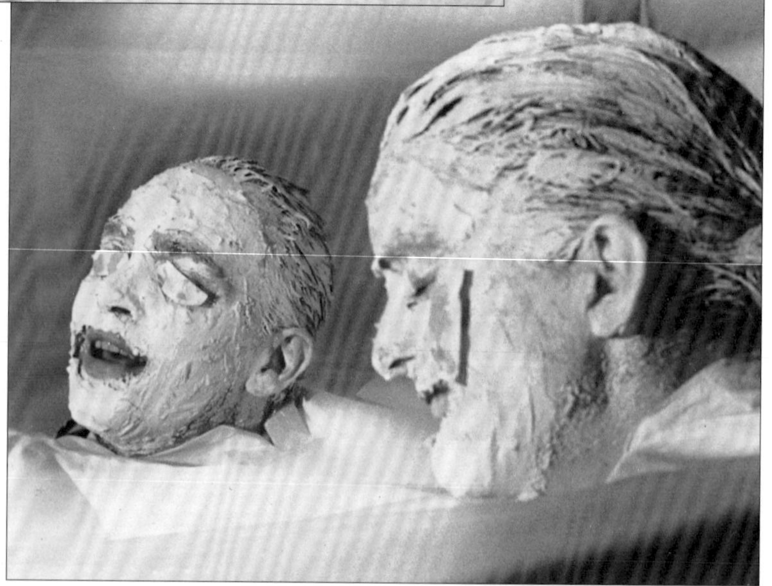

Envy (1993)
(Photo: Brian Tarr)

Song from a Forgotten City (1995)
(Photo: Brian Tarr)

Song from a Forgotten City (1995)

(Photo: Brian Tarr)

Song from a Forgotten City (1995)

(Photo: Brian Tarr)

Song from a Forgotten City (1996)
(Photo: Brian Tarr)

Song from a Forgotten City (1996)
(Photo: Brian Tarr)

Edward Thomas and Russell Gomer: *Flowers of the Dead Red Sea* workshop, Theatr y Werin, Aberystwyth (1997)

(Photo: A. Parry-Jones)

Gas Station Angel (1998)

(Photo: Pau Ros)

HWD: *What, then, is that particular theme?*

ET: I suppose my main aim is to try to discover what mythology means in contemporary society and especially in contemporary Welsh society. I'm happy to be a Welsh writer, but there also has to be universality as well. I'm content to work from a small area in South Wales as long as my plays have relevance to, say, Barcelona or to Ohio where we're having this conversation. It gives me considerable confidence that people choose to translate my plays into other languages, although no one to date has done a translation into Welsh of *House of America*.[2] The British Council don't pay for my plays to be translated so I'm delighted that people from different cultures in France, Germany, Spain and Montreal choose to translate my plays when they have a wide range of international plays from which to choose. And when they do translate it they place it within a Welsh context. They don't adapt it to a Catalan or Quebec context. So the central theme, the central metaphor of my plays means something to them; the themes therefore are universal and not locked into a parochial view of the world.

But on the question of 'theme' I'd have to add that I'm pretty obsessed in my plays with absent fathers. I can't analyse that. Playwrights aren't the best people to deconstruct and describe the nature of their plays.

HWD: *Why do the Catalans, although they like* House of America, *prefer* East from the Gantry*?*

ET: *House of America*, as I've often said, felt for a time like yet another albatross around my neck. I'd written one good play in *House*, but the subsequent ones were not as good, but they were different. *House of America* is easy to get your head around since it's heightened naturalism, but the plays I wrote subsequently don't follow the same strong narrative. Rather, they experiment with form and style. The Catalans, although they liked *House of America*, preferred *East from the Gantry* because of its shape and the gaps it had. What I mean by 'gaps' is that in my theory of 'drama of possibility', they found more possibilities of fitting their own Catalan version into my text. In *House of America*, because the metaphor and narrative are so strong, you take it or leave it, so there's less room for manoeuvre. When I work with Y Cwmni, now Fiction Factory, the plays serve me and we work within our own interpretation. When other people and nations do the play they are free to see other possibilities within the text. It pleased me that the Catalans chose to do *East from the Gantry* rather than *House of America*. That albatross has also finally dropped from my neck.

House of America is the least translated work of all my plays, and the French translation, to be performed in Montreal this summer, will be the first translation of *House of America.* To come back to your question, I think the Catalans relate to the themes of my plays – the theme of shifting identity, of how to be a small but significant voice in a changing Europe and a changing world, and maybe, how to reclaim and reconstruct the past and make it your own, and also how to create an attitude and a confidence. I'd probably argue that all my plays have the same theme and that I probably will have to put up with that theme for the rest of my career, but I don't think that's necessarily a bad thing. The important thing is to have variations on the theme.

HWD: *You're clearly not prescriptive about the way your plays should be produced. What is it, then, that makes your plays 'plastic' or 'dramas of possibilities'?*

ET: Part of the explanation is that the process of writing plays is a journey of discovery for me. When I begin writing I have no idea *what* I want to write. Initially, I just write three to four hundred pages of dialogue without male or female characters. The characters, then, are sexless and stateless. What I have are words and rhythms and at least two hundred pages have to be scrapped. I might start with a landscape. Often that's enough of a kick-off. And I like having deadlines. But even after writing the three hundred pages I don't know exactly where I'm going. I construct a narrative out of those pages and after that I do a careful re-write. It's very rarely that I'll use more than probably a page of complete dialogue from the initial pages.

HWD: *Indeed, there's no such thing as a 'final re-write' in your case. The plays are continually updated.*

ET: Yes, I'll be updating *House of America* for the 1997 Autumn tour and, who knows, I may revise it even during the tour. *Flowers of the Dead Red Sea* started with six characters and that's how we did it when it opened in The Tramway, Glasgow. There was a whole sequence about linking art and killing, but I saw that the strength of the play was the landscape and the two slaughtermen. In the original play I had an artist who was the lover of one, or possibly of both, of the slaughtermen. But I didn't think that the scenes with the artist worked. So when I directed and adapted it to a radio version, I had two men and a woman. The woman was the conscience, the chorus. When it came to publishing the play I felt that what I was really after were the two slaughtermen. And they weren't really two slaughtermen. It was a much stronger metaphor than that. *Flowers* could be set anywhere because it's about story-telling, memory. What I was conscious of doing was developing a dialogue which takes us beyond the rhetoric of '*Ni yma o hyd*' (We are still here). I wanted to say that Welsh identity is as fragile as Tom Jones's dicky-bow. I also wanted to convey that we were living in a world we don't comprehend and I wished to explore the idea of being good as opposed to being bad. Mock and Joe could be two men in hell or two men in heaven. When we staged *Flowers* in The Tramway, it was absolutely slated by the Scottish critics. We then took it to London and back to Glasgow again. The second time the play was transformed.

HWD: *What did the critics have to say about* Flowers *the first time round in Glasgow?*

ET: Rough, tough, brutal, violent, nasty – they used all those adjectives. They also stated, 'it grapples with the guts of theatre'. I have no idea what that means. *Flowers* isn't a well-made play. I think my plays are well-made from another point of view. I don't like 'well-made' plays that have an argument and a counter-argument and a message relayed to a sheep-like audience. I find that very problematic. I like layered plays that suggest possibilities, plays that are open to different interpretations from different audiences and cultures. For example, *Flowers* was performed at the Castle Theatre, Aberystwyth last year and two women played Mock and Joe. I'm really pleased when somebody produces an unexpected and fresh version of my play. In Barcelona, Madrid and Montreal people do my plays in different ways. They are all equally valid. It means that my plays can be about different things to different cultures while still maintaining a coherent flow. I hope there's something in the text of the play that liberates the imagination. My job as a writer is to write about the world I know, and if the themes and metaphors become universal, that's for someone else to decide. In some productions of *House of America*, for example, the names I gave the characters are retained. In Barcelona they kept the Welsh names and Welsh places even though the play was in Catalan. In the Montreal production they changed the names to Jean Claude, Alvarez, Maria and Maman; they appropriated the play to their culture. In Quebec they think *House* is the play that Quebec never wrote because they're surrounded by North America, and the American Dream is far more pertinent to them than it is to us. They thought it very strange that a Celtic country across the Atlantic should be obsessed with the American Dream. Small nations understand the themes of *House of America*, they understand the invisibility, they understand what a huge culture like the American one can do to small cultures and nations. But if, during performances in various countries, the play loses its Welshness, it probably gains in some other way. I distrust art that tells you what to think. If my plays are only the assertion of my point of view, then they cannot be good plays. I, as dramatist, am a flawed man and I'm as confused by the world as any watcher of my plays. I am a fiction-maker and I don't claim to be prescriptive. My job is to be imaginative, to make things up. Maybe the way I work has been conditioned by the fact that I was interested first of all, not in the character, but in the actor.

HWD: *In writing your plays are you thinking of particular actors?*

ET: Yes, maybe. It has something to do with the way 'Y Cwmni' was established. We were all unemployed, and the first play we did was *House of America*. I was lucky enough to have a body of actors who were committed to my way of looking at things and who wanted to do my plays. In collaboration with people like Russell Gomer and Richard Lynch I learned certain theatrical possibilities. They never treated my text as if it were a 'new play' or 'new work'. There's nothing more off-putting than 'New Writing'. It means, 'Don't go to see that play, it will be crap'. Members of 'Y Cwmni' collaborated to solve acting and directing problems, and we didn't cut the text willy-nilly. But we weren't overprotective of the text, either. The main thing was that we never sat down and discussed 'the meaning of the play' or the policy of 'how can we work together?'. Indeed, when we started doing workshops three or four years ago we felt quite nervous and diffident about it because we were trying to respond to people who were asking us to 'describe our process'. But we didn't have a process, except the one that declared, 'I'll throw it, you catch it'. My process has got to have hips. I'm the scrum-half, and I like actors with hips. By that I mean that I like actors than can glide through defences with an ease. My job as director is to release that 'ease'. What pleases me is that, in the plays I've written, the actors have been free to see that there are enough clues in the text to construct the characters that they want to enact on stage. That, of course, is often based on the kind of people the actors are. So, inevitably, there's a Richard Lynch part and a Russell Gomer part. I hope that in my plays there's a gap for the actors to take on board the possibilities of the play, and to feel that they're expressing their own words, rather than using their acting skills as a vehicle for expressing Edward Thomas's world-view. My world-view is as confused as anybody else's. Richard Lynch and Russell Gomer have used their own voices in constructing characters.

HWD: *Russell and Richard are now working for the RSC, and you will have to work with new actors. Is your process of writing going to change?*

ET: Not radically, but I will of course have to work with new actors. I've just had a play accepted for the Royal Court. I have ten actors, and when we did the reading in the Duke of York I deliberately chose people I hadn't worked for before. I chose Philip Madoc, Sharon Morgan, Jason Hughes, Simon Harries, Michael Sheen – people I hadn't worked with before. We did a very quick private reading in the morning and we had only an hour and a half to discuss the plans for the 'official' reading in the afternoon. The afternoon reading was terrific and Stephen Daldry thought it was the most exciting reading he'd heard for two or three years. I'm thankful the actors got the spirit of the play. Working with new people therefore will be a welcome challenge. We all have to grow up and move on.

HWD: *In moving on you've reinvented your company. It is now 'Fiction Factory'.*

ET: In 1989 we were called 'The Company'. Then we changed our name to 'Y Cwmni', because we were a Welsh Company. But because the scale of our work was increasing, and because on our travels to Germany, Australia and England, and indeed within Wales, people couldn't pronounce 'Y Cwmni', we had to re-think. Anyway, what did the name mean? 'Fiction Factory' seemed to be an umbrella name for all our work. If you place the emphasis on 'factory' it appears as if we churn things out willy-nilly and make nuts and bolts. The word 'fiction' changes all that. We've often re-invented the focus of the company, and changing its name was actually much easier than I thought it would be.

HWD: *Tell me about the play that has just been accepted by the Royal Court.*

ET: At the moment it's called *The Aces of Gaerlishe* or '*Where we go when we drive a blue-tinted glass Marina 1800TC into the heart of a Saturday Night?*'. Or the title might be *Gas Station Angel.* I'll probably stick to the third title. It's probably the closest thing to a straight narrative I've written since *House of America.* It's a kaleidoscopic road journey between a man whose house has fallen into the sea and a dancer who has missing brothers. It's a strong story, the language is heightened and it's got a voice-over. In fact the whole play is heightened. I like the absurd. All you have to do to see absurdity is to look out of the window. But I wouldn't define myself as an absurdist writer in the Ionesco sense. What I like about the absurdist tradition is its enquiry about the world, between order and chaos. In art, we're not recording reality; we as dramatists are not journalists discussing the issue of unemployment in the South Wales valleys or the use of heroin or ecstasy in Cardiff or London. As dramatists we don't discuss issue-based things. We weave fictions, reveal issues which exist only in fiction, but fictions which contain possibilities of telling certain truths or reflections about the world. Take *Song from a Forgotten City*. If I'd put a narrative to that play I'd say it was about a lonely smack addict who lives in this city, hasn't got any confidence, but wants to become a hero, to be centre-frame. The only thing he knows about the films he's seen, like the film noir, is that you start at the end and work back, so if he places himself in his own fiction, 'Man shot dead in a hotel room and discovered by bell boy', he naturally becomes a hero. The narrative interest of the play, therefore concerns itself with the question of 'How did this character get to be shot in this hotel room?'. You realise at the end of the play that it's all fiction anyway. But, during the course of the play, that doesn't stop you from believing that what you are watching is something with which you can legitimately engage.

HWD: *Recently Seren published the play* Hiraeth *in a volume of selected one-act plays. Do you think* Hiraeth *could be performed without the context for which it was first written?*

ET: I certainly wouldn't be comfortable about performing it without that particular context, although the editor of the selection of the volume of one-act plays must have been of the opinion that it could stand on its own two feet. *Hiraeth / Strangers in Conversation* was an installation piece, a collaboration between myself and the artist Iwan Bala. When *Flowers* was first produced Iwan painted seven canvasses for the production and in 1993 he suggested to Jenny Spencer Davies that he and I should work together. My play would be there, not to describe his paintings but to recreate imaginatively what the themes were. He'd done a lot of work in Zimbabwe and when he was there he had a dream about Wales being the mainland that he could never reach. And then, when he was in Wales, he had a dream about Zimbabwe in ruins, and again he couldn't reach it. The dream had mythic meanings. In his work he tried to convey the sense of 'hiraeth', of never being in a place, but always longing for it. In the background you might see a canvas he had painted three years previously, and then he'd pull the glass a foot or two away from the canvas and start painting on the glass. It became something like a palimpsest. I had to write something about that gap between the canvas and the glass. The only thing I could come up with was this idea of two disembodied heads that appear above a parapet in a landscape of nothing. These heads don't know who they are. In forty-five minutes they have to make up a past for themselves and imagine a future. They have to invent on a blank canvas. They begin to talk and express fear of the landscape in which they find themselves. One of them tells a story about a trip in America and both have visions of absence and presence. In Iwan's work there were, as I said, canvasses he had painted three years previously, and I therefore deliberately used characters from my previous plays *House of America* and *Flowers of the Dead Red Sea*. It was a self-conscious mélange, and I shall probably never perform it again. I directed a Welsh-language version of the play, and acted in it. We performed the play in Oriel Gallery, Cardiff and then took it to Swansea.

HWD: *You've just mentioned that you're a director and an actor as well as a playwright. Do you find that your skills as actor and director have helped your work as a dramatist?*

ET: Well, I use the term 'actor' loosely. I'm not a very good actor and I don't enjoy it. I became an actor through financial necessity. Although I'd never acted before, I was offered a job in *Pobl y Cwm* and I did it for three years. But, yes, my experience as an actor has helped in practical terms. Knowing my limitations as an actor means that I'm well aware of what's difficult about acting. Also, in order to allow me to make a living as a writer, I've been lucky enough to have had the opportunity to direct a lot of television and I've directed three films. This means that I can cross-fertilise my ideas between film, television, radio and theatre. I've done an opera with John Hardy and Music Theatre Wales, and I've worked a great deal with John since then. He scored *Double Indemnity* which we did in the Royal Court and which we'll do in the West End next year. He also created the soundtrack for *Song from a Forgotten City*. We're lucky in Wales because we can cross-fertilise between the different media without self-consciousness.

HWD: *In the case of your work, of course, you've adapted your plays for radio, television and film. Is it difficult for you to transpose a theatre piece into a film?*

ET: *House of America*, for example, has a strong narrative but we had a hell of a battle to make it acceptable as a film. I wrote the script but the director Marc Evans collaborated closely with me inasmuch as he and I worked on realising the film and defining the images. The film we both imagined became the script. Marc Evans is probably the only director I'd trust with my work, and it would be great if we could collaborate every two or three years. Marc was probably more protective of the words of the original play than I was. We worked on the film for six years and eventually we got the money to make it. What attracted Marc to *House of America* was the metaphor that the play says more strongly than the film – the metaphor concerning the American Dream and the lack of contemporary Welsh mythology. There is in *House*, too, the idea of Welsh characters being cool dreamers. There is nothing wrong with Sid, he just selects the wrong dream. But the quality of his imagination is terrific. In the play the choice of the wrong dream becomes a tragedy. In the film, however, as soon as you put Sid Lewis on a motor-bike, the loser becomes the hero. We use the South Wales landscape in the film and Wales appears as the big little county. Wales is shot in colour and America in black and white, and America appears quite small. While complaining about Wales's lack of heroes, we have in the film created one. Wales wins by doing a double-con. In the first production of *House of America* it was a case of 'Let's make something up before it's too late.' But my autumn production of *House* will be fuelled by the ideas and the thinking that were developed while making the film. The film and the play will co-run, and at the same time there will be a Galician version, a Spanish version and a French version. What puzzles me is that nobody is particularly interested in doing a Welsh version of it.[3] I'd like to do most of my plays one day in Welsh, but I'd be interested if somebody else translated some of the English texts into Welsh. In fact, one-eighth of *Aces of Gaerlishe* is in Welsh. I don't know whether the Royal Court will use sub-titles – they've never had the Welsh language on that stage before. There's another 'first' in the play. It's the first time that anybody has good heterosexual sex in a play of mine. So being a heterosexual man, I am, after seven years as a fiction maker, writing good heterosexual sex! At the end of the new play the characters re-invent a sex language in Welsh which is very healthy I think. I've yet to meet anybody who can have exciting sex in Welsh – it's either overridden by guilt or it's completely unromantic.

HWD: *How would you define yourself – as a writer or a Welsh writer?*

ET: Oh, as a Welsh writer with international aspirations. A Welsh writer is primarily one who writes about his own square mile. For me, the idea of Wales as an imagined nation is a really interesting one. But in Wales, and certainly in Welsh-language theatre, there is still a perverse kind of naturalism.[4] In the seventies naturalism was big in Britain, and in Welsh-language theatre it is still the dominant factor at the end of the nineties. And naturalism isn't the best model to express Welsh ideals, especially in the Welsh language. If you watch *Eastenders* or *Coronation Street* you can accept the premise on which they're based, you can accept that life can be like that. But I've said to you before that in *Pobol y Cwm*, the reality is so selective that it's almost like Fantasy Island. If in *Pobol y Cwm* a hooker turned up to see a gynaecologist and wanted legal representation, that scene would be a brilliant absurdist scene because you couldn't identify the reality of it. It would be Theatre of the Absurd at its most brilliant, and I think that's liberating rather than confining. In Wales only about a fifth of the population speak Welsh and so the premise on which *Pobol y Cwm* is based is completely unbelievable. If you dropped the sound boom into the frame and revealed the cameras, then potentially you've got an interesting way of showing what the real Wales is. In the Welsh-language, real Wales probably exists in the Television Studio rather than in the rural areas.

It needs a master of style to liberate the Welsh language. On S4C the language is made into a laughing stock because it has no mastery of style. S4C style is borrowed and copied from elsewhere and appropriated to a Welsh context and expression that ridicules the language. That offends me greatly. If you create fictions you have to know what style means in terms of culture, expression and in terms of your reality and perceived reality. Style is the most important thing. People who practise in the Welsh language need to understand what style suits the language in order to liberate it. Let's not ridicule the Welsh language with the use of naturalism. Naturalism is a joke.

HWD: *You said to me earlier that you enjoy creating pictures on the stage and that you will aim at this in your future directing ventures. Is this because you've been involved with film, which is picture-driven?*

ET: The dynamic of cinema is the picture, the dynamic of the stage is still the picture, but the words have to carry more weight. I enjoy writing for the theatre because I like words, but words without a picture are meaningless. I think my directing for the stage is getting to be more cinematic and more sophisticated. I know how to construct a screen play and I know how the cuts work. You can use the same techniques in theatre and have numerous narratives going on at the same time. Many people think that *Aces of Gaerlishe* is cinematic and I'm very keen to do a cinema version of the play. The landscape, characters and narrative will be the same, but I will provide a different dynamic. Some people will call it an 'adaptation' of the play. I call it 'a pretty much full realisation of something woven around the same theme'. Working on a film has taught me a great deal. You have to communicate ideas very clearly to fifty or sixty people and you've got to prepare carefully. It's no good going on the set at 8.00 a.m. and saying 'Oh, wouldn't it be a good idea if we had this or that prop here?'. I think theatre people could learn a great deal from the rigour, the preparation and the communication that is needed to work on a film. You've also got to be pretty humble about yourself and your abilities, and you've got to find a system whereby you can creatively gloss over the weaknesses and maximise your strengths. It's much more rigorous than theatre or television.

HWD: *You have often described television as 'the bastard child' Why?*

ET: What I mean is that film and theatre have become the forum of adventure and ideas. Television doesn't interest me that much, not because of any snob value, but because of the nature of broadcasting at the moment. It's more formulaic than it's ever been. It needs international sales to sustain a thirty minute drama or a fifteen minute sit. com. And television drama needs world-wide sales. That means that it *has* to be formulaic, and the individuality of the author is submerged. There are some talented writers who can survive this straight-jacket, Jimmy McGovern in particular.

HWD: *Will you, while over here in America, go to the theatre in, say, Boston or New York?*

ET: Theatre is dead in America. I'm amazed how low it's sunk. Broadway is fast disappearing and 'Real Estate' is taking over. Independent American cinema is taking over the role of our fringe theatre. The forum for powerful and exciting ideas in America is not the theatre but the Independent American Cinema. In Britain, however, I think that theatre is undergoing a renaissance. There's a buzz there. Stephen Daldry is doing a great job at the Royal Court. Welsh theatre, however, is in the doldrums.

HWD: *Is that why you are looking beyond Wales, to Europe?*

ET: Yes. In Wales, there's not enough investment in theatre. Maybe it's not the fault of the Arts Council of Wales. It's probably to do with the Welsh Office. Seven years ago when Y Cwmni was starting out we were the young Turks. In Welsh theatre there were people who were more experienced than us – Moving Being, Made in Wales and Brith Gof. They were funded as revenue clients. We were not. We were not 'The Establishment'. In the last seven years Volcano, Brith Gof and Y Cwmni, were the companies that toured most extensively outside Wales, but these three Companies cannot, in reality, be regarded as 'Establishment' Companies, by the very nature of their work. What worries me is that there are no young Turks coming up behind our companies now. There is no energy, no enthusiasm, no bright young things with gusto and élan. There's no 'New Wave'. I think that theatre in Wales is an abject failure, or rather the reception of theatre *within* Wales is depressing. The Companies I've mentioned have received acclaim, not by touring Wales, but by presenting their work in Europe and the U.K. There is, after all, only a limited number of theatres in Wales where we can tour. The cost of productions prohibits doing things from the back of a lorry. I'd much rather be a Welsh artist plying my trade in the world than belong to a struggling 'Welsh Theatre Company' with access only to touring Wales. In Wales, too, it's a failure of the imagination from venue managers. More worrying, perhaps, is the fact that dramatists in Wales have not been able to attract the imagination of Welsh audiences. Sustaining an audience in Wales has always been a problem. Do Shakespeare and the classics, and you have a full house. Do something challenging and new, and you have half-empty houses. I myself am an optimist as long as I can tour internationally.

HWD: *You talk of 'empty houses' in Wales but you yourself aren't a great frequenter of the theatre.*

ET: No, I'm not. Classical theatre doesn't appeal to me. Too often I see plays that are journalistic in their expression. What I've enjoyed are circus groups, Theatre de Complicité performances and the scale of Brith Gof's work. I'm not a Thespian. I like the 'possibilities' of theatre. I think that theatre should release the imagination for people who want to be taken on a journey. I don't think anyone wants sensible footwear. Nobody wants to espouse mediocrity. Nobody wants to part with ten quid for an evening that doesn't take them to a landscape or fire them up. I dislike the kind of theatre, represented by the theatre of the 70s and the 80s, that tries to bring everything down to ordinariness. Theatre of the ordinary is like washing up. Nobody likes washing up unless he or she is high on drugs. Washing up isn't interesting.

I enjoy the theatre of the imagination, the theatre of possibilities. Bridging the gap between the actor and the audience to me is paramount. The actor knows what is going to happen next, the audience doesn't. The actors are the fiction-makers and the audience are the collaborators. To refuse to acknowledge this fundamental difference is to create the theatre of the ordinary. In my kind of theatre I aim at the extraordinary.

Notes

1 In 1997 Edward Thomas was invited to deliver a lecture on Welsh Theatre at the annual conference of the North American Association of the Study of Welsh Culture and History, held at the University of Rio Grande, Ohio.

2 In October 1997 Iwan England translated *House of America* into Welsh (*Tŷ'r Amerig*).

3 The Welsh version, *Tŷ'r Amerig*, was performed by Cwmni Seithug at The Cabin, Aberystwyth, 14 and 15 December, 1997. The performance was reviewed in *Y Cymro*, 24 December 1997, in *Golwg*, 8 January 1998, in *The Big Issue Cymru*, 26 January 1998, and in *Barn*, March 1998. See also Iwan England, 'Lladd America', *Golwg*, 11 December, 1997.

4 Hazel Walford Davies, 'Wanted: A New Welsh Mythology' [interview with Edward Thomas], *New Welsh Review* (Winter 94-95), p. 55.

Caught in the Act: On the Theatricality of Identity and Politics in the Dramatic Works of Edward Thomas

Heike Roms

. . . a whole language, a way of life, a people drowning . . .
She said art can save culture.[1]

Mock the butcher could have spoken these words about his own creator, Edward Thomas. Thomas's entire *œuvre* has been motivated by the ardent belief that the art of theatre may have the capacity to save a culture from drowning in insignificance. In Thomas's case, this hope of rescue is aimed at the culture of Wales, a culture which in his own words has been 'paralysed by lack of self-esteem and lack of confidence'.[2] In an early programmatic essay on 'Wales and a Theatre of Invention'[3], the writer drafts his vision of how a new Welsh theatre could contribute to the future of Wales and Welshness. Echoing the influential thesis of historian Gwyn Alf Williams on the need for a constant reinvention of Wales in the face of a permanent threat of extinction[4], Thomas closely connects the fate of political reinvention with that of theatrical inventiveness:

> In a Wales that only exists in the hearts and minds of those who desire it and who see that existence based on constant re-invention, any new Welsh theatre must be a theatre of invention, with its own new language, form and style. It is a theatre based on a life imagined rather than a life reproduced; and naturalism can play no part in it. The argument for a new Welsh theatre of invention is part of the argument for a new and invented Wales.[5]

The commitment to a political cause like that of the reinvention of Welsh identity must not be mistaken for a simple dramatic blueprint for political activism. Edward Thomas's plays have nothing in common with the often crude literalness that characterized the agitprop theatre of the 1960s and 1970s. A 'theatre of invention' suggests instead a more complex understanding of the 'political' in theatre as a reaching over of art into life, fiction into reality, via the force of the imaginary. Thomas attempts nothing less than turning the conventional notion of the 'political' in theatre on its head. What interests him is not so much the way in which the theatre may be able to reproduce a political reality, but the way in which reality is able to accommodate the models for identity and political action that the theatre has imagined into being. This has made Thomas the most stylistically conscious playwright in Wales, whose interest in the political implications of form and style sets him apart from the British dramatic convention of social realism.

Thomas's concept of a 'theatre of invention', however, is not without its contradictions. Despite the writer's passionate wish to create reality in fiction's image, his plays often show us the reverse and problematic side of this wish, the tragic repercussions when art is mistaken for reality. They recurrently explore models of Welsh identity and politics through such theatrical notions as role-playing, visibility and memory. They confront the fictions that constitute Thomas's political vision with the realities of theatre making and its limitations. In his dramatic writings Thomas betrays a more ambivalent attitude towards the actual power and influence of theatre than his model for a 'theatre of invention' allows him to acknowledge.

In the framework of this essay I want to discuss this model as it emerges from the written and spoken testimonies of Edward Thomas, before tracing its manifestation and its refutation within his play-texts.

Caught Between Reality and Fiction: The Paradox of a Theatre of Invention

> I don't think of myself as a playwright. I am not that interested in "Edward Thomas, playwright". I prefer to be an imaginer, I am paid to imagine things.[6]

To speak of Edward Thomas as a playwright does not do justice to the wide range of theatrical activities in which he himself is involved. Thomas not only writes and directs his own plays, he also runs his own company, Y Cwmni, now renamed Fiction Factory, which was formed in 1988 for the purpose of staging his work.[7] Thomas has emphasised on numerous occasions that the written play for him is only part of the larger artistic machinery that is theatre. A drama for him is a mere potentiality which needs the transformation onto the stage to achieve its full effect: 'without actors and without a stage, plays are dramas of possibilities rather than dramas of certainties.'[8] Thomas has also claimed that he hates to think of his plays as finished versions:

> The text doesn't mean anything. Only the theatre means something – it is flesh and blood. The writing only becomes interesting when the text isn't served and the writer isn't served but the idea which the text suggests is brutally, ruthlessly, beautifully, magically interpreted . . . The actors aren't representative of the ideas of the text, they are the ideas in 3D.[9]

For someone thus embracing the full spectrum of theatrical means, from the written text to the staging, the failure of Welsh theatre is one of style and form. The present Welsh theatre is what he calls a mere 'theatre of adoption' in as much as it has adopted the style, structure, form and management of the established English stage. Its main artistic form of expression is naturalism, a style which 'reproduces everyday reality as closely and authentically as possible: it is a drama based on life reproduced rather than life imagined or invented'.[10] In Thomas's view, the style of naturalism is deeply inscribed in English culture and therefore inappropriate for a representation of the complexity of Welsh reality:

> Because only a fifth of the Welsh speak the Welsh language, not one village, town or city in Wales is a hundred per cent Welsh speaking. So the 'reality' of Welsh-speaking Wales can only be reproduced in the theatre of naturalism by being economical with itself (ignoring a part of the community in the interest of writing only in Welsh to the exclusion of English words), or by writing in a mixture of Welsh and English (Wenglish). Either way, the naturalistic style is insupportable . . .[11]

Thomas creates his own artistic vision of a Welsh 'theatre of invention'[12] in opposition to the naturalist 'theatre of adoption'.[13] He thereby produces an interestingly paradoxical model which shifts between the poles of 'reality' on the one end and 'invention' on the other. Theatrical naturalism, usually associated with a truthful reproduction of reality, in his view produces an invented and distorted image of Wales, whereas the 'theatre of invention' is truly representative of Welsh reality. What we have here is a theatre of naturalism which supposedly reproduces reality, yet which in truth is an invention, and a theatre of invention which is reality's truthful representation. The 'theatre of invention' has thus set itself a difficult task: rather than reproducing an actual Welsh identity, it seeks to represent a Wales that does not yet exist.

This is, however, not the only reality that the 'theatre of invention' needs to take into account. The theatre, as we have seen, is for Thomas a medium of 'flesh and blood,' where the inventions of dramatic writing are transformed into the realities of the stage. The paradox between the 'theatre of invention's' political mission to invent and imagine a reality that does not yet exist and its artistic reality as 'flesh and blood' constitutes a tension that fuels all of Thomas's work. In the following section I will show how this paradox has left its marks on the form and style of Edward Thomas's own dramatic writings.

The 'New Wales Trilogy': Dramatizing the Paradox

> . . . the individual plays in his trilogy are linked by the attempts of his characters to find in their memories, or create in their imaginations, stories through which they can reinvent and assert themselves.[14]

Brian Mitchell and David Ian Rabey have identified a number of leitmotifs that run through the dramatic writings of Edward Thomas: the search for identity, the role of memory, the creation of a personal mythology, the activities of playing and of storytelling.[15] In the light of Thomas's above-mentioned ideas on theatre, I want to emphasise the theatrical aspects of these motifs: Thomas depicts characters not merely searching for identity, but acting out that search through a form of theatrical role-playing, assuming a fictional persona as if they were actors on a stage (which, of course, they are). The characters imagination is being set limits by the actual reality of the stage as well as that of their fictional reality. And the tragedy of their pursuit does not arise from their invention or replication of stories alone, but from their attempt to re-enact the narratives, to translate them into their own 'flesh and blood'. The ambition of all of Thomas's dramatis personae is not so much to become 'the reader and writer of your own life' but rather the actor and the spectator.

The following discussion will focus on three areas where, I want to argue, Thomas has chosen the exact points where theatre serves as a model for personal identity and political activity in order to explore its suitability for such purpose: firstly, the problem of identity as role-playing; secondly, the question of visibility; and thirdly, the role of memory. Though all three aspects are present in all of his writings, albeit in degrees, I want to discuss each one of them in relation to the plays in Edward Thomas's *New Wales Trilogy*, the trio of plays consisting of *House of America*, *Flowers of the Dead Red Sea* and *East from the Gantry* with which the author first made his name.

House of America: On the Paradox of Acting

> Boyo: Pretending to be somebody else for a living, lies, all lies.[16]

In *House of America*, (1988) Thomas' first full-length play, the writer explores the way in which the identity crisis of a nation manifests itself first and foremost as the identity crisis of an individual. In his own words,

> *House of America* explored the ideal of modern mythology in non-Welsh-speaking Wales, a schizophrenic community where most popular images of heroism are derived from American models.[17]

The community is represented by a family of four whose father is believed to have left their isolated house in the Valleys years ago to go to America – only later will it be revealed that his own wife has killed him and buried him on a mountain near the house. Two of the children attempt to escape from the reality of unemployment and deprivation into the fictional world of Jack Kerouac's novel, *On the Road*. In a world without confidence in itself, the American Dream of Kerouac becomes a seductive substitute for a self-defined identity, its heroes standing in for a lack of home-bred role models. But the characters' desperate search for identity leads to incest, insanity and murder.

Thomas organises the theme of identity around a very theatrical notion:

that of acting. In an early scene in the play, in which the family is gathered watching a video of *The Godfather*, Boyo, the younger son, delivers a definition for acting: 'Pretending to be somebody else for a living, lies, all lies'. In their search for identity, all four main characters in *House of America* adopt or reject forms of acting/pretending. Mother's identity, which defines itself through the absence of the father, is put at risk when an open cast mine threatens to uncover the body of her murdered husband. In anticipation of her discovery, she begins to act differently, but is suspected by her children of merely 'putting it on'. She herself admits that 'I'm not myself'. When she finally reveals the truth about her husband's death to her sons (after re-enacting the burning of clothes that followed her murderous act) the two brothers still accuse her of 'telling lies'. In the end, Mother puts on the best act of all. By feigning madness, she provides herself with a new identity: she is no longer Mother in the House of America, but 'Mrs Lewis in the house of fools':

> Every time the nurse or the doctor comes in here for something, I've been pretending to eat my cawl, and you know what? Not one of them has told me there's nothing in it, not one of them. Do they think I don't know that, uh? What would you say, Boyo? Don't you think I know there's no cawl in there, but do they say something? No. Because they don't want to upset me, because I'm mad, that's why. Tell me, Boyo, who's joking who here?.[18]

By pretending her madness, Mother remains not only conscious of the essential difference between reality (no *cawl* in the bowl) and pretending (to eat it), she actively plays with this difference. Respect for the difference between reality and pretence plays a vital role for Boyo. Though it is he who first introduces pretending into the play when he impersonates a Gerry Anderson puppet and later Marlon Brando, he, as his sister puts it, can only do 'bad impressions of film stars'. He refuses to join in his sibling's subsequent play with identities, claiming 'no fucking tinpot dreaming for me', and 'It's not my size'. For him, pretending to be somebody else remains a lie, and the border between reality and fiction must remain fully intact.

This border is being severely violated by his brother and sister, Sid and Gwenny. They both mistake fiction for reality, pretending for being, though to differing degrees and with different consequences. Sid first expresses his wish to have been 'born someone else, somewhere else . . . Jack Kerouac' after having been rejected for a job on the mine. For him, assuming the identity of a character provided by fiction is paradoxically born out of a sense of reality: 'It's called facing facts, wus, telling the truth about the way things are . . . from now on I'm going to do things my way . . . The Sid Lewis experience'. He finally sheds his old identity after meeting the labourer who got the job he applied for, the person he would have been: 'Sid Lewis, R.I.P.'. Yet Sid begins to act his new identity without considering the physical consequences of this act of embodiment (incest and pregnancy). When he finally calls the game off, 'Hey, come on, don't play games . . . game's over . . . we were only playing', and insists 'I am, I am', it is too late.

If Sid temporarily mistakes pretending for being, his sister undergoes a full and irreversible change of identity. Her transformation from Gwenny to Joyce is the most interesting in the play because it manifests the theatricality of the act. It is Sid who first gives her a new name, Joyce. After spending time 'in my room reading [*On the Road*], and trying on clothes', she begins to transform herself into her new role by changing her appearance, emphasising the importance of costume change: 'And then all you need is a pair of faded old jeans and like a lumberjack shirt and I could call you Jack'. The transition is completed after she learns about the death of her father. She reassures herself: 'Are you really Jack Kerouac?', to which Sid responds: 'Look in my face, can you see the truth in my face? Feel'. From then on, Gwenny ceases to exist, and Joyce takes her place.

Gwenny's change of identity, and to a certain extent Sid's, follows the process of character acquisition familiar from the medium of theatre: starting from a written text (*On the Road*) which provides the *dramatis personae*, the actors first acquire the names of their roles, then change into a costume. The final transformation into the identity of a character is completed when there is 'truth in the face' and the emotional identification or 'feel' is right. The tragedy of the siblings is that they ignore what acting theory has called the 'double nature' of acting, most prominently articulated by Diderot in his 'Paradox of the Actor': the difference between the fictional character and his feelings and the actor's 'real' emotions.[19] The identity of a character on stage, rather than on the page, is composed of this paradox of a reality of fiction. This shifting of acting between pretending and being has posed a problem for a modern world view which seeks fixed and stable identities. In the world of politics, this has frequently led to a moral damnation of theatre (Plato for example saw in acting a dangerous play with identity which could potentially threaten the stability of the state).[20] Modern acting theory has often attempted to counteract the potentially destabilizing force of acting by focussing on the actor's self rather than the character he or she is playing.[21] Edward Thomas articulates a similar privilege of the actor's self over the role for his theatrical practice:

> I have always said that I am more interested in the actor than the part he or she is playing. In traditional theatre actors often speak of 'my Hamlet'. I am not interested in their Hamlet, I am just interested in them. And in the rehearsal room, the play can only be shaped through that raw material. I want the actors to think that they wrote the play, that it belongs to them.[22]

Yet, the problematic relationship between acting and identity does not stop at the doors of the theatre. Various theories on identity have used the model of the theatre with its concepts of role, person, character and mask to describe the way in which identity is formed individually and socially.[23] For most modern identity theory, identity can only be successfully formed if the 'self' and its social 'role' (the character it is acting) are being brought into balance. This position has been criticised in recent theory which has begun to question the existence of a self outside the role he or she is playing, and has pointed out the potentially subversive effects of extreme role-play.[24]

House of America, however, remains clearly within the parameters set by the pretending-being divide. It emphasises the limits of the play of identity, its pathologies, traps and shortcomings, and shows the tragic repercussions when the border between fiction and reality is broken down. The drama betrays a highly sceptical attitude towards the concept at the very heart of Edward Thomas's 'theatre of invention': the power of the theatre to provide a model for identity, whether personal or communal.

Flowers of the Dead Red Sea: On the paradox of seeing

> Joe: I KNOW WHAT I SEE.
> Mock: What do you see?
> Joe: Look for yourself.
> Mock: I know what I look like.
> Joe: Then look again!'[25]

The second play in the trilogy, *Flowers of the Dead Red Sea* (1991), continues the theme of identity, acting and pretending that was introduced in *House of America.* This time, the drama is set in a slaughterhouse where two butchers, Mock and Joe, are trapped in a fierce exchange of words and stories, while the world is quite literally falling on their heads. The language of the play is of prime importance, because through that language the characters affirm and deny each other's identity and that of the world. 'Must break the silence, speak . . . speak . . . SPEAK . . . SPEAK', demands Mock from himself, a silence he earlier described as 'Horrible silence, horrible, hanging silence . . . a whole language, a way of life, a people drowning . . .'. Memory is another recurrent theme: Mock repeatedly asks his companion 'What's happened to memory, Joe?'.

There is, however, another theme that runs through the play and determines a large number of its metaphors: that of seeing. The discourse between the two characters revolves time and time again around the issues of seeing, watching and witnessing. Seeing and being seen are thereby closely linked to identity: in his dream of being a bucket, Mock denies Joe an existence on the grounds of his invisibility: 'You were nowhere in sight, you never featured', and later, even stronger, 'you never featured, you weren't in it, you were invisible'. Joe responds by revealing that whilst Mock was asleep dreaming a dream in which he was invisible, he himself was watching Mock sleepwalking. And he is able to tell Mock the things he had done whilst sleepwalking because: 'I saw you'. He discloses a side of Mock's identity that remains invisible to Mock himself, because when sleepwalking 'your eyes were open but they were dulled and glazed'.

The intrinsic relationship between identity and seeing, or more precisely between identity and being seen, is played out several times in the drama. It reappears, for example, with regard to the identity of Mock's father: Mock: 'You knew my father?', Joe 'I watched him play darts in a pub', and Joe: 'He's dead, Mock, I saw him fall'. Being seen constitutes identity and seeing is an instrument of knowledge: 'Joe: I KNOW WHAT I SAW'.

But seeing also has its limits. Joe remarks about an object fallen from the sky: 'I CAN SEE IT'S A PRAM, BUT WHY DOES A RUSTY OLD PRAM FALL DOWN FROM OUR SKIES'. Seeing the object does not explain the reason behind its existence. The world of the characters is delineated by its visibility which guarantees identity and knowledge. Beyond the limits of visibility lies incomprehension: unknown sounds come from the darkness beyond the visible world (a splash indicating water which the characters can hear but not see). Later, however, Mock claims to understand this world: 'Because there is a difference between us, I see the mystery where you see only ignorance'.

Like acting, the problem of seeing and being seen constitutes an area where the realms of theatre, identity and politics overlap. The seeing/being seen distinction may be called the very foundation of theatre, the 'looking place' (Greek: *theatron*). Our modern theatre is founded on a clear architectural separation between the visible (everything on stage) and the invisible (the theatrical apparatus, the auditorium, the outside of the theatre),[26] thereby equating the visible with the meaningful. This creates the need for a particular form of perception on behalf of the audience which we again may call paradoxical: the necessity to filter out everything that lies outside of the clearly marked visible area of the stage as that which is incomprehensible or meaningless, even if we may actually be able to see it. This paradox has helped the theatre to separate the realm of 'fiction' from that of 'reality'.

Many theories have highlighted the link between the articulation of visibility/invisibility in theatre and our modern understanding of power, knowledge and identity.[27] It is seen to hold the spectator in place, providing him or her with the illusion of a stable identity through a unified view point. Accordingly, the theatre of our century is full of attempts to break with this arrangement by revealing the theatrical apparatus (Brecht), breaking down the audience/stage divide (Artaud) or moving the theatre out of its enclosed buildings.

Edward Thomas, however, chooses a different way to mark the ideology of the visible and its limitations: he creates a form of complicity between the characters on stage and the audience by emphasizing that the world that is mutually visible to them is the world delineated by the stage. Beyond the stage is darkness, which remains incomprehensible to both the characters and the spectators. Thomas also shows the limits that visibility poses on the understanding of our own identities: in the same way that Mock is unable to see himself dreaming, a part remains in ourselves that is never fully comprehensible to us because we are unable to see ourselves seeing.[28] A short dialogue towards the end of the play reiterates this point:

> Joe: I KNOW WHAT I SEE.
> Mock: What do you see?
> Joe: Look for yourself.
> Mock: I know what I look like.
> Joe: Then look again! Mock: Nothing . . .
> Joe: Look at your eyes.
> Mock: Clear.
> Joe: Not as clear as they used to be . . .
> Mock: What's in my eyes, Joe? What can you see? . . .
> Joe: YOUR SOUL IS IN DECAY.[29]

Even more than its predecessor, *Flowers of the Dead Red Sea* is a self-conscious play with its own status as a theatre piece, in which characters exist as long as they are being watched and the world stretches only as far as the boundaries of the brightly-lit stage. And again, this problem extends into the realm of politics, where the power of visibility plays an important part, not least for Thomas's own concept of a 'theatre of invention': In Thomas's play *Hiraeth* we find the character 'Gwenny' declaring that 'There's nothing worse than invisibility'.[30]

Flowers of the Dead Red Sea proves, however, that it is impossible to get a full view of the world, of each other and of ourselves, in the limited space of the theatre. But without such a view, the creation of a proper reflection in the mirror which the theatre holds up to society must be so much more difficult.

East from the Gantry: On the Paradox of Memory

> Ronnie: Have you got a home, Trampas?
> Trampas: Not any more. The home I knew has gone forever.
> Ronnie: Time to make a new start then.
> Trampas: Something like that. The first thing I'll do is change my name.
> Ronnie: What's your real name?
> Trampas: My real name is Billy.
> Ronnie: Call yourself Billy then.
> Trampas: I guess I will.
> Ronnie: Hello, Billy.
> Trampas: Hello, Ronnie.
> [They shake hands].[31]

East from the Gantry (1992) is a fitting play to conclude the *New Wales Trilogy*, a tragicomedy of reconciliation and recovery that attempts to resolve some of the conflicts posed by its predecessors. In the surreal setting of a burnt-down house on a snow-covered mountain under a blue moon, we witness the meetings of three characters: a couple fallen out of love, Bella and Ronnie, and Trampas, who calls himself after a television character. *East from the Gantry* maintains numerous links with the two previous plays: concepts such as imagination, lies and memories make a reappearance, and again we find references to acting and seeing. Only here, the threads unfolded in the earlier dramas are tied together in a more hopeful manner. Like Sid in *House of America*, Trampas has taken on a fictional identity. But unlike Sid, he is able to resume his original identity in the end ('My real name is Billy'), having realised that 'Superstars, even legends, can be so thoughtless sometimes, so unpredictable'. Bella and Ronnie replay the bitter exchanges over true and false memories that we know from *Flowers of the Dead Red Sea*. But whilst the two butchers in the earlier play find no reconciliation, Bella and Ronnie finally achieve something like a joint accommodation.

The main focus of East from the Gantry lies in memory and the role it plays in making up the past that constitutes our identity. Memory appears in different forms, however. On the one hand there are the more extended personal reminiscences of Trampas and Bella, which often begin in a similar way: 'It was a Sunday night', 'It was a Saturday afternoon', 'It was a Wednesday night'. These are stories formed out of real or invented personal memories, told by one person, listened to by another. In the encounters between Bella and Ronnie, which alternate with those between Bella and Trampas, personal stories become the object of doubt and dispute: Ronnie: 'I'd like to believe you, but I'm afraid I just can't, Bella'. The end of the play achieves a balance between the need for acceptance and that for dispute: Ronnie and Bella begin to agree on the memories of their joint past (if only to fall out again immediately afterwards), and Trampas and Bella have moments of disagreement: 'You're not listening to me'.

The status of memory is again an obvious point of contact between the theatrical, the personal and the political. Memory is essential to the act of theatre, whether it be the actor's memorizing of a role or the audience's memory of a performance, the place where theatre survives. And the construction of a narrative out of memory is not merely the task of the playwright, but that of each individual in her or his search for a stable identity across the passing of time, and that of each society in its attempt to make history out of the past.[32]

In *East from the Gantry*, memory is first and foremost a memory told, listened to or disputed. Edward Thomas shows that it is the performance of memory, not memory as an entity locked away in our brains, that constitutes the narratives out of which individuals and societies construct their past. Yet the performance of memory also activates what could again be called a paradox: the need to transform memory into a consistent story with a beginning and an end is constantly being subverted by the impossibility of containing memory within the limits of a story. Thomas plays with this paradox when he stimulates the memory capacity of his audience in a self-conscious game of quotes and references. *East from the Gantry* is full of cross-references within the play which encourage the spectator actively to remember what has been said before: the accidental shooting of his aunt by her husband, remembered by Trampas at the beginning of the play, reappears in a later encounter between Bella and Ronnie; the French underwear Bella throws at Tom Jones unnoticed by the singer becomes an object of desire between Bella and Ronnie. But the references also extend beyond the narrative of the play into previous plays by the author. *East from the Gantry* revives not only characters from earlier plays but also motifs and metaphors. There are references to a house, a killed cat, dreaming, lying, books, television etc. which link the play to its predecessors. Mitchell claims that 'knowledge of the earlier two plays gives us guidelines for interpretation'.[33]

East from the Gantry consistently breaks through the attempted closures of narrative by activating its audience's memory. This is precisely the empowerment of an audience that Thomas has so often demanded:

> As a writer, I am to engender the possibility for imagining, allowing the audience to make sense of interesting moments'.[34]

A politics based on narrative, on the will to 'play out, listen to and tell stories', which Rabey has identified for Edward Thomas's work[35], is therefore at the same time affirmed and contested. Stories are no longer either true or false, fiction or reality; they are in themselves never completed, always open to antagonism, to disagreement from the audience. This is the limitation a 'theatre of invention' faces when embarking on the project of re-inventing a Welsh history through story.

Acting Out: The Politics of a Theatre of Invention

In their consideration and marriage of the nature and status of Welshness and the nature and status of theatre, Edward Thomas and his company have often been compared to another group in Wales, the physical theatre company Brith Gof.[36] And a comparison between the two indeed sheds an interesting light on the different theatrical strategies with which the political project of reinventing a cultural identity may be achieved. Both companies reject the orthodox form of theatre, the conventions of the well-made play and those of stage realism and naturalism, as a style that is deeply inscribed within the mainstream English culture and therefore inappropriate for a new theatre of Wales.[37] But their attempts at defining such a new, relevant, contemporary Welsh theatre with a distinctive style and form of its own has led them to very different artistic solutions. On a more obvious level, they both represent opposite theatrical genres, the large-scale physical spectacle (Brith Gof) and the more intimate dramatic chamber play (Edward Thomas).

The main difference between the two, however, lies in their very different attempts at achieving political impact by establishing a close relation between 'fiction' and 'reality'. Brith Gof aim to dismantle the borders which the institution of theatre has erected in their view to separate art from life by introducing reality into the fiction, thereby hoping to place their work amidst the historical, political and cultural realities of Wales: they stage their works mainly in non-theatrical sites with a history of usage in work or worship; they set real physical tasks for the performers; and they force the audience to engage actively with or flee from the action that is happening all around them.

Edward Thomas's theatrical works, on the other hand, aim to establish a link between art and life not by dismantling the border that divides them but by articulating its fragility. Thomas has never attempted to move out of the representational framework of theatre, out of the conventions of theatre buildings, role acting and the stage-auditorium divide. This does not mean, however, that the framework has gone unquestioned. As I hope I have shown, Thomas subjects the theatrical conventions of play, perception and narrative to relentless scrutiny. His awareness of the political implications of form makes him cautious also of his own theatrical project, a 'theatre of invention' which demands a politics of identity based on theatrical imagination, visibility and memory.

But Edward Thomas understands that only by addressing the inherent paradoxes that structure his own model of theatre is he able to envision a new model for a theatre which has set itself a difficult task: to represent something which does not yet exist, the future of a new Wales.

Notes

1 *Flowers of the Dead Red Sea* in Brian Mitchell (ed.), *Edward Thomas: Three Plays: House of America, Flowers of the Dead Red Sea, East from the Gantry* (Bridgend: Seren, 1994), p. 135. Hereafter cited as *Edward Thomas, Three Plays*.

2 Hazel Walford Davies, 'Wanted: A New Welsh Mythology' [interview with Edward Thomas], *New Welsh Review* 27 (Winter 1994-5), p. 56.

3 Edward Thomas, 'Wales and a Theatre of Invention' in Neil Wallace (ed.), *Thoughts and Fragments about Theatres and Nations* (Glasgow: Guardian Newspaper Publications, 1991), pp. 15-17.

4 Gwyn Alf Williams, *When Was Wales?* (Harmondsworth: Penguin Books, 1985).

5 Edward Thomas, 'Wales and a Theatre of Invention', p. 17.

6 See Heike Roms, 'Edward Thomas: a Profile' in this volume, p. 186.

7 David Adams has noted that 'the fact that Edward Thomas has his own company is important, because part of his philosophy – and the crux of Y Cwmni – is that Welsh theatre has to find a new form and style'. See David Adams, *Stage Welsh* (Llandysul: Gomer, 1996), p. 52.

8 Hazel Walford Davies, 'Wanted: A New Welsh Mythology', p. 58.

9 See Heike Roms, 'Edward Thomas: a Profile' in this volume, p. 186.

10 Edward Thomas, 'Wales and a Theatre of Invention', p. 17.

11 Ibid.

12 In Thomas's writings this 'theatre of invention' also appears as 'theatre of possibilities', 'theatre of uncertainty' or 'landscape' plays.

13 The important role which Edward Thomas grants the theatre is in fact constructed out of a series of oppositions. For example, it defies the minor role that the theatre played in traditional Welsh culture. He has claimed that, 'because there is no real theatrical tradition in Wales, we have tended to inherit naturalism as a subconscious model, though our own traditions are of oral poetry and myths . . .' (see David Ian Rabey and Charmain C. Savill, 'Welsh Theatre : Inventing New Myths', *Euromaske 1*, 1996, pp. 73-5). Thomas has pointed out on several occasions that he himself is a theatrical autodidact and that his career was purely accidental: 'I am self-taught, which has big advantages and disadvantages. Sometimes I think the flaws in the work are more interesting than the things I am good at.' (see Heike Roms, 'Edward Thomas: a Profile' in this volume, p. 186). See also Thomas's acount of his early theatrical years in Manon Wynne Davies, 'Cymru yn fy mhen – yng nghwmni Edward Thomas', *Golwg* 4/50 (27 August 1992), pp. 22-3 and Hazel Walford Davies, 'Wanted: a New Welsh Mythology', pp. 54-61.

14 *Edward Thomas, Three Plays*, p. 14.

15 See David Ian Rabey, 'Why Can't This Crazy Love Be Mine? an introduction to Edward Thomas and Y Cwmni' in Pamela Edwardes (ed.), *Frontline Intelligence : New Plays for the Nineties* (London: Methuen, 1993), pp. 262-4.

16 *Edward Thomas, Three Plays*, p. 37.

17 Quoted in David Ian Rabey and Charmain C. Savill, 'Welsh Theatre: Inventing New Myths', p. 75.

18 *Edward Thomas, Three Plays*, p. 18.

19 Denis Diderot, 'The Paradox of Acting', in Toby Cole and Helen Kirch Chinoy (eds.), *Actors on Acting* (New York: Crown Publishers, 1970), pp. 162-70.

20 Plato, *The Republic*, trans., H.D.P. Lee (Harmondsworth: Penguin, 1995), pp. 383-6.

21 The privileging of self over character is expressed in such diverse modern acting theories as those of Stanislavski, Brecht and Grotowski. See Philip Auslander, 'Just be Your Self' in *From Acting to Performance* (London: Routledge, 1997), pp. 28-38.

22 See Heike Roms, 'Edward Thomas: a Profile' in this volume, pp. 186.

23 Erving Goffman, for example, uses the metaphor of theatrical performance extensively to discuss the operation of identity and role playing in social situations. See Erving Goffman, *The Presentation of Self in Everyday Life*, (New York, Garden City: Doubleday, 1959).

24 See, for example, Judith Butler, *Gender Trouble – Feminism and Subversion of Identity* (London/New York: Routledge, 1990).
25 *Edward Thomas, Three Plays*, p. 161.
26 The French philosopher Jean-François Lyotard describes this architectural separation as the two limits of theatre: 'For all theatre is an apparatus duplicated at least once . . . thus made up of two limits, of two barriers filtering the coming and going energies: one limit (1) which determines what is exterior to the theatre ('reality') and what is 'interior', a second limit (2) which, on the inside, disassociates what is to be perceived and what is not to be perceived (underneath, stage lights, wings, chairs, people . . .)'. Jean-Françoise Lyotard, 'The Tooth, the Palm', *Sub-stance 15*, p. 110.
27 In his influential study on the birth of the modern prison system, Michel Foucault, for example, likens the disciplinary design of Bentham's *Panopticon* prison to the spatial arrangement of a theatre building: 'By the effect of backlighting, one can observe from the tower, standing out precisely against the light, the small captive shadows in the cells of the periphery. They are like so many cages, so many small theatres, in which each actor is alone, perfectly individualized and constantly visible' (Michel Foucault, *Discipline and Punish* (Harmondsworth: Penguin, 1979), p. 200). For the audience the effect is as follows: 'The frame provided by the proscenium arch, and the containment of the action within the framed stage, offers a single, unified point of view for the audience, a comprehensive vision of the events dramatized, which is also a comprehensive and therefore authoritative vision . . .' (Catherine Belsey, *Critical Practice* (London/New York: Routledge, 1980), p. 97).
28 The relation of gaze and identity in psychoanalysis is illustrated in Jaques Lacan's theory of the 'mirror stage'. See Jaques-Alain Miller (ed.), *The Seminars of Jaques Lacan. Book 1: Freud's Papers on Technique, 1953-1954*, trans. John Forrester (New York/London: W. W. Norton & Co., 1991).
29 *Edward Thomas, Three Plays*, pp. 161-62.
30 See Phil Clark, *Act One Wales: Thirteen one Act Plays* (Bridgend: Seren, 1996), p. 172.
31 *Edward Thomas, Three Plays*, p. 212.
32 See Paul Connerton, *How Societies Remember* (Cambridge: Cambridge University Press, 1989).
33 *Edward Thomas, Three Plays*, p. ix.
34 Chairman C. Savill, 'Wales is Dead', *Planet* 85, February/March 1991, p. 88.
35 David Ian Rabey, 'Why can't this crazy love be mine? – an introduction to Edward Thomas and Y Cwmni', p. 262.
36 David Adams has emphasised the corresponding politics of the two companies: 'With Brith Gof, it [Y Cwmni] could only exist in present-day Wales because the nature and status of Welshness is what it is all about. Virtually everything Thomas writes addresses itself to the problem of cultural identity and he echoes Gwyn Alf [Williams]'s ideas about an invented Wales'. David Adams, *Stage Welsh* (Llandysul: Gomer, 1996), p. 52.
37 Brith Gof's artistic policy reflects views and ideas embraced by Edward Thomas. In its booklet *Brith Gof – a Welsh Theatre Company* (Aberystwyth: A Brith Gof Publication, 1988) the aim of the company was set out: 'to develop a new, vibrant and distinctive theatre tradition in Wales, one which is relevant, responsive and challenging to the perceptions, experience, aspirations and concerns of a small nation, and not just a pale reflection of English theatrical conventions. Our object is a theatre so vivid that it communicates across linguistic borders' (p. 2).

Edward Thomas: Negotiating a Way Through Culture

David Adams

Celtic cultural identity? Ask Edward Thomas. A Welsh arts renaissance? Wheel on Edward Thomas. The referendum debate? Cue Edward Thomas. Edward Thomas, soundbites supplied. Instant summaries of the problems of inferiority and self-deprecation. And delivered with authentic Welsh lyricism and eloquence. Many more people have heard Edward Thomas talk about re-inventing Wales, rebuilding confidence in the Welsh voice, breaking the silence, than have ever seen his plays; and they might think that this is a one-idea man, a sort of dramatised and simplified version of Gwyn Alf Williams, classically Celtic good-looking, never at a loss for words, witty . . . yet at best a committed but hopelessly romantic rent-a-gob.

Of course, Edward Thomas's plays are certainly part of that dominant postmodern late twentieth-century obsession with identity and memory. They refer in detail to the worlds of family, nationality and individuality that inform an exploration of identity. But Edward Thomas tells us more: he tells us about that other much-used complex word, culture. We may find, as some suggest, that Edward Thomas's creative life has a limited time-span, that he has less than a dozen good plays in him (he has produced nine to date), but he is more than a quick-quote nationalist, more than an exciting, inventive and original playwright. He is a cultural phenomenon. He sees that culture is not simply roots but offers routes, not just about origins but about futures. Culture is where Edward Thomas comes from and what he uses as a way forward. His work deconstructs and dissects the past and the present as surgically as the butchers in one of his plays divide the carcass (his father was the family butcher of Cwmgiedd) and is created into a product for later consumption. Thus Edward Thomas, media purveyor of instant Welshness. Thus, also, the Edward Thomas industry because the product stays the property of the makers. Edward Thomas is part of a cultural practice that is not just concerned with origination and performance but packaging and selling, not just with theatre but with radio, television and film. He and his colleagues (and we will see that we cannot ever really separate the playwright from the company) have taken control of the means of production of their dramatic art. They are part of the cultural continuum.

It is as a figure in this landscape that I want to look at Edward Thomas in this essay. I cannot but fail to examine his themes but it is his distinctive position within the various cultural contexts – in other words, the work as productions rather than scripts, as products of a particular culture and contributions to (another) culture – that interests me. I will offer a brief chronology and description of the work, then try and locate it in the playwright's geographic and social background (often foregrounded in the plays), identify the contemporary cultural references, from rock music to food, before outlining the very positive positioning within the culture industry and the ideologically materialist objectives of the producers of the work. Finally, I relate this to the question of identity that is the heart of Edward Thomas's work.

History

As I write Edward Thomas and his company – originally known as Y Cwmni, but more recently renamed Fiction Factory – have several projects. The film version of *House of America*, Edward Thomas's first full-length play and regarded by many (though not by himself) as still his best, has just opened across the UK to reviews that range from the ecstatic to the uncomprehending, with Siân Phillips in the central role. *The Aces of Gaerlishe*, the working title of a new play commissioned by Stephen Daldry at The Royal Court, is about to be staged in London. *Gas Station Angel*, a film version of the play written in tandem with the theatre script, is ready. (The stage play will probably also be called *Gas Station Angel*, but I shall here use its working title to differentiate it from the film.) New, young, trendy, Welsh author James Hawes's best-selling novel *Rancid Aluminium* is being developed as a film. *Satellite City*, the offbeat television sitcom series written by Boyd and Jane Clack and produced for BBC by the company, has just finished its second series and will certainly get a third. A new radio comedy series by the Clacks, *What a Wonderful World*, is being recorded before an audience for transmission within a few months. The so-called *New Wales Trilogy – House of America, Flowers of the Dead Red Sea and East from the Gantry* – may be restaged to tour nationally and *House of America* is in rehearsal as I write, opening to coincide with the film version, and *Flowers of the Dead Red Sea* (probably retitled simply *Flowers*) is being prepared. *House of America* almost simultaneously has premieres in Montreal in French and in Santiago de Compostela in Galician. *East from the Gantry* tours Spain in a Catalan version. A German translation of *Song from a Forgotten City* is due to open in Berlin and a Danish one has been mooted. The reinvention of Y Cwmni and Edward Thomas has been achieved with remarkable success.

The Edward Thomas Show opened in 1988 when *House of America*, a tragedy with much comedy, ostensibly a mythic tale of murder and incest within a doomed family but also about a country and its people, was booked by Geoff Moore, perspicacious director of Moving Being, as part of a radical writing season at his St Stephen's Theatre Space in Cardiff's Butetown. Based on a piece for Made in Wales's new writing festival, *Write On!*, *House of America* was staged by a small group of actors mostly from Welsh-language television impressed by Edward Thomas's writing and including familiar faces like Sharon Morgan and newer performers like Richard Lynch and Russell Gomer. The production was stunning, the effect electric, the response ecstatic. The company, calling themselves simply Y Cwmni, realised they had something special and announced themselves as a new force in Welsh theatre with a manifesto, a programme and a commitment to new work, to quality and to an exploration of Welshness. The ball had started rolling.

House of America became a cult hit. It toured the Welsh Valleys, went to London (where it won a Time Out award) and Edinburgh and has been revived several times since, including a production directed by Jamie Garven that treated it as a modern classic. In 1989 Edward Thomas wrote, not for Y Cwmni but for Dalier Sylw, his only Welsh-language play, *Adar Heb Adenydd*, which outraged traditionalists as it harnessed symbolism and the language debate to create an absurdist satire. *The Myth of Michael Roderick* the following year was an adaptation that perhaps lost some of the bite by being in English, but it was nevertheless hugely entertaining and anarchic.

Flowers of the Dead Red Sea (1991), set in an abattoir where two manic skilled butchers argue about memory and reality as the world crashes (literally) about them, maintained the one-a-year pattern of play production but was more interesting since it underwent several revisions and the final, published version (in 1994) trimmed the cast from six to two and deleted a major plotline. Edward Thomas directed it in the first and third versions, while Janek Alexander offered another variation in-between. The process was significant in that it set a pattern whereby the play was never seen to be in any final form, either as a theatre script or as any other dramatic medium; *Flowers of the Dead Red Sea* not only underwent several stage versions, it was adapted for radio in 1992 and made into an opera in 1995. *House of America* had also changed, of course, not least with recasting; it was rewritten as a film in 1996, but with *Flowers of the Dead Red Sea*, perhaps because the writer was less satisfied with it, the product itself was seen as something changeable and mutable. The next stage was abortive: Edward Thomas and Y Cwmni announced an ambitious project, *The Seven Deadly Sins*, but never got beyond the first, *Envy*, the story of a bitter outcast determined to show the world his prowess by appearing on *Mastermind*, which was performed as a 50-minute monologue by Russell Gomer in 1991 and has only toured on and off since then. *East from the Gantry* (1992) divided critics: I confess I thought (and still do) that it was the playwright's most interesting work to date, an eloquent abstract exploration of the now-familiar themes of memory and place , with some beautiful as well as funny writing, and he himself prefers it over anything else. It opened, like *Flowers of the Dead Red Sea*, at The Tramway in Glasgow and was published in Methuen's *Frontline Intelligence* in 1993; by 1994 a new, revised version opened at Chapter and was published later that year. Meanwhile *Hiraeth* (given the English title *Strangers in Conversation*) was staged as part of an event at Oriel art gallery together with paintings by Iwan Bala. A thirty-minute two-hander, it worked within the context and the text won him a BBC Arts Award. *House of America, Flowers of the Dead Red Sea* and *East from the Gantry* were then repackaged as the *New Wales Trilogy*: Y Cwmni had discovered marketing.

That flirtation with hype came to a head the next year, 1995, with *Song from a Forgotten City*, when Cardiff was covered not just with posters but with yellow AA signs. The posters, cards, stickers and flyers all featured a red-lipped recumbent woman in bra and panties – a character quite absent from the play (which has an all-male cast). To some of us the play, centred on a novelist in a hotel room just after another Welsh rugby defeat, didn't say much that was new, and Edward Thomas felt it was to an extent a resumé of his messages about inferiority, reliance on myths, the need to reinvent. Allegedly based on Thomas's five years in London, it did have some sharp, funny dialogue, an interesting use of film techniques (Y Cwmni was becoming more involved in movies), a shocking buggery scene and some excellent performances from Dorien Thomas, Russell Gomer and Richard Lynch. It played in London, at the Royal Court (where it won an award) and Donmar Warehouse, and in Romania, Bonn and Melbourne. It was rewritten, recast, restaged and repackaged and toured again to great acclaim. The only problem was that Y Cwmni had decided to dissolve itself. Over the next couple of years it folded, reformed, collapsed and eventually transformed itself into Fiction Factory.

Location

I want to suggest that Edward Thomas's plays are not just about 'cultural identity', a catch-all phrase of dubious meaning, especially when hitched to the nationalist 'Welsh'. They are about family, the author, memory, myth, madness, nation, language – all part of 'identity', of course, but making it a more complex subject than straightforward politics. Throughout his plays he refers not so much self-consciously as naturally to his background. Thomas comes from Abercraf in the Swansea Valley and moved to Cwmgiedd, the 'by-pass' town referred to so often in the plays. So the Cwmgiedd of *East from the Gantry*, where Shinkin's butchers shop has become an old people's home and the school a place to buy DIY and cheap furniture, no longer a village but part of Ystrad, is real, 'a bypassed South Walian one horse Welsh Western town' in *Song from a Forgotten City* and, in almost identical words, in *Envy*. Edward Thomas's father was the village butcher: hence the setting of *Flowers of the Dead Red Sea*, an abattoir with two craftsmen-butchers. When Humphrey Jennings chose the place to film his classic 1942 *A Silent Village* (prompting not only a new television documentary from Edward Thomas but a viewing in *East from the Gantry*, a play much concerned with location in place as well as memory), Edward Thomas's father and grandfather were in it. As a ten-year old boy seeing the film for the first time, Edward Thomas saw them as film stars: his characters have been spotting film stars ever since – Telly Savalas, Burt Reynolds and others. As a boy, Thomas nearly drowned: hence there are drownings in *Aces of Gaerlishe*, where place and family are at the core, especially relationships between siblings, in *Adar Heb Adenydd, East from the Gantry* and *Song from a Forgotten City*; in *House of America* there is incest; lost brothers and fathers are there in *Flowers of the Dead Red Sea;* madness is ever-present, as in some form or another it is in any small community. The Drum and Monkey is not only real but was the scene of the darts match where a player died and they laid him on the bar and finished the game – 'It's what he would have wanted . . . at least he died when he was ahead' – a story told in both *Flowers of the Dead Red Sea* and *Envy*. Of course, most of the characters are based on real people, though not necessarily by name, and they reappear: Wymff, Boyo and Gwenny are all in *House of America* and *East from the Gantry*, Gwenny also in *Hiraeth*; there is a Scon in *Envy* and *East from the Gantry*; a birdman appears as the eponymous *Michael Roderick* and as Martin Bratton in *East from the Gantry;* Sid Lewis is one of the brothers in *House of America* and is the invisible other character in *Envy*. Some of the seedy characters in *Song from a Forgotten City* were allegedly based on people the dramatist knew during his 'missing' London years. There's some of Edward Thomas, who went through an early-twenties period thinking he was Jack Kerouac, in Sid and Boyo. Why is there a pizzaman in *East from the Gantry* and *Aces of Gaerlishe*? Because at the time of *East from the Gantry*, during one of the sex scandals that beset the Conservative Government, a minister, David Mellor, was exposed for having an affair with an ex-porn star who had starred in one steamy classic with a pizza delivery man called . . . Ed Thomas. The joke almost became documented fact when one newspaper was convinced (thanks to some overzealous PR and a wicked sense of humour) that the porn actor and the playwright were one and the same. And, of course, the notion of a pizza delivery service in somewhere like Cwmgiedd is so bizarre as to be funny.

The real is also the metaphorical, reminding us that theatre may be essentially metaphor but may also need to rely on the real. The Lewises' house is Wales, with all its secrets and lies and false ambitions, and a house perhaps in the Jungian sense of the house as a person, but it is also a real house (indeed, hyperreal in the movie). The landscape of *East from the*

Gantry is a landscape of memory and imagination but it is also precisely located ('We're in Southern Powys . . . In Wales . . . A country . . . On the west coast of Great Britain . . . Conquered in 1282 . . . Its economy is mainly agricultural . . . With an old industrial area down here in the south . . . And quarries and stuff in the north . . . With holiday destinations . . .' is an early quasi-erotic dialogue between Bella and Trampas). Mock and Joe are uncomprehending souls who are unsure of their identity, but they are also well-defined real butchers, real craftsmen. Ted John, Scon, is the Welsh psyche, epitome of a national sense of inferiority and impotence, but is also a recognisable real figure, a loser, a man racked by envy. Only in *Hiraeth* are the characters, two disembodied heads, deliberately unreal, although their conversation is commonplace. Perhaps in *Song from a Forgotten City* the characters are less convincingly real, credible people, partly because they are people living on the edge, a smackhead, a transvestite, urban misfits rather than dotty rural families.

What we have in the work, though, is a further level: the real is not simply fictionally real, realism in terms of its genre, but actually real in an unfictionalised sense. Cwmgiedd is a real place inhabited by real people; it is also a synecdoche for Wales and a metaphor for a culture that has been made invisible. The various references to drowning are because the playwright was nearly drowned as a child (an experience no-one is likely to forget); Marshall's story in *Aces of Gaerlishe* is exactly what happened, and there are other immersions and submersions – in *Adar Heb Adenydd/The Myth of Michael Roderick* a jester tries to drown himself in a water-butt and in *Song from a Forgotten City* Carlyle tries to drown in a sink (which also represents a lake in a rural idyll) the 'white Welsh trash' coke-snorting literary agent Jackson. In *East from the Gantry* we are offered another significance: 'I once had a brother who fell into a river, he drowned . . . I tried to save him but . . . this is very difficult for me . . . He was my own flesh and blood and I couldn't save him . . . I cut my feet badly, my blood turned the river red,' says Bella; 'That's really symbolic,' says Trampas, 'A red river rising.' More obviously, however, there is a familiar historical reference: drowning as representing the submersion of Wales and Welsh culture is a metaphor that has immediate popular resonance for a nation where a history of domination and abuse was symbolised by the flooding of villages to create reservoirs for water supplied to English homes and English regions.

Does it help to know that the young Edward Thomas nearly drowned? That his father was a butcher? That Cwmgiedd really does have a by-pass? That characters, incidents, are actual memories? Yes (*pace* 'The Death of the Author' school of criticism), insofar as culture, family, friends, place, local gossip and myth, real lived experience, give the work an authenticity (another discredited term, of course). We know, without any biographical searching, that it is true – or at least true in the sense that for those that tell the story it is true. Truth itself is a far more slippery question, of course. Edward Thomas constantly engages with memory and myth, areas of uncertainty and territories where fact and fiction are inextricable: the Lewises of *House of America* are trapped by a lie; the butchers of *Flowers of the Dead Red Sea* can never decide on what has actually happened and what has not; everyone in *East from the Gantry* inhabits the past as much as the present, never certain what is imaginary or real, invented or established; the loner-loser of *Envy* has a head full of facts ready for *Mastermind* but can't tell the real world from the imagined; the central character of *Song from a Forgotten City* is a novelist surrounded by fantasists, the story told in flashbacks that give it a fictional framework; events in the past dictate the present for the characters of *Aces of Gaerlishe*, while the real tragedy happens because an imaginary world of fairies and angels impinges on actuality. All these stories, especially *House of America* and *Aces of Gaerlishe*, are basically Greek tragedies, complete with hubris but maybe lacking catharsis. Not just Oedipus and the rest, either: Biblical and Celtic mythology is there – consciously but not deliberately – for example, in the fratricide of *House of America*, the severed heads of *East from the Gantry* and *Hiraeth*, and in the Fisher King motif (fishing itself features in *Hiraeth, Song from a Forgotten City* and *Aces of Gaerlishe*). In that constant debate between the universal and the specific, Edward Thomas's plays work so well partly because they are located in the particular – geographic, cultural, temporal, personal – but by working in classicly mythic terms they are also universal. The self-conscious awareness of the question of myth (as in the title *The Myth of Michael Roderick* but also in the recurrent jokey concerns about heroes, for example) is another postmodernist spin of which the playwright would, I suspect, deny all knowledge. The tracking of myths in Edward Thomas's oeuvre is an exercise that would be fascinating but one for which we do not have space here.

Popular Culture

But the popular mass culture of his generation also permeates the work. Edward Thomas is a soccer and rugby fan: Johann Cruyff, the Dutch footballer, is hilariously confused with Vincent Van Gogh by the craftsmen-butchers in *Flowers of the Dead Red Sea*; the defeat of the Welsh rugby team by the All Blacks in 1974 is recalled in *East from the Gantry* and their defeat by England is the starting-point of *Song from a Forgotten City*. He listens to popular music: 'Crash into Suede's *White Trash*' says a stage direction in *Aces of Gaerlishe*, while Sid and Gwenny in *House of America* listen to The Doors, Hendrix, Lou Reed, Sam and Dave, Dionne Warwick, Elvis and Patti Smith; Georgie Fame gets a mention in *Hiraeth;* Marc Bolan and T Rex and the Manic Street Preachers in *Aces of Gaerlishe*. (Tom Jones is, of course, a constant point of reference, not just as a singer but as an icon, and music is also used ironically – Dean Martin's 'Memories are made of this' and 'Beth yw'r Haf i mi' in *East from the Gantry*, Henry Mancini's 'Theme From a Summer Place' in *East from the Gantry*; Frank Sinatra in *House of America* and *Hiraeth*). Literature is Kerouac, Burroughs, Camus, *Zen and the Art of Motorcycle Maintenance* (attributed, in *Song from a Forgotten City*, to Barry Sheen!). The central figure in *Song from a Forgotten City*, Austin Carlyle, is named after a car; *Aces of Gaerlishe* has a central image of a tinted glass blue Marina 1800 TC; cars, from a souped-up Capri to a beat-up Robin Reliant, and bikes (an old Harley, though not the *Easy Rider* model) are dominant visual imagery in the film of *House of America* .

Edward Thomas comes from a television soap background, (he was once an actor in *Pobol y Cwm*) and Welsh-language television drama is parodied in *Adar Heb Adenydd*; in *East from the Gantry* a character takes on the role of Trampas from *The Virginian*, an older American series. Magnus Magnusson, the questionmaster of *Mastermind*, and Fred Housego, the taxi-driver champion, are referred to in *East from the Gantry* and Ted John, the solo character in *Envy,* desires only to be a contestant. Television weatherman Michael Fish is an alleged and unlikely sexual fantasy figure in *East from the Gantry*. The Lewises mime *Thunderbirds* characters before getting involved in deeper role-play in *House of America*; the two talking heads in *Hiraeth* remember *Blue Peter*, *Magic Roundabout*, *Star Trek* and *Crossroads*. In *East from the Gantry*, Celtic mythology and Gnostic symbolism meet movie idolatry in a severed head that looks like Burt Reynolds, and Telly Savalas is also sighted and *The Hustler*, *Citizen Kane* and *Deliverance* are mentioned. Telly Savalas is also sighted in *Envy*. *Song from a Forgotten City* is a stage version of film noir; in *House of America* the family's personal gazetteer of imagined America is compiled from Westerns and Marlon Brando movies and the screenplay of the film has the mother wandering among the ten-foot high letters of the operators' name above the open-cast mine, looking for all the world like the famous sign above Hollywood.

The characters inhabit a popular working-class culture of a wider sort, too. Pizzas are a favourite treat, but Tyrone and Gwenny in *Hiraeth* long for kebab, curry, sausage-and-chips, lager, tea and shortbread biscuits dunked until they're soft; Boyo demands Jaffa cakes with his beer in *House of America*; Bella and Trampas in *East from the Gantry* dream of new-season lamb on a Sunday with mint sauce, buttered new potatoes, honey-glazed carrots cut into rounds not strips, cabbage and a little gravy, followed by home-made rice pudding with the skin on top. Beer and pills are the chosen intoxicants of the children in *House of America*, while drugs dominate in *Song from a Forgotten City* and *Aces of Gaerlishe*.

Language is a fascination, both in the playwright's own discourse and in the concerns of his characters. An interest in Welsh (the playwright is a first-language Welsh speaker, although he has written only one play in his mother tongue) permeates *Adar Heb Adenydd* (with its English version, *The Myth of Michael Roderick*) and *Hiraeth* and emerges in *Aces of Gaerlishe*; the vernacular, especially swearing, can seem almost overpowering in *Song from a Forgotten City* and is there too in *Flowers of the Dead Red Sea* and *East from the Gantry*; 'slang,' agree Carlyle and Night-Porter in *Song from a Forgotten City*, 'means we're connected . . . part of something.'

This emphasis on language – explicitly in *Adar Heb Adenydd* and its English version, *The Myth of Michael Roderick,* where after a long passionate kiss with a woman who claims to be his mother a character rejects her because, he says, his mother 'lost her tongue' – is just one reason why we also have to address the question of nationality in Edward Thomas's plays. And while we recognise the familiar self-referential, self-conscious, ironic, eclectic postmodernist style, the detail in the cultural references, naturally, helps situate and define the work within a specific culture. In many ways Edward Thomas is far more about Welshness than *Trainspotting* is about Scottishness or Friel about Irishness, although we may want to question more rigorously the precise nature of this Welshness. That concern about nationality may turn out to be transient, a vehicle for more interesting and enduring explorations of identity. It is a question to which I shall return.

Welsh theatre practice

We need, briefly, to place the work within the very important context of Welsh theatre in the late twentieth century: it is, after all, the crucial artistic milieu within which Edward Thomas the playwright operates. As I write, in 1997, theatre in Wales is in the doldrums. I can count on one hand the theatre companies I would get out of bed to see (were I not a professional critic and so bound to see all of them). Ten years ago, when Edward Thomas's first play, *House of America*, was written, it was different – an exciting time, a new wave of Welsh theatre companies emerging from the still developing Welsh-theatre culture.

We have to remember that there was, quite literally, no professional Welsh theatre before the 1960s. There may have been an age-old non-literary performance tradition that came to manifest itself in folk custom; perhaps an element of staging in the oral bardic tradition that died in the middle ages; the so-called Interludes of Twm o'r Nant and his eighteenth-century contemporaries briefly offered an alternative to the all-pervasive Anglo-Irish drama that occupied theatre in Wales as much as England; and there was a strong amateur movement in the first half of this century, modelled on English bourgeois and social realist drama. But there was no continuous tradition of theatrical writing and performance such as can be found in virtually every other European culture. Welsh theatre had to be invented. And so it was, by the English-based Arts Council. Theatre buildings were erected with no Welsh product to put in them; theatre companies were formed with no trained actors, technicians or playwrights; drama provision was organised with no audiences identified. But from the original plantings – community and theatre-in-education groups, building-based mainstream companies, removed London-based practitioners – an indigenous theatre started to grow. Geoff Moore's Moving Being multimedia company not only transplanted to Cardiff but increasingly took on the concerns of Welsh theatre and became promoters as well as producers – it was during their 'radical alternative' seasons that Edward Thomas's first two plays were first seen. Mike Pearson, an archeology graduate of the University of Wales, Cardiff, founded first Cardiff Laboratory Theatre with Richard Gough (now of the Centre for Performance Research), then Brith Gof with Liz Hughes-Jones. Dek Leverton and Vanya Constant made Pauper's Carnival a small but unique influence. Jeremy Turner, another Grotowski-influenced practitioner of Cardiff Lab, made Aberystwyth his base and is now running Arad Goch. Political theatre was prominent, thanks to the usually ultra-left committed workers in Theatre in Education but also to small short-lived groups like Unity Too – and, later, Volcano Theatre, whose life has been contemporaneous with that of Y Cwmni. Within this often physical-based theatre the playwright generally was little encouraged: community groups commissioned (and still do commission) fine writers like Larry Allan, Greg Cullen, Dic Edwards, Lucy Gough, Gareth Miles and Charles Way, but that was about it. More muscular and literary writers like Edward Thomas and Ian Rowlands, of Theatr y Byd, had to form their own companies.

There was, however, another newcomer to the fledgling professional Welsh arts scene: S4C and its BBC and HTV counterparts. It has been pointed out that Wales must be the only country that had television before it had theatre – and the spectre of television drama still looms over the stage. It is on television that actors and writers earn their bread, and it was here that Edward Thomas and Y Cwmni also had their origins. That early background in screen work obviously influenced Edward Thomas's interest in television and film but there was also a more pressing reason: there was not enough funding from public bodies to ensure that he and his company, founded specifically to perform his work, would succeed. The Arts Council had by the late eighties targeted its funding to well-defined areas of dramatic activity, with the emphasis on provision – in other words, ensuring that perceived audiences were being catered for in terms of geography, interest and language by a range of companies that varied in size and style. Thus there was a mainstream building-based theatre sector, a community and Theatre in Education sector, and a Welsh-language sector. Where did new writing like Edward Thomas's fit? Only in the tray labelled 'development', and ten years later the company (and hence Edward Thomas's plays) is still designated 'development' work – with the accompanying low-level grant.

There was a further problem. While Y Cwmni were immensely popular in Cardiff, elsewhere, they often emptied theatres. Audiences had not been developed and the requirement by the Arts Council that funded companies had to tour in Wales meant that *Flowers of the Dead Red Sea*, for example, while subsequently a success in various forms and in various countries, lost money in Wales. Arts policy was moving towards a bums-on-seats subsidy approach – calculated on how much it cost in subsidy for each seat sold – and any work that was experimental, dangerous, challenging, was at risk. Hence the imperative to give the work different lives and for the playwright and his company to look away from the parochial Welsh theatre scene, towards Europe, towards repackaging existing work, towards new markets and new media forms – creating a product-based cultural enterprise based on the unquestioned creative talents of Edward Thomas.

Product

With the Edward Thomas industry, cultural context does not end, as with so many playwrights, with the finished script. In fact there is no such thing as the finished script. Nothing is fixed; form is fluid. As I have said, *House of America* has been produced as a stage play in several versions and as a film. It has been translated into French and Galician for productions in Quebec and Spain. The latest version for the theatre has, inevitably, been influenced by the film script, which is considerably different from the original play. *Flowers of the Dead Red Sea* went through three different versions when it was first written, changing from six characters and a complicated plot to a three- and then a two-hander and no plot; as an opera it had three characters (including the one woman recovered from the first version) and a much-pared-down script; it was produced as a radio play; Edward Thomas is working on yet another version. *East from the Gantry* started out as three actors playing various characters in a landscape that was both the inside of a semi-derelict house and an imaginary terrain, with sheet-covered props being gradually revealed like memories, a television set that showed *Silent Village* and a disembodied head in a box; it was restaged with three characters round a table; a Catalan version was a huge hit in Barcelona, where it was set. *Song from a Forgotten City* started out in the studio space of Chapter and was revised to tour on main stages; in another version, it opens in German in Berlin. *The Aces of Gaerlishe/Gas Station Angel* was conceived as simultaneously a play and a film and while sharing the same characters and basically the same plot they are different products. So just as the plays themselves are about invention and reinvention so is the work (and the company) itself, its production and packaging, subject to the same invention and reinvention. The play is quite emphatically not a final product, not even a permanent script, but part of an endlessly changeable process. Any play, of course, changes in production, changes with each production, but Edward Thomas's plays mutate in text, in form, in medium.

This process is a clear example of what postmodernists mean when they assert that all writing is a rewriting, that there is no beginnning and no end to a work, essentially no *closure*. The feeling of suspicion against closure has been supported by the evidence that there are at least two distinct and different scripts of *King Lear*, for instance. If Shakespeare could revise his work, as he clearly did, so can Edward Thomas, and a 'differential' reading of the plays would, I am sure, also be rewarding to explore, if we had the space. But Edward Thomas can do this, of course, only because he and his company retain control over the whole process, from origination to any future development – like Shakespeare but with more potential outlets. You cannot discuss Edward Thomas the playwright without recognising Edward Thomas as a cultural entrepreneur; Edward Thomas the purveyor and marketer of a cultural product can only be understood within the context of the business. Y Cwmni started with a group of committed theatre practitioners who all contributed to the ethos of the company; actors Russell Gomer and Richard Lynch, for example, were inseparable from the work not only because they were regular performers (with parts specially written for them) but because their *ideas* were there, too. There is not only a company 'mission' ('We only do work that stimulates and challenges us, work that we enjoy, work that we are passionate about') but a company image (various, from 'sex and drugs and rock'n'roll' through 'good as gold, mad as hell' to 'respected for originality, imagination, style and passion'). The actors (Gomer and Lynch are currently in London, with the National and RSC) are not now always so close but their ghosts haunt new productions with other performers. Ian Hill ensured a high level of technical and imaginative production. Nearly ten years on, Fiction Factory does not include actors in its core company but Ian Buchanan, who succeeded Ian Hill as production manager, has been joined by musician John Hardy (who wrote the score for *Flowers*), designer Jane Linz-Roberts and lighting designer Nick MacLiammoir (the three who came together for *Song From a Forgotten City).* Neil Wallace, onetime director of Chapter Arts Centre before moving to Glasgow Tramway, is not only a great fan but their producer – a concept most theatre companies would never entertain, or need. Edward Thomas's business partner and full-time producer is Mike Parker, who initially joined when the company was flirting with film and television. What marks all these individuals out is quality, and it is this concern for quality that defines the work. (Hence, presumably, the reference to Robert Pirsig's *Zen and The Art of Motorcycle Maintenance* in *Flowers of the Dead Red Sea*; Pirsig's odyssey in search of quality was like that of the master craftsmen in the abattoir and the theatre practitioners gathered around Edward Thomas.) We cannot any more see Edward Thomas as simply a playwright; he is an integral – indeed pivotal – element in a cultural industry. But, without a sense of direction, a desire to explore whatever cultural-product media and market there might be, to be in control of every stage, the work would not be as it is. That fluidity, that flexibility, that placing of the play within a broader cultural-materialist context, that confidence that product quality can be ensured throughout, that ownership of the means of production, is essential to an understanding and appreciation of Edward Thomas the playwright.

Identity

Welshness, however, is what Edward Thomas *seems* to be about. *House of America* may have been a startling drama about family secrets but its impact was as a state-of-the-nation play: here at last was a play that discussed cultural identity, albeit from an apparently pessimistic perspective. The Lewises stood for the Welsh nation. The truth about Welsh history was that it was dead and buried; a new Wales had to be invented. Sid and Gwenny's obsession with America was an escapism and an acknowledgement of the replacement of Welsh culture by imported forms. Mam's mental disintegration was due to a guilty secret compounded by lies, like Wales and its past. Dreams and myths – Greek, Celtic and Biblical – make it more universal, of course, but the play spoke to the people of Wales very powerfully about their national identity. The film, while now relating guilt to the absence of the father, and the dream to the son-father re-uniting, substituting a Cain-Abel ending for another, still spoke eloquently (and in two voices, because it augmented Edward Thomas's voice with that of director Marc Evans) about Welshness. Industrial South Wales was shot in Eastman colour, America in grainy black-and-white. The film worked for audiences anywhere, but for people in Wales it had another layer.

The argument seemed based heavily on Gwyn Alf Williams's *When Was Wales?* and Edward Thomas's public utterances made him a spokesman for the 'reinvention' project. *Adar Heb Adenydd/The Myth of Michael Roderick* addressed the question of identity directly: Welsh attachment to romantic ideas, the addiction to the return-of-Arthur dream, the resort to mythology, all expressed in a form that was a parody of Welsh-language anti-naturalism. The original *Flowers of the Dead Red Sea* had a parallel debate about art and identity but the revised version concentrated on the two butchers and their verbal duelling over memory, individual and communal. The very use of the word *Hiraeth* as the title for a play suggested more identity-seeking. It was staged as part of a joint production with artist Iwan Bala in the Oriel art gallery in Cardiff with an exhibition of paintings on the same theme.

East from the Gantry, more abstract and lyrical, at last talked more about the unreliability of memory without linking memory specifically to nationalism. *Song from a Forgotten City*, though, seemed a return to the issues of Welsh defeatism, what Edward Thomas calls 'miserablism', the clinging-on to false ideas and rural myths. Only, perhaps, in *Aces of Gaerlishe*, do we see the playwright escape from the 'Welshness' debate and deal with what much of his work is really about: families. (It is also the first play, I think, that is not expressly male-centred – women are important but altogether physically absent from the revised *Flowers of the Dead Red Sea* and *Song from a Forgotten City*.) That does not mean that the questions of culture and identity, of memory and false consciousness, of secrets and lies, are absent. They are, but the subject matter is, as it was in *House of America* (although, as noted, the film of the play shifted the emphasis to the father and his absence, a post-structuralist psychoanalytic interpretation not so evident in the original), the family. That, to me, is what Edward Thomas's plays are about, rather than the more non-specific, though obviously interconnected, question of identity: the real as well as the metaphorical *family*

The concern with identity and its related problematic is, it should be stressed, not an intellectual exercise. Indeed, the playwright insists he is not responsible for any intent. With a university degree behind him and an obvious wit and intelligence, Edward Thomas may be disingenuous when he disclaims any conscious meaning; but he would not want scholarship to compromise his assumed naturalness and spontaneity. So the concern is symptomatic, then, of our postmodernist culture, as is the work's 'deferral', its sense of irony, its self-reference, its mixture of classical myth and popular culture, its depiction of the instability of life and the slipperiness of truth – and, perhaps, his playing with the notion of the Welsh as the 'Other'.

We may look at Edward Thomas within a postmodernist context – the use of irony, the self-reference and knowingness, the playfulness with language and the elusiveness of meaning, the questioning of memory, the mistrust of authenticity, the suspicion of closure, the spurning of metanarrative, its deferral, the sense of the Other, and so on. The point is that while Edward Thomas's work is about identity (and, as a whole, about *family* as a signifier), and not simply about Welshness, it is also about negotiating a way through culture, admitting the difficulty of making sense of it. But in practice Thomas is an evangelist and entrepreneur of cultural products, looking for opportunities to produce, to sell and communicate. Edward Thomas and his agency – Fiction Factory – but I use the word *agency* in a loaded sense – have positioned themselves to make a powerful contribution to the culture.

Edward Thomas: Geography, Intertextuality, and the Lost Mother

Katie Gramich

What at first seems strange in the work of Edward Thomas is that, despite his many grand, public pronouncements expressing a desire to create a new Welsh mythology, to reinvent Wales, to galvanise Welsh people and make them reinvent themselves, the canvas of his works is not lavish but restricted, the atmosphere of his plays fetid with a sense of claustrophobia and a kind of internecine nihilism. The dramas are played out within the family, in a closed-in space, often in an overtly Oedipal scenario, as in *House of America* (1988), which echoes the Sophoclean tragedy, Freud's appropriation of its central figure, and Shakespeare's *Hamlet*, or at least Ernest Jones's Freudian interpretation of the character of Hamlet. The spatial restriction is thus exacerbated by the obsessive intertextuality, which seems to enclose and re-enclose the text in a series of ever more stifling referential boxes.

The dramas are littered with dead, buried, or lost fathers, with questing sons, rival brothers, mad mothers, and sexually-troubled, father-fixated daughters. Edward Thomas seems to be dissecting the corpse of a dead culture (like the father's body in *House of America*) or, more gruesomely perhaps, a moribund one. But in this apparently rigid imaginary world of patriarchal inheritance and parricide, what is the role of the mother and the female in general?

Edward Thomas figures the malaise he diagnoses in Welsh cuture and society as a familial neurosis. Often, his aspiring male characters, the dreamers, have a continuing attachment to the mother which is nothing short of obsessional, preventing them from forming relationships with other females. Their aspirations are warped and diminished into an almost infantile desire to please 'Mam'. An example of this is the character Ted in *Envy* (1993), who becomes obsessed with winning the Mastermind title (special subject: Cwmgiedd Miners Welfare Hall, the complete and comprehensive history from 1918 to the present day!) ultimately in order to present his Mam with the winner's trophy of a glass bowl, which she had once, in an offhand remark, admired. The obsession continues even after the mother's death. Significantly, when Ted fantasises about his success, he imagines 'a model' to wear on his arm but what he visualises her performing in his hotel room is not a sexual act but the repetition of his last, triumphant Mastermind answer. Ted has failed to grow up and acquire adult sexual drives; he remains arrested in the oral stage of infant sexual development, failing to emerge from the infant's fixation on the mother as the source of all satisfaction.

Adult sexual relationships in Edward Thomas's *oeuvre* are incestuous, over, or completely random. A good instance of the latter is the relationship between Bella and Ronnie in *East from the Gantry* (1994). Here Bella explains to Trampas how she first met Ronnie:

> It was a Saturday afternoon. It was raining. I was watching greyhounds chase a fake rabbit round a track in the name of sport on TV. I'd just had a bath. I felt warm and good. I felt horny. I dreamt I was in a hotel room with Martin Bratton in a large bed, champagne, sex, heat. He was stroking my breasts with long, delicate fingers and kissing the back of my neck. I could feel the heat from the inside of his thigh and his breathing heavy. I wanted to fuck him there and then, on the bed, on the floor, on a chair, crazy, biting, clawing his back, making me come, again and again and again. [*Pause*] But I was alone in my room, with the rain and the greyhounds, the fake bunnies and a phone. I picked up the phone book and flicked through the pages. I picked a number, any number at random. I lit a cigarette, and dialled.[1]

In addition to the singularly aleatory nature of the human contact figured here, there are hints of intertextuality, for Martin Bratton, the dead lover remembered from Bella's youth, is reminiscent of Michael Furey in Joyce's well-known story 'The Dead'.[2] Thomas seems to intensify this echo deliberately, reminding us of the snowy images at the end of Joyce's story in lines such as: *Bella*: 'They say it's general.' *Ronnie:* 'What is?' *Bella:* 'The snow.' Thomas seems not only to be echoing the potent atmosphere of frustrated longing which characterises Joyce's story, but also that work's juxtaposition between the east (Dublin) and the west of Ireland. The dead Michael Furey's grave lies in the west, which is the unvisited country of the past, fulfilment, belonging, authenticity; in the Irish context, true Irishness, the peasant, the land, roots. Thomas borrows this binary opposition for his Wales. In *East from the Gantry*, characters look to the east as a place of escape, east to England, but at the same time this escape route is figured as bogus. Martin Bratton attempts to fly 'east from the gantry' and kills himself in the process. Conversely, Sid and Gwenny in *House of America* look west to America as the place of salvation. That too, is revealed as a false dream. What Edward Thomas seems to be suggesting is that the only place of salvation and fulfillment is not west, not east, but here. In R. S. Thomas's words:

> It is too late to start
> For destinations not of the heart.
> I must stay here with my hurt.[3]

Other instances of intertextual reference abound: Thomas's work is haunted on the one hand by Oedipus and by Hamlet, and on the other by Tom Jones and Lou Reed. Sid in *House of America* is Thomas's version of Hamlet, as well as of Jack Kerouac, while Gwenny is a kind of Ophelia (as well as a Joyce Johnson) with her vulnerability and her eventual madness. Just as Shakespeare has a play within the play, so Thomas has a text within a text, Kerouac's *On the Road* being Sid and Gwenny's Holy Book, their genesis, their blueprint for reinventing themselves as others.

Intertextuality is not just a literary embellishment in Edward Thomas's plays. It is central to the idea underpinning the drama: stories are made and re-made out of other stories, myths and cultures are re-invented. The ideology of Thomas's work is thus anti-Romantic, denying the validity of Romantic originality or inspiration. However, many of Thomas's characters evidently wish to be Romantic heroes, individualistic, dissident, extreme. But their inspiration is other texts, other cultures: Sid transforms himself into Jack Kerouac, reinvents himself as American. Thomas reveals the potency of a self-engendered myth and its potential destructiveness. Myth can be empowering, endowing one with a sense of identity and belonging, or it can be emasculating and destructive. Or, as the great American poet Wallace Stevens wrote: "just as there is a romantic that is potent, so there is always a romantic that is impotent."[4] The romantic myth of Sid and Gwenny remains impotent. But, as in the most traditional of tragedies, we as an audience admire the heroes even as they are defeated.

Classical tragedy revolves around a secret which is revealed at the climactic point in the play: the revelation of Oedipus's true identity, for example. Edward Thomas has recourse to this device of classical tragedy but he divests the secret of its grandeur and dignity by figuring it again and again as a dead cat in a bag. Thomas deflates the tragic potential of his own characters by infusing their circumstances with a crass comedy. The common cliché for revealing a secret is 'letting the cat out of the bag'; Thomas gleefully uses this cliché but makes it absurd by taking it literally. Thus, in the opening scene of *House of America*, Mam tells the story of the accidental death of the cat, Brando, 'washed to death' in the washing machine, consigned to a Tesco bag and eventually buried in the garden next to budgie Billy.[5] This farcical tragedy occurs at the same time as the disappearance of the father, Clem, and in the mother's deranged mind Clem and the cat become identified. The dead cat in the bag is the dead body of the father so that when Mam makes her confession, she declares 'the cat's out of the bag now'.[6] But what can a dead cat do? Not a great deal. Thus Thomas, like his namesake Dylan, transforms clichés into vivid and troubling new images ('once *below* a time' . . . 'let the *dead* cat out of the bag'). This is an example also of the way in which Thomas habitually destabilises the heroic ideal by means of humour.

Mam in *House of America* is a multiple parody: of the Welsh Mam, of Clytaemnestra, and of Jocasta. A murderess who (allegedly) kills her husband because of his infidelity and his neglect of her, she nevertheless lacks the grandeur, the ruthlessness, and the overwhelming passion of Clytaemnestra. While Clytaemnestra is strong, capable, calculating and formidable, Mam is weak, vulnerable, pathetic and mad. Mam has no Aegisthus in her bed but, as a version of Jocasta, she may well have, or at least desire, the presence of one of her own sons there instead. While Clytaemnestra sacrifices everything for her own sexual passion for her lover, ignoring the feelings of her children, Mam devotes herself to her children, virtually incarcerating them in her House, smothering them with a love which is both maternal and sexually charged. There are also Shakespearean echoes in her characterisation; like Lady Macbeth she is obsessed by the indelibility of blood which no-one else can see.

The House is strongly identified with the mother. Thomas seems to be toying again with the iconic image of the Welsh Mam, queen of her hearth, powerless outside it. Thus, Mam wants to keep her children at home, to keep the house intact. Its physical structure is now threatened by the coming of the open cast, which is encroaching upon it every day. The house is fragile, tottering, like its image, the house of cards which Boyo and Sid separately try to construct. Boyo's house of cards is deliberately knocked over by Mam, while Sid attempts to cheat by gluing the cards together. The house's fragility indicates the vulnerable state of its inhabitants; far from being a solid 'castle' which invests the family with a sense of security and belonging, the house crumbles around them, an image of their own disintegration and homelessness. (A similar use of the house image may be seen in V. S. Naipaul's masterpiece, *A House for Mr. Biswas*.)

Just as the traditional Mam is identified with her house, so is she with the home fire which burns within it. Again, Thomas takes this cliché and transforms it into something threatening and nightmarish. For Mam in the film of *House of America* is nothing less than an arsonist, who wants to deploy fire not in the welcoming maternal grate but as an agent of universal destruction. Thus, when the boys bring home firewood Mam's words 'keep the fire burning' and 'mustn't forget the fire'[7] are invested with menace. Mam at times becomes a raging Fury, an agent of vengeance.

Yet the images of burning found throughout the play are not simply destructive. Sid, too, dreams of burning, the intensity and catharsis of the burning he sees in Kerouac's novel. But Gwenny's words early on in the play suggest that Thomas conceives of the characters caught up in an entropic culture, heading slowly but inevitably for a burning destruction:

> Gwenny: Heard it on the radio I did, the earth is travelling at eighteen miles a second round the sun . . . But if all the planets.. like earth right, decide to slow down, well, we'd just fall into the sun and burn.[8]

As Ernest Jones has shown[9], Hamlet's peculiar behaviour can be convincingly explained as an impasse brought about by powerfully repressed Oedipal sexual feelings for his mother. Similarly, Sid's apparent antagonism toward his mother and his identification with the absent father can be seen as a cover-up for a continuing maternal obsession from which he is trying, but failing, to extricate himself. In this case, Gwenny, his sister, is the eventual substitute for the mother, a woman as close as possible to his mother, a relative, but not quite his mother. If the father really is dead, we suspect that the murderer may well be not Mam but Sid, who is being protected and shielded from memories of his own Oedipal violence by his doting mother. Boyo's maternal obsession is altogether more overt, and the rivalry between the brothers may well be ultimately over possession of the mother; ultimately, the rivalry culminates in fratricide. Sid is forced to admit his dependence on his mother when probed by Boyo:

> Boyo: Well, Jack, did you find your American dream? . . .
> Sid: No, I went half mad in 1967, and died in my mother's arms.[10]

'My father wasn't my real father . . .'[11] says Carlyle in *Song From a Forgotten City* (1995); in Freudian terms it is easy to see Thomas's male characters ridding themselves of their fathers (and thereafter making excuses for having done so) in order to have sole access to the mother and to fulfill their infantile sexual desires for her. However, the longing for Mam is never, can never be, truly fulfilled. The violence and murder therefore has to continue, in a futile effort to delete the past.

Mother in Edward Thomas's plays (perhaps in a gruesome echo of the film *Psycho*) always has to be pleased and placated by her inadequate sons, in order perhaps to cajole her because she, as the Mother, is the only one capable of engendering a new world. She alone can give birth, can reinvent her own sons. This motif is made explicit in *Song from a Forgotten City*, which ends with a mock nativity scene in which the mother is about to give birth to a country. This of course elevates the figure of the mother to monumental proportions but unfortunately the mother characters in Thomas's plays seem just as flawed, fallible and inadequate as the rest of the *dramatis personae*. Most, in fact, are clearly 'bananas.'[12] Thomas seems to take a perverse pleasure in divesting the revered icon of the Welsh Mam of her dignity. Mam in *House of America* wanders around with a plastic daffodil in her self-parodic Welsh hat, while Edna Davies, the 45 year-old vicar's wife in *Envy* seduces a 16 year-old boy during a performance of – inevitably – *Mother Goose*. These hints of the sexuality of the mother are deliberately disquieting, particularly since the would-be heroes of the plays are the doting sons, the dreamers, the Hamlets who don't want to be reminded of their mother's sexuality. And yet, deep down, that is all they *do* want.

If Sid and Boyo have Oedipal tendencies, it is tempting to see Gwenny as an Electra figure, writing letters to her absent father at an obviously bogus American address. She hankers after him, and takes Sid on as a substitute for him. At the end of the play she is pregnant but she is also mad; Gwenny is being transmuted into the parodic Welsh Mam. But she remains fundamentally a child, as is made clear by the speech she makes to her brother Sid before they make love:

> Come and make us a baby, Jack, a sweet pea dream baby that runs in the Florida sun in winter, sleeps all night and smiles all day: a baby to be proud of, a baby to sing and dance and fly in the air . . . How many b's in baby?[13]

Nativity scenes, even bizarre or unnatural ones, may herald new beginnings. Perversely, however, scenes of murder, particular the killing of one's parents, may be seen as a hopeful symbol: one of the rejection and discarding of the past, the assertion of autonomy and independence, and the reforging of new identities. Because Thomas's plays consistently eschew naturalistic modes, it is possible for them to figure such violent and unnatural acts as potentially liberating and even necessary. However, what is crucial in the recurrent acts of parricide and matricide (in *Envy*, for instance, Mam's mam is shot dead accidentally by her son, while Benny in *Song From a Forgotten City* is also responsible for his parents' deaths) is self-realisation and acknowledgement, what the Greeks would have called *anagnorisis*. In other words, killing your father is all very well, but the most difficult task is digging him up again and recognising him and yourself.

Traditionally, anagnorisis has been the preserve of the tragic hero, his qualification for a kind of tragic apotheosis at the end of the play. It is questionable whether any of Edward Thomas's protagonists ever achieve the status of tragic hero, precisely because they fail to attain anagnorisis. This is by no means a failure in the dramatic oeuvre of Thomas; on the contrary, he is a playwright who writes with an awareness of the impossibility of tragedy in a postmodern age. He can allude to tragedy, plagiarise it, play with it irreverently or longingly, but he can't have it. Neither can we. This generic impasse may be seen as a mirror of the thematic one of which the plays treat. Thomas's characters, Thomas himself, even we as a Welsh audience, may long for a version of Welshness, Welsh identity and Welsh history, which achieves the dignity of the tragic mode, but we are all aware that we can never fully achieve it: 'everything round here is Mickey Mouse, wus'.[14] Thomas's Disney-Cymru is not a nation of heroes and authentic action but a shifting site, an open-cast mine, of imitation and sham.

The adoption of an imitation American identity as a substitute for a lost Welsh one is an attractive option for characters like Sid and Gwenny in *House of America*. Nor is Thomas the only Welsh author to exploit this possibility: one thinks of Gwyn Thomas's American models for his heroes in *Oscar* and a number of short stories, or of Duncan Bush's protagonist in the novel, *Glass Shot.* In *House of America* Sid alludes to a real role model, an individual who has succeeded in re-inventing himself as American – John Cale of the Velvet Underground.

> Sid: I don't care if Cale came from fucking Ystrad, he's living in New York now, and I bet you that's where he'll stay . . .[15]

America symbolises all that Wales is not: young, new, rebellious, iconoclastic, populist, secular, materialist. At the same time, there is a strong parallel between Wales and America as they are imagined in the plays: both are frontier, Western lands, pioneer country, cowboy country, fit for outsiders and dreamers like Sid and Gwenny.

Another character who adopts an American persona is Trampas, in *East from the Gantry* (1994), who has adopted the name and image of a character from a 1960s television western, *The Virginian.* Yet Trampas, the outsider/drifter figure, is ultimately more realistic and constructive than Sid in *House of America;* moreover, Bella tells him exactly where they are:

> *Bella:* We're in southern Powys.
> *Trampas:* Yes.
> *Bella:* In Wales.
> *Trampas:* Yes, Wales.
> *Bella:* A country.
> *Trampas:* On the west coast of Britain.
> *Bella:* Conquered in 1282 . . .
> *Trampas:* Could be a good place in the right hands.[16]

Significantly, by the end of the play, Trampas reveals his real name, which is Billy. The play ends with the three characters toasting each other and 'ready for something good to happen'.[17] Generally, the two later plays in what has been called Thomas's trilogy 'of national reinvention'[18] tend to offer a glimmer of hope that the reinvention which he desires and advocates might take place, in contrast with *House of America* which ends in death and darkness. Interestingly, the film of the play, directed by Marc Evans and scripted by Thomas himself, also holds out more possibilities of hope than the published play.

Thomas's plays are postmodernist in the sense that they exhibit the way in which a global popular culture erodes cultural difference and a sense of national identity. Most references in Thomas's plays are in fact to popular culture, rather than to high-point literary texts. A trawl through the one-act play *Hiraeth* (1994), for example, unearths references to Max Bygraves, *Star Trek*, *The Magic Roundabout*, *Crossroads*, and Georgie Fame, as well as to Orpheus and, indirectly, Oedipus. Edward Thomas's plays are populated by obsessional characters who are constantly searching for heroes, who are almost invariably figures drawn from popular culture, and frequently strike one as pathetically inadequate, for they range from Telly Savalas and Tom Jones to Barry John and Fred Housego. Yet these figures and the global popular culture which they represent is by no means entirely ridiculed or condemned: Lou Reed (in *House of America*) and Tom Jones (in *Flowers of the Dead Red Sea*) *are* presented as heroes. But they are somewhere else, not here. They are names, myths almost, absent elsewhere, in New York or Las Vegas. Tom Jones's dicky bow, which was probably never really his, is an icon, a trophy, a semi-sacred object which holds the promise that heroes do exist, somewhere. The dicky bow is a deliberately absurd and trivial object but to its owner, Mock, it is like a saint's relic. Joe's mockery of it is equivalent to blasphemy. We as an audience feel a mixture of admiration and pity for Mock in his reverence for this pathetic object. Similarly, in *Envy*, a Mastermind glass bowl containing Mam's Turkish delights becomes for Ted a holy grail, forever desired, quested for, but forever unobtainable.

Thomas's treatment of popular culture is thus never entirely mocking. He recognises that the lyrics of Velvet Underground songs are a much more significant part of the identity of many Welsh people of Thomas's (and my own) generation than, say, the words of the *Gododdin* or even Welsh hymns or *hen benillion*. The fact that the Velvet Underground can hardly be described as indigenous Welsh culture (apart from John Cale!) does not necessarily mean that devotees of the New York band are doomed to a life of mimicry and inauthenticity. The problems arise when dreamers like Sid want to transform Ystrad into New York.

In tandem with a willed mimicry goes a willed forgetting. In *Flowers of the Dead Red Sea*, Mock is told by Joe that his beloved father is dead; Mock grieves:

> Everything floats by past my ears, past my lips, a million words passing, a whole language, a way of life, a people drowning, a mother, father, grandmother, grandfather, daughter, son, sister, brother passing by. Silent, sad, unmarked, peaceful, mad but sad, dead sad. I don't know who I am. Where am I?[19]

The dead red sea is the sea of blood which flows from the slaughter house but it is also a sea of oblivion; Mock reiterates the phrase 'What's happened to memory, Joe?', while Joe, a Mephistopheles-like denier, is concerned only with his own triumph over Mock. Mock doesn't even recall his own father's death, nor does he know where his brother has gone. This is 'the last place', a place of oblivion, of bewilderment, of buried secrets, where the individual like Mock, aspiring, a dreamer, is adrift as in a dead red sea. This is a despairing and bleak play, though at the end Mock, hanging like an animal carcass from a hook, still asserts 'I AM STILL HERE.',[20] while a painting of a woman dancing on a red sea is seen hanging above the set.

Clearly, the cultural references here are Welsh ones. Mock's last words are a translation of the well-worn, defiant Welsh phrase '*yma o hyd*'. The sea of oblivion is, at least partly, the drowned Welsh language and the generations of Welsh people who once spoke it. Similarly, the Welsh word used as title for the one-act play *Hiraeth* suggests not so much homesickness in the sense of a geographical exile but homesickness in the sense of a longing for the past, identified with wholeness and belonging. But Thomas easily avoids the sentimental clichés of Welsh hankerings after a past golden age. Though he advocates in various ways the remembrance of the past, even its excavation from oblivion, he never suggests that the past actually was an ideal place. Most of his characters are precariously poised in besieged 'last places', on the edge, on the frontier: they are remnants (and again that word has specifically Welsh reverberations) of what was once a people with a culture and a sense of identity.

Emyr Humphreys has stated[21] that the Welsh condition in the late twentieth century is a paradigmatic one. Edward Thomas seems to be indicating something similar in his depiction of characters at the end of their tether, hanging like Mock from a hook in a slaughter-house, and yet still asserting their survival: *yma o hyd.* Thomas's plays are, like Emyr Humphreys's novels, explorations of tragic themes and possibilities in a contemporary Welsh world which appears to have been orphaned of its own history. Both authors present a bleak fictional world and yet both are evidently committed writers who still offer belief and hope in the future of Wales and the possibility of cultural redemption or re-invention. Thomas's dedication of the volume of plays published by Seren in 1994 'Iddyn Nhw, Wrtho Fe' (To Them, From Him) is indicative both of a necessary distance and of an undoubted commitment to 'Them'.

Thomas's eschewal of naturalistic modes has been a progressive one. *House of America* (1988) is perhaps the most naturalistic of the plays discussed here, while *Song from a Forgotten City* (1995) is arguably the most absurdist and self-referential. Thomas has often expressed his admiration for American playwrights, in particular Sam Shepard, but there is also a clear debt to the experimental theatre of Samuel Beckett, as is most evident in the one-act play, *Hiraeth*, as well as in the better-known *Flowers of the Dead Red Sea*. On stage in the former are two blind, disembodied heads who speak of their bewilderment, neurosis, and anguish. The initial description of the heads, 'as if being born', suggests, however, a glimmer of hope in what is fundamentally a bleak and apparently nihilistic play. As in his longer works, Thomas's characters' fates seem gender-determined: the female characters go mad, while the males become murderers. *Flowers of the Dead Red Sea* is, very much in the mode of Beckett, set in an abbatoir which is periodically showered with random falling objects. There are only two male characters in this play, but there are significant references to a woman, who is viewed as an agent of potential salvation. The macho rivalry between Mock and Joe and their bloody trade of butchery are counterpointed by an image Mock sees in a dream:

> Mock: She is an artist. She paints with oil on canvas. Sea horses and a heavy sky, a moon or sun of red. She is naked, but she dances on the sea, her long hair flows, her arms reach up, perhaps she is laughing, perhaps she is free. She is sprinkling yellow flowers on a dead red sea.
> [*Pause*]
> She turns and looks at me, I feel I should know her . . . I think that I used to love her . . . She said art could save culture.[22]

Edward Thomas seems to believe in the tragic potential of the cliché. Far from eschewing the usual clichés of Welsh identity, Thomas with apparent perversity collects and liberally spatters his plays with them. Tom Jones, song, coal mines, rugby, *cawl*, daffodils, Mams, they're all in Thomas's plays, but he defamiliarises them and makes them absurd. *Song from a Forgotten City* takes place on International Day in Cardiff – and Wales, inevitably, has lost. The tone of the play is savage. And most of the savagery is directed against the tired old clichés of Welshness and against the Welsh who allow themselves to be content with the clichés. In Carlyle's first monologue he tells of the pubful of grieving Welshmen finding themselves unable to sing, at which the barman goes crazy and slashes his wrists:

> He bled. Nobody stopped him. He bled and bled. Somebody called the ambulance. But it never came. We watched him die. We never sang. (PAUSE) Then somebody switched on the TV. To watch the highlights. In the Welsh language. A bloke with a moustache. 'Anelu at y pissed' he said. Don't know what the fuck it meant but it sounded like my head. We all watched the highlights in a language we don't understand.[23]

Like *Flowers from the Dead Red Sea*, *Song from a Forgotten City* has no female character among the *dramatis personae*. Focusing around the macho ritual of International Day, the male characters reveal their despair and inadequacy partly through their inability to relate to women. The first female we witness in the play is a doll called Cindy. The fisherman who owns her calls her his 'comfort and joy', his 'ideal woman.'[24] To console himself for the fact that Wales is losing in the rugby match he masturbates onto the Cindy doll, 'burying his Welsh face in platinum blonde dolly hair' and declaring 'I'm Welsh and I'm fucked in the head'. The scene is deliberately crass, though not devoid of humour (when the bellboy shows little interest in looking up Cindy's skirt, the fisherman says: 'You queer? . . . Cos if you're queer, I got Ken in the car. Ken will shag anyone.').

The picture of the Welshman as a defeated, pathetic wanker (literally) is a savage one. This play seems much more angry and devastatingly bleak than, say, *House of America*, and I would argue that is partly because of the absence of real female characters. Though Mam and Gwenny in *House of America* and Bella in *East from the Gantry* are decidedly flawed characters, they are invested with a symbolic significance by their menfolk. Human connection, love, is a possibility and even a consolation. In the macho world of *Song from a Forgotten City*, the only female characters are either dead or made out of plastic.

The defeat at rugby is seen in the play as the final humiliation. The Bellboy laments 'THE WHOLE FUCKING WORLD IS BEATING US AT OUR OWN GAME'[25] while the Night-Porter puts it even more poignantly when he says: 'I was part of a nation that was fucking good at something.'[26] Even the language, with its high proportion of four-letter words, especially the word *fuck*, is indicative of a macho world in which speakers show their bravado and their carelessness by the incontinence of their swearing. In the absence of womenfolk, some of the characters try desperately to assert their connectedness with one another. The Night-Porter states that the use of slang connects them, and Carlyle is convinced: 'We're connected then . . . connected by the way we speak. We speak the same language as dentists, man.'[27] Yet this assertion of linguistic community has already been contradicted by the scene quoted above, where the barful of men watch the rugby highlights in a language they don't understand.

Song from a Forgotten City is in many senses a more experimental and self-referential work than any of the preceeding plays. The protagonist, Carlyle, is himself 'a writer and a dreamer' and, possibly, a murderer; at one stage he declares 'I am the writer of this fiction' and at many points in the play we become aware that he sounds very much like Edward Thomas himself in declamatory mode:

> Our voices must be heard Night Porter, we must play our part on the world stage. We've got to show that the way we live, love and die means something, that we are part of the world, not unique but similar, universal, like small countries all over the world![28]

If there is an element of self-parody here, there is also an echo of the playwright's sincere belief and commitment.

Like so many of Thomas's characters, Carlyle has lost his parents; he himself is a foundling and his name is a false, a contingent one. 'Do you know what it's like to feel cheated, man . . . like on a permanent basis?'

Unlike the isolated, one-horse Valleys towns found elsewhere in Thomas's plays, *Song from a Forgotten City* is set very explicitly in Cardiff. Yet it is a play in search of a city. As Carlyle complains:

> I came to the city and found only Cardiff. This ain't the city for dreamers, man. Sometimes I'm not sure it's a city at all, more like a place waiting for something good to happen. Like it hasn't been invented yet. Like it doesn't believe it exists.[29]

The search for a city is emblematic of the quest for a new, modern, urban, Welsh culture, not one based on an outmoded rural idyll, still redolent of Arthurian myth. At one point in the play, Carlyle pulls out a 'dead, poisoned, plastic fish and a hand holding a sword out of a bucket' and this again can be seen as a parody of one clichéd version of Wales. Search for the rural idyll, as voiced by the character Jackson in the play, is exposed as futile and inauthentic.

Just as the idea of a past Welsh golden age is mocked, so any notions of absolute value, truth, and hierarchical structures are questioned, even ridiculed, in Edward Thomas's plays. His characters exist in a landscape of radical dislocation, where everything is unstable, memory has been lost, and things fall mysteriously on them from the sky. These objects are random: a rusty pram, a bottle of Fairy Liquid, a radio (in *Flowers from the Dead Red Sea*). Some of them might come in useful, but they can't be rebuilt into a former whole. As Gilles Deleuze and Félix Guattari put it in *Anti-Oedipus*:

> We live today in the age of partial objects, bricks that have been shattered to bits, and leftovers. We no longer believe in the myth of the existence of fragments that, like pieces of an antique statue, are merely waiting for the last one to be turned up, so that they may all be glued back together to create a unity that is precisely the same as the original unity. We no longer believe in a primordial totality that once existed, or in a final totality that awaits us at some future date.[30]

Edward Thomas's plays certainly seem to embody this postmodernist ideology.

If none of the characters in *Song from a Forgotten City* goes about wearing a crash helmet as Joe does in *Flowers of the Dead Red Sea* because the random falling objects are so hazardous, the Cardiff of the play seems just as dangerous and potentially violent as the settings of Thomas's other works. And particularly perilous for women. Though no female character appears on stage, two are referred to by name in the version of the play I have read (Draft 4 – this may well not be definitive): Yvonne and Rosie. Both are described as 'cut up' or mutilated, bleeding from the stomach. A recurrent motif of rivalry among the male characters is seen, with the reiterated question put by the neurotic Carlyle: 'Did you fuck Yvonne?' When Benny sees Yvonne in the burnt out shell of an Austin 1100, bleeding from the stomach, he sees her as his own mother, remembering the crash in which his parents were killed. When he 'sees' Yvonne in the car:

> I wanted her to be my mother . . . I looked at the way she held on to her stomach man with the blood dripping through her fingers . . . I wanted to be in her fingers . . . with her holding me tight . . . like I remember my mother doing man . . . like mothers do . . . making me feel safe.[31]

Carlyle then pontificates: 'The world is full of dead or missing mothers man.' The images here are troubling, for the female is simultaneously both victim of violence and nourisher of the young. It is almost as if she is suckling her child with her own blood. The image is one of selfless sacrifice, a traditional maternal image, but one taken to its bizarre and gory extreme in the characteristic style of Edward Thomas.

Towards the end of the play, Carlyle invents his Welsh city and, interestingly, he figures its creation as a mock nativity scene:

> Somewhere on the outskirts of the city a man and a woman are making their way to a hotel. The Angel Hotel. On the way to the same hotel are three men who bear gifts. They are travelling by train. Above them is the moon which connects them to the world. To happiness and pain. Out at sea a foghorn blows. Can you hear it? (PAUSE) The woman is heavily pregnant. They arrive at the hotel to shelter from the wind and the snow. She wants to give birth in the city. She wants it to happen in the city because she wants to give birth to a country. Without a city she can't have a country.[32]

The play ends with the sterile old tradition ('singing, dancing, winning at rugby') being buried under snow and 'heavy falls of Welshmen'. This, together with the mock nativity quoted above, suggests a triumphant end, indicative of a new beginning, a new invention. But the play actually ends equivocally, not only because Carlyle finally shoots himself in the head but also because his final monologue is a memory of his father wearing his mother's clothes, 'her underwear, wig, make-up, the whole jamboree' and dying when caught unexpectedly so dressed by the mother returning home. She 'plants' him in his bed and tells the doctor he died 'on the job'. Carlyle's last words are 'Funny things families, Funny things heads. (PAUSE) Why the fuck wasn't I born in a Merc Mam?'.[33]

In this play there are two episodes of transvestism, where men wear women's clothes and act out female roles. From one point of view, these can be seen as instances of one of Thomas's favourite motifs of pretence and inauthenticity (analogous to Sid and Gwenny pretending to be Jack and Joyce in *House of America*). But there are further implications to these scenes in terms of the depiction of gender in the plays. Thomas is always mocking machismo and the particular characteristics of Welsh machismo. In *Flowers of the Dead Red Sea*, for instance, Joe says 'You must never forget your trousers' and Mock replies 'No, a man doesn't know who he is without his trousers'.[34]

In *Song from a Forgotten City*, a play from which females are absent, where the moribund remains of a culture are rigorously macho, the image of the father dressed as the mother is an image obviously of the unnatural but, tellingly, an image of the abrogation of the female's role and status by the male. Thus, it could be viewed as a symptom of what has been wrong with existing Welsh culture: the mother is repressed and even expunged, but the repressed returns in unexpected and often violent ways. Carlyle's plea 'Why wasn't I born in a Merc Mam?' could be understood as a complaint about his lack of social status (he is, by his own admission, one of the 'fuck all squared's), but might also be construed as a lament about gender stereotyping. If he was named after the car he was found in, why couldn't it have been the female name, Mercedes, and therefore the female identity, that his mother bequeathed him?

The roles assigned to women in Edward Thomas's plays could be regarded as reactionary in that they tend to refer to clichéd notions of female identity: the succouring mother, the slut with a heart of gold, the dutiful but deranged daughter. Moreover, the playwright tends to assign the central role of the active, questing dreamer to a male character who is, in some senses, a version of the playwright himself. On the other hand, from a feminist point of view, Edward Thomas's habitual mockery of macho roles and behaviour and his parodying of clichéd icons such as the Welsh Mam effect a destabilisation which can only be threatening to the patriarchal status quo.

Notes

1 *East from the Gantry* in Brian Mitchell (ed.), *Edward Thomas, Three Plays: House of America, Flowers of the Dead Red Sea, East from the Gantry* (Bridgend: Seren, 1994), p. 184. Hereafter cited as *Edward Thomas, Three Plays.*
2 James Joyce 'The Dead' in *Dubliners* (London: Triad Grafton, 1977), pp. 199-256.
3 "Here" in R. S. Thomas, *Selected Poems 1946-1968* (London: Granada, 1973), p. 77.
4 Wallace Stevens, quoted in M. Wynn Thomas, *John Ormond* (Cardiff: University of Wales Press, 1997), p. 65.
5 *Edward Thomas, Three Plays,* p. 14.
6 Ibid., p. 57.
7 Ibid., p. 50.
8 Ibid., pp. 17-8.
9 Ernest Jones, "Hamlet and Oedipus" in John Jump (ed.), *Shakespeare Hamlet: A Casebook* (London: Macmillan, 1968), pp. 51-63.
10 *Edward Thomas, Three Plays,* pp. 74-5.
11 Edward Thomas, *Song from a Forgotten City* (photocopy labelled Draft 4, dated June 1995), p.22. Hereafter cited as *Song from a Forgotten City.*
12 Edward Thomas, *Hiraeth* in Phil Clark (ed.) *Act One Wales: Thirteen One Act Plays* (Bridgend: Seren, 1997), p. 164.
13 *Edward Thomas, Three Plays,* p. 90.
14 Ibid., p. 41.
15 Ibid., p. 32.
16 *Edward Thomas, Three Plays,* pp. 182-3.
17 Ibid., p. 213.
18 *Edward Thomas, Three Plays,* [Introduction], p. vii.
19 *Edward Thomas, Three Plays,* pp. 134-5.
20 Ibid., p. 166.
21 Emyr Humphreys, Preface to the new edition of *Outside the House of Baal* (Bridgend: Seren, 1996).
22 *Edward Thomas, Three Plays,* p. 135
23 *Song from a Forgotten City*, p. 7.
24 Ibid., p. 10.
25 Ibid.
26 Ibid., p. 11.
27 Ibid., p. 15.
28 Ibid., p. 21.
29 Ibid., p. 22.
30 Gilles Deleuze and Félix Guattari, *Anti-Oedipus: Capitalism and Schizophrenia* (London: Athlone, 1984), p. 42.
31 *Song from a Forgotten City* op. cit. pp. 58-9.
32 Ibid., p. 60.
33 Ibid., p. 63.
34 *Edward Thomas, Three Plays,* p. 138.

Tryweryn of the Soul: Edward Thomas's *Flowers of the Dead Red Sea*

David Ian Rabey

Brendan Kennelly has noted how the particular insularity and history of repression has assisted the breeding of a world-renowned drama in Ireland, through a continuous re-creation of that history:

> This insularity breeds a particular kind of intensity in talk, humour and human relationship. It nourishes gossip rather than thought, encourages anecdotes rather than philosophy. It creates an atmosphere of congestion that is frequently bitter and, more often than not, bitterly articulate. It helps to spawn what is known in Ireland as 'begrudgery', that is the state of envying other people whatever progress they may make in their lives, particularly in Ireland. One may be forgiven for improving one's lot abroad, but not at home.[1]

Does this sound familiar to anyone in or from Wales, apart from me? I include it because I think it catches the disposition of a traditionally repressed and reflexively repressive sociality – 'reflexively repressive' meaning that it seeks to anticipate and forestall repression by dividing internally against part of itself and seeking validation from the panopticon[2] of repressive scrutiny: some external or externally-delegated internal 'higher power'. Hence, an external policing mechanism of systemized scrutiny appoints such deputies as will seek status for themselves by identification with the values and practices, if not the incontrovertibly different details of identity, of the presiding power base. The granting and maintenance of such status depends upon the internal deputy fulfilling in anticipation the presiding power base's demand for the sacrificial identification of an 'enemy within' – a representative offender against dominant values, from whom the deputy can be further distinguished and thus publicly vindicated.

England, a confounded, nostalgic, imperial power, seeks to rationalize its own depression at its own waning status by identifying and blaming such 'enemies within' its ostensible jurisdictions; Wales has historically responded to its neighbour's foibles either with a defiance borne of a sense of alternative possibilities and values or with an enervation – a direct consequence of repression – which has sought accommodation within that repression through incorporating and extending processes of normalization, categorization, disqualification and invalidation. Hence the status of such deputies who have become self-disciplining and self-identifying with the hegemonic forces which define 'reality' by submission to an invisible and inaccessible process of appraisal; thus, 'reality' is defined by the hegemony of the power base which decrees that individuals cannot claim or own their work or environment, rather that they make products within and for an externally defined structure, without being allowed to create a practice on their own terms.[3]

As Ruth Shade has observed, Wales has often been viewed as a region rather than a nation, and a region to be scrutinized in terms which are ostensibly utopian but effectively disciplinary. It is not entirely surprising that many of its institutions have discounted the imagination which might permit them the development of terms which might replace their effective function, which is fundamentally (self-)disciplinary, maintaining status and validation at the expense of some foolishly visible or avowedly different individuals which might be designated representative cases for abjection.

What are the alternatives? Well, to start with, there's Performance, which Richard Schechner describes as 'Behaviour heightened, if ever so slightly, and publicly displayed: twice-behaved behaviour'; 'Performance is amoral . . . This amorality comes from performance's subject, transformation: the startling ability of human beings to create themselves, to change, to become – for better or worse – what they ordinarily are not'.[4] There's theatre, described at its most powerful by Simon Callow as 'a mythical medium, a mythifying medium . . . not a naturalistic medium. It's not a medium of verisimilitude, it's one of *intensification*'.[5] Both of these propositions suggest that things are not always what they seem under the terms of systematic disciplinary scrutiny, and that it may be possible to change them. And there is the innate comedy of anarchy, which is not a normalising or societising palliative based on recognition of inevitabilities like lesser forms of comedy, but which encourages active choice through the development of imaginative alternatives. The vicious slave-mentality of the deputy constitute what Brendan Kennelly terms 'the drab decencies' on which such comedy 'declares hilarious war'; 'Comedy brings us in contact with the frightening possibilities of amoral freedom . . . This contact which we permit ourselves to establish with the free, amoral images of our buried irresponsibility, even criminality, creates laughter of a special kind and of a special energy . . . the full irresponsibility of whose anarchic being is an insult to the concept of duty, the idea of work, the notion of altruism, the chastening, changing power of suffering, the commitment to familial and social responsibility'[6] – all terms which are rhetorical weapons in the arsenal of social discipline. Augusto Boal's praxis of the Theatre of the Oppressed identifies how 'the oppressor produces in the oppressed two types of reaction: submission and subversion. *Every oppressed person is a subjugated subversive*. His submission is his Cop in the Head, his introjection. But he also possesses the other element, subversion. Our goal is to dynamise the latter, by making the former disappear'[7] – or by making the fear of freedom transparent in his sense of shame. Thus, theatre is a good place to *start* – not to end, in the reinscription of fatalism and determinism which are at the heart of naturalism – but to start, in the free play of possibilities which may illuminate the protagonist's and spectators' spectrum of *desires* – 'which may or may not concur with her *will*; the will is a conscious decision, the desires are amoral forces'[8] – to dynamise the enfusal of desire into will. It's a good way to make a living.

I have written elsewhere on Thomas's drama some words which still seem pertinent:

> Some say that a man or woman is made up by memories. But memory is a selective process, drawing on imaginative experience. Memories might revolve around something that can be verified by so-called objective witnesses; but, also and equally, they might not. Thomas's plays show how relationships break down when one person insists on the exclusive truth of their own point of view, and in so doing blocks their partner's capacity to play, in the full and most vital sense, which is a large factor in human dignity. When people limit other people's abilities to dream and transform, they limit their own: they sacrifice strangeness, preferring familiar, reiterative patterns of possibility which mount up in the form of depression.[9]

Indeed, in *Flowers of the Dead Red Sea* there is a palpable sea of depression swelling around Mock and Joe's shrinking island of diminishing possibilities. However, the drama is counter-entropic. In conversation, Thomas has likened the play to 'a fifteen-round prizefight in which the protagonists have to spend the first fourteen rounds in a dance' of verbal empowerment, hurtling back and inwards to find something or someone to hold on to, amidst the grim sense of time running out; then, says Thomas, 'the last round becomes a matter of knockout'; Joe and Mock plunge into vicious cancellations of their selves and each other, volatile and self-destructive in their lack of any other sense of release, like the 'Rumble Fish' in Francis Ford Coppola's film of that name.

Richard Pine identifies a spirit of national accommodation-within-defeat in Brian Friel's *Translations*: 'a Chekhovian dream of national hope focussed on tomorrow, an introspection on the part of the dispossessed, a second-class citizenry, on the glory and wealth of that which they once held, and which they dream of regaining: language, identity, self-respect. That such a demeanour should be servile, and yet eloquent, is a characteristic of depression'.[10] Pine proposes 'The Irish psyche, and the nature of the Irish past, are subject to – and demand – divination, but not definition. Both Friel and Heaney dig below the everyday surface to show us . . . the tensions which hold some parts of people, and society, together and keep others apart. Eventually, however, they return us to the surface in a closure which often resembles the coda of an archaeologist's exposition'.[11]

Friel's work depicts and formally reiterates this closure, in a self-consciously classically Chekhovian delineation of endurance; a closure and endurance which might be identified by a dislocated outsider as resignation. Thomas's work, in contrast, pursues the plunge inwards and onwards, cutting free of obligation to surface, closure and resignation; the spirit of Mock in *Flowers of the Dead Red Sea* becomes ultimately a hopeful determination to make a life lived at full pelt, a last bid to fire on all cylinders, to confront, to grasp and to throttle once and for all the taunting spectre of eloquent but servile depression, or to die trying.

Flowers of the Dead Red Sea is a unique play within Thomas's canon, not least in its bleakness, which is nevertheless vehemently opposed to the prospect of resignation. This prospect is effectively incarnated in the figure of Joe, who shows himself to be a buoyant, witty, persuasive, shrewdly tactical, even likeable and partly inventive personification of resignation – but a personification of resignation nonetheless. Within the shrinking arena of the play, he is literally all that Mock has left to hang on to – and Mock finds that, like everything else that he has tried to hang on to, his friendship with Joe can be turned against him, in a vicious climate which seeks to transform strivings for joint strength and respect into signs of weakness and forms of vulnerability.

As Richard Taylor has commented, Thomas's plays derive as much energy from contradiction as from elucidation (Thomas describes himself as working towards 'epiphany rather than comprehension'[12]) and thus denying simplistic meaning at every turn. As Taylor puts it:

> *Flowers and East from the Gantry* for example deny the didactic and realistic continuation and elucidation of narrative, and instead work around a dreamlike ephemeral structure, demanding of the spectator not just concentration, but active interpretation. As such, the experience of the plays, rather than being one of intellectual satisfaction, is one of denial. The spectator is denied easy meanings and structures, and is instead confronted by the plays, whilst simultaneously being moved by the subtly affecting nature of the language, through which the characters have assonance and resonance with one another. In Thomas's theatre, the agreement, that the spectator will watch and the actor will act, is stretched to its intellectual limits: the dependency between the actor and the spectator is vast yet fragile, more vital because of its tenuous nature. The performer is unusually reliant on the spectator's response to create the performance, and the spectator's only point of contact is the humanity of the actors, and their act of giving. The experience is not detached nor empathetic, as with television or film, but electric, tenuous and potent.[13]

A good example of this mutual vulnerability is provided by Trampas's last major speech in *East from the Gantry*, which begins 'I thought I could be somebody' and goes on to enfold the experience of 'the bitter silence of now'. Trampas effectively hymns the splendour and imminence of an unspecified revelation, a missed experience: the onus is on the performer to imagine and respond towards that which is undefined, and indefinable, but to do so with a personal investment and vulnerability that may invoke a similar trajectory from personally specific experiences of disappointment to an unspecified imagination of hope (thwarted, but attempted) on the part of the spectator. This is an imaginative experience which the spectator is required to construct for herself or himself, but in response to the demands of the vulnerable character/performer, and the respect he (they?) can command. But whereas *East from the Gantry* edges comically and poignantly towards a fragile but attainable sense of cooperation and festive generosity, *Flowers* remains regularly and extensively porous to imaginative howls of anger, outrage, pain, despair, and separation, called forth in and by all concerned: dramatist, characters, performers, spectators. *Flowers* is the most profoundly painful and angry of Thomas's plays, and perhaps thereby his most profound, potentially his most emotionally accessible in terms of its depressive yet defiant extremity, but also his most discomforting and unpalatable in the stark immediacy of the despair, and the *grounds* for despair, which it confronts with an unflinching insistence which acknowledges its own possible loss of sanity (a sanity which might *possibly* also have been a contributory route to, or manifestation of, that despair).

D. Robert Storr identifies the pertinence of the play to the 'pivotal moment' of contemporary Wales, 'caught by its image of its past, yet needing to define itself if it is to have a future',[14] and quotes Eugenio Barba on problems of definition:

> When the delineation of borders is lost, identity is threatened. And insecurity over identity leads to rigour, to an exasperated attempt to give oneself a profile by opposing others. Intolerance, xenophobia and racism come out into the open.[15]

Storr proposes *Flowers* as a dramatic presentation of antagonism and its self-begetting consequences:

> We have Mock who is constantly searching for an authentic heritage and culture to identify himself with, opposed to Joe, who can only look to shallow icons and authorities such as 'Cragg' to identify himself with. We see them constantly asking, 'Who are we?', and the question is only ever answered by silence. The play is 'plastic' in Charles Way's sense, that it 'takes its cultural meaning from the culture that receives it'; having said that, it is not difficult to find an echo of Wales in the dwelling place of Mock and Joe. They inhabit a tiny isolated space that somehow suggests infinite and self-imagined boundaries if only they could lose their fear and go beyond. In the theatre, it is, interestingly, the audience that forms part of the fearful darkness which restricts Mock and Joe. By the end of the play, Mock and Joe have worn each other down and neither has gained any real identity; Joe has acquired an

> assumed identity through submission to Cragg. As in Charles Way's *Dead Man's Hat*, the play ends with the small state submitting to the larger. Their world, and the reflection of our own as we see it in the play, are shown to have no grounding. Each of the myths is exploded and we are left with a cultural clean slate. At the end of this play we may feel in a position of despair. However, from Thomas's point of view, Wales is now a playground of the imagination, free to construct itself out of the myths that the current generation can imagine.[16]

The play opens with Mock and Joe '*counting sheep*' – which may well be played out as counting members of the audience. And '*Tom Jones's "It's Not Unusual" may play*': if it does, the audience is immediately confronted with a seductive performance of vulnerability familiarized by its status as pop record until its exuberance is mistaken for archness. The pinnacle of Jones's vocal performance is a fracture of his strenuous attempts at worldly wisdom into an extrapolated, bemused yet defiant, virile bellow at possibility itself – '*Why can't this crazy love be mine?*'. Nothing in the situation narrated by the song *is* unusual: from outside the song, the experience of desire is stereotypical even to the man in the centre of it; from the inside, it is unique, painful and volatile because *he* is in the centre of it.

Mock does not trust Joe's story, about his dicky bow belonging to Tom Jones, because Joe is not at the centre of it – as Joe acknowledges, he was not part of the crowd to which it was thrown, or the woman to whom it was given in Las Vegas, or part of the queue in New York; whichever the story, Joe has literally 'bought into' it, for the fee of £20, and seeks to defuse Mock by directing his attention to the material, 'Fuck the story, feel the velvet'. Mock maintains his own sense of essence and story: he is a killer in a slaughterhouse, tone deaf and too busy to sing like Tom 'to hide the stench', or hum or whistle. To Mock it is the situation that is impossible – not, as to Joe, Mock's unwillingness to 'cope' with it. Mock believes that the onus is not only on him to either break or adjust: the sheep must revolt against their silent or bleating complicity. Joe believes that the sheep have either never possessed, or lost touch with, will and desire: 'There is not a bone of revolt in their bodies . . . it is all silence, meek submission. They would rather starve in a crowded pen than revolt'.

Mock opposes the incontrovertibility of the power and status of Cragg, who controls and invisibly scrutinizes the slaughterhouse: 'FUCK HIS POWER AND ANGER, I HAD A DREAM'. Crucially, it is Mock's dream, from which he dismisses Joe's fears and voyeuristic, semi-envious assistance: 'This was *my* dream, Joe . . . You were nowhere in sight, you never featured'. In the dream, Cragg's kicking of Mock, who was 'only trying to breathe', becomes fatal to the oppressor because Mock has transformed himself into a bucket and thereby made Cragg 'kick the bucket' – a scenario which demonstrates that scenarios can be devised by Mock and not exclusively by Cragg, and which turns Cragg's oppression back against him so that 'When I came round he was flat on the floor as dead as dead, but I was still here . . . I AM STILL HERE!'. Mock's absolute play has unsettled the serious into a joke, and the joke into the serious, and rewritten possibility through the carnival of dream; Joe does not dream, he is a 'light sleeper'.

However, Mock's dream is, like the carnival, ultimately short-lived and contained, as is shown by his own vulnerability to being unsettled when Joe tells how rats appeared in the night, unbeknown to Mock in 'the land of the dead' ('I AM NOT DEAD'; 'How do you know?'). Mock's terms of faith in his own identity remain precarious, acknowledging he may be asleep even now but insisting 'AT LEAST I DON'T SLEEPWALK' – an apt note of desperation for Joe to seize, to insist that Mock does sleepwalk, and that Joe has to chain him up for his own protection, to quell his abject behaviour of howling wolfishly and running at the wall shouting 'shame, shame', 'WHAT'S HAPPENED TO MEMORY' and 'HAVE I DROWNED? AM I DEAD?'. Apparently, Mock's only means to 'Break the silence' in this somnambulistic state is to sink his teeth into his own arm: Joe's report of his actions would seem to be merely the sensationalism of moral panic, were it not borne out by teethmarks on Mock's arm, which makes Mock query the extent that he might also have internalized reflexes of shame, unconsciously and self-destructively, and is therefore a justified subject of some form of dispossessive policing.

In this climate of (self-)divisive mystification that calls into question the very existence of individual will, Joe likens himself and Mock to 'two men in a boat', Joe the one who accepts the apparently incontrovertible elements, Mock the one who is nauseated and debilitated by them. Joe challenges Mock's knowledge of Joe's capacities: Mock emphasises his function, status and limitations ('Your name is Joe, you salt the skins, you wash the floor, you put the feet and guts in the bin'), but Joe aptly challenges Mock on his inability to recall how many months or years Joe has worked there, or how they met. Mock dissociates himself from Joe: 'The only shame I have is that I gave you the job' when 'I wanted someone with dignity, self-respect'. These are obstructive abstractions to Joe, who proclaims 'Fuck self-respect, fuck dignity' and risks ridicule rather than remove his crash helmet, to which he clings as to a protective talisman, secure at least in the fearful intimations of his own childish dependency ('these are dangerous times, things falling apart at the seams'). Icons of conformity and consumer rewards fall from the skies about them: pram, cooker, washing machine, frozen chicken, hair drier, microwave, chair (which, Joe claims, Mock bolstered his own status by requisitioning). They agree on the desperateness of the situation, but differ in responses to it:

JOE: THIS CRASH HELMET PROVIDES ME WITH MY ONLY PROTECTION FROM THE RAVAGES OF PROGRESS AND THE GENERAL GOOD.
MOCK: We are not progressing.
JOE: No, we're fucked.
MOCK: And I hate the General Good.
JOE: So do I , but this helmet will protect me.[17]

Whereas Joe sees no alternative to fearful accommodation within the utopian promises which even he recognizes as disingenuous and destructive, Mock confronts him with the consequent probability that the anthropomorphised General Good, who slaughtered red Indians and buffaloes from his shiny white stallion of Progress, will entertain such attempted ingratiation for only so long as permits him to charge onwards and away, leaving Joe his precious helmet containing the crushed good bit of his brain. Joe resents Mock's superiority even as he accepts the pertinence of his story, acknowledging that only 'the bad bit' of his brain remains but claiming an ancestry, fraternity and lineage even in this self-conscious reductive determinism: 'I am the progeny of crushed good brain, the history of crushed good brain, I am the future of a million crushed good brains, now give me back my helmet before the rest gets crushed for good'. Thus Joe's vicious slave mentality is driven to deny any possibility of, let alone take pride in, difference; Mock conflictingly asserts that he himself might yet be 'good' on his own individual terms, 'a good man born with high hopes'. However, Mock cannot immediately realize any such hopes, such as the possibility of being a boxer, within the climate of depressive pressure: he feels incapable of moving and is reduced to crying 'IF ONLY THINGS WERE DIFFERENT'. Joe claims this as a sign, like Mock's inability to be happy or smile convincingly, that he is not good; that the alley cat in his head has eaten the fresh fish of happiness and left only rattling bones 'all in the name of the Lord'.[18] To emphasise the centrality of his own contribution, Joe claims to have brought Mock his distinctive knife from Saudi Arabia. Mock is grateful, but unswerved in defining the terms of his own use of it: 'I WON'T KILL MORE THAN 40 A DAY', explaining 'this is a craft taught me by my father, he was a good teacher, Joe'. Joe hijacks the vision of the father by fabricating the image of a heroic pub darts player and then adding the detail of his death, relegating Mock to the role of an impotent griever, sundered irrevocably from an ideal which he himself cannot recall despite his insistence on its centrality to his own sense of identity and pride; Mock is driven to moan, in the way Joe either reported or foretold, 'What's happened to memory?'.

This inflicted, and mutually inflictive, climate of the unfeasability of desire and the impossibility of will drives Mock into a vision of a town and an incoming tide, a contemporary Tryweryn of the soul where 'I look around but I don't recognise anyone and no-one recognises me', at the centre of which is a child on a swing crying, saying he's lost his brother ('It could have been you, Joe'): 'a million words passing, a whole language, a way of life, a people drowning . . . Silent, sad, unmarked, peaceful, mad but sad, dead sad'. Opposed to this oppression into complicity in erasure is the promise expressed and embodied by Dotty, an artist 'who paints with oil on canvas', conflated with the subject of her own painting: 'She is naked but she dances on the sea . . . sprinkling yellow flowers on a dead red sea . . . I think I used to love her . . . She said art can save culture'.

Mock reawakens to the dispossessed exclusion of the funeral scenario developed by Joe and asks 'WHERE THE FUCK WAS MY BROTHER' who might have kept him abreast of such developments, the sunshine boy who went East 'to flower away from his roots' and whom Mock suspects of stealing his dicky bow. Mock and Joe edge into a mutually invented scenario of male in/security where 'a man doesn't know where he is without his trousers' (with comic precariousness, they both check that they are wearing trousers before they can smile). Joe initiates the challenge of hypothetical eroticism, a 'naked woman, lying on a silk sheet bed' which Mock incorporates into a scenario of being 'watched' in a way that was 'good' (an exchange of personalized, inviting and appreciative gazes crucially opposed to the inscrutable inequalities of Cragg's mysterious surveillance) – a woman he met, not in the depressive familiarities and restrictions of 'town', but somewhere good, and who took him somewhere good. Joe fearfully recoils from the vision of a woman without trousers as 'A WOMAN WHO DIDN'T KNOW WHO SHE WAS', probably the artist Dotty, which Mock denies in a flustered manner, shouting to Joe 'YOU'VE MADE IT UP' as if coerced into a scenario he cannot recall or negotiate with conviction. Joe dismisses Dotty's offer to paint Mock and his craft, 'I FUCKING HATE ART', leading Mock into a desperate defensive play climaxing in the flustered assertion 'VAN GOGH SHOULD HAVE BEEN A FOOTBALLER' because he was born in the wrong age 'Like me . . . I'm a good craftsman . . . I PAY THE BEASTS RESPECT, THEY DIE WITH DIGNITY'. Joe crucially opposes such notions, 'They are dull bastards I'm glad to see dead, NOW BUTCHER THE REMAINING LAMBS OR LET ME DO IT'. Their mounting quarrel is deflected by the incoming tide, a realisation of Mock's vision that threatens to redefine the slaughterhouse as an island. Joe is again fearful about discovering the extent of this supposed impossibility; Mock admits he is also afraid but determines to discover the difference between fantasy and reality ('I once read a dictionary from cover to cover then threw it away . . . Because it ended in Z . . . Z is where the known ends and the unknown begins'), insisting that even in this dangerous place, and not knowing where or who they are, they are not alone in their fear – a pitch of shared desperation that seems an apt moment for Mock to share his hunch that Joe might be his brother. Mock describes a hunch as when 'you know something because you feel it', but Joe dissociates himself and maintains 'I feel nothing', insisting on Mock's unconscious reiteration of 'shame'. In the face of such odds, Mock is driven to concede 'There is no opposition in me', and to wonder if his disintegration is indeed the result of his own enervated deathwish: 'Am I suffocating memory? Am I suffocating myself? Am I already dead?'. Joe sees Mock's frank exhaustion and despair as a weakness, and an opportunity to prove his own continued resilience and willing instrumentality to the demands of the externally imposed schedule. Mock holds to the ideal of the two of them working as a co-operative team, based on Mock's direction:

MOCK: STAY AWAY FROM ME, JOE. This house has no room for two craftsmen. We would compete, the competition would lead to a race, the race makes us tired, we would get sloppy, sloppy work is dangerous, accidents will happen . . .
JOE: I don't care about accidents, I don't care about craftsmanship, sheep, people or beasts, I care about fuck all, I JUST FEEL LIKE KILLING, THAT'S ALL.[19]

Here Joe is exposed in his fundamental colours as the licensed philistine and institutionalised vandal, relieved by the prospect of jettisoning autonomous thought and making his aggression the instrument of a dominant ideology, the only terms on which he can conceive of any betterment or personal advancement, no matter if it depends on his rising on the mounds of corpses, including that of someone who might be his brother. Mock insists on a 'mystery' in the eyes of the dying beasts which he must 'respect' rather than treat them as part of a production line, but Joe dismisses this as an inflexibility that conceals guilt and shame. Mock counters 'I WILL NOT LIVE IN SHAME', implicitly ascribing shame to Joe in his lack of sense of (personal, human or animal) worth and relief at external regulation. The very expression of this alternative possibility is anathema to Joe, who maintains that this is an age of shame and Mock has no choice (thereby excusing his own) beyond that of slavish nominal participation in the cynical but dazzling lottery of systematic dispossession: 'FOLLOW THE FLOW TILL . . . BINGO! BINGO! BINGO! HE WINS ALL THE SILVER IN TOWN. COLLECT. COLLECT'. Mock seeks to prevent the spiritual collapse which Joe assumes has already occurred, and clings to the hope 'I am not the only one asking questions, there must be others who lurk', and the opposition between them amplifies:

MOCK: I WILL NOT SUBMIT.
JOE: WE HAVE ALREADY SUBMITTED.
MOCK: I WILL FIND A SOLUTION, WRESTLE FOR AN ANSWER.
JOE: IT IS IMPOSSIBLE! WE ARE AN EXCITED HORSE WHO'S UNSEATED HIS JOCKEY RUNNING HEADLONG INTO A VOID . . . WE'LL SHOOT THE HORSE!

MOCK: WHAT?
JOE: PUT IT OUT OF ITS MISERY.
MOCK: WE CAN'T SHOOT THE HORSE.
JOE: WHY NOT? IF IT'S AIMLESS AND EXCITED IT'S. . .
MOCK: WE ARE THE FUCKING HORSE.
JOE: A CAREERING HORSE IS A CAREERING HORSE.[20]

This exchange illustrates the systematic self-denial of the 'careering' Joe, tricked into identifying with those who would 'progress' towards his own extermination, applauding the opportunity for licensed aggression, literal and spiritual murder, afforded by the promise of imposed discipline, finally acknowledging himself part of the 'meek crowd' who 'live in shame', counter-defined by Mock as the 'servile herd' akin to predatory lemmings, whose only pride lies in the short-term exhilaration of their brief status in a mutually destructive nihilism. Joe is driven to insist that Mock must also live in shame, 'YOU ARE THE SAME AS EVERYONE ELSE', and *'begins to beat Mock mercilessly'*.

With Mock apparently subjugated, Joe stands supremely alone as the vessel for Cragg's will, blithely assuring over the phone 'I'll kill as many as you want, I'm the main man now'. Nevertheless, Joe is *'stopped in his tracks'* by Mock's voice and the revelation of Dotty's painting, expressing a dual insistence, 'I AM STILL HERE'.

Thus, *Flowers of the Dead Red Sea* insists on the individual's right to the dignity of his/her own terms, however crude, lonely and heart-driven they be. A further quotation from Eugenio Barba seems pertinent to the play's questions: 'Our dissatisfaction with the present is nourished by . . . profound dialogue with what was different in the past. This dissatisfaction is what we call our "spiritual life".[21] *Flowers* confronts the effective doomsday scenario that this possibility of spiritual life, and those 'lurking' who would seek it, might all be dismissed and drowned by Welsh complicity in the monetarist and philistine reductive cynicisms of 1980s and early 90s English Conservatism. The dramatic ferocity of *Flowers* is stinging, but potentially cleansing. D. Robert Storr sees it as a means towards a goal sketched by Jerzy Grotowski, 'confrontation with myth rather than identification':

> whilst retaining our private experiences, we can attempt to incarnate myth, putting on its ill-fitting skin to perceive the relativity of our problems, their connection to the "roots", and the relativity of the "roots" in the light of today's experiences. If this situation is brutal, if we strip ourselves and touch an extraordinarily intimate layer, exposing it the life mask cracks and falls away.[22]

In the meantime, we are still here, left to deal with those like Joe who have sold the best part of their brain and land in exchange for 'pram, cooker, washing machine, frozen chicken, hair dryer, microwave, chair'. Those who prefer to become thus repressively instrumental in externally defined processes of policing and discipline might maintain that 'We have no choice' because 'This is the way the world is'. However, they deserve only one thing: to be asked 'On whose terms and in whose interests?'. And this may be the most important part of making a living, because there are even more sheep in Wales than you might think.

Notes

1 Brendan Kennelly, *Journey into Joy*, ed. Åke Persson (Newcastle: Bloodaxe Books, 1994), p. 72.
2 My choice of the image of the panopticon is informed by Ruth Shade's as yet unpublished research paper, 'English-language Theatre in Wales: Panopticism, Hegemony, Ownership and Self-Identification', presented at the University of Aberystwyth Department of Theatre, Film and Television Studies in November 1996, to which I refer by her kind permission.
3 The terms I employ to describe the disciplinary aspects of this process are again informed by Ruth Shade's analysis, to which I wish to acknowledge my indebtedness.
4 Richard Schechner, *The Future of Ritual* (London: Routledge, 1993), p. 1.
5 Simon Callow, 'Who the Fuck Are We?', in *Live 2: Not What I Am*, Interviews by David Tushingham (London: Methuen, 1995), p. 2.
6 Brendan Kennelly, *Journey into Joy*, ed. Åke Persson (Newcastle: Bloodaxe Books, 1994), p. 215.
7 Augusto Boal, *The Rainbow of Desire* (London: Routledge, 1995), p. 42.
8 Ibid., p. 154.
9 David Ian Rabey, 'Why Can't This Crazy Love Be Mine? An introduction to Edward Thomas and Y Cwmni' in Pamela Edwards (ed.), *Frontline Intelligence : New Plays for the Nineties* (London: Methuen, 1993), pp. 262-3.
10 Richard Pine, *Brian Friel and Ireland's Drama* (London: Routledge, 1990), p. 41.
11 Ibid., p. 51.
12 Hazel Walford Davies, 'Wanted: a new Welsh Mythology' [interview with Edward Thomas], *New Welsh Review* 27 (Winter 1994-5), pp. 54-6.
13 Richard Taylor, unpublished essay, University of Aberystwyth Department of Theatre, Film and Television Studies, 1997.
14 D. Robert Storr, unpublished essay, University of Aberystwyth Department of Theatre, Film and Television Studies, 1977.
15 Eugenio Barba, letter to Richard Schechner printed in *The Paper Canoe* (London: Routledge, 1995), p. 142.
16 Storr, op. cit.
17 *Flowers of the Dead Sea* in Brian Mitchell (ed.), *Edward Thomas Three Plays: House of America, Flowers of the Dead Red Sea, East from the Gantry* (Bridgend: Seren, 1994) pp. 121-22. Hereafter cited as Edward Thomas, *Three Plays*.
18 The refrain of the song 'Dem Bones', parodied here by Joe, is actually 'Now hear the word of the Lord'. Joe's garbling of this line to 'All in the name of the Lord' may be unconscious, but permits an ascription of pseudo-divine vanity to Mock and refuses any revelation or faith in any cosmological absolute beyond Joe's own resignation to entropic doom.
19 *Edward Thomas, Three Plays*, p. 156.
20 Ibid., pp. 162-63.
21 Eugenio Barba, op. cit., p. 150.
22 Jerzy Grotowski, *Towards a Poor Theatre* (London: Methuen, 1968), p.23; quoted by Storr, op.cit.

Edward Thomas: A Profile[1]

Heike Roms

Prior to the Welsh Referendum in September 1997, Heike Roms met Edward Thomas, to talk about theatre, devolution and the 'new Wales'.

When *The Observer* invited Welsh writer and theatre director Edward Thomas to comment on the prospects of devolution for his country, the author responded by hailing the dawn of a new Wales: 'Old Wales is dead. The Wales of stereotype, leeks, daffodils, look-you-now-boyo rugby supporters singing Max Boyce songs in three-part harmony while phoning mam to tell her they'll be home for tea and Welsh cakes has gone . . . So where does it leave us? Free to make up, re-invent, redefine our own versions of Wales, all three million different definitions if necessary, because the Wales I know is bilingual, multicultural, pro-European, messed up, screwed up and ludicrously represented in the British press . . . So, old Wales is dead and new Wales is already a possibility, an eclectic self-defined Wales with attitude.'[2] These are surprisingly confident words from a man who had become a passionate yet pessimistic commentator on a culture which he not long ago diagnosed as being 'paralysed by lack of self-esteem and lack of confidence'.

But Edward Thomas has good reason to be optimistic. This autumn sees the general cinema release of *House of America*, a feature film based on his award-winning play of the same title, directed by Marc Evans with a star cast (Siân Phillips, Steven Mackintosh, Lisa Palfrey, Matthew Rhys). The energetically performed and stylishly shot movie about a family in the South Wales valleys, whose desperate search for identity leads to incest, insanity and murder, has already played to critical acclaim on the film festival circuit. Thomas himself is currently directing a new theatrical version of the drama which will première at the Sherman Theatre in Cardiff in October before going to Australia. For 1998, he has secured a prestigious commission from the Royal Court Theatre, London's premier venue for new writing. A film based on the new play is already in the planning stage. And as if this wasn't enough, Thomas also produces *Satellite City*, BBC Wales's successful television comedy. *Fiction Factory*, the new name for his Cardiff-based company which has replaced the more prosaic *Y Cwmni*, seems to reflect not only Thomas's move out of the theatre into producing narratives for a wider range of media, but also hints at the enormous productivity of its director.

I went to meet Edward Thomas to talk about the new culture of optimism that he has discovered in Wales, and the role that the theatre may play within that culture. To my utter surprise, however, Thomas opened our conversation by revealing plans to move to London. 'If all the money is going to come from London for the next two years' worth of projects I think I will have to move there', he stated very matter-of-factly. 'There is no work that I've got left which is funded from Wales. We only receive project money from the Arts Council, so we have to rely on co-productions. And if we do well at the Royal Court, we will continue the relationship.' It seems that optimism can't always make up for lack of provision – or for lack of a stimulating climate. When the Cwmgiedd-born writer returned to his native Wales in 1989 after a decade in London, the theatre scene he found in Cardiff was particularly vibrant, with companies such as Moving Being, Brith Gof and Volcano at the height of their creative output. Subsequently, this theatrical scene has been seriously eroded through movements of migration, either into other professions or away from the Welsh capital. 'Some people go West, to Aberystwyth for example, others go East, but only a few stay here. There are no natural allies left here any more, nobody that I would like to collaborate with.' Thomas's closest artistic associates, actors Richard Lynch and Russell Gomer, have both accepted offers to work in London – a huge loss for a company that has always built on the strength of its ensemble acting.

Moving away from Wales, however, would in Thomas's view not compromise his commitment to the project that has so far dictated his entire *oeuvre*: the reinvention of Welsh identity in a new Welsh theatre with a distinctive style and form of its own. 'For me it is as exciting to do a Welsh play in London as it is to do it in Cardiff. We'll have to be fast on our feet, the actors have to be brilliant. This Welsh energy and drive will show an otherness. I hope it will define itself as something which is not English theatre, not Irish theatre, so it must be Welsh theatre.' Irish theatre provides the best-known model for the creation of a theatrical identity 'in exile'. But the wave of new Irish writing talent which is currently sweeping the London stage can look back on a long history of theatrical self-reflection. 'I envy the Irish writers sometimes. They fall right into a tradition. What we haven't got is a tradition. Sometimes I find that emancipating, but when you want to set ideas into a context, especially for a foreign audience, it is more difficult. Some of the work I am interested in doing is in danger of falling apart because you don't have an exported myth.' Yet the absence of an exportable image of Welshness has not prevented Edward Thomas's work from gaining popularity beyond the British Isles. His own company has toured extensively throughout Europe, and his plays have been translated into German, Rumanian, Spanish, Galician, Catalan and Canadian-French. But will an English audience accept his project of Welsh reinvention as readily?

Thomas thinks that the time for such a project has never been better. 'What I think is the source of the current optimism is that the old stereotypes which are still placed upon Wales by the English, particularly the English press, have become in the last five years completely laughable to us. They are not even insults any more. And the next step has to be self-definition. We Welsh have to prove that we are dignified enough for tragedy, funny enough for comedy and good enough lovers for romance.' A new Welsh self-definition is already taking shape in Thomas's view. 'When a young actor comes out of a large drama school in London nowadays, he can do a feature film in his own Welsh accent. In his CD collection, there are five, six, seven Welsh bands. He can go from making a film to working in the National Theatre, where for the first time in almost thirty years they produced a contemporary Welsh play (Peter Gill's *Cardiff East*). The Wales that a twenty-year old Matthew Rhys (one of the actors in the film version of *House of America*) inherits today is fundamentally different from the Wales that I was born into.' Only three years ago, Thomas prophesied that unless the Welsh were to produce a wide range of art works which reflect the culture back at itself and which have currency across the border and beyond, there could be no Welsh identity that expressed itself in confidence. Today it looks as if this prophecy has at least been partly fulfilled. For Edward Thomas, the current attempts at self-representation in Wales, however, are mostly taking place outside the establishment in what he calls the 'despite culture'. 'This "despite culture" is beginning to define Wales in eclectic ways. Everywhere I go I am aware that there is a generation behind us, who manifest themselves as musicians or actors who are Welsh in the world. The "despite culture", however, is down to individuals rather than organisations and to their desire to do Welsh work. It is almost like a punk ethics revisited in Wales – let's not throw stones at the establishment, let's create a condition by which the establishment is really rattled because they don't own any of the new culture. They don't own *House of America*, they don't own *Fiction Factory*, they don't own actors like Richard Lynch, they don't own any of the bands.' This new culture has mainly taken root in the Welsh music and film scene, which have recently met with unprecedented excitement, leaving the theatre lagging behind. Thomas puts this down to a widespread reluctance within Welsh theatre to depart from the conventions of the English dramatic tradition. 'The most exciting theatre in Wales has been happening within physical theatre, with companies such as Brith Gof and Volcano. Even I would have to be dragged along to see a text-based play . . . and I write them myself. I haven't seen an interesting new play for ages. I want to be taken to a landscape of imagination where I am forced to question. I need magic, I need dramas of possibilities. But a lot of the time, we have been guilty of dramas of certainty, built on argument, counter-argument and a message. People must know that a facile message is finished today. The answer is not in the message, the answer is in the magic of doing it.' Behind these words of disillusion with the theatre's current state of affairs hides a playwright who believes deeply in the power of the theatre, its ability to move us emotionally and politically and its vital role as a forum for cultural intervention and reinvention. His quest for a new Wales has been inseparable from his quest for a new Welsh theatre. This has made Edward Thomas the most stylistically conscious playwright in Wales, a passionate crusader against the conventions of naturalism and the well-made play – in spite of, or maybe because of, his non-theatrical background. 'I am self-taught, which has big advantages and disadvantages. Sometimes I think the flaws in the work are more interesting than the things I am good at.' It comes as no surprise, therefore, that the self-confessed theatrical autodidact does not seem to care much for the traditional rôle of his trade. 'I don't think of myself as a playwright. I am not that interested in "Edward Thomas, playwright". I prefer to be an imaginer, I am paid to imagine things.' This is not merely a polite self-deprecation on his part. Thomas's theatrical imagination extends far beyond the written word. He is one of that rare species of writer-director-producer which once dominated the British theatrical system but of which only few are left in our times of artistic specialization. A play for him only truly comes to life when transformed from page to stage. 'What I hate is this old fashioned idea that if you do text-based theatre you are serving the text. The text doesn't mean anything. Only the theatre means something – it is flesh and blood. The writing only becomes interesting when the text isn't served but the idea which the text suggests is brutally, ruthlessly, beautifully, magically interpreted.' Thomas's plays thus appear in as many versions as there are stagings of them. This is also due to the large influence the performers take on the process of staging. 'The actors aren't representatives of the ideas of the text, they are the ideas in 3D.' As a director, Thomas has always encouraged his actors to deliver energetic and visceral performances that draw their strength from the actors' personalities as well as from the lines of their characters. 'I have always said that I am more interested in the actor then the part he or she is playing. In traditional theatre, actors often speak of "my Hamlet". I am not interested in their Hamlet, I am just interested in them. And in the rehearsal room, the play can only be shaped through that raw material. I want the actors to think that they wrote the play, that it belongs to them.'

And Edward Thomas's commitment to the theatre remains strong, despite his engagement in other media. 'The theatre is my obsession. I am interested in theatre and film for different reasons. You cannot create catharsis on celluloid because people aren't real, they aren't breathing there and then. In theatre, when people are made flesh and blood in front of you, tragedy becomes real, tragedy as celebration, as catharsis, as uplifting. I think that only theatre can achieve that.'

The formal difference between theatre and film has also informed a change of ending for the film version of *House of America*. Whereas the stage play spirals towards a tragic climax of death and fratricide, indeed strongly reminiscent of the cathartic force of Greek drama, the film concludes on a more positive note. But one may suspect that this change might have also been informed by a change in Thomas's attitude towards the central theme of the play, the search for identity. 'The play was written as a backlash against my days in London when I thought I was somebody else. I tried to suppress my Welsh accent, I wanted to be just a South London boy. This is why I wrote the play. I hated its main character, Sid Lewis, a bloke who took on the iconography of somebody else. But when we were working on the film, we realized it was Sid's story after all. So that shifted the film, and that will also shift the way I direct the play. It won't be played with the same moral correctness as the original stage version.' When Edward Thomas wrote *House of America* in 1988, he placed his South Walian family in a world without confidence in itself in which the American Dream became a seductive, but fatal substitute for a self-defined identity. If he was to write the play again, would the characters now be listening to Super Furry Animals instead of Velvet Underground, and would they find their role-models in films like *Twin Town* rather than in the writings of Jack Kerouac? 'Super Furry Animals, Catatonia, Gorky's Zygotic Mynci and the Manic Street Preachers – the soundtrack we have for the new stage version will be scored in relation to this new Welsh musical counter-culture. So the question will come up why these people don't get their act together. What I want is that these characters have a lot of imagination and resilience. I am not going to give them a row for dreaming and for making up their own narratives within the given frame, what I would give him a row for is buying an American Dream off the shelf.' Today, this ready-made utopia may have finally lost its allure and the valleys of South Wales may have started to create an identity in their own image. 'There is a fundamental difference between post-industrial South Wales and rural North Wales. The Welsh language is a living reality in North-West Wales and therefore you need to take a defensive standpoint, but in the culture where I come from it was eroded before I was born [though Thomas is a first-language Welsh speaker]. North Wales has a tourist problem – we don't have any tourists. Nobody wants a *pied-à-terre* in the Rhondda valley. What we had was lost ages ago: the mining industry, the steel industry, everything which held the community together has been destroyed. Therefore all we can do is reinvent, and that goes right up to the Gwent valleys now. There is also a reinvention of the Welsh language.' This has encouraged Thomas to experiment with bilingualism in his writing for the first time. So far, his only attempt at writing a play in Welsh, *Adar Heb Adenydd*, is regarded by himself as having failed to establish an appropriate dramatic style for the language.

'Naturalism in the Welsh language is impossible. It kills the language rather than sets it free. The only way to liberate the language is to find the right form for it.' Thomas seems to have found a suitable form for it now as the the new drama for the Royal Court will contain large sections in Welsh. 'The Welsh language, as interpreted by an old couple in their seventies, is much more muscular and magical when you know that the generation that follows has lost it all. That is a really good texture.'

The reinvention of the Welsh language also presents a strong political force for Thomas. 'A shift in mentality is happening which realizes that the presence of the language is not a threat but a benefit. And if you look towards Europe, where bi-, tri-, quatro-lingualism is a normal phenomenon, you find forms of regional self-government and devolved accountability everywhere.' 'I would like to thank the Tory government', Thomas concluded ironically, 'for creating the conditions whereby it's now obvious to everyone that we are not democratic, that our government is not accountable, that the Secretary of State for Wales was never voted in by the Welsh people, and they might have created the confidence and the stubbornness to say, this can't go on anymore. A new optimism in Wales may have more to do with 18 years of Tory government than with any of the fictions that any of us may have contributed to.' Whether confidence and stubbornness are strong enough to decide in favour of devolution will have been decided by the time this profile appears. What is certain is that Edward Thomas will continue his project to imagine the future of a new Wales.

Notes

1 This profile has been adapted from 'Making it New', *Planet* 125 (October/November 1997), pp. 10-16. Reproduced with the kind permission of the editor.

2 Edward Thomas, 'A land fit for heroes. (Max Boyce excluded)', *The Observer* 20.7.1997.

Reviews

HOUSE OF AMERICA

House of America (Wales Tour, Preview)
Western Mail, 18 November, 1988.

House of America, a new play by Edward Thomas, is to tour South Wales.

The young playwright from Abercrave, whose father is a butcher, wants to give voice to ordinary Welsh people. He is concerned at the way American culture dominates the means of expression of English-speaking Welsh people.

'If we believe in our Welshness we've got to express it and express it well,' he said. 'If we believe it is unique, we must make sure it bears our trademark. its uniqueness made as apparent as its universality. We have to find voices which are authentic, original and true.'

House of America focuses on a divided family living in a South Wales mining town torn by unemployment. The mother tries to hold on to an old way of life, but two of her children are attracted by the American Dream, represented by the rebel culture of Brando, Ginsberg, Kerouac and 60s music.

It's an explosive tale that had a successful premiere at the Radical Writing Season at Cardiff's St Stephen's Theatre Space earlier this year. It's the third play written by Thomas, who is well-known to television viewers as Dr Gareth in S4C's Welsh-language soap opera *Pobol y Cwm*.

After taking a degree in English at University College, Cardiff, he started his career as actor and director on the London fringe. Since then he has worked in radio, television and theatre.

He recently finished a tour with Hwyl a Fflag in *Elvis y Blew a Fi*.

The Company, a group of professional actors, have come together specially to tour *House of America*.

The cast includes Richard Lynch, who starred in Karl Francis's acclaimed film *Boy Soldier*; Russell Gomer, recently seen in Theatrig's *Hamlet*; Sharon Morgan, who will soon be seen in an HTV children's series *The Snow Spider*, and Catherine Tregenna who is currently appearing in *Pobol y Cwm*.

House of America (St Peter's Civic Hall, Carmarthen)
Carmarthen Times, 22 November, 1988.

Rumours that a play about the South Wales Valleys and due to be performed in Carmarthen tomorrow evening (Wednesday) contains scenes of incest have been quashed by one of the promoters.

Val Hill, a member of the Carmarthen-based Society for the Promotion of Theatre, said the play – which she has seen – 'is more to do with unemployment, poverty and a search for identity'.

Alarm that rumours of discontent about the play were growing was voiced by Carmarthen town councillor, Geraint Thomas, chairman of the Council's finance committee, which controls lettings for St. Peter's Civic Hall.

He commented: 'I have been approached by people worried that the play – *House of America* – contains scenes of incest, murder and drunkenness.'

Clr. Thomas said: 'To my knowledge, none of the complainants have seen the play. It would be blind censorship if the production did not go ahead and a great loss to Carmarthen.'

House of America (St Peter's Civic Hall, Carmarthen)
Carmarthen Times, 29 November, 1988.

Mam stands centre stage, telling how she killed the cat in the washing machine.

'I put it in a Tesco bag . . . and then later I buried it in the garden, next to the budgie.'

Thus opens Edward Thomas's *House of America*, a tale of a South Wales family beset with the problems of unemployment, and poverty.

The bleak stage and sleazy lighting set the scene for the inevitable plunge into the squalor that follows. In an attempt to shut out the reality of their existence, Boyo turns to drink, Mam to insanity and Sid and Gwennie to an escapist, incestuous relationship based on the 1960s American Dream.

But like Gwennie's card house, the dream tumbles down, their lives filling with wretcheness as the stage fills with litter.

The house shakes with the blasting from the mine – especially when it is discovered that Dad, who, 'ran off to America with a floozy' has been lying dead under the tip waste for 15 years. The 'cat' is out of the bag: Mam killed him.

The performances were powerful but the implications behind the script were too depressing to make it comfortably enjoyable.

Rumours that it contained incest and bad language were true – yet people unhappy about its showing might be reflecting the escapist theme of the play.

When Hijinx Theatre staged 'The Decline and Fall of the Roman Empire' containing blatantly incestuous scenes, not a murmur was raised in protest. *House of America* was a little closer to home.

Judy Stenger

House of America (St Peter's Civic Hall, Carmarthen)
Carmarthen Journal, 1 December, 1988.

Brother and sister incest marked the destruction of a Welsh family whose 'roots flew out the window a long time ago' in Edward Thomas' disturbing new play, *House of America*.

The play, acted in true professional style by touring theatre group, The Company, threw up a number of challenging ideas which seemed to register with the Carmarthen audience.

Set in an old South Wales mining town the focus is on a family at first dominated by a mother's secret and a long-absent father.

Sharon Morgan, a native of Brechfa, plays the demented mother who is not quite as mad as her delight in watching Mr. Snow, the interference on the telly, might suggest.

Indeed, although it turns out that she has murdered her husband, she is the only one who seems to recognise the obvious malaise in the air her children breathe.

Fantasy starts taking over in the family home. With the mother tucked away in the hospital, Sid, and his sister Gwenny begin to lose themselves in an American dream world.

He seeks his escape from unemployed boredom in Jack Kerouac's semi-autobiographical novel *On the Road*, and takes his sister with him into the world he has created.

Brother and sister lose themselves in the Bible of the Beatnik generation. American accents, Jack Daniels and 60's music suffuse the little Welsh home, whilst the down-to-earth brother tries desperately to keep a grip.

Boyo fails to break through Sid's dominating vision and can only look on, or get drunk down the pub, as Sid and Gwenny merge into the roles of Jack and his lover.

The American Dream comes to an untimely and violent end when Gwenny tells Sid she's about to have his baby.

It is good to have a professional group performing in Carmarthen, although the venue St. Peter's Civic Hall leaves a lot to be desired.

It was a pleasure to see Richard Lynch as Boyo, and Sharon Morgan displayed the experience she undoubtedly has.

The performances of Russell Gomer and Catherine Tregenna as Sid and Gwenny I would not fault.

The Company must be congratulated for coming out to what a lot of people regard as 'the sticks' and putting on such a convincing performance.

I suppose it is a clever play rich in levels of meaning and political symbols but it didn't really do a lot for me, perhaps because it failed to create through the dialogue (despite the acting) the sense that these were flesh and blood human beings on stage and not just pieces of varying weight in a construction.

Jayne Thomas

House of America (Bloomfield Centre, Narberth)
Western Telegraph, 7 December, 1988.

House of America, written and directed by Edward Thomas and performed last week at Narberth's Bloomfield Centre by The Company/Y Cwmni, is a play about lies and their destructive power.

Mother lies to the audience when she tells how her husband left her to go to America: the same deception she passes off on her three children, Gwenny, Boyo and Sid, in order to keep the family together.

Sid and Gwenny, devotees of Jack Kerouac and all things beat, fantasise about following in their dad's footsteps. Oppressed by their circumstances in economically depressed South Wales, it is a dream of escape to a new life. All that prevents them leaving, it seems, are the same crushing conditions which make their idealism burn so brightly: unemployment and lack of money.

Diggers at a nearby opencast coal pit unearth the body of their father – murdered by their mother who admits all. Instead of puncturing the illusion that escape is possible, this event only drives Sid and Gwenny on to deny its reality. The first lie gives rise to a second, greater one, a self deception in which brother and sister come to believe they are Kerouac and his lover, Joyce Johnson.

They have sex. Gwenny becomes pregnant. Sid is brought back down to earth. But it is too late. He is killed by Boyo and his sister commits suicide. The message is clear – reality will always catch up. The strain of maintaining her deception has already driven mother mad, whilst Sid and Gwenny are destroyed by the unavoidable fact of pregnancy. At the end, the only character intact is Boyo. And he is the one who managed to keep his feet – if a little unsteadily due to the alcohol – on the ground.

The performance was given in the Bloomfield Centre's sports hall. In that small space and with no stage and minimal set, all attention was on the acting. It stood up to the close scrutiny with powerful and convincing performances by the four central characters. Professional at all times and in places outstanding, it was the talent of the cast that made the difference between a complicated plot of heavy symbolism and a play that convincingly captured and portrayed the mixture of frustration, confusion, fear and idealism caught up in the Lewis household. Particularly memorable was Sharon Morgan's Mother, and Boyo, the younger brother, played by Richard Lynch, who gave a stunning performance at the play's shocking climax. Sid was played by Russell Gomer; Gwenny by Catherine Tregenna and the labourer by Wyndham Price.

House of America (Battersea Arts Centre and Chapter Arts Centre, Cardiff, Preview)
South Wales Echo, 29 December, 1988.

January sees the London debut of a Cardiff-based theatre company in a new play that highlights concerns about Welsh culture.

Following a successful tour to Welsh community centres in November. The Company now take Edward Thomas's *House of America* to the Battersea Arts Centre, bringing wider exposure to the play's themes – closely tied to the breaking down of stereotypes that still shape people's perceptions about Wales.

The show can also be seen at the Chapter Arts Centre, Cardiff, from January 9 to 11.

Formed earlier this year, the six-strong company are aiming to stage home-produced theatre work to high standards, but work that also possesses an extra edge by serving a purpose that goes beyond theatre – reflecting Welsh experience.

For their first production – premiered as part of a radical writing festival held in Cardiff in May – this purpose is met by juxtaposing life in a depressed South Wales town with the American Dream, here embodied in a romantic escapist fantasy acted out by a brother and sister played by Russell Gomer and Catherine Tregenna.

The imported culture represented by Kerouac's beat novel *On The Road* and a soundtrack made up of music by Lou Reed, The Doors and Frank Sinatra, is shattered under pressures that are peculiar to a particular family living in a Welsh mining town, a family experiencing unemployment and harbouring guilty secrets.

Reactions from Carmarthen to Abergavenny were favourable, particularly from people coming to see theatre for the first time, and now the cast want to generate a similar sense of excitement in England's capital city.

'We want to stun London audiences,' says Russell Gomer.

He has no doubts that the ideas and concerns in the play will transfer into an English theatre – and be taken up by audiences who might be unfamiliar with developments in Welsh culture.

The debate about national stereotypes, he argues, tap into a wider regional movement.

'It could easily be a group of English working-class people breaking down the American myth – or the German or Italian myth. The brother and sister, Sid and Gwenny, could well be living near an open-cast mine in the North of England.'

But roots remain important to The Company.

'Community awareness is an intrinsic part of Wales finding its voice', he adds. 'In this respect South Wales would seem to have more of a problem than North Wales. Fewer people speak Welsh and there is not the same awareness of history. Identity has been buried by a mish-mash of Americana and English. Some people we met on tour would say why whinge, or complain about yet another radical play, but the fact is that they were excited by what they then saw, the contrast to the television screen. After all theatre is dangerous. You cannot tell what is going to happen.'

Future plans include the production of a new work by Edward Thomas – this time in Welsh – and a workshop with Welsh language theatre company Dalier Sylw.

Penny Simpson

House of America (Chapter Arts Centre, Cardiff, Preview)
The Gem, 7 January, 1989.

One of the most powerful pieces of new writing ever seen in Welsh theatre is to be presented at Chapter Arts Centre from Monday, January 9, until Wednesday, January 11, 7.30pm.

House Of America, written and directed by Edward Thomas (better known to Welsh TV viewers as Dr Gareth in *Pobol y Cwm*) was first performed at the St Stephens Theatre Space Hall in May 1988.

Such was the success of the play with audiences and critics alike, the performers calling themselves The Company/Y Cwmni decided to tour with the production taking in venues throughout South Wales.

They round off the tour with dates at the Battersea Arts Centre in London and Chapter in Cardiff.

This play, set in an old South Wales mining town focuses on a family dominated by a mother's secret, a missing father, and a brother and sister dream – all happening as work begins on the open cast behind their house.

It is an explosive mixture of their attempts to hold onto a culture and a way of life, contrasted with the attractiveness of the American Dream represented by the rebel culture of Brando, Ginsberg, Kerouac, Jimi Hendrix, The Doors, and The Velvet Underground.

All members of the cast are well known faces both in film and television.

Russell Gomer was recently seen in *Journey's End* and Catherine Treganna is currently appearing in the popular Welsh Soap *Pobl y Cwm*.

Richard Lynch is best known as the star of the highly acclaimed film *Soldier, Soldier* and Sharon Morgan has long been established as an actress of great talent and versatility in theatre, film, television and radio.

What is extraordinary about this group of well established Welsh professionals is that they receive virtually no funding and have financed much of the project themselves through their work in film and television.

Their total commitment and belief in the play's worth as an expression of Welshness make this outstanding drama a signpost for the future of theatre not only in Wales but Britain also.

Highly recommended.

House of America (Battersea Arts Centre Preview)
The Times, 9 January, 1989.

Edward Thomas, author of this overheated drama, has written elsewhere of a difficulty that faces Welsh theatre outside Wales. Like black theatre, women's theatre, Irish theatre and, he could have added, gay theatre, it carries the burden of being expected to speak for its defined culture within a larger community.

Thomas avoids creating a state-of-the-nation piece by taking the extremest course available. As his South Wales family disintegrates beneath the hammer blows of incest, fratricide and open-cast mining, it ceases to be representative of any likely community. Eventually, so little happens to the mother, sons and daughter except what makes their troubles worse, that even as a family representing only itself the drama forfeits belief.

This is the more unfortunate because it begins well, first with a curious reminiscence by Mrs Lewis, addressed directly to the audience and spoken by Sharon Morgan under fierce top-lighting, as a compound of honesty and oddity. Her account of how her absent husband disappeared for America – on the same day the cat Marlon stepped into the washing machine ('He was washed to death') – convey the sense of being just faintly askew from the way someone quite sane would tell it. Both writing and performance artfully suggest this.

The next few scenes carry the impetus forward, seeding details about the unfulfilled lives of her children: Sid (Russell Gomer), skint and pushing 30; Gwenny (Catherine Tregenna), too eager to collude with his Jack Kerouac fantasies; and Boyo, the eventual lone survivor, nimbly played by Richard Lynch.

Directed by the author for Y Cwmni (The Company), the cast take hold of their roles with conviction, darting about a black stage almost bare of furniture and giving exuberant reality to their party scene. But Thomas never shifts the focus beyond his intensely inward-looking plot. The only outside character is a labourer up on the hills (Wyndham Price), and even he digs up something of theirs with his bulldozer.

Good use of music, though, beaten out at the side of the stage on percussion. And an author to watch, certainly.

Jeremy Kingston

House of America (Battersea Arts Centre)
Time Out, 11-18 January, 1989.
To include murder, incest and fratricide in a play which proffers a portrait of our times by a relatively inexperienced writer might seem overweeningly ambitious, but the only sense of hubris that emerges from Edward Thomas's stunning, angry, anguished drama about a South Wales family is that which emanates from the actions of his protagonists. The Lewis family live deep in the valleys in a house which is posed on an open-cast mine, but their lives, castrated by unemployment and the putrefaction of the environment, are caught up in furious fantasies of the American Dream. The music of the Velvet Underground, Hendrix, Elvis and Sinatra eloquently counterpoints the drama of Mam, dottier by the day; elder brother Sid, who's only ever worked digging graves and who finds incestuous solace with his sister Gwenny as they play out the roles of Jack Kerouac and his sweetheart Joyce; and Boyo grimly aware of Mam harbouring her guilty secret some 15 years after Dad left for America with his floosie. In the manner of Greek tragedies, this punchy, poignant play moves tautly and inexorably to its sensational and violent climax. Thomas's own production which superbly marries a visual physicality and '60s music, makes this the most exciting new play I've seen in a long time.

Ann McFerran

House of America (Battersea Arts Centre)
City Limits, 12 January, 1989.

The ghost of Jack Kerouac looms large through this tale – a brother and sister take their identification with Kerouac's Jack and Joyce a little too far – but I wouldn't be surprised to discover that Edward Thomas was influenced by other, somewhat different American authors. Like Shepard and O'Neill, perhaps, for this tale of family troubles aspires to as much trauma as you'll find in either. *House of America* though is about dreams of the American Dream via a contemporary Welsh nightmare. Father is absent, mother is rapidly losing her sanity and three offspring, trapped in a small house next to an open cast mine, are all jobless. Grainier than fields of Southern wheat, some of Thomas's realism is predictably bombastic, but in places his dialogue has the clanging precision of a steel works. He directs too, and some interesting production features give a pleasing non-naturalistic edge: hard, useful lighting; a sparse set and some apposite drumming effects thrown in for good measure. Promising work then, but as the play crashes through to an overblown denouement the concern with Anguish-American-Style calls for some fairly heavy sacrifices. Whatever happened to good old-fashioned characterisation and plausibility?

Andy Lavender

House of America (Harry Younger Hall, Edinburgh)
London Theatre Record, 27 August – 9 September, 1989.

'Look at Wales. Where are our Gods? Where are our heroes? We haven't got any.' Herein lies the meat of Edward Thomas's modern tragedy for a neglected nation.

A redundant Welsh family kills time in a windswept cottage, while the opencast pit marches remorselessly ever closer. Mother goes quietly mad to the accompaniment of television interference, and unable to find work, her children create an American Dream of their own – their only means of escape from lives of such mundane and perpetual suffering. But fantasy invades reality and their childlike game bears adult consequences in a chaotic and distressing climax.

Thomas's directing is as restless and as rigorous as the acting. The performances left me humbled. My only criticism, and a major one, is that this play travels beyond its natural conclusion, and robs this piece of much potential power.

Nevertheless the claustrophobic orbits of the characters, and the uncompromising anger of their message makes *House of America* a master work. To witness, along with *The Scam*, two Welsh productions of such pride and pain is too much of a coincidence. There's a small revolution brewing in the valleys. Check it out.

William Cook

House of America (Chapter Arts Centre, Cardiff)
South Wales Echo, 5 October, 1992.

When Ed Thomas's play, *House of America*, was first performed in a disused docklands church it threatened to raise the belfry roof.

A blistering attack on deprived South Wales Valleys communities, the play took in murder, incest, drugs, sex and rock 'n' roll in a fast moving narrative that echoed the blood drenched dramas of the Jacobean period.

The audience sometimes recoiled from the frenetic pace, and it is the same for the actors.

Jamie Garven, who directs Y Cwmni's revival at the Chapter Arts Centre this week, points out that it takes its toll on the actors too:

'In rehearsal I'm finding it's taking them a while to recover from some of the scenes, the emotional impact is that strong. It is very demanding, never boring, and it seems to get you in its grip and just does not let go.'

He is also convinced that it is as topical as ever as unemployment figures rise and more and more communities are facing the kinds of problems meeting Ed Thomas's dysfunctional family in *House of America*.

It's very much the opposite of the neat, well-packaged theatre play. It retains its power thematically and is still a strong image of late 20th century Wales. There are going to be many more new plays staged over the next six months, but you will find very few that are going to better this one. It's got strong characters, cracking dialogue and a compelling story. It's loud, sexy and exciting.

The very qualities that got councillors in Carmarthen hot under the collar – they were on the verge of banning it when it began a Valleys tour after its premiere – were enough to win its writer a prestigious Time Out/O1 award and glowing reviews at the Edinburgh Fringe Festival.

This time round, *House of America* is being teamed with two other plays by Ed Thomas, all being shown around England, Wales – and the Ukraine – in coming months. The New Wales Trilogy tour is being supported by Cardiff Marketing Ltd, giving audiences a chance to assess the damage being done to the collective Welsh psyche through Thomas's anarchic and sometimes near inscrutable musing about national identity.

House of America (Chapter Arts Centre, Cardiff)
Cardiff Herald and Post, 8 October, 1992.

Y Cwmni – The Company – has stunned another set of theatre goers with Ed Thomas's *House of America*, running at the Chapter until Saturday.

To date this has to be among the experimental (but loyally Welsh) group's best productions.

If the first-night performance was anything to go by then *House of America* and its author should storm not only the current Cardiff Festival but Wales, the UK, Europe . . . it's a play which should grab the world by the throat so it takes a proper look at Wales.

The dark background but sharp lightwork picks up on first the happiness of a Valleys' family anywhere between Merthyr and Ystrad Mynach. Surprisingly the jokes were fired quick-pace and with laughs in equal measure, lambasting everything from Tom Jones to Harry Secombe.

But with the opencast looming the family are not concerned about the Valleys' heroes but the image of their father in the US of A, walking in the footsteps of Jack Kerouac and Marlon Brando.

Eventually the dreadful truth about the dreaded opencast is dug up throwing everything into disarray.

Highlights such as these are caught excellently by the cast, from Eluned Jones as Mam to Lisa Palfrey's Gwenny in her most poignant dying moment.

Martin Donovan

House of America (Chapter Arts Centre, Cardiff)
Western Mail, 9 October, 1992.

Anyone doubting the vitality of Welsh theatre should be forcibly led to this production. Its passion and fury practically burnt a hole in the roof as a highly talented cast turned in a searing performance. They made the most of a disturbing and sometimes shocking play – the antithesis of the cosy Welsh drama of yesteryear.

The entire action takes place in and around a Valleys house where an opencast mine is being developed. It threatens not only the house itself but the sanity of Mam (Eluned Jones), who is firmly opposed to her sons Boyo (Rhodri Hugh) and Sid (Russell Gomer) getting jobs there. This is because it holds a family secret which is gruesomely uncovered in the course of the mining operations. The play turns, however, not so much on this revelation as on the disintegration of the family.

The broad humour of the opening scene, when Mam recalls the day when her husband supposedly ran off to America, gives no hint of the darkness ahead. It is only slowly that Sid and his sister Gwenny (Lisa Palfrey) lose themselves in fantasy to such an extent that they become lovers, imagining themselves to be the Sixties beat hero Jack Kerouac and his girlfriend Joyce.

Thomas confirms his reputation as a writer with a sublime gift of invention, who follows his intuitions to give us work rich in symbolism. He is well served by director Jamie Garven and a cast with energy and imaginative sympathy, who create an impressive atmosphere.

If you're anywhere within range, don't miss this memorable production.

Herbert Williams

House of America (Tramway, Glasgow)
Glasgow Herald, 13 October, 1992.

Edward Thomas is a difficult writer with whom to get on terms. He makes a moving target of himself, never returning to the same ground twice. His New Wales Trilogy, performed all this week at The Tramway, reveals a restless search for form. When his *Flowers Of The Dead Red Sea*, the second of the trilogy opening tonight, was seen in the version that came to The Tramway last year it was like two separate plays competing for a single space.

House of America sometimes gave that same impression last night, but for an entirely different reason. It works on at least two fundamentally different levels. You have a play about a family, a household, threatened by dissolution, madness, incest, and fratricide in a tragic chain of events triggered by the establishment of an open-cast mine in the neighbourhood. But another seam is the fracturing of a culture, Welsh culture, by the intoxicants of American dreams, Jack Daniels and benzedrine.

That open-cast mine assumes a new significance as a repository of fragile roots exposed to ultimately destructive Beat generation hallucinations of Jack Kerouac, and diluted by the often ironic sounds of Lou Reed, Jim Morrison and Aretha Franklin. It is a play that serves a warning that a people who lose their voices (as characters do here, losing their accents by a mimicking of role models), lose their identities, and then their minds. That is pertinent to a Scottish audience.

No-one could accuse Thomas of a lack of ambition in these three plays, brought by Y Cwmni (The Company), but in purely theatrical terms he may still not have found his direction. *House of America* has plenty of powerful moments, and it is easily the most absorbing of the trilogy, but in both the measure of the writing and the scale of the conception I see a potentially great novel, and an over-extended stage play.

John Linklater

House of America (Chapter Arts Centre, Cardiff)
Gair Rhydd, 19 October, 1992.

Without art a nation lies soulless. With another's culture pulling the strings, a nation is corrupted, but as *House of America* implies, spiritual quest will result in survival. The twentieth century has marginalised live theatre, forcing much of it into a non-sensical cul-de-sac. Y Cwmni are fighting back.

House of America is built on sturdy foundations allowing the walls to reverberate with cultural conflict. The family of Sid, Boyo, Gwenny and Mam are ensnared by a changing Wales. They are on the cusp of historical shift. Mam and Boyo resist through rituals, Sid and Gwenny embrace the new, namely America.

Within the conflict, Edward Thomas, the writer, craftily reclaims Welsh stereotypes and ultimately, exposes cultural imperialism. His weapon is humour. The first half teems with earthy jokes; the humour of a community that has repelled many attacks. Boyo (Rhodri Hugh), a die-hard valleys' lad, remarks, 'Hard life being a sheep, innit?'. He is as much talking of his own life.

The dialogue shines with a plethora of anecdotes and one-liners. The timing is immaculate. Director, Jamie Garven, and the small cast, react superbly to Thomas's writing. Boyo and Sid (Russell Gomer) act out a break-neck brotherly relationship. Sid, his fantasies in America, bemoans Wales's lack of heroes. 'You wouldn't queue and laugh in the rain for hours for Harry Secombe', he says. Boyo, resigned to his life, retorts that Secombe does not claim to be a hero. 'And he'd be fucking right', replies Sid. Mam, astutely played by Eluned Jones, is embittered by the past, scared of the future. The open-cast mine where Sid and Boyo half-heartedly seek jobs symbolises cultural invasion and the family's exposed situation. It also holds a horrific secret.

House is played on a minimalistic, but adaptable set. The music of the Doors, Lou Reed and other American Rock Gods crashes around the action. Sid and his younger sister Gwenny (Lisa Palfrey) become embroiled in a perverse fantasy of themselves as Jack Kerouac and Joyce Johnson. This provokes a family row of palpable proportions. Mam unable to grasp Gwenny and Sid's 'game' suggests they are having an incestuous affair. Her vicious cruelty aches with maternal concern.

The clash of reality and fantasy is the furniture in the *House of America*. At times it is difficult to distinguish between the two. Sid and Gwenny visit the mine as pseudo-Beatniks, where a demonic labourer (Wyndham Price) has lost his head. The final stages are awash with heart-tearing emotion. Sid is demoralised. Gwenny's closing monologue is startling. It exposes the Beat mentality as shabby within a late twentieth century context. Youth culture has gone much further than Zen and high-art.

House of America catches you unaware. It urges Wales to survive. The valleys are teeming with tales to be told, but while America grips popular art by the throat Sid's stories will go relatively unheard. It is moving to the point of emotional overload. Ears and eyes understand far better than words can express it. *House* coaxes its audience to journeys beyond the physical. The world has been mapped, the mind lies dangerously uncharted.

Gareth J. Ledbetter

House of America (Sherman Theatre, Cardiff, preview)
The Western Mail, 11 October, 1997.

The favourite room of Wales's foremost playwright, Ed Thomas, has had a major impact on his life.

What goes on in it got him noticed, led to the formation of his own stage and television production company and has now propelled him firmly into films.

Perhaps 'room' is not quite the right word. We are talking about the set of his play, *House of America* which he first staged in Butetown, Cardiff back in 1988.

He built on the play's success (*Time Out* reckoned it was that year's best play) by forming what is now called Fiction Factory (Y Cwmni, as was), based at Chapter Arts Centre, Cardiff.

And now, more than half-a-dozen stage productions later, all written by him, the company is about to present his first play once again.

It opens for 10 days at the Sherman Theatre in Cardiff next Wednesday before setting off for Australia, on the way visiting Warwick, Brecon, Swansea, Cambridge and Belfast.

The theme of US and home cultures on collision course has struck a chord abroad and next week will see the play opening in French in Montreal and in Galician in Santiago de Compostela in northern Spain.

House of America is now also a film (Mr Thomas wrote the screenplay, Marc Evans directed) in which Siân Phillips plays the mother. It opened in UK cinemas yesterday and the arts pundits can't recall when a Welsh film and play last rode out together.

The last time it happened elsewhere in the UK was with much-acclaimed *Trainspotting*.

House of America is about a family, or more particularly the father trying to live the American Dream in Wales. The clapboard house he builds alongside an encroaching drift-mine is like something out of the American prairies. Central to the play is the lounge – as wide and as spacious as any you'll see in US sitcoms, dominated by the inevitable giant sofa.

In and around the house, the iconography is suggestive, with the likes of James Dean, the young Brando, beat generation guru Jack Kerouac and baseball helping relay the American look. But one of the points of the play is that it all misses the mark.

'The house ends up looking like American "poor white trash" but with a Welsh dimension,' said Mr Thomas. 'The vehicle in bits in the front yard is more likely to be a Reliant Robin than say a Dodge pick-up. It becomes the home of someone up against it.'

Then suddenly the father is gone, presumably to chase his dreams at first hand across America and the family are left to pick up the pieces.

In the film the American Dream not being what it is cracked up to be is summed up by the US scenes shot in black and white and the Welsh ones in colour.

'Wales is the hero, not America', said Mr Thomas. Mr Thomas's favourite room works hard for its living. When we spoke, the 'room' existed only in model form, though it had been partly constructed, giant sofa and all, in a cavernous rehearsal studio at Chapter, and Mr Thomas proudly used the model to show me how the various transformations would be achieved.

Set designers, in this case Jane Linz-Roberts, are ingenious people.

So, seven busy years separate the early and latest versions of Mr Thomas's ground-breaking room. The extent to which he has come a long way in that time can be shown by the finances involved.

The film version of the play cost around £1.5m to produce, a fleabite compared to some Hollywood blockbusters but a far cry from what it cost him to stage *House of America* in Butetown eight years ago – just £26.

John Williams

House of America (Arts Theatre, Belfast)
Belfast Telegraph, 26 November, 1997.

Be careful what you wish for – you might get it! and who hasn't wished to live the American Dream? To hit the road in an open top car, with the wind in your hair, radio on, and bottle of bourbon in hand . . .

Clem Lewis left his dilapidated Welsh village in search of the Dream, leaving his wife to bring up their three kids. Now his son Sid, and daughter Gwenny are set to follow in their father's footsteps – and those of their hero, Jack Kerouac.

Ed Thomas has written a Welsh drama with a universal theme – there are towns everywhere filled with people who have never worked, who fill their days dreaming of a better life.

Performed on a disordered, dysfunctional set – a fair depiction of the minds of the Lewis family, and interspersed with a soundtrack to die for, the play is directed by the author at such a pace that the actors bounce around like basketball players, ducking and weaving, with nowhere left to go when the tension is stepped up.

Richard Harrington's Boyo is the eye at the centre of this storm, and even he is given his head in the overlong climax, when the dream turns into a nightmare.

Fast, furious, and at times very funny, this House could do with a bit more order – to better illustrate the mess it's in.

Grania McFadden

House of America (Arts Theatre, Belfast)
Irish News, 26 November, 1997.

The award-winning *House of America* makes its Belfast debut at the Arts Theatre.

Written and directed by Edward Thomas the internationally-acclaimed company, Cardiff-based Fiction Factory, gives striking performances. The bleak set mirrors the uncompromising humour. The atmospheric lighting gives a dramatic backdrop to the gritty realism. There is a disturbing and intense ambience interspersed with moments of hilarity. All this combined with the wonderful soundtrack makes for an innovative piece of theatre. This angry and anguished play is an unforgettable evening at the festival. Definitely a highlight and will stay in the memory long after the festival has finished. I strongly recommend seeing this production.

House of America (Arts Theatre, Belfast)
Irish News, 27 November, 1997.

Some plays can be classed as pure escapism while others reflect hard-hitting reality, yet both elements are permanent residents in Fiction Factory's *House of America* at the Arts Theatre this week.

This stunning production of Ed Thomas's ten-year-old play remains fresh with universal themes and issues relevant to any small community where hope and employment have decreased. Getting away from the reality of the situation – the core of this frantic family drama – may not necessarily be the answer, even if the other man's grass does appear to be greener.

Ducking between reality and the fantasy of dreams, the players are trying to escape from their mundane existence as the two drug-taking teenagers become victims of an incestuous relationship while living out their obsession with the characters in a book. The boy, who inherits the dream of his missing father to go to a new life in the land of milk and honey, accuses their mentally unstable mother of emotional blackmail while her nervousness is really related to her obsessive objections to the open-cast mining in the area which threatens to uncover a dark secret from her past.

The action throughout is fast paced and in-your-face as much as the loud and vibrant soundtrack (Lou Reed, The Doors, etc.) is in your ears, which should attract older teenagers.

However, no matter what your age, be prepared to experience something totally different which will leave you shocked, uncomfortable and drained as this two-hour play builds to a gripping and tragic climax.

Performed with vigour by this excellent Welsh company – Jams Thomas, Shelley Rees, Richard Harrington, Helen Griffin and Steve O'Reilly – this intensely physical piece is powerful, passionate and poignant.

Damien Murray

House of America (Arts Theatre, Belfast)
Ballyclare Gazette, 3 December, 1997.

Watching *House of America*, showing at the Arts Theatre during the Belfast Queens Festival last week, was more like going on a ride, than going to see a play.

This vital and crazy production crashed through themes as way out as those in *Hamlet*, in an environment similar to the film *Twin Town*, only with a better story.

In 1990s Wales the Lewis family are unemployed, skint and bored with their lot, but their eccentric Mam has held the family together since their father ran off to America.

When a new open cast mine is started in their town, the two brothers, Sid played by Jams Thomas and Boyo played by Richard Harrington think this is finally their chance to get a job and make enough money to go to America to find their Dad. But things don't go as planned and the digging starts to send their Mam (Helen Griffin), crazier than ever, until they are not too sure that their Dad did go to America after all.

To make things worse Sid and the boys' sister Gwenny (Shelley Rees) seems to be getting a little too serious about playing make-believe they are characters from a Jack Kerouac book, so that pretty soon Boyo can't decide if it's the drugs or something more sinister which is making them act so strangely.

The cast, a Welsh group called Fiction Factory, bang out their characters with great enthusiasm. Mam especially, is brilliantly schizophrenic and although you get a strong sense of Wales with strong Welsh accents, unemployment and pride in their stars like Tom Jones, the themes of the play are universal and you realise it is portraying the life of any deprived and depraved family in anytown.

Written eight years ago by Ed Thomas for the company the play has also been made into a film of the same name. In the Festival production the dynamic action was complimented with a boisterous backing soundtrack to beat *Trainspotting* and although the set is bare it provides the cast with great opportunity to move around. Parts of the play were very funny and parts intentionally made you cringe. But although the family are totally screwed up you also enjoy their ability to make their own fun and throw a party with nothing but a few cans and themselves for entertainment.

Jane Bardon

House of America (Stage and Film Version, 1997)
New Welsh Review, (Winter 1997-98).

Suddenly, last October, as the days grew danker and shorter, the long-awaited Welsh cultural renaissance drew nearer. Just a few days after the narrow Yes vote for an assembly brought a quickening of the heart and spirit, this turned into a rush of exhilaration, sheer joy, as Marc Evans's stunning movie, *House of America*, hit cinema screens – and Ed Thomas's play, its glorious source, began a new tour in yet another reworked version, eight years after its first staging at Chapter.

'And of course I needn't have worried about disturbing the corpse of the original play because it never died. Unlike the film, the play can be revisited again and again', wrote Evans in the programme for Fiction Factory's production under Thomas's direction. And it's true: the two media are as different as chalk and cheese. The only thing they have in common is the soundtrack, the haunting Manics' 'Motorcycle' Emptiness most of all.

Evans's film, first shown on HTV, works, weaves its magic, on myth and image. Sid and Gwenny, the would-be Kerouac-style beats, are virtually mythopaeic figures. In the stylised if movingly human performances of Steven Mackintosh and Lisa Palfrey (so good she deserves an Oscar) they could be from anywhere, Seattle or South Dakota, rather than specifically from South Powys. This universality is heightened by the breathtaking black-and-white cinematography of Pierre Aim which dissolves the landscape of the South Wales valleys into a desert-like terrain and the village into a strangely deserted street as in a Leone Western.

This sense of unreality is heightened by the choice of Siân Phillips as Mam. It's in some ways a compelling performance but, as the Scots would say, *nae real*; she's such an archetypal figure of Mother, in her pain, disillusion, love and delusion, it scarcely matters she's more Richmond than Rhymney. And, above all, the overall effect, despite the vitality and humour, is to present the dysfunctional family – and nation – as victims of forces beyond their control. Evans has escaped from one outmoded stereotype of Wales via the American Dream into myth.

Ironically, given its unreal nature and the spare set of designer Jane Linz Roberts, the theatre in Thomas's new production is more grounded in reality. It's not just that Helen Griffin's Mam is so obviously more rooted in the Valleys; nor that she lets us know early on that she killed her unseen husband (a visible road-movie drifter in Evans's film); not that Sid clearly kills himself because of his incest with Gwenny; nor even that Richard Harrington's Boyo is the dominant stage-presence.

What is more, the stage version's impact is livelier, more humorous, more approachable, more celebratory. Would it be fanciful to surmise that Thomas's reworking of his original scripts reflects the slow-burning, hesitant rebirth of Wales as a self-confident nation, anticipates even the devolution result with its promise of a half-baked legislature?

Certainly, the national symbolism behind the tragedy of Sid and Gwenny, Mam and Boyo, remains seared into the memory but the overall effect is uplifting . . . Either way, these two versions of one man's accomplished vision confirm what we have long known: Thomas is a major writer; and Wales, in the shape of Evans, can compete filmically with the best. They prove that the constant force in Wales for cringing self-denigration, persistent self-laceration, is redundant.

David Gow

House of America (Perth, Australia)
New Welsh Review, (Spring 1998)

Screeching twenty-eights, traffic-light coloured parrots, are having conniptions high up in the canopy of the paper-bark gum trees. The tawny sand-coloured brickwork of the Octagon theatre, set on the Swan River-hugging campus of the University of Western Australia is backlit, pinkened by the weltering sun. It is opening night for Ed Thomas's *House of America*, which he has been erecting and dismantling these past ten years. This time his home for dysfunctionals was built in Perth, a house down under . . .

The Perth Festival performances by Fiction Factory were a long way removed, both theatrically and literally, from those I'd witnessed in Cardiff and Brecon during their run last autumn. This was due, in no small measure, to a deal of pre-tour work by assistant director Steve O'Reilly, bolstered by some whip-cracking attention from the playwright himself in Perth. Sitting in on the rehearsals was revealing in the extreme as Ed Thomas covered the hoops in razor-wire and torched the petrol before getting the actors to jump through them. He is a demanding director, instigating changes even at the dress-rehearsal, where the mainly under twenty-five-year-old cast showed their mettle. Shored up by their necessary confidence, the actors took the changes in their stride, coming up with their own refinements from time to time. Realising this 'drama of possibilities' is very much a two-way traffic.

During some workshops and masterclasses during the Festival Ed Thomas reminded us of the genesis of this piece, of a time when he found himself thinking he was Jack Kerouac in a London where people probably only knew Wales as home to the boxer Colin Jones and the place where they went rock-climbing when they were in Borstal. Since which time, he admits to having cultivated an obsession with Wales, that sort of relationship. The play started with a blank page which was then filled in, starting with a rhythm. Thomas admits to being good at putting words next to each other but freely admits to 'having nothing to say but everything to discover'. He writes signifiers not characters. There is latitude for experiment, actors bringing what they have to the party.

Some of the relationships inherent in the play had changed greatly, had spun round on their axes, since the Welsh run. The brothers, Sid and Boyo had homo-erotic bent, if you pardon the pun. Where, in Wales, a kiss between them had been greeted by an *ych a fi* wiping of the mouth by Boyo, in Australia the lips met for more than a fleeting moment of tenderness and when one brother leaped onto his brother's back, much as he would mount a motorbike, that sex thing reared its head, a smokescreen, seemingly, for the later incest between Sid and Gwenny as they transform into Jack Kerouac and his lover, Joyce Johnson. Shelley Rees as Gwenny was deeper into her character this time around, her delusional self a palimpsest over the scared little girl within, sending her hopeless missives to a father she has to believe is in America but whose corpse is, in truth, about to be disinterred by the open-cast. Indeed the entire cast had plumbed the psychological depths of their characters, knew them as family. Richard Harrington as Boyo was the Jaffa cake-loving epicentre of things, a man of good heart who tries to take the place of the missing father but who's also taken to the point where everything breaks. This was a rocket-fuelled ride, the actor not on auto-pilot but rather steering his own unwitting course for damnation.

Sid, whose dreams are expansive enough to ride a Harley Davidson across, became, in Jams Thomas's latest incarnation, a testosterone-saturated celibate, a choreographer of the sexual come-on, and from his very first strutting entrance he held the audience much as Claude Mesmer must have himself first done. This black-leather-clad fantasist, a man who drinks Campari and soda down the rugby club, is the character Ed Thomas himself has the least sympathy with, because he buys into other people's dreams. But in Perth he was the audience's hero. They felt his hurt as their own.

The plaudits – the palm, the oak and the bays as Andrew Marvell put it – went to Helen Griffin who, as the murder-haunted Mam seemed to actually break down in front of us. If Lady Macbeth saw her hands drenched in blood then Mam put on seven league boots before going a step further by redecorating her room in blood red. Any clinical psychiatrist in the audience would have put Mam in a rubber room long before the play put her in the 'mental'.

A play which started its road-movie journey a decade ago as an explosively iconoclastic affair, it is now itself iconic, from a writer whose work stands out as a cathedral amongst booths. But it still has the power to provoke, at times to dynamite, a cliché. In this production there is a moment when Mam takes off her black hat and uses it as a chamber pot before casually putting it back on her head. This was rupturingly funny.

It was a standing ovation for Fiction Factory on opening night and with 3,000 tickets sold it promised to be an Antipodean success. Audience members I spoke to seemed in competition for bigger and better superlatives. Newspaper reviews described the entire spectrum, from a splenetic tirade in the provincial *West Australian* under the heading 'Over the Top Down in the Valleys', which sent one cast member round the city looking for a Kalashnikov, to the national broadsheet *The Australian*, which saw it as a 'screamingly funny and grotesquely morbid', offering a 'wild, extravagant and violent picture of modern Wales' with 'acting that stays as high as Snowdon and stays there'. Me? I thought it worth travelling to the other side of the world to see.

John Gower

ADAR HEB ADENYDD

Adar Heb Adenydd (Sherman Theatre Arena, Cardiff).
The Guardian, 20 June, 1989.

Ed Thomas set the Welsh theatre world alight last year with the remarkable House of America, a play he both wrote and directed and which went on to give Londoners a taste of the muscular, critical self-evaluation that can occupy the stage west of Offa's Dyke and the Severn Bridge.

Adar Heb Adenydd is his first Welsh-language play, and the touring production by the new company, Dalier Sylw, gives him a chance to explore more directly the issues of language and nationality.

Thomas is also an actor (though not here) and earns a crust with appearances in notorious Welsh-language soaps. The fascinating mixture of dramatic work in Welsh, from those soaps to the stylised work of other companies, when wedded to Thomas's almost surrealist sense of humour and love of symbols, is evidenced here.

Adar Heb Adenydd (Birds Without Wings) both revels in and mocks the conventions. In an aggressively anti-naturalistic production, the characters are out of Beckett, a mercenary struggling to learn Welsh and whose uniform has been stolen by a Fool, a guru-cum-piano tuner, a spurned bride complete with wedding dress, an escaped prisoner and a pregnant girl who gives birth to a beach ball. A skeleton taken to be the remains of a national hero turns out to be a railway worker.

It is all very amusing – the more so if you speak Welsh, although an English synopsis and some upfront performances mean that it attracts non-Welsh-speaking audiences, too, important to the play's concern – but it points up the seriousness of what Thomas is saying about the nonsense that attends nationalism and the general question of freedom in a prescribed world.

David Adams

Adar Heb Adenydd (Harry Younger Hall, Edinburgh)
The List, 25-31 August, 1989

Wales – plagued by images of green valleys, lilting harps, male-voice choirs and a dying mining community – has a message for all Festival Fringe visitors. Through new writing, adaptations and explosive, confrontational theatre, a series of new voices can be heard.

Having found their new and authentic voices, Dalier Sylw, The Company and Made In Wales Stage Company, profess to be 'Raiders of the Western Shore' and offer a stimulating and challenging picture of Wales and its contemporary culture.

The new self-confidence and faith of Welsh-language theatre is demonstrated by Edward Thomas' first full-length Welsh-language play, *Adar Heb Adenydd*. This aggressively anti-naturalistic, physical piece breaks down the barriers between those who do and do not speak Welsh. A tragic farce with its roots firmly in the circus tradition, *Adar Heb Adenydd* confronts its audience with new exciting characters who make anything happen and are far removed from the dross of Welsh kitchen sink drama or the usual, stereotypical profiles perpetuated in both mainstream and Welsh television.

The International and Fringe Festivals are no strangers to foreign language plays, yet there is a feeling that *Adar Heb Adenydd* offers more than even Macbeth in Japanese. With no reference points for the audience to cling onto, this play demands that they watch and think. Using only the concept of the mythical hero, which spans continents and cultures, Thomas feels that his play wasn't easy for Welsh speakers either – but once they had overcome their expectations of mediocrity, they were able to adapt to the play's enjoyable, contemporary style.

Thomas has also written (in English), *House of America*, an angry new drama about a disintegrating South Wales family which also purports to be a portrait of our own times. Well received in London, *House of America* joins with *Adar Heb Adenydd* to be performed by a bi-lingual company for the last week of the Festival.

Claire Davidson

Adar Heb Adenydd (Harry Younger Hall, Edinburgh)
The Guardian, 30 August, 1989.

The Raiders of the Western Shore have arrived. With Peter Lloyd's play, *The Scam*, at The Traverse, and two films, Carl Francis's *The Angry Earth*, and Peter Edwards's *Mwg Glas, Lleuad Waed* (Blue Smoke, Blood Moon) expected, there seems no doubt that contemporary Welsh culture is experiencing a resurgence and breaking out of national boundaries.

The playwright, Edward Thomas, has brought two works to Edinburgh. His *House of America*, presented by The Company, portrays a South Wales family fighting for identity against a background of the American dream, played out to the music of Hendrix, Sinatra and Lou Reed.

This play, in English, which toured Britain earlier this year, deservedly won him a Time Out/01 For London award.

It is, however, Thomas's challenging new play in Welsh which will cause a stir. In *Adar Heb Adenydd* – Birds Without Wings – various characters interact round a table and two chairs, helping themselves from a cocktail cabinet made out of a disembowelled television set. Against a background of fields and rolling hills, they subvert all clichés and stereotypes of Wales.

An army captain, without name, reduced to long johns having lost his clothes, who cannot remember where he comes from but thinks he may be Greek, tries to speak Welsh. Dan, a dosser, is looking for a scholar in order to pass on his wisdom, and later manages to teach a headless doll how to play Greig's Piano Concerto on a child's baby grand. A skeleton hanging side-stage is thought to be Michael Roderick, a National Hero who might impart wisdom.

But heroes, says Beti, a double for Miss Haversham, are always a disappointment, created out of inexperienced material.

If all this sounds nonsense, that seems to be the intention. What is startling about the play is the spontaneity of its exploration of non-narrative form. Drawing freely on the magical realism of Marquez and Isabel Allende, Edwards is trying to create Welsh characters whose identity is not tied to tall hats, leeks or the past legacy of bards. They do not speak the rural, Land Of My Fathers lilt of Dylan Thomas but spit out an urban Welsh, conjured up between lip and tongue.

In this world, spoken language, that traditional way of asserting nationhood, is limited, for it is questionable that it can make sense of reality. When Bran (once called Tracy Bogus, 'But my husband, who turned into a great white bird, asked me to change it to Bran for the sake of symbolism') gives birth to a beach ball rather than her expected son she is ready to give it away; if it gets pricked with a pin she will not know whether to visit a doctor or get out the puncture-repair kit. And this is a child, probably fathered by the nation's saviour, which can be easily deflated, stuffed away, possibly lost.

If there is a message in this play it is that identity has to be built out of the present, whatever the origin, vulnerability and seeming oddness of the material. The aggressive, vivid performances, which give the play its feeling of logic and conviction, state that these Welsh people, at least, know who they are and where they are coming from.

Edwards's farce is by no means yet in the highest league. He has yet to learn how completely to bring his Welsh magical realism beyond the experimental, how to make his wry jokes more visual for a non-Welsh-speaking audience, how to direct the violent edge that is present. But there can be no doubt that the company is well named. In English, Dalier Sylw means Pay Attention.

Jan Fairley

Adar Heb Adenydd (Harry Younger Hall, Edinburgh)
The Scotsman, 31 August, 1989.

Don't let the fact that this play is in Welsh deter you from going to an adventurous, colourful production. The theme is one often touched on in Scotland: national identity in crisis.

The story is rather convoluted and inadequately outlined in the synopsis, but essentially is a parable about the regeneration of Wales through the agency of a convict, a soldier minus uniform, a tramp, a fool and two women. That reincarnation, however, can only happen by shaking hands with the skeletons in the nation's cupboard, by coming face to face with cultural decline and fragmentation. The tools in this endeavour are a little eccentric: a toy piano, a doll, a beachball, a lampshade, lots of booze and, of course, the Welsh language.

The production and acting are superbly original and full of explosive energy, This young exciting company has much to teach us about how to make political theatre gripping and dynamic.

Joy Hendry

THE MYTH OF MICHAEL RODERICK

The Myth of Michael Roderick (St Stephen's Theatre Space, Cardiff)
Plays and Players, February 1991.

There is no trout in my trousers. Well, search me. I don't know what it means. It is just the best of a whole list of phrases scribbled by the blind-drunk dyslexic who took over my notebook as soon as the lights dimmed at St Stephen's Theatre Space. As to who said it and why, I can't help you. But as a source close to the cast whispered to a fellow member of the audience at the interval: 'It all comes together more in the second half.'

Bewildering, yes, but *The Myth of Michael Roderick* is bewitching and beguiling as well. The action is frenetic and the able cast play it very fast. It's a bit like a sick cartoon, where warped and one-dimensional characters bugger each other, gouge out eyes and wave severed tongues in full and glorious onstage technicolour. To begin with, it is all chaos as daft idealists clash with brutal cynics, but by the high camp of the ending Edward Thomas has drawn all his strange and gaudy threads together.

The mad, fragmented passing of this vicious slapstickery debunks the idea of myth and the dreamers who support it with their steadfast refusal to see. 'How can I prove it? It's the naked proof in front of your blind eyes', says Beti (Sharon Morgan) to her rediscovered son the Captain (Russell Gomer), a suspender-clad *Rocky Horror* refugee who refuses to believe she is the lost mother he thought raped and de-tongued years earlier. The tongue he carries as a memento turns out to be a red pepper – but Beti has to fry it and let him taste it before he will believe she is his mam and not the idealised, tragic victim his imagination has created.

This is typical of the warped logic of a play where characters are forced to think up ingenious ways of snapping the idealists out of their self-delusion. Dan The Maestro (Owen Garmon) gets his cold shower of disillusionment when the headless doll he has been training as a musical genius to express the nation's 'tragedy of music' fails to perform before a sceptical audience. But at least he gets to deliver the best line of the play, while his rapacious landlord (the excellent Timothy Lyn) buggers him in lieu of rent payment: 'This place has no room for your naked capitalism – find yourself another arse!'

Another spidery note in my book: *Romance instead of reality – the disease of a suffocating country.* The Welsh accents leave us in little doubt which country is implied in this Mamiaith/Mother-tongue production: it's a country where arsonists style themselves as the sons of a part-mythical prince in their struggle with holidaymakers, isn't it! Fervent lunatic Tommy Janes (Richard Lynch) convinced he is on a mission to resurrect a hero, chooses Michael Roderick after reading he has dedicated his life to fighting for freedom. Tommy goes off to usher in a new age with his resurrectionist's wares – trolley and tomatoes – even though the slim newspaper reference is the first time he has heard of Roderick. The corpse he set to work on turns out to be John Hughes, a dead and not very glamorous railwayman. Heroine Tracey Bogus (Catherine Tregenna) tells a different tale of Roderick – he has turned into a white bird to avoid responsibility for her pregnancy.

The entrance of a ludicrous, glowing white being leading a startled dog to end the play debunks Tommy's romantic quest. So too does the birth of the Bogus/Roderick progeny: it's a beachball, and poor Tracey worries that she will never be able to visit the coast again. *The Myth of Michael Roderick* is Thomas' third play, and it is an imaginative tour de force. There's no trout in his trousers.

Robin Williams

The Myth of Michael Roderick (Theatr Mwldan, Cardigan)
Planet, February 1991.

'The problem is that there are too many bastards dying in this forgotten country either heavy with nostalgia for a golden age there never was and they never saw or pregnant with indifference, either way they're playing havoc with our arms.' So say the stretcher-bearing porters at one point in *The Myth of Michael Roderick*, Ed Thomas's third play, performed by Y Cwmni in Cardiff and Cardigan in November and December, 1990.

The play develops the notion of 'bastards heavy with nostalgia', who eventually cause the porters' arms to drop off, but more importantly it demonstrates characters breaking through indifference and nostalgia, wrenching and distorting themselves in efforts to create or sustain their own individual myths, so preventing the incipient putrefaction of their souls and delivering themselves into a state of vibrant rebirth. They follow the journey mapped by Joseph Campbell in his analysis of mythological struggles for identity in *The Hero with a Thousand Faces*: 'When our day is come for the victory of death, death closes in; there is nothing we can do, except be crucified – and resurrected; dismembered totally and then reborn.' *Michael Roderick* also explores the fears articulated by Gwyn A. Williams in his article 'A Pistol Shot in a Concert' (*Planet* 84) that 'We seem to want to create a cosy Welsh world in a Wales whose predicament is singularly uncosy . . . this is a badge of subordination . . . it represents the diminishing and sometimes debilitating shorthand of a subordinate people cultivating a reassuring self-indulgence in the interstices of subordination.' Y Cwmni breaks through the 'interstices of subordination' with its theatre of brutal and enlivening images, forcing a rupture and relocation of previously held notions of Welshness and identity.

Y Cwmni's first production, Ed Thomas's more naturalistic play *House of America*, grew out of Moving Being's season of radical writing in May, 1988. They toured south and west Wales, playing to capacity houses, and won a *Time Out* theatre award, following a two week residency at Battersea Arts Centre. In January, 1989, the *London Magazine* commented: 'To include murder, incest and fratricide in a play which proffers a portrait of our times by a relatively inexperienced writer might seem overwhelmingly ambitious, but the only sense of hubris that emerges from Edward Thomas's stunning, angry, anguished drama about a South Wales family is that which emanates from the actions of his protagonists. The Lewis family live deep in the Valleys in a house which is posed on an open-cast mine, but their lives, castrated by unemployment and the putrefaction of the environment, are caught up in the furious fantasies of the American Dream.'

House of America played at the 1989 Edinburgh Festival in tandem with Thomas's subsequent play *Adar Heb Adenydd* (Birds without Wings), commissioned by Dalier Sylw Theatre Company. The premise of *Adar* was Thomas's sense of the absurdity of his own position, as someone commissioned to write a play in Welsh yet unable to express himself in a classical sense through the medium of that language. Described by Ed Thomas as 'a circus of a play', it suggested none of the resonance associated with its ensuing adaptation into the English language play *The Myth of Michael Roderick*; nevertheless, *Adar Heb Adenydd* was still the most exciting Welsh play of its year, surging with anarchic imagery and vigour lacking in many of its more naturalistic rivals.

The Myth of Michael Roderick is scattered with pithy, self-reflexive exchanges which expose the style and structure of the play, and which license performer initiative and audience response:

> *TRACY:* *It's not an everyday story.*
> *BETI:* *Don't fool yourself, the world is full of extraordinary everyday things.*
> *TRACY:* *But it's not naturalistic.*
> *BETI:* *What's naturalistic about an earth that's burning and a sea that's a cesspit of bad ideas?*

The play is a consciously chaotic exploration of style and form, connecting with Ed Thomas's enthusiasm for chaos theory and his statement that 'the world is as miraculous as it is cruel and full of inconsequential happenings – Joyce's *Ulysses* and Bruce Chatwin's *The Songlines* are fascinating investigations of this. Chaos theory gives hope through refusing reductionism; similarly, naturalism and absurdism are essentially tyrannical forms of theatre because they reduce the world to a received view. The ideal of the well-constructed play is an idiocy: flaws are more important, and the avoidance of constructing reducible meaning, to permit connections between art and life. As a writer, I aim to engender the possibility for imagining, allowing the audience to make sense of interesting moments. The tyrannical shape and style of television is a lack of vision: it destroys language and reduces the world. Instead, the juxtaposition of meaningful and meaningless moments frees the writer and the actor. Myth dismantles the tyranny of style and permits the individual to blow life up to what they want to make it – as Gwynfor Evans once said, start by imagining you are free.'

Watching *The Myth of Michael Roderick*, a precisely constructed labyrinth delving into possibilities of salvation, is like experiencing jazz: the technical virtuosity of the writer and performer sweeps the sensibilities into free-fall, the provocation to think and feel anew. The disruption of order leaves the audience with no sense of where the play will take them. 'Catastrophe is also birth' – a line from Howard Barker's *Women Beware Women* – provides an apt description of the experience.

Growing out of the complex play of separate realities in the closing stages of the tragic *House of America, Michael Roderick* acts as an expansion, as well as an adaptation, of Thomas's *Adar Heb Adenydd*, embracing a non-naturalistic, expressionist style, where a sense of ritual reveals the spinning vibrancy of each character's separate world. The resulting disturbingly humorous events shatter ideas of what is possible in theatre: a fool has his eye cut out as an attempted trade-in for wisdom, a businessman buggers a self-crippled artist in search of genius, and a woman gives birth to a beach ball. In a public seminar following Y Cwmni's performance at Cardigan, a woman member of the audience observed that the bombardment of pain serves to reawaken: 'an arm comes off, an eye comes out, but we make ourselves, we say "I AM"' and David Ian Rabey (Lecturer in Drama, UCW Aberystwyth) noted a principal difference between *Adar Heb Adenydd* and its new English adaptation: '*Michael Roderick* pushes further in exploring the pain and dignity of the characters and what their searches cost them. There is a tragic humour generated by the misplaced but deathly seriousness of their pursuits: this is opposed to the irony and superficiality by which most characters and performers elsewhere conventionally strive for comedy.' Asked if he thought the form of *Michael Roderick* suitable for discussion of themes such as language and identity, Rabey repudiated any criteria of suitability, or discussion: 'The play is infinitely more dramatic than a discussion, it's a rampage through spurious notions of imaginative circumscription, determinism and integration into the fictitious cult of normality, exposing them all as essentially fears of freedom.'

Charmian C. Savill

The Myth of Michael Roderick (Chapter Arts Centre, Cardiff)
South Wales Echo, 23 November, 1991.

Michael Roderick is a pretty odd sort of a hero to believe in. One minute, he's a dead man in a bathtub, the next a great white bird.

These are the kinds of outlandish transmutations which are worked into Ed Thomas's latest drama, *The Myth of Michael Roderick*, a very irreverent – and a very funny – black comedy, which sense up in no small measure the way in which a culture can become badly distorted when empty rhetoric takes a hold over the imagination.

Those who are familiar with Thomas's plays will instantly recognise the terrain – a world that sets its own rules . . . one where a man can easily turn into a lampstand and a one-eyed pianist will wholeheartedly believe in the powers of a plastic doll's torso to revive a lost art.

Whether you think this is all inspired or just plain daft, the carefully-crafted craziness of it all demands a hearing – and it gets one too, thanks to the excellent performances delivered by the members of Y Cwmni, who have returned to Cardiff's Chapter Arts Centre for a two-week residency after showings in Glasgow and London.

A Captain dressed in suspenders discusses semantics, a Fool submits to being blinded in order to learn wisdom from a spiv with a kipper tie, who in turn has designs on the one-eyed Maestro.

And if that seems a bit tame, then what about the newly-christened Tracey, who gives birth to a beach ball?

Their search for some meaning is given a kick-start by an escaped lunatic, whose discovery of a figurehead, the mythical Michael Roderick, seems to suggest an explanation for all that is going on between these argumentative and volatile characters. The playing style is challenging – like the writing – and it immerses the spectators deeper and deeper in the convoluted twists and turns of Thomas's arguments.

The poetry, the farce and the violence escalate into what is really an outrageously creative show which somehow manages to retain some thoughtful and haunting moments among the comic invention.

Penny Simpson

FLOWERS OF THE DEAD RED SEA

Flowers of the Dead Red Sea (Tramway, Glasgow)
Glasgow Herald, 10 September, 1991.
When I was forced to leave this at 11.15 last night to bring you this notice things were shaping up pretty ugly. Three of the cast were down to bare torsos, two smeared in blood, the other daubed in paint. A clerical sort of fellow in a white hard-hat had been strangled. There was a man on scaffolding, stage right, taking a hammer to a piano, and a couple on scaffolding stage left. The woman was eating spaghetti. The man had his head in a plastic bag. He was dead, too. Suffocation. The play was going the same way.

All around there were objects which had either clattered from the flies to the stage, or had been flattened by monotonous acts of violence. What we had seen, I think, was the corruption of a young man in a slaughterhouse. He doesn't want to slaughter lambs any more. His mate works him over with a series of jibes, fantasies, blows, word-games, and strings of associations. Disconnected gibberish, mainly. The most glaring problem is that the energy expended by the performers is not worth Edward Thomas's puerile text. Neither does he, as director of the piece, make much intelligent use of the Tramway space. It is an extremely unpleasant experience, cacophonous, frenetic, brutal and virtually unintelligible. This is the second in the Theatres and Nations season. A huge risk has been taken in inviting the company, Y Cwmni from Wales, to bring a new, untested piece. It does not come off.

John Linklater

Flowers of the Dead Red Sea (Tramway, Glasgow)
The Scotsman, 11 September, 1991.

Edward Thomas's new play, performed by Y Cwmni at the Tramway in Glasgow this week, is a spluttering, incoherent, self-indulgent tirade with sporadic bursts of violence to relieve its very considerable monotony. But like any flop, its root failure seems to lie in a poor sense of its own purpose.

Flowers is mainly set in a slaughterhouse, where two young butchers with apparent amnesia invent for each other, and for themselves, past triumphs and miseries. Some of the opening dialogue was leavened with humour, but this relationship was not significantly explored.

The two figures became noticably bloodier as the evening wore on. We were almost certainly being told something about erosion of culture and the subsequent loss of community. At least, that's what the programme note said.

For diversion a secondary plot cavorted windily around the conflict between elite and popular cultures. On a three-level set a dumbstruck artist painted in her attic while the glib programme producer watched telly in the basement. There's symbolism now. The playwright (who also directed) must surely be fresh out of art school after discovering Beckett and Genet.

But no, Mr Thomas has written three previous plays which have been performed by the same company apparently to great acclaim. So this piece can only be dismissed as a disastrous error of judgement.

The cast, particularly Richard Lynch and Russell Gomer give their all, but at an early stage they should have realised this to be an expense of spirit which might well undo their previous achievements. At least one member might also have felt what she was asked to do was both demeaning and pointless.

The indispensable Tramway programme revealed Mr Thomas's talents to be high and wide. At 30 he has already flourished in many media – last year he wrote and directed ten plays for Welsh Channel Four. My advice, for what it is worth, is to stop spreading himself so thinly or people might just start to see right through him.

Simon Berry

Flowers of the Dead Red Sea (Tramway, Glasgow)
The Scotsman, 14 September, 1991.

What is a minute to a good man who has lived in hope? asks Mock, one of the slaughterhouse workers in Ed Thomas' bold, vibrant and driving play *Flowers of the Dead Red Sea* (part of Tramway's reopening Theatres and Nations season). Well, it usually takes a lot less than a minute to know whether a hope has been raised or dashed, and that was certainly the case with Simon Berry's review (Wednesday, 11 September).

His outright dismissal of the work (the views of his colleague John Linklater in the *Glasgow Herald* weren't much kinder) leaves me confused, startled and a bit angry. I found the play, and after several viewings still find it brilliantly intelligent, its poetic rage lifted by exemplary performances from just about everybody. Its setting is a Beckettesque nightmare of designer-abattoir exotica.

Metaphors of every kind – universal, individual, visual, and from the stance of an embattled nation with an identity crisis – pour from the production. And it is funny. So how are such collisions of interpretation possible?

Such polarised reactions do remind me that hope is one of the essential commodities for a producing organisation like Tramway, or any other, when they chose to present artists who work in new contexts, who may be wilfully controversial or unpredictable, but whose work one believes in before just about any other consideration. 'It's like feasting with panthers', Oscar Wilde said, – 'the danger is half the fun'.

We value the past work of *Y Cwmni* and that's why we're excited by what it wants to make in the future and the source of our artistic loyalty. Not uncritical loyalty, but sufficient to extend an invitation to co-produce the piece here – to use Tramway in which to build, rehearse, and open. In other words, to act as a *host*.

I'm very pleased to confirm my unswerving commitment to *Flowers of the Dead Red Sea*. It's not perfect, but it does have an almost perfect place in the season, an appropriateness which I believe has been missed. It's not just the rhythm, colour and rippling energy which only natural writers like Thomas can produce, it's the excitement at what the play's inner voice adds to our opening season.

The most important moment in the work, and such a moving one it is too, occurs towards the end. Called upon to speak by his rejected artist-soulmate Dot, the broken, dispirited Mock, in a breathtaking silence, utters only a penetrating cry of anguish. In Ed Thomas' theatre that cry is for a nation and its partly self-inflicted loss of purpose, the powerlessness of its own bastardised culture to rescue it.

In my view, a distinguished, articulate and exciting visiting company from Wales has suffered gross misinterpretation by someone for whom we hoped this message should ring clearly, richly and with a familiar resonance. This makes me very sad.

Neil Wallace

Flowers of the Dead Red Sea (Chapter Arts Centre, Cardiff)
South Wales Echo, 27 September, 1991.

Bloodstained abattoir workers discussing the meaning of love, life, religion – even Tom Jones . . . it's a bizarre concept, but powerfully executed in Ed Thomas's extraordinary new drama.

Black humour, philosophical questioning, and physical acrobatics are all pushed to illogical extremes to portray a culture under threat.

Workers in the abattoir are under attack from strange phenomena – a collapsing world of battered prams, buckets and torn bow ties – but also from their failing memories.

Maybe Mock and Joe are brothers, maybe Dottie the painter is a real artist, but the goal posts keep shifting in verbal sparring matches that show off Thomas's unmistakable wordplay – a brilliant mix of poetic and scatological references that embody so well the sense of unease experienced by these disparate characters in search of an identity.

But finding a voice, searching for definitions, leads only to brutal, wordless despair, a feeling that finds its way into the striking canvases of Iwan Bala, which line the theatre walls.

The performances more than match up to the demands of Thomas's complex, surreal script, particularly the abrasive confrontations acted out between the suede-head Mock (Richard Lynch) and his sidekick Joe (Russell Gomer).

If anybody doubts that theatre can still give a radical and vital assessment of our times, they should make a point of seeing Y Cwmni in action. Theirs is a style of theatre where politics, dramatic experiment and visual imagery meet in explosive and exciting ways, cracking open old, stultified arguments about what exactly drama should be about.

Penny Simpson

Flowers of the Dead Red Sea and *The Myth of Michael Roderick* (Watermans Arts Centre, London)
Brentford Chiswick and Isleworth Times, October 1991.

Two men argue in a slaughterhouse while domestic objects crash from the sky, an artist torments another into a murderous rage, a religious maniac walks a non-existent dog through an exploding town: Edward Thomas's play *The Flowers of the Dead Red Sea* is, I suppose, surrealistic.

The finale is reminiscent of watching a Beckett play performed on amphetamines while having a piano dropped on your head.

The Cwmni Theatre Company, under the direction of the author, has produced a remarkable double bill that could only work as theatre, full of that electricity unique to a live performance. Among the strong cast Russell Gomer and Richard Lynch were especially notable as the arguing slaughterhouse men, who spoke at such a furious pace I couldn't always keep up with them.

The comparison to Beckett is perhaps misleading. In these plays, communication is possible, and even hope. At the end of the first play, art is seen as a positive force that can rescue people from inarticulacy and nihilism. They are also very funny in a bizarre way, in fact *Michael Roderick* gets some rather easy laughs from nudity, sodomy and a sword wielding army officer in women's underwear. But I recommend this double bill to anyone not offended by swearing, and who wants to see what live theatre is capable of.

Ben Francis

The Myth of Michael Roderick and *Flowers of the Dead Red Sea* (Chapter Arts Centre, Cardiff, preview)
Venue, 15-29 November, 1991.

Ed Thomas is no stranger to controversy, but even he reeled slightly at the reception given in some quarters to his new play *Flowers of the Dead Red Sea* when it opened in Glasgow in September. Reeled, but smiled with satisfaction. What he really didn't like was when he couldn't get the *Guardian* to even see it when it played in London. *Time Out* did, though, and gave it a rather bewildered but positive reception.

We'll be getting a chance to see it at Chapter at the end of the month when it returns as part of Thomas's company Y Cwmni's two-week residency. *The Myth of Michael Roderick*, a production that again divided audiences when it played at St Stephens last year, opens on Tuesday 19 November.

Chapter, who premiered *Flowers of the Dead Red Sea* earlier this year, are certainly hyping up Ed Thomas and Y Cwmni. 'Is this Wales's best theatre writer?' their programme asks rhetorically. 'This is theatre hot from the forge based on a will and a passion to communicate', they proclaim. Well, Venue called him 'probably the most exciting and significant playwright in Wales' and his first (and, ironically, most widely admired) play, *House of America*, won Y Cwmni a fringe award in London and raves in Edinburgh.

Since *House of America*, a startling play that first revealed the writer's violent concern with Welsh cultural identity and integrity, the more conservative commentators have been less enthusiastic. His Welsh-language play *Adar Heb Adenydd*, written for the Dalier Sylw company, outraged many Welsh-language critics, who somehow saw it as an abuse of the tongue. Interestingly, its English-language version, *The Myth of Michael Roderick*, won more admirers. They maybe felt more objective about the mother-tongue issue, brought from metaphor to absurdist humour as one character kisses a woman, finds she's his mother and bites off her tongue. Symbolic or what?

In fact, Ed Thomas pushes such ideas to the limit and beyond, taunting his audience with over-the-top images and characters. *The Myth of Michael Roderick* features a mad piano-teacher, a man in a basque, a scantilly-clad policewoman and an escaped lunatic, among others. *Flowers of the Dead Red Sea* is about two slaughtermen and a dickiebow that once belonged to Tom Jones. Or rather, they're not about those at all, but about the false gods, self delusion and pomposity of Wales. What Ed Thomas and Y Cwmni do is ask questions, not offer answers.

Flowers of the Dead Red Sea the company describe as a tale of sex, lies, love and power. Y Cwmni were invited to take it to The Theatres and Nationhood Festival in Glasgow. 'The play', says Thomas, 'was born of an overwhelming feeling that the country in which I live only exists in spirit and the realisation that those who speak of this spirit were not speaking about a country but essentially about themselves.'

Since *House of America*, Ed Thomas's plays have certainly got more extreme, less naturalistic, more abstract – and funnier. In both senses. They may be serious, but *The Myth of Michael Roderick*, for instance, really is great fun. I don't know about *Flowers of the Dead Red Sea*: set in a slaughterhouse, it doesn't sound much of a laugh – but who knows?

David Adams

Flowers of the Dead Red Sea (Chapter Arts Centre, Cardiff)
The Guardian, 2 December, 1991.

Ed Thomas is fast getting a reputation as Wales's most exciting new writer and his new play for Y Cwmni shows why.

It's a brilliant, explosive display of verbal pyrotechnics from a playwright who revels in language and in particular in the rhythmic patterns of South Walean English. And in this mainly Welsh-speaking company, especially Russell Gomer and Richard Lynch, he has a group of actors who have both the delivery and physicality to make *Flowers Of The Dead Red Sea*, currently at the Chapter Arts Centre, an electrifying production.

Gomer and Lynch dominate the stage as a couple of workers in a slaughterhouse, debating the artistry of a clean slit of a lamb's throat, arguing over a dicky-bow that may have belonged to Tom Jones, and ducking strange objects that fall from above. They may or may not be brothers and/or ex-lovers of the same woman. She, an artist, and her partner, a comedy writer, live somewhere else and it must be said that Clare Williams and Mark Knight tend to get dwarfed by the performances of the other pair.

The wordplay, at one moment like a Pinter throwback, at another like Barker, with inevitable reminders of Genet and Beckett, but essentially startlingly distinctive, tends to dazzle enough to obscure what Thomas is talking about. Sense is difficult to find among this rich word-dominated play, but somewhere there is an anguished debate about Armageddon and art, language, sex and power, conducted through rituals of blood and conflict and expressed through the medium of the absurd.

It's pure theatre, and the obliqueness of the content is part of the appeal of a play like this, but there is a danger that Thomas's fascination with language can deny access to his fertile ideas. Superb acting, excellent direction by Thomas, and a fine set and effects by Ian Hill, make the production outstanding.

David Adams

Flowers of the Dead Red Sea (Chapter Arts Centre, Cardiff)
Western Mail, 10 September, 1992.

Welsh identity is stripped of its cosy myths in Edward Thomas's self-styled 'theatre of invention'.

Mr Thomas, who seeks to redefine Welsh identity could not be more bleak or uncompromising in *Flowers of the Dead Red Sea*. This is a new version of *Flowers*, part of a trilogy of his plays which has just embarked on a Welsh tour.

He forbids any illusions in his portrayal of a claustrophobic small town void of warmth, hope and joy. The setting is a workshop behind a slaughterhouse. The characters include a slaughterman, his girlfriend and two mates.

What develops is a powerful study of aggression bred of living in an unhealthy environment. The characters, lacking the will or unable to control their stifling circumstances, physically and psychologically attack each other. It's like watching battery chickens peck out each other's eyes.

Thomas assaults us with coarse descriptions and violent imagery as characters explode with resentment. We're presented with a study of social dynamics where tensions rise, erupt and subside in an outpouring of language so rhythmic and densely-textured that sound takes precedence over meaning. It's not an easily accessible play; Thomas's message isn't completely clear. But we get clues: it's about the importance of dreams, the dangerous assault of the material on the spiritual, the need for moral human behaviour.

The slaughterman Mock (Russell Gomer) represents faith and the spirit, declaring 'I will not submit' to the nihilism of Joe (Wyndham Price) who asserts 'We're no longer dignified; we live in an age of shame'.

Thomas has fun playing around with that icon of Valleys culture Tom Jones in a hilarious scene where the three men strip to their underpants and gyrate to *Viva Las Vegas*.

There are fine performances from Y Cwmni and punchy direction from Janek Alexander.

Nicole Sochor

Flowers of the Dead Red Sea (Tramway, Glasgow)
Glasgow Herald, 14 October, 1992.

Y Cwmni has been touring this play for a year now yet it retains the feel of work-in-progress. At times stimulating, at times stultifying, it has a hesitant air about it. In running full throttle at an intellectually perplexing dilemma – what is memory? – it occasionally stumbles, or, to adopt its own imagery, drowns under the steady flow of writer Edward Thomas's relentless rhetoric.

The absurdist action focuses on three misfit characters – Mock, a tortured soul who insists he is a craftsman not a butcher, Joe, his vengeful, frustrated apprentice, and Dottie, an artist – and switches between the cold grimness of a scaffolded slaughterhouse to a red, bleeding dreamscape.

The characterisations are solid but all are untrustworthy narrators. Ridiculous rants about dogs, dickie-bow-ties and death send them all spiralling into self-doubt. The dramatic drive becomes an existential struggle to hold on to the memories which aid self definition.

Thomas has written an ingenious exercise in mind games – often involving word plays which could be crass yet surprisingly triumph and manage to be witty – but while his play does often show the power to be disquieting it is too often disappointing. It comes across as a series of sketches connected by only the wispiest of threats.

There are many absorbing moments, both funny (and the male striptease to the exuberant anthem of ZZ Top's 'Viva Las Vegas' treads a fine line between macho posing and parody) and painful, but the isolated pleasure serves only to emphasise how much any overall cohesion is lacking.

Sara Villiers

EAST FROM THE GANTRY

East from the Gantry (Tramway, Glasgow)
Glasgow Herald, 16 October, 1992.
The lights come up white and glaring on a stage littered with shapes concealed by sheets – a snowy landscape. Gradually the covers are cast aside, dramatically, as if in an act of revelation, yet there is no sense of any demystification process. In fact, the reverse happens as we are presented with a bemusing array of objects; a window frame, a television, sculptures, a Hoover, a severed head . . . this gruelling mish-mash builds up an increasingly perplexing picture, constantly forcing us to re-adjust, re-focus.

So it also is with Edward Thomas's script for this, the final play in his loosely connected trilogy. It is a many layered narrative, constantly peeled back to reveal the increasingly obscure lifestories of its protagonists.

Thomas is an inventive and audacious writer. In his work, a constant tension can be discerned, a pull between accepted truth and outright lies. Everything he gives us he snatches back – thus, each piece of information he dispenses immediately contradicts itself, becoming crafty disinformation. This can be an irritating device but while *East from the Gantry* is both wilfully perverse and playfully obscure it is also surprisingly entertaining.

Thomas's characters talk in amusing Pinteresque riddles; he is skilled at capturing day-to-day absurdities and then inflating them to hilarious levels. But while there is a slack humour and smart intelligence rippling away here, there is also a self-indulgence which constantly threatens to kill the joke. This play could be greatly improved by some ruthless editing.

Sara Villiers

East from the Gantry (Tramway, Glasgow)
The Scotsman, 16 October, 1992.

My heart sank on reading the programme's description of *East from The Gantry* as 'a confusing play . . . (that) may put together a complete jigsaw or provide a finished picture, but it may simply represent a series of possibilities of how . . . the individual self can be re-claimed'. It sank even further on realising that this pre-emptive muddying of the waters was penned by the play's author Edward Thomas. If it is confusing to *him*, I thought, then we are in trouble.

East From The Gantry is more entertaining than the modish drone of this blurb suggests, largely due to winsome performances by Boyd Clack, Richard Lynch and Ri Richards. But the faults of the Y Cwmni's production are at least as noticeable as its strengths, and at times during its one-and-three-quarter hours (without an interval), strong memories of an indifferent night on the Fringe came drifting back.

Clarity or coherence are lacking in this playful examination of individual and Welsh identity (it is part of this company's *New Wales Trilogy*), and given the absence of real compensatory qualities in the direction – for example strong or original visuals, or interesting movement – the play looks slight and gimmicky on the Tramway stage. The performances are rich in whimsical and surreal humour and there are some very funny moments, but, like many productions directed by the author, the production is badly organised, indulgent and too long.

Colin Donald

East from the Gantry (Wales Tour, 1994)
The Independent, 8 February, 1994.

This will be the last tour we'll do in this way. In the past we've done lots of one-night stands, some in city art centres, others in rural areas. But it doesn't work any more, trying to take shows round briefly. As we've grown, the set design has improved and we no longer feel that we can do a proper show in a small venue. Ideally it would be great if we could go to an old chapel in mid-Wales and stay for 10 nights, but we can't afford it.

We did play a converted chapel for two or three years in Pen-y-graig in the Rhondda Valley. It was a great venue, with the audience sitting on pews. The best place though was Ystradgynlais, in an old miners' welfare hall. It was a small mining community yet 300 people came both nights. The last show that had been there was *The Cat and the Canary* in 1963.

I suppose playing in rural Wales has affected the writing. So far none of the plays has been set in a city, but that doesn't mean the writing is naturalistic. They are set in a reinvented Wales.

The profile of a theatre company which is Welsh is pretty low. It's not the same as having an Irish, a gay or a black identity and it is hard to find affordable venues in London. It might appear that we're Celto-centric because we're not playing London, but really we'll go anywhere if we can.

Our worst night? It had to be when an actor refused to die at the end of a performance. It was at the Edinburgh Festival in 1989, and he insisted on a happy ending. We had a chat about it and decided that he would die the next night and he did.

Edward Thomas

NEW WALES TRILOGY

New Wales Trilogy: House of America, Flowers of the Dead Red Sea, East from the Gantry (Y Cwmni, 1992 Tour)
South Wales Echo, 28 August, 1992.

Once upon a time, Y Cwmni added up to little more than a script, a lot of determination and a borrowed docklands venue. Four years on, they are preparing to launch their new play, *East from the Gantry*, in Glasgow's Tramway with a host of civic dignitaries joining art workers in the stalls.

It's a remarkable achievement, but there's no room for complacency. The company still exist with a core group of theatre makers struggling on with the idea that strong Welsh theatre can be forged with a lot of imagination, if not hard cash.

'You could say our situation is desperate, not serious', says playwright Ed Thomas, whose wry understatement is in contrast to the flamboyant, often surreal dialogue in his plays.

The cash flow may have silted up, but the company is about to launch a major tour, taking a trilogy of his works across Wales and into Scotland – a project backed by Cardiff Marketing.

These plays lie at the heart of Y Cwmni's success to date, beginning with the award-winning *House of America* staged at St Stephen's Theatre Space in 1988.

The play, set in a South Wales Valleys town devastated by unemployment, used the music and moods of the American Dream to tell a story of a family with secrets and hopeless ambitions.

Later plays have moved into less normal terrain – strange worlds where abattoir workers chew over half-forgotten memories and dispute the ownership of a bow tie (*Flowers of The Dead Red Sea*), while in *The Myth of Michael Roderick*, a woman gives birth to a beach ball and a soldier dresses up in suspenders to discuss semantics.

It is a bizarre, sometimes controversial departure from what audiences expect from contemporary theatre. It challenges anybody who relies on comfortable stereotypes to conjure up a picture of 20th century Wales – a swipe at the view of Welsh life portrayed by the heritage industry.

'There's no longer a collective spirit – only a ragbag of individual ones here in Wales', says Ed.

Experimentation with form, style and language has helped Y Cwmni sketch out a new perspective on Welsh culture that is winning them audiences far and wide. Kiev theatre workers caught one of the shows in Chapter and now want the company to visit the Ukraine.

Another key is the commitment and invention of the core of regular players, who return again and again to re-shape old texts and create new works.

This is an important aspect of this new tour – the access to a real memory of the past three years or so joined with the perspective of two new directors, Janek Alexander and Jamie Garven.

'There are going to be connections between the three plays, but we are not really a company with a message, rather one of infinite possibilities that we want to expand on', says Thomas.

Because Y Cwmni is not just concerned with stage presentations, already there are plans for film and TV work that will take the experimentation into new fields.

Says Janek, 'They have broken a mould of a writer producing one goodish play, followed by a slightly better play and then come the television commissions. The next cycle is wooing that person back into the theatre.

'Y Cwmni just seemed to arrive from nowhere and were doing what they needed to do. They avoided the easy option of re-staging a hit and tried new experiments.

'*Flowers*, for example, is a re-mix of the original stage play with elements drawn in from the version commissioned by BBC Radio Wales earlier this year. But the actors have different roles and the script is changing. It is still an adventure, not merely repetition.'

Penny Simpson

New Wales Trilogy (Tramway, Glasgow)
The List, 25 September-8 October, 1992.

The last time Cardiff-based theatre company Y Cwmni played in Glasgow, it got such a round slating from *The Herald* and *The Scotsman* that it used the juicy quotes to lure in audiences on the rest of the tour. Playing the Peter O'Toole *Macbeth* card, the company continues to boast about the notices – 'considerably monotony,' 'extremely unpleasant', 'disastrous error of judgement' – to promote the restaging of the show, *Flowers of the Dead Red Sea*, and its two companion pieces, *House of America* and *East from the Gantry*.

Actually, we here at the level-headed *List* were considerably more enthusiastic about Edward Thomas's play. True enough, it lost its way, and its argument was convoluted, but its relentless poetic barrage was performed with mesmerising intensity and self-destructing set onto which shopping trolleys were liable to fall from the ceiling at the most unexpected moments. Funny, striking and intriguing, the production had too much going for it to dismiss out of hand.

Thomas admits that a good deal of the play was changed after its Tramway debut and explains that it was rewritten again for radio transmission earlier this year. When it returns as part of Y Cwmni's New Wales Trilogy, it will be as a hybrid of the previous versions put together by its new director, Janek Alexander. But revisions or not, it's clear that Thomas, the writer of all three plays and director of *East of the Gantry*, loves the idea that he might be unsettling his audiences. 'The company doesn't espouse naturalism', he asserts, 'and when you have action that doesn't depend on a narrative so much, you're bound to have people who feel one way or another. All over Wales some people think we are brilliant and other people think we are crap. I welcome criticism.'

'The plays are not meant to be constructed by the audience as a collective,' he continues, 'they're meant to affect the individual. Howard Barker talks about honouring an audience. You make arguments that are fragments, some of which are convoluted, some of which are contradictory, some of which will be beautiful, but the principle is that in a fragmented world you can't as an author think that your work provides a thesis or a message – you require a large ego to do that. What I'd rather grapple with is how difficult the truth is, how you re-create a reality from memory, otherwise theatre becomes a vessel for mediocrity. Our work is not mediocre.'

Key words in Thomas's conversation are 'invention' and 'fragmentation'; the first because he is setting about creating a theatrical tradition in a country which does not have one, the second because that tradition needs to be rich in its diversity. And it seems natural for the playwright, who contributed to Tramway's *Theatres and Nations* season last year, to look to Ireland and Scotland to see nations defining, redefining and asserting themselves. 'In Wales', he says, 'we don't have a strong theatre tradition. We have a theatre of adoption. I've argued before for an invented Welsh theatre in language, form and style, rather than re-hashing old ideas.'

Each play in the trilogy stands on its own, but the directorial, textual and acting links between them justify sitting through all five hours. 'The three plays have a big U-shape', says Thomas. '*House of America* is like a Greek tragedy in form, then we end up in a no-man's land, a shrinking land, in *Flowers of the Dead Red Sea* where memory is brittle, and we develop the arguments about not submitting, not living in shame. Then in *East From the Gantry* we pick up the end pieces of *Flowers of the Dead Red Sea* and create possibilities through story-telling. It's not a narrative but it's a bit more accessible. Maybe through story-telling you can connect with memory and that can be treacherous, harmful, false or completely made up, but somehow, through confronting a fragmented memory, we may be able to come up with the possibility of a future. It's far more optimistic – not in the sense of "hey let's go out and ring the bells" – but I suppose it's the most optimistic thing I've written.'

Mark Fisher

New Wales Trilogy (Tramway, Glasgow)
The Evening Times, 6 October, 1992.

Murder, incest, love and lies.

That's what Tramway audiences can expect next week when the Cardiff based theatre company Y Cwmni presents three works by the contemporary playwright Edward Thomas.

Entitled *New Wales Trilogy*, these very diverse pieces each highlight the author's assault on the stereotypes and clichés which often surround and obscure attempts to define 'Welshness'.

Set in the depths of winter, *East From The Gantry* examines a tangled web of sex and passion, at the centre of which is a woman, in love with a contract killer, whose name she chose at random from a telephone directory. (Oct 10 – preview and Oct 14 & 16 at 9.0 pm).

In *House of America* tragedy stalks the Lewis family, as the past and present are set on a collision course across the dole, drugs, death and the American Dream. (Oct 12 & 15 at 8.0 pm).

Flowers Of The Dead Red Sea takes place in 1999 and is a dark tale of deception and power in which truth and desire are set in contention, as two slaughterhouse workers wrangle over the art of butchery.

New Wales Trilogy (Tramway, Glasgow)
South Wales Echo, 16 October, 1992.

Welsh playwright Ed Thomas's surreal vision of the world seems to get darker with each play he writes.

Over the past few weeks, it's been possible to see the method in the madness – nothing less than a startling re-invention of Welsh cultural icons.

The revival of his early plays, first at the Chapter Arts Centre and now at Glasgow's Tramway, and the commissioning of a third drama, has confirmed in no uncertain fashion the stature of a body of work that has challenged head-on the expectations of new writing produced here in Wales.

Texts that are soaked with violent, often passionate claims and counter-claims about identity are acted out in bruising, muscular performances that have left audiences often deeply divided between ridicule and hyperbole. Seeing *House of America* and *Flowers of the Dead Red Sea* performed back-to-back has simply heightened the debate.

Jamie Garven's new production of *House of America*, an award-winning drama about a family trapped in a recession-hit Valleys town, is quite simply explosive. He has drawn out electrifying performances from the cast, who also double up to perform in *Flowers of the Dead Red Sea*. If the Lewises moved in next door you would worry: mum is burdened by a heavy secret and has put the cat Brando into the washing machine, while brother and sister, Sid and Gwenny, are living in a fantastical world that is supposed to replace their boredom with the trappings of the American Dream, but instead leaves them confronting the reality of incest.

It's not just the open-cast mine which threatens this happy home, but the anger of dispossessed people who no longer have a hold on what they are or what they can hope for. They are left punching the air with half-realised reams. It's a relentless piece of work, full of rage and fury, and, unexpectedly, deep black humour.

Flowers of the Dead Red Sea has been substantially re-worked since its premiere in Cardiff last year. A claustrophobic and cluttered set provided the atmosphere of the piece, life on the edge as experienced by three abattoir workers and a woman artist. That they are all adrift in a harsh, disintegrating sort of world is something of an understatement. Characters come into focus, only to blur again, often within the time span of just one sentence. Holding on is a problem, not just for the wild, dreaming characters, but for the audience too, who find the play's pivotal points of reference as off-beat and obscure as the disputed ownership of a dickie-bow.

While there is much to be admired in Janek Alexander's production, there is the overriding feeling that the tension and pace of the original performances has been lost. The tense dynamic set up in the early portrayals of the relationship between Mock and Joe has shortcircuited – maybe an outcome of the fact that the writing has become a little too dense for the actors to adapt into a very physical performance style?

A third play, *East From the Gantry*, will move audiences into even stranger terrains – take a Danish pastry, a fanbelt and a lawnmower up a snowy mountainside and you get some idea of what to expect when it is unveiled at Cardiff's Sherman Theatre next month.

Penny Simpson

New Wales Trilogy (Tramway, Glasgow)
The Guardian, 21 October, 1992.

Metropolitan Britain had better watch out for a roar of energy from the periphery. Glasgow this month is playing host to some electrifying new work from Wales, and to a whole season of new Irish theatre.

All three countries have produced impressive dramatic work in the past decade, but when they get together, the resonances – and the implications for the cultural future of these islands – are terrific.

The New Wales Trilogy of the young Cardiff company, Y Cwmni, written by director Ed Thomas and playing at the Tramway, is at the cutting edge of this process, a fast-moving three-part reflection on the cultural formation and identity of modern Wales that evolves like a piece of modern poetry, fragmented, allusive, metaphorical, difficult, full of breaks in the time-sequence, and shifting, fluid characters.

In the trilogy's final play, *East From the Gantry*, premiered in Glasgow this week, Thomas tries for a lighter, more comic-surreal effect than in the earlier pieces, *House of America* and *Flowers of the Dead Red Sea*, bringing the mood sharply up to date, while keeping all the thematic elements of the trilogy in focus.

The action takes place mainly in the memory of a woman called Bella, a tired thirty-something in Derek Jarman-punk clothes, who, in the process of separating from her jealous husband Ronnie, relives her first encounter with him, some past affairs, some possible future scenarios.

In the background, big black-and-white photos emerging from dust-sheets conjure up images of old Wales – rugby teams, stone farmhouses, pitheads. A flickering TV screen shows a film of mining-village life circa 1945, and there is a single, understated passage in the script – extraordinarily powerful, this week – in which the two male characters discuss how the whole mining culture 'just disappeared; amazing really'.

In the foreground, the characters drift around like any other inhabitants of the modern consumerist West, discussing their sex lives, their yearning for perfect happiness, and the relative merits of artichoke or anchovy on their pizzas.

The meaning of Thomas's play is rarely distinct, and sometimes its absurdism wavers into silliness. But it gives an unforgettable sense of the mass-produced experience of the late-20th century – films, TV, junk food – lying thinly over an older language, and a recent history of more distinctive and rooted experience, from which we could draw strength, if only we could find truthful and unsentimental ways of connecting with it.

The specifics of Thomas's work are absolutely Welsh. But the trauma of physical and cultural dislocation he describes with such explosive energy is the common experience of our time; and one which is now provoking a frightening kind of reaction, against which Thomas's loud, streetwise, pluralistic modernism – deeply aware of its cultural roots, but never confined by them – is the best defence.

Joyce McMillan

New Wales Trilogy (1992 Wales Tour)
Western Mail, 2 November, 1992.

Coal mines, male voice choirs, women in tall black hats, Tom Jones crooning *The Green, Green Grass of Home* – all icons of Welsh culture, parodied but nonetheless potent – and all are anathema to Valleys-born playwright Edward Thomas.

These are stereotypes which, to his mind, have stifled the emergence of a truer expression of Welshness.

His answer is nothing less than to develop a new style of theatre, his self-styled 'theatre of invention'. The result – his New Wales Trilogy of plays is currently touring Wales to acclaim.

Performing the plays is Y Cwmni, a young Cardiff company which along with such as Brith Gof, Moving Being and Dalier Sylw, represent the new voice of Welsh theatre.

It is fashionable for Welsh nationalists to see Wales languishing under the yoke of British imperialism, and for Thomas this may be truest in a spiritual sense.

The 31-year-old's work reflects the uncertainties of the age. At a time when the demise of coalmining shattered the economic foundations of the Valleys, Thomas considers the state of mind of the dispossessed. His plays are set in empty, dislocated settings in which the anguished cries of his characters rail in anger and despair at the meaninglessness of their lives.

Above all the plays hint at a sense of loss – be it loss of nationhood dating back to Edward I, the outlawing of the Welsh language or the more recent effects of the recession.

However, Thomas, son of a butcher who once wanted to be a rugby player, dislikes the patronising tone of suggestions he is the voice of the people. 'I hate people who claim to be voices of the dispossessed', he retorts. 'The dispossessed are more than capable of speaking for themselves. I am only speaking about my own sense of loss.'

Thomas is an iconoclast who believes 'Wales desperately needs to be reinvented, its outmoded stereotypes need to be crushed and a new self-image created'. He kicks out the props from under his characters so they sway, uncertain where to go.

He neither avoids the abyss nor poses neat solutions which can make for depressing viewing – but entertainment seems to be less important than confronting issues for Thomas who says 'My job is not to give audiences puerile messages. I'm looking for truth in a confusing world and I am as confused as anyone else.'

Feelings are given explosive force in physical theatre and raw dialogue so rhythmic and fast-flowing the meaning behind the words can be irritatingly obscure. But there's nothing obscure about Thomas's concern to 'reclaim' Welsh identity.

To him that means evolving a new vision of Welshness, which may be fictional but one which has emotional truth. It means 'inventing new forms, language and style' in theatre and developing Welsh TV and films. That ambition is being realised as Thomas and Y Cwmni have been hired to film a BBC documentary on Thomas's childhood home of Cwmgiedd near Ystradgynlais.

The Ukraine beckons when the company flies to Kiev on November 9 to perform *East from the Gantry* (to be recorded in an S4C documentary). The actors will also perform in an off-beat Russian-Ukranian-Welsh-English co-production. Bizarre as the show sounds, the pervading theme of cultural identity is the Nineties' key issue, as the EC, USSR and Yugoslavia disintegrate before our eyes.

The empty promise of the American Dream is examined in the first play in his trilogy, *House of America*, set in a Valleys town wrecked by unemployment and involving a family afflicted by incest, guilt and secrets.

The sequel, *Flowers of the Dead Red Sea*, weirdly set in a Valleys abattoir, is perhaps his bleakest play peopled by lost, hopeless characters clinging to Tom Jones' songs for support.

His latest play, *East from the Gantry* is, he says, more positive and suggests several avenues forward.

Nicole Sochor

HIRAETH/STRANGERS IN CONVERSATION

Hiraeth/Strangers in Conversation (Oriel, Cardiff)
Gair Rhydd, 8 November, 1993.

Shout 'Brown Nose' if you will, scream it if you prefer but the only disappointing thing about this play is that it is only half an hour long; the dialogue is so dynamic that you barely have time to breathe let alone fall into that deep slumber usually reserved for Monday morning lectures.

They say that first impressions count and the first impressions of Edward Thomas's *Hiraeth* hit you like the old cliched but well loved 'ton of bricks'. If you're looking for convention don't bother, this play is bizarre – even the audience resembled a revival of Woodstock love children. The set itself is enough to send any self-respecting claustrophobic running to the fridge for that can of cheap lager that's been lurking there since joining the music society in freshers week. Those who stay to be engulfed in white sheeting became witness to the banter of two grotesque, zombie-like heads which ooze from the sheets of ethereal blue light to the strain of Louis Armstrong's *Wonderful World*. Get the picture? So it's not conventional drama but it works nevertheless. Hilariously funny in places, *Hiraeth* is pervaded by a poignancy which captivated the entire audience.

Thomas' play has a haunting quality evoked by the strength of the two actors' performances and enhanced by the lighting which changed colour subtly yet startingly powerfully, to swing the mood of the audience from joy to despondency in seconds. According to the programme, the writer's aim is to 'explore questions of identity in Wales' but it goes further than that. Hiraeth's theme can be interpreted according to whoever you are and whatever your outlook might be, becoming a cry not only for a national identity but also for the importance of the individual voice.

Rowan and Sara

Hiraeth/Strangers in Conversation (Swansea Arts Workshop Gallery)
The Guardian, 19 November, 1993.

Not many people know this, but the *Guardian* discovered Paul Merton. Or Paul Martin as he was then, 11 years ago. And discovered is the word, hidden as he and John Irwin were in the crypt of St Jude's Church in what must have been the most obscure venue of the Swansea Fringe. And here he is now, a superstar headlining this year's Fringe with his own sell-out show at Swansea Grand Theatre.

It would be churlish to say I prefer Goff Morgan, a South Walian comic who pedals a droll line in surreal anecdotes, but I guess I like my comedy intimate. The use of the city's biggest venue as a Fringe venue is utterly bizarre – but there are few St Jude's Halls this year.

That the Fringe has lost a lot of its offbeat appeal doesn't mean there isn't interesting work. Y Cwmni's *Hiraeth*, for example, a short play to accompany an exhibition of paintings by Iwan Bala at Swansea Arts Workshop Gallery, was premiered at Oriel in Cardiff, although it is just the sort of thing for a Fringe. Two disembodied talking heads in limbo frantically ransack mythology, fantasy and memory to create their identity and history, a history that aficionados of writer Ed Thomas will know from his previous plays.

David Adams

FLOWERS

Flowers (Music Theatre Wales, Chapter Arts Centre, Cardiff)
The Independent, 19 March, 1994.

If the test of an opera is that you would pay to see it again, then John Hardy's new chamber opera *Flowers*, commissioned by Music Theatre Wales and premiered by them in Cardiff's Chapter Arts Centre on Thursday, is for me a failure. It's a biggish 'if', though. While neither agreeable nor amusing, *Flowers* is a strong piece that seems to do what it sets out to, which isn't the case with many first operas. Its defects lie in the intention, and intentions – like tastes – can't be discussed.

Or can they? *Flowers* is another of those first-operatic 'statements' which pin their drama to a social metaphor. Hardy's microcosm is a slaughterhouse faced with ruin because of the reluctance of its old-world-ethical manager to meet modern production targets which threaten his quasi-mystical relationship with the animals he has to kill.

The work concentrates on the slaughtermen, ending with a fight in which first one, then the other, falls victim to the methods of the trade. Intercut with this allegorical round-up of today's main news-stories is a series of monologues for an Ophelian soprano – the victim, so far as one can understand her, of a failed love affair (alias the modern world's failure to allow for human feelings). Her narrative linkage with the plot is obscure until she appears at the moment of ritual slaughter and unexpectedly falls into the would-be slaughterer's arms.

Hardy's problem with this material – or is it just mine? – is its unrelenting, agonising grimness. Known in Cardiff for theatre and film music of a certain rhythmic ferocity, he hasn't sought to lighten *Flowers* with popular – still less vulgar – elements which might set the feet tapping while the emotions seared. Instead his musical metaphors are all too well integrated with the scenic ones, and from the ear-splitting imitation of knives being sharpened which makes up the prelude, to the hubbub of the culminating fight, the little seven-piece band rarely does anything but insist that life is a discordant mess.

The fact that it does so with terrific conviction, with a flair for torturous sonic imagery, and with no hint that the composer is not in complete control of his materials, is a redemption only in hinting at what Hardy might achieve once he decided that opera is drama (and maybe fun) as well as metaphor. For all this, *Flowers* is eminently stageable, and MTW do it with their habitual energy and concentration. Michael McCarthy's production (designer Richard Aylwin) pulls no punches but avoids gratuitous viciousness.

The singing and playing are likewise admirably focused. Gareth Lloyd and Michael Bundy are finely matched as the two slaughtermen: the tenor pragmatic but sensitive, the baritone idealistic but capable of brutality. Eirian Davies sings with much warmth and involvement in a part which offers nothing dramatically. Michael Rafferty conducts a fiercely controlled account of the disagreeably impressive score.

Stephen Walsh

Flowers (Music Theatre Wales, Chapter Arts Centre, Cardiff)
Western Mail, 19 March, 1994.

John Hardy's new work *Flowers* is music theatre on the edge, provocative, disturbing and extremely enjoyable.

Based on a play by Ed Thomas, his first opera is a focused and highly charged piece, concentrating on three skilfully drawn characters.

The opera by John Hardy, former music director of *Brith Gof* and composer of *Pax* and *Haearn* who earlier this year won a Bafta Cymru award for best original score for the film *Hedd Wyn*, forms an auspicious start to Music Theatre Wales' New Opera Writing Initiative.

The work opens with the sounds of knives being sharpened. We are introduced to the bloody slaughterhouse and the symbolic dilemma of butcher Mock, a proud, skilled craftsman struggling against the pressures of mass production.

Directed by Michael McCarthy and designed by Richard Aylwin, the opera is performed with passion by a strong cast of actor-singers clearly committed to this new creation.

Eirian Davies sings a chilling and thrilling Dotty with fine characterisations from Gareth Lloyd and Michael Bundy as the slaughter-men Joe and Mock.

The singing and music, from a chamber opera conducted by Michael Rafferty, is emotionally searing, challenging but accessible.

The drama, set in a highly effective minimalist staging, will have you on the edge of your seat and the disturbing, powerful images will linger well after the sound of knives being sharpened has faded from your ears.

Mike Smith

ENVY

Envy (Cardiff Summer Festival)
The Guardian, 14 August, 1995.

Amid the impressive range of theatre events mixed in with the busking, cabaret, pyrotechnics, music and mayhem that makes Cardiff Summer Festival so much more than the street festival it was, the events in the Red Tent next to Burgess's mock-gothic Cardiff Castle, have been fascinating. It was here that the Ukrainian Theatre an Podol performed their amazing *Midsummer Night's Dream*, where the comedy becomes a tragedy, a chilling metaphor for the powers of the ageing ruling forces to awake and take revenge on those who dare dream. It was here, bizarrely, that the company were also forced to do their swimming-pool-set *Iago*, rejected at the last minute by the Marriott hotel – a last-minute re-staging obviously missed out on the symbolism of the water but was still stunning. A small country's theatre will in Wales always seem to express a critique of a dominant neighbour's cultural colonialism.

I was as grateful for Ian Hill and Y Cwmni's enterprise in this programme under canvas as much as anything for another chance to see Ed Thomas's *Envy*.

It's a scintillating monologue given a riveting performance by Russell Gomer as one Ted John, the near-psychopath loser from West Walian valleys town whose ambition is to get on Mastermind. To which end he kidnaps the local hero who qualifies and forces him to go through a mock contest in the village hall where the audience is hand-painted and a crude stuffed dummy of Magnus Magnusson's face is the question-master. Thomas's black humour and ability to write about the personal and the political (even if the autobiographical content sometimes seems unnecessary and self-indulgent) is impressive, and *Envy* is far more than a black comedy with the desperate Ted John another of the author's voices of a repressed and depressed nation that relies on false dreams and fake myths.

But what makes the piece work so well is Gomer's performance: he can always realise Thomas's characters perfectly here from the sniggers to the telling crack in the voice when he speaks of the 'uncle' he was brought up by, as swaggering smugness degenerates into sweaty desperation. He brings to life a character who is both human and allegorical, in a virtuoso performance. It's a good bit of writing and a brilliant piece of acting.

David Adams

SONG FROM A FORGOTTEN CITY

Song from a Forgotten City (Chapter Arts Centre, Cardiff)
Wales on Sunday, 12 February, 1995.

Y Cwmni have scored a coup with their latest production, *Song From a Forgotten City*, written by Ed Thomas. It will be the first original Welsh play to be staged at the Royal Court Theatre in London.

The theatre, a stronghold of innovative writing, has earned a formidable reputation for showcases of bright new work. The play will be produced there from June 6-10 but it can be seen in Cardiff first.

Ed Thomas, one of Wales' best known writers, won a BAFTA award last week for his screenplay, *Fallen Sons*. He has also been short listed for a Dennis Potter Award.

Song From a Forgotten City has a complex theme. It is set in a doomed metropolis. The three main characters are lost souls who believe themselves to be poets.

They eulogise an idealised city which exists in their minds but bears no comparison to the reality around them.

The drama has melancholic overtones, but is lifted from despondency by the powerful thread of humour which runs through it.

Y Cwmni spokesman, Phil Hamilton, describes it as a thriller, a raw, tense, violent work which exudes power. The brutality of this lost city, however, is defused by humour.

'It's very strong, very funny, very sexy and soulful', he says.

The play is accompanied by an atmospheric musical score devised by John Hardy. He recreates the real sounds of a city and the music is mixed during the performance.

'By doing this we create the atmosphere of a live event. It feels like the story of the play is really happening and the audience is part of it. The sense of involvement is very strong. We also have very good lighting effects and a good set.' Publicity photographs for the production have been devised by Cardiff based photographers Clanger & Boink. They are suitably arresting, and complement the disturbing and imaginative nature of Ed Thomas's work.

Nerys Lloyd-Pierce

Song from a Forgotten City (Chapter Arts Centre, Cardiff)
The Big Issue, 13 February, 1995.

I'm not at my most quickfire before noon, expecially on the telephone, but Ed Thomas, writer and director of Y Cwmni Theatre Company, sounds like his imagination is on some kind of caffeine rush. He is warming to his subjects with admirable passion, and his quota of soundbites per minute is soaring at a dramatic rate. Y Cwmni's latest work, *Song from a Forgotten City*, is shrouded in intrigue and mystery.

'I'd call it a darkly mischievous, tragic farce', says Ed. 'Is it very black humour?', I ask somewhat stupidly. He laughs knowingly – 'It owes most to David Lynch and Quentin Tarantino, rather than to Max Boyce.'

Does he write to be realistic then? 'No, I'm the most inauthentic writer in Wales, hopefully.' But surely black humour indicates social comment, I counter. 'Being a Welsh man is the argument for being invisible. What I know from travelling around the world . . . is that Wales has a very low profile – particularly in the performing arts. It's very difficult to get the press to come to see anything in Cardiff – they expect nothing good to happen. And we've got to prove to them and to our own people that we can cut it and we have an attitude.'

He agrees South Wales is a rich source of subject matter: 'The proof that we're here recording films, making plays, is an argument for making marks. If I was a visual artist, by putting my hand in a bit of blood and putting it on canvas. It's a sophisticated way of saying *Kilroy was here*. Because we haven't got a benchmark, work which is internationally recognized, we consistently have to prove ourselves. We're not the most confident culture. I think we're very imaginative, but I come from a bypass town in a bypass country and that's pretty much everything I've written about.'

'I would like a different Wales, based on the past with an imagined future. I really like Catalonia being imagined through Barcelona. The focus of Catalonia is very much Barcelona – it's pride and soul and energy. It's proud of its architecture. It's proud of its different traditions. I don't envy them, but I would like it if Cardiff would feel confident enough to speak for Wales, and if Wales could be confident enough for Cardiff to speak for itself.'

Should Cardiff be on the 'Map of Cool', as it is called in the play? 'It should be. I think it's a fine city. But the play is very much a downer on Cardiff. It's making the possibility for an agenda where people automatically think "Cardiff – Wales, London – England or Paris – France".'

Cardiff he feels, needs to liberate itself: 'It's got to be internal. If you're a prisoner you've got to free yourself. We're not that far away, but we've got to make a collective leap of faith into a demanding and different city. A city that speaks for you. And if the city cannot do that, then it's got to be forced to do it – it's a question of attitude.'

Ed explains how the 'forgotten city' of Cardiff is an imagined landscape – one he'd like to visit. 'I've got to think we've got a metropolis in Wales for my own sanity, and that people are excited about coming here. When I first went to London, I felt a buzz going over Hammersmith flyover . . .' Whereas in Cardiff? 'There's no myth. But the myth is capable of being created.'

Councillors, artists, citizens of Cardiff take note. Great things are afoot at Chapter Arts Centre. Agendas are being set, lines are being drawn. A cosmopolitan metropolis is there to be made, but as yet it's a romantic notion. Perhaps we should drag Cardiff kicking and screaming and make the metropolis a reality.

Colin Dallibar

Song from a Forgotten City (Chapter Arts Centre, Cardiff)
South Wales Argus, 16 February, 1995.

Carlyle dreams of 'a Metropolis, a place where something good might happen', a city where everyone feels alive and nobody is invisible.

But the city of Carlyle's dreams bears little relation to the imaginary Cardiff where *Song From a Forgotten City* is located. Here Cardiff is a bleak, decaying place peopled with the downtrodden and hopeless.

Carlyle, played brilliantly by Dorien Thomas, is the central character in this uncompromising visual and verbal tour-de-force penned by award-winning playwright Edward Thomas.

The Welsh rugby team has just been beaten 33-3 and the sense of shame and loss voiced by the play's three main characters symbolises the failure of reality to live up to Carlyle's dreams.

His nightmares are lived out on stage as characters who appear real in one scene are revealed as figments of Carlyle's imagination in the next.

This is not an easy play. Edward Thomas uses strong language to get his message across and some might be offended by that. But there is humour here as well, a black humour which brings much-needed light relief.

Award-winning theatre group Y Cwmni perform with confidence and inventiveness and Edward Thomas proves he is worth the accolades he has already earned.

The play will be performed tonight and tomorrow and from February 21 to 25 inclusive at Chapter Arts Centre, Cardiff, before going on a tour which will include five nights at London's Royal Court Theatre.

Song from a Forgotten City (Chapter Arts Centre, Cardiff)
Western Mail, 17 February, 1995.

'This ain't heaven man . . . this is Cardiff' drawls one of the characters in Y Cwmni's latest offering. Set in seedy backstreets, shabby hotel rooms and dingy bedsits with trains thundering overhead and rain pelting on the ceiling, this is no thriving metropolis but a bleak and warped figment of the writer's imagination.

Which writer? – Carlyle, the troubled writer at the centre of the plot or Ed Thomas, the BAFTA winning author.

The play's three central characters Russell Gomer, Richard Lynch and Dorien Thomas turn in stunning performances but ultimately it is the words – from a machine-gun volley of brutal accusations to a crescendo of previously unspoken dreams – which steal the show.

The audience is taken on a violent roller-coaster of emotion: the wonderful euphoria of the writer's drug-induced inspiration plunging into the darkness of crime, passion and betrayal.

No emotion is left untouched. Simultaneously shocking, touching, funny; it's by no means an easy ride and poses a host of questions about identity and upbringing which will haunt you for days.

Pauline McLean

Song from a Forgotten City (Chapter Arts Centre, Cardiff)
The Independent, 1 March, 1995.

'I have yet to see recorded anyone having good sex in the Welsh language', says Edward Thomas, playwright and self-appointed inventor of the modern Welsh nation. As one of the characters in Thomas's play *Flowers from the Dead Red Sea* proclaims, 'Art can save culture', and it is through the theatre that Thomas is embarking on his idiosyncratic mission. It is a serious mission, born of a passion for his country, yet one whose grandness is constantly undercut by the playwright's debunking irony. 'I don't want a country based on nationalism, I want a country based on desire. We need two people behind the bike sheds experimenting with the birth of a nation', he says.

For Thomas the lack of any representations of good sex in the Welsh language is a cultural tragedy of the same magnitude as the fact that Wales has no heroes other than Tom Jones and Harry Secombe. 'Damned is a nation without heroes', said Thomas, knocking back his pint of Guinness in the bar at the Chapter Arts Centre in Cardiff before the performance of his latest play, *Song from a Forgotten City*. To redress the balance, sex occurs in most of his own plays (he writes in English and in Welsh), though never without an edge of darkness. In *House of America*, his first and most frequently performed work, a sister and brother, who have escaped from the reality of a depressed 'by-pass' Welsh town into the fantasy that they are Jack Kerouac and Joyce Johnson, are seen *in flagrante*. In *Song from a Forgotten City* it's the enigmatic figure of the Writer who, in a drug- and drink-fuelled moment of confusion seduces his friend, believing him to be a lost lover because he happens to be wearing her suede mini-skirt.

The power of Thomas's playwriting lies in the fact that the madly imaginative, chaotic, lyrical stories he tells present themselves instantly as metaphors. The dysfunctional sex could be seen as an expression of the fervid desire of the Welsh to be united with the country they love, thwarted by history and circumstance. At least, though, his characters are making the attempt. All the depressing reality of 1990s Welsh life is there in the writing – the open-cast mines, the blood-swilling abattoirs, the abandoned houses, the cold, rainy hills – but Thomas's aesthetic and cultural agenda is to create an imaginary new Wales. Wales only exists in the imagination, he argues, so it's up for grabs for anyone and everyone to fashion as they will.

Song from a Forgotten City is the most unabashed effort to create this imaginary land to date, exploring the relationship between a country and a city, between civic and national pride. It is set in the metropolis that Wales lacks, on the evening of an international match that Wales have lost, and it opened in Cardiff in the week of the international match that England had won. The character referred to as the Writer waxes lyrical in the imaginary metropolis: 'The city is yours. You know that people from all over the world want to come and visit it . . . to feel it for themselves. They want to share your city with you for a day . . . or a week . . . then go back home and tell their people that they never knew such a city existed, man. Your city. Your country's city. You aren't invisible.'

They say that on rugby international days, Cardiff is as close as it ever gets to feeling like a major city. The streets throng with people, the bars are full to overflowing, grown men wear daffodils in their lapels and the rain-soaked wind at about two o'clock carries snatches of the Welsh anthem, sung by hundreds of supporters in full throat. But by the next morning, Wales have lost (Wales have only lost twice to England at the Arms Park in the last 30 years), the streets are deserted and, despite the bi-lingual signposts, the shops in the main street are the same as you would see anywhere in Britain. As one of Thomas's characters laments: 'I came to this city looking for a metropolis, but all I found was Cardiff.'

'I don't want to be a Welsh miserablist,' Thomas professes, 'but it's hard: if Wales had won the international, it would have done more for Wales than five of my plays. If we had an English-language sitcom set in Wales that we exported, or a soap-opera, or a Welsh hero and heroine on the big screen . . . Cardiff has all the potential dancers and painters and poets to make an impact culturally, it's just that their work isn't recorded, there's a huge lack of confidence.'

The son of a butcher, born in Abercraf, Swansea Valley, Thomas studied English at the University of Wales in Cardiff before leaving for France and then London, where he worked in fringe theatre and began to write. An appealingly ravaged face bears testament to some wild living in his youth, before he moved back to Cardiff and became a serious writer, forming Y Cwmni in 1988, a theatre and television company with whom he has written and directed six productions. Thomas's plays used to receive more enthusiastic support in Glasgow, Dublin and even London than in Cardiff. But *Song* (the first new play in 10 years to run for more than 10 nights at Chapter Arts) sold out for its whole run. Thomas still expresses pleasure at seeing an audience comprised entirely of strangers, rather than friends and family, and welcomes the current cultural vibrancy in Cardiff. With the opening of The Point there will be 40 theatre openings in Cardiff in 10 weeks. And even the mysterious disappearance of the Manic Street Preachers' lyricist, Richey James (his abandoned car was found by the Severn Bridge) gives the dour reality of contemporary Welsh life a romantic, Kerouac-like edge.

In fact, James could almost be a character from an Ed Thomas play. After the burlesque comedy and theatrical tricks of the first half, *Song from a Forgotten City* degenerates into a troubling vision of a group of friends getting by on drugs and drink when everything they have cared for has been brutalised and destroyed, and all their aspirations have been mocked into nothingness. For all his romantic fervour, Ed

Thomas's vision of a Welsh nation is unsentimental, urban and very contemporary. And it is articulated in a new urban Welsh vernacular which is arguably more relevant, and more exportable, than the Welsh language itself.

'Wales has never had a modernist era, or a post-modernist one, or any bloody thing', says Thomas. 'I hope my plays are a way to bring Wales up to the modern world', he says, then checks himself. It's easy to mock, but Thomas is torn between a natural subversive tendency and protectiveness towards his fledgling country. 'We've inherited a glasshouse culture. All sacred cows should be attacked, but ours is so fragile. *Song from a Forgotten City* is the most autobiographical thing I've written yet', he says. 'If we can record the way the Welsh live, love and die, then at least we've made a step.'

Clare Bayley

Song from a Forgotten City (Theatr Clwyd, Mold, Preview)
Daily Post, 1 March, 1995.

Song From A Forgotten City which opens at Theatr Clwyd, Mold, on Thursday is set in a doomed metropolis, a bleak Kafkaesque environment with undertones of menace.

From the opening moments of the play the audience is drawn into a black whirlpool of impending disaster as the original music by John Hardy brings the sound of the city alive.

The clatter of a train, the thrum of rock music, reverberate around the auditorium, sucking the observer inexorably into this intense narrative.

Despite its message of defeat, this is not a depressing play. The dialogue is sexy and sassy, its delivery raunchy and upbeat. Writer Edward Thomas weaves a faint hint of promise into the gloom.

This may be a lost city, focal point of a forgotten nation, but it is one in which something good might happen: it is also very funny.

The full emotive power of the production comes in the second half, the most dynamic scene revealing two lost souls, Carlyle and Jojo, penning poetry. In their drug-raddled euphoria the words flow and the two are exultant.

But when reality seeps in Carlyle is overwhelmed by despair and he fulfils the tragedy of his destiny. For Jojo, the brutal exposure of his self-deception destroys his personality.

Russell Gomer's Jojo veers alarmingly from sexy self-confidence to the broken babbling of a shattered psyche, a portrayal of the disintegration of the deluded poet that is utterly convincing.

Thomas, who directs his own work, has come up with a daring production: the strong language, homoerotic scenes and dark passion of the text destroy Welsh stereotypes.

When the production opens at the Royal Court Theatre, London, in June, it should force a wider audience to sit up and take notice of the cultural revolution which is currently taking place in Wales.

Nerys Lloyd-Pierce

Song from a Forgotten City (Chapter Arts Centre, Cardiff)
Socialist Campaign Group News, March 1995.

Y Cwmni's performances of writer director Edward Thomas's new play *Song from a Forgotten City* sold out in Cardiff during February. After a tour of Wales,

England and Bucharest it will arrive in London in June. It is a startling dramatic embodiment of the prolonged crisis of confidence in which Cardiff is gripped: is it Welsh enough to be Wales' capital? Is it big enough to be a European City State?

Service industries have replaced much of Cardiff's manufacturing business as employers. A determined effort to stem that tide is essential for the city to regain anything like the mercantile swagger of its heyday (1880-1950). While there are various economic, historic, and social pointers to a positive, distinctive, cultural future, they have yet to be translated into any readily accessible form. *Song from a Forgotten City* reflects with frightening wit the despair in the absence of available hope.

We are introduced to the slightly sinister surreal world of the play by a bellboy and a night porter. Despite the cuteness of their uniforms, their dialogue is redolent of generations of excitement-seeking Americanised South Wales males. They discover the corpse of Carlyle and through a series of dream sequences and flashbacks reconstruct the events leading to his suicide.

Carlyle and his lover Yvette had both sold their bodies to live. Yvette has been killed. Carlyle dreams of his city growing into a neon pulsating metropolis that the world will want to visit. Searching for consolation he asks a taxi driver to take him to somewhere good in the existing city; but, not only has Wales lost at rugby again, the supporters in the pub he enters have forgotten how to sing. Digging deeper, Carlyle's friend, Jojo, puts on Yvette's sinister mini-skirt and after simulating Carlyle and Yvette's old dance routine the men make frantic love. Lust provides no answer to Carlyle's agony.

This is a high-energy production, with performances from all three actors, Dorien Thomas, Richard Lynch and Russell Gomer, combining dynamism and subtly defined characters which more than make up for the occasional lack of focus in the text. It would have been good to have the poignant anecdote of Carlyle's father's dying wish, 'Whatever you do don't let him get hold of the binoculars', expanded, as it seems to tap into a well-spring of frustrated humanity. In the figures of the bell boy, the night porter and the mildly transvestite Jojo, Thomas flirts with deconstructing Welsh masculinity but stops tantalisingly short. With a little more daring *Song* like Y Cwmni and Cardiff themselves would be on the road to being a major artistic force. Y Cwmni's daring should include expanding their repertoire to perform seminal texts of the European theatre companies with whom they are forging links.

Whether they will want to address current economic and social issues any more concretely seems doubtful but other theatre companies and playwrights in Wales should consider this. To this end, later this year Made in Wales Stage Company is organising a forum of playwrights, theatre companies, politicians, academics and the media. In the meantime it is staging an impressive season of four new plays. This began with Dic Edwards' *Utah Blue* in February, which reworked the life and death of Gary Gilmore as a challenging examination of the co-existence of artistic sensitivity and latent violence.

Lloyd Trott

Song from a Forgotten City (Royal Court, Preview)
Time Out, June 17-24, 1995.

'I find silence embarrassing. It's not very good to be silent if you come from nowheresville. The aim is to say something with attitude but without being declamatory.' There's no room for embarrassment as the words spill out of playwright Edward Thomas's mouth, little time for breath either. If, in spite of what he says, his talk borders on the soapbox, it also smacks of the crack that flows in what Thomas describes as the by-pass towns of South Wales, where the people come up with stories that have never been heard before. His missionary zeal comes from the belief that the image of Wales is faint to the point of invisibility, providing the opportunity for today's artists to scrawl new pictures on top; preferably urban, contemporary fictions in contrast with the folksy, rural ones of the past. Tired of artists who drink themselves to death (he points out that he hasn't had a drink while waiting in the bar next door), of Eisteddfods, Tom Jones and Harry Secombe, the grey-haired 34-year-old is engaged in creating something else. His passionate, violent plays demand visibility.

He's in London because his play *Song From a Forgotten City* is about to be staged at the Royal Court. Oddly, it will be performed as part of the Barclays New Stages Festival, more noted for its support of performance art than text-based plays. Formed in 1988, Y Cwmni is based in Cardiff and has produced shows for theatre, radio and television, most of which have been written by Thomas, a founder member. *House of America*, a passionate play about murder and incest that won a TO award when it played at the BAC, will be filmed in the autumn. Trips to London have been rare, but Thomas's reputation is growing. What must have convinced the selectors that *Song* was appropriate for the Festival was both its rejection of naturalism and its Welshness. *Song* comes from a different cultural perspective.

What Thomas doesn't want to do is fall into the trap of small-minded nationalism and parochialism, the curse of many a tiny country. 'I don't want to be a Welsh miserablist. I work from the particular all the time. If that fails to make the leap from the particular to the universal I will have failed. Then it will always be landlocked in Wales.' But, if it is true, as Thomas repeatedly affirms, that Wales has no iconography, why is it that it's not had the confidence to create its own culture when the Scots and the Irish so vigorously promote theirs? 'Wales is only an idea. It is a fragmented nation. It cannot be defined as a country, because it doesn't rule itself and has very few institutions, so it's there to be redefined. There's no soap opera or sitcom or film that's been shown consistently. How do you speak, have confidence in the way that you live, love and die if it's not reflected back at you in any muscular form?' Thomas points out that a soap opera in Welsh would be only 'a boom shadow away' from being an absurdist play, because there is no community that speaks entirely in Welsh.

Song is engaged with all these issues, but not as an issue-based play. It's no surprise to discover that Thomas's favourite playwrights are Sam Shepard and Howard Barker. Like many Welsh people, he looks west rather than east and envies Shepard the American mythology against which he sets his characters. *Song* is ostensibly a thriller, with a soundscore to match, in which a writer called Carlyle creates a series of violent stories. He is in a hotel in Cardiff, topically, on the night that the Welsh rugby team has lost to England. 'A lot of people in Wales thought it was about the nature of cities. That's only one theme. It's about a lonely man who doesn't like where he lives, but it's not a treatise on Cardiff. It's a theatrical form of Kilroy Was Here. What Carlyle does is to create his own fiction and then find that he is one of the heroes in that fiction.' There's a strong feeling that Cardiff is failing to live up to its role as a metropolis. 'Sometimes', says one of the characters, 'I'm not sure it's a city at all, more like a place waiting for something good to happen.' He can't do it on his own, but that's something Thomas is determined to change.

Jane Edwardes

Song from a Forgotten City (Royal Court, London)
The Independent, 8 June, 1995.

'Inside my head,' proclaims the hero of *Song from a Forgotten City* (a head also often awash with chemicals), 'there's a city of 2 or 3 million people. A Welsh city of opportunity.' Outside his head, in so far as such a place can be said to exist in this work, there is Cardiff, capital of a country that only has 2 or 3 million people *in toto*, whose idea of a national tradition is the Eisteddfod and whose pantheon of heroes would be sorely reduced were Tom Jones and Harry Secombe ever to cop it in the same air crash. No letters, please: I'm merely reporting the view implied in Edward Thomas's zanily imaginative, often very funny play which takes us, via a spoof thriller premise, into its protagonist's weird, violent mental scenarios on a day when Wales has lost to England at rugby.

One of the refreshing things about this drama is its wild freedom from the kind of parochial humbuggery brilliantly satirised in Kingsley Amis's Swansea-set *Old Devils*. A character in the Amis remarks: 'Do you know they have wrestling in Welsh now on that new channel? Same as in English oddly except the bugger counts *un-dau-tri* etc. Then the idiots can go round saying the viewing figures for Welsh language programmes have gone up. To four thousand and eleven.' In Thomas's play, such satire collides with surrealism, as in the hero's account of the pub after the match, where the barman, freaked out by the first no-singing silence he's heard in 40 years on an international day, breaks all the glasses, slashes his wrists and dies, whereupon the customers calmly turn on the TV 'to see the highlights in a language we didn't understand'.

Beginning and ending with the sight of the bald, smiling corpse of the protagonist Carlyle (Dorien Thomas) standing upright like a statue with a gun in one hand and a row of faxed manuscript in the other, the play shows both his desperate need to make 'connections' (a word much harped on) and his compulsion to blast them apart, a tendency that climaxes in his suicide. Thomas to a degree shares Carlyle's cultural aspirations. The fact that he makes this semi-surrogate a deluded smackhead whose garbled writings spew from a fax and who winds up topping himself is a measure of the self-debunking irony that aerates *Song*.

The loopy, dark humour is projected with tremendous chutzpah by the cast of three, with Richard Lynch and Russell Gomer versatility playing the bell boy and night porter of the cod Hotel Angel where Carlyle fetches up, and all the other figments in his fantasy. Often the chaotic verbal comedy seems radio-inspired and it gets side-tracked into riffs of exuberant, eccentric irrelevance, as when the night porter talks of never sitting on toilet seats since the day he sat on one as a child and heard a cat purring down the bog. But in a work obsessed by 'connecting', there is also a strange lattice-work of correspondences that seem too private for an assured interpretation. What's the link, say, between the episode when a drug-confused Carlyle sodomises a friend who happens to be wearing his deceased lover's miniskirt, and the climactic account of his father falling down dead when discovered wearing his mother's clothes?

Search me. What you can say with certainty is that here is an arresting voice and that a more accurate title for this piece would be *Songs for a Not Yet Invented City*.

Paul Taylor

Song from a Forgotten City (Donmar Warehouse, London)
The Times, 21 March, 1996.

If you think Edward Thomas was a First World War poet who wrote quirky verse about the Wiltshire countryside, you will be mightily surprised by the dramatist of the same name currently represented in Covent Garden. He lives in South Wales, founded a theatre company called Y Cwmni in 1988 and has more in common with Sam Shepard and the Irvine Welsh of *Trainspotting* than with A.E. Housman or Wilfred Owen.

This Edward Thomas's *Song from a Forgotten City* is a surreal play about the trials of being Welsh, with a tormented, dragged-out writer as its main character.

That summary is unlikely to lure Londoners in hordes to the latest arrival in the Donmar's 'Four Corners' season. But I suspect that this will not vastly surprise Thomas nor send him into storms of resentment at Anglo insularity. He himself feels that Wales is the British Isles's forgotten corner and, though he laments its sidelining in vivid, even violent style, he does not act the victim nor offload the blame. Indeed, the play comes across as an exasperated attempt to shake, rattle and roll his compatriots out of their own enervated, enervating habits.

Though it took me time to succumb to his idiom, I came to feel he was fulfilling this task in the best way possible by displaying a high-voltage imagination. He pulls us into a lurid, sinister world where, as the writer-protagonist says, it isn't clear 'where my life ends and my blur begins'. The stage furniture consists of a toilet bowl, crushed Coke cans, cages filled with urban detritus, towering pipes, neon lights. At times this represents the streets of Cardiff, a run-down hotel where the night porter wears a frock coat and a plastic skirt, the flat where the writer snorts cocaine, and his own disoriented head.

Though characters merge into each other, and some events are hallucinated, the drift is clear. After all, you don't need a Dada phrasebook to interpret the scene in which a sneering publisher urges Carlyle (as the writer is called) to pen saleable pastoral, only to get his head shoved in the lavatory in reprisal. Neither the protagonist nor his author are into nostalgia. Quite the contrary, 'I came to the city in search of a metropolis,' says Carlyle, 'and I found only Cardiff.'

Feeling as he does that 'without a city you can't have a country', he is preoccupied with the urban future, not any rural past. Though the dialogue free-associates this way and that, taking in everything from Barbie dolls to dentistry to car crashes, it is never more passionate than when Carlyle imagines taking a taxi-ride through streets that buzz with human excitement.

Sometimes the humour gets facetious – shirts plastered with 'World of DIY' – but the invention and energy don't flag. Nor do Patrick Brennan, Jack James and Russell Gomer, a three-man cast who ably perform the work of ten. If Cardiff remains Cardiff, and Wales Wales, it won't be Y Cwmni's fault.

Benedict Nightingale

Song from a Forgotten City (Royal Lyceum, Edinburgh)
Scotland on Sunday, 26 May, 1996.

We Scots tend to be quite proud of our survival – as a nation, as a culture – into the late 20th century. Look, we say, 290 years of uneasy union with one of the most powerful and centralised nations on earth, and yet we are still here; what a plucky people, how stubborn, how strong. But by that same measure, the Welsh – despised youngest brothers in our island family drama – have done many times better. Seven hundred years of total defeat and absorption into the English state; and yet Wales is still there too, confused, impoverished, divided as to language, yet still able to say, in so many different voices, 'We are Welsh and we are here; ni yma o hyd'.

And since 1989, the writer/director Ed Thomas and his company Y Cwmni – whose *Song from a Forgotten City* played at the Royal Lyceum last week as part of Kenny Ireland's bold 'Best of the Rest' season, featuring radical drama from England, Wales and Ireland – have established themselves as the ultimate poets of the Wales that is 'still here' in the 1990s. It has to be said that their work often seems, in conventional terms, like a kind of postmodern theatrical car-crash, in which the whole evolution experienced by Scottish drama in the last quarter-century – from the post-industrial lamentation of plays like *Willie Rough* to the 1990s urban burn-out of *Trainspotting* – is smashed together into a single mind-blowing evening. *Song From a Forgotten City* is set, after a fashion, in a run-down Cardiff hotel, on a Saturday night after another notorious Welsh rugby defeat at Cardiff Arms Park. 'Heavy falls of Welshmen', says one character lugubriously, of the scene on the streets, 'and a lot of drifting.' A would-be writer called Carlyle checks in, talks to the Bell Boy and the Night Porter about pain and defeat and Welshness and dentists, relives his traumatic relationship with quiet hard man Benny and skirt-wearing smack-head Jojo, and shares his dream of a real Welsh metropolis, a city of two or three million people, a world city, a Barcelona of a city, a city and a country no longer invisible. The piece is staged like a kind of rave in a warehouse nightclub, with a fierce sound-track punctuated by monologue, dialogue, incident; and the sheer elaborate noisiness of it all sometimes threatens to overwhelm the brilliant stream-of-consciousness text, to irritating effect.

But for all that, this strange and powerful piece of theatre manages to say more in two hours – about national identity and its loss, about masculinity in the age when DIY superstores and drug culture have replaced the old heavy-industrial certainties, about the interface between global commercial culture and intensely local lives and memories – than many writers manage in a lifetime; and it's also, at the same time, extremely funny. Patrick Brennan as the hero Carlyle, Jack James as the Bellboy, and the brilliant Russell Gomer as Jojo and Night Porter, give the kind of performances – unforgettable, witty, heroic, right on the edge of theatre and its possibilities – that ought to win awards; but, alas, never do. The only question is why the young rave audience that packed the Lyceum for *Trainspotting* was not even willing to give a passing glance to this show, so similar in preoccupation and mood. No magic Irvine Welsh brand-name, I suppose, no cheery buzz of wha's-like-us Scottishness, and so even the under-25s remain in comfortable ignorance of just how 'like us' they are, our brothers the Welsh, and every other small nation on earth.

Joyce McMillan

Gas Station Angel (British Tour Interview)
Western Mail, 16 May, 1998.

. . . And of course, there is *Gas Station Angel*, the first play to be commissioned by the Royal Court for 30 years.

It reflects his new-found optimism about Wales—indeed, he seems to have surprised himself with its positive tone. 'It's a new kind of play for me. It's very optimistic. I don't know if it sits very happily with me but I feel optimistic.'

House of America explored the dangers of attempting to define identity through a borrowed culture. The pursuit of the American Dream by its dysfunctional Valleys family leads to insanity, incest and murder.

The protagonists of *Gas Station Angel*, however, come to realise they've got their own mythology to discover. Not that you'd know this from the suitably cryptic flyer, which mysteriously reveals: '*Gas Station Angel* is set in a shrinking land by a tantrum sea where the past is faced up to and overcome, where a people recover and where magical things can still happen in a cruel world.'

Thomas elaborates: 'I was going to call it *Where Do We Go When We Drive A Tinted Glass Blue Marina 1800cc Into The Heart of Saturday Night* but that didn't trip off the tongue!'

'It's boy meets girl on a beach, his house is falling into the sea, she's chucked her job in as a checkout girl. The boy's mother thinks he's a changeling and that their house has collapsed because her husband dug up a field that belongs to the fairies. The girl's part of the James family, he's part of the Ace family. Both families are linked by a tragic past. In 16 hours 48 minutes, their lives change. They find out about their pasts, which include fairies, angels and succubae, missing brothers, dead chickens, axed sheep. It's very dark, very strange, very Welsh—a kind of love story with magic realism.'

Magic realism on stage is an ambitious enterprise but Thomas has no qualms. 'You've got to avoid Welsh whimsy. It's not whimsical but it is optimistic. *House of America* was the first thing I wrote. It was about "damned is a nation without heroes", you can't buy the American Dream off a shelf and call it Welsh. You've got to make up your own heroes, your own contemporary mythology.

'*Gas Station Angel* is about how these two people—white trash, I call them—make themselves up and realise they've got their own mythology. The future is theirs, if they come to terms with the past. Instead of the past destroying them like in *House of America*, they survive the past, so it's quite hopeful.'

Carolyn Hitt

Gas Station Angel (The Sherman Theatre, Cardiff)
South Wales Echo, 28 May, 1998.

I'd have liked to have said *Gas Station Angel* is the most amazing new play I've ever seen.

It is incredibly exciting, vibrant, funny, and challenging.

Following the fates and fortunes of two Welsh families—author and director Ed Thomas has created a tour de force exploration into what it means to be human (and Welsh) in the late 20th century.

There are the Aces, whose house is slowing falling into the sea, and the James' whose son Marshall is treated like an angel after he nearly drowns.

And as the action weaves its way in and out of their lives, a great mystery which fundamentally links both families is revealed.

The cast turned in outstanding performances, particularly Simon Gregor as Dyfrig, Keith and Mr Entertainment, Richard Harrington as Bri, and Valmai Jones as Mary Annie.

The direction was truly inspired, and the sound, lighting and set construction people (Mike Beer, John Buswell, and Miraculous Engineering) all deserve big slaps on the back.

And the but? Well, the play was far too long—some judicious pruning would do it wonders. And there was no need to spell out Ace's new found optimism about being Welsh and European. But apart from that it was a joy to watch.

Sarah Roberts

Gas Station Angel (The Sherman Theatre, Cardiff)
Western Mail, 29 May, 1998.

So much hype surrounds Ed Thomas it's difficult sometimes to see his work beneath the veneer of publicity, and the opening night of his opening play at the Sherman Theatre was certainly something of a cultural event—the return of the hero with a major new commission from the Royal Court in Cardiff before heading for London's West End.

So is *Gas Station Angel*, written and directed by the man himself, the latest step in their progress in world domination by his company Fiction Factory (formerly Y Cwmni)?

With reservation I would say Yes. As a piece of live theatre it is stunning, but high production standards have always been a hallmark of this company's work and having designer Peter Mumford (once with Cardiff's Moving Being) and composer John Hardy (ex Brith Gof) ensures quality.

You never expect a straightforward story with Ed Thomas, his first play and recent film *House of America* being the nearest to naturalist narrative, and this tale of two Welsh families linked by love and a terrible secret is in many ways a semi-abstract piece of theatre that speaks as poetry does, lyrically but obliquely.

It is on a very real level about the Jameses and the Aces and their dysfunctional members about a love story, a killing, a house falling into the sea—but it is also about families in the broader sense, the balance between imagination and reality, ritual, Wales, language, the unreliability of memory, secret and lies.

Essentially it is, like much of the playwright's work, mythic. His obsession with heroes, with dynasties, with madness, with fate is here again, with echoes not just of Greek tragedy but of the Bible and Shakespeare.

Myth, though, does require a clear plot—and in the transition from page to stage the plot has been lost, it seems to me, and we are left with some brilliant words where poetry and ideas come tumbling out incessantly. Great staging, flying metaphors, lots of humour, impressive performances, but an unnecessary lack of clarity in the storytelling.

But since the play has changed a lot so far, it can evolve further. That, after all, is the strength of theatre.

Meanwhile I still found it one of the most exciting, richest, cleverest and most theatrical productions to have come out of Wales for some time.

David Adams

Gas Station Angel (Royal Court Theatre Upstairs)
The Times, 11 June, 1998.

To be Welsh at the end of the century you need imagination. So says a supermarket checkout girl called Bronwyn, or Bron, near the end of *Gas Station Angel*; and she speaks both for her fellow characters and for her author. Ed Thomas and his Fiction Factory recently brought London *Song From a Forgotten City*, which was set in a lurid, sinister metropolis that turned out to be dull old Cardiff as it had been reinvented, complete with hotel porters in plastic skirts, by a tormented, drugged-out dreamer. Their latest offering (sponsored by Barclays New Stages) is less surreal but not a lot likelier to appeal to those with linear minds and geometric spirits.

If you unpick Thomas's play, which takes some effort, you find a simply if slightly sensational story. Years ago Bri saved his brother Marshall from drowning in some South Wales estuary, but his initiative was not recognised by his father. With Marshall more the family favourite than ever, Bri went to the bad, taking an axe to a neighbour's lambs and forcing Marshall to strangle the chickens belonging to a farmer who already had troubles enough, since coastal erosion was inexorably pushing his house over a cliff.

Grim stuff, and worse is to come. Bri vanishes, leaving a disconsolate Marshall to mooch besides the water with a fishing rod whose hook, line and sinker remain firmly on dry land. What has happened to him? I will reveal nothing except that a batty farmer's wife with a shotgun plays a part in the mystery. But we are left with a little warmth and hope in the form of an affair between Bron, who is Bri's sister, and Ace, who turns out to have been largely responsible for Bri's disappearance.

This rustic tale could be told in many different ways. Martin McDonagh, Irish author of *The Leenane Trilogy*, would pack it with scorching satire; David Harrower, Scottish author of *Knives and Hens*, would reduce it to an hour of dour monosyllabic grunts; the current batch of young English dramatists would emphasise everyone's social and economic alienation. Not Thomas. He plays somersaults with time and dramatic structure and allows his people's fancy to burrow into the underworld, vault into the sky or, weirdly, do both at once.

In this corner of modern Wales a middle-aged woman can explain disasters as acts of revenge by angry fairies, while her husband can turn on the sea and accuse it of taking out its tantrums on his family. Even cool young Ace sees good and bad angels all around, and not only when he is smoking dope. You can describe this as ingrained feyness, or the remnants of paganism, or an escape from the boredom and brutality of contemporary life, or a refusal of personal responsibility, or a sign of national weakness. For Thomas, it is being Welsh.

His writing can get cluttered and the acting of his cast (Richard Lynch, Siwan Morris and Richard Harrington among the exceptions) escalates from the intense to the overwrought. But there is talent behind the fuss, and concern for a mini-country still fighting for its identity, still in spiritual turmoil. Will a Welsh parliament make a big difference? No, not really, not on this evidence.

Benedict Nightingale

Gas Station Angel (Royal Court Theatre Upstairs)
The Independent, 11 June, 1998.

Ed Thomas, leading light of the Welsh theatre scene, believes in fairies and angels. And he's not ashamed to admit it. Thomas is no fool, though: he knows that a modern audience—especially an audience at a hip joint like the Royal Court—would scoff at any literal-minded attempt to represent a sprite, winged or otherwise, on stage.

Evocative though the title of his new play may be, *Gas Station Angel* isn't about the life and times of Robin Goodfellow, elf pump attendant. A quartet of very 20th century-looking seraphs flit in and out, dressed in business suits with tiny blue wing markings etched on their shoulders, solemnly holding up black umbrellas.

But like the throbbing soundtrack they're more for decorative effect than anything. Thomas tries to suggest another world by abstract means, on an empty stage, a world which may be solely a figment of the human imagination, or simply a convenient metaphor, or even a joke.

Unfortunately, he overburdens both his able cast and his audience with the task of making sense of the play's all-pervading ambiguities. The piece probably contains more references to fairies and angels than Shakespeare's entire canon. The very first line is 'I saw an angel' uttered by Ace, a young man with his head in the clouds and his heart set on the ethereal Bron. It's a perfect match (as Ace's constantly spooked-out, doddery mother, excellent Valmai Jones, informs him: 'You were a baby made by fairies.') together they are going to leave the dreariness of Small Town behind them and drive 'a blue tinted glass Marina 1800 TC into the heart of Saturday night'. The only obstacle is the past—the two come with some heavy emotional baggage, which we watch being stacked up, and finally jettisoned as the narrative loops back and forth in time.

Ace and his folks, have been driven over the edge by the imminent destruction of their cliff-top home through the combined forces of 'a tantrum sea' and the local council. Bron meanwhile is missing her brother, Bri, the black sheep of the family that has not got over the shame of being blamed for the senseless slaughter of 24 new-born lambs.

The play's main problem is that for all their dreams of flight, Ace and Bron never stand out from the rest of the crazy-talking town. Simon Gregor steals the show as both a gruff pub landlord (a sort of Welsh Begbie) and a frustrated checkout assistant who wails 'Let me get pregnant by the spunk of a fairy!'

Thomas can write dialogue that is sometimes as excruciating in its whimsy as that of another Thomas, Dylan. But there are times when you hear something funny, stirring, and original. Better luck next time.

Dominic Cavendish

Gas Station Angel (Royal Court Theatre Upstairs)
The Guardian, 13 June, 1998.

Fiction Factory is a Welsh company devoted exclusively to the work of writer-director Ed Thomas. Watching Thomas's *Gas Station Angel* at the Royal Court's Theatre Upstairs, I felt it might be a good thing if this particular factory started turning out alternative products. There is a wild and whirling talent here, but also an incredible verbal self-indulgence.

As in *Songs From a Forgotten City*, Thomas casts a critical eye over his native land. Modern Wales, he suggests, is a strange mix of Celtic superstition, tribal loyalty and family fission. He presents us with the burgeoning young love between Ace and Bron, both overloaded with inherited problems. Ace's family home is symbolically falling into the sea through soil erosion. Bron, meanwhile, has two brothers, one of whom, Bri, has disappeared apparently in protest against the family sanctification of his sibling. What we see is young love triumphing over the twin burdens of antique myths and domestic bonds.

'Words are beautiful,' cries Ace at one point. 'They conjure up things.' But they can also obscure things. And Thomas so over-stuffs his text with references to angels and fairies that we lose sight of the key point: that the young, looking to the future, see themselves as Welsh Europeans rather than as twilit relics, and eagerly embrace their national identity without being enslaved by it.

The production itself, despite over-loud bursts of music to create an air of excitement, makes good use of the space. Richard Lynch plays Ace with skill, Siwan Morris is a sexily appealing Bron, and Richard Harrington makes his mark as the blond, bolting Bri. But the text could be cut by a third with no great loss.

Michael Billington

CHRONOLOGY

EDWARD THOMAS – STAGE PLAYS

House of America	Y Cwmni	Wales Tour	1988
		Chapter Arts Centre, Cardiff	1989
		Battersea Arts Centre, London	
		Harry Younger Hall, Edinburgh	1992
		Wales Tour	
		Tramway, Glasgow	
	Fiction Factory	UK Tour	1997
		Perth, Australia	1998
Adar Heb Adenydd	Dalier Sylw	Wales tour	1989
		Harry Younger Hall, Edinburgh	1989
The Myth of Michael Roderick	Y Cwmni	Wales Tour	1990
		St Stephens Theatre Space, Cardiff	1991
		Chapter Arts Centre, Cardiff	
		Watermans Arts Centre, London	
Flowers of the Dead Red Sea	Y Cwmni	Tramway, Glasgow	1991
		Chapter Arts Centre, Cardiff.	
		Watermans Arts Centre, London	
		Wales Tour	1992
East from the Gantry	Y Cwmni	Tramway, Glasgow	1992
		Kiev, Ukraine,	
		UK and Ireland Tour	
		Wales Tour	1994
New Wales Trilogy	Y Cwmni	Wales Tour	1992
		Tramway, Glasgow	
Hiraeth/Strangers in Conversation	Y Cwmni	Oriel Gallery, Cardiff	1993
		Swansea Arts Workshop Gallery	
Envy	Y Cwmni	Wales Tour	1993
		Cardiff Summer Festival	1995
Song from a Forgotten City	Y Cwmni	Chapter Arts Centre, Cardiff	1995
		Wales Tour	
		British Festival	
		Royal Court, London	
		Bucharest, Romania	
		Donmar Warehouse, London	1996
		Royal Lyceum, Edinburgh	
		Bonn, Germany	
		Melbourne, Australia	
Gas Station Angel		Euro Theatre, Brussels	
		UK Tour	1998
	Fiction Factory	Royal Court, London	

TELEVISION

A Silent Village/Pentre Mud	BBC/S4C	1993
Fallen Sons	BBC	1994

RADIO

Flowers of the Dead Red Sea	Radio 3	1992
East from the Gantry	Radio 3	1997

FILM

House of America		1997

PUBLICATIONS

Edward Thomas, *East from the Gantry* in Pamela Edwardes (ed.), *Frontline Intelligence* (London: Methuen, 1993).

Brian Mitchell (ed.), *Edward Thomas Three Plays, House of America, Flowers of the Dead Red Sea, East from the Gantry* (Bridgend: Seren Books, 1994).

Edward Thomas, *Hiraeth/Strangers in Conversation* in Phil Clark (ed.), *Act One Wales* (Bridgend: Seren Books, 1997).

Ed Thomas, *Gas Station Angel* (London: Methuen, 1998).

Charles Way

Dead Man's Hat.

Charles Way

Dead Man's Hat is a play set in the American West. That alone does not make it a 'Western'. To my mind a 'Western' contains certain stock ingredients which form part of a storytelling tradition which goes back, long before the advent of the cinema, the medium with which the Western is now generally associated.

The character of the western hero began life as a frontiersman, a trapper living in harmony with nature and the Native Americans. James Fenimore Cooper wrote *The Pioneers* in 1823, in which his 'Leatherstocking' character moved from the mountains, and took up the life of the farmer, not only living in harmony with the land but also taming it. In fiction therefore the way west was being prepared. The character of 'Leatherstocking' helped establish a philosophical view of the frontier that justified the taking of land – by presenting characters who 'found themselves' in a quasi-spiritual sense – through their experiences in the wilderness. This idea seeps into modern westerns such as *Dancing with Wolves* in which the central character escapes the Civil War and goes west to find-the frontier – but instead 'finds himself'. It is a romantic view, and contradicts the experience of many pioneers who 'found themselves' in perilous situations. It does however reflect a lasting desire for some communion with the natural world. Ironically, as we advance into the wilderness we destroy it. Thus the need for justification is very strong. Writers paved the way. The advance of agricultural settlement was a theme central to the literature of the early nineteenth century. At the heart of this was the issue of 'old forest freedom' versus the new needs of a community which must establish the sovereignty of law over the individual. The clash between individual rights and the needs of the new societies is a theme which, with its moral, cultural, economic, spiritual and political aspects, runs through many great Westerns. In Zane Grey's *Riders of the Purple Sage* (1912) the Mormons represent a strict and over-structured society, trying to dominate the mind, heart, spirit and purse strings of the beautiful Jane Withersteen. She must take them on to prove that America is the land of the free while at the same time staying morally clean. Enter Lassister – a stranger with smouldering eyes and very big guns. Lassiter represents the other side of Jane Withersteen's nature, the individual who can act unfettered by the demands of society. The only obligations he has are to a mysterious past and his horse. This theme emerges, transformed, in the classic Jack Schaefer western *Shane* (1953), in which the individual rights of homesteaders to occupy land the government has sold them contravenes the old prairie rights of Cattlemen trying to keep an open range for their stock. The 'Lassiter' character is taken over by Shane, a gunslinger caught between his past and the hope of reaching forty.

Jack Schaefer's book was made into a powerful film in 1955, the year I was born. My father said it was the best Western ever made and I have seen the film over twenty times. The story is simple and yet profound and is the basis of *Dead Man's Hat.*

SHANE and DEAD MAN'S HAT.

In the film a gunslinger, Shane (they only ever seem to have one name) rides into a valley in Wyoming and stops to water his horse at a small homestead. He stays a couple of days and helps out the farmer, Starrett. Together they take out an old root of a tree in the yard. There is heroic music to accompany this male bonding which results in the tree losing its grip on the land. Nature is subjugated for the betterment of mankind. The action is watched by a young boy who idolises the stranger, who is softly spoken, stylish and mysterious. The local cattleman is trying to force the homesteaders off the land, and they are forced eventually to hire a gunman, Wilson (played by Jack Palance), an act which ultimately condemns them in the eyes of the audience. Wilson is mean, dressed in black and quick on the draw. He enjoys killing people. Only Shane can equal his skill with a gun. One cannot help wondering if Shane too enjoys his craft, only finding fulfilment in the moment of conflict and death. Shane is drawn into the fight despite the fact that he is trying to find a place where he can live peaceably – rather like the eponymous outlaw in the film *The Outlaw Josey Wales*. This dream place seems to exist only in his, and our, imagination, in the promise of somewhere west of civilisation, toward the setting sun. In order to reach this paradise he must slay the spectre of the evil man within himself. In many Hollywood movies and in *Shane* the duality of man's nature was represented by two separate characters – Shane and Wilson. In *Dead Man's Hat* both personae exist in the one character, Clay.

Dead Man's Hat is a reworking of *Shane*, drawing also on an historical conflict known as The Johnson County War and introducing into the narrative two characters with one foot in history and one in Western Legend: James Averill and Kate Watson, also known as Cattle Kate, the only recorded white woman ever lynched in the west. She was called Cattle Kate because she ran what was euphemistically known as a 'Comfort Station' for cowboys. Legend has it that if a cowboy couldn't pay for his 'comforts' he used to rustle a cow for her instead. In this way she is reputed to have built up quite a herd.

The introduction of such a woman into the story marks a huge shift in tone from *Shane* which reflects a 1950s sensibility toward sex and human motivation. *Dead Man's Hat* in contrast is cynical rather than elegiac. The characters are motivated by psychological maelstroms, sex, power and politics, all of which are dimly present in *Shane*, but never examined. In *Shane* narrative is everything. This is not so in *Dead Man's Hat*, which gains power the slower the action goes, allowing us into the inner worlds of the characters. The pre-pubescent boy who idolises Shane in the film, becomes Anne, a seventeen-year old girl who would like to get out of the valley. The homestead, in which Starrett's wife bakes a huge apple pie for the 'good gunslinger', becomes a converted brothel or 'comfort station'. Starrett, the hard working but uneducated farmer, becomes Jim, liberal and apt to quote Walt Whitman at any opportunity. His philosophical allegiance drives him west, and thus to his death. Shane himself becomes Clay, a killer who hears voices in his head, who can be charming or deadly, who can be anything the other characters and indeed the audience want him to be. Cattle Kate, Jim and Anne hope that he will help in their conflict with the cattlemen. These men, represented in *Dead Man's Hat* by Quinnel, are not like the cowmen in *Shane*, but are more powerful, omnipresent businessmen who ply their trade in Washington and New York.

And as for Clay, he does not save the family as in *Shane*, but destroys it from the inside, despite the fact that to belong to a family is the one thing he desires above all else.

Shane is a narrative told in flashback. Jack Schaefer's story is already made into myth by the narrator. He can draw an image of Shane, not as he really was but as the narrator remembers him. In doing so the book acts as a conduit for the collective American memory of the West which is more persuasive than any reality. In *Dead Man's Hat* the narrator is Anne, not a bystander to the action but someone centrally involved and affected by it. The violence in *Shane* is ultimately cleansing, despite the fact that Shane has to move on in order to fulfil his mythic function. Violence in *Dead Man's Hat* is not so liberating.

Westerns are a genre in which violence is generally acceptable and in the revenge tradition often redeeming. Within the first five minutes of *Dead Man's Hat* the audience witness Clay shoot another man in the back. This sets up a working tension between expectation and reality. Clay's position in the narrative marks him out as the 'Hero' and the audience is interestingly inclined to forget what they have actually seen. They want him to fulfil the needs of the story they bring in their hearts and minds.The play operates by deliberately exciting this need and confusing it. The audience share their expectations of Clay with Anne, the storyteller. She fills Clay with her own hopes and dreams. He is Anne's American Dream. When Clay turns out to be her nemesis, not her saviour, she is forced to kill him. This act does not release her however – it is not redemptive – it is tragic and debilitating, because she also loves him. The story is told from the porch of her house where the main action took place forty-three years previously. She has never moved on. She is trapped by the past.

The Past

The story of *Dead Man's Hat* is released by the arrival of a young man called Dickson who wants to find out about the past. He is writing a history of the west – but is more interested in trying to find out what happened to his grandfather. In short, he is searching for his identity. He hears Anne's story and is moved by it, but one wonders how he will interpret it. Is it the history or the myth that gives him a sense of self that he will find useful? At the end of the play he is given the theatrical symbols of Clay's past – the white hat, the buckskin suit and the fancy guns – a circus outfit. When he puts on the white hat which Clay shot his grandfather for – and smiles – the audience often laugh recognising the need for the myth.I find it one of the more sinister moments in the play, but I laugh too. One senses that young Mister Dickson will ride off on his bike toward Hollywood where he will write a plot outline for a movie that one day will become *Shane*.

Play as Metaphor.

The best Westerns are always metaphors. *High Noon* is seen as an examination of fear in McCarthy's America of communist witch hunting. The trouble with metaphors is that sometimes people just don't get it. It requires of the audience a way of seeing and thinking about art, about stories and symbols and why the story is being told. In countries with repressive governments the use of metaphor becomes a means of dissent. Arthur Miller's *The Crucible* was popular in China just prior to the democratic rising in Tiananmen Square. The audience recognised the metaphor. In the television age popular drama such as *Eastenders* eschews metaphor with great success. It's about what it's about – its open, accessible and powerful. I hope that *Dead Man's Hat* can be enjoyed as a straightforward tale of love and revenge, but I would also describe it as a metaphor. A metaphor for what? It's a metaphor for the way we – non-Americans – perceive and use and interpret America and its culture.

I have ambiguous feelings about the power of American culture which dominated, through Westerns, my boyhood imagination. I saw more of Monument Valley than of Scotland or Wales. The culture was loud, attractive and always harked back to a time of wide open spaces and a clear moral view of the world. Later, as a teenager, Westerns also helped politicise me. The myth of America as the 'Good Guys' imploded with the Vietnam conflict, and some Westerns reflected the anti-war feeling. *Soldier Blue* graphically showed an Indian massacre in which the American flag was seen proudly flying over a scene of murder, rape and infanticide. This was not a time for myth, but for a new reality.

And yet the myth always seems to reassert itself, fulfilling some deep need in us for archetypes, and storylines that are not burdened by social reality. (See Sharon Stone in *The Quick and the Dead.*) The idea that the

American character was forged on the frontier has long been rejected in favour of complex theories of social development concentrated in the highly populated cities of the east. This was the market for stories about the West and its great opportunities. In *Dead Man's Hat* the myth, and indeed America itself, is represented by Clay, simultaneously attractive and corrupting – a man who lives for the opportunity life throws his way without moral unease.

If Clay represents American culture then the other characters represent ways of seeing and dealing with American culture. Jim represents the failure of liberals to see clearly the power of the forces against them. He completely misreads Clay's nature:

> *Jim: He's a good man Anne. Straight out of the great glowing west is our Clay. But don't get to liking him too much, because he'll leave one day the same as he came.*[1]

This does not mean that Jim is a weak character, or that liberalism is a useless political position. Jim is the person most people identify with and his early death within the play comes as a shock. His nature and his fate highlight the moral dilemma America and the West have about freedom. How do you protect freedom and people like Jim, without using the weapons which will turn you into everything you hate in your enemy? This is very much at the heart of *Shane*, whose hero utters the evergreen cliché 'A gun is as good or as bad as the man who uses it'. *Shane* was written when America was the most powerful nation in the world, armed with the atomic weapons to be Sheriff of the World, but also shouldering the guilt of Hiroshima. Jim loathes guns and sees them as the curse of the nation. He is ready to 'shake hands with the devil' and use guns if he has to, but his inner belief in the dream of free land and fresh starts leads to a romanticism which allows Clay to creep up, quite literally, and murder him. His wife, however, sees the darkness or coldness in Clay. She is more realistic about life but has also bought into Jim's dream – our own dream – and she does not understand the power of the new force in the land, which is capital. She cannot believe, therefore, that a man she once knew (Quinnel) has become a businessman capable of ordering the death of people he once worked with, but who now stand in his way.

Play as Narrative Theatre.

I have recently directed a production of *Dead Man's Hat* and was struck by the difficulty the play presents in being both a narrative epic and a psychological drama. The former demands pace, so that the story does not lose shape; the latter needs space, time for the actors to play the scenes, moment by moment. Eventually, the production veered towards the psychological approach, allowing time for the tension to build, and because of the construction of the play the story seemed to hold its own. It also gave us time to create a sequence of filmic images that affects the audience in a subliminal way.

Not long ago, I heard it said that narrative theatre was dead. I have yet to see the corpse. The drive in an artist to create a structured narrative, rather than deliberately break down form, probably comes from the same psychological root, and is not contradictory. It is a matter of artistic choice and intent, which reflects different ways of understanding the world. I'm rather suspicious of art that is random, in which, from a critical point of view, the only thing that matters is how each individual receives the art and the intention of the artist is not up for debate, because he or she was not conscious of it. I struggle to achieve form, structure, because art is not life. Life, I perceive to be disparate, unfair and illogical, where death strikes the good and the bad without discernment. In my plays to date (and this is not to say I will hold this view forever) I strive for order in the universe, not in content – since bad things happen in my plays, sometime without clear meaning – but in the way the story is told, in the form, in the act of theatre. Writing plays is somehow compensatory, a chance to talk back, to re-order, a right to reply. In *Dead Man's Hat* I am re-ordering the influences of childhood and in its 'story' form I am trying to create something which is not transitory, not fractured, not disparate. The enjoyable irony and tension in *Dead Man's Hat* comes from the fact that its central male character has the opposite view. He would like to break out of the play and shoot me dead, because structure runs opposite to his dream of freedom.

The story, once set in motion, has to go the way it goes: there is a kind of inevitability which writers who feel the world differently from myself will consciously struggle to break. In doing so, they will inevitably create a new structure, to be deconstructed by someone else. I am interested in this but not drawn towards the process for its own sake. Older forms of 'telling' seem to have a strong hold on me.

There is a 'Greekness' in the inevitability of the tragedy and the use of myth in *Dead Man's Hat*, and this leads to possible accusations of conservatism. But 'The point of any myth is to provide a known element as a starting point and preserve us from the vacuum of absolute novelty'[2], as Eric Bentley has noted.

Each of the characters in *Dead Man's Hat*, gives off a sense of impending doom that is more than their own. What is doomed is not just them, but their idea of America:

> *Jim:* *The government sold this land to all these homesteads along the river, and if you think we're going to let a handful of crooked, powerful men throw us off you are wrong. An' you know why, Frank? Cos that ain't the kind of country we want to live in.*[3]

The difference between Greek and Modern drama is that in a Greek drama fate is used to describe whatever is outside men and women. In *Dead Man's Hat*, fate resides in both; it is inside the characters, but also in the landscape itself, the sunsets, the wind, the wilderness.

The conservative form is one which the audience are at ease with, in which they are lulled into a sense of security by their own expectations, particularly when the play is performed in a non-theatre venue. In *Dead Man's Hat* I am trying to have my Western and eat it, because the content is quietly subversive and bleak, while the form is recognisable and enjoyable. This isn't new; Sergio Leone's brilliant film *Once Upon a Time in the West* uses form and content as warring factions, not partners. This even went into casting. The American public were shocked to see Henry Fonda, so often representing liberal America, cast as the villain. His first act in the film is to murder a child. This produces in the audience an inner conflict, which I try to harness in *Dead Man's Hat*, the notion being that the drama does not truly happen on stage but in the consciousness of the audience. I explored this idea more fully in a recent play, *The Dove Maiden,* (Hijinx Theatre 1996). This is a play about denial, which takes the form of a Russian folk tale to explore the moral turmoil in the mind of a soldier (Petrushka) who believes himself to be the hero of the tale, a belief he shares with the audience. As the story unfolds it becomes clear to him and to them that he has committed some terrifying acts of ethnic violence, which he has blocked out from his mind. Or has he? The problem for the audience is that this character is genuinely likeable and surely a folk tale is a safe place for an evening's entertainment – don't they always end well? Form and content are being played off against each other.

Dead Man's Hat and *The Dove Maiden* both take a steady gaze at the presence of 'evil'. In both plays it becomes a palpable force – a force that I approach consciously through story rather than naturalism. A narrative drama must first create a spell, which binds an audience into the heart of the play by committing them, not only to the outcome of the story, but more crucially, to the meaning of the outcome. In *Dead Man's Hat* this works by a clear invitation to the audience to listen to a story, an old trick, but psychologically a comfortable place to be. The actors, rather than the characters, lead the audience into the heart of the play, as if through a series of doors, transporting the audience from the venue to the play, and thus to the themes. The opening pages illustrate the theatrical language that will be employed throughout the evening. It is not social realism. It involves music, sound, image, movement and so on. A contract is made between the audience, the actors and the play. An actress who is obviously not sixty years old tells us that she is, and begins to conjure up for us images of her past. Within a few moments a play within a play begins that takes us back in time to the place of the main action. By the time Clay arrives, circa 1892, and the actress playing Anne has told us she is now sixteen-years old, a spell should have been woven. It is perfectly legitimate to create such a spell and then break it, thus challenging the audience in a different way. Here I choose not to break the spell. The play continues to build itself, and each building block carries an extra layer of complexity. The play accumulates meaning and resonance as the story unfolds. Narrative is about structural eloquence, it is about not allowing story threads or character traits to outstay their welcome, it is about the themes being carried by the whole structure and not shoved into the mouth of one character.

Play as Psychological Drama.

I have in press notes described *Dead Man's Hat* as a psychological western. I am now forced to confront what this means since all art must have a psychological root, conscious or not. I assume that it is all about motive, and the connection between my motives as playwright, the characters' motives and the audience's understanding of both. It is as if the stage were a physical representation of my mind and the struggles that exist on it are therefore the struggles which exist in my mind. The play is a debate with myself – a struggle for clarity which I endeavour to share with the audience in an entertaining fashion. This play has its roots in my childhood and I am using material I was exposed to before I had the intellectual means to decode it. This does not mean that the play is therapy – it is theatre.

Society is reflected within the play by the characters, who are motivated by sex, money, politics, culture, law, everything in fact that makes up 'society'. The characters themselves are not in control of the action; events happen and the psychological make-up of each character forces the action into a particular shape. Narrative theatre therefore is not about writing-by-numbers. It is about providing a structure for the inner struggles of each character. Each, like myself, is involved in an inner debate which the audience sense and are held by. What does each character want? Are they going to achieve their desires, and at what cost? These are the questions that keep an audience in their seats and any number of empty action-scenes unsupported in this way will eventually bore them. The playwright's job is to throw as many obstacles in the path of the characters' objectives, frustrating and giving meaning to their desires. From this comes the storyline, the journey.

An actor playing Clay has to draw up his own psychological profile of the character. There are clues, but no blueprints. It is possible that Clay is a schizophrenic, and therefore out of touch with reality. Such unknowability in *Dead Man's Hat* is not, however, a medical proposition but a philosophical one. It is a reflection of the human condition, a lostness. What matters is how Clay tries to make sense of himself in the world, in the universe:

> Clay *It don't matter, Frank. What you or me, say or do 'cos, it'll all be lost on the wind by tomorrow. That's the truth, Frank – nothing matters 'cos we're all just passin' through – an' none of us is happy in our skins. And the moment you know that – there's nothing to be or belong to you can be free. Hell, its a free country.*[4]

Clay is connected to an idea, born out of the myth of the frontier (which ironically was officially pronounced closed in 1892, the year the action takes place). Beyond the frontier is a place where morality is meaningless in any social sense because the law/society cannot reach you. Whatever you do means nothing. Because there are no consequences you can ride away and reinvent yourself. This is also what Shane desires. In one sense it is a reflection of paradise – an American utopia – forever a land of fresh starts. Clay is therefore maladjusted to the reality of the new society with its schools, churches and courts, but perfectly adapted to the myth of that society. Therefore he has contradictory voices in his head, telling him to ride on and yet settle down. This is his maelstrom and the source of the tragedy in *Dead Man's Hat*.

Cinema.

Part of the fun of *Dead Man's Hat*, for audience and actors, is in trying to find a theatrical language for a cinematic genre. Cinema has changed the way people receive stories and they are used to fast, short scenes and flashback structures. Cinema has influenced the way plays are written. There are many images in *Dead Man's Hat* that are designed to trigger the filmic memory of the audience. Actors in the play often say that they can see themselves as if in the film. They can recall many films with an evening scene on the porch, a campfire scene, and of course a shootout. I have tried to weave these clichés together, piling one on top of another so that – combined with the use of familiar western talk such as'You start walking or I'll start shootin' – the style becomes pure cliché, an art form in its own right. The story should be gripping enough to stop it becoming pastiche or parody.

There are of course no horses in *Dead Man's Hat*, only saddles. But, like the movies, we do have music. Music and song in *Dead Man's Hat* provide the audience with a soundscape which is both emotional and pictorial, replacing the wide open spaces of the movies themselves. It is also a storytelling mechanism and can describe the action of a group of cowboys pulling up fences and allow the story to flow between place and time like a film, without the play having to stop. I hate plays that stop. I hate watching stage managers in black, reordering the furniture between scenes as if they were not really there. Every moment is significant because it can enlarge the theme of the play, and if content and form are linked then the way you get from one scene to another is important. Some playwrights leave this to the director, but I think that the theatre writer needs to have a good grasp of this spacial stage craft. This is nothing to do with stage directions. Nor does it mean the director must follow the stage directions. I don't include many stage directions and the ones that do exist are there for the reader – to make sense of the play, in the first instance. What distinguishes playwriting from other forms of writing is the need to be aware of the notion and potential of 'the empty space', as proposed by Peter Brook. In this space, words have a physical reality, they can hang in the air. They are given weight by silence. And yet they are only part of the potential of total theatre, which combines narrative, music, movement, light and sound. None of these elements can be ignored by the playwright. He or she is a creator of possibilities.

The music for *Dead Man's Hat* is written by Tom Nordon, and he has used old ballad forms to construct music which helps tell the story, reaching into an emotional landscape which might otherwise be unobtainable. The song 'Oh it's hard on this land', works on several layers. It is personal to Anne, and yet carries the weight of the play in lyric and music. The narrative may appear on paper to stop but the emotional story and overall theme of the play is being developed:

Anne: *Oh its hard*
On this land
To make a living I know
It raises your hopes
Then it brings 'em down low
An' it don't give a damn
For right or for wrong
The land looks away
As we struggle along.

Chorus: *Oh the West, oh the West*
Where the wild winds blows
Nobody knows, nobody knows
Nobody knows.[5]

Other songs work within the action, notably the wedding song, 'That Sweet Little Gal', a traditional ballad during which the wedding scene is set up. Much interplay can happen between the characters during this scene. The story does not stop. The verses themselves are all about romantic hopes and desires which in one moment support the action and in the next act in juxtaposition to it.

The use of song in *Dead Man's Hat* comes out of many years of working in the community theatre in Wales in the nineteen-eighties, with small groups of professional actors touring plays to village halls, community centres and working clubs. The companies developed skills as actors and musicians to tell stories to audiences who often had more direct reference to Music Hall and Variety than to theatre. Music was a populist form that linked the two worlds. Intellectually, the companies took much inspiration from the direct approach of Brecht to the use of song in plays. There is in *Dead Man's Hat* a strong Brechtian influence, particularly in the saloon scene where a ballad begins and ends the action as if the gunfight itself were part of the song. In the most recent production, I have rewritten this song so that the published version disappears. It is now a song which a saloon singer could have actually sung. It still comments upon the action, but in a more integral way.

The Future.

Despite the fact that I have now spent some several thousand words chewing over the nature of this play, I actually do not make any claims for it. That is up to others, and the play has provoked wildly different critical responses. All I can say is that it has still, after five years, the power to hold an audience for two hours in very uncomfortable seats without the benefit of great special effects. That is something that gives me satisfaction. But I am not satisfied. When directing the play I was able to look at the moments which seemed to need more work – and this would be ongoing, because each production stresses different elements of the story. A production has yet to happen which is large enough to capitalise visually on the play's potential. The play can be performed by five actors, making it seem like a small scale piece – but there are eleven speaking parts. The challenge would be in retaining the intimacy of the storytelling format.

Nor do I set its chosen way of telling above any other forms of theatrical expression. This is not a disclaimer. It is a belief in a culture strong enough to absorb and explore a whole range of theatrical forms, not just plays, but not to the exclusion of plays, either. What interests me at present is further adventures between text, movement, sound and image. I said recently to a designer that the play could be designed as if it were a dance piece. Most designers in small scale theatre are hindered by the need to raise the action so that the audience can actually see what is going on, and the notion of the empty space therefore has less potential. Several more recent works (notably, *The Dove Maiden*) moved in this direction under the influence of Theatre de Complicité and Cheek by Jowl. In Wales, because of a lack of theatre criticism, the experiment went largely unnoticed and one feels driven back to more conventional forms.

What, then, as a playwright in Wales would I ideally wish for? For several years I was able to work with Hijinx theatre in Cardiff, creating theatre in which every element was given full attention. The plays wove narrative, music, movement, dance and design into 'miniature gems'. This was possible because of the attention given to the creative process and desire to release each person's creative potential. It created small scale, total theatre. The opportunity still exists to continue and develop the process on a larger scale, creating a company which is mature, strongly led and the equal of companies that have been given a larger canvas to work on, and are now known throughout the world.

Notes

1 Brian Mitchell (ed.), *Charles Way, Three Plays: Dead Man's Hat, Paradise Drive, In the Bleak Midwinter* (Bridgend: Seren Books, 1994), p. 35. Hereafter cited as *Charles Way, Three Plays*.
2 Eric Bentley, *The Life of the Drama* (New York: Atheneum, 1979), p. 53.
3 *Charles Way, Three Plays*, p. 40.
4 Ibid., p. 80.
5 Ibid., pp. 59-60.

Charles Way

(Photo: Simon Chapman)

On the Black Hill (1986)

On the Black Hill (1986)
(Photo: Phil Cutts)

On the Black Hill (1986)
(Photo: Phil Cutts)

Paradise Drive (1989)

(Photo: Keith Morris)

Paradise Drive (1989)

(Photo: Keith Morris)

In the Bleak Midwinter (1990)
(Photo: Brian Tarr)

In the Bleak Midwinter (1990)
(Photo: Brian Tarr)

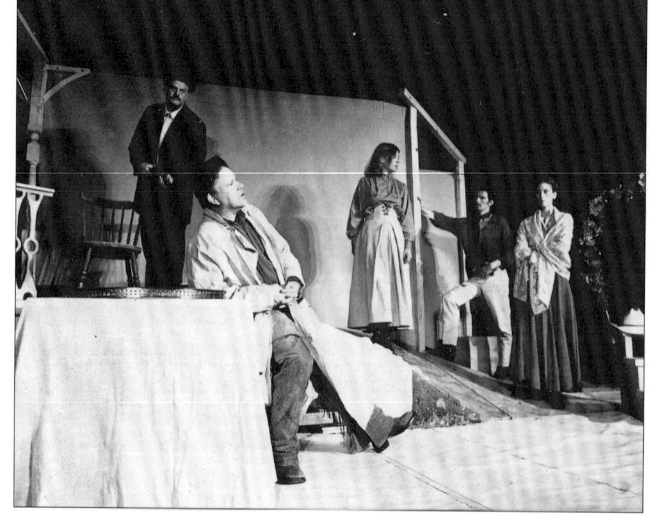

Dead Man's Hat (1997)
(Photo: Brampton Studios)

Dead Man's Hat (1997)
(Photo: Brampton Studios)

Dead Man's Hat (1997)
(Photo: Brampton Studios)

Eye of the Storm (1995)
(Photo: Brampton Studios)

The Search for Odysseus (1993)
(Photo: Brian Tarr)

The Search for Odysseus (1993)
(Photo: Brian Tarr)

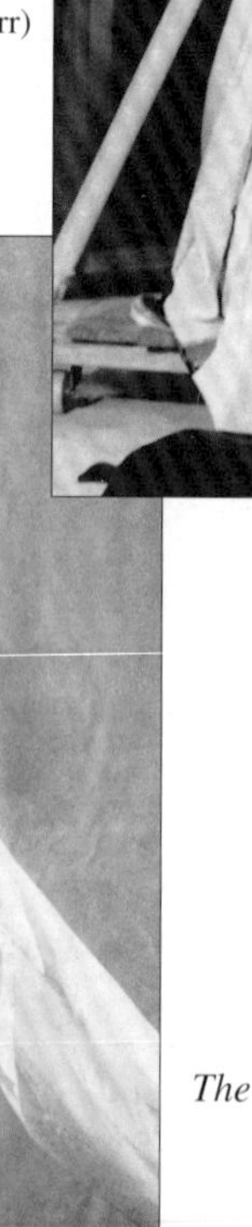

The Search for Odysseus (1993)
(Photo: Brian Tarr)

Ill Met by Moonlight (1994)
(Photo: Brian Tarr)

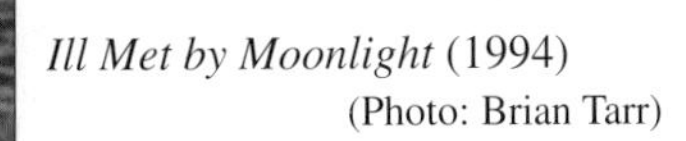

Ill Met by Moonlight (1994)
(Photo: Brian Tarr)

The Dove Maiden (1996)
(Photo: Brian Tarr)

Charles Way: *Dead Man's Hat* workshop, Theatr y Werin, Aberystwyth (1997)

Charles Way's Professional Journey

David Adams

(1)

It is a cold, late autumn evening and while earlier even the bleak beauty of the Glamorgan Heads of the Valleys heights was muddied by a dirty drizzle it has now become particularly dismal. In the functional community centre of a post-industrial village a troupe of actors entertain a packed and attentive audience, most of whom will be here for the bingo tomorrow night and were here for the jumble sale on Saturday. The play is performed in a range of acting styles with some emotional moments and some humour and some songs. The story is about a family trying to cope with their life over the previous ten years: a father who has probably been unfaithful, a daughter who escapes by marrying someone she doesn't love, a son who feels undervalued as an artist and kills himself, a wife and mother who tries to keep it all together.

The time is November 1989 and Margaret Thatcher has been in power for ten years; the play, *Paradise Drive*, is a commemoration of the fact. It could offer more depression, and certainly little comfort, to an audience who have suffered in economic and social terms as the fictional family in the play has. The lives they see portrayed may not be directly recognisable – an entrepreneurial daughter, an artist, a middle-class family who have bought a villa in Spain – but there is little doubt that they represent for this demoralised, bereft, abused, demeaned community of a once-thriving working-class mining centre, the downward spiral of fragmented despair initiated by Thatcherism.

This is a gritty but poetic kind of social realism. What is important is that it is essentially about the lives of those in the audience, that somewhere in the pessimism is a shout of hope based on the power of the collective spirit. It is a far from typical example of community theatre in terms of its poetry, its obliqueness. But in many ways it has all the other ingredients: an audience-friendly presentation, an inclusivity, a mix of drama and music, laughter and tears, an assumption of shared values and political perspectives.

In this production by Hijinx Theatre, which played in dozens of such community venues, the relationship between drama and audience, the function of the drama, the situation of the audience, is one that is archetypal, but it is in particular that of a form that was theatre in Britain until the flowering of humanistic Renaissance theatre. It is essentially medieval theatre, the ironic title echoing the Biblical theme of the loss of innocence familiar from the mystery cycles: allegorical struggles of Good and Evil, moral tales, examples of sinfulness and repentance, pedagogy, performed in a mix of the vernacular and the poetic, direct, accessible – 'a good night out' with a message. The popular and populist tradition of carnival, the mystery, miracle, folk and morality plays and interludes is replicated in present-day community theatre. And just as critics have spurned the medieval drama and insisted on seeing it mainly as an historical and social phenomenon, so some mistakenly relegate late twentieth-century community theatre to the status of non-literary non-durable cultural expression.

Unusually and surprisingly for such an ancient European culture, there is in Wales no tradition of professional theatre provision, and theatre here only properly got off the ground with the establishment of county-based Community and Theatre-in-Education companies in the 1970s. Three of the four playwrights discussed in this book have been closely associated with these companies, but Charles Way was there at the very beginning, turning out populist plays for Gwent Theatre, seven between 1980 and 1984. Twenty years later he is still associated with Hijinx, another and very different community theatre company, for whom he has written five plays, although there is a world of difference between, say, *Humbug* (1980) and *The Dove Maiden* (1996). He has also been associated with large-scale community plays (a genre quite different from community theatre, the latter being plays professionally performed in the community, the former plays professionally produced for performance by the community) in Cardiff and Monmouth as well as the West Country. He has been particularly committed to work with young people, writing children's plays, working for BBC Education and latterly as writer-in-residence with the Sherman Youth Theatre in Cardiff, and he has several awards for his work in this area. He has written extensively for radio and television, including a film-poem for BBC2. He has also worked with Made in Wales Stage Company, Theatr Clwyd, Diversions Dance and the Welsh National Opera as well as the community/TIE companies Spectacle, Theatr Iolo and Theatr Powys. Outside Wales he has had his work performed by Buster YPT, Dukes Playhouse, Lancaster TIE, Library Theatre Manchester, Mercury Theatre, Leeds TIE, M6, Polka Theatre, Rent a Role Theatre, SNAP, Theatre Centre, Theatre Royal Stratford East, Tyne and Wear Theatre, Unicorn, Wilde Theatre and ZAP; he has a long-term relationship with Orchard Theatre and Perspectives (now New Perspectives). His plays have been produced in Wales, England, Russia, South Africa, Germany and Canada. He has adapted Charles Dickens, R. D. Blackmore, Bruce Chatwin, The Bible, Greek myth, Arthur Ransome, Dannie Abse, Mary Shelley and Shakespeare. Today he has taken a renewed interest in directing and suspects that television may be the most appropriate medium for his plays. His full biography makes impressive reading.

Charles Way is a product of community theatre practice, a prime exponent of it, but he is also a playwright who has exploited the qualities and conventions to create a corpus of work that retains the values but transcends the impermanence of community theatre. Yet as an individual he is all but invisible; his work may not in any obvious regard be about Welshness, his politics are never worn on the sleeve, he has never been trendy, never been called radical, does not deal in controversy. He is not Welsh (he was born in Devon), speaks no Welsh, has lived in the quiet border town of Abergavenny since 1980; he comes from a middle-class background and went to public school before training as an actor. He has written around sixty plays, all but three of which have been staged, and I would guess that more people in Wales have seen a Charles Way stage play than one by any other writer working here. He has also been produced in the rest of Britain more than any other living Welsh-based playwright.

The key to his success – and also the reason for his low profile – lies in his unfashionable concern to be accessible. That does not mean simplistic: his plays can be complex, subtle, elusive, metaphorical, mythic, magical. But it does mean that the audience is always present in the process of playmaking – and that the essential art of storytelling is at the core of the play. These strengths comes from his apprenticeship with, initially, Leeds Playhouse TIE (for whom he wrote his first professional play in 1978) and Theatre Centre in London, and then with Gwent Theatre. Liz, Charles Way's wife, from Aberystwyth, was an actor with Gwent Theatre and Charles Way himself was soon involved in the company's familiar devising process: the plays were varied, and of variable quality, but started with the company's brief to offer 'a good night out', coloured by the inevitable left-wing bias of all TIE/community companies, often structured around the associated predilection for Brecht's epic style, and crucially informed by the demands of the popular audience. The thousands who enjoy (and still do enjoy, despite cuts) Wales's unique provision of community theatre are not traditional theatregoers. They typically live outside urban areas and fill rural village halls, schools, community centres, pay little for subsidised tickets, sit on hard chairs, have tea and biscuits in the interval and dress up only to keep warm. The product has to be engaging, resonant, affective, not too long and premised on the belief that any political consciousness-raising came not from didacticism but from a more subtle and often unacknowledged acceptance of metaphorical meaning. Gwent Theatre, perhaps more than any other of the eight county-based TIE/community companies, was careful not to preach to audiences or to disrupt too much: the shows had to work first and foremost as entertainment.

The experience was to inform Charles Way's playwriting for the next decade and beyond. Community theatre, crucially, is *about* something – sometimes basic issues, as in young people's theatre, sometimes immediate social matters, sometimes broader concerns. Thus *Inner City Limits* (1980) was specifically about the Toxteth Riots; the unperformed *Black Parlour* (1984) and the play *Hitting Home* (1986) were about the miners' strike; two short radio plays, *The Old Country* and *A Journey in Hell* (both 1986), were about the famine in Ethiopia; *Paradise Drive* (1989) concerned the effects of ten years of Thatcherism; *In the Bleak Midwinter* (1990) touched on the Poll Tax, and *The Dove Maiden* (1996) was indirectly, but essentially, about Bosnia; *Humbug* (1980), adapted from Dickens's *A Christmas Carol*, was about the evils of capitalism, *She Scored for Wales* (1981), based on Aristophanes's *Lysistrata*, about sexism; *In Living Memory* (1983) about the spirit of community in Gwent's mining villages; *Behind the Lines* (1983) about the power of the press; *Bread and Roses* (1983) was about the Spanish Civil War and the need to combat fascism today; *Witness* (1985), about the Rosenbergs, also concerned the demonisation of trade unions in Tory Britain; *Trade Winds* (1998) was about young people and their job prospects, and *Playing from the Heart* (1998) about Evelyn Glennie. Not one of them, despite the issue basis, not even the sometimes crude populist early plays for Gwent, is a message-play that foregrounds the politics at the expense of theatricality or storytelling.

And, although plays like *Paradise Drive* get pretty close to domestic drama – albeit in a knowing, ironic way – none is straightforward naturalism. While community theatre may be about something, it rejects mainstream bourgeois-theatre conventions, and the plays in general are a fascinating catalogue of innovative stagecraft techniques that exploit the necessities of the form: doubling-up, songs, audience involvement, in-view scene changing, cross-genre experimentation, topical references. The community theatre aesthetic still applies, whether it is a small-scale production like *The Dove Maiden*, a sweeping main-stage epic like *On the Black Hill*, a musical like *Sweeney Todd* or a large-scale play for young people and professional actors like the latest, *Carlo's Luck*.

Charles Way's professional journey from issue plays to the more philosophical spiritual work of the nineties is one I want to track. But the range and volume of his output are so big that I intend being selective and specific: in terms of the playwright's role to make theatre mediate reality I will look at what is special about the work, not so much in terms of form, but in terms of content and audience. Where his theatre is *located* is of the essence.

(2)

Just to discuss Charles Way as an outstanding writer of children's plays would take a chapter. In the past few years he has won awards or nominations for Best Children's Play from the Writers' Guild for *Sleeping Beauty*, *The Search for Odysseus* and *A Spell of Cold Weather* and, in a genre where the work is often regarded as ephemeral and disposable, he has had his plays taken up and restaged year after year. Of his impressive output, twenty are stage plays specifically for children, fourteen television or radio programmes, nine are adaptations; but I want to discuss the rest, most of which are set in non-urban locations and generally are about non-urban communities.

I want both to explore how the work of this prolific and underrated playwright is in the direct tradition of popular theatre, with its roots in medieval drama, and to explore what I think is the most distinctive of the playwright's qualities: as the mediator of the ordinary, non-metropolitan people, the working class of the rural areas of Devon and Wales and of the industrial valleys of Gwent. He is, of course, not working-class himself, neither by birth nor by profession, but he is undeniably not an elitist; he has, of course, written works that are not about life outside the city – indeed, *Inner City Limits* was specifically set in Liverpool and *A Song of Streets* was the community opera of Splott – but the urban landscape is not his natural milieu.

Of the four playwrights discussed in this volume, Charles Way is the only one brought up and still electing to live in the country (Abergavenny is, after all, a very small market town). Dic Edwards and Greg Cullen both moved to the country from cities, and Ed Thomas moved from the country to the city. Charles Way's work, it seems to me, is deeply rooted in non-metropolitan values and experiences to an extent that no other playwright's is that I can think of, in Wales or England. He has a rural sensibility, he writes often for rural audiences, he is little concerned with urban issues – and that is a rarity.

I think Charles Way now sees himself as a Border person, someone very aware of living in an area of Wales that in some ways is not deeply Welsh, certainly where little Welsh is spoken and where issues of Welshness have little resonance, somewhere he sees

> The English and the Welsh
> like an old married couple
> pulling the blankets off each other's back
> jostling for space
> kissing and cursing
> in the long bed of history[1]

– not a very hard-line political perspective, but very 'Borders'. Perhaps *Dead Man's Hat* (as the author hints in his own essay on the play in this volume) is in some ways about Wales: the invention of tradition, the reinvention of a culture, the otherness of those over the border, and so on;

but these are not foregrounded in the narrative or the metaphorical subtext. His rugby players and wives in *She Scored for Wales* are recognisably Welsh but their fight is universal (it was, after all, based on a Greek satire); the same can be said for his striking miners and their communities. The shepherds of *In the Bleak Midwinter* come from Old Radnor and speak more like Herefordians than Welsh people; the characters of *Ill Met By Moonlight* may joke about Anglo-Welsh (indeed, Hereford-Welsh) rivalries but are actually also not very Welsh and the folklore with which the play is imbued is drawn from Herefordshire tradition; *Bordertown* is about Monmouth, a town notorious for its political ambivalence but probably more English than Welsh. His work, then, inhabits that area described in Bruce Chatwin's *On The Black Hill* – Charles Way's adaptation of which was a great success for Made in Wales and Theatr Clwyd in the mid-Eighties. Slightly extended from the valleys of the Wye, Monnow and Usk to the Rhymney, the Ebbw and the Sirhowy, it is an area of rolling hills and now-derelict coal mines, of farms and rows of terraced houses, of market towns and heritage sites, of Raymond Williams and Arthur Machen and Idris Davies and W.H. Davies – and not so far from Dennis Potter and Leonard Clarke. I used to live a few miles over the border from Charles Way's home in Abergavenny and I would challenge anyone to tell by accent, language, culture, landscape or tradition where the boundary between Monmouthshire and Herefordshire lies – except from bilingual road signs.

That is not to say that there is no division – but it is one, the dramatist suggests, that is negotiated by the people and the landscape. The spirit of place for the most part is implicit in the plays but in the recent *No Borders* (1997), a piece written as a television 'film-poem' for BBC 2, he deals in more depth with the idea. The lines quoted above are from the opening section, where he describes birth as 'the first border breached' and in the section on schooldays he asks

> What unseen border in our souls
> must be traversed
> before our sense of belonging
> becomes a sword
> we turn against our closest friend?[2]

And the dichotomy is not just one of nationalism but of modern identity, where tourists have changed the nature of towns like Monmouth, Hay, Knighton and Abergavenny:

> On a Monday afternoon
> the rain slides down a border town
> (the eyes of commerce, closed)
> and the church bell tolls the hours
> across an empty market square.

> This is the borderland of farmhouse B&Bs
> waitresses in black and white,
> in hushed tea rooms,
> waiting for the dying light
> to send them back to clubland.[3]

But essentially he sees it as a welcoming place, this Borderland:

> Here it's true that radical
> is next to ridicule
> but the border has long been home
> for those on the fringes of acceptability.
> Preachers, poets, painters, lovers and
> authors of every description
> find refuge here,
> breathing the soft air of tolerance . . .[4]

It is, he concludes,

> A generous forgiving landscape
> where the rich concoction
> of temperament, climate and history
> is bold enough to take in all who come,
> until they belong to the place
> and the idea of the place
> and all its possible lives.[5]

That, really, is Charles Way. A rural man, a simple man, a tolerant man who is nevertheless fired by injustice and angered by intolerance.

Both *Ill Met By Moonlight* and *A Spell of Cold Weather*, written in 1994 and 1995 respectively, are set on the Welsh borders and feature local folklore, notably mischievous Puckish spirits, Gwarwyn-a-Throt in *Ill Met by Moonlight* and Tomos Trickman in *A Spell of Cold Weather*. Both represent the sense of collaboration between mankind and nature but in the first, a family show for Hijinx, the spirit, a cantankerous force for good and evil, is about to disappear with the coming of modern farming, and in the second, a children's play for Theatre Centre and The Sherman Theatre, the spirit wins over a couple of farmers who have lost their sense of fun, with the magic literally gone out of their lives. Both fairy characters come from the same group based on a Tom-type name – Trwtyn-Tratyn is another Welsh variant – the first exclusive, it seems, to Monmouthshire and Herefordshire.

The specialness of the rural border country, and in a country which is itself on the Celtic edge, is not just evident in the tolerance of the people, the landscape and the folklore. It is an in-between-land. 'A place . . . has the power to change a personality, to bring out the best or worst in us,' says a character in *Ill Met By Moonlight*. In a very different play, *Dead Man's Hat*, we see the same message: the Wild West, frontier country, land of myth and movie, but also a very real locale, impacts on the characters in different ways. The play, based on the film *Shane*, has particular resonances in Wales, as I suggested above, although it was written for Orchard Theatre, a Devon company, and last toured the Midlands. It is an allegory of freedom and capitalism, of individualism and collective responsibility. A stranger, a gunslinger, appears to defend a remote poor homestead against the incursions of the neighbouring greedy landowner but proves to be more morally ambivalent than the celluloid good-guy. There are, in fact, no heroes in this story, although we have again, as in *In the Bleak Midwinter*, a couple who represent the (female) pragmatic realist and (male) naive liberal idealist – opposites found also in medieval drama, notably in the division of the whole person into polarised attitudes represented by God and the Devil. The contradictions are symbolised by the earth itself, both unforgiving and supportive:

> Oh the land
> Is a killer so cold[6]

while under the disturbing challenges to tradition there are the stable images familiar from Westerns and musicals:

> The farmer is the man
> Lives on credit till the fall
> But if you'll only look and see
> I think you will agree
> That the farmer is the man that feeds them all[7]

they sing, in a refrain that would be supported by most audiences in rural Wales. The land of *Dead Man's Hat*, though, is deeply unsettling; it is certainly one of the author's most intriguing and thoughtful plays, where myth, narrative, character, morals, are all subverted. This is real frontier country, a land beyond the law – a topographical version of the medieval period of Carnival, where values are turned topsy-turvey and people can wear disguises and do what they want.

(3)

It would be hopelessly nostalgic and romantic, of course, to equate the rural with the simple and thence to hark back to Fernand Braudel's *longue durée* of medieval plebeian life. But there is a timelessness about the Welsh border country, a pattern still imposed by the necessities of farming, that cannot have changed much over the centuries. Calendar customs are still celebrated in the Marches and the seasons are important and prescriptive to an extent incomprehensible to urbanites. The notion of community is different, too: in towns and cities it is all too often a sociological designation, ideological and idealistic, in rural areas it is a reality. Crucially, in our context, the rural areas of Wales and the West have been relatively untouched by sophisticated post-industrial modes of live performance: television, radio and, now, video have all become important contributions to the culture but theatre, especially in its bourgeois form and acknowledging the occasional forays into the provinces of touring companies from Shakespeare to the Unity Theatre, has played little part in mediating reality from the medieval period to the community theatre provision of the last thirty years.

In fact there was probably a wider range of live performance in rural medieval Britain than today: the miracle cycles, folk drama, carnival, morality plays, mummings, sword dances, pageants, interludes and, particularly in Wales, performances that we might not consider 'theatre' and which have become labelled as folk custom, such as the Mari Lwyd. And while the major 'mystery' cycles were confined to the cities and towns (the 'mysteries' were named after *mystères*, or guilds, which existed only among urban artisans), single plays from the cycles were, we know, performed in smaller towns and rural parishes. In broad terms, this medieval performance work is strikingly similar to what we call community theatre. The staging could involve a touring set, a booth or trestle stage; the language was vernacular, multi-register, a mix of poetry and crudity; the narrative was documentary, universal in the miracle plays, individual in the moralities; the style a non-naturalistic mix of slapstick and declamation; actors were close to and would mingle with the audience; the content could be debate, polemic or satire; the audience was popular; the purpose didactic and to entertain; in carnival, to mock and subvert authority; in interpretation, not only clerics would appreciate the four levels of literal, moral, allegorical and analogical. Today's small-scale community companies, with their set stacked in the back of a transit van, their accessibility, their ideological messages, their rejection of conventional forms and styles, their combination of music, comedy and social realism, their commitment to provide 'a good night out' while offering a multi-layered experience, would recognise that medieval theatre ethic. Performance was essentially festive and political, a celebration of collective life. The traditional view of medieval drama as something of historical interest but unworthy of serious critical attention is also an attitude community theatre practitioners would recognise.

If much contemporary community theatre is similar to medieval theatre, then Charles Way's plays can often seem a modern replication of those miracle and morality plays. The mystery cycles, dealing with stories from the scriptures, are in fact (as we shall see) used by this dramatist directly in plays like *The Flood*, *The Nativity* and *In the Bleak Midwinter*, which incorporates the story of Mak the sheep-stealer and his wife Gill from *The Second Shepherds Play*. The basis of the morality plays, that humans are sinful but that repentance is possible, and their purpose, the acknowledgement of confessions and forgiveness of sin, hence a sacrament of penance, can be seen in Charles Way's plays (as, in some ways, it can in Ibsen and Brecht, of course): Charles Way's characters are all too human, flawed, but capable of change – not so much through conventional religion but through other more humanistic processes. Stock characters like Cain, Joseph, The Wife Taken in Adultery, Mary Magdalen, are alive and well and living under assumed names in these modern moralities. The battles between Vice and Virtue are still fought, but more recently with less determinism than in his early plays and as conflicting qualities within each individual. The pedagogic morality plays, with their basis in social conditions and emphasis on addressing the problems of the young (Youth, Lusty Juventus, Nice Wanton and The Disobedient Child, for example), have their equivalent in young people's theatre today – less rigid and Calvinistic in their teaching, of course, but with a common aim of alerting the young to the perils of life. (We might note with interest that the only evidence of Welsh drama before the late 1900s consists of some medieval miracle plays and the eighteenth-century moral interludes that Twm o'r Nant and his colleagues performed at fairs. CharlesWay's work could, then, be seen to be in that fragile Welsh tradition.)

In the late Seventies and early Eighties, when Charles Way was serving his apprenticeship, albeit turning out some engaging, accessible and durable scripts, the didacticism common to medieval drama and community/TIE work drove such plays as *Humbug*, *Inner City Limits*, *She Scored for Wales*, *Bread and Roses*, *In Living Memory*, *Behind the Lines* and *Funny Boys* – all written for and devised with Gwent Theatre; it was the period, as Charles Way says today, when his work was determined by Welsh theatre provision – but good populist theatre for all that. His first play for Gwent Theatre, *Humbug* (1980), revealed his penchant for taking an original and using it rather than simply adapting it: Dickens's *A Christmas Carol* is given an ideological spin by having not Scrooge reforming but a militant Bob Cratchit realising his revolutionary potential (and I will always remember how in the interval, with Scrooge feigning sleep as we trooped out for our tea and biscuits, an old lady in the audience continually poked the actor with her umbrella until he responded !). *She Scored for Wales* (1981) similarly used a classic, though one less familiar to community audiences – *Lysistrata* – and in Dario Fo-style farcical mode had the women take action to get equality in that bastion of Valleys boyoism, the rugby club. And it was actually toured round the rugby clubrooms of Gwent.

Crucially, many of Charles Way's plays deal with specific moral issues of the day through history, allegory, memory and myth. *Bread and Roses*

(1983) was one of three plays running concurrently in South Wales that dealt with local people's participation in the Spanish Civil War, but it was by far the most potent, not least because it was not simply about history and nostalgia but about the constant need for working-class opposition to fascism. Much of the play exploited the similarity between the thirties and the eighties: local communities had experienced wage cuts, and were still reeling from the swingeing employment cuts in major industries like the all-important steel works. Fearing the drift to the extreme right they joined in unemployment marches, like the March for Jobs that followed the old Chartist route down the Valleys to Newport and on to a huge rally in Cardiff.

In the same year, *In Living Memory*, which I saw staged in a makeshift performance space in The Big Pit mining museum at Blaenavon, followed a family through three periods, in 1913, 1926 and the (then) present, 1983, with the central character starting as a young schoolgirl and ending as an old lady watching removal men pack away her history in crates before she goes to an old folks' home – an achingly poignant scene but one that had acquired even more import as what was to be the last fight by the miners was about to start in the few remaining pits in the South Wales coalfield. I recall being struck by the conflicting messages of the venue. There was obvious irony in the fact that the venue was a heritage centre converted from a working pit, albeit one where the miners' struggle was well represented. Also, to get to the show audiences – many of them people directly affected by the destruction of the coal industry, their lives a continuing battle with private and public pit owners – had to pass under the shadow of the long-stilled big wheel and through an exhibition where grainy photographic blow-ups showed posing miners whose eyes, ringed with white in the coal-black weary faces, seemed to stare out accusingly. Conceived as a play for junior schoolchildren bussed in from throughout Gwent (in the days when not only did Gwent exist as the local education authority but also paid for an ongoing comprehensive theatre-in-education provision as a necessary part of young people's education), *In Living Memory* was recognised as a play that should be seen by adults too. I confessed then, and can still recall, that it left me emotionally drained by the finely-wrought description of that battle of social values.

Plays like these, with their contemporary social relevance, the debate between good and evil, the mixture of directness and metaphor, are clearly in the popular tradition of plebeian drama that has its roots in the middle ages. Crucially, medieval drama existed only through actual performance – indeed, its value as theatre rather than as historical phenomenon has only recently been acknowledged because of performances of some of the mystery cycles. To a greater or lesser degree medieval plays may work on the page but they are patently written to be performed and not to be pored over as literature. Many of Charles Way's plays repay critical attention to the written text but for their qualities to be properly recognised all (with the exception of the television work) they have to be produced and seen as part of the collective experience of popular theatre. For example, just as the medieval mystery cycle *Second Shepherd's Play*, with its introduction of a classic comic villain in Mak the sheep-stealer and the parody of the Nativity, really needs to be seen for its dramatic muscularity to reveal itself, so *In the Bleak Midwinter*, first produced by Hijinx (directed by Ros Hutt) in 1990, came alive through its performances. It is actually a subversive challenging of Biblical assumptions and in particular of the Commandments against murder, stealing and adultery, with a conflict between idealism and realism ultimately resolved in the marriage of the two shepherds Zac and Miriam, but theatrically it is a vibrant popular knockabout comedy. Staged in the round, it opened with the cast of four singing the familiar carol 'In The Bleak Midwinter' before the actor playing Mak comes forward and addresses the audience:

> Ladies and gentlemen
> Once upon a time
> Somewhere in the Black Mountains
> Not far from Bethlehem[8]

- a witty way of associating with the local audience in just the same way the medieval original introduced Wakefield references, with here the added political piquancy of having the shepherds going to Bethlehem not for the Nativity but to register for the so-called Poll Tax, the community charge which had been introduced by the Thatcher government that year. The rural audiences of South-East Wales laughed just as the Yorkshire audiences did at the Wakefield Master's original – and both could appreciate the complaints of the shepherds at an unjust tax. The spirit of the original, rife with outspoken social comment, is retained. Charles Way's play conflates the shepherds into one comic character, Zac, and his long-suffering wife Miriam (another miracle-play character), retains the subversive comedy of the sheep-stealing, and keeps the device of Mak and his cloak and the scene where the other shepherds toss him in a blanket as punishment for stealing the sheep. The playmaking process was devised cooperatively with the company, resulting for example in the blanket scene having an unscripted comic addition ('There then follows an improvised section of horseplay' says the script) when Miriam, who has given her 'baby' to a member of the audience to hold, suddenly remembers it; while she is doing this an imaginary thirty-five tosses have taken place, one for every year of Mak's age. The others look exhausted from the effort while Mak looks as if he's enjoyed it.

Many of Charles Way's plays are in fact based on the assumption of the improvisation process not only leading to a final script but also being integral to any future productions – and that device of directly addressing the audience, drawn from medieval practice, is common to many of his plays. *Ill Met By Moonlight*, for example, amusingly plays with the conceit with an opening with the stage direction that '*The following lines may be shared out among the actors*':

> Ladies and gentlemen
> Welcome
> Aye – very welcome
> We are . . .
> Very very welcome – you are – indeed
> We are storytellers
> And this is a Faery Story
> It is – and you're very welcome to it . . .
> Yes! There's no need to say it more. They be welcome. That is the end of the welcoming . . .[9]

and so on for a full page of the script.

The dramatist tackles the same story in his verse version of *The Nativity* (1995), adapted from his 1987 Devonshire-accent mystery cycle for Clwyd Youth Theatre, where he conflates several miracle plays in his nine-act epic, including again the *Second Shepherds Play*, with Mak and Gill, the sheep-stealing parody and the tossing in the blanket; but he introduces a different note of rural politics and anachronistically (another feature of the original plays) anticipates enclosures, mechanisation and new technology:

> For lo the end of shepherding is nigh,
> First they will enclose the moor,
> our work be done by fences.
> Then industry will do us down
> till all folk speak of shepherds in past tenses.
> Man-made fibres hold the folk in thrall
> new fangled cheenes do our work withal
> All we may do is weep without why,
> for no-one yet pulled nylon over foolish eyes.
> Tis called progress, all men bow to it . . .[10]

That ambiguous Luddite strain could degenerate into the romantic rural idyll. Personally, I don't feel it does, and there's a healthy ambivalence about technology in *Ill Met By Moonlight*, set at the end of the nineteenth century. Here the subtext of the clash between tradition and progress surfaces when the last of the Bwcha, the spirits of the countryside, complains to the farmer: 'If only you had honoured me so many times I helped you, sow seed, mow hay, thresh corn . . . But you forgot these yester ways an' put your faith in all that's new. Your cider is bought in the barrel and the press rots in the barn. With this flail I earned my keep with one household to the next for eight hundred years and now 'tis better hung upon the wall for folk to question at its use. Even the moon weeps, for she have shone kindly on many a kiss. But you no longer need her, now that you have lit the world so wonderfully well by artificial means . . .' And the play ends as the last of the Bwcha, who lives disguised as a tree, hears the farmer say 'You know that old tree at the bottom of plovers' field . . . I reckon we should cut it down . . . I'll need a gate by there for the new mechanical reaper . . .'

(4)

In the Nineties, there has been a discernible move away from the political in Charles Way's work. He has, of course, become as sceptical as the rest of us about the old certainties, less willing to take sides or see things in that quasi-medieval Good/Evil binarism. He himself says he has become more (w)holistic, more introspective, more spiritual.

But he still uses the same means to explore ideas, to mediate life: in his most recent stage work he still goes back to popular medieval drama, to myth and to folk tales and in general is still a storyteller. *Dead Man's Hat* is a reworking of Wild West mythology that also questions our own liberal ideas and our ambivalence towards American culture; *The Search for Odysseus* is a challenge to received ideas about heroes and universal truths; *The Nativity* is another version of a mystery cycle play where the dramatist offers an original alternative ending with the Devil having the last word.

The Dove Maiden (given in 1996 an excellent and imaginative production by director Jamie Garven and Hijinx) incorporates the usual techniques – storytelling, song, magical transformation – but also touches on more sinister matters. The soldier hero, Petrushka, has to undertake a series of tasks but lurking in his past, repressed and denied by the hero, is a secret that we recognise from the horror stories of Bosnia. This distinctly places it in a time and culture: I suspect the reference, at the core of the work, may go unrecognised in years to come, when I am sure the play will still be performed. But for us at this time the folk tale becomes a story about uncertainty, ambiguity, a suspicion again (as in *The Search for Odysseus*) of war heroes and a guilt over atrocities in which we may feel complicit.

But it is still about Good and Evil. I get the impression that part of the playwright's journey has been, not only a disllusionment with ideological certainties or progress, but also a nagging doubt about the eventual triumph of Good over Evil, resolved to some extent by the acceptance that the two are opposing sides in a kind of Manichean psychology: the old Christian morality-play battle is that which goes on inside each of us rather than between external forces. *The Dove Maiden* is a result of Charles Way's unease with his inability to understand many recent events across the world which have all been described as 'Evil', according to his own programme notes for the production. Evil in earlier plays is represented by witches; here it is a folk hero, Petrushka. In *Ill Met By Moonlight*, *In the Bleak Midwinter* and other plays that also draw on folklore and morality, hope triumphs over despair. good over evil, the likeable over the dislikeable. *The Dove Maiden* has its lighter side but is essentially an attempt to confront the reality of evil acts that seem to make no sense, certainly not to a liberal humanist. It stands with *Dead Man's Hat* in its sense of open-ended perplexity at human nature. It is a long way from the rather determinist message-led plays of basic community theatre to this sophisticated, ambivalent, spiritual and more lyrical writing.

But those skills, that concern about the ideological transaction that is performance, that 'good night out' ethic, is what underscores *The Dove Maiden* as much as *Humbug*.

Notes

1 An unpublished film-poem, *No Borders*, broadcast by BBC 2 (1997).
2 Ibid.
3 Ibid.
4 Ibid.
5 Ibid.
6 Brian Mitchell (ed.), *Charles Way Three Plays: Dead Man's Hat: Paradise Drive, In The Bleak Midwinter* (Bridgend: Seren Books, 1994) p. 60. Hereafter cited as *Charles Way, Three Plays*.
7 Ibid. p. 28. This is a traditional American folk-song. See Irwin Silber (ed.), *Songs of the Great American West* (London: Macmillan, 1967), p. 236.
8 *Charles Way, Three Plays*, p. 140.
9 *Ill Met By Moonlight* (1994). Unpublished.
10 *The Nativity* (1995). Unpublished.

The Creative Process of a Theatre Writer

Graham Laker interviews Charles Way

GL: You've written for television and radio, but most of your work has been for the theatre, which makes you one of those rarities in Wales: the full-time theatre writer. How easy is it to earn a living from writing for the stage at the end of the 1990's?

CW: Well, it's changed since I first came to Wales in 1980. Nowadays, there are not many small-scale companies which employ writers on long-term contracts: they just can't afford it. When I first worked with Gwent Theatre, the company had six actors, a designer, a director, a writer and two stage-managers, all working more or less full-time: it was quite a sizeable outfit. And it was just one of a number of small companies (Theatr Powys, Spectacle, Action Pie), all growing and expanding. In my own case, the long-standing relationship that I had with Gwent Theatre enabled me to practise the trade, earn a living, and become sufficiently established here to be able to buy a house – writers have to live somewhere like everybody else! And it was important to me, as a writer, to have a strong base, and develop relationships with one or two companies again and again so that they have formed a kind of nucleus for earning a living, having a life in Wales and not being drawn outside. But that depends on these companies being funded sufficiently to work in this kind of way: to develop close, long-term relationships with writers, and in the last ten years, all these companies have been forced to contract.

So the way I manage to earn a living now is by gradually increasing the range of work that I can do. I started off writing for Theatre-in-Education, which developed into Children's and Young People's Theatre, adult plays, community plays and so on. The pool that I'm swimming around in has gradually got bigger! By now, what stabilizes me and allows me to continue to do theatre work are royalties on plays I've already done, particularly Christmas shows, like *Sleeping Beauty*, which has had five productions. It's just been done at the Library Theatre in Manchester so the cheque I shall be getting in the next few days will pay for Christmas. Without that happening, it would be very hard; you can't earn a living just off commissions because you only get four or five thousand pounds per script, and even if you are lucky enough to write two full-length plays a year, your annual income would not be much more than ten thousand pounds.

GL: What a lot of writers in your situation do, of course, is to subsidize their theatre work by writing scripts for television. It pays proportionately better for work which is in many ways easier, particularly if you're writing for a series, and simply following a story-line which has been provided by your producer or editor. So from a financial point of view, television might be attractive, quite apart from the fact that it would give you the opportunity to reach far larger audiences than a stage play can.

CW: That's playing the numbers game which makes one's work seem more important because more people see it. I'm not against television – in fact I'm writing a drama series for BBC Wales this year – but I didn't want to write other people's story-lines. It's not that I'm a control freak – you can't be a control freak in theatre – it's just that the writer in the televisual process didn't seem to me to have enough say in what the end-product was going to be. So I've waited until now, when, with twenty years writing behind me, television producers are gradually beginning to come to me, and are happy for me to approach the work in much the same way as I do in theatre. So, I say: 'I want to do a play about this', and I send them a first draft and we talk about it and I'm able to develop the same sort of collaborative relationship with the director, producer and actors as I do in theatre. *No Borders*, the film poem I did for BBC 2, was hugely collaborative – between the sound man, the lighting man, the camera man, the director, and myself, but in terms of the actual intellectual content of the material and the philosophical and dramatic structure, I still felt that I owned it.

GL: You have talked about needing to work in a wide range of genres in order to earn a living, and it's one of the most impressive things about your C.V. – the fact that you write for such very different audiences: young children, teenagers, adults; you've written for small-scale touring companies, community shows, TIE projects, 'main-stream' houses and so on. I'm wondering whether we're hearing a single voice emanating from all these different genres or are you, as it were, a different writer when you sit down and draft a play for these very different audiences?

CW: To me, obviously, I'm one writer doing one thing, but it's multi-faceted. In a linguistic sense, of course, I work with a variety of voices. If you're doing a Western like *Dead Man's Hat*, you have to use a totally different vernacular; you have to be fully inside the boots of someone who talks in a completely different way to how a shepherd might express himself in *In the Bleak Midwinter*. Putting yourself in another person's shoes is at the heart of being a playwright. You have to be able to do that in your head, in the sound of the words, emotionally, intellectually in order for the characters to have a complete life outside of you. I think that's part of the job. And it's something which comes with experience: allowing each character to have his own voice and not to put your own thoughts into their mouths because you want to change the world and say something marvellous that everyone will want to hear. At the same time, of course, you need to keep control, so that the characters don't witter on themselves and stop the play moving on.

GL: So different voices, but what about common themes and common techniques?

CW: If you look through the six or seven of my plays which I consider are worth reading and worth doing again and again, what I hope binds them to each other is a sense of humanity: giving the people in the plays a fair chance to say why they're there, and making the whole experience of the theatre into a positive thing. And the structure of the plays relies on a number of techniques and rules that I've learnt over the years. I believe in structure very strongly. I think people can recognize a Charles Way play in the way that the story is told – short scenes which fold into one another, or the use of song, or perhaps a thread of poetry and magic which runs through quite a number of them: *Ill Met By Moonlight*, for example, or *The Dove Maiden*.

GL: I'm interested in what you say about the importance of structure, the way the story is told. Can you say more about that?

CW: First of all, I believe you have to engage the audience instantly in the type of theatre that it is, and the type of questions being asked. And that can be centred on the characters, who have certain ambitions or things that they want; and what provides the structure is putting obstacles in front of them, which they need to overcome. Where experience plays a part is being able to let go and allow the narrative to develop organically under its own momentum, but, at the same time, keeping control so that scenes don't outstay their welcome, once they've made their point. It's a dual thing: control and release, control and release. The first several drafts are concerned with finding the structure, and discovering what the play is about, because if you know what you're writing before you've written it, I think you're into something quite prescriptive.

GL: So the structure of the play, and even the story, may undergo considerable change as you are writing. How does the original stimulus or idea for play manifest itself? As a social issue? An image? A snatch of dialogue?

CW: It depends where the impulse for the play comes from. Sometimes people phone up and say 'We'd like a play about this, or an adaptation of that'. If I'm left to my own devices, I find it a great help to look at other writers' materials: it gives you something to argue with. So if I'm interested in writing a play about sibling rivalry, I'll look at the story of *Cinderella*, and see what's in that. I do this a lot. *Ill Met By Moonlight* is based on *A Midsummer Night's Dream*; *In the Bleak Midwinter* is a re-working of *The Second Shepherd*'s Play; early on, *She Scored for Wales* was based on *Lysistrata*. These other works give me a basic structure, and a set of themes that I can both engage with and debate with. What I then do is to open up a note-book and fill it with ideas; I'll have a particular 'eye-in' when I'm doing a project so that everything I read and see, conversations with people, television programmes, newspaper articles, may spark off other ideas. It's a gradual process of collating material which eventually forms itself into the broad outline of a story which I can write out in a couple of pages. Then I'll do a scribble draft, fleshing out the scenes, not so much in terms of dialogue as a series of actions: what is going on here? what are the characters' intentions? For me, dialogue is not the impetus: my plays are not generally driven by dialogue, by people saying clever things. My plays are not like Oscar Wilde's . . . if only they could be!

GL: I'm interested that you should say that it's action that drives the dialogue in your plays, because I can hear the actor talking. As you know, one of the first things an actor does in rehearsal is to 'action' the play; discover what the character's intention is behind each line, what the character is trying to achieve in the scene. I wonder whether this perspective has come from your own actor training?

CW: Yes, but it also comes from working in the theatre for so many years. You've got to be aware of all the possibilities within a scene, not just the dialogue. To know something about the process of acting and directing, of how plays work on stage visually as well as aurally, makes you a theatre writer rather than any other sort of writer.

GL: I know that sometimes your collaborative process with actors, designers and directors begins even before you've written the first draft. With Hijinx, for example, you workshop an idea for a play before beginning the writing process.

CW: I have to really trust the actors and know the nature of their commitment to the project for this to work. They need to know something about my process as a writer. I watch actors stumbling through the read-through and first rehearsals of a play of mine and I don't expect a full performance – which is the classic mistake of writers in rehearsal. I know that I have to allow the actors their journey. Similarly, in a collaborative situation, I need to work with actors who know something about my journey as a writer, and how I get to the final script. Working regularly with a group like Hijinx enabled us to develop a mutual trust and an understanding of each other's creative processes. So the starting point might be that I would arrive with some material and perhaps a few pages of script, and the group would say: 'Let's focus on these ideas or themes and let the play come out of the centre of us all'. But I've found that you can only really write well what is inside yourself, something which is philosophically close to your heart. Now it's very difficult when you're working in a group to write something which is philosophically close to everyone's heart. Because the actors in Hijinx understood the writer's process, they enabled me to do my job more fully: they didn't expect me simply to record their improvisations, for example. So the collaboration was about finding a meeting place where the form of theatre which the company wanted to stage could marry the theatre script that I wanted to write. But these preliminary workshops can certainly help with the writing process. Say I have an idea that I want to explore (the theme of adultery in *In the Bleak Midwinter*, for example), then we can all have a discussion about relationships and extra-marital affairs and that can be immensely stimulating. When I'm on my own that intellectual journey takes longer; I have to debate the issues with myself. Working collaboratively, you get material that you would never be able to find on your own. And you can test ideas immediately, and say: 'That's a great idea; let's try it out in the rehearsal room right now.' Then, if I see the actors do something that really works, I can put it in my notebook and, lo and behold, in the scenario there it is. It may survive right through to the final script.

GL: So you've workshopped the ideas behind the play with the actors and director, and you go away to write the first draft of the script. Would you then bring that draft back to the same company and the same actors for further development?

CW: Certainly this was the way I worked with Hijinx, which had a more or less permanent company. And I think that here something has changed, particularly theatre in Wales. The number of actors who have longer-term commitments to particular companies, and can follow the whole creative process through, has shrunk. I've always found that if the actors have an investment in the creation of the material, the nature of their performance is different to actors who simply learn the lines, do the show and disappear. Of course, in the end it's about putting a play on, and hoping that audiences will gain something from it. But if there's been a genuine collaboration in the creative process between people who are emotionally and intellectually generous, then that process will be tangible within the play, and will somehow communicate itself to the audience.

GL: I'm sure that's true, but I'm also aware of a problem that can sometimes arise through very close collaboration between author and actors. There's a danger that the cast, in their excitement and enthusiasm, will try and hi-jack the play, or at least, pull it off its tracks during the workshop process. They'll see all sorts of new ways in which the play might develop, and new relationships between characters. They'll say things like: 'Wouldn't it be interesting if my character did such and such?' or 'What about writing a scene between me and X?' Are you familiar with that sort of discussion in rehearsal?

CW: Yes, it does happen. 'My character wouldn't say this' is the classic comment. To which the answer is 'It's not your character, or my character; each character belongs to himself and the laws of the drama!'. And then you go on to discuss the laws of the drama. The most difficult thing is when there's a clash about what the play should be saying, and that's something you just have to work through. What developed with Hijinx over the four or five plays we worked on together was a more mature sort of relationship. Just because an actor did a great improvisation didn't mean that it necessarily had to go into the play. It's a case of letting people do their own job: listening to what other people have to say, but remaining true to yourself. If I'm going to write the play, I'm going to write it! In the same way, the designer doesn't want me saying: 'Well, actually, I don't much like your design.' It's all about trust: if everyone trusts one another, then, occasionally, it all comes together.

GL: So, moving on a bit, we come to the start of the rehearsal period proper. The script will have gone through several drafts by this time, and there may be further changes to the play before opening night. I know that you regularly attend rehearsals, quite often as an assistant director. How do you see your role in rehearsals for a play that you have written?

CW: Maybe the term 'assistant director' is not quite right. The job is one of assisting the director rather than helping to direct the play. For me it's more about trying to explain what the heart of the play is, and what it's trying to express. The closer the theatre writer is to the 'nuts and bolts' of the production, the more likely it is that the heart of the play will be revealed in performance. This is quite interesting in terms of my experience with *The Dove Maiden*. It was a difficult script, a sort of double-layered fairy story. The impulse for writing it had been the situation in Bosnia, but I needed to find a way of translating this into a form that could be taken on by a small-scale touring company. I came up with a story, based on a Russian folk-tale, of a soldier who is seen as a hero, but has actually been involved in a crime which even he denies that he has committed. So it was very tough material and it was very hard to find the right tone in performance. The director was Jamie Garven, with whom I've worked a lot and whom I trust very much. But, on this occasion, the rehearsal process led to the production being more about what the actors did in the rehearsal room than what was at the heart of the play. What was put on the stage was, if you like, the subtext – what lay behind the fairy story – rather than the story itself. I had stepped out of the process early on, because I didn't really feel that, with this particular group, I could function in a really creative way. I just had to say to them 'O.K. – you get on with it'. Part of the problem was that I'm not sure that I knew what the play was trying to say, and if you have a writer who is not clear about his intentions, who is still on the journey himself, he's probably better off out of it! As a result the play was not universally liked. But there have been other occasions when Jamie and I have worked together, and when the play has been, perhaps, simpler, when I have been able to give very clear guidance on what I'm trying to achieve.

GL: So one of the writer's roles in rehearsal is to help ensure that the production remains true to the play, as written. From that, it seems a small step to directing the play yourself.

CW: I recently directed *Dead Man's Hat*, and enjoyed being able to make the final decisions about the nature of the production. And I think that the early worries that the actors had about the writer being the director were rapidly dispelled because of the years that I had spent in the theatre, gaining an understanding of the acting process. In that particular production, having seen other people direct it, I was able to use all their ideas and take them on further. Now, as I'm moving into areas of work which combine dance, movement, music, and song – more of a 'total theatre' approach – I'm even more attracted by the idea of trying, as director, to merge all these disparate elements – and text – into one story, and give the whole a narrative drive. That would be really interesting.

GL: So the play finally opens, and let's say it's a success: text and production have welded together. However, the life of a play-script shouldn't end there, with a single production. I've heard writers say that the only thing more difficult than getting the first production of a new play is getting the second production. How important is this for a writer?

CW: It's fantastically important, because you realize that the play isn't just one thing. When you're involved in its first production, you think you are seeing its entire life. When you see a second production by a different company, you realize that the play can be interpreted in a wholly different but equally valid way. And that's an important lesson because you begin to appreciate that what seemed, in the original creative process, so subjective actually has an objective existence as well. In practical terms, it gives you the opportunity to re-define and improve things in the script, and, of course, in financial terms, it's crucial if you want to make any sort of living.

GL: Your own plays have been performed very widely: *Sleeping Beauty* and *The Flood* in Russia; *The Search for Odysseus* in Germany: *A Spell of Cold Weather* in Canada; not to mention productions in Britain. How does a writer go about getting his plays into the wider theatre market?

CW: The problem is getting the play, together with the name of the writer, into the consciousness of the theatre world so that when it lands on someone's desk, it's not mentally 'binned'. In Young People's Theatre, there are a number of organizations which publish information about new plays across the world. The most important one at the moment is, probably, ASSITEJ. It is largely through such networks that my plays have been revived by other companies in Britain and abroad. I think those working in Young People's Theatre are connected more openly and less competitively than in the case of main-stream drama. They are less bound by traditional criteria of success. If you have a play running at the National Theatre, you are more likely to be able to sell it abroad because of the National Theatre connection. Young People's Theatre is less concerned with that sort of kudos. It still needs to be a very good play, of course, and to survive translation. But there are a lot of people in Europe looking towards Britain for new plays. Unfortunately, I don't think we look the other way very often; maybe we need to redress that.

GL: A lot of what we've talked about so far is relevant to the business of earning a living as a theatre writer almost anywhere in the world. I'd like to focus a little more now on the particular challenges of creating theatre in Wales. One of the most distinctive things about Wales is that, until very recently, it had no tradition of professional theatre: you can't trace Welsh theatre back over the centuries as you can in the case of England or France or Italy; there is no canon of 'great plays'; no history of influential companies or great theatre buildings. Do you think that the lack of a theatrical tradition in Wales is an advantage or a disadvantage as far as the writer is concerned?

CW: When I came to Wales for the first time, that notion never entered my head. I was new to the country, didn't know anything about it and certainly wasn't weighed down by a sense of 'history that wasn't'. I just went forward: the whole atmosphere was one of expansion – each county had its own theatre company – it was great. It's good to have a sense of history but a sense of the future is ultimately more important. Ensuring that the companies that we have now can expand and diversify and roll on rather than cutting them down is what matters. After all, that's where the opportunities for writers lie.

GL: As far as the future is concerned, you said in an interview with Hazel Walford Davies recently that 'the theatre is set to return as a vital force in people's lives'. It's a very positive prognosis, and I wonder what grounds you have for such optimism, given the current financial climate and its impact on theatre activity?

CW: I suppose it's partly that I can see television possibly going in the direction of 'fifty channels and nothing on', accelerating the process of social fragmentation. More and more, we will need to go to places where we can sit with other people and join in an experience which binds us together rather than splits us apart. The nature of the social event will become even more important. It may be that fewer people will go to the theatre than used to go to the cinema, or now watch television, but, as I said before, we mustn't get hooked up in the numbers game. Theatre offers something different: a live event: something an audience can have a direct relationship with. However brilliant a film or television programme is, it's a 'cold' event: you're not dealing with flesh and blood. In Wales, we have the opportunity to develop a philosophy towards theatre, which would be quite different to theatre structures in larger cities or the West End. What I have found really interesting in my time here has been the relationships that can develop between a theatre company and its immediate community: groups of actors who are known to local people, actively engaged in the life of the small towns in which they are based. Maybe we need to rethink the distinction between professional actors who perform, and local people who watch, and initiate more work which brings both groups together to create theatre. The Knee High Company in Cornwall has created quite a stir by doing highly popular and populist work which involves the community and is presented outside the theatre building – in the harbour for example. Maybe that's a way forward.

GL: One of the big debates of the last few years has been concerned with the establishment of a National Theatre for Wales. From what you've been saying, I would infer that you would regard the creation of a large, highly-subsidized company, based in one of the larger cities, and touring major-scale shows to the main theatre venues, as not really all that relevant to the needs of Wales.

CW: If it meant that it syphoned off resources from other forms of theatre, then that would be a bad thing, but I don't see that this necessarily has to be the case. The fact that Cardiff is to have a massive new sports arena in the Docks should not mean that, say, Wrexham Rugby Football Club should lose its sports ground. You can surely have both. If a National Theatre was an institution which raised the profile of theatre in Wales, by presenting its best work, then it could be very exciting. Wales would no longer be a country without a theatrical tradition, and the status of theatre work in general in Wales would be enhanced. But it would have to live and breathe off those actors who spend their life touring with the smaller companies, and offer to those companies a space to show their work. All too often in the past the best work originating in Wales has disappeared without trace because there has not been a national or international platform where it can be seen. So if there's going to be a new impetus, the so-called National Theatre might be it, but who knows . . .?

GL: And, finally, to turn to that other perennial topic: how best to encourage new writing for the stage. In your view, what single initiative would be most helpful in terms of developing play-writing in Wales?

CW: It would be to maintain the companies that already exist and to create new ones with the particular aim of working with writers on a long-term basis. The companies would need to be strong enough to be able to take risks, so that if a play failed, the world wouldn't collapse round everybody's ears. Writers need to be bound into the heart of theatrical life, rather than being outside it, having to send their scripts to people who don't read them. They need to be part of the whole process of making theatre as much as an actor or a director. It's in this context that theatre writers can be born and nourished, and the proof of that is the number of theatre writers, most of them now in their forties, who came out of the expansion of theatre companies back in the 1970's. I'm one myself! Unless we can re-create those conditions, there is no-where for today's 'twenty-something' writers to learn their craft.

Reviews

SHE SCORED FOR WALES

She Scored for Wales (Community House, Newport)
The Guardian, 17 December, 1981.

It's a neat idea. Gwent Theatre's new community road show: an update of Lysistrata, the local rugby club replacing Athens as the citadel of male chauvinism, with a finale set in Cardiff Arms Park, the very Acropolis of Welsh machismo, as the leader of the striking women parleys with the Pope, Prince Charles, Carwyn James and Barry John.

Community theatre shows, all too often, get no further than being neat ideas. But this time Gwent Theatre have a very strong show, lively, funny and performed with just the right combination of the energetic and the flip. Charles Way's script steers clear of the temptations of polemic, getting its points across effortlessly and effectively and the cast have now been together long enough to give some good ensemble playing.

She Scored for Wales is touring Gwent before and after Christmas and perhaps Community House in Newport was neither the best nor the most typical of venues; I'd like to see how it goes down in a real lion's den, like the Pontypool Clubroom. All right, I suspect, for there's plenty to enjoy without taking the politics too seriously. Indeed, it's almost too inoffensive at times, its barbs often blunted rather than sharpened by the humour.

Most gratifying to see, though, is that even at the less than suitable Community House, the audience do actually respond, if only to the instantly recognizable stereotyped characters and attitudes.

David Adams

BREAD AND ROSES

Bread and Roses (1983 Tour Preview)
South Wales Argus, 18 March, 1983.

The valleys of Wales and the olive groves of Spain have never come closer than they did during the days of the Spanish Civil War in the 1930s.

Gwent Theatre's new play, *Bread and Roses* by Charles Way, is based on interviews with people who can remember those far-off and troubled days.

It tells the story of Tom, a Welsh miner, and Adela, a young woman from Northern Spain who falls prey to Franco's repression when the mining community in which she lives rises up against poverty.

She flees to Wales. Tom leaves behind the depression at home to fight for the ideals of democracy against the Spanish Fascists.

Their paths cross but world events sweep over them.

Brian Jarman

Bread and Roses (Abergavenny)
The Guardian, 4 April, 1983.

It is by coincidence rather than design, I am assured, that there have been three new plays by Welsh companies in the past few months all on the subject of the Spanish Civil War. Charlie Way's *Bread and Roses* was written for Gwent Theatre and is currently touring community centres after opening at the company's Abergavenny base.

There are many good things about the play, not least its directness of approach and its determination to see working class opposition to fascist policies as a continuing necessity, but so far the group seem a little unsure of the strengths of the play. But that's the way with community groups; when the interaction with audiences, and non-theatre going audiences at that, is so important, the performance takes a while to settle in.

Evident so far are the raw bones of a good play that certainly says a lot more about why Welsh miners uprooted themselves from their families, homes and their own fight against oppression, to take that bizarre journey through France and over the Pyrenees to fight a war in which many were to feel more like pawns than Theatre Wales's recent *The Blood that Sings* suggests.

Much of the play is about the similarities between the Thirties and today; unemployment marches, wage cuts, anti-union legislation, the drift to fascism. At times the author seems a little too anxious to present a balanced view but by the end there is little doubt as to what he is saying. On the way there is maybe a bit too much said and done, with a script that still needs working on and pruning and action that could do with a bit of simplification. I fancy, though, that within a week or so *Bread and Roses* will be a show well worth seeing.

David Adams

Bread and Roses (Nantybwch Senior Citizens Hall, Tredegar)
South Wales Argus, 19 April, 1983.

Just a bunch of fresh-faced Oxbridge boys, enjoying the biggest student rag of their lives?

That's how I'd tended to imagine the British members of the International Brigade who fought with the Republicans in the Spanish Civil War of the mid-1930s.

How wrong I was. More than a hundred working-class Welshmen were among them.

One such volunteer is Tom Richards, a soap-box orator and newly converted Communist.

Another is his friend Ellis Morgan, whose decision has as much to do with bitterness at losing his pit job and getting a black eye in the Battle of Cable Street as with any idealism. This is their fictional story.

And superbly told it is too, with Charles Way's eloquent, uncomplicated script and six tremendous acting performances.

Diana Cox is excellent as the Spanish refugee lodger who first converts Tom to the cause; an intense gawky, Garbo-like figure in beret and flat shoes.

Artistic director Gary Meredith, stalks around most menacingly in various roles of sinister authority – policeman, social security snooper, Black Shirt, commissar – while Christine Blanchard and Trudy King are painfully good as the wife and mother left at home to wait and hope.

But the real triumph belong to Andrew Rivers as hero and narrator Tom and Simon Scott as Ellis, completely convincing as the men who fought because – as one of them says – Hitler, Mussolini and the dole queue 'somehow all seemed part of the same darkness'.

Anne Hegerty

IN LIVING MEMORY

In Living Memory (Big Pit, Blaenavon)
South Wales Argus, 29 June, 1983.

With British theatre going through some of its darkest days since the war, it is strange to hear of a play with a waiting list of people who cannot get in to see it.

And it is even stranger when you hear the play is being performed at a Gwent colliery – namely the Big Pit mining museum at Blaenavon.

Since this unique experiment opened in April the numbers who have flocked there have amazed even those who were most optimistic about the venture.

Some 30,000 visitors from all over the world have already paid to spend an hour tramping through the dusk and dust of this underground world.

For most people, it is their first glimpse into the shadowy life of our mining ancestry.

But while the guides – former workers at the pit – can illuminate the tour with facts fascinating and fearful, the one slight criticism has been that it lacks that spark of life . . .

But meanwhile they have found another way of bringing to life the dead pit – and now every day some hundred schoolchildren follow a tour underground by watching a play about a mining family from 1913-1983.

It was the idea of Gwent Theatre – the county's education theatre group funded by the County Council, the Welsh Arts Council and the South East Wales Arts Association.

They specialise in on-side projects for schools with 'teachers' packs' for follow-up work in the classroom and questionnaires about the play.

In the past they have done similar work at Newport's Tredegar House, which turned out a huge success.

But the Big Pit project has surpassed even that.

Aimed at ten- and eleven-year-olds, the performances, running twice a day until July 15, were fully booked almost by return of post . . .

And as each day the coaches roll in to see the hour-and-a-quarter long play in a room near the pithead baths, excitement mounts in everyone involved.

'The children are enthralled', says the pit's assistant director Anne Griffiths, a university graduate born in Cwmfelinfach. 'We're getting dozens of calls from people who want to come and see it . . .'

Called *In Living Memory*, the play was written by Crickhowell writer Charles Way with the aid of the company themselves, and music specially composed by Christine Blanchard.

Their last production told of South Wales miners' involvement in the Spanish Civil War and so they already knew many of the horrors of mining life.

But there has been more research – with the actors talking to locals in Blaenavon and working closely with the staff at the pit. 'One miner's widow in a Blaenavon old folks' home could not believe people were paying to go down the pit', says Gary.

Everyone had their say in the way it developed. Diana Cox, for example, has recently joined Gwent Theatre from the Midlands and was interested in the extensive role women played in the pits . . .

Tracing the life of one Megan Powell [the play] opens in 1913 when she is thirteen years old and her grandmother can remember working down the mine.

She tells Megan that she once saw a woman give birth to a baby underground but her family was so poor she was back at work within a week.

The themes of the play are mining and education, mirroring the idea of the project itself and seen through a multi-location set . . . Her mother dies giving birth to sister Bethan, her older sister Ceinwen has to leave home to find work after being sacked for swearing at a foreman who refused to get a doctor to see to the crushed hand of a fellow woman worker, and their father eventually dies of the dust.

Bethan turns out to be a brilliant scholar and wins a place at the local grammar school. Her family are overjoyed at this escape route and promise to work even harder to find the money.

But it is the time of the General Strike, and although her father is tempted to go on working to fulfil his promise, he is won over by the arguments of Megan's new husband Wil, who points out that if pay is lowered any more starvation will mean some children will not need education.

Bethan is forced to leave for London to become a chambermaid.

The play avoids any of the sickly-sweet sentimentality of outside views of the valleys such as the Hollywood film of Richard Llewellyn's *How Green Was My Valley*.

It shows Megan's family battling on, with an unfailing dignity, courage and compassion that is difficult to understand given the appalling conditions in which they were forced to live and work.

The cast are not entirely happy with the last part, which shows an 83-year-old Megan leaving the old family home for an old folks' home. They feel it is rather a flat end.

But I felt this was also its strength – a sad and undramatic end to a life full of drama and tragedy.

There are two public performances of *In Living Memory* on July 5 and 6 and the hundred or so people who manage to get in to see it should consider themselves very fortunate indeed.

The fact that so few will is in itself a tragedy . . .

Brian Jarman

In Living Memory (Big Pit, Blaenavon)
The Guardian, 11 July, 1983.

Charlie Way has written his latest play, *In Living Memory*, for Gwent Theatre as a piece aimed at young stars at junior school. I don't know what they made of it, but by God, it certainly got at me.

It's the most emotionally draining work of theatre I've seen for some while. Conceived initially for schoolchildren, it has also been playing to adults who, like the daytime younger audiences, cram into a makeshift theatre space at The Big Pit mining museum in North Gwent to see three linked playlets about a local family.

Perhaps it's the context, the drive up past the disused workings under the shadow of the big wheel, through an exhibition where grainy photographic blow-ups show posing miners whose eyes, ringed with white in the coal-blacked sweaty surfaces, seem to stare out accusingly, the fact that in the audience are bound to be ex-miners, miners' families, people who lived through the great strike, whose menfolk coughed their way to death, who were part of the continuous battle against private and public owners.

It's all in the play. Not in any dogmatic way, for Gwent Theatre know well enough that youngsters don't respond like middle-class lefties to agitprop dramas. The tale of the mining family that starts in 1913, goes on to 1926, and ends in 1983, is too near home truths to be a mere documentary.

It is, inevitably, the story of working-class struggle, but against social values rather than any simple class war. In the final scene, as the old lady who we first saw as a schoolgirl sits in her cottage while removal men shift her history into crates on their way to an old folks' home, the poignancy is almost unbearable.

The one great shame is that not enough people can get to see this marvellous show. It's still on at The Big Pit and I would urge anyone within travelling distance to insist that it opens its doors for more community shows.

David Adams

In Living Memory (1986 Re-Tour preview)
South Wales Argus, 7 March, 1986.

Going east along the Heads of the Valleys road, the drama centre at Abergavenny is presenting Charles Way's *In Living Memory* on Thursday 13 and Friday 14, before the production goes off to do the rounds.

In Living Memory, performed and devised by Gwent Theatre, the county's only professional theatre company, is the story of the rise and decline of a mining village seen through the eyes of one of its inhabitants, Megan Powell.

First performed in 1983, it received enthusiastic reviews from this paper and its power should have been enhanced by memories of the miners' strike which ended just over a year ago.

FUNNY BOYS

Funny Boys (Drama Centre, Abergavenny)
Abergavenny Chronicle, 15 March, 1984.

Gwent's own professional theatre company has this week opened with an exciting new play for adults at the Drama Centre, Abergavenny.

The first night of *Funny Boys* by Charles Way took place last night and it is being staged again tonight (Thursday) and tomorrow night at the Drama Centre, before it goes on a tour of the county.

It's a bitter-sweet comedy that follows the fortunes of Twp and Tom, a Welsh comic duo, as they struggle for stardom in the hard world of showbusiness in the early 1960's. The play contains some lively songs which have been set to music by Chrys Blanchard and the production is being directed by Bob Tomson from Theatre Powys . . .

Funny Boys (Newport, Baneswell Community Centre)
The Guardian, 23 March, 1984.

Community theatre audiences are much like those on the Northern club circuit – unwilling to take any nonsense, but ready to respond when the material hits home.

Gwent Theatre are well used to community venues in South Wales, so they must wonder at the wisdom of taking out a show about a couple of stand-up comics with heavy political overtones. And in Baneswell Community Centre they died a death such as inadequate performers suffer in all tough gigs and for the same reasons.

They lost their audience – literally, since a couple of rows didn't come back after the interval tea and biscuits, but also very profoundly in terms of the material and their performance of it. Charlie Way's script, which attempts to link the language issue with popular culture by having a stooge who's a Welsh Nationalist, comes across as at best misguided, at worst patronising irrelevance. The performances suggested a lack of belief in the script – and, and more crucially, an inability to make anything of the characters.

Gwent Theatre have rightly earned themselves a fine reputation for their community work, but in their new show they seem to have made all the wrong decisions and it suffers sadly from the contradictions between a script and devised work: between audience appeal and characterisation; between slick production and the economics and constraints of community touring.

In brief, *Funny Boys* reveals the weaknesses of community theatre. As a play, it tackles in a desultory way issues that, in Gwent at least, are not seen to be the concern of community audiences. It's also too long, too wordy, and not funny enough. In performance, that rejection of character portrayal and projection that makes community theatre so effective because it's so direct and accessible here leads to a flatness that is wholly inappropriate.

David Adams

WITNESS

Witness (Duke's Playhouse TIE Company)
The Guardian, 21 February, 1985.

Witness, a new play by Charles Way looks at the treatment which the State hands out to those individuals it perceives to be a threat. It is being shown in the studio by the Duke's Playhouse Theatre in Education company for fifth and sixth formers, complete with a follow up pack for teachers.

But like so much schools work the play is both in the way it is written and the way it is staged, by director Sheryl Crown, an intensely watchable drama. It's not just deserving of an adult audience, which it will get for a special performance tonight. It's actually a lot better theatre than much of the stuff that repertory audiences are routinely offered.

Witness is about the trial and execution of Julius and Ethel Rosenberg after the last war when America was convinced that someone had leaked the secret of their atomic bomb to the Russians.

The play does not begin to try to establish the innocence which they protested to the end. It demonstrates the irrelevance of actual guilt or innocence when an embarrassed government needs to find a scapegoat. The commies who were killing our boys in Korea were also catching up on nuclear technology. Despite the objections of eminent scientists that the atom bomb was 'an industry, not a recipe', J. Edgar Hoover's suggestion that 'the unknown man has to be found' led to a spy fever that could only be satisfied with a human sacrifice.

Charles Way's script relies heavily on contemporary documents such as the transcript of the trial and the Rosenbergs' letters written from prison. But it carefully avoids manipulating the audience too obviously towards sympathy for the victims of an official conspiracy by the distancing device of following a reporter covering their case.

The play's relevance to both the McCarthyite witch hunt of communist infiltrators in the film industry and to Mrs Thatcher's bogey man of 'the enemy within' is left for an adult audience to work out for itself. In the teachers' pack the connection is explored by reference to John Proctor's speech at the end of Arthur Miller's *The Crucible* – another occasion when the American government offered the option of confess (and co-operation) or die.

Robin Thornber

ON THE BLACK HILL

On the Black Hill (Theatr Clwyd)
The Guardian, 4 February, 1986.

This, rather than West End trouser-farce, is what Theatr Clwyd should be doing. Fine, sharp, powerful writing, compellingly, sympathetically staged, and most of all tellingly relevant to the concerns of a Welsh identity.

I hadn't read Bruce Chatwin's book, *On The Black Hill* (although it won the 1982 Whitbread award for a first novel), but after seeing Charles Way's stage adaptation I want to go out and buy it tomorrow.

It's a richly satisfying account of rural life in the Marches country straddling the Radnor-Hereford border during the first half of this century. Lying somewhere between *Cider With Rosie* and *The Hired Man*, it paints a fond but unsentimental picture of a world that is almost gone but still recognisably real.

And in chronicling the history of one quirky family, it celebrates the values – timeless and probably fairly universal – of the people who live on and off and for the land. Amos Jones got his tenancy by marrying Mary, a missionary's daughter touched by travel and refinement, and that opened a draughty window on the closed world of the Black Hill.

Their twin sons suppress their dreams of escaping the predetermined pattern – Benjamin's slightly feminine traits like baking cakes, Lewis's fantasies of flying – but the younger daughter, Rebecca, leaves tainted with a townie cloud of pregnancy by an Irish Catholic.

The impressionistic saga of rooted certainties knocked by land feuds within the village and torn by strange notions from outside – like classical learning and the Kaiser's war – is brought to vibrant, vivid life by Jamie Garven's superbly powered, meticulously focused production, economically fluid but catching the pace and colours of rural life.

The playing is so consistently strong that it seems unkind to single out Terry Jackson's tense, terse father, Susan McGoun's gently suffering mother, and Andy Rivers and Sion Tudor Owen as the twins, sharing their parents' quilt for 40 years.

All the performances were more than good, in depth and in detail, catching a stillness and self-possession that's rare these days. And the whole company joined in the music, composed and directed by Philip Thomas, which with Keith Hemming's sensitive lighting on Kim Kenny's rustic set made the show so warmly evocative.

Robin Thornber

On the Black Hill (The Sherman Arena)
The Guardian, 11 February, 1986.

It was an inauspicious opening to what was to be a three-hour marathon at the Sherman Arena: folk dancing and a tableau suggested we were in for the usual corny country nostalgia extolling the virtues of natural living. The first act was bitty and too long. But then, by golly, the thing really got going and we ended up with that rare sense of emotional exhaustion and a feeling that we had witnessed a remarkable production – a unique and marvellous work that was epic in scope.

I haven't properly read Bruce Chatwin's best-selling novel of life on the Herefordshire-Radnorshire border, an area that yields a surprising amount of creative work. But clearly the book isn't a voyeuristic documentary, or in any way patronising. Charles Way's adaptation for the Made in Wales Stage Company, which changes the emphasis quite noticeably, is if anything even more respectful.

It's the story of a family made exceptional only by the presence in it of identical male twins. It is their life we follow and, really, there's little in their tale to hold us – except that it's realistic and everyday like Hardy, and it is his rural world with which *On the Black Hill* must inevitably be compared.

It isn't perfect, and I suspect there will be some changes after the first night, but it is something quite special, a work of intensity, compassion, humour, and tragedy, where the immediacy is enhanced by the intimacy of the studio performance space.

What makes the production ultimately such a triumphant evening is the way that all the elements work so well together – Way's script, Jamie Garvin's direction, Philip Hazelwood's music, Kim Kenny's set and ensemble performances that are quite extraordinary, notably from Tudor Evans and Andy Rivers as the two brothers, Terry Jackson as their surly father, and Eleanor Thomas as the patient, middle-class mother.

David Adams

PARADISE DRIVE

Paradise Drive (Windhill Community Centre, Bridgend)
The Guardian, 24 February, 1989.

The latest work from that most distinctive of Welsh touring companies, Hijinx, is without doubt the most depressing piece of theatre I have seen for a long time. It deals with a pretty depressing period, the last 10 years, and offers periodic snapshots in the generally unexceptionally depressing life of a family.

If we care to see it as an allegory of a decade of the more subtle effects of Thatcherism then it's a depressingly accurate catalogue of disintegration, compromise, entrepreneurialism and the triumphs of material values over the artistic and the spiritual.

Unrelenting nihilism, though, makes for a pretty dire evening's entertainment. Those that packed Windhill Community Centre on the outskirts of Bridgend probably came on the strength of earlier Hijinx shows, where the realities of life were never shielded but an energeric, fun show was guaranteed. Of late the company have been concerned with darker subjects explored with a discomforting, controlled anger.

Ros Hutt's production of *Paradise Drive* is full of nervousness, of the signs of a world falling apart. An attentive mother verges on the neurotic, father is having an affair, daughter has an unhappy marriage, son feels there is no place for the artist in today's Britain. It is the familiarity with these sketchy lives that makes the story (devised by the company and scripted by Charles Way) so disconcerting.

It is also, perhaps, the emptiness that makes it, for me, an almost unwatchable piece. With no attempt to flesh out any of the characters, we neither understand nor care about them. They are, in the words of one of the plaintive songs by Phil Thomas in the production, four strangers bound by blood, and they remain strangers to us as to themselves with the audience often seeming intruders on private family relationships that make no sense.

Performances were also unsettling, sometimes suggesting unrevealed intimacy, sometimes inexplicable remoteness. The characters' lives make no sense because life itself is being drained of purpose but also because we simply don't know them well enough. Paradise Drive is an elusive work and it can all too easily slip away.

David Adams

Paradise Drive (Theatr Clwyd)
The Guardian, 7 November, 1989.

This is a lovely nugget of a show, far better than any show preceded by the sinister words 'devised by the company' has a right to be. Perhaps for this we should thank Mr Charles Way who apparently put the words down on paper. We should also thank Rosamunde Hutt who directs the four members of Hijinx Theatre Company with elegant economy, and Philip Thomas, whose plangent music does so much to promote Paradise Drive from the status of thoughtful sitcom to reverberant sound sculpture.

The subject is the dissolution, or evolution, of a family. This is familiar territory; Hijinx's triumph is that they manage to explore it without, largely, slipping into the usual potholes of the form. The son does something spectacular with himself in the last 15 minutes, tangentially involving the Home Secretary and society, but by this time the company has earned the right to one grand gesture.

Events are spread over 10 years. The family – 'four strangers bound in blood' as the script nicely puts it – exchange deceits, disappointments, confidences and optimism round and over a darkened dining room table. The mood is intimate, whimsical and sad. The central sadness is the dying of human love. Nothing else matters.

Mr Way's dialogue is a pert, neatly posed, affair. 'I haven't felt like this since my driving test', sighs crewcut Sally on her wedding day. 'You passed your driving test', consoles Mum. Below the words swirls an extraordinary acoustic undertow. Lipstick is rattled on mirrors, keys swung from palm to palm, heels click nervously. Saxophones, guitar and violin exchange melancholic harmonies. The characters launch into a kind of Celtic acapella whenever the going gets particularly tough. The effect is stunning.

The acting is first rate. Richard Berry's neurotic executive, Gaynor Lougher's anxious wife, and Matthew Bailey's artistic son are sympathetic, slightly heroic, individuals. Eddie Ladd's Sally – punk-cum-advertising-mogul – is a superb creation, and a perfect vehicle for Ms Ladd's extraordinary brand of contained menace. Imagine a ferret with a wrenched neck playing Lady Macbeth and you're about half way there.

Erlend Cloustron

THE FLOOD

The Flood (The Unicorn Theatre, London)
The Independent, 7 March, 1990.

Charles Way's new play for children wrestles the deluge from its biblical context, transposing it, alarmingly aptly, to contemporary times. Dad is too busy making money to listen to the prophetic dreams of his long-suffering wife. He is livid when she blows the joint account on a boat, and his refusal to throw his briefcase overboard threatens his family's survival. A beautifully choreographed storm finds them shipwrecked on a bountiful desert island, where ecological issues come to the fore. Despite such seminal subject-matter, this show is distinguished by a tender comic touch, epitomised by children sublimely portrayed by actors old enough for pensions. This is a profound, pleasing play for all ages.

The Flood (The Unicorn Theatre, London)
Time Out, 14-21 March, 1990.

'After the rain came the wind; after the wind came the sun'; softly, and uninvited, the audience of nine-to-twelve-year-olds joined in the litany of elemental hazards faced by the family who survived the rain that just started one day and didn't stop until the world was covered with water. The Unicorn's production opened in a week when flooding in Britain hit the headlines and the country was yet again battered by unusually strong winds, ironically reinforcing the relevance of the play's theme. In *The Flood* Charles Way has come up with a piece of theatre of the same calibre as the Unicorn's award-winning production of *The Red Chair*. Way doesn't write down to his audience, and this play makes for sometimes uncomfortable watching, but the tension is broken at intervals by nicely judged humour. The plot is simple: Martha, the mother, intuitive, perhaps psychic, insists that the rain isn't going to stop, ever. Martha's workoholic husband thinks she's neurotic and her children are frightened – of the endless rain, and by their parents quarrelling. A world in which nothing remains but water is convincingly conveyed by a set that features acres of blue drapes, with lighting and sound effects further enhancing the apocalyptical illusion. When she fails to convey her certainty of impending disaster to her family Martha blows the family savings on a boat which the family are persuaded to board in the nick of time – but a tidal wave is only the starting point of a voyage which tests the family, individually and collectively. The play's ending is movingly hopeful but does not discharge the concern generated by the frighteningly plausible plot. Recommended as a foundation for a lasting enjoyment of the theatre.

Sara O'Reilly

The Flood (M6 Theatre Company)
The Guardian, 20 June, 1992.

In a cupboard-size drama studio with nothing but an upturned table, two chairs and sound effects, M6 Theatre Company vividly confronted a group of schoolchildren with profound questions about the quality of their existence and the threat of global destruction.

Charles Way's provocative and moving play is modern Noah, only Noah is female and her husband is a smug executive with no time for his wife's 'neurotic' premonitions about impending ecological doom. Even her children are disbelieving, torn between fear and anger and their parents' conflict.

But the family soon find themselves afloat, lone survivors on a sea of never-ending rain, possessing only life's essentials and thus evolving a new relationship with each other and the land they eventually find.

Magical, haunting, funny and tearful, M6's skill in conveying so huge a theme in such a limited setting is the stuff of real, discomforting, involving theatre and, as the accompanying teacher's pack indicates, the potential for social and personal exploration for children lucky enough to see it is considerable.

Francesca Turner

IN THE BLEAK MIDWINTER

In the Bleak Midwinter (The Sherman Arena)
The Guardian, 25 September, 1990.

If you want small-scale perfection, try Hijinx Theatre. Their shows are with almost uncanny reliability little masterpieces, miniatures where every aspect of the product is finely crafted – direction, acting, music, singing, design, and, in their latest play just starting on their UK tour, the script.

In the Bleak Midwinter is a reworking by Charlie Way of the Shepherds' Pageant, with Wakefield (or York, Chester, or wherever) transported to home territory, somewhere above Abergavenny but still near Bethlehem, a piece of writing that is quite delightful in its fidelity to the spirit of the mediaeval miracle plays and yet utterly contemporary.

Way has written something that matches perfectly the company's unique style that mediates the ground between community shows and precision-made physical theatre. Using the characters of the shepherds' plays, the production uses the same vernacular to ask, without necessarily being religious, more immediately moral questions: Herod's census becomes the poll tax registration, for example. As with the miracle cycles, Way uses circular material in a familiar Biblical context to comic purpose.

The company, under the excellent direction of Ros Hutt, made good use of the Sherman Arena space, moving from the performance area up into the audience and round the back, but the focal point remains Richard Aylwin's set, a classically simple amalgam of the religious and the pagan that can be both a shepherds' camp and the Nativity stable, a design enhanced by Ian Buchanan's lighting. The music, by Paula Gardiner, and singing is similarly both reverential and full-blooded, a kind of mixture of gospel and liturgical; ever a strong point in Hijinx productions, the only criticism is that there was not enough.

David Adams

In the Bleak Midwinter (The Sherman Arena)
South Wales Echo, 3 October, 1990.

Hijinx Theatre's new show *In the Bleak Midwinter* is far from being an unseasonal offering.

Writer Charles Way has taken the Nativity story for his starting point, but has transformed it to create a captivating contemporary piece of theatre that explores the theme of friendship, its ties and its bonds, in a refreshing and lively manner.

The writing is sharp, humorous, and at times very moving, given full impact by the four-strong cast.

Between them they have developed a spellbinding method of telling their story about two shepherds, a thief called Mak and his partner Gill, staged on a beautifully simple set that frames the quartet like the fabulous painted architecture does characters found in Renaissance paintings.

The opening scene is set on a hilltop where you can well believe 'frosty winds do moan'.

Shepherds Miriam and Zachariah are en route to Bethlehem, their flight interrupted by a dispute over a stolen sheep, which Mak and Gill attempt to pass off as their new born son in a hilarious piece of farce that sets the tone for many of the exchanges.

Elements of the original story are cleverly interwoven into this dispute between two feuding couples, shifting blame and misunderstandings in imperceptible ways until you arrive at a final scene of reconciliation.

Along the way, the audience at the Llanover Hall Arts Centre became a herd of sheep, a baby minder, and witnesses to a vision.

But the world is out of joint too – the couple are being forced to pay an iniquitous poll tax, a King in silken finery has been robbed, and the city is a threatening, unfriendly place.

This is a superb evening's entertainment relying on a few tricks to offer up the kind of magic that a consummate storyteller can weave.

Penny Simpson

In the Bleak Midwinter (Mold Alun High School)
The Guardian, 18 October, 1990.

Hijinx Theatre from Cardiff is currently barnstorming Wales with a most satisfying evening of theatre. Writer Charles Way has taken the sheep-stealing scene from the Nativity in the Wakefield Cycle of medieval mystery plays and projected this specific, localised comic gem onto a universal, timeless plane.

The shepherds have been summoned from watching their flocks on a black hill, somewhere in the Marches t'other side of Hereford, to Bethlehem to register for the poll tax. Robbing a wandering king of his myrrh on the way, they find the crowded city's inns all full and end up sharing a stable with an unmarried mother.

As with the Wakefield original, it is the interplay of strongly-drawn, instantly-recognisable characters that gives the piece its power: Zachariah (Richard Berry), the plodding, dreaming shepherd with more principles than there are stars in the sky; Miriam (Erica Eirian), his pragmatic, grumbling wife; Mak (Peter Rumney), the wily, sheep-stealing chancer and Gill (Helen Gwyn), his free-spirited girlfriend.

All four give immaculately-detailed performances in a richly-textured production, directed by Rosamunde Hutt.

It is enriched with acapella music by Paula Gardiner – a totally original style of unaccompanied harmonising that draws on jazz scat singing, gospel and early church music in a way that is bewitching and entirely apt – and an arena setting designed by Richard Aylwin that combines earthy realism on the ground with a Gothic canopy overhead that comes straight from the Duc de Berry's Book of Hours.

Deeply rooted, warmly human, funny and moving. *In the Bleak Midwinter's* spellbinding magic was strong enough to overcome even the dismal forbidding context of Mold Alun High School, which seems to be designed for the incarceration of students rather than the liberation of the spirit.

Robin Thornber

In the Bleak Midwinter (Llanover Hall)
Western Mail, 22 November, 1990.

In the Bleak Midwinter is a re-working by Charles Way (*On the Black Hill*) of a Nativity play that has been touring small venues around Wales.

Just as the famous story is here-placed in the familiar setting of the Black Mountains, so questions of right and wrong behaviour are posed in a way that the many young members of the audience as well as adults can appreciate them.

Ethics and religion are worked into a heart-warming story full of comedy and humanity as we follow the progress of a shepherd, his wife and their newborn son as they travel to Bethlehem to register for what else – the poll tax.

On the way they meet a thief and his girlfriend and all suffer the consequences of the moral choices they make. Like sheep they go astray but ultimately find the path of righteousness and a reconciliation.

Zachariah the shepherd is a simple soul who loves his flock and trusts mankind. Richard Berry is appropriately gormless-looking with his ears sticking out from under a bowler hat. Erica Eirian gives a spirited performance as the sharp-tongued wife Miriam who has the best lines. 'I'm driven to my wits end', cries Zach. 'A shortish journey', she retorts. Peter Rumney is the conniving thief Mak and shows his versatility in other smaller roles. The girlfriend Gill (Helen Gwyn) is a cheerful, brazen liar who discovers the error of her ways.

Woven into the play are attractive bits of singing that put across the Ten Commandments in a mixture of gospel music and plain-song. Rosamunde Hutt directs a lively show with many humorous touches.

The simple imaginative props like the stuffed sheep are one of the charming features of this unpretentious production.

The talented designer Richard Aylwin here creates a gazebo-like set that could equally be a manger or a heavenly crown. He combines meticulous attention to detail with an eye for fantasy to create such delights as a little black rock dotted with miniature sheep which represents a bird's-eye-view of the Black Mountains.

Nicole Sochor

In the Bleak Midwinter (Wales Tour)
Western Mail, 15 October, 1993.

The revival of this topical comedy from Charles Way has begun an extensive tour of Wales and England.

Set in the Welsh hills 'overlooking Bethlehem', the play uses biblical analogies to remind us of the world's suffering.

A shepherd, Zac (Richard Berry) takes his wife Miriam (Firenza Guidi) to Bethlehem for the census, complaining about taxes and poverty.

Zak's simple faith in human nature is tested by the thief Mak (David Murray) and his lady Gill (Helen Gwyn).

This is far from being a sombre play, however. It is an entertaining and down-to-earth comedy with a fast and furious dialogue.

The cast performs flawlessly throughout, making light of tongue-twisters and country accents. Three of the performers double up roles, creating an illusion of scope it is hard to credit to a cast of four.

Not content with just acting, the performers add musical harmonies, and turn scene-changing into an art.

An intriguing set designed by Ian Buchanan gives a theatre-in-the-round setting. This enables the audience to become sheep on the hillside, or the crowds thronging to Bethlehem for the census.

The comedy raises many smiles, touches the conscience and provides an outstanding theatrical experience. Try to catch this production when it visits a venue near you.

Noel Lacey

In the Bleak Midwinter (Withernsea High School Drama Studio)
The Holderness Gazette, 26 November, 1993.

Theatregoers in Withernsea had an enchanting preview of Christmas at the Withernsea High School Drama Studio last week.

Hijinx Theatre Company, who are based in Cardiff in Wales, are currently touring England with their award-winning play 'In the Bleak Midwinter'. Their itinerary takes in venues as far apart as Devon and North Yorkshire. Once again there was a packed house and a very appreciative audience.

Charles Way who wrote the play recalls his own experiences of school Nativity plays and the joy of being chosen for a part. This motivated his delightful story.

The performance employs the techniques of Shakespeare's theatre in the round. The location is somewhere on the Black Mountains not far from Bethlehem. Hijinx Company is noted for its music. The play opens with the four members of the cast, Richard Berry, who plays Zac a shepherd, Firenza Guidi as Miriam his wife, Helen Gwyn is Gill, a girl who is involved with Mak, a rogue played by David Murray, giving an unforgettably poignant rendering of the carol 'In the Bleak Midwinter' in their spellbinding acapella style. The music runs throughout the play with some carols and some songs specially composed for the play by Paula Gardiner. This is magical, along with the carols are foot-tapping lively numbers which delighted the audience.

The theme is the traditional journey to Bethlehem to pay the Poll Tax or Community Charge. The story is woven round these four people. It brings out all the characteristics displayed by people in troubled times. There is warmth and love, and in Zac the trusting optimism and honesty of the simply country shepherd who cares for his wife and baby and also his sheep (not forgetting Barnaby the lamb).

There is stealth and craftiness from Mak who has a strong sense of self-preservation, in a world where hunger and violence are rife.

He, like all rogues, has a charming side and, though stealing the lamb and Zac's blanket whilst they sleep, shares his cider and gives Miriam's baby a present. He hopes to share his ill-gotten gains with Gill.

The theft is discovered and she is thrown upon the mercies of Zac and Miriam. She travels with them.

There is a beautiful scene where Miriam finds Mary, Joseph, and the Christ child in the manger. Mary gives her gold which is later to save the life of her baby, Moses, from Herod's assassin.

From a mutual hatred love grows between Miriam and Gill as they show sisterly concern for each other.

The play closes as it opened with the beautiful Welsh voices of these four talented people filling the theatre with the poignant sound of the carol once more.

Local people of all ages, from the very young to elderly, enjoyed the play, but an interesting reaction came from three young Withernsea drama students; Amy Ward and Amanda Harmann were enthralled by the different approach to the story and loved the singing; Kiera Thomson thought the show was well prepared for presentation in a small theatre. They are pleased to be able to see good theatre locally at affordable prices.

Grateful thanks were expressed to Gordon Beastall for his usual hard work in securing this company for Withernsea, in spite of a very full itinerary.

M.C.

In the Bleak Midwinter (Bradford Peverell Village Hall)
Dorset Evening Echo, 16 December, 1993.

A Nativity play which is described as a family comedy requires investigation, an exercise with which half the village population of Bradford Peverell presumably concurred since they piled into the hall in prodigious numbers to see the Hijinx Theatre Company at work.

Based upon the sheep-stealing scene from a medieval mystery nativity play, this new work by Charles Way uncovers the essential humanity and timelessness of the Bible story and gives it an altogether delightful yet challenging edge.

A shepherd, his wife and infant son are dispossessed of their home and take themselves off to Bethlehem at the behest of Herod's census.

But the dreamy-eyed shepherd Zac and his ferocious wife Miriam find their path a thorny one as they meet up with all kinds of temptations in this morality play with a chuckle at every turn.

First there's Mak, who says he's a friend but isn't then, there's Gill, who says she's not a temptress but is. What with bogs and babies to contend with, it's no wonder Miriam is driven to distraction by her star-gazing husband as they struggle to reach Bethlehem only to be separated in the crowded streets.

Still Miriam is lucky enough to get shelter for the night in a stable with a young couple who've just had a baby but her troubles are not yet over, as she soon discovers.

The cast of four actors recreate marvellously and with amazing economy the power yet simplicity of ordinary lives touched by tremendous events. Funny, touching and sometimes horrifying happenings are brought magically to life by dialogue, songs and acting of an exceptionally high order which transformed a small Dorset village hall for a while into a far distant land of long ago. Brilliant.

Marian Cox

ASH ON A YOUNG MAN'S SLEEVE

Ash on a Young Man's Sleeve (The Sherman Theatre)
Western Mail, 1 March, 1991.

Dannie Abse's semi-autobiographical novel about a Jewish boy coming of age in World War II Cardiff is also a resonant document of Welsh social history.

So it was fitting for Charles Way, who specialises in bringing Wales's past and folk memories to the theatre, to adapt it for the first time for the stage.

His sensitive interpretation retains the poetry and Dylanesque imagery of the original and focuses on key elements in the plot: the bonds of friendship and family, budding sexual awareness and growing consciousness of the devastating events on the world political arena.

The play is like a stream of memories in which events unfold as a sequence of fragmented scenes experienced by a young Dannie, bound together by a narrative from a grown-up Dannie and an emotive accompaniment of original piano music by Paula Gardiner.

The play preserves the fragile balance of the moods of the book.

Brother Leo is a live-wire, irreverent and passionate about left-wing causes and pretty girls alike. Brother Wilf is weighed down by the cares of being a doctor. Mother clucks and fusses about her sons' welfare as she admonishes them to stay clear of shiksas. Father frets about Dannie's poor marks in school and keeps the Sabbath holy.

As the comedies and tragedies of domestic life unfold, so the atrocities of Fascism impinge on their lives: a Welshman's death in the Spanish Civil War, news of the Holocaust, and finally the Blitz which shatters Dannie's innocence.

But it's also a funny piece, with odd characters like Uncle Isidore spouting obscure aphorisms, and Dannie's chum Loll – 'He's an idiot, and he lives in Splott!'.

This ensemble piece saw all in the Sherman theatre Company carrying their weight. Director Phil Clark created a seamless flow of action.

The set was a disappointing jumble of incongruous bits and pieces – trees and lamp posts jostling with furniture – unified by a messy length of gauze.

The props weren't moved so we had the peculiar spectacle of Dannie camping on Ogmore beach next to a dining room table and chair. Lighting should be used to define segments of the set more sharply, or better still, the set should be simplified.

This aside, *Ash on a Young Man's Sleeve* should move anyone who recalls their youth and idealism.

Nicole Sochor

Ash on a Young Man's Sleeve (The Sherman Theatre)
The Guardian, 4 March, 1991.

Phil Clark has transformed the Sherman Theatre from prime evidence of the imminent death of mainstream drama into a vibrant and exciting venue by enthusiastically importing many of the values of community theatre on to the main stage.

Ash on a Young Man's Sleeve, based on the semi-autobiographical novel of poet Dannie Abse, has no star names in its cast but instead boasts a quality of ensemble playing and a directness that is the inheritance of Wales's thriving community theatre tradition.

Charles Way's adaptation chronicles faithfully the poet's early years in Thirties Cardiff, focusing on a boyhood friendship but capturing within its range the socialist, Jewish, South Walean culture in which Abse grew up.

It's a technically very complex production, with lots of short scenes – again, the sort of format that touring community groups are used to but which, when transferred from the limited resources of village-hall gigs to the larger dimensions and greater ambitions of a main-house stage, can get messy. In fact, the Sherman Company do amazingly well, even if in these early days it is slightly ragged.

With adaptations taking the place of original new writing it is rewarding to find a work that is marvellously theatrical in its own right.

Charles Way tells Abse's story with sensitivity and a lightness of touch that make the emotional climaxes all the more effective, with evocative music from Paula Gardner and an expressionist set from John Elvery – perhaps too diverting in that a raked table, for example, is so angled that we expect the candles and bowls to slide off into the front row.

David Adams

Ash on a Young Man's Sleeve (The Sherman Theatre)
South Wales Echo, 4 March, 1991.

Ash on a Young Man's Sleeve – Dannie Abse's account of a Jewish boy's adolescent years in pre-war Cardiff – has been imaginatively transferred to the stage of the Sherman Theatre.

Playwright Charles Way has captured the spirit of Abse's original text with a judicious selection of incident and character.

The voices are intercut with childhood rhymes, snatches of song, and poetic description that weld together unforgettably the domestic scenes set around the Abse kitchen table with echoes of the wider social and economic upheavals of the 1930's.

These characters are in constant movement, criss-crossing their way across John Elvery's magnificent dreamlike set of broken picture frames, discarded chairs and a park bench overshadowed by a large fringed lampshade.

These surreal elements underscore Phil Clark's direction, which has shaped from Abse's written past a strong visual vocabulary that strikes a chord for anyone remembering their own childhood experiences and the world events that may have left some small scar.

For Dannie, it is the treatment of Jews in Germany and the invasion of Poland that leave a jarring note after the summer swims in Ogmore and the wooing of Lydia Pike – information we glean from two striking vignettes that change the scene to Spain and Paris.

An older Dannie (Andy Rivers) acts as narrator, a master of ceremonies in crumpled cords, who also transforms into the wonderful Uncle Isidore – a philosopher playing on a badly strung violin.

Gareth Potter plays Dannie's young self with a fine touch, developing from an awkward slouch into the Brylcreemed Casanova found outside the old Empire cinema.

The rest of the ensemble adopt different roles effortlessly, with some fine comedy playing from Rhodri Hugh as would-be-filmstar Loll and Nina Holloway's purse-lipped mother anxious to keep her three sons free from the clutches of other women.

Penny Simpson

Ash on a Young Man's Sleeve (The Sherman Theatre)
The Stage, 4 April, 1991.

The pleasures and pains of adolescence set in a context of local events and historical perspectives – such is the stuff that can make for an absorbing play.

It certainly does in the Charles Way adaptation of Dannie Abse's semi-autobiographical novel *Ash on a Young Man's Sleeve*, as given in its world premiere by the Sherman Theatre Company.

Dannie the poet and his brothers Doctor Wilf and Leo, long-time Labour MP, grew up in the thirties in Cardiff. In an affectionate Jewish family atmosphere, they viewed the Depression, the rise of Hitler, the Spanish Civil War, the bombing of their city, as a backdrop against more immediate personal concerns.

In a expressionistic setting by John Elvery, this Phil Clark production roved through time and location with self-assured fluency. The ensemble playing by the cast of ten, tackling with a minimum of props and costume changes a score of well-defined characters, was admirable, underpinned by the evocative piano music of Paula Gardiner.

Here were outstanding performances by anchorman Andy Rivers as the older Dannie commenting throughout, and Gareth Potter as the young Dannie. The many notable cameos included Nina Holloway and Terence Dauncey as the mother and father, Geraint Morgan as best friend Keith, Russell Gomer as Leo and Rhodri Hugh as Loll. Support came from Bill Bellamy, Erica Eirian and Paula Gardiner. Full of social comment and gentle humour, Ash on a Young Man's sleeve is in no way confined by its Welsh perspectives and is worthy of a wider audience.

Jon Holliday

DEAD MAN'S HAT

Dead Man's Hat (The Plough, Torrington)
The Stage, 29 October, 1992.

Having rescued Mary Shelley's Frankenstein from the embellishments imposed on it by Hollywood, Charles Way has performed a similar service for the Wild West.

Dead Man's Hat had its first performance by the Barnstaple-based Orchard Theatre Company at the Plough, Torrington's arts centre, on Thursday, thus embarking on a tour of over 20 venues.

Way's plot, set in the Wyoming of the late 19th century, has its share of shootings and lynchings. But the role around which it revolves – a drifter named Clay admirably interpreted by Andrew Howard – has more credibility than many of the archetypal heroes portrayed on the screen by such actors as John Wayne.

He wanders into the small town of Brandonsville and takes a job with a family of homesteaders who have staked a claim alongside the Sweetwater river. Almost immediately he is caught up in a classic confrontation between farmers and cattlemen, which inevitably results in a kind of open war.

Bill Buffery's production is full of innovation. Actors spin from one character to another and there is a stimulating moment when Gill Nathanson, as the farmer's wife, gallops an imaginary wagon across the open stage.

Andrea Gascoigne plays her daughter, disenchanted with a pioneer existence. Other roles are taken by David Plimmer and James Lailey, and atmosphere is heightened by the music of Tom Nordon. Meg Surrey designs a simple but effective set. But it is Gill Nathanson, first as a determined settler and then in a cameo as saloon barmaid, who deserves the award of player of the night.

Frank Kempe

EYE OF THE STORM

Eye of the Storm (Snap Theatre)
The Times Educational Supplement, 19 March, 1993.

Under attack, huddle together or strike back. Essex theatres are doing both in a lean time for the arts and a desperate one for Theatre in Education. Snap Theatre combines its experience of performance and workshops in schools with three major theatres – repertoires at Colchester and Westcliff-on-Sea, and touring Harlow Playhouse. The larger companies can claim increased access and community responsibility, while Snap has extra resources for its area of expertise.

This, the consortium's first project, has especially close links with Westcliff's Palace Theatre. It has to be said that, in the past, none of the county's main theatres have made outstanding contributions to young people's work. Now though, Westcliff provides rehearsal space and technical input. In future, more theatres may become involved and take such support in turns.

Aimed at the 13 to 16 group, each day's residency brings up to 100 young people to the appropriate theatre's studio (a much friendlier space than a main house). Bringing together people from more than one school is an advantage of the scheme, and the 80-minute play which starts the day off shows the extra scope a theatre setting allows.

This is particularly the case with Dawn Allsopp's setting. A circular revolve with an arched ladder crossing its diameter, the stage suggests an island or boat. Curtains are skilfully manoeuvred by the actors to vary the focus of the playing space.

Based on *The Tempest*, it is anything but Prospero's story. Rather it focuses upon a sulky, bored teenage Miranda whose rebellion against her father is activated by a storm she raises, marooning the other two characters, Trinculo and Stephano. Both are given their own histories, but Trinculo does not grasp that his mate is his ex-girlfriend Stephanie in disguise. He treated her as badly as he plans to treat Miranda. Meanwhile Miranda comes to see that it is *she* who is going to have to be brave in the new world for which she sets sail.

Much of Charles Way's script is a skilful blend of the poetic and colloquial and Andy Graham's production uses the limited area well. Among the cast, Hélène Batchelor and Beaux Bryant present strong women characters as Miranda and Stephanie, while Alistair Schofield manages Trinculo's sexploitation tactfully.

Timothy Ramsden

ILL MET BY MOONLIGHT

Ill Met By Moonlight (Splott East Moors Community Centre)
Reviewed for *The Guardian*, but unpublished, 20 November, 1994.

Storytelling can seem a lost art in postmodernist theatre but I've just seen two touring productions from smallscale companies that entrance, intrigue and delight in two quite different ways.

Cardiff's Hijinx Theatre have an unassailable reputation for accessible, immaculate, theatre, their community shows honed with the attention to detail and clarity that defines their less visible but invaluable work with and for audiences with learning disabilities. In Charlie Way's *Ill Met By Moonlight* they have a script of great beauty and skill, a passionate tale of love and magic that is classically simple but which evokes, as do the best stories, layers of archetypal response.

Set in the Celtic borderland as the twentieth century was seeing the end of superstition, where the Pycha, Shakespeare's Puck, is fighting a rearguard action against modern machinery and organised religion, the play draws on Ella Mary Leather's classic *Folk-Lore of Herefordshire* (long a treasured book) but imbues the natural magic world with a humanity as two ordinary, plain people find a love that inevitably defies the scheming of the last brownie. Les Miller's production catches beautifully that mixture of magic and humanity with impressive economy, creating in the everyday performance venues (I saw it in Splott's East Moors community centre) a world of mischief, passion and change. Charlie Way wrote an excellent stage adaptation of *On the Black Hill* and his knowledge and appreciation of the Border culture is again evident here as he takes also the opportunity to show his lyricism and ability to explore the spiritual in everyday life.

Bristol's Public Parts, whose tour of *Stuffed Shirts and Marionettes* is confined to England but did get to within a stone's throw of Wales with visits to the Forest of Dean and the Wye Valley (I caught it at Coleford's College Theatre), offer a story that is a far cry from the world of hobgoblins and rural culture but is set in the same period and is no less about human passion. Based on Claire Tomalin's book *The Invisible Woman*, it tears apart the urban Victorian world of hypocrisy and pretence as it follows the life of Ellen Tierney, actress, mistress of Charles Dickens and respectable wife and mother.

But where Hijinx rely on simplicity, Public Parts tell their stories obliquely, insisting on a multifaceted impressionistic narrative. We are led gradually by the four performers into the interwoven themes of sexual deviancy and violence, double standards, the ambiguous interface of Dickens's fact and fiction, the world of pretence that was both the theatre and Victorian England. Like Hijinx, Public Parts are strong in voice and make powerful use of music, with the songs expressing in tone as much as in words the harshness and contradictions of the story. The show is an exhilarating, searing, mind-teasing piece of consummate theatricality, performed with staggering energy and commitment and, like *Ill Met By Moonlight*, is totally engaging.

David Adams

Ill Met By Moonlight (Llanover Arts Centre, Canton)
The Stage, 19 January, 1995.

The course of true love rarely runs smoothly, especially if the faery folk intervene with their mischievous tricks.

So it proved when a shy middle aged bachelor decided it was time he had an heir to leave his hill farm to and fixed his romantic gaze on a neighbouring widow, struggling to keep her own farm going.

Set on the borders of Wales and England towards the end of the last century when many remote rural people still believed faeries were a force to be reckoned with, *Ill Met By Moonlight* provided an evening of rare enchantment at Llanover Hall Arts Centre, Canton.

With more than a nodding acquaintance with Shakespeare's *A Midsummer Night's Dream*, this excellent play by Charles Way was full of intriguing twists and turns, poetic imagery, laced with humour and a little malicious fun and most appealing tenderness.

Directed by Les Miller in a cleverly evocative setting by Bettina Reeves, with charming music and songs by Paula Gardiner, the cast of four showed just how effectively a small ensemble group can people a stage with colourful and convincing characters.

As the faery folk, Richard Berry and Helen Gwyn were quite delightful, while Robert Lane and Erica Eirian extracted every bit of humour and pathos from their roles as the unlikely lovers.

A fine performance in every way.

Jon Holliday

Ill Met By Moonlight (Community Centre, Rhydyfelin)
The Pontypridd and Llantrisant Campaign, 27 January, 1995.

On Thursday 15th December, the award winning theatre company, Hijinx, brought the latest hit show by Charles Way *Ill Met By Moonlight* to Llan Community Centre in Rhydyfelin.

Superb acting performances by Rob Lane, Richard Berry, Erica Eirian and Helen Gwyn, excellent music by Paula Gardiner all aided by a magically effective set, lighting and sound effects, kept an audience of over 50 people spellbound for two hours. The story tells of two reluctant lovers struggling to fall in love and of the interference in their already difficult lives by the mischievous fairie folk of Puck resulting in some hysterical and some very sad moments, but needless to say everything finished happily.

Little wonder that this Cardiff based company are in great demand up and down the country and picking up awards.

SLEEPING BEAUTY

Sleeping Beauty (The Sherman Theatre)
Western Mail, 2 December, 1994.

The idea of introducing a prince who is black into one of the best-known fairytales immediately raises suspicions of a moral lesson in political correctness.

But in the Sherman Theatre company's production of *Sleeping Beauty* there is no room for such jaded observations.

This production is inspiring, because it shows that in these world-weary, often too nostalgic times, there can be an exciting and new approach which produces brilliant family entertainment.

By telling the tale in his way, writer Charles Way (who adapted *On the Black Hill*) has put paid to the idea of the good old ways being the best, and has shown that the most hallowed and successful stories can be improved on and even given a Welsh flavour – all in the best possible taste.

With his material the cast and director Jamie Garven, have produced a play which lightens the most cynical hearts, and enthrals young ones. Everybody knows the story, but few could be prepared for the surprises.

Good and evil are portrayed by Branwen and Modrun, the fairy sisters whose movements lend a new dimension to the spells they cast.

The King and Queen ('Gwen Bach') are Edwardian in dress, and Sleeping Beauty in a froth of pink and white showing the mixture of spite, impatience and kindness that children do.

But it the prince, Owain son of Owain son of Owain etc., was the character that children will probably learn much from.

His passage from a dithering, 'can't do anything', to a confident man via the challenges he has to face cannot be missed.

On top of this add Gryff, half-man half-dragon – one of Branwen's spells gone wrong – the Spider King and the Tylwyth Teg, and you have a rich play which loses none of the fairytale elements of the original.

The sets are imaginative – hanging whirring bicycle wheels marking the passage of time for example – the costumes terrific and the live music uplifting.

The Sherman has built a national reputation over the past years for its Christmas productions.

I doubt there will be one anywhere to match this.

Judith Davies

Sleeping Beauty (The Sherman Theatre)
Gair Rhydd, 5 December, 1994.

This pantomime will wipe the floor with its more traditional counterparts at surrounding theatres. The age-old story of sleeping beauty is revitalised and given a Welsh twist by playwright, Charles Way.

The main concern of the tale is whether the inept Prince can overcome his fears and flaws to save Sleeping Beauty. The story is narrated by Branwen and Modron, two omniscient witches: one good, one evil. The author expertly weaves them in and out of the tale creating two levels on which they move. Meanwhile the audience is kept laughing by Gryff, the half dragon, and the extremely clumsy Prince.

The production evokes a rustic quality that is echoed throughout the play. Rickety scaffolding covered in tethered materials makes up much of the set and old bicycle wheels are spun to produce the clicking sound of spindles. An excellent musical score blends well with the action on stage, reinforcing the ethereal atmosphere and provides an extra dimension to the performance.

A pantomime is not the easiest of styles to work in, yet none of the cast fell short of the play's demands. Gryff, the half dragon (Russell Gomer), has the sort of comic timing Harry Enfield can only dream about, while Modron (Melanie Walters) delivers a refreshingly original evil witch.

Like all good theatre this is simple. Jamie Garven, the director, builds a wonderful storybook world of pastel colours and subtle stylised acting. This has none of the clichés of the traditional British pantomime. There is almost a sense of parody as Branwen tries to launch into a pop song or when one character says 'We must hurry, we only have 100 years'.

The ending is somewhat of an anti-climax and lines like 'love laughs at locks and keys' do tend to churn the stomach. I'm not sure whether it would suit the majority of Rob Newman-loving students, although the accidental line from the Spider King, 'I'll suck you dry,' would no doubt raise a laugh. Overall this is a beautiful production worth seeing. Definitely a pantomime for the Nineties.

Richard Mackey

Sleeping Beauty (The Sherman Theatre)
The Guardian, 4 January, 1995.

No, not the panto – or even a seasonable musical in the usual sense.

Charles Way's fairytale adaptation is smashing holiday entertainment for young people but to label it would diminish what is simply a well-targeted piece of theatre.

The story of Briar Rose and her prince still provides the narrative, but it's set in Edwardian Wales, the dragon is only half a dragon, the heroine is a rather spoilt girl and the prince is not unlike a black Jerry Lewis on a bike.

True to the moralistic original, this Sherman Theatre Company production offers a lesson in perseverance, self-confidence and honesty as the hapless hero has to conquer his discophobia (two left feet), arachnophobia and sheer lack of skill in princely pursuits from swordfighting to solving riddles.

Way can work on many layers and can create dialogue that is almost epic in style – and he is also a superb storyteller and can write very good young people's plays that are neither patronising nor over the heads of the audience.

Sleeping Beauty, while perhaps not delivering all its promises, handles the ingredients of witchcraft, romance, comedy and adventure with an impressive assurance and keeps that perfect balance between magic and reality.

In an utterly engaging and entertaining production, there are some nice performances from leads Joseph Jones and Lynne Seymour, Jamie Garven's direction moves it along well and Matthew Bailey's Ravelesque music is a delight, but what's really stunning is Jane Linz Roberts's design – beautiful greens and bronzes, cranks and wheels and striking costumes, a feast for the eyes.

David Adams

A SPELL OF COLD WEATHER

A Spell of Cold Weather (Theatre Centre and The Sherman Theatre Company, Riverside Studio)
Time Out, 14-21 February, 1995.

When Holly arrives to stay on her aunt and uncle's farm while her mother's in hospital she finds herself in miserable company. Her relatives have dim memories of a time when the farm was a happy place and they don't really know why life got so gloomy. It takes the arrival of a child to initiate a process of change which begins when Holly acknowledges the presence of Tommy Trickman, a fairy whose antics the audience can see all along even although he's invisible to Aunt and Uncle.

Drawing on ancient tales of household spirits responsible for the fortunes, good or otherwise, of humans, 'A Spell of Cold Weather' has much magic of its own. A set seemingly created from found materials conceals a series of ingenious surprises; there are some simple but enchanting visual effects; comic moments hit the spot for both children and accompanying adults and there's one lovely, haunting song.

It's quite unusual to come across a company with the confidence to create a show that addresses children's intrinsic sense of things unspoken and their capacity to embrace the realm of enchantment. What radiates from this show by Theatre Centre and the Sherman Theatre from Cardiff is an ethos that values children, celebrating them as a healing force.

Sara O'Reilly

A Spell of Cold Weather (The Sherman Theatre)
South Wales Echo, 18 December, 1995.

Little ones sat spellbound – and there's not much finer praise for an under-sevens' show than that!

There's much to amuse and entertain in this Sherman Theatre Company production.

Abergavenny playwright Charles Way's play tells the story of Holly, a little girl who changes the lives of her grumpy uncle and aunt when she stays at their farm over the New Year.

A vital ingredient in the working of this spell is Tom, a fairy who performs wonderful tricks including making animals talk and turning milk to cream.

But for me, his most magical gift of all is captivating such a young audience and making them chuckle. Magic indeed!

Lauren O'Beirne

A Spell of Cold Weather (The Sherman Theatre)
The Stage, 21 December, 1995.

Catering for large audiences of children of seven and under is a highly specialised undertaking and the Sherman Theatre Company (this year teaming up with the renowned Theatre Centre for a four month tour) proves yet again they are masters at it.

A Spell of Cold Weather, by Charles Way, is a simple tale of a grumpy farming couple (Michael Jasper and Hazel Maycock), who through their round-the-clock toil have lost the knack of actually enjoying themselves.

But a visit from their young niece Holly (Vicci Jade Smith) and some tricks and treats by the rural fairy Tomos Trickman (Neil Thornton) eventually convinces them that all work and no play makes Bob and Betty a dull couple. The farm animals find voices through the efforts of Tomos and are all soon joining in games, songs and dances. The farm may have ignored Christmas but the New Year party makes a magical night to remember.

Director Matthew Bailey ensures there is plenty of physical action, lots of surprises, tricks and knockabout fun in the imaginative setting by Dominie Hooper, with the music provided by John Hardy.

A Spell of Cold Weather is a little gem of a seasonal show that sparkled for the whole of its 60 minutes in the Sherman Arena.

Jon Holliday

NO BORDERS

No Borders (BBC Wales)
New Welsh Review (Spring 1997).

My problem is that although I have a television I rarely watch it . . . I still haven't read *War and Peace*, to say nothing of *Bywyd a Marwolaeth Theomemphus*, and if there is time to be frittered at the end of a day I'm inclined to do so with neglected bits of last week's newspapers. That said, I recognise it is possible from time to time to be ambushed by a televisual treat.

One such was BBC Wales on 2's 'themed' evening on the border, a multifaceted examination of the perennially indeterminate zone between Dee and Severn that negotiates the transition from hard Welsh highland to fruity English plain. Ten programmes, from Roy Noble's wacky canter through two thousand years of border history to the 1988 film version of Bruce Chatwin's *On the Black Hill*, enacted in their variety the exuberant diversity of character and event that invariably issues from this borderland's gentle (these days) frottage of cultures.

The pick of this rich bunch was Charles Way's sympathetic and profoundly moving 'film poem' *No Borders* which, focusing on the mid-border territory of Presteigne, Knighton and Montgomery, was a meditation both on the submerged tensions of life in what is now 'a generous, forgiving landscape', and on the various borders between cradle and grave which we all have to cross. Frenzied editing and screaming arguments seem increasingly to be the characteristic form and content of contemporary TV. It is rare, in this culture of inarticulate grunts and the glib soundbite, to find a programme that has the confidence to trust both the human voice (forty minutes of poetry in a primetime slot) and its audience's ability to attend to the subtle, magical relationships set up between words, visual images and music – and not only the words of the poem, spoken by the actor Bob Peck, but the jokes, songs and shards of anecdote of a host of actual border people: a brandied, irresistible gruel of Radnorshire, Shropshire and Montgomeryshire. Directed by Dafydd Lyr James, with music by Andy Price and stunning visuals from Jimmy Dibbling and his team, it was a collaborative labour of love.

Having known the work of Charles Way the dramatist, it was a pleasure to encounter Charles Way the poet – deft of touch, incisive of wit, warm and non-judgmental of heart. Take, for instance, his portrayal of small-town adolescents, 'Strange inhabitants of a distant planet/called 'thirteen'./ These juveniles beguile themselves/with shy insurrection;/rebels from an unrelenting civil war,/being neither very young nor old enough/to buy a drink, or vote – /armed to the teeth with boredom./Time passes slowly for the young/in these dull towns, until that kiss,/that lifts the gate/and lets them through/leaving the child staring back . . . /That's you.' Like Raymond Carver's poems from the sidetracks of American Life, *No Borders* was at once intensely local and effortlessly universal. It should be shown all over the world.

Nigel Jenkins

CHRONOLOGY

CHARLES WAY – STAGE PLAYS

Feed the World	Leeds Playhouse T.I.E.	1978
When You Were Sixteen	Theatre Royal Stratford East	1979
Don't Just Sit There	Theatre Centre, London	1979
Inner City Limits	Gwent Theatre	1980
The Monkey and the Crocodile	Theatre Centre, London, Buster Y.P.T.	1980
	Zap Theatre Company, Mercury Theatre, Chester	
	York Theatre Royal Y.P.T.	
Humbug	Gwent Theatre	1980
Don't She Look Funny	York Theatre Royal Y.P.T.	1980
She Scored For Wales	Gwent Theatre	1981
	Retour	1985
Dying For a Living	Newcastle Playhouse Y.P.T.	1982
Farm Dance	Theatre Powys	1982
Behind the Lines	Gwent Theatre	1983
In Living Memory	Gwent Theatre	1983
	Retour	1986
Bread and Roses	Gwent Theatre	1983
Funny Boys	Gwent Theatre	1984
Witness	Dukes Playhouse Lancaster	1985
	Retour	1986
	Gwent Theatre	1990
Hitting Home	Dukes Playhouse Lancaster	1986
The Fall of the Roman Empire	Hijinx Theatre	1987
Oh Journeyman	Made in Wales Stage Company	1987
Paradise Drive	Hijinx Theatre	1989
	Retour	1990
The Stone Throwers	Spectacle Theatre	1989
The Flood	The Unicorn Theatre	1990
	Theatre Iolo, Rent a Role Theatre,	1991
	Snap Theatre, Theatre of the Young	
	M6 Theatre Company	1992
	Spectator, Rostov on Dan, USSR	
	Theatre Iolo (Welsh translation)	1993
	Watershed Productions, National Tour	1995
In the Bleak Mid Winter	Hijinx Theatre	1990
	Retour	1993
	New Perspectives Theatre	1994
Dead Man's Hat	Orchard Theatre	1992
	Gwent Theatre	1994
	New Perspectives theatre	1997
Eye Of the Storm	Snap Theatre	1992
	Gwent Theatre	1993/4/5
The Search for Odysseus	Made in Wales Stage Company	1993

	Theatre of the Young Generation, Dresden, Germany	1998
	National Theatre of Mannheim	1998
Ill Met By Moonlight	Hijinx Theatre	1994
Looking Out To See	Sherman Theatre	1994
A Spell of Cold Weather	Theatre Centre and Sherman Theatre, Cardiff	1995
	Les Coup de theatre, Montreal	1998
	New Perspectives Theatre	1995/6
Somebody Loves You	New Perspectives Theatre	1995/6
The Dove Maiden	Hijinx Theatre	1996
	The Sundance Playwrights Forum, Utah, USA	
The Nativity	Theatr Clwyd	1996
Playing from the Heart	Polka Theatre	1998

ADAPTATIONS

Lorna Doone	Orchard Theatre	1982
The Chimes	Perspectives Theatre	1982
On the Black Hill	Made in Wales Stage Company/Theatr Clwyd	1985/6
Frankenstein	Orchard Theatre	1991
Ash on a Young Man's Sleeve	Sherman Theatre, Cardiff	1991
Sleeping Beauty	Polka Theatre	1993
	Sherman Theatre	1994
	Market Theatre, Johannesburg, SA	
	Theatre for Young Spectators, Novgorod, USSR	1995
	The Wilde Theatre, Reading	1996/7
	The Library Theatre, Manchester	
Sweeney Todd	Orchard Theatre	1993

LARGE SCALE COMMUNITY PROJECTS

A Song of Streets	WNO, Cardiff	1985/6
Bordertown	Monmouth	1987
A Mystery Cycle	Exmouth	1989
One Giant Leap	Diversions Dance Company, Cardiff	1995

TELEVISION

Thinkabout Science	BBC Education	1990
Thinkabout Science	BBC Education	1991
Numbers Plus	BBC Education	1993
A Figure of Eight	BBC2 Scene	1996
No Borders	BBC2	1997

RADIO

Funny Boys	Radio 4	1985
The Old Country	BBC Radio Wales	1986
A Journey in Hell	BBC Radio Wales	1986
In Living Memory	BBC Radio Wales	1986
A Sea Change	Radio Wales (schools)	1988
On the Black Hill	Adaptation, BBC Radio 4	1988
Merlin	Radio Wales (schools)	1989
Swallows and Amazons	Adaptation, BBC Radio 4	1990
The Flood	Radio 5	1994
Telling the Sea	Adaptation, BBC Radio 4	1997
Trade Winds	BBC Radio Wales	1998

PUBLICATIONS

Charles Way, *The Flood* (London: Collins Educational, 1992).

Brian Mitchell (ed.), *Charles Way Three Plays: Dead Man's Hat, Paradise Drive, In the Bleak Midwinter* (Bridgend: Seren Books, 1994).

Charles Way, *Looking Out to See* in Phil Clark (ed.), *Act One Wales* (Bridgend: Seren Books, 1997).

Charles Way, *The Search for Odysseus* (London: Aurora Metro Press, 1998).

Greg Cullen

I Paint Me in the World and the World in Me

Greg Cullen

A sung Catholic mass in concrete Stevenage new town; 1960s. An altar-boy sits bored with the performance. Last week he'd taken a severe hiding from his dad for chewing gum on the altar and laughing when someone farted. Around him the priest invokes the God in an ancient language. Other altar-boys who have learned this language by rote get the good parts, they waft the incense burner and jangle golden bells as the miracle happens; bread, which tastes like ice cream wafers, and wine are transformed into the body and blood of Christ and we have to devour them. An electric organ is forcefully pounded to suggest passion as the only woman who thinks she has a voice swoops between notes projected from a cavernous balcony at the back of the church. Beneath her are the sheepish men who want to make a quick escape to the pub afterwards and only attend to set a 'good example' to the children. The bored altar-boy looks around at various parishioners, the violent, the self righteous, the repressed, the terrified, and contorts his face and body until he can feel what it must be like to be them. This was my first theatre.

It is hard to pull apart the strands which cross each other within my plays, as hard as dissecting who I am. At any given moment aspects of my personality come to the fore, my interpretation of the past changes, my view of the future shifts a few degrees towards optimism or pessimism. I am only writing this at this moment; tomorrow I might be saying something different. Each time the earth goes round the sun it takes a slightly different orbit. I am in a process, still busy feeling.

DIEGO: Even here in the Park
If one treads carefully
The motions of the earth can be felt[1]

I suppose the only way to make myself do this exercise is to look at what repeats in my plays. Formalistically, I have always tried to make the stage as theatrical as possible. There is a love of poetry, stylised speech and action, two or more things happening on stage at once. My principle collaborator, the musical director Steve Byrne describes them thus: 'They use dance to tell their tale, music to underscore action, visual imagery to beguile and disturb. Characters suddenly speak directly to you, implicating you. Time becomes elastic and the folds between this world and the next are broken down. History is still happening and the future is suddenly here, lurching and blinking stupidly in front of you.'[2]

I rarely obey the dramatic unities because I want to make 'associations' between things which at first seem unrelated. They are perhaps anachronistic, or suggested in the mind of a character. The associations are webs of ideas, phenomena, implications. Perhaps they mirror how we actually form concepts, they despair of the linear. 'Associations' reveal and build meaning alongside the plot. In *Frida and Diego* they drive the play, causing it to change direction as the two protagonists, in the presence of death, summon scenes to punish, inspire, arouse and challenge each other's view of the value of their lives. 'Which way now?', Diego constantly asks. As the associations draw together at the end, emotional responses to the story are given force by the intellectual sense of realisation. There is an inflamed desire to act, for justice. Sue Glanville who directed *Taken Out* in the mid eighties described this process in that play as being akin to 'rolling a snowball, it gathers more snow as it goes until it's huge and comes to rest at the door of the British State'.

Content-wise, lots of people die in my plays. In fact, in *Raging Angels* everyone is dead. The opening scene of *Frida and Diego* is on the morning of Frida's death. Even chimpanzees die in *Tarzanne*. *Taken Out* was about some dead soldiers. I like births too, although they don't always go too well. Frida Kahlo miscarries and in *Mary Morgan* Mary cuts her baby's throat having just given birth to it. I'm not sure where this is leading:

> FRIDA: There are so many things. Trying to cluster them all together in one place is like herding sheep into a field with no fence. Far better to paint![3]

Far better to see the plays.

I know some people tend to think of me as a 'serious writer', but then I see them laughing. In 1997 I wrote a play called *Whispers in the Woods* which is about a tailor and his daughter who falls in love with a wolf. Well, anyway, people were ecstatic because it had a 'happy ending'. They teased me about it. Mind you, they were all in tears before the happy ending. Maybe it's the order in which these things occur that determines whether or not one is a 'serious writer'.

I love stories. It seems to me that the only way to understand anything anymore is through metaphor, but then the people who write the Bible and folk stories understood that. I wanted to write my political agenda at one point. My duty was to serve the revolution. But then something happened. I think it was the birth of my son. The moment he flopped out like a glob of latex a new and huge energy shot from my body into his. My first thought was 'If you die now, I don't want to live'. Why? I didn't even know him.

Something more intense then sex, or drugs or revolution had happened. I was brought up a Catholic, but this remains the only religious experience I have ever had. I suddenly felt myself 'astride the grave'. History seemed such a short space of time. The Eastern bloc was crumbling. Apartheid was ending. The miners had just been defeated. Thatcher was eating up my time on earth. Within this context, I was transformed by this one fundamental gesture.

HEFINA: (SUNG) The future's in my daughter's hands
To make of it what ever she can.
I'll say to her and without fear,
Take the world by the hair my dear.

You will find in the world turned upside down
A place where a childhood can be found
Together you'll be a central piece
In the central peace
Of a world turned upside down.[4]

After that I was always in a rush for some reason and yet life itself seemed slower. Since the birth of my son I have been able to feel the bass line through the floor not just the electricity in the atmosphere. I want to bring beauty into the world alongside my rage and disgust. In *Cherubs*, a family's self-destructive relationships are transformed when the corpse of an incredibly beautiful man washes up in the river besides their apathetically run farm.

NATHAN: I'll plant an avenue of fruit trees leading from the house, so when we walk up to the grave his abundance will nourish us.[5]

I've not gone soft, *Cherubs* is about self-mutilation, betrayal, incest, suffocation by history, it just has a keener sense of the beauty of people, the possibility of redemption. It's a play about Wales, but I hope it is very simply a play about what it is to be human – as all good drama is. I began in a tradition where theatre had to have a direct political purpose. Whilst I still seek commissions for plays like *The Whistleblower* which came as a response to the *Sea Empress* disaster, or *Tower* based on Tower Colliery, those plays are set in a world of metaphors which themselves ask questions of our existence. They are poetic constructs which, whilst performing a political function, which can be as bald as giving information, have a spiritual voice which comes from my own sense of being alive. Where previously I might never have entertained such 'self indulgent whimsy' it is what makes my voice my own.

SHOSTAKOVICH: (To Stalin) There are sounds inside me which must be heard. Different sounds, perhaps to those inside you.
STALIN: This is the problem, I think.[6]

I keep meaning to write small plays, but to hell with it! If I'm going to be broke all of my life, then I'm certainly not going to skimp on-stage. I want to give the audience a roller-coaster ride, something which will resonate in their heads and hearts for ages afterwards. I want theatre that wrings you out and leaves you wanting to do it all again. There's still a large part of me which is a working-class yob who wants to 'have it large'. Collaborators like the designers Meri Wells and Steve Mattison, musical director Steve Byrne, choreographer Michelle Gaskell and Alison Saunders the costume designer, share that. We create huge shows each year with the Mid Powys Youth Theatre. Perhaps, like Diego Rivera I want to paint public murals instead of still life.

In my plays you will find that I range from an epic sense to a domestic reality on the turn of a page. In *The Informer's Duty*, one moment we are in the midst of a choreographed Soviet street parade, the next we are in bed with Shostakovich, his wife and baby, the next we've gone in even closer and are inside Shostakovich's conscience. Then I get clever and make all three happen at once. Why? So that we can explore the interior life of characters, their immediate social world, and the larger political environment to see what 'associations' interact across all three and transform the characters' fortunes. My forms try to capture human beings as social animals. 'I paint me in the world and the world in me' said Frida Kahlo. *Frida and Diego* gave me the chance to be both a muralist and a self portraitist, as they were. The play enabled me to look from the vantage point of the character projecting outwards to transform the world and to look from the world projecting inwards upon a character and transforming them. One day, I'm going to write a monologue for a man with a pipe who likes his slippers, but not quite yet, not quite yet.

When dubbed a surrealist, Frida Kahlo replied 'I paint my own reality'. I'd go along with that. As with the birth of my son at a time of great political realignment, the world comes along and turns us over. Frida's life was transformed by a bus crash, and more:

> FRIDA: I suffered two grave accidents in my life, the second of which was Diego Rivera.[7]

However, Frida was also a product of her times. In *Mary Morgan* the birth of Mary's child jeopardises an alliance which reaches to the King himself. She doesn't know that. We often don't know why things happen; we just find that the world has changed and that we can't do what we used to anymore. The poetess Anna Akhmatova describes her life thus in *An Informer's Duty*: 'This cruel age has diverted me like a river/From its course'.

I don't yet share her resolution at this juncture,

> . . . But if I could step into
> The life I should have had
> And contemplate the person I now am,
> Then at last, I'd know what envy is.[8]

Writing is a somatic activity at the moment of gestation. Too much thought clogs the works. You end up able to justify every comma, but bore the pants off everyone. My plays often strike me as magical – where do they come from? I can't believe that this solid chunk of paper is me. There is a sense of wonder. When I direct my own work I am as intrigued by the play as if it were by someone else. I see beneath the surface of what I have written. Then I will rewrite it or leave it undisturbed as long as the resonances are right.

The Catholics knew how to stage a big mass, especially when I was growing up. It was in Latin so you had no hope at all of understanding it, but it was all to do with the mystery; people didn't want to *know*, they wanted to 'believe' and that frightened me. Besides, I was growing up in 'rational' England, not Ireland, after, not before the war. I resented the priests and the nuns having this objective. They were also quick to back it up with physical violence if they thought your 'faith' was weakening:

> HARDWICK: These are the easy things, Anne, little things. What are the difficult things you can do?
> ANNE: I never make chimp talk. Never walk chimp.
> HARDWICK: More Anne, there is more.
> ANNE: No, there's not. I'm a good girl.
> HARDWICK: There is more! And how dare you speak back to me!
> ANNE: Never think chimpanzee.
> HARDWICK: Never think chimpanzee. But do you mean it Anne? God needs to know that you mean it.[9]

The tyranny of 'belief', with its necessarily hypocritical underbelly, is something which emerges elsewhere in *Mary Morgan*, *New World in the Mourning* and *Raging Angels*. It's everywhere in my writing. Half the time I don't even notice it, I just feel something emotional when I am writing and there it is, that's what the powerful thing I felt was.

I think it was Dennis Potter who said that he'd spent his whole life writing about betrayal. I don't think I write about one thing, but being told who one is, how to behave and what to think, incite violent rebellions in me. This is the chip on my shoulder and it is not just derived from the imposition of belief and guilt structures, but from class. Growing up in the working-class does not bestow 'street cred', or reverse glamour unless you become a rich pet, a court jester, kept to outrage and amuse the establishment. Its real bequest is that I am cursed both by people who underestimate me and by my own lack of confidence to do anything about it. Sometimes I can deal with it diplomatically, at others I can erupt with frustration, but then like a rioter, I return next day to life amidst the ruins of my own neighbourhood, not theirs. The worlds I occasionally inhabit – theatres and the BBC – are not my own; I keep expecting a security guard to challenge me. The resistances that class self-consciousness sets up feed my dramas with anger, frailty, humour, repression and liberation.

In *Tower*, based upon the experiences of mining families at Tower Colliery, the characters are held in time, their potentials trapped and suffocated by history in their personal and political lives. They follow false trails along the way to redefining themselves in a new era. They succeed, but not all my characters do any more than I do. I have no message, just a fascination.

I sometimes think that I still am an Irish Catholic by culture. Stories are crucial, songs and images also, miracles happen like the pigeons who fly to reunite the mining family on Hirwaun common in *Tower*, or the boy in *Birdbrain* who can place his consciousness inside that of a buzzard's and so free himself from his parents. In *Whispers in the Woods*, the Tailor's daughter eats stolen snippets of cloth, then in private she regurgitates them as sewn together. She takes the sewn cloth and makes a dress for herself, the first dress her father has not made her. In *Cherubs* the arrival of a sublimely beautiful corpse shames and inspires the family to a better life. They deduce that he must be a fallen angel as he rids them of their sins. 'From death comes life' is a Mexican expression which I adore, but it is also evocative of the 'Christ who died so that we may be saved'. The infiltration of these ideas into my psyche is dangerous but also a deliciously rich vocabulary which I can reissue with new meaning.

> DIEGO: . . . In my eyes, last night they took Cauhtemoc's life
> And now Montezuma can but sit and wait himself to die,
> And helpless, watch the conqueror,
> Our images and temples downcast
> And from the ruins build a new image of the past . . .
> Which way now?[10]

In Mexico, I saw in paint what I was trying to do on stage. In his epic murals, Diego Rivera recalls simultaneously the mythology and history of Mexico alongside, and in dialogue with, the present and hoped-for future. In his mural in the Chapel of Chapingo, Diego paints a material and spiritual symphony devoid of God. Just as the Spanish knocked down the Aztec pyramids and built churches on top of them from the rubble, replaced human sacrifice and cannibalism with Christian symbolism, Rivera was usurping the imagery of the Catholic Church and defining a modern mythology for post-revolutionary Mexico.

I'm not sure my aims are that grand, but I am using a vocabulary which belongs to a culture from my childhood. I cannot be other than Judaeo-

Christian. It is an absurd idea that we can revolutionise our thinking to ever remove that fact from our unconscious associations. Marxism cannot do it because it is itself quintessentially Judaeo-Christian. Far better employ our dominant cultural metaphors, take them on, define our age.

Within some of his greatest works Diego also paints himself; rarely without humour. 'A Dream of a Sunday Afternoon in the Alameda Park' is one such masterpiece. Diego is central as a boy of twelve amidst his memories and personal relationships, but surrounded by the great villains, heroes and clown princes of Mexican history. This painting leaps across time, juxtaposes icons, ties each single character into a web of relationships to create a human process:

> DIEGO: We shall walk in the Alameda Park and dream a little . . .
> There a moment is not an instant – isolated, lost, without cousins,
> But a prism through which all history can be focused and
> Cast onto a surface.[11]

It was his last great work. It is also gloriously beautiful to stand before and feel the colours permeating through your clothes to stimulate your skin. I would love to think that someone would experience all that from one of my performances. To have painted this mural would have been both a personal need and an act of great generosity, a contradiction which I encourage others to engage with in our working practice. The play is subtitled 'A love story' for this reason.

The play explores Frida Kahlo's and Diego Rivera's relationships to each other, the world and their art. It attempts through its form to mirror the devices used in the paintings. On one level they are conversations with the people of Mexico, so I have the paintings, when depicted on-stage by actors, come to life. Frida's exquisite simultaneous depictions of both her external and her internal being in her self-portraits (or are they portraits of Mexico?) are mirrored through soliloquy and a visual unravelling of the contradictions which motivated her. Their lives become a metaphor for marriage, for creativity, but perhaps most of all for what it means to struggle with the temptations of both life and death. The play ends with Diego (Frida has just died) offering a paintbrush to the audience to take up the challenge to describe their lives, their times. His are nearly over. It is my most treasured gesture from any of my plays.

I don't think I'm doing anything more than anyone else does. I'm somewhere between birth and death and one has to work out how to live and what, if anything, has meaning. All I want to do is talk about life, bring big questions back in front of us because they are the best questions, the most entertaining and the most natural obsessions for me. They sensitise us to life again, we sense the fragility and the thrill, the need to make each life count for something and never mind the bollocks.

FRIDA: Everyone seemed crazy to me after the crash. All searching for something, but I knew then what we have is life. We already have it. And I loved it. 'A wonderful investigation of space'. Hey, without the accident, I would never have sat still long enough to paint. Maybe this way I have been a little use in this world, eh? Do you think?[12]

Notes

1 *Frida and Diego* in Brian Mitchell (ed.), *Greg Cullen, Three Plays: Mary Morgan, Tarzanne, Frida and Diego* (Bridgend: Seren Books, 1998) p. 179. Hereafter cited as *Greg Cullen, Three Plays*.
2 Personal correspondence.
3 *Greg Cullen, Three Plays*, p. 169.
4 Ibid., p. 56.
5 *Cherubs* (unpublished). BBC Wales recently commissioned a Television version of *Cherubs*.
6 *The Informer's Duty* (unpublished).
7 *Greg Cullen, Three Plays*, p. 180.
8 *The Informer's Duty*.
9 *Greg Cullen, Three Plays*, pp. 138-9.
10 Ibid., p. 168.
11 Ibid., p. 167.
12 Ibid., p. 186.

Greg Cullen

The Snow Queen (1983)

Past Caring (1984)

The Bride of Baron Duprav (1984)

Taken Out (1985)

Tarzanne (1987)
(Photo: Charlie Baker)

Frida and Diego (1993)

Frida and Diego (1993)

Frida and Diego (1994)

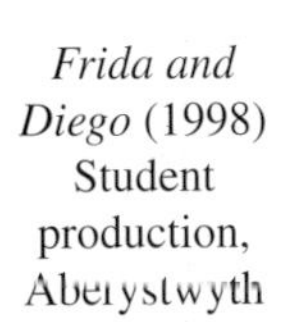

Frida and Diego (1998) Student production, Aberystwyth

Silas Marner (1996)
(Photo: Phil Cutts)

Silas Marner (1996)
(Photo: Phil Cutts)

Bridbrain (1996)
(Photo: Sgrîn/BBC)

Whispers in the Woods (1997)

Greg Cullen: *Mary Morgan* workshop: Theatr y Werin, Aberystwyth (1997)
Photo: Keith Morris

Greg Cullen: *Tarzanne* workshop, Theatr y Werin, Aberystwyth (1997)
Photo: Keith Morris

Greg Cullen's Drama: Spiritual Realism and Chaotic Necessity

David Ian Rabey

If Greg Cullen were a Latin American novelist, like Isabel Allende or Gabriel Garcia Marquez, he would be rapidly acclaimed because categorizable as a 'magical realist'. Cullen, like Allende and Marquez, weaves artful subversive fables grounded in the visceral realities of political repression, identifies the fear at the heart of control-orientated social presumptions and sytems. Furthermore, like these writers and their closest British fictional relative Angela Carter, Cullen purposefully testifies to the irrepressibility of the human spirit through narrative methods that are vitally surprising, if not conventionally respectable within the mainstream of British intellectual culture: the persistent attempts of ghosts and spirits to intervene in human affairs; the demonstration of the possibility of transformation through some 'rough magic' which is both pragmatic and unrationalizable; a frank recognition of the essential centrality of love and sexuality in people's powers to surprise themselves, their peers and those who would maintain a fundamentally deadening social orthodoxy; and the sheer imaginative nerve to propose that the drift of universal forces might be life-enhancingly, radically chaotic rather than tending towards entropic conservatism and stasis. All in all, these are very unBritish qualities, perhaps better identified by the poet Gwyneth Lewis as 'spiritual realism', a phrase reported by Richard Poole as putting 'backbone into the over-used "magical realism"'.[1]

However, Cullen is not a Latin American novelist; he is from the Irish community of London, lives in Llandrindod Wells and works as the Artistic Director of Mid Powys Youth Theatre. If the last piece of information strikes any reader as negligible, marginal or illegitimate within the context of a book like this, then they should be informed that, since Cullen's setting up of the company at Builth Wells Wyeside Centre in 1987, Mid Powys Youth Theatre have successfully demanded recognition as a youth theatre initiative and company as startling and potent as any in the British Isles. They have won the Lloyd's Theatre Challenge, and the BT National Connections Award, making two appearances at London's Royal National Theatre; also a BBC Arts Award for company excellence, a Barclay's Youth Action Award, and a Health Promotion Wales award. Evidently, something unusual, indeed unique, and of national significance (or, more properly, given the recent workshop collaborations with Monaghan Youth Theatre in preparing the latest show, *inter*national significance) is happening in Builth Wells under Cullen's leadership.

However, Mid Powys Youth Theatre and all who create that theatre are a cultural and theatrical phenomenon which deserve a historic survey and critical appreciation in their own right. My brief in this essay is to consider the distinctive and important qualities of Cullen's drama, which sometimes crucially overlaps with, and constitutes the major work of MPYT, but which also sometimes extends beyond it to other stages, those of radio and film. After working for six years as a dramatist, actor and director in the East End of London and then as writer-in-residence at Theatr Powys, a period which Cullen describes and documents in the interview with Hazel Walford Davies, 'Discovering a Theatrical Landscape',[2] Cullen came to national prominence with the play *Taken Out*, which was in 1985 performed onstage by Theatr Powys and broadcast twice as the vanguard entry in a Sony Award-winning season of Welsh radio plays on BBC Radio 4, later performed by Spark Theatre at London Drill Hall in 1987 and published in Germany the same year.

First, a reflection on dramatic technique: for there *is* a tradition of magical realism within English popular writing, but it is to be found in drama rather than in fiction. The magical, or spiritual, realism of drama lies in its demonstration that anything can happen that the imagination permits. Marlowe's *Dr Faustus* is a good example, in the ways it harnesses the energies of the medieval and Elizabethan popular theatrical forms, and imbues them with a spirit of enquiry which problematizes the absolutes of its age. Marlowe's play invites its audience to consider the possibility and appeal of limitless power, and then to dissociate themselves from Faustus because of the limitations and fundamental mediocrity of his ultimately conventional imagination. For in the theatre, imagination becomes the medium of magic, to manifest the invisible and to realize the impossible, as by depicting God; to demonstrate the simultaneity of alternatives, as when the Good and Bad Angels speak; and to explore the entirety of a person, such as Faustus, onstage, not only in his physical presence, but in his imaginative life and significant past, challenging and rewriting the habitual effects of time. Marlowe permits the audience to enjoy such imaginative range, that any fixed position of orthodoxy is revealed as the limitation of possibility which it fundamentally is.

Cullen uses all of these techniques at various stages of his work, and sometimes together. The 'spiritual realism' of his drama suggests and demonstrates the importance of imaginative awarenesss to augment basely material considerations and evaluations of people, places and events.

However, the plays are never abstracting, escapist or other-worldly; on the contrary, they are purposefully realistic in terms of how the potential of that awareness might be expressed and realized in immediate social and political terms, amidst recognizable forces which significantly strive to restrict the unpredictability and, therefore, ungovernability of any informed and delimiting imagination at play.

Taken Out permits the voices and wishes of both living and dead, distant and proximate, to jostle and overlap, but never to combine except in the audience-member's consciousness: the effect is both ironic and poignant, sometimes almost unbearably so, in its emotional rather than merely factual informing of events. The play depicts the visit by two Welsh women to the Falkland Islands, where their son and husband Barry Brooks died aboard the Sir Galahad during the 1982 war between Britain and Argentina. Their reminscences, and arguments as to whether Barry died 'for his country' or 'because of his country', are interspersed with other questioning voices and presences. As they attempt to comprehend Barry's experiences and contact his memory through visiting the site of his death, by way of counterpoint Barry's ghost re-enacts childhood war games with his friend Paul; in the name of 'fairness', they are both obliged to 'die' and their game ends in a deadlock, with the boys calling out to any adult passerby 'Help! We're dead! Release us!'. Meanwhile, though now safely in Britain, Ex-Captain Peter Sommers finds his memory automatically recalled to unbidden recollections of the fatal battle, particularly a hellish central image and its shattering conceptual reverberations: he recalls how the bombed men aboard the Sir Galahad had:

> lips burnt away, white teeth showing. They looked like bunnies. Tortured bunnies. How do you explain something that isn't a set of facts? Looking into the torture, seeing those men, flames plucking their faces into another grimace, you were filled with a sense of what they had been. Suddenly, in a flash, you saw them in their entirety . . . You were aware of what had been lost . . . My whole life had brought me to that point: school, cadets, Sandhurst. Everything that made me a man was there at that moment and . . . I burst into tears. I couldn't help it. Being a man just didn't work anymore.

Most non-combatants have their sense of a war constructed by the mediation of facts and pictures. Just as Sommers strains to explain the non-factual, he is aware that 'You're not really human when you look at a picture; you can't smell it, you're not feeling it through your skin'. Whilst images and abstractions may permit non-combatants to countenance war, as I have remarked elsewhere,[3] Cullen's dramatic method denies the audience such insulations, either by pitching the audience or listener into the scrambling desperation of battle, or by probing fluidly the thoughts of both living and dead, the scorched emotions of fragmented beings, drifting in and out of focus, an orchestration of pain which is both delicate and unflinching in its invitation to the audience to unite, imaginatively, the various intimacies of articulated personal griefs, and to realize how these griefs can be traced back to political causes which depend on such connections being thwarted. One such connection occurs in the uneasy meeting between the Welsh forces and a Patagonian-born Welsh-speaking Argentinian prisoner; when an officer quizzes the prisoner, he has to ask a sergeant to translate, permitting them the brief ironic exchange: 'How come you're fighting for them?' 'I could ask the same of you'.

Cullen keenly identifies how the limitations of gender roles are instrumental in separating and manipulating interests: one mother asks 'Why do boys – what makes them go to war?', and is reminded 'It's you that packs their sandwiches, Joan', whilst the ghost of her son comments 'It's you we're heroes for'. The pregnant widow Christine tells Barry, the dead father invisible and inaudible to her, 'Everyone wants it to be a boy now you're gone'; only the audience hear his reply, 'I'd rather it were a girl now'. As Peter Sommers recognizes in the aftermath of his discovery 'being a man doesn't work anymore'. Institutionally-instilled 'Pride works in favour of discipline': 'go against' the terms of the institution, 'and you're a wimp'. He is flown back early from the war, separated from other men, because he 'asked questions'. The word and sense which tolls throughout *Taken Out* is 'Waste', strategically concealed from the victims by means of forcible separations and spurious sentimental associations. This is highlighted by the final, self-consciously contradictory stance of Joan, who recognizes that Margaret Thatcher and her ministers decreed the Welsh forces on the Sir Galahad expendable: 'She put a price on them, a value. It grieves me to have to vote for her. But she's the only one who's said she'll keep the islands British. I'll not have Argies walking here. For Barry's sake'. The audience have been made privy to army hierarchy's influence in prioritization: other troops and equipment are removed from the Sir Galahad because 'They've got a colonel, we've only got a major'; later, even ammunition is removed from the more vulnerable ship rather than the men. Joan is denied access to such information, and her misguided bid to bandage her loss by investing it in specifically Conservative necessities is doubly pathetic. The play concludes with a triptych of perspectives on the dead Barry: Peter Sommers's fazed, blunt, neo-factual report to an unsuspecting colleague that '49 Brooks was taken out'; Joan, riven by the memory of Barry as a baby, struggling to rationalize the destruction of the 'soft flesh' she made and 'kissed all over', but determining to 'start again' somehow; and Barry as part-ghost, part-boy, forcibly abstracted into watching the proceedings with ironic but hurt bemusement, reiterating the cry 'We're stuck here . . . Hey! We're dead! Release us!'. As in other Cullen plays, the cumulative effect of the final convergence of initially disparate narrative seams creates an emotional effect in which characters progress *through* language *into* a crisis of emotions; they become consciously placed beyond rational boundaries, where language itself has its sufficiency called into question: here, Cullen's interrogation of the terms and interests behind the so-called 'national interest' is startlingly thorough, poignant and indicting.

Mary Morgan (Mid Powys Youth Theatre 1987, Red Shift Theatre Company 1988 and winner of the City Limits Award for New Expressionism that year, BBC Radio 4 1991 and 1992) is based on a true local story of a serving girl who was hanged for the murder of her illegitimate baby daughter, whose father, her employer, sat on the jury which convicted her. The play shows a bewildered, volatile King being undermined by the ambitious, *nouveau-riche* Wilkins, at a juncture when the women of a shanty town are becoming revolutionary in their anger. The play is nominally set at the time of the Napoleonic wars, but the script specifies '*The set and costumes should be an eclectic mix of periods and cultures, recognizable but unfamiliar*'. Unable to pay for bread with their men away at war, the women of the shanty town vividly express the sense of the King and gentry's effective theft of the heat and flesh which belongs to them and their children (with a similar vehemence to the disenfranchised characters in Edward Bond's *The Fool* and Caryl Churchill's *Light Shining in Buckinghamshire*). The King finds the seeds of another war on his own soil, and Wilkins amasses troops:

> KING: By what right do you raise armies on my soil?
>
> WILKINS: The right which says my home is my castle. I shall protect it, and of course, you, your Majesty.
>
> KING: Now I see you! A little Bonaparte.
>
> WILKINS: You send your lads to fight against revolutions to ensure that no revolution breaks out here. The war impoverishes and displaces the populace and so in turn they renew their reasons for revolution. Ultimately, I'd say you were in a bit of a bind. . . . if you should ever have need to re-establish order in your Kingdom, do not hesitate to call upon my services.[4]

Wilkins's son Walter begins a dalliance with Mary Morgan, who is resented by her peers and labelled 'proud and ambitious'; Wilkins himself is complicit in the philandering of his powerful friends, such as his cousin Judge Hardinge, and advises Mary 'Learn discretion, my girl, and you'll be cared for'. Ostracized by other women, Mary feels propelled towards Walter: 'You're all I got left, Walter. You better love me'. Moreover, she is assaulted by the resentful local boy John (who justifies his actions by saying 'Let him stick to 'is own kind. You're one of us, Mary Morgan. I'm only taking what's mine'). When Walter tries to finish the relationship, Mary informs him that she is pregnant. Walter assumes the attitude of being protective towards the child to license his control of Mary ('From now on, you'll do as I say'), though she appalls him by considering abortion and vaguely reporting an association with John. The King's dependence upon Wilkins increases. Later betrayed by Walter, Mary gives birth and recoils from her confused emotions, including an emergent love for the baby, by slashing its throat. Wilkins seeks to accelerate Mary's execution for murder, in order to leave Walter's character unblemished and without impediment to a respectable society wedding. One of the women, Bethan, serves as executioner, for a fee. When Mary is killed, the women round on Bethan and wrap her in petrol-soaked sheets to be torched. The helpless King begs Wilkins to bring in the troops, and the play ends with the women and soldiers on the point of confrontation, and the King fearful of, and beholden to, Wilkins, who triumphantly exclaims 'The world changes!'.

More precisely, *Mary Morgan* shows how the terms of 'the world' – traditionally defined by the rhetoric of those in power – change, but the nature of power, and the repressions on which it depends, remain, though their command be effectively transferred from the King to Wilkins. The final execution and the incorporation of motifs from a range of periods recalls Bond's *Restoration*, a similar salutary vision of the mechanics of social sacrifice, which subverts associations of period melodrama and comedy. However, *Mary Morgan* is distinctive and original in the natural yet apocalyptic poetry with which Cullen imbues the gathering sense of the 'trial of worlds clashing', particularly in the chorus of the shanty town women:

> HEFINA: A hard winter. Stone against skin.
> SARAH: A freezing. Shards of ice cut light into the gloom. The sky plays patterns on the surface, tempting us to rise up into the light.
> HEFINA: An ice without compassion.
> WOMEN: Burn it![5]

Cullen's next play, *Tarzanne*, has been refined through the several different versions,[6] a powerful dramatic metaphor to which he has returned, with new questions and discoveries, from a Mid-Powys Youth Theatre version in 1988, to a joint production by Theatr Powys and Footloose Dance Company of a revised text in 1990, and a third version again for MPYT in 1995. The jokesome title, with its associations of subverting (whilst recalling) popular films, should not lead the casual reader to dismiss the play as a casual or negligibly populist work. Cullen has variously developed the core story of a 'wild child', abandoned in the jungle and raised by chimpanzees, then captured by humans and returned for re-integration into Victorian Welsh ruling-class society. However, Anne retains an ability to question the social expectations for which she is being groomed, and the prejudice, snobbery and, ultimately, persecution she encounters. The insights of the play are developed through startling juxtapositions of images from the human and chimpanzee societies, and vivid expressionistic intercutting from Anne's perspective, from which the humans become increasingly degraded and malign (the traditional associations of the term 'bestial'), to that of the wilfully uncomprehending society around her. Cullen's programme notes to the 1995 version of the play pithily identify the issues at stake:

> Young people are animals. I know, I work with them. Animals have limits. Each year the pressure upon young people to concentrate solely upon getting exam results increases and it is straining their limits. The pressure comes from worried parents, schools who are competing with one another for results and individual teachers who fear that their pupils' results will 'let them down'. This combination of competition, fear and pressure is set against a background of ten million living below the poverty line, graduate unemployment, youth unemployment and a lack of security for those with jobs, including parents and teachers. Whilst we all collude to apply this pressure we all want 'the best' for the young. In my experience this increase in pressure is damaging them. Not only does it lead some to the desire to 'get out of it' for a while with binges of alcohol and drugs, but in the long term it is destabilising their lives and damaging our culture . . . If the Arts become even more marginalised, shoved to the corner of our national consciousness, then we will increasingly become a nation who cannot make sense of its own experiences. The Arts give us the opportunity to be still, to enjoy, to reflect and wonder, to understand life better. If we teach our young that this is extra curricular, luxurious and non-essential, then what have we become? Machines, perhaps? Or chimpanzees? Unless we think and imagine we will not give voice to our desires.

The radio plays, *Spoiled Papers* (BBC Radio Wales, 1986) and *A New World in the Mourning* (BBC Radio 4, 1988), return to immediately contemporary settings, specifically the South Welsh valleys during and after the miners' strike of the early 1980s, during which the Conservative government's explicitly forceful policing and covert surveillance of the miners and their communities caused the supposed impartiality of the principle and forces of law and order to be not so much *called into question* as *shown to be instrumental* to the ambitions of government and the financial interests of government allies (a historical moment recently dramatised with pungency by Peter Flannery in his BBC television version of his play *Our Friends in the North*), an exposure of the polarization of power akin to the final confrontation scene of *Mary Morgan*. *Spoiled Papers* recalls the method and strengths of *Taken Out* by dramatizing the experiences of a cross-section of characters in a mining community, showing how traditional relationships change and – perhaps even more challengingly than *Taken Out* – showing how an encroaching disempowerment can drive people to the ultimate desperation of violence, only to find themselves further isolated beyond law and morality. However, the characters wonder, what alternatives exist for them, apart from humbled submission. The naked anger of *Spoiled Papers* is transmuted in the style and 1987 setting of *A New World in the Mourning* into ironic comedy which nevertheless shows Cullen at his most subversively inventive. *New World* takes place during the 1987 election campaign, when it was generally considered that the Conservatives were so smugly secure as to have 'written off Wales as surplus to their voting requirements', whilst Labour were distrusted, accused of not supporting either side in the strike with sufficient conviction. The well-meaning but nonplussed Labour candidate Emlyn tours his prospective constituency, seeking to present an appealing liberal-humanist impression, but finds his polite arguments stonewalled by 'fear' – 'That's all I hear' from the consituents, he complains, '"It's safer for the kids", "It's for my old age"'. His friend and agent Billy counsels him with a cynicism dressed up as pragmatism: 'people don't understand debate, it looks shabby on TV, our prime objective is to get elected'. In the case of one constituent, former policeman and current right-wing fanatic Eric, fear has warped the man into a paroxysm of moral indignation and vicious paranoid crusading, to the extent that he believes God addresses him directly. However, God accords less and less with Eric's expectations of Old Testament vengefulness, expressing rather a whimsical intrigue in human events and a predisposition towards wonder and playfulness rather than moral absolutism; as He remarks to Eric on his first appearance, 'Oh, don't mind me, do what you like'. Meanwhile, Billy's schoolgirl daughter Shirley rejects her father's despairing injunctions to her to leave 'this slag heap built on hollowed ground'; she also rejects a double period of religious education at school as 'An hour and a half of being told things that don't exist are more important than we are'; in defiance, she is constructing a terrorist glamour for herself, and a bomb for representatives of the government. Her accomplice is Maldwyn, a gay ex-miner – 'The only one who came out twice in the same strike' – who is picked up by Duncan, Emlyn's commodities broker son, who is also gay, but whom Maldwyn finds increasingly appalling. Eric spies on Duncan, self-styled 'prodigal son of the Eighties', and Maldwyn with outraged fervour, photographing their assignation. Duncan justifies his flippant ostentatiousness, 'It's my money, I'll decide what it's worth'; when Maldwyn protests at his impulsive callousness, 'Do you decide what I'm worth, too?', Duncan snarls 'Yes I do, get out'. God watches the whole scene with childlike pleasure, not least in Eric's zoom camera lens: 'Why didn't I think of that? I could have given everyone zoom eyes . . . human beings have such *potential!*'. Even Emlyn's wife Sian becomes impatient with his conciliatory posturings, including his willingness to implement a no-strike deal, virtual Toryism which drives her to ask him 'On what grounds do we become someone else's?' – a keynote question throughout Cullen's drama. God becomes increasingly disconcerted (exclaiming 'Blimey!') by Eric's fundamentalist frothings of moral panic. Eric blusters, 'But you're supposed to know everything!'. 'Well, I don't know how that rumour got started', replies God, who goes on to tell Eric how He is in form akin to an amphibian, with flippers rather than wings or a beard like Santa Claus or Karl Marx. He tries to defuse Eric's Manicheism further by explaining 'Satan doesn't exist, it's just Me in a bad mood. I'm a complete being, you see. I try to, y'know, keep happy, but I lose my temper sometimes'; the mythical 'Wrath of God' is, moreover, attributable to PMT:

> GOD: I'm a bit of both, aren't I, man and woman, sort of androgynous only I don't need a partner. Sometimes I wish I did, mind.
> ERIC: Disgusting!
> GOD: Typical. And people wonder why I choose to remain a mystery!

Emlyn narrowly escapes a campaign-endangering scandal, for being the father of a homosexual in a climate of homophobic populism. With Shirley's bomb, he blows up the local ex-mine-owner's house bought by Duncan as a showy plaything – 'If things are going to change, this is one bit I don't want left standing' – and Duncan publically pledges money for a community centre on its site. Eric is arrested on suspicion, and God appears instead to Maldwyn, who protests 'I'm not religious'; God, who is planning some 'adventures' they can have together, replies 'That's exactly what I thought. We're made for each other'. The play closes by 'panning back' to the general electoral situation, in parody of a football commentary, in which Thatcher rewrites the referee's rules and has the rival team, Labour, ordered off the pitch; team captain Kinnock advises his men to abide by the rules, 'Well, that's true British sportsmanship for you . . .'.

Cullen's purposeful, mischeivously surprising dramatizations of a cosmology are further exemplified by two plays for MYPT. *Raging Angels* (1991) is a play about sexual feelings, fantasy and behaviour in the light of AIDS and HIV stigmatization and moral panics. Five hapless humans find themselves in the Arrivals Lounge in Heaven. Like a comic version of Sartre's *In Camera*, their antagonism leads them to reveal their past lives as sexual beings, involving challenges to pride, moral superiority and presumptive homophobia. In *Little Devils* (1994), four young people find themselves accidentally transported to Hell along with a retired magistrate. Hell is in decay as human beings can no longer define good and evil. The young people plead for the safe return of a deceased friend's soul.

Frida and Diego: A Love Story was first produced by Red Shift Theatre Company in 1989, touring nationally after winning a Fringe First at Edinburgh, and subsequently produced in Stockholm, San Francisco, Houston and Mexico; rewritten for Mid Powys Youth Theatre in 1993 and performed by them at the Royal National Theatre, London, in 1994. The play charts the stormy relationship and artistic careers of the revolutionary Mexican painters Frida Kahlo and Diego Rivera, in the context of international political events. An important stylistic feature of the play is the constant onstage presence and wry counterpoint of the *Calaveras*, animated skeletons who are familiar irreverent figures in Mexican native traditions of art and celebration, presences described by the script as '*playful reminders from a close friend of one's own mortality*', suggesting the constant presence of death, both as a limitation to the power of human systems and as the source from which life springs anew.

Cullen, at a workshop at the University of Wales, Aberystwyth (17 November 1997), has expounded the importance of the cultural and iconographic background to the play, how Catholicism was grafted onto the originally Aztec culture of Mexico (much as it was onto Irish paganism), which naturally tends towards a dialectical view of relationships, process and progress – for example, the sensibility embodied by the Calaveras that you cannot be alive unless your death is with you. The Calaveras are originally Aztec figures, re-animated and popularized in the artwork of J. G. Posada, of whom Rivera regarded himself as the artistic heir. One particular variant of the figure is Calavera Catarina, a skeleton affecting the fashions and doomed vanity of a European lady, who features in Rivera's Alameda Park mural and, in Cullen's play, as a sinister alter ego of Frida, and a mocking representative of Western values. Rivera's murals were initiated by the first post-revolutionary Mexican government, huge expansive works painted at great speed and scale, intended to teach a largely illiterate generation about their experience of the revolution and urging them to look forward to a future and the place which Mexico might have in the world. Like Rivera's work at the Chapel of Chipingo, the murals refer to religious iconography of sacrifice and redemption to present a primarily atheistic, humanist and scientific perspective on world development. But Rivera never denied or removed himself from his painting, and many of the murals depict scenes from his own life; Kahlo, also in many ways a self-mythologizing self-portraitist, probably developed his confidence to locate himself in his work. Thus, their work testifies to how a sense of spiritual values has to augment that of social process in any secular belief that might seek to displace Catholicism. Kahlo's art goes even further than Rivera's in imaging the history of her nation through the kaleidoscope of her own experiences, with the context and interior of her own largely impassive features depicting the pressures and breakthroughs of sociality; again, the Aztec base of Mexican culture directly informs both the dialectical materialism of the couple's Marxist beliefs and Kahlo's expressionist images (painting the inside, as well as the outside, of the head is an idea which springs consciously from the Aztec tradition of iconography rather than the contemporary adjacent European school of surrealism). Even the way Kahlo constantly paints herself in Mexican-Indian (implicitly working-class) clothes distinguishes her from the non-indigenous pretentions of Calavera Catarina, and forms part of Frida and Diego's re-evaluation of their culture and popularization of the image of a non-European, new Mexican race. Another of Kahlo's personal developments of indigenous influences was her use of the form of the *retablo*: small votive images done by street painters, commissioned by the purchaser to intercede to a specific saint on behalf of an ill or distressed loved one. Many of Kahlo's images assume this form, illustrative messages to those she loved, figurative recordings of her own experiences of anguish, from which the traditional presence of the Saint is absent (as in the portait of her miscarriage, 'The Henry Ford Hospital'). Thus, both Frida and Diego's paintings might be defined as secular forms of prayer, should we accept Brendan Kennelly's definition of prayer as 'anger at what is and longing for what should be'.[7]

Cullen's *Frida and Diego* is a social dreamplay, asking, like Rivera's murals, that the audience look not at one thing in isolation, but at the relationship between several. In staging, one half of the play is usually identified as Diego's province, the other Frida's, with the action oscillating and bouncing between the rival claims and versions, attractions and antagonisms, expressed and enacted. Cullen's 'Notes on the Play' draw attention to how the characters 'had many strongly felt wants and embodied within these wants is the desire not to have to want it any more, to wish you had never started wanting it in the first place. Duality makes things whole rather than singular and isolated as in our dominant perception. To describe love as good and hate as bad is to deny love a wholeness . . . To really love means at times wishing one no longer loved, that one had never started loving in the first place'.

As in their artwork, the presence and arguments of Frida often help Diego to *locate* himself when he expresses doubts. His opening, wilfully puzzling invocation of Cauhtemoc is a reference to the Mexican Aztec General who saw through the blandishments of Don Cortes and alerted Montezuma: Diego associates himself with Montezuma, and Frida with Cauhtemoc, an agent of unique, crucial imaginative resistance now lost. Yet he clings to his own will to insight: a moment that is 'not an instant, isolated, lost, without cousins. But a prism through which all history can be focused and cast onto a surface'. Diego's feelings about Frida's death are characteristically unruly: 'Why can't we just feel one thing at a time? One thing purely . . . to feel remorse, to rage and scream'; yet he also acknowledges 'And yet I also feel relief', and in this admission of contraries is placed more in touch with the voice and ghostly presence of his recently deceased wife. In flashback, the play tells their story, but also dramatizes the imaginative impact of their art, exposing the terms of industrialist society as in the animation of Diego's Detroit mural 'The North Wall', in which the character-participants realize the didacticism of their own self-representation and move to destroy the mural in rage. At one point, Frida asks a doctor to cut off her head, 'Then I will only do what my body wants'. However, despite this reflex towards an idealized simplicity, her imaginative triumphs are demonstrated by her imagistic self-transformations (from *'Christ. To an Aztec human sacrifice. Then Christ again. Calaveras transforms similarly, acting out the rituals'*), which are also part of her strategy to command erotic pity, as when Diego succumbs to the power of her Christ postures and Frida '*smiles knowingly*' to the audience, unseen by him. The transmutability of everything is recognized in retrospect, such as the sense that even Frida's miscarriage is painfully informative: 'From that death came Frida's life / In painting, painting, painting'. Beset by problems of integrity and compromise, Diego holds fast to the image of the former conquest of Mexico and determines to identify similar contemporary disastrous self-deliverance to a supposed foreign saviour: 'Our culture erased / We are gone./ We cannot think / We cannot remember / We are beholden to Rockefeller for the truth'. Frida emphasizes the importance of the artist's pride in and use of subjectivity: 'An artist never draws an object, they draw their feelings for it. In this way we make a strong relationship with the world'. *Frida and Diego* is a heroic, even romantic, play, but never simplistic or sentimental, thanks to its aliveness to the contrary self-revolutionizing viewpoints on and natures of the protagonists, the 'Beauty and savagery' which they simultaneously contact and express through their strong, because insistently personal, relationships with the world. Diego's final offer of his paintbrush to the audience provides a concluding image similar to that of Howard Barker's *No End of Blame*, inviting participation in and development of the artists' scenes of (self-)overcoming. Diego asks 'Which way now?' and invites the audience to take on the task and responsibility of creating artistic statements and expressions of their own.

The Informer's Duty (Welsh College of Music and Drama 1992, BBC Radio 3 1994, MPYT 1996, in three consecutively refined versions) continues the exploration of the artist's role in society, in this case the careers and tribulations of the composer Shostakovich and the poet Akhmatova under the tyranny of Stalin. The play opens with Akhmatova's forceful image of repression which crystallizes its mechanics and intended consequences in many Cullen plays: 'The condemned were marshalled into the railway yards like cowering asylum inmates, startled by the urgent whistle song "Say farewell to your desires"'. However, the play is perhaps more concerned to demonstrate the internalization of social terror, as bred by Stalin's paternalist rhetoric and assumption of the right to infantalise and 'discipline' his people, and by the moral-perceptual superiority which an interrogator assumes, through scriptural invocation of social theory, in talking to Mandelstam after detailing his wife's rape: 'You appear recklessly unable to comprehend the objective truth. You exist only within your subjective reality'. By such tortuous pseudo-logic emerges a blackly comic episode in which artists are driven to 'transcend themselves' by donning 'the Archbishop's Bag' and shooting themselves in the head. At one point, Stalin confronts Shostakovich, with the ownership of the imagination itself at stake:

STALIN: Why this constant desire to hear sounds that should never be heard?
SHOS: Because there are sounds inside me which I must find. Different sounds perhaps to those inside you.
STALIN: We are not concerned with introspection . . . We seek to transcend ourselves to serve the collective need.
SHOS: My experience is the collective experience.
. . .
STALIN: Fear is a sign of guilt.

Akhmatova reflects on this manipulation of fear, and the institutionalization of the envious dismantling of personalities in the name of what Zoshchenko terms 'superior political doctrine': 'This cruel age has diverted me like a river from its course', deduces Akhmatova. Shostakovich asks his wife Nina 'Do you think the people are ashamed of what we are allowing to happen to each other?'; she recognizes they are, 'Because they smile in the daytime, but not at night'. However, as another character remarks, 'Cynicism is a form of apathy', and the play ends with Stalin '*triumphant*' on one stage level, but the artists triumphant on another, identifying and defying the totalitarian ideology and base materialism of the Russian Stalinist state as Frida and Diego identify and defy the same tendencies in Western capitalism.

'Even pumpkins can be transformed' remarks Big Bryn on his unpromising son in Cullen's radio play *Tower*. Indeed, the ability of people to transform themselves in the face of the onerous demands of social crisis is a theme common to *Tower* (BBC Radio 4 1995) and *The Whistleblower* (BBC Radio 4 1996). *Tower* introduces the audience to a beleagured South Welsh colliery community similar to that in *Spoiled Papers*, ten years on (specifically, the Tower colliery in Hirwaun, Glamorgan, successfully bought out by its workers; also the subject of Alan Plater's more recent film *Towards the Light*). Cullen's play artfully adopts the narrative frame style of a fairytale, established with the opening 'An old King lay dying'. The king in question is not a literal monarch, but Big Bryn, family grandfather and spiritual patriarch to a community, representative of traditional certainties regarding male identity and social role. However, Big Bryn's ghost remains a witness to, and narrator of, the events immediately following his death; like the ghosts of *Taken Out*, he is unable to contact those he cared for and can only watch, as if awaiting release into final freedom by their actions; however, the tone of *Tower* and of Big Bryn's bewilderment is more comic than the painful exploration of severance in *Taken Out*, though *Tower* retains a serious social concern at the heart of its ironic comedy. One character voices his opinion, 'When you died, Big Bryn, you took this place with you', as if Big Bryn were, in both life and death, the spiritual guardian of the community and the unchanging miner's lodge with its unchanging music which has soldiered on for ten years since the strike. His son Bryn acknowledges his major achievement: the Pit continued unclosed because 'the union was stronger, thanks to Dad' and his efforts. When Big Bryn's daughter-in-law Sally chucks her husband's reverently hoarded miner's lamps and Welsh landscapes, the ghost is more phlegmatic than his son, recognizing 'The first thing you realize when you're dead is that you only have one life'. However, Big Bryn is frustrated by being reduced to the role of a passive onlooker when there is a new initiative to close the pit: 'They are closing my pit and I'm not able to be there, to do something; this is hell'. The community is divided ('It was as if the dragon had caused people to turn on each other, making the job of devouring them that much easier'). The meetings of the men are rendered in a gently mock-heroic style ('The knights met to pledge themselves') and critically framed by the voices of the community's women, principally Sally, who identifies a slide back to the gender polarizations which the community resistance during the strike had done much to dissolve. Bryn challenges the allegation, 'You haven't the imagination to be anything other than your father', with the assertion, 'And you haven't the imagination to see that there isn't anything worth being in this community other than my father'. Sally responds by going to Cardiff to seek work: 'If you can't face the future, I will'. The community seems in the grip of one-eyed monsters dispensing 'facts' (though one inhabitant asks 'Facts? Who are they to treat us like facts?'), and Big Bryn bewails his 'ineffectual parody of being' which even denies him access to beer ('No testing of the truth profound forgotten by the morning? No *beer*? Then this death is not worth living!'). Bryn and Sally separate under the pressure also felt by many couples around them ('pumpkins and white mice all around, the land fell under a spell of silence'). Nevertheless, the Old King rediscovers 'an inextinguishable fire within his people he could trust', significantly kindled by the next generation, his grandchildren, who start their own revolution to attack the domestic deadlock with determined interventionist spirit ('We have nothing to lose but our ignorance'; 'Our pocket money?'; 'Exactly, a say in the domestic economy'). Even Big Bryn seems to manage an intervention of sorts, when the flight of his pigeons is interpreted by his other son Robbie to be a portent, with the consequence that Robbie owns up to an embezzlement of the miners' funds. When Bryn and Sally confront each other in Cardiff, their acknowledgement of each other's resourcefulness and ability to effect change make them spring to a position of mutual defence against Sally's new employer, who is frankly out to sell 'fantasy' as a way of life through her exorbitant furniture designs. The sympathetic will of Big Bryn, the pragmatism of the children, and the adults' acknowledgements of the ability and need to redefine oneself truthfully to oneself and others, combine with the effect that 'a new kind of kingdom had begun to appear', and that Big Bryn's two sons can shed their inferiority and rivalry and bury 'the sins of their father'.

The title of *The Whistleblower* recalls Akhmatova's image of the whistle song that calls the condemned to 'say goodbye to their desires' in *The Informer's Duty*; it also carries the associations of referring to a surreptitious informer. Like *Taken Out* and *Spoiled Papers*, the play is a good example of Cullen's ability to dramatize a complex response to a contemporary and immediate social issue, in this instance the environmental disaster constituted by the oil tanker, *The Sea Empress*, running aground at Milford Haven and generating a huge oil spillage. Jenny, a Cardiff schoolteacher, has her pregnancy confirmed, amongst wry warnings from her colleagues that there is 'no such thing' as a painless birth. Her romantic excitement is shattered when one of her pupils, Sally, dies of an asthma-triggered heart attack as the playground whistle blows, and she is prevented from telling her husband Geordie about the pregnancy when he is called in to try to rescue the tanker which has run aground. Jenny's pupils initiate an anti-pollution research project which discovers an alarmingly poor air quality at the school site, compounded by the surrounding architectural designs and recent road works; however, the headmistress clamps down on the project and its findings, lest they jeopardize the 'competitiveness' of the school. At Milford Haven, Jenny meets a local fisherman, Huw, as they participate in a voluntary beach-cleaning exercise, and witness the many corpses of birds who have died of heart attacks in the oil, unable to move or breathe; a huge slick awaits the unsuspecting migrating birds at Skomer because of the spillage. Jenny and Huw speculate how the views of the harbour pilots might have been overridden, and security measures neglected, because of the power of the oil companies. Huw explains how 'if the port authorities throw their weight around, the companies leave and jobs are lost'. One consequence is that harbour radar facilities have been 'left to rot'. However, as Huw says, 'no one person's to blame for this: it's endemic to the whole business'. 'Business' is also a key consideration for Jenny's headmistress, who orders her pupils to return to 'national curriculum' (rather than project) work because schools inspectors are coming to check attainment levels. Jenny objects to how the needs of her pupils to come to terms with their bereavement are being compromised by the order to return to curriculum teaching, and vociferously identifies the larger safety consideration at stake, and realizes 'what a corrupt, cowardly, insidious world I live in'. The headmistress deems her 'unfit to teach' for expressing such concerns and convictions, and suspends her. In defiance, Jenny begins an imaginary dialogue with the child Sally, who died the day before the tanker ran aground (akin to the addressed soliloquoies of the mother and wife in *Taken Out*, though Jenny is sharing an engaged activity with the ghost of the deceased – for example, how stealing the pollution figures from the headmistress's handbag 'felt right' – rather than a bereft expression of severed isolation). Geordie is unsympathetic to her decisive action and unwilling to disclose any harbour circumstances which might identify blame (he objects, 'We have a mortgage to pay, two cars to run, a holiday to pay for, you can't run around doing "what feels right"'). Jenny claims his attitude as further evidence that morality is disappearing into 'subtle self-interest and petty competition' and acknowledges how he, like most employees in most businesses are governed by 'one big fear: open your mouth, and that's it, for life'. Jenny presses on with her investigations, determined to discover and demonstrate that 'there is a reason to believe in the future, even if we have to fight for it'; her increasing isolation and shared passion brings her closer and closer to Huw. Together, Jenny and Huw find out that a harbourmaster can only be overruled by a government minister or his representative, suggesting the full implications of the negligence and the financial interests for which it might have been condoned. When Geordie attempts a reconciliation with Jenny, he can do little to change her impression of him as 'gutless', another paid-up servant of the maintenance of normality. She tells him, 'You have valued employers above family, been complicit in mass murder'. He protests, 'I've done what was asked of me' and she replies, 'Exactly'. When Geordie discovers the existence of her unborn child and tries to claim it as his own, to exercise control over her life, she tells him how working on the oil dispersals has damaged his own fertility, that the child is not his: 'you're not a fit parent anymore . . . a child needs courage'. Contrastingly, Jenny expresses the liberation of discovering 'I don't have to play by the rules' and 'I can't live anymore in the old complacency'; she has 'run adrift . . . on instinct', and takes her dialogue with the unborn child, whom she calls 'little Sally,' with her into their joint future.

The Whistleblower is a strong example of Cullen's mastery of the Ibsenite 'forensic' form and technique, identifying as surely as does *Pillars of the Community* how misplaced investment in the apparent normality of capitalism places at risk the lives and futures of the future generations on whose behalf those instrumental in the system's maintenance ostensibly but short-sightedly claim to be working. And like *An Enemy of the People*, *The Whistleblower* does not shrink from depicting the strain and isolation involved in standing apart from 'gutless' unison to identify complicity in potentially murderous consequences. However, Cullen imbues the form with his own distinctive qualities: informed analysis, shrewdly provocative deductions, a keen awareness of the paradigms we create for, and impose upon, children, and a spiritual sense of imaginative possibility which must manifest itself in purposeful direct social action to 'break the rules' of complicity in fear.

The other side of Cullen's writing, the mythic settings of such themes, is aptly illustrated by his two most recent major plays, *Cherubs* (1996, as yet unproduced) and *Whispers in the Woods* (MPYT 1997). *Cherubs* is perhaps Cullen's most originally and impressively poetic work, maintaining a fiercely unsentimental and unflinching exploration of the tangles of power and sexuality in a domestic Welsh setting (the play was commissioned but rejected by Made in Wales Stage Company). The introduction of three sisters who live on a remote farm with their morose father Nathaniel invites but subverts expectations both of a *Cinderella*-like fairytale and of an ultimately reassuring saga of charming idiosyncratic endurance such as *On the Black Hill*. The youngest daughter Sam is sexually aware but reclusive, engaged in a clandestine sexual relationship with her widowed father, knowing that 'the only way / To douse the raging of the fire / Was sacrifice of self', following each incestuous intimacy by cutting into her flesh to 'thereby silence its desire'. The eldest sister, librarian and the only wage earner, Gwen, finds the moral high ground of her own seniority compromised by her awareness of Sam's activities and her own almost erotic fascination with her youngest sister's inscription of her own body. This tight-lipped, involuted and self-loathing stasis holds the entire family in a thrall of complicity until the middle sister, the most sheltered and naive Megan, discovers the corpse of a large, handsome man in the nearby river. Megan retrieves the corpse and adopts him in her imagination as a romantic fantasy husband to care for. When the other two sisters discover the corpse, they also develop a fascination through the simultaneously Christ-like and erotic washing and tending of the corpse, which is marked only by two wounds on the back: they conjecture that he was an angel, his wings burnt off as punishment for his giving way to temptation. Sam is particularly empathetic with this notion, '*especially transfixed as if she recognizes his expression from her own in the mirror*' (Cullen's stage directions specify that the face of the naked actor playing the corpse should never be seen). In grieving for their 'fallen angel', the girls grieve for themselves, their own longing for some 'peace and dignity' such as their ministrations attempt to give him: 'Everyone deserves somewhere they can be forgiven'. Their sense of the man's lost power and wasted beauty ignites a despising of their father 'for his idleness', until they challenge his power together, unafraid of his reviling their care for the corpse as a 'pact with the Devil'; 'witches we are' replies Sam, sensing the power that lies beyond 'breaking the rules'. Gwen is turned from her suicidal impulses by her contemplation of the corpse and a tacit promise at the heart of her attribution to him of the sense of the importance of all life, including hers. Nathaniel tries to reassume power in significantly paternalistic terms ('now I'm taking charge to protect you from each other'), but discovers that the women are no longer under his command. He blames a curse lying on the site and the stones from which the farm is constructed, having formerly belonged to a castle, but determines that 'no man, especially not a dead one, will drive me from this place'. Sam achieves her own breakthrough into self-acceptance when she reaches orgasm sitting astride the corpse, then tells her father: 'I've given myself to him. And he let me be. He knew everything and let me be it all . . . Reached inside to all that pain and said that I was beautiful. He reached inside and left a little beauty there. And I don't need you anymore'. Nathaniel lunges for the corpse with an axe, but also finds himself transfixed by the face: '*It is as if he sees within the corpse all that he could have been. He recognises himself*'.. He breaks down in contrition. The sisters improvise a candlelit ritual invoking the 'mourning' of the stones, their 'remembrance of defeat / Of abandoned wives and children' and 'innocents slaughtered', in which even Nathaniel assumes a role, joining the incantatory procession by insisting on carrying the corpse to burial on his own back: 'This is my due and I shall pay it'. They commit their strange adult foundling to the earth, in a new shared sense and anticipation of the purification of the soured atmosphere of their land, which future local legends might attribute to the tale of how 'They buried an angel there'.

Cherubs is startlingly theatrical in its insistence that characters, performers and audience alike acknowledge the body – not just the 'character' of the mysterious corpse, but the physicality of all involved in the occasion of performance – and the challenge that its sensuality presents to fearful dismissal and souring involution. Its combination of searching liturgical poetry, purposeful frankness and physical immediacy distinguish it as one of Cullen's most powerful and original works for the stage; a skilful production might realize it as his finest stage play. Its careful excoriation of vital energy warped into envious vicariousness, sexual hypocrisy, fearful self-loathing and social sterility might constitute a salutary challenge to the incestuous tendencies of the Welsh imagination, theatrical and otherwise. This remarkably resonant and haunting poetic drama invites a national psyche to confront its own potential for adulthood and grow up accordingly.

Whispers in the Woods terms itself 'A fairy story for all ages', akin to Angela Carter's liminal tales of individuation in *The Bloody Chamber*, *The Magic Toyshop* and elsewhere. Cullen's progamme notes alert the audience to the manner and theme:

> Fairy tales gave us a world of impossibilities in which we could express realities . . . our work was, we have realised, a play about prejudice, coming of age and the desire to know who we are; borderlines . . .
>
> On the border we bring up our children to behave in a world as we wish it to be, then expect them to cope with the world as it is.

> On the border we try to build castles around our children to protect them from the warring armies who sweep across the boundaries. We build the walls so high that they cannot see above them . . . we do not want their beautiful eyes to see the carnage of our lives.

A tailor and his daughter live on a shop on the edge of a forest, where he makes clothes which are able to release the surprising potential of the wearer. However, he prefers to give his daughter clothes which hark back to her girlish past rather than acknowledge her emergent womanhood. She visits her fairy godparents and friends in the forest, and develops an interest in the socially ostracized Wolf, who makes witty allusions to the possibilities of wearing what she hastily dismisses as 'nothing'. Questions pervade the daughter's head. She goes so far as to secrete and eat some of the magic cloth which the Tailor is given by the fairies, unlock the trunk containing her dead mother's wedding dress, and wear it herself; meanwhile the Tailor is beset by Bad Thoughts (personifications of malice voicing repressive fears reminiscent of those which patrol Blake's *Songs of Experience*). He spies on a meeting between his daughter and Wolf: as they dance, *'Wolf pulls brightly coloured fabrics from her dowdy dress. The Tailor sees the colours the Wolf can bring forth from his daughter, colours that he cannot match'*. Furious, he encases his daughter in a dress of poisoned pins (so startlingly realized by Allie Saunders's costume design for the MPYT production as to become the unforgettable central visual image of the show) which immobilizes her and makes the Wolf die when he finds contact with her irresistible. The Bad Thoughts propose and develop images of suicide ('Once we have tasted paradise / There is no point to further life'), and the daughter stabs herself. The Fairy King and Queen grieve with the Tailor, revealed as the parents of the girl's mother, who shunned her for her liaison with a human outsider. They commute the young couple's death to a hundred year coma, but their power can stretch no further. The other half of the spell is broken by the Tailor's grief, not just at the loss of his daughter, but for the death of the Wolf. The couple revive. The human and fairy parents reflect upon the self-defeating effects of their possessive jealousy and fearful bids to control:

> We keep laws which violate
> In seeking to preserve, we annihilate . . .
> The truth has an enriching pain
> Whilst wishful thinking cheats in vain.

Granted three wishes, the couple choose 'to remember' their experiences, 'to know' the immanence of love, and 'to look forward'. Thus expressed, the parents' realization, and the young people's will for a future, are apt crystallizations of the threshholds which are crossed in many of Cullen's plays.

Seen from one perspective, Greg Cullen's ability to write daringly direct and immediate drama about the recent past and present – tough, funny, moving plays which are angry, urgent responses to the waste of human potential – suggests he is Wales's equivalent to Peter Flannery and Jimmy McGovern, who also identify moments when being a (wo)man and playing by the rules don't work anymore, necessitating significant explosions within a corrupt and cowardly world. From another perspective, he is a theatre poet creating resonant social myths and artful fantasies which are too shrewd, worldly and generous to forget the playfulness which is essential to life and theatre. But, as he has remarked, an awareness of duality makes things whole rather than singular and isolated. Both facets of his work generate stirring reminders that unless we think and imagine we will not give voice to our desires; and that the recognition of desires is a crucial factor in forging reasons to believe in the future, even if we have to fight to express those desires and thereby make that future. In all of these important and valuable ways, his work looks forward, and encourages others to do the same.

Notes

1 Richard Poole, 'Spiritual Realism', *Planet* 125 (October/November 1997), p. 75.

2 Hazel Walford Davies, 'Discovering a Theatrical Landscape' [interview with Greg Cullen], *New Welsh Review* 38 (Autumn 1997), pp. 78-83 and *New Welsh Review* 39 (Winter 1997-98,) pp. 76-81.

3 David Ian Rabey, 'On Being Dispossessed', *The Listener*, 27 February 1986, p. 28.

4 *Mary Morgan* in Brian Mitchell (ed.), *Greg Cullen, Three Plays, Mary Morgan, Tarzanne, Frida and Diego,* (Bridgend: Seren Books, 1998), p. 18. Hereaftercited as *Greg Cullen, Three Plays*.

5 *Greg Cullen, Three Plays*, p. 70.

6 Greg Cullen discusses the amendments to the scripts of *Tarzanne*, and the reasons that impelled them, in the interview with David Ian Rabey in this volume.

7 Brendan Kennelly, *Medea* (Newcastle: Bloodaxe, 1991), p. 42.

Inner Need and External Demand: The Plays of Greg Cullen[1]

David Adams

(1)

Playwrights do not operate in cultural vacuums. We have to identify their locus: where do they write, about what, to whom, for whom, when? In Wales in particular, with the lack of a major commissioning and producing theatre and with a tradition of small-scale touring, in order properly to evaluate their work and contribution, we must situate the playwright within specific contexts. We may acknowledge Sanchez Vasquez's insistence (quoted as a caution by John McGrath) that 'the artist can only create in response to an inner need to express and communicate – freely, not on account of an external demand'[2] so as not to be simply subject to the laws of supply and demand; but in practice the playwright in Wales generally writes to commission, for a specific company that in turn has a specific brief to a geographical area, a community of interest, a defined audience, and at a specific point in time, and the contexts of production determine this 'external demand'.

How much drama these days starts with the playwright? In Wales, theatre is in general provision-led and playwrights are part of the ecology of theatre but a part that might well be by-passed without any noticeable collapse of the ecosystem, despite the Arts Council's insistence that new writing is at the heart of Welsh theatre. Why else are there so few good playwrights, a dearth of new plays, a handful of Welsh works worth reviving? Apart from the writers' company, Made in Wales Stage Company (who, incidentally, rejected two of Greg Cullen's best plays, *Frida and Diego* and *Cherubs*) the only way playwrights can really 'create in response to an inner need' is to start their own company.

Greg Cullen differs from the other writers in this volume in that his apprenticeship was outside Wales and his work since he moved here in 1983 seems to me to be that of an outsider, a city radical transferred to the middle of rural Powys, a visitor from another culture. He loves Wales, feels Wales was the country he had adopted, he said to me, but Wales had not adopted him. His background, his upbringing, his beliefs, are those of a working-class Londoner steeped in urban conflict politics. Until relatively recently, with exceptions like *Taken Out* in 1985, his plays looked like the product of a professional and creative life run to a political agenda; even his move to Theatr Powys from Hackney was, I would guess, politically motivated or even politically engineered.

So: a playwright without a locus? Hardly. The 'external demands' are not only the commissions but also the place (Mid-Wales) in which he has chosen to live; the job (running a young people's theatre company) that he has chosen to do; the events in the real world, from the Falklands War to the Sea Empress spillage; the social relationships of postmodernist capitalist society. He has survived, prospered and matured because, simply, he is a good playwright. As with most politically-driven artists, age and the times have had their effect. He was for years a good playwright in the service of a political ideology; he has since become a good playwright in the service of no-one except his own drive to explore the problematics of personal and social relationships.

(2)

I take theatre to mean live performance: the synchronicity of play, audience and venue. Each of these three has its own context and each is essential to the generation of meaning. I want to examine the journey of a playwright who knows all this, who has learned his craft and has found a voice but without ever losing sight of the role of the audience and the significance of where a production is enacted.

Of the four playwrights here, Greg Cullen has made in every way the longest journey. From Cockney to would-be Welshman, from far-left activist to contemplative socialist, from agit-prop interventionist to complex commentator. What hasn't changed is that he still has the concerns of young people at heart, having founded and run Mid Powys Youth Theatre, and he is still obsessed with the nature of justice and freedom. He can also still turn out a piece to order as a journeyman playwright. Unlike the other playwrights under scrutiny (and indeed unlike most playwrights), and with absolutely no disrespect to them, Greg Cullen is also a doer, an activist in the real sense (and theatre is part of that urge to make people take on life). If he now accepts it's that much harder actually to change the world then the least he can do is help people understand it.

Talk to Greg Cullen today about his radical youth and he tends to dismiss the importance of the factional world of Marxist protest politics. Theatre then, of course, and youth and community theatre especially, was riddled with left-wing internecine squabbling. Most practitioners who came into the profession were politically committed and the variety of post-60s Marxist activity was reflected in the work of young theatre groups: Maoist, Trotskyist, Leninist and other dogmatic variations drove and destroyed radical theatre. The Workers Revolutionary Party, the Socialist Workers

Party and the International Marxist Group battled with each other as well as the straight Communist and Labour Parties and unaffiliated socialists more than with the real enemy. Like many who have come through those years, Greg Cullen affects to have been outside party politics: he insists he has never been part of any 'movement', but he was there and, crucially, in London where the conflict was more acute. Disrupting neo-fascist marches was part of everyday life in the East End, part of a tradition, part of the culture.

Greg Cullen was not a practitioner first and a revolutionary second. Born in Kilburn in 1954, he came from a non-academic working class London-Irish background, and the education system failed him first time round as he found himself in a secondary modern school in Stevenage New Town. He did, however, prove selection wrong by getting ultimately to St Mary's University College London to study drama and art – and activism. He gained a Bachelor of Education degree – after a hiccup, when he was kicked out for union activities – and he carries with him the enduring mark of a secondary modern success, the missionary zeal to bring out the potential in others who are not natural scholars. As a student activist he was also involved in Anti-Apartheid and support for Third World freedom fighters and paid his way at college by working for a cargo airline. After graduating he got a job with them in Angola so that he could experience African revolution at close quarters. His first play, *The Flyboys*, never produced, came out of it. He became an actor (and I guess for him the very word carries with it a responsibility to play a positive role in society) as part of direct community action, a reclaiming of community resources by squatting in a disused library in Hackney until the local authority let it be converted to an arts centre they called Chats Palace. At the same time he was running a youth theatre and an adult devising company that staged large-scale community shows. He worked for East End Theatre Group, Harlow Theatrevan and The Grove Theatre, Hammersmith. Radical groups all. Not one of them has survived.

Cullen was active in theatre in London from 1979 to 1983, when he came to Wales. Those few years were a crucial time: Thatcher came to power, unemployment increased by 140% and there were inner-city riots. The community ethic of the Seventies was challenged by the new ideology of individualism. Local authorities' rearguard action against central government was gradually destroyed, as was trade union and student power. In 1983 there were 45 community theatre companies outside Wales in the British Alternative Theatre Directory; in the 1996 British Theatre Directory there were just 23. He wrote *The Bar*, showing tourists as cultural imperialists, and *Spiv*, about the emergent entrepreneurial ethic, for The East End Theatre Group; large-scale multi-media community shows for Chat's Palace; youth theatre shows. Were they any good? I don't know because I didn't see them – and of course you can never evaluate this work from scripts, for community theatre has to be seen to be appreciated. As I say, his first play, *Flyboys*, which he wrote in 1979, was unproduced, but it is a play that he himself recently dusted down and thinks has merit. His last work in London was with Harlow Playhouse Theatrevan, a small scale community company funded entirely by Harlow District Council whose seven members worked collectively for an equal wage under Equity TIE contracts under the management of the Playhouse.

He left London at a time when "alternative" theatre, which had emerged some twenty or so years before, was in a state of crisis, strong enough to have its own annual directory and its own listings sections in magazines but riven by internal conflict and finding it hard to face up to the new order in British politics. It was a time when some did try to look objectively at the area. Playwright Dusty Hughes, in the 1981-82 *British Alternative Theatre Directory*, could openly criticise the distressingly low quality of some of what passed for 'radical theatre' in Britain and my then Guardian colleague Joyce Macmillan, in her rigorous foreword to the 1983/4 issue of the *Directory*, castigated the movement:

> Insofar as British alternative theatre has been identified with radical politics as well as radical theatrical styles, its development has been patchier and less happy . . . The problem is that, contrary to what some of our more imaginative dissidents seem to imagine, we are not – yet – living in some kind of totalitarian society where the mere fact that a voice is raised against the establishment is enough to guarantee its owner's courage, integrity, radicalism and inquiring spirit. We are, in fact, living in a pluralistic culture, where anti-establishment groups are often allowed to flourish to the point where they develop little establishments and power-structures of their own; and the pressures which they can exert on artists and theatre companies which they regard as 'theirs' can be fully as destructive and distorting as the demands of any other hierarchy . . . In the situation we face now, it seems to me doubly-important that alternative theatre in Britain should avoid the easy option of playing to the already-politically-committed, or of becoming the automatic mouthpiece of an established 'alternative' politics which clearly, for one reason or another, has very little appeal for the majority of British voters . . . It's this position of smug, self-validating impotence that British alternative theatre must struggle to avoid over the next five years.[3]

In fact, of course, the struggle dragged on for nearly twenty years, by which time the whole ethos of 'radical', 'alternative', 'community' theatre had changed, where postmodernism in theory and in crude reality had thrown into doubt the old ideological certainties and established processes of protest, where Chaos Theory and the pulling-down of the Berlin Wall, New Labour and Lottery Funding, all combined to change the scene dramatically.

(3)

At the centre, or so they would like to be seen, of the debate about revolutionary theatre was an organisation called the Standing Conference of Young People's Theatre, a Trotskyist 'forum for discussion' set up in 1975. Harlow Theatrevan were active members, and so were Theatr Powys; other Welsh community/TIE companies varied in their enthusiasm, often depending on the company personnel at the time. Greg Cullen regards SCYPT as a 'lions' den'. But it was through Theatrevan's involvement in the organisation and SCYPT's concern to use Theatre-in-Education as an agency of revolutionary change that he decided to apply for a six-month writer-in-residence placement with Theatr Powys. He got the job, and has stayed in Llandrindod ever since.

The quality of the work for Theatr Powys varies, inevitably, but few would disagree that he delivered: family shows, Theatre-in-Education work, youth shows, musicals, all written with commitment and a rare sense of balance between the accessible and the political. In fact he had moved away from the didactic nature of much TIE/community theatre. Not only was there a playfulness, almost, in some of the politically-correct shows like *The Bride of Baron Duprav* (1984), *Aladdin* (1984), *Beauty and the Beast* (1986) and the Thatcherite allegories suggested in *The Snow Queen* (1983), for example, but crucially there was also a rapidly-acquired maturity of vision that emerged in *Taken Out* (mooted as part of his application for the Theatr Powys job in 1983 but not produced until 1985). Theatr Powys, as a company, were committed to consciousness-raising through theatre but while musicals-with-a-message like *The Snow Queen*, his first play for the company, and *Aladdin* and challenging schools shows like the impressive *Past Caring* (1984) fitted the bill, a play that did not take any clear ideological line on the Falklands War was problematic. *Taken Out* represented a link between Cullen's former life as an activist in Hackney and his new-found Welsh responsibilities. The germ of the idea for the play had come while he was still living in east London and heard Dafydd Elis Thomas try to get a public enquiry into the sinking of the Sir Galahad and the subsequent death of fifty Welsh Guardsmen on board. He wrote a poem which actually formed part of his application for the job at Theatr Powys – a not inconsiderable factor, perhaps, in the appointment to a left-leaning theatre company of a London playwright with just a handful of slight scripts under his belt! By chance or otherwise, a company colleague at Theatr Powys was (contrary to what one might expect) in a long-term relationship with a Guards officer who had been on the Sir Galahad. On reading the poem, the officer agreed to talk to Greg Cullen and the idea for a play developed. *Taken Out* became a play that felt authentic, offered no easy interpretations or solutions, and was all the better for it. But social realism or agitprop it was not.

There are, of course, several subtexts to the *Taken Out* episode. First, I think it is an early sign of the playwright's ambivalent attitude to his new home. His urge to write a play about the Sir Galahad incident came from his outrage at just one atrocious action in a war that was notable for such incidents, an outrage based on a natural ideological opposition to the Falklands War and the coincidence of a personal contact with someone involved with the actual event. Theatr Powys may have been a politically-motivated company but at the time it was relatively 'soft', dealing with anti-militarism in a gentle way – not least because they depended for their funding on a local authority not known for its radicalism, and for its audiences on a population made up mainly of farmers. When *Taken Out* was first proposed, the leading voice in the company's board of management was a colonel whose son was a major in the Welsh Guards. The company would not give the playwright the support he needed for the commission to write the play and the project was shelved. Instead, Greg Cullen wrote a play about fascism. Not long afterwards, I recall him admitting to me that he felt he had left one form of racist politics for another and that on a personal level he felt he suffered from discrimination as a Londoner in rural Mid-Wales. He still has difficulties with a country he sees as colonial-minded, medieval, feudal, class-ridden, prejudiced, narrow-minded and reactionary. He has, however, located his work here. *Sherlock Gnome and the Egg Snatchers* (1985), which he wrote for Masquerade Theatre, a Cardiff-based company mixing mask, puppetry and actors, was a play for 5-8 year-olds about a gnome and a pair of Red Kites who have their eggs stolen – a Welsh-based environmental parable. Both *Aladdin* and *Spoiled Papers* (1986) were about the 1984 miners' strike, the latter a radio play researched in and dealing with issues raised in communities in the Neath, Swansea and Dulais Valleys. *A New World in the Mourning* (1988) was a radio play about Labour during the General Election in Wales. *Tower* (1994), another radio play, was commissioned for the tenth anniversary of the miners' strike and was about the Mid-Glamorgan mining community's decision to buy the Tower pit for themselves. He wrote *The Whistleblower* (1996) to discuss the implications of the Sea Empress oil-spill disaster in Pembrokeshire. I know he was particularly hurt when both Theatr Powys and Made in Wales rejected *Frida and Diego* because it wasn't somehow 'Welsh' enough. Yet it seems obvious enough to me that there is a direct (and, I assume, deliberate) analogy in its theme of a post-colonial drive towards cultural independence by an emergent nation. His latest play for MPYT, *Whispers in the Woods*, covers themes he feels are essential to living in Mid-Wales: prejudice, a closed attitude, a meanness of spirit, the love and warmth of a community, the need to be different.

Secondly, and more evidently, we can see an assured move from agitprop and rather issue-led work to non-prescriptive drama. It was a move that antagonised hard-line political colleagues and undoubtedly came out of the twenty hours of taped interviews with someone actually involved in the Sir Galahad incident. *Taken Out* became a play with real voices, those of people who were confused. They were not characters created to state anything that would lead to the playwright's own truth, to prove his own hypothesis. Greg Cullen had become disillusioned with such didactic drama. What *Taken Out* revealed, then, was a different approach to theatre, using it as part of a process of interaction, a contribution to a debate rather than the case for a specific perspective. Further, it broke through the social-realist barrier by being based on that 'inner need' rather than 'external demand'. The play, says Cullen, was full of himself and liberated him from any guilt he had felt about putting himself at the centre of his art. That was something that was to explored further, most obviously in *Frida and Diego* and *The Informer's Duty*.

Thirdly, the controversy about the play, which moved from the reactionary right's reservations prior to production to the revolutionary left when it was shown at a SCYPT Conference, left deep scars. It is impossible, I think, to overestimate the effect this had on Cullen's development. He felt he had made a major leap forward as a dramatist and, presumably, as a writer working from a Marxist perspective, and in the socialist tradition, though not in the social realist tradition. Many colleagues felt he had betrayed his principles by not taking a straight condemnatory line, by apparently siding with the British Thatcherite government against the Argentinians, by being racist in his uncritical depiction of the soldiers' attitudes, and so on. That conference, he says, was a breaking-point: a break with SCYPT, a break with vulgar Marxism, a break with any remnants of social realism, a break with his past in many ways. Theatre from then on was not simply consciousness-raising, an agency of social change, but a debate with an audience using a plurality of voices. That struggle, which I detect as one that has never been altogether resolved in favour of plurality, is what, ever since *Taken Out*, much of his work has been about.

(4)

The period of conflict over *Taken Out*, the mid-1980s, was also when qualitative leaps were made in Greg Cullen's other area of interest – theatre for young people. He had, of course, been heavily involved right from the beginning of his theatrical career, running a youth theatre at Hackney Chats Palace and also writing for the Grove Theatre before moving to Wales. But Theatr Powys's remit, and the reason they were relatively generously funded by Powys County Council as well as the Arts Council of Wales, was that they produced work not only for community audiences but also as part of the local education authority's Theatre-in-Education provision and Greg

Cullen's placement responsibilities meant he had to target his audiences very specifically. *The Snow Queen* actually toured outside Powys and was a successful and entertaining version of the Hans Christian Anderson fairy story with a political bite that I suspect did not really come across – but basically an accessible, colourful, well-produced family Christmas show. The second of the two shows he had to write as part of the attachment was the replacement for the temporarily-aborted *Taken Out* project, another busy, sharp comedy with lots of politics, this time not so deep beneath the surface of a mock-Gothic horror. A classic piece of artistic subversion, *The Bride of Baron Duprav* was the result of a commission by Powys Young Farmers' Clubs who, in return for a cut of the box-office, had guaranteed an audience for 'something funny'. Was a critique of sexism with a central character based on Nietzsche really such a hoot? I remember it as a rather obscure political parable that was undeniably funny in parts but, to be honest, probably not the fare expected by the YFC. Both *The Snow Queen* and *Baron Duprav* lacked a clear through-line and lacked a personal voice except in the slightly chaotic style; but both did nevertheless instil a sense of application, of writing to a specific brief for a specific audience. And also, with hindsight, both reveal a development in the playwright's craft.

In the same year, however (1984), although he had finished his six-month attachment with Theatr Powys, Cullen was asked to stay and help devise a TIE piece. The result, *Past Caring*, written and directed by Cullen, was as important in some ways as *Taken Out* for playwright and company. Theatr Powys, under new director Louise Osborne, based an enhanced reputation for TIE work on this watershed production that was acclaimed by the international young peoples' theatre organisation, ASSITEJ, and played all over the world. For Greg Cullen it was a hugely successful project that reinforced any ideas about the importance of work with young people. Two years later, he formed Mid Powys Youth Theatre.

He had in the meantime been made writer-in-residence with Theatr Powys and written a string of shows for them, not all of which fulfilled the promise of less dialectic political explorations. *Aladdin* was a reworking involving Chinese myths, inspired by the 1984 miners' strike and the threat to communities; *Swashbucklers!* (1985), was another Christmas show, though this time a bit nearer home with the story of a farmer's son who discovers all about the control of food markets and poverty; *Hard Times* (1986), one of several versions that toured Wales, was his first classic adaptation (*A Christmas Carol, Germinal* and *Silas Marner* were to follow); and *Beauty and the Beast* (1986) was another accessible double-edged Christmas community pantomime where music and comedy are employed in the best Brechtian tradition to get political messages across. He was to continue in similar tradition with another panto pastiche for Christmas, *Robin Hood* (1987), again enjoyable and witty, but still rather confusing: it was the last of its kind and was already a theatrical anomaly in a developing oeuvre that had gone from *Taken Out* to a response to the miners' strike, *Spoiled Papers* (1986), a radio play that was full of questions rather than answers, *Hard Times* and *Mary Morgan* (1987), an award-winning historical drama based on the true story of a servant hanged for the murder of her illegitimate baby.

Mid Powys Youth Theatre, for whom he wrote *Mary Morgan* with a commission from Theatr Powys, was part of a natural progression for someone who had become impatient, it seems, not only with the internal politics of the TIE movement and its domination by the Workers' Revolutionary Party, but also with small-scale touring and the role of journeyman playwright. MPYT gave him the opportunity to become, in his words, a 'theatre-maker' rather than just a playwright and director. (It is worth noting that the latter role, while outside the brief of this book, started with a degree-production of Edward Bond's *Saved* at the Edinburgh Fringe and included various large and small-scale community shows in London as well as the highly-praised *Past Caring* for Theatr Powys; and that he has also directed Dürrenmatt and Brenton.) *Mary Morgan* had a company of 40 – unthinkable outside youth theatre – and a full orchestra. It also involved a promenade audience – mixing with the working-class characters, caught up in the middle of the trial scene – as part of an ambitious staging that emphasised the class theme, with the action on three levels with the king at the top of a tower, the family on a raised stage, and at ground level – well, the groundlings, the people, the audience.

MPYT also crucially freed-up the playwright to be able to make shows not to another company's commission brief, but according to 'that inner need' rather than the 'external demand' referred to in the Sanchez Vasquez quotation with which I started this essay. In truth, Greg Cullen had been writing from an 'inner need' since *Taken Out* but the 'external demands' had sometimes got in the way. Nevertheless, some of his best work has been done for MPYT, although interestingly it is also in the production rather than just the writing. *Mary Morgan* and *Tarzanne* were written for the company but *Frida and Diego* and *An Informer's Duty* had both been done before, and in this respect it was in his new staging that he fulfilled his 'inner need'. Ten years on, as he told Hazel Walford Davies, 'the real Greg Cullen is in the plays I write for myself'.[4]

(5)

The theme of *The Informer's Duty* is (to oversimplify) the role of the artist in society. The same theme is also at the core of *Frida and Diego*. It is something that has always been at the heart of Greg Cullen's work. He admits that for the first few years of his professional life he didn't really know why he was writing. For the next few years, he hardly had time to think further as he churned out (his phrase) community plays for Theatr Powys. The problems over *Taken Out* – projected in 1983, not supported by the company, rejected by the management board, then (when it had been selected to be part of a BBC radio season of new plays) supported by the company in 1985, creating another furore at the SCYPT conference that led to more months of rancour, reworked in 1987 and subsequently published – seemed to put a partial break on what was clearly important in the playwright's artistic development. It was really only when he became his own master, in 1987, as the director of MPYT, that he was released and tried to get to grips with his motivation and purpose.

Frida and Diego, a dense and well-researched study of the lives of Mexican artists Frida Kahlo and Diego Rivera, when it was first produced by Jonathan Holloway for Red Shift in 1989 may have won an Edinburgh Fringe First but it was not to the playwright's liking. He thought it too stylised, too confusing. When MPYT staged a rewritten version in 1993 Cullen, as director, could make it more rounded and coherent and leave us with a question on the future in a postmodernist world. The play was also more clearly about love and passion – and about dualism, another theme that has occupied the playwright. The stage is divided in two, one half Frida's, one half Diego's; love is celebrated as being both good and bad; the artists' truth to themselves and responsibility to society. The 'inner need' and 'external demand' has to be reconciled but without compromising – a lesson learnt by Greg Cullen five years before at that SCYPT Conference and from which he was obviously still smarting. Dualism was to reappear in several plays, for example in *New World in the Mourning*, where God declares that 'Satan doesn't exist, it's just Me in a bad mood'!

The Informer's Duty was commissioned by and presented at the Welsh College of Music and Drama in 1991 and I can remember Greg Cullen being amused and shocked at the students' utter lack of knowledge about the historical context – the suppression of Dmitri Shostokovitch's music by Stalin and the subsequent dilemma for the composer. Indeed, Cullen tells the story of his conversation in the WCMD bar with the then head of drama, Paul Clements, when he expressed this surprise at the students' lack of political awareness and history. As they looked out on to the busy main road a demonstration by environmentalists was holding up the traffic. The two men looked to their students for signs of solidarity and support for the demonstration: the drama college students were standing in the bar laughing at what they saw as the stupidity of the protest. 'There you are,' said the head of drama, 'students have changed'. A few years later Greg and I were despairing at the same lack of political awareness as we read that Cardiff could not support a single coach to take students to the demonstration in London against the new Labour Government's decision to charge student fees. Inevitably, the WCMD production was essentially a showpiece for the student actors and musicians – a large cast and full orchestra creating an impressive theatrical event, and one that I still treasure. I suspect that the playwright could sympathise with the composer's frustration at the simple-mindedness of Stalin's crude interpretation of social realism: this was also Greg Cullen versus the mindless marxists of SCYPT. But what happened to the play when MPYT staged it in 1996 was something quite startling. A play about a specific predicament and the more general question of the artist's responsibility, distant and abstract issues to young people today, became something more for the thirty young performers on the Wyeside Arts Centre stage. And for all of us it happened as the glorious, tragic orchestral sounds of the Fifth Symphony that was Shostokovitch's response to Stalin's suppression changed to a contemporary techno sound. The music became not that of a remote experimental Soviet composer of the 1930s but that of a generation who had been told that this infamous music with its 'repetitive beats', so-called rave music, had just become illegal under the new Criminal Justice Act, the enforcement of which could lead to forced entry, search, confiscation of goods and equipment and maybe imprisonment. Shostokovitch and his friends would have recognised the crude oppression of a misunderstood, subversive culture by an authoritarian state. The theme of cultural repression as a form of political control needed young people to bring it alive today. No wonder Greg Cullen is still very actively involved in the rave culture in Mid-Wales. And as such he is, of course, continuing his oppositional political activity. In Mid-Wales, he asserts, the great and the good are waging a war against the culture of young people, a war which he first explored in *Mary Morgan*.

(6)

Political commitment does not, of course, preclude poetry. Cullen is also concerned about the spiritual: he believes that poets and playwrights are not only the unacknowledged legislators of the world; they (rather than scientists) offer the only way of understanding it. There is a lot of lyricism and much poetry in his work, in spirit but also actually in the script. I find it surprising that so much of many of the plays I had seen had been written in blank verse. One of his most recent plays, *Cherubs* (1996), as yet unproduced, seems to me to express most eloquently the playwright's use of lyricism to express his sympathy, his questioning of moral absolutes, his interest in sexuality and his willingness to explore sensitive areas.

Anyone who knows Greg Cullen appreciates how he can be almost disconcertingly passionate about his beliefs, yet able also to laugh at himself and so thoroughly enjoy life. While this essay is not biography, the playwright's own life – at a more personal level than political and artistic activity – clearly informs much of his work and is, I suspect, an unrevealed part of that 'inner need' which can be in conflict with 'external demand'. We do not have to look too deeply into *Frida and Diego* to see the artist and political animal as a man who has suffered the agonies and ecstasies of love.

The spiritual side of life had been important in *Frida and Diego*: it was basically, as its subtitle declares, a love story. But it was the very passionate love not only between two people but a love of life, of art, of justice. Cullen says the play is about what it is like to be alive – not just a material evaluation of their lives. It's an allegory about a spiritual relationship with the universe.

In many ways, lyrically, poetically, mythically, sexually, *Cherubs* goes further. On the surface, it is a story about a father and his three daughters, with one of whom he is having a passionate incestuous relationship and another of whom finds the body of a beautiful man washed up on the shore. They bring the body home, strip and wash him, note his beauty and the marks on his back, and give him a ritualist burial. The play reads almost like an extended spontaneous poem. Where it came from, Cullen says, he doesn't know. 'Left to my own devices,' he laughs, 'this is what I come up with'. Inner need, obviously.

The text – without a staging as I write, so perhaps we cannot talk of a play yet – is full of symbolism. Behind the family house is some 'higher ground' occupied by the moralistic elder sister on which stand the ruins of a castle. The stones of the house weep for the 'sins' committed therein. And so on. There are hints of the Fisher King, of King Lear, of the Crucifixion. The man is, presumably, a fallen angel – fallen because he, like the family, disobeyed the laws of nature. We never see his face but the daughters are as interested in his penis. The playwright's notes insist that the casting must ensure that the family are played by small actors so that the angel can appear superhumanly large. The supposed angel embodies a possible range of meanings: even, I think, that of standing for ideology.

While I have just said that this essay is not biography, equally it is not literary criticism. When I say I am concerned with the relationship between the playwright and his plays, by plays I do mean performed texts, acknowledging that a script has no theatrical life until it becomes a shared experience with an audience; and so I leave textual analysis of the script-text to others. But I do find it interesting how much Greg Cullen puts into his stage directions. In *Cherubs*, either because the playwright is unsure as to whether the words can reveal the motivations of the characters, or simply because, since it is an unperformed play, we can only read the script text, we are told much by the words between the dialogue: 'Nat is suddenly overcome with shame. Perhaps he is breaking yet another resolution that this incest must stop. He despises his own weakness . . . He starts to undress Sam as she undoes his trousers. He is urgent, she is in control; he the child, she the adult. She may even be amused by his desperation to uncover her breasts . . .'

What is shocking about Cherubs in not simply the sexuality – and desire simmers throughout the play – but the fact that an incestuous relationship is dealt with sympathetically and even enthusiastically at times – with the 'abused' seemingly challenging the passive role. Sam, the daughter who enjoys sex with her father, also practices self-abuse in the form of ritualistically cutting herself and simulates sex with the corpse 'You can say he should never have started me/ And that was the original sin, / But ever since, my love, / I have gladly sinned with him' she tells the dead angel. While she is portrayed as a strong character in some ways, and while guilt and opposing the laws of nature are at the heart of the play, such pleasure in what is conventionally seen as abuse inevitably makes for uncomfortable reading.

(7)

From their titles, you might think *Raging Angels (1991), Little Devils (1994) and Cherubs* (1996) represent a trilogy. Not quite: but they do reveal a fascination with Christian cosmography and the moral ironies therein. (They are also furthef skirmishes in that war between the establishment and young people, especially *Little Devils*, where an old-guard pillar of society is put on trial.) *Raging Angels* deals with AIDS and sexual feelings, *Little Devils* with problems of defining good and evil, *Cherubs* with incest and sexual desire – all at root about moral attitudes, a subject relevant to young people, of course, but also increasingly the area being occupied by the playwright. That uncertainty about moral absolutes which is of course inherent in Marxism's relativity was getting a brush-down with the dominance of postmodernism and its suspicion of meta-narratives. For the socialist, such uncertainty could provide a challenge to ideological belief – something Greg Cullen knew only too well.

That is not to say the years of apprenticeship in London and, more importantly, with Theatr Powys, altogether lacked direction or integrity. But they did lack complexity, perhaps, coming as much from external demand as inner need. What Greg Cullen said to me recently was that while he has his own agenda he now sees his drama as a platform for voices that are not necessarily his own. He is on an equal basis with the audience – in his plays he wants to go out and have a chat with them, he says, and while *Frida and Diego* and *The Informer's Duty* may have not been so, he wants his plays not to go above people's heads. And, yes, he is *driven* to create. But the presence of an audience – not necessarily a congregation to preach to or a proletariat to politicise, but fellow human beings to engage in debate – is central, and awareness of it crucial to the work.

The point is that Greg Cullen is an activist as well as an artist. I get the feeling that he went into theatre to change the world, to make his contribution to socialist revolution. TIE is the natural habitat for such activity, and it has to be said that some TIE practitioners are better at political than at theatrical activity. For Cullen, the limited scope of political parables and consciousness-raising drama became a constraint. *Taken Out* perhaps brought home the fact that matters can be more complex than crude Marxism allows and that the playwright has a responsibility to tackle contradictions and make the political personal, to serve communities that are not necessarily in agreement with yourself, and to acknowledge that the dramatist cannot actually explain everything.

However, at the same time as writing *Taken Out*, he was the local organiser of a miners' support group during the '84 strike. His political activity led to research into the mining communities he was working with and to a play, *Spoiled Papers*, which dispelled any doubts that he might have lost his socialist fervour as he produced a paean to the power of working-class people to organise and oppose, even if they lost the actual war. In both *Taken Out* and *Spoiled Papers* there is also notable support for the women, usually subordinate in both wars and miners' strikes. Greg Cullen may no longer be – if he ever was – a Trotskyist; he is no longer, as he certainly was, a Marxist; but he is undeniably still a socialist.

I return to the premises with which I opened. That constant artistic dilemma, the resolution of the potential conflict between 'inner need' and 'external demand', whether to write from inside or to respond to outside forces, the balance of artistic integrity and social responsibility, is a dualism that emerges in various forms throughout Greg Cullen's work. He says that the real Greg Cullen is in the plays he writes for himself: powerful, poetic plays like *Frida and Diego*, *The Informer's Duty*, and *Cherubs*, where an audience can be almost irrelevant. But years of writing audience-led plays inevitably make a playwright conscious of the symbiotic relationship between play and audience so that the shared experience transcends that of product-consumer to become transactional. I suspect Greg Cullen is nowhere near the end of his journey and that his best plays are yet to be made. When they are, I also suspect they will evidence a lyrical and political poetics that will encompass the dualities of 'inner need' and 'external demands'. This poet, this lover of life, this man so full of ideas, so full of humanity, wants to 'have a chat' with an audience: and he can be a persuasive talker.

Notes

1 I have drawn on my own experience of seeing Greg Cullen's work since he came to Wales, my own published views of productions, records of my interview and conversations with him, scripts of plays, and the interview with Hazel Walford Davies in *New Welsh Review* 38 (Autumn 1997), pp. 78-83 and *New Welsh Review* 39 (Winter1997-98), pp. 76-81.

2 John McGrath, *A Good Night Out* (London: Methuen, 1981), p. 79.

3 See Joyce Macmillan's Foreword in Catherine Itzen (ed.), *British Alternative Theatre Directory 1983-84* (Eastbourne: John Clifford, 1984), p. 7.

4 Hazel Walford Davies, 'Discovering a Theatrical Landscape' [interview with Greg Cullen], *New Welsh Review* 39 (Winter 1997-98), p. 76.

Love, Anger and Money

Greg Cullen in conversation with David Ian Rabey

DIR: *As* Tarzanne *has been a recurrent touchstone in your theatre work, I'd like to start by asking you about the changes that the script went through in its different versions, for Mid Powys Youth Theatre in 1988, for the joint production by Theatr Powys and Footloose Dance Company in 1990, and in the third version for Mid Powys Youth Theatre again in 1995. The 1988 show ended the most romantically with the wild child's rejection of human society and a return to a more natural jungle life; the 1990 show considered Anne's life posthumously, after she had been committed to an asylum; the 1995 show went even further against the grain of any wish for a romantic ending with a significantly appalling image of the mother's incarceration and separation from her child.*

GC: People have said to me that the end of *Tarzanne* became more bleak, but I never really agreed, because Gwydion, Anne's son, survives, and will be well cared for by Sophie,who has herself gone through a remarkable transformation from an upper-class bitch to a suffragette in the course of the play. Sophie has become a new kind of independent woman who earns her own living; Gwydion will be brought up by her, and I don't think that's a negative ending. At the same time as wanting a positive ending, I could not ignore what happened to women in real historical situations. Within this century and even now, women have been incarcerated and demeaned by society because they have stepped outside our morality, and when morality defines sanity we have a real problem. Many women were put into mental institutions because they became pregnant, and that is their story. In the play, a girl who starts her life in a playpen is subsequently caged as a wild animal, and ends up caged again at the end. The whole point of the process of the play is that human society can transform itself; it's through Sophie and Gwydion that we look for the next transformation to take place. Rather than a bleak ending, it's one which begs resistance from the audience to what has happened to Anne, questioning what is and is not allowed. In the first version of the script, Anne made a return to the jungle, where she felt she could be most human, taking with her tools which belonged to the gardener Jenkins, who had become her father not in literal but in social terms, so that she could cultivate the jungle. That ending was, as you quite rightly describe it, somewhat romantic; it also applauded Anne's divorcing herself from human company, preferring that of chimpanzees. Some people felt that constituted a rejection of humanity, which was not what I wanted at all! The landlord of my local pub, for example, was quite gruff after the show, and asked 'Well, what was I supposed to get from that? That human beings are shit and chimps are great?'. That troubled me, and led me to challenge that ending myself. Such comments are the best monitors of my work. I don't write for a critical fraternity or some *Time Out*-style fringe audience, I want to tell stories to a wide audience, move them and thereby make them think. I changed *Tarzanne* because of my audience.

DIR: *The characterisation of God in* A New World in the Mourning *is a particularly joyous and farcically anarchic moment in your work.*

GC: After *Taken Out*, I was invited to write a play about the Labour Party in Wales. *Taken Out* had genuinely emotionally moved some people in the higher echelons of BBC radio, and I was briefly hailed as some working-class prodigy. The commission seemed to reflect a feeling amongst the intelligentsia at the time that some sort of sea-change was occurring in Wales, that the Labour majority and community concensus was about to crumble (how little they knew!). I researched and toured with a Labour candidate in the late 1980s, at a time when the Left in the Labour Party was very much stronger than it is now, so that the activities of the Militant Tendency in Liverpool were being disowned by Neil Kinnock in his search for a 'respectable' identity for the party. My research experiences made me find the whole election campaign entirely farcical. I wrote a very serious scenario which actually bore no resemblance to the play I later handed in, to which the BBC in London objected strenuously. The producer Adrian Mourby defended the play, and the principle of respecting the way the writer chooses to develop the original idea; nowadays few producers are prepared to make that argument for trusting the writer, or if they do, they are unlikely to get anywhere. So the play emerged in a healthy spirit of sceptical irony.

DIR: New World *nevertheless seems a positive play to me, in that, even while the final parody of a football match commentary depicts the Tories rewriting rules of procedure around Labour's polite bemusement, an anarchic gleeful God is proposing a deliberately unlikely alliance with a gay miner for the prospect of further 'adventures'. Your consistent challenges to homophobia are a feature of your work which I find particularly admirable.*

GC: I don't really do that consciously, though sometimes I do find that a gay character will, in an Ortonian way, ignite a play, in the same way that gays and lesbians ignite life and its possibilities. Gay culture is very enjoyable to me, a heterosexual man. If I go clubbing, I hope to find a gay club that permits a mix because I find such places more refreshing, sexy and shameless in their showmanship than the sad hypocrisies of most heterosexual culture. I enjoy the mix of life; and I enjoy the mix in my plays as well. If you put a homosexual character in a play, then all of a sudden you have extended possibilities. And I love upsetting notions of what is, or might be, normal, as a means to challenging a culture to grow up. This nation – and I mean Britain, not only Wales, though there are certain things I think Wales specifically has to get hold of – is so stultified and anally retentive and immature in its culture, for example in its continuing dependence on a monarchy. It represents a lack of desire to take responsibility or to grow up, to be adult.

DIR: *The gay miner's question to the stockbroker in* New World *as to how the latter decides what the former 'is worth' also seems to me to be central to* Taken Out, *asking why certain human lives are valued above others.*

GC: It's essential. I myself am one of the first wave of working-class people, mostly men, who came through the education system and were given a crack at going on to university or further education. In this, I think we're looking at people like Dic Edwards and Charlie Way as my contemporaries. We're a first post-war wave of writers coming through. I failed my Eleven Plus exam to enter grammar school, and so was put into a secondary modern, with all the immediate attendant implications that life has its limitations now because you didn't 'make it'. But I accepted it, and thought I would do what I could to do well there. There were many people there who were brighter than me, had wonderful gifts and talents, and left school at fourteen or fifteen. But it was suggested that the best I could hope for would be a manual or technical apprenticeship, and that was the way my life was going to be – my father was keen that I join him in the Post Office as a steady job for life. But at the same time the whole hippy culture was emerging, and some people were suggesting, interestingly, that you are not defined by these parameters alone. Then when I reached the fourth year, the Labour government changed everything over to the comprehensive system! My school suddenly had to build laboratories and language suites, replacing the traditional empahsis on woodwork and metalwork. Teachers suggested 'Never mind CSEs, do the O levels, then the A levels'. We were bewildered and said 'We can't do this, we're secondary school kids, fuck off, you're putting too much pressure on'. BUT we DID IT. And I was so angry. At the way I'd initially been dumped at eleven, and at the waste of all my mates at school who had so much intelligence, so much heart, so much soul, and who never got to the point where they believed in themselves. If someone had believed in them in the first place, everything would have been different. That experience was really important for me, because all my plays are about people's potential, whether we release it or not, and the ways in which our society prefers to waste people.

DIR: *'Waste' is perhaps the most resonant word in* Taken Out, *in which there is a terrible sense of failed or aborted breakthrough as the ghosts and the living try to contact each other in vain – a diametrically different effect to that in* New World, *in which God effectively crashes through the ceiling of characters' presumptions to proclaim that human beings have such potential, are capable of ingenuities he never anticipated, but that they prefer to ignore that potential.*

GC: God's alliance with the gay miner reflects the way I like the idea that God might reside in good souls, who don't necessarily have to be Christian or even religious. Without wishing to get woozy about spiritualism, I think that the dominant preoccupations with materialism and rationality have missed the point. Science cannot explain the wonder of the universe.

DIR: *Much as I love many of Bond's plays, I find it hard to embrace his sense that all contradictions can or should ultimately be resolved by rationality.*

GC: I can't accept that, either, because, despite however many essays theorists write, human beings will never behave completely rationally; life doesn't work like that. Life is more like a series of interconnected cogs, you turn it on and so many things start moving further on down the line, but there are so many cogs you can't know about all the ramifications. I'm very interested by the recent story of how the New York telephone system has gone out of control because there are so many wires and connections that strange things are starting to happen, suggesting that past a certain limit the thing has discovered its own autonomous vocabulary! It's reached a point where critical mass has transformed into chaos, which I love. I think that reflects our point at the end of the century: we've reached critical mass, and are destroying the environment, our days are numbered, and all the firm old beliefs, be they the Catholicism which I grew up with or the Marxism that I had in my youth, cannot explain everything away, and that discovery has been the major experience of my middle age. I struggled with it, but now I rejoice in the idea of chaotic necessity: it's where I exist, it's where I have truly always existed, the rest of the time has been an institutional mad clawing for some kind of certainty which I no longer need, and that's great! I love confusion. *Taken Out* was in this respect the most important play of my career, in that in the face of everyone around me telling me what I could and couldn't do, I just said 'FUCK OFF!', and in so doing produced the first play in which I could recognize my own case and the personal way in which I had argued it; this was how I felt and how I identified the reasons why. It's been the inspiration for everything subsequently, in that I must try to do that every time. I don't always manage it, the way I want to.

DIR: *You might say 'Our days are numbered', but I don't sense any fatalistic despair in the plays. Even* The Informer's Duty *chooses to end by depicting Stalin triumphant on one level – one literal level of the stage – but Shostakovich triumphant on another.*

GC: I added a further stage direction to the end of that play which I think is missing from the copy you read – which is '*AKHMATOVA also triumphant*'. It wasn't until I directed the final scene of the play that I realized that was what was missing. Stalin thinks he's won the war, the world, Shostakovich's obedience, that he is supreme; and in a way he was, but where is he now? What is his lasting victory? Akhmatova's poetry is now translated into English, she has been the subject of two recent books by Lydia Chakovskaya; Akhmatova is going to be to poetry what Frida Kahlo is to painting. She and Shostakovich have survived in ways they knew they would. And that's what we as artists and citizens have to remember about our political so-called masters, that the *citizenry* continue when the political masters come and go, and no matter how much they persecute us, there is our ability to triumph within their disaster. Nelson Mandela, in prison for twenty-seven years, triumphed *within* the absolute apex of apartheid's success. Where was he? *Winning*. Year after year, all down the line. All he had to do was *wait*. And his persecutors knew it. So, yes, there is a real positive will in my work and life.

DIR: Mary Morgan *is an intriguingly strange play, not only in the archaisms that it deliberately throws together, ranging through time; it's also specifically based in place and time and on a dilemma of social class. At the end of the story, many of the characters revert to their class types, significantly and disconcertingly, with the pivotal character Wilkins finally exultant, like Stalin, at his control. But Wilkins is a King's Minister, pleased that issues have been played out into the fundamental conflicts and contradictions of power, and finally proclaims 'The world changes!'.*

GC: I think it is Wilkins who wins in the end – the bourgeoisie triumph over the aristocracy. That was the transformation of the time: that the gentry, the *nouveau riche*, rise and change the structure of society, not through revolution, but through metamorphosis of what we accept as social structure. I wrote that play when I was very close to the Socialist Workers' Party and very much into street politics, concerned with how change manifests itself on the street, and so there's a lot of street imagery in there, for example the threat of burning 'necklaces' as an image of revolutionary street violence that I was calling up for the audience to question in this context. The question as to when violence might be justified was very close to my concerns then – less so *now* – and I'd be interested to re-direct that play now, ten years on, to see what I might make of it. But there is a kernel of truth in the play which remains for me, which is that in all revolutionary situations it's never the working-class who inherit the earth: it didn't happen in Russia, it didn't happen here, rather there is the revolution of another class system. So yes, Wilkins gets what he wants, but the women are still in the shanty town.

DIR: Whispers in the Woods *is a disarming but no less powerful demonstration, in its fairy tale form, of how the institutionalization of fear sells the future's potential down the river: a recurrent tendency which your work identifies and challenges. The Wolf's final wish to 'Look forward' is also very characteristic, because, no matter how desperate the situations you depict and dramatize, the importance of looking forward is always expressed somehow.*

GC: I almost cut that last scene from the play . . .

DIR: *I'm glad you didn't! For a moment in performance, I did think you were going for a* Romeo and Juliet-*type ending, which would have been too easy and too familiar, as well as an uncharacteristic submission to fatalistic determinism . . .*

GC: Oh, I wasn't going for a tragic death, I was going to end with the Faery Queen's pronouncement of the Tailor's Daughter, 'Now, a woman whose past was clear,/ At last she felt her mother draw near', which I felt was a powerful uplift. But then I thought we needed to hear once more from the characters, but I didn't know how to end it or what they would say. But in the workshops for the play, as part of our exploration of fairy-tale forms and motifs, we'd naturally tried the question, 'What would each character ask for if you gave them three wishes?', so I asked this of the actors, who replied, *to remember, to know* and *to look forward.* I immediately thought, I can't end with that, it's too *naff*, but I left it on the page for a couple of days, and then asked myself, 'Well, what do *I* want?'. And the answer was, *to remember, to know* and *to look forward.* I want to remember where I came from in order to know why I'm here. Memory is very important in all the plays; you'll notice I'm always flipping to the 'back story', going backwards to discover, and I don't do this just as a theatrical convention but because the role of memory is so important in the work. I don't want to simply open a lens and present a situation without deriving some sense of *why* people are doing what they're doing, and then close the lens again.

DIR: *I'd also like to make the point that no one is going to sense the full measure of what you do just by reading your scripts on the page – they would have to come to the Wyeside centre in Builth Wells and see the multiple-national-award-winning Mid Powys Youth Theatre in action under your direction, to see how you've helped to create what you termed in your last programme notes 'a safe place in which to experiment and be dangerous', and to develop what one current member calls an 'unfathomable capability to meet any challenge with a war cry'.*

GC: It is a unique place, partly because it's my personality that dominates the atmosphere; and I'm not going to be ashamed or shy about that. If it were someone else's, the place would be different. I've made loads of mistakes with the Youth Theatre, but the point is that in a fully professional situation, you'd be *cauterized*; in the Youth Theatre, they accept you as a human being, with all your failings. And what artist could ask for more? In a professional situation nowadays, everyone is in such a psychosis of fear about 'the product', and about seeming ridiculous, that you often can't find a proper artistic flexibility in people. People arrive at the Youth Theatre with no technical skills whatsoever, but with hunger, passion, conviction, commitment, loyalty, a willingness to work beyond standard hours, and they express an incredible amount of satisfaction when they achieve what they've worked for. And over the years there have been so many fantastic people to work with. And as long as I envy them the experience that they've had, at their ages, then I know I've done my job. I needed and would have loved something like the Mid Powys Youth Theatre when I myself was growing up.

DIR: *What keeps you going?*

GC: Love, anger and the need for money!

Reviews

THE SNOW QUEEN

The Snow Queen (Theatr Powys)
The County Times, 9 December, 1983.

Theatr Powys is poised to go back on the road with another spectacular Christmas show; this time bringing to life Hans Christian Anderson's famous children's story of *The Snow Queen.*

The Christmas shows have become increasingly popular as the special effects involved get better every year.

Last year, more than 15,000 saw 'Pinocchio' and the company hopes to top that in their eleventh birthday year.

The show-piece of this year's production is likely to be the great ice palace of the Snow Queen at the finale, but along the way there are plenty of other magical effects to be enjoyed. These are all currently being perfected by the cast at the Drama Centre at Llandrindod Wells.

The story has been adapted by Greg Cullen, the company's resident writer.

The play is narrated by the Trolls – the slaves of the evil Snow Queen who plans to turn the world to ice. Kay is kidnapped and held prisoner by the Snow Queen, and his only hope of rescue is his friend, Gerda, who must follow the trail across the ice flats to the final show-down.

There are 28 characters involved in the story and the players include many new faces to Theatre Powys audiences.

Caroline Staunton is the Snow Queen, Shaun Waller is Kay and Bernadette O'Brien is Gerda.

One familiar face will be that of David Coslett, in his tenth year with the company, who plays the Grand Master Troll.

This year's show will also feature an original stereophonic soundtrack including seven new songs written by James Mackie, previously a member of the pop group, The Selector.

The Snow Queen (Theatr Powys)
The Express, 22 December, 1983.

The Snow Queen, this year's Christmas show from Theatr Powys, played to a near-capacity audience seated in the fine new seats and staging at Brecon's Guildhall last Friday.

An instant success with children and adults, the show displayed the characteristics one has come to expect from Mid-Wales' premier touring company – versatility, energy, startling light and sound effects (the latter at times competing with local police messages) and a plot easy to follow without becoming boring.

Based on a story by Hans Christian Andersen, the play bore clear allusions to the threat of world domination by an evil power. The main lessons to be drawn are that those who make the bombs (mirrors, in the story) are as guilty as those who authorise their use – 'We just makes 'em. It's not our business what use they puts 'em to.' The inexorable progress of evil needs to be opposed by practical goodness, not just apathetic indifference. In the words of Edmund Burke, 'All that is necessary for evil to triumph is that good men do nothing.'

It is essential that local children continue to see such excellent theatre and the reaction of one speaks for all, 'That was ace that was!'.

Breconians now eagerly anticipate the performance of 'Charles Dickens Esq.' at the Castle Hotel on 28th January.

The Snow Queen (Theatr Powys)
The County Times, 5 January, 1984.

The Theatr Powys 1983 Christmas entertainment, *The Snow Queen*, which was performed at Newtown's Theatr Hafren, is a magnificent electronic son-et-lumiere with endlessly dissolving and re-forming sets and backdrops, ever changing colours, and remarkable sound effects.

Seven players between them covered the 18 characters in this version of Hans Andersen's story which was adapted by Greg Cullen. These players are all tremendously versatile, or they would not be able to do this, but it does lead to a certain amount of identification difficulty at times.

This play about a boy and girl playmates, Kay and Gerda, is really an allegory on the two conflicting outlooks on the world, the despairing and the hopeful, and it carried overtones of nuclear menace and a parallel with today's worldwide violence. It is thus particularly apt and topical both seasonally and politically.

It is also an oblique commentary on the theme of love and ambition.

But as a multicoloured extravaganza of a fairy tale it also made a wonderful spectacle for children out of Gerda's search for Kay, and the stories she was told by the flowers and animals on her journey to the realm of the Snow Queen to rescue him.

The book took a number of liberties with the original text, introducing a band of Trolls, goblin-like creatures who do not appear in Andersen's original story, and who had allegories of their own to impart. And it was rather a pity that they spoke in broad Mummerset which was not always easy to follow.

Most of the cast were recent recruits to the Theatr Powys company, but the 'old guard' David Coslett, as the Grandmaster Troll, was the anchor-man who virtually compered the story and held it all together.

There was some very clever miming, as in the scene where Gerda is drawn in a cart, and where the reindeer actually carries her on his back. The scenic and lighting effects were a tour de force, especially in the final scene where metallic sheets shone and shimmered in ever changing colours, from green to gold and red to silver.

The sound effects too, were brilliantly rendered, notably the forest sounds of birds and animals.

Bernadette O'Brien played Gerda with a nice simplicity. Shaun Waller, as Kay, played as coldly as the splinter of distorting glass which had pierced his heart and frozen it; while Caroline Staunton made a Snow Queen as regal and ruthless as her name.

Jonathon Morgan and Bob Tomson jointly directed the production and kept it at the high professional level which Theatr Powys always achieves. The way they kept it simultaneously on two levels, as a children's spectacle and an adult allegory, was a remarkable achievement . . .

'The Snow Queen' may not rank as the cleverest of the Theatr Powys plays –

that title surely still belongs to the 'Great Egg Scape' – but it will undoubtedly be remembered as the most brilliant spectacle and extravaganza to date.

Cynric Mytton-Davies

The Snow Queen (Llanelli Entertainment Centre)
The Guardian, 12 January, 1984.

There are a few good shows in South Wales at the moment and Theatr Powys's *The Snow Queen* is one of the best, with a tour (until the first week of February) that takes them round most of the principality. I caught them at the Llanelli Entertainment Centre, squeezed between 3D Jaws and adult movies. A good thing, too, because we need to see the likes of Theatr Powys who have a massive home county to serve but who manage, amazingly, to have two productions at once on the road, and still set an example of polished, adventurous smallscale theatre.

The Snow Queen may be playing in schools as well as theatres but it's a beautifully dressed production that's competently and confidently done, with a direct approach that brings in the young audience but one that has admirable standards of direction (from Jonathan Morgan and Bob Tomson), music (from ex-Selector James Mackie) and design (from Clare Southern).

The one worrying thing, it seems to me, is the philosophy of the piece. That the Snow Queen bears an uncanny resemblance to a certain present-day icy lady who also creates a frozen uncaring world is fair enough, and I guess the temptation to draw analogies was too much. But Greg Cullen's script at times could well leave the children behind.

Indeed, that the evil Snow Queen was defeated by the power of popular united action did, I'm sure, pass most of the audience by. For them, the fun and enjoyment was in the crisp production, the upfront performances, the sheer variety of characters, with seven actors playing nearly two dozen roles, and the excellent sound, lighting and effects.

David Adams

THE BRIDE OF BARON DUPRAV

The Bride of Baron Duprav (Newtown Youth and Community Centre)
The Guardian, 28 March, 1984.

Frankenstein meets Dracula in the Castle of Otranto for Theatr Powys's latest community show touring mid-Wales, *The Bride Of Baron Duprav*. It's high Gothic camp with not only ghosts of dead brides, but sexual transplants, crows instead of vampire bats, and the almost mandatory social politics virtually lost in the showers of blood and screams of horror.

Greg Cullen's script mixes the madness and the message well. Because the evil Nietzschean philosopher wants a wife but not with a woman's brain, the mad scientist puts a man's brain inside a woman's body: and so as not to waste anything puts a female brain in a male body.

Fears that the dialogue would be splattered by feminist role reversal polemics are, however, groundless and the situation is instead used for a host of witty, rude and telling jokes. It's a little cameo of a comedy – even the creaking of the doors is vocalised by whoever is opening or closing them and Clare Southern's neat little set works a treat.

It's that emphasis on entertainment rather than raising social consciousness that makes it a typical Theatr Powys production, this time directed by Harriet Landsowne with pace and panache.

The performance skills mean that the small cast can play with relish the caricatured roles, whip it all along at a sometimes quite manic speed and still reach out to an audience who are not used to theatre and are often seated in a venue singularly unsuited to performance. Newtown's Youth and Community Centre is far from the worst gig but it does take a lot to make a show work there, and here it certainly did despite a smallish audience.

David Adams

The Bride of Baron Duprav (Theatr Powys)
The County Times, 9 June, 1984.

The Bride of Baron Duprav is stalking the stages of Mid-Wales again as Theatr Powys revives their madcap horror story spoof.

On Monday the cast will make their first appearance at the Powys Theatre, Newtown, home of the town's Amateur Dramatic Society.

The amateurs and the professionals will meet each other and *The Bride* is assured of an enthusiastic reception.

The play toured extensively earlier this year to rave reviews and the company decided to revive it for eight more performances ending on Saturday at the Wyeside Arts Centre, Builth Wells.

The company's writer, Greg Cullen, has brought together many of the elements of the old Gothic horror stories, and woven them into a manic send-up, as a bizarre experiment and a family curse involve the players in an hilarious romp.

The English maid, played by Louise Osborne, and a young American, David Coslett, are at the centre of the fiendish experiment cooked up by the crazy Baron and scheming doctor, Ian Kerry and Roger Wooster, while the lovely femme fatale, Bernadette O'Brien, tries to make sense of it all and the butler (Grant Stevens) shuffles mysteriously on.

The Bride of Baron Duprav (Theatr Powys)
The Stage, 19 July, 1984.

In the entertainment business every new genre spawns its own parody, and the Theatr Powys may well be first in the field with a version of the video nasty.

Their recent touring production (*The Bride of Baron Duprav*) has all the right ingredients. The blood spurts freely as the scalpel bites, defenceless women are preyed on by crows in human guise and depravity stalks the chill corridors of the Transylvanian castle.

The odd thing is that this farrago of nonsense is rather gripping. Greg Cullen's story of an aristocrat who wants to father an heir by a wife with a man's brain is original and intricate, while director Harriet Landsdowne has devised a taut, unflagging presentation that allows no time for questioning its plausibility.

It helps that the company has turned out its first 11 for the occasion, and there is a fine array of extrovert talent on show. Veteran Roger Wooster plays the perverted doctor with an incongruous jokiness that is very funny indeed. As the Baron, Ian Kerry teeters constantly on the brink without quite going over the top. Bernadette O'Brien seizes gratefully on the chance to wear a preposterous mauve dress and thus upstage almost everyone as the doctor's mistress. In the end, however, the hardest task falls to Louise Osborne and David Coslett, acting out the intricate technical consequences of a mental sex-change – no doubt something previously unattempted on stage or screen, and very impressive too.

One of the greatest assets of the production is Clare Southern's miniature Gothic set, and as always the technical effects cannot be faulted. I should add that Grant Stevens spends the evening bent double as the butler, but in the concluding minutes he – well, I won't go on because this is a show that Theatre Powys may well want to revive.

Lawrence Garner

ALADDIN

Aladdin (Cefn Coed Community Centre)
The Guardian, 11 January, 1985.
Theatr Powys, despite changes in artistic direction, somehow managed to maintain an amazing consistency of style. Their *Aladdin*, currently touring Mid and North Wales, has the same flair, colour and exuberance that marked their previous seasonal shows.

It has, of course, some of the same company as last year's Snow Queen. Greg Cullen's script is again witty and works on two levels – one for the children and one for the adults. It's set in China (more authentic than Arabia, apparently, and using ancient Chinese myths) but it somehow also involves a bemused Irish lady cyclist lost in Wales after landing from the Dublin ferry. Otherwise the characters are much as we are used to, and Aladdin's mother, the dame of traditional pantos, gets a topical cheer as she demands a T-shirt saying 'Twanky Goes To Holyhead.'

For the adults there are anti-police cracks, some nice fun with meditation and even a visual joke about H blocks. But the cleverness never gets in the way of the enjoyment, and at the crowded Cefn Coed Community Centre the youngsters were in the pockets of the cast in no time.

Tam Neal's music was notably good and the whole cast performed with gusto. My only complaint is that it is a show designed to be seen in its entirety, not just what's visible above the heads of the people in the row in front: a lot happens at floor level and in community centres that don't have ramped seating (and that includes most of them) a lot of the fun is missed.

David Adams

SWASHBUCKLERS

Swashbucklers (Theatr Hafren)
The Guardian, 3 January, 1986.
One really did want Greg Cullen's new show for Theatr Powys to work, a neat idea with capitalists depicted as latter-day pirates, written on two levels that should have satisfied the ideological conscience of the adults and the inquisitive sense of adventure of the younger one.

But it didn't, at least at Theatr Hafren it didn't, although it's fair to say that in the sort of community venue that the company are more used to, *Swashbucklers* would probably at least get the audience more involved.

I have to admit that I totally missed the bit where we all blew the baddie into the avaricious monster food mountain because I glanced down at my programme. This may have been because there's a two-page children's guide to colonial imperialism and Third World repression through famine: admirable, and one hopes elucidating reading for after the show.

In a different venue with a less polite audience it may well be that the fights, the songs and the fun and games would be more engrossing than the message.

Such a theme shouldn't need detailed justification, of course, and the main fault of the show is that the injustice, the exploitation and the cynicism just don't come across in the script.

The plight of young Thomas Morgan, a local farmer's lad who can't understand why his farm is going broke when there are starving millions in the world, is neither entertaining enough nor presented interestingly enough to grab minds or hearts.

We're used to Greg Cullen's children's shows working on two levels and to his political acumen and stylish writing, but *Swashbucklers* doesn't ever quite gel.

I liked Alison McCaw's designs but the rest of the production was disappointing, especially by Theatr Powys standards. The cast throw themselves into it but there just isn't enough action or enough of a story line to pull us into the moralistic role.

David Adams

Swashbucklers (Theatr Powys)
The Western Mail, 2 January, 1986.

'The stale bread used in this production is donated waste' said a prominent note in the programme for *Swashbucklers*, the Theatr Powys Christmas show.

The reason for this prim defensiveness becomes clear when we find the young hero Tom Morgan, pestering his parents and teachers with questions about starvation in the Third World and asking why the family farm will have to be sold because of food surpluses in the West.

As the story develops he joins a band of pirates dedicated to the task of eliminating the owner of a food mountain.

I found this combination of buccaneering entertainment and Geldof economics slightly embarrassing, but no doubt this is an adult niggle. With any luck those children who are not *Guardian* readers will let the moralising pass over their heads and revel in what Theatr Powys is best at – exploiting every technique available to produce vivid theatre.

Tessa Gearing, Ian Heywood, Adrian Lockhead, Bill Lynn, Carol McGuigan and the perennial Roger Wooster hurl themselves around unstintingly in a variety of resplendent costumes, conjuring up some dazzling visual effects.

Pirates emerge from a school desk, ships engage in a battle at sea, a cook disappears into his own stew and sailors fall off the edge of the world.

The scenic artists have been busy too, and their masterpiece is undoubtedly a grisly, animated food mountain that roars and gurgles revoltingly and eventually eats the villain. Parents may cringe but the children will love it.

Ian Heywood's original music is catchy and spontaneous, and the best of it relies on solo voice with vocal accompaniment by the rest of the cast. Refreshingly nobody grabs a microphone to sing.

Director Sue Glanville has done wonders with a Greg Cullen script that gets dangerously po-faced in places, and the result is a show that should be a revelation to any child used to regarding television as the last word in entertainment.

Lawrence Garner

Swashbucklers (Theatr Powys)
The County Times, 11 January, 1986.

The big blue lorry has been embellished with Theatr Powys and *Swashbucklers* signs. It is packed with rostra and lighting equipment, puppets and props, musical instruments and costumes – a melee of colour, the sternly practical scaffolding bars alongside the extraordinary products of design fantasy.

The lorry sets off from the Drama Centre in Llandrindod – the Theatr Powys Christmas Show is on the road.

Record advance ticket sales this year have confirmed the company's feeling that all through Powys, children and grown ups have come to have high expectations of them at Christmas time.

Despite the curtailing of resources, which means fewer performers and stage managers, and stringent limits on budget for set and costume compared with previous years, somehow they must devise a way of satisfying the demand for a show that entertains all ages, is visually exciting, full of laughter and excitement but with the capacity to move people and involve them with the drama.

Theatr Powys draw on the oldest pantomime tradition for their Christmas shows – strong, clear heroes and heroines and villains, lots of knockabout and lively participation with and from the audience, bright colours in design and performance, no limits to imagination and fantasy.

Greg Cullen, the resident writer, for whom this is the third Christmas show for Powys, has worked with designer and performers to weave these elements into a story which has its roots in reality – in Wales and the world where many starve while farmers are told to produce less and often cannot sustain their livelihood.

To a child, the logic of economics which allows food mountains to rise while thousands die for lack of food, is incomprehensible, especially if the child's parents are farmers whose livelihood is threatened by this situation.

Swashbucklers takes Thomas, a boy whose roots are in such a farming family, into a dream world, a fantasy peopled with pirates and full of fun and adventure, in which he can explore his desires and his fears, bring them to a satisfactory conclusion, and grow in confidence and effectiveness.

So swashbuckling and seabattles, defeating the villain and defending the weak, a whole fantasy world beneath the floorboards, 'a world that has no history', a food mountain and Ophelia the Octopus, music, magic and laughter, all combine to reinforce the still relevant Christmas message expanded by Bob Geldof's *Feed the World*.

The writer and performers are now planning their next projects even while on the road in *Swashbucklers*. Greg Cullen's next piece of work will be his second play to be broadcast by BBC Radio in conjunction with Theatr Powys, after the extremely successful *Taken Out* earlier this year.

He then applies himself to a community theatre play for the company next autumn, all the while bearing the next Christmas show in mind.

Sue Glanville

TAKEN OUT

Taken Out (BBC Radio 4)
The Listener, 28 February, 1986.

In Greg Cullen's play *Taken Out* (Monday R4 8.15-9.30pm), Captain Sommers of the Welsh Guards struggles to explain his Falklands War experiences. 'You're not really human when you look at a picture; you can't smell it, you're not feeling it through your skin.' Summers wonders if this purely visual sense has enabled noncombatants to countenance and condone war. Adrian Mourby's production permits the radio audience no such insulation. It pitches us into the mess and desperation of battle through the gulfs of sound which periodically emerge from Sommers's ticking nerves, in uncontrollable 'automatic recall' of air-strike conditions. At other times, the play's method is fluidly psychic as it probes the raw sense of loss experienced by family dependants. For asking questions about the fate of the Welsh Guards in the Falklands War, Sommers and other soldiers in the play are judged to be 'embarrassments' and military ranks are closed against them.

Mourby's BBC Wales Radio Drama Unit has been committed to fostering new plays for Wales about aspects of the country lacking or denied a dramatic voice – and presenting contemporary images to replace the folksy landscapes and musty associations of *How Green Was My Valley* and *Under Milk Wood* which still hang over much writing and thinking about Wales. The Unit has been correspondingly concerned to work with new authors and new methods of producing plays. *Taken Out* was jointly commissioned by BBC Wales and Theatre Powys in radio and stage versions, and the play's authoritative articulation of local feeling demanding wider expression makes it an apt and urgent choice as part of the Unit's 'Plays for Wales' series for Radio Four.

Cullen researched *Taken Out* by interviewing relatives of Welsh Guards who died aboard HMS *Sir Galahad*, as well as survivors from the South Atlantic. Its characters are scorched and fragmented by their experiences. The reminiscences of living and dead drift in and out of focus, teasingly short of successful communication with anyone bar the radio audience, who are invited to unite the almost unbearable intimacies of their griefs. We struggle with Sommers to manage the implications of warfare, to complete and deal with details like the burning deckhands who resemble 'tortured bunnies' in their disfigurement and agony.

Taken Out is remarkable not only for its delicate and unflinching articulation of personal loss, but also for the immediacy of its pursuit of this loss back to political causes. *Edge of Darkness* took a similar route into an imminent ecological disaster. But Cullen's play is even more indicting for its basis in recent military fact and its fundamental questioning of government defence strategy – seen as continuing the historical process by which Welsh interests are placed secondary to English benefit. *Taken Out* and the other plays in Radio Four's Welsh Drama Week – *Three of Swords* by Mike Dorrell (Saturday R4 8.30-10pm), and *The Penrhyn Summer* by Alison Leonard (Tuesday R4 3-4pm), all reflect a sense of disenfranchisement and isolation, energy robbed of direction and characters marginalised into eccentricity for conflicting with centralised interests. Dispossession is seen as the fate of those who do not reinforce officially sanctioned notions of national pride and national 'interest'. Cullen's forthcoming radio play on the miners' strike, *Spoiled Papers*, promises a similarly telling 'unofficial' view of the effects of political events on Welsh communities.

David Ian Rabey

Taken Out (Drill Hall Theatre, London)
The Guardian, 9 January, 1987.

Greg Cullen's *Taken Out* detonates a forceful charge against the military planners whom he believes responsible for the loss of British lives at Bluff Cove, during the Falklands war and it attempts to convey the impact of Bluff Cove upon one bereaved family, the wife and parents of an 18-year-old Welsh Guard who went up in the smoke and flames of that ghastly conflagration nearly five years ago.

It is a daring theatrical enterprise for a tiny theatrical company, and the scope and the scale of the piece is very large. The author also provides a fascinating seven and a half page essay within the programme, based upon his own researches and interviews with staff from the Welsh Guards and relations of those killed. He suggests that the guardsmen were victims of belated planning. They sailed to Bluff Cove, moored at Fitzroy, stayed there several hours in light of day as sitting targets for the Argentinians in an already bomb-damaged ship with no air protection.

The details provided in his programme are far more expansive and rather more gripping than those in the play itself. But even so Cullen's technical ingenuity and inventive organisation of large themes, and the extent to which he reveals the nature of loss in war, is very strong.

He has set the play within the frame of the arrival of Barry Brooks's parents, with his pregnant wife, at a Falklands Island memorial service for the fallen. He then ranges freely back in time, with the dead private and his best friend brought back to life to recreate their fatal hours.

The fashion in which the dead and the living converse may not be altogether new but it is, in Cullen's script, poignant with its sharp sense of outrage, desolation and grief. And that sense of waste and loss grows inexorably through the process of the play. Sue Glanville's production, with an ugly, sparse and unfunctional set by Sarah Pulley, and lighting and a sound track which are not very evocative, is not consistently lucky with the cast, who are uneasy with complex emotional demands required of them. But this remains an emotionally power-packed occasion.

Nicholas de Jongh

Taken Out (Drill Hall Theatre, London)
The Socialist Worker, 17 January, 1987.

Good socialist plays are hard to write.

But Greg Cullen has done it, and done it well. His play *Taken Out* is on at the Drill Hall in London this month.

Taken Out is about the Falklands War in 1982.

Cullen is a Socialist Workers Party member who lives in Wales. Before he wrote the play he talked to Welsh soldiers who had fought in the Falklands, and to the families of boys who had died there.

He wrote the play with them very much in mind.

He doesn't tackle the war head-on. Instead he focuses on one little incident – the bombing of a ship, the *Sir Galahad.*

The play focuses on two Welsh boys killed in the bombing.

The family of one of the boys comes to the Falklands for the memorial service with their daffodils, their flask of tea and their grief. (Arbel Jones is stunning as the mother.)

Running alongside is the story of the major in charge of the boys (John Cillet –

wonderful). His bewildered anger at the waste of battle interweaves with the family's mixture of rage and wish to feel their boy died *for something*.

Behind their feeling lurks the question, why?

And there is a Welsh-speaking, Patagonian-Argentinian, rugby-playing revolutionary with an answer to that.

Taken Out is sometimes funny, sometimes moving, always sensitive, always angry. And it's well acted.

If you're in London and you want a good, satisfying socialist night out, go and see this play.

Jonathan Neale

Taken Out (Drill Hall Theatre, London)
The Independent, 20 January, 1987.

As Barry's parents and pregnant wife ask questions at a memorial service in the Falklands, Captain Sommers agonises because although he knows why the Welsh Guards were left for six hours on the Sir Galahad in full view of Argentine positions, he has quit the service and can take no action. Barry's family feel that his death has no dignity so long as the authorities conceal the truth, and his mother (Arbel Jones) swears that she will live another 30 years just to see the declassified papers. Greg Cullen has united the political with the tragic, personal element of war and is well served by excellent acting from Spark Theatre in their debut. This play rescues the Falklands war from television news, and sets a new agenda for theatrical debate.

Paul Arnott

SPOILED PAPERS

Spoiled Papers (BBC Radio Wales)
Planet, June/July 1986.

There are now several very promising dramatists in Wales. However, like dramatists everywhere, they are dependent on being performed and on getting play commissions: and the practice in Wales, it appears, is still to favour productions of well-known imported plays or, where new commissions are given, plays with an identifiably 'Welsh' subject-matter and pre-approved 'relevance'. In the minds of the minders and paymasters of contemporary Welsh drama in English, stage Welshness is sometimes very much still with us.

The situation in radio broadcasting is the same, if not worse. Indeed radio, like television – because of the size of audiences, the cachet of success that comes from having work broadcast, its more centralised cultural power – bears a particular responsibility in this respect, and one that it has usually failed in.

So, in this context, it was not with unmixed optimism that I approached the recent Radio Wales series of plays *Six On Saturday*, mostly work newly-commissioned by producer Adrian Mourby. I was not reassured by the BBC's pre-declared intention of finding 'new images of Wales and Anglo-Welsh experience'. Why not just 'new images of experience'? Wouldn't that be enough? And 'Anglo-Welsh', as I've suggested, is already a self-characterising (if not self-colonialising) placard of the kind that fewer writers now would willingly hang around their necks . . .

Probably the most widely-anticipated play of the six was the last. Following his success last year with *Taken Out*, a controversial play about the Falklands, Greg Cullen had now researched and written a play about the 1984-85 miners' strike. *Spoiled Papers* was set in a South Wales mining community recognisable as the Dulais and Swansea Valleys to those who know the area and its support group. The play dramatises the pressures and passions of the long strike and its effect on both strikers and scabs in the same community, with tragic consequences that make a cross-coalfield reference to the Shankland and Hancock case. Yet the play is about much more than that one event and what led to it. The strike was a profound political experience for many thousands of men and women. These were often heady days. And all this comes through in a succession of scenes of great dramatic force and cinematic brevity: the police offering to drive miners from the pub to the picket-line in the strike's early days, to make sure of their own overtime pay; the women of the Neath, Dulais and Swansea Valleys' support group occupying the Cynheidre pithead baths; or that infamous, long day in the sun at Orgreave, where police on horseback, with helmets and riot-sticks, charged miners 'in daps and T-shirts' in a bloody rout of infantry by cavalry which had been pre-planned in some police operations room with Clausewitzian care . . .

Spoiled Papers was a remarkable example of dramatic pace and concision, condensing as it did a strike that lasted a year into an hour of radio time, without Greg Cullen's treatment ever seeming sketchy or tendentious. What held the whole thing together was its immense narrative drive and, frequently, the edge of rawness, fear and urgency of events in the strike itself – not forgetting the resilience, too, the tenacity, the humour. This was a fitting play to finish with and, if I may say, a fitting tribute to the men and women of the community in that small area of the coalfield whose experiences Greg Cullen has so carefully listened to, collected, selected from, reshaped and used verbatim too, with such dramatic clarity and purpose.

Overall, as I've suggested, the season was very much a mixed bag, not only in terms of style and subject-matter but in quality. Yet we have to commend Radio Wales and series producer Adrian Mourby for their commitment in mounting this season of new Welsh drama – after all, nobody in theatre or television in Wales is providing this kind of outlet for new writing in the English language or looks likely to. And you have to take the risk of doing bad and middling plays if you want to find the good ones.

Here, it was interesting, finally, that the two best plays by far dealt with events in specific tight, local communities: that of Spanish and Italian immigrants in Dowlais in Alan Osborne's play [*Mestizo*] and that of a small mining community to the west of the coalfield in Cullen's. You can't get much more local than that. These two plays, coincidentally, were also probably those which ran most risk of stereotype: boxers and miners are the archetypal heroes of industrial South Wales. Yet perhaps these plays gained their wider relevance from the fact that for their characters, as for their respective authors, what was happening here, in this place, in this time, was genuinely more significant than what was going on anywhere else in the world. These plays came crackling with the tension of real dramatic experience. Perhaps in writing you can deal with anything afresh – even archetypes – as long as you start in a real place in a real time, with a living language, and with people.

Duncan Bush

HARD TIMES

Hard Times (Roses Theatre, Tewksbury)
Berrow's Journal, 26 September, 1986.

Dicken's classic tale of poverty and prejudice among the mill workers and the masters of northern Victorian England could so easily have been hard going for this year's Tewkesbury Festival.

Indeed, everything pointed in that depressing direction during the first fifteen or so minutes of opening night in the town's barely filled theatre.

The Mayor, sat just along the row, must have been wondering what he'd let himself in for . . . a sadly depleted audience. Dickens at his drabest and the odd notion that the evening's entertainment was being performed by members of a travelling circus.

Not just any circus, you understand, but Sleary's Circus, no less – star of Mr Dickens' novel, *Hard Times*.

Confusing? It was, trying to assimilate tellers from tale and acts from actors.

Doubly so when each of the six circus members took on three or four roles, two took on one, women acted as men and men acted as women!

Come to terms with all that and the production was all the more impressive.

Theatr Powys took this adaptation by Greg Cullen and turned it into pure entertainment.

They used mime, they used magic. They used quick-change routines and shifted scenery. They used Dicken's dialogue and a few passages he didn't write.

'Hard Times' may have seemed a strange choice for the Festival play and the organisers may have had a hard time packing in the punters, but the loss was by those who missed out on a faultless piece of theatre.

David Chapman

MARY MORGAN

Mary Morgan (Mid Powys Youth Theatre)
Mid Wales Journal, 6 November, 1987.

To be quite frank it was the last thing I wanted to do that Thursday night. You know the feeling, hard day at work, travelling 30 miles, good film on the telly.

Well, tough luck on those of you that didn't make it to see the first production from Mid Powys Youth Theatre, *Mary Morgan*.

It was gruelling, moving, atmospheric and entertaining.

To begin with the set was magnificent. It transported its audience into a market place, study, kitchen and river bank of the 19th Century.

The ability to be able to walk around the set exploring different angles and perspectives though, proved to be too much for many of the audience.

There were large gaps in front of some of the scenes, particularly in the first half, because people were rooted to the spot.

The script, by Greg Cullen, was in the first half a little too complex. I found at times that I was becoming confused with characters and the story-line became a little blurred.

However, by the second half it developed and produced some enormously powerful scenes.

Guy Roderick's innovative direction drew from the cast a versatility both in the style of their performances and in their depth of characterisation.

The musicians played a vital role in this production. Under the direction of Steven Byrne assisted by Janine Sharp, they managed to heighten tension and emotion throughout the play by some extraordinary haunting music.

But what was most important about this production was its relevance to young people who are growing up in a world where the division of the classes is becoming wider and more apparent.

The debate on capital punishment is being discussed over and over again in parliament and Mary Morgan is a reminder of how this form of punishment cannot be reversed.

It is also a reminder for us not to return to Victorian times in our quest for morality. Greg Cullen in the programme notes asks for the young everywhere to recreate a world in which the nurturing of human life is central. After seeing *Mary Morgan* I can only echo that plea.

Ian Kerry

Mary Morgan (Wyeside Arts Centre)
Golwg, 3 October, 1987.

Every Tuesday night at the Wyeside Arts Centre about thirty young people get together to hold drama workshops, under the directorship of Theatr Powys members and teachers from local schools. This new company voices the fears, hopes and needs of young people in the area and widens their experience by introducing outside influences. They are taught the skills of theatre and communication, and are also able to entertain the community.

We in Mid Wales are familiar with the work of Theatr Powys, a professional company whose work is always varied and of a high standard. I knew therefore to expect something special from this group. The story told was that of Mary Morgan who lived in the old county of Maesyfed during the last century.

The history of Mary Morgan happened between September 1803 and April 1805 in the parish of Llanandras. She was a servant girl in the service of Mr Wilkins. He was a wealthy member of parliament who made his money in India in the grain industry. It is said that 3 million Indian people died of starvation due to his high prices. When he came back to Britain he bought land and opened a merchant bank in Aberhonddu – later to become Lloyds Bank. It was his wealth that assured him his seat in parliament.

A cousin of Mr Wilkins was one George Hardinge, M.P., and judge in the case of Mary Morgan. He was also a poet of very little importance who held a high opinion of himself. After he had caused her death it is said that he wrote poetry in her memory. 'Inspiration'?

Mary was hanged for murdering her baby and there was much protest in the parish of Llanandras against her hanging. Her body was laid to rest in the garden of a local priest and on her grave stone were written these words

> He that is without sin amongst you
> Let him cast the first stone

The play was written by Greg Cullen and directed by Guy Roderick. It was evident that they had worked hard and had inspired the young people. The script was created and developed from the workshops on Tuesday nights. A note in the programme mentioned Greg Cullen's and Guy Roderick's attempts to show how class struggles can change society, how class can effect all of us and how our morality does not correspond with humanity and human needs but with an artificial culture based on wealth. 'Morality demands that we condemn Mary Morgan as an evil individual for the murder of an innocent child. However, to do so removed our responsibility for perpetuating an unnatural world. Our morality is trapped in a contradiction of creating the violence it purports to condemn.'

Eight simple sets were created in the Market Hall, and the happenings switched from one to the other. One set was lit whilst the others were in darkness. The audience were free to move from one set to the other to follow the action. This was not a problem as there was plenty of room, and adequate time was given between the scenes. The music was provided by a group of very young musicians playing string, wind and percussion instruments. I found it hard to believe that these were school children playing as they made such a beautiful lovely sound.

The actors expressed themselves with clarity and energy. The scenes ran smoothly without fuss and the cast moved swiftly through the audience to the next scene. In the middle of the floor was the gentry's parlour where we met Wilkins (Neil Thomas) and his son Walter (Chris Davies). The audience were drawn to the charismatic young Walter at the beginning, but as the play went on the animosity towards him grew. Chris Thomas gave a crafted performance and enchanted his audience.

Libby Davies' performance as King George was wonderful. She and her servant (Andrew Sterrey) were perched on top of a high tower. The quickness of her speech, her use of pauses and her way with gestures were superb to watch.

Samantha Evans was the cook of the house and her very Welsh face suited the part. Her stance and movements were that of a middle-aged woman, which is a lot for a fifteen year old to achieve. Claire Rogers must also be congratulated on her portrayal of Maggie Harvard, the head maid, and the way in which she soft-soaped her mistress.

But it is Lynne Seymour in the leading role of Mary Morgan that I give most praise to. We watched how this tender character grew in confidence through her love for Walter, how she gained self respect and altered her behaviour to suit the surroundings. She is betrayed by Walter when she is expecting his child. She finds herself in a hideous predicament and has to choose between life and death. The audience were completely captivated by her experience and sympathised with the play's message. Mary Morgan is another example of how the Welsh have been badly treated by the English gentry. The character of Mary Morgan condenses the whole history of the Welsh working class.

A powerful performance was had by all in a very professional manner. Obviously, they had had to think, discuss and analyse their attitudes and standpoints in society today. This is Mid Powys Youth theatre's first public venture and it can be positively said that the future for this energetic company is a shining one. Good luck to them!

Siân Hawkins

Mary Morgan (Riverside Studios, London, preview)
Mid Wales Journal, 15 January, 1988.

Mary Morgan has been selected to be read at Wordplay '88, a festival of new writing at the Riverside Studios in London, at the end of this month.

Mary Morgan was written by Greg Cullen, writer-in-residence with Theatr Powys and was premiered by the newly formed Mid Powys Youth Theatre in October last year.

The play was subsequently submitted for the competition organised by City Limits magazine and was one of three plays to be chosen for reading as part of Wordplay '88.

The play is based on the true story of local servant girl Mary Morgan who was hanged for the murder of her illegitimate baby.

Eight members of the Mid Powys Youth Theatre who were part of the original production will be going to London to participate in the festival.

The play has a cast of 23 characters.

The parts will be read by Youth Theatre members performing alongside professional actors and actresses, members of Red Shift Theatre Company.

Organised by the new Playwrights Trust and the Playwrights Co-operative, the festival features the work of other companies producing new work, and is intended as a showcase for the best new writers and plays.

Mary Morgan is the only play in the festival to be produced by a Welsh company, and a Theatr Powys spokesman said it was exciting to be given this opportunity of showing some of the new work that is produced in Wales.

ROBIN HOOD

Robin Hood (Theatr Powys)
The County Times, 2 January, 1988.

Theatr Powys are on the road with their annual pantomine, this time *Robin Hood*, and have already performed at Llandrindod Wells, Newtown and Brecon. The tour continues until February 11.

Described as 'a riotous mixture of music and magic, bubbling over with energy and originality', it is, in fact, a send-up of the Sherwood Forest adventures of Robin and his band. For instance, instead of Friar Tuck we were given Friaress Tuck, an exuberant Dame part; also a very strange character whose head was missing from its proper place and replaced his right hand. Continually panning and zooming like a television camera, it had a somewhat flesh-creeping effect. But what its significance was quite eluded me.

Seven players between them took 11 parts, and the inevitable doubling up made identification difficult. Only Shaun Waller, playing Robin, had a one-part interpretation.

There were no self-contained scenes. All the action was continuous, and by no means confined to the stage. At times the players came into the auditorium, and even among the rows of spectactors, chasing each other or trying to escape capture. At one point there were archers aiming arrows from the audience on to other players on the stage.

Half-life-size puppets added to the crowd, magnificent 'horses' pranced about on and off the stage, 'ridden' by equally magnificent riders.

The topical jokes, inevitably, with bowmen, included a reference to Jeffrey the Archer.

The star of the show was the design team responsible for the set and the effects. They did a brilliant job.

There was plenty of audience participation and fast-moving slapstick, singing and dancing. And one must not forget a speaking frog who contributed cryptic observations from time to time.

Cynric Mytton-Davies

Robin Hood (The Guildhall, Brecon)
The Guardian, 11 January 1988

There is a curious custom in Wales during the Christmas period. It's a competition, unacknowledged of course, to produce the most Ideologically OK Children's Show. Now this is usually infinitely preferable to the dreadful conventional competition over the border to find the oldest living comedian who can ad-lib his way around a tacky script with the maximum number of blue innuendos. But dutiful Welsh critics tend to enter the new Year feeling like they've been on an Open University course in restructuring the Dandy.

Usually, the I-OK competition is won hands down by Theatr Powys, whose anti-fairytale *Beauty And The Beast* last year (yes, you guessed: the white fairy was a prissy bitch and the black witch the goodie, etc.) was terribly smart in upending stereotypes but about as appealing to kids as sugarcoated cod liver oil tablets.

This year, though, Theatr Powys have ended a fine year of community theatre in mid-Wales with a sparkling, fun version of *Robin Hood* that actually avoids the obvious social message. Greg Cullen's script is lively, fast and accessible; Steven Byrne's music simple and effective; Ali McCaw's masks marvellous; the playing full of energy and well-judged.

It does involve the kids but still has enough to make the adults smile, like the portrayal of Robin and Marion as a pair of medieval yuppies – they exit hand-in-hand talking about the derelict country cottage they'll snap up and the secondhand Aga they've found.

David Adams

TARZANNE

Tarzanne (Wyeside Arts Centre)
The Guardian, 8 November, 1988.

No, you read it right. *Tarzanne*, however, is no easy upending of the Edgar Rice Burroughs macho story but a deeply provocative play from Greg Cullen, one of the best workers writing in Wales, for Mid Powys Youth Theatre.

His first piece for MPYT, *Mary Morgan*, is about to be recorded for Radio 4 and was also performed in collaboration with Red Shift at the Riverside. Clearly Cullen and his company Theatr Powys, treat youth theatre seriously. And indeed this production at Wyeside Arts Centre, directed by Guy Roderick, is a truly rewarding theatrical experience with the young cast performing with remarkable commitment and skills. The centre itself has been transformed into a marvellous jungle.

Tarzanne herself (Amber Dibling, managing the evolution, or perhaps degeneration, from a chimp-like innocent to corseted Victorian miss beautifully) gradually learns the upright stance only to revert at a coming-out ball in a memorable scene where all the guests appear as animals.

The production is replete with such striking images – change from jungle to industrial mill to the discordant tune of Rule Britannia, for example – as the theme of nature versus nurture is expounded. Such theatre is not only exciting for the audience but revels in a corporate sense of achievement from the company.

David Adams

Tarzanne (Grand Pavilion, Llandrindod Wells)
Mid Wales Journal, 18 May, 1990.

On May 4 at the Grand Pavilion as part of their 18th birthday celebrations, Theatr Powys in collaboration with Footloose Dance Company, premiered *Tarzanne* by Greg Cullen.

The Powys company's resident writer ends his association and he plans to go freelance, and has already received further commissions from the BBC to write plays for Radio Four and one for television. He told me one project involves a research material trip to California – it is difficult to think of a better place to visit!

Judging by the standard of his past 18 plays for Theatr Powys including *Taken Out* about the Falklands War and *Spoiled Papers*, set in the Ystradgynlais area about the miners' strike, and *Christmas Carol* based on the Charles Dickens' classic, and after penning this series of wide ranging high standard material I am sure we will hear more of Greg Cullen and his writings in the future when he becomes more widely known.

Tarzanne, the latest Theatr Powys, offering extends and revives a production by Greg Cullen for the Mid Powys Youth theatre, one of the many groups helped by the company. It is directed by Martin Jameson, designed by Janis Hart and has an original score by Matthew Bailey.

Tarzanne is based upon the Tarzan myth and follows the socialisation of Anne Breckner who, reared by chimpanzees, is returned to her 'rightful' place in the world as heiress to one of Powys's aristocratic families.

As seen by the two performances the company members must have been training hard during rehearsals to bring the chimpanzee colony to life and as promised it was one of the most unusual evenings of theatre seen in Llandrindod Wells for many years – possibly ever.

Of the individual performances it is difficult to pick out anyone in a professional company effort. Suffice to say that Jane Scott-Barrett in the title role showed unbelieveable energy and enthusiasm which was followed by her colleagues, with at times very powerful versatile acting.

With future performances in different parts of Powys to come in the next two months it would be unfair to spoil readers, anticipation of an evening of gripping theatre, and culture supporters will obviously go and see for themselves. The play uses a magical blend of drama, dance and music . . .

The power of the pen is great, and the writer is able to bring his thoughts to the audience, on a number of very wide ranging issues, including in this case the transition from feudalism to capitalism in a hanging world. The relationships between gentry and servant members, the rise of the unions and the comparison between the environment of chimpanzees and mill workers, Victorian punishments and values and the problems of educating Anna in human relationships, her own vividly expressed views and her adaptation between the animal and human kingdoms – their differences and similarities are all covered by the writer's thoughts on the ruling classes and the implications of their past, present and future actions on society.

The occasional reappearance of chimps at important times in the play brings the audience back to reality, or is it to the origins of civilised society itself?

Just a mention of the adaptable central 'catwalk like' stage of the type Theatr Powys have used previously and must be ideal for Community Centres, and the versatility of the performers playing different parts and the movement of the scenery to suit different conditions . . .

These factors about Theatr Powys productions have often impressed and intrigued me, but to further review the production would either state the obvious for those who have seen or spoil the enjoyment for future patrons.

CB

FRIDA AND DIEGO

Frida and Diego (Assembly Rooms, Edinburgh)
The Guardian, 12 August, 1989.
He was the revolutionary artist and polemicist. She was one of the finest painters of the century. He was a muralist painting vast pictures for public places. She, crippled in a tram crash in 1925, painted small works shining with humanity.

His art was defaced and battered but still shouts from the walls of Mexico City. Her works are almost all in private hands, selling for millions of dollars.

He was the friend of Stalin, she the lover of Trotsky. He was shot at by the Nazis, threatened by the Russians, attacked by the Mexicans. She became a symbol of the early feminists.

Diego Rivera and Frida Kahlo were married, divorced and then remarried.

They shared a passion for politics and Mexico's rich Indian culture. Together they helped throw off the restrictive legacy of bourgeois European art, delving back to Mexico's rich rural traditions that lead straight to the Aztecs.

And together they have emerged as icons of cultural, social and political opposition.

Two biographies and a couple of recent exhibitions have pushed them both into postmodernist fashion.

Madonna now collects Kahlo's paintings, popular magazines offer DIY Frida Kahlo interiors and in time there will be Rivera furnishings and Kahlo clothes.

In a way, they were always fashionable. The couple were lionised and then rejected alternately by Left and Right. When Kahlo first went to Paris, she was a sensation and a major fashion house exhibited their Mme Frida Kahlo collection.

The two mixed with the Rockefellers, the Bretons, the international socialists and socialites of the day.

'There's a lot of glamour there', says Greg Cullen, who has just been to Mexico to research the story for a new play. 'Nothing can take that away.'

'On the other hand, these people were in a very dangerous situation for much of their lives. Rivera had to carry a gun, even while painting. They managed to offend with great courage.'

Winkling out relatives, old friends, former students and colleagues and going through the archive material, Cullen has pieced together the remarkable story of their relationship.

'It's impossible not to add to the myth', he says, 'you're bound to add another layer; its accrues with time. Rivera was like a rock star of today, he enjoyed the myth and never denied the lie.'

'I have tried not to turn them into emblems, which is the danger when you have a visual style.'

Cullen wrote the remarkable *Taken Out*, about the slaughter on the *Sir Galahad* during the Falklands War.

He first heard of the pair a few years ago and was immediately attracted to the underlying theme of the place of art in people's lives.

His own working class background – 'where art was not for us' – and his professional life spent with the same people, gave him, he says, a vehicle to reaffirm in theatrical terms why art is so important. Especially in these atrophied times.

'What attracted me was their differences; Rivera with his huge exposition of history, Kahlo with her internal relationship with the outside world.

'What united them was their concerns, with society, its health and the role of art.'

Mexico was revelatory. Everyone from intellectuals to cab drivers have stories of Rivera and Kahlo. Twenty women's groups, he found, use Kahlo as an example and as a focus for the debate about the role of women in Mexican society.

Kahlo's students, now all in their sixties or older, all still paint. The grandchildren are involved with the Kahlo gallery, the Blue House where they lived is almost a shrine, the Mexican Government wants to turn Kahlo into a National Treasure.

He talked to Ella Woolf, Stalin's former secretary and Frida's best friend, now in her nineties, and Rina Lazo, who worked with Rivera on the murals.

But above all, Mexico City, loaded with Rivera's great hymns of praise to Revolution, gave him the insight into the culture of the couple.

The play spans almost 40 years from 1916 to Kahlo's death in 1954. Written in epic style – at times naturalistic, at times poetic – to mirror Rivera's painting, the major problem in the writing was which of the two should be the lead character.

The performance is played against the massive backdrop of Rivera's famous 'Sunday Afternoon In The Alameda', which is painted by the actors as the narrative progresses.

Characters come out of the painting to tell their tales, the cast of seven playing 20 parts.

It should have been a two-hour play. Cullen says he has enough material for five plays. In the end the turn round times at the Assembly Rooms demanded that it be only 90 minutes. 'Bloody criminal', says the author. In the wall-to-wall art of the Edinburgh Festival the role of commercial practicality is supreme.

John Vidal

Frida and Diego (Assembly Rooms, Edinburgh)
The Guardian, 15 August, 1989.

Greg Cullen's new play *Frida And Diego* – presented by Red Shift at the Assembly Rooms, in a blazingly vivid production by Jonathan Holloway – is a bold, dedicated, impetuous attempt to tell us everything we need to know about the lives of these two most remarkable artists of the 20th century in the space of 90 minutes;

it's hardly surprising that its success as drama is compromised by its ambition as biography.

On a richly coloured set by Charlotte Humpston – the background from Rivera's great mural of the Alameda Park, all deep burnt-earth tones and brilliant Mexican blue – the seven-string cast play out the whole panorama of Frida and Diego's life together, his role in the Mexican revolution and in government, his great commissions in the USA, his affairs; her crippling early injuries in a bus accident, her struggles towards and away from motherhood, her passionate commitment to Mexico, her sexuality, her relationships with men like Trotsky.

Their marriage is therefore only one of half-a-dozen themes on which Cullen touches. He could have written a tremendous play about the impossibility of marriage between two such free spirits; he could have written one about art and politics. He could – given Anna Savva's wonderful, wiry, flashing performance as Frida – have written a beautiful and poignant piece about the life of a woman artist, about the cruel paradox by which failure in the conventional female fulfilment of motherhood becomes linked with a magnificent sensuous achievement in painting; he comes close to writing one about the relationship between art and life, the pity and horror of things and the beauty artists can create out of it.

In fact, the weakness of *Frida And Diego* is that instead of choosing to write one of these plays, Cullen has tried to write all of them; he has pruned his material like a historian trying to cut a long story short, rather than an artist choosing incidents that are central to his preoccupations, and there are some embarrassing docu-drama moments of the 'Hallo Rivera, this is Trotsky' type.

But for all that, the text contains some brilliant writing about sex and marriage, art and politics; Holloway's production is heavy with the hot, passionate atmosphere of Mexican life and politics that sustained and obsessed both artists.

And the script lets us see clearly, amid all its twists and complexities, how Frida and Diego – who married, divorced and then married again – in the end found a way of loving without trying to possess one another; not without pain, but with enough strength to see them through to the threshold of death.

Joyce McMillan

Frida and Diego (Assembly Rooms, Edinburgh)
The Independent, 18 August, 1989.

Written by Greg Cullen for the respected Red Shift Company, this play tells the story of the torrid marriage between the revolutionary artists, Frida Kahlo and Diego Rivers, the great Mexican muralist. A physical ruin, Frida was evidently a woman of huge spirit, unflagging in her belief in her appallingly lecherous husband. A whistle-stop tour through the wreckage of their domestic lives is staged by Jonathan Holloway, the imagery is trowelled on and skeletal figures emerge periodically from the closet. The epic sweep of the piece finally dilutes the dramatic impact of this warts-and-all love story. A shame, since Charlotte Humpston's painterly set is just gorgeous.

Robert Gore-Langton

Frida and Diego (Assembly Rooms, Edinburgh)
Financial Times, 19 August, 1989.

Red Shift's *Frida and Diego* is an ambitious biographical study composed by Greg Cullen in bright primitivist blotches, relating Diego's pathological sexuality to

Frida's under-rated artistic competence and sad, crippled physicality. Charlotte Humpston's beguiling design, and the broad-brush acting, capture perfectly the Mexican muralist's style, with direct quotations from the great Alameda Park painting. Taking a cue from Sondheim, you might say this was 'One Day in the Park with Frida and Diego.'

Anyone who has visited Mexico is drastically changed by the experience. My affections for the country were gaudily aroused by this spirited compendium of politics, passions, and images of death (there is a lovely mini-chorus of dancing skeletons). We also meet the André Bretons and the Trotskys – at the same lunch party! Anna Savva and Nicholas Jeune are superb as the twice-married (to each other) indivisible rivals.

The play comes straight to the Croydon Warehouse after Edinburgh, for most of September, before embarking on a long tour. Catch it.

Michael Coveney

Frida and Diego (Assembly Rooms, Edinburgh)
Scotland on Sunday, 20 August, 1989.

There is a rash of biographies on the Fringe. The best have been the iconoclastic, while the uninspiring have kept on the kid gloves. But this, it has to be said, is just as much a reflection of the subject under scrutiny. Some people just fail to shine under the spotlight.

Artists inevitably provide ideal raw material for the stage, but it requires skilled hands to work it into something genuinely theatrical. Greg Cullen has succeeded in doing just this with *Frida and Diego – A Love Story*. And Red Shift's remarkable production at the Assembly Rooms completes what is an explosive account of a tempestuous love affair.

Diego Rivera and Frida Kahlo fed off each other's volatile emotions to produce some of the most artistically striking and politically charged images of this century. Their lives were just as tumultuous as the times in which they lived and just as haunted by betrayal, prejudice and death. And it is the way in which Cullen has interwoven the two that gives the play its power and vitality.

Both director Jonathan Holloway and designer Charlotte Humpston share this vision, creating a vibrant, seamless parade of tableaux that draw their inspiration from the monumental works of Rivera and the surreal, intimate imaginings of Kahlo.

The lovers fight, rage and make love while mortality, dressed as skeletal grotesques, carousel about them. And it all happens before a set full of exaggerated perspectives and distorted familiarity mirroring the obsessive preoccupations of Frida and Diego.

Not only do Anna Savva (Frida) and Nicholas Jeune (Diego) revel in all this with unabashed commitment but they also expose the vulnerability and fallibility of those frustrated by circumstances they desire to control. Savva seduces and suffers with equal subtlety. Jeune philanders with consumate bravado and hectors like a soap-box pugilist.

Animism, revolution, and an uncompromising humanism animated their lives and all are captured by a company that relishes the voluptuousness of art as palpable passion.

Frida and Diego (Assembly Rooms, Edinburgh)
Observer Scotland, 20 August, 1989.

André Breton said 'the art of Frida Kahlo is a ribbon around a bomb'. In her extraordinary person she was as decorative as the one and almost as explosive as the other. Greg Cullen's new play for Red Shift Theatre Company, *Frida and Diego*, demonstrates this vividly and poignantly at the Assembly Rooms.

Rivera's revolutionary murals and monumental canvases are the stuff of artistic and political history. Frida, revered in Mexico, collected in the United States, has until recently had little or no recognition in Europe. Cullen's play is about their art and their tempestuous life together, but it is Frida's masochistic paintings, the pains of her doomed life, her passions, her eccentric duality, and – despite everything – her love for Diego which fuels his text and sets it alight.

This emphasis, amounting to an acceptable imbalance, owes nothing to Anna Savva's uncanny likeness to Frida, whereas I doubt if Nicholas Jeune comes within six stones of Diego's grossness. The illusion of Frida's reincarnation is heightened by the timbre of Ms Savva's contralto voice, her physical bearing, her costume – Frida dressed and painted herself like a Mexican folk doll – and by the way her dark eyes address us; she is trying, as Frida did in so many interrogatory self-portraits, to see herself as we might see her.

Jonathan Holloway's direction compounds the magic. A cluttered set suggests, without attempting to reproduce, the great Alameda Gardens and backgrounds to Frida's canvases; its artefacts include the strange props of her paintings; we are inside the blue house at Coyoacan which Diego turned into her shrine when she died in 1954. But this imaginative production, which deserves more space and better technical resources, goes well beyond the material and physical. Choral skeletons chant runes of death. Exuberant dancing echoes Frida's last dying scrawl – 'viva la vida' – yet the heels could be thundering on her coffin lid.

A clever cast playing more than a score of parts – from Leon Trotsky to Helen Wills Moody – galvanise this black carnival with intelligence and commitment. They deserve the accolade of full houses from now till 3 September.

Frida and Diego (Assembly Rooms, Edinburgh)
Daily Telegraph, 23 August, 1989.

I was less impressed by Greg Cullen's much-touted *Frida and Diego – A Love Story*, presented by Red Shift Theatre in the Assembly Rooms. This is a breathless biodrama about the Mexican painters Diego Rivera and Frida Kahlo whose lives seem to have been spent in a determined attempt to live up to the conventional image of the artist as bohemian.

Both embraced revolutionary politics, but seemed even keener on pursuing a succession of torrid affairs. The crippled Frida got Trotsky into bed. Diego had a fling with Frida's sister, the couple divorced and remarried. Jonathan Holloway's production is busy and colourful, with a set based on one of Rivera's own murals, complete with dancing skeletons played by the actors; and Anna Savva as the husky-voiced Frida makes the most of an affecting death-bed scene.

In the course of an hour-and-a-half, however, one learns a great deal about the couple's sex lives, rather less about their characters and virtually nothing about their art. That's showbiz, I suppose.

Charles Spencer

Frida and Diego (Croydon Warehouse)
Time Out, 30 August, 1989.

Frida Kahlo and Diego Rivera's lives together were exotic and turbulent enough to fill a five-hour epic film. Faced with such a cornucopia of material, dramatist Greg Cullen has tried to edit and eradicate, but still has too much happening to make a satisfying play; instead of digging deep he only skims the surface of the characters of these fierce Mexican artists fighting for a socialist revolution who found themselves caught between Stalinists on the one hand and capitalism on the other. While death stalks the stage in the shape of a chorus of skeletons (an intrinsic part of Charlotte Humpston's vibrant designs, which are a fitting tribute to the protagonists), Rivera struggles to complete his large-scale murals, and Frida battles heroically against the ghastly consequences of a road accident to produce her surreal, often masochistic self-portraits. They are incapable of fidelity; Frida even having a brief flirtation with the exiled Trotsky. Director Jonathan Holloway and Red Shift were lucky to find Anna Savva to play Frida, an actress who looks convincingly at home in the folkloric finery of Kahlo's country. The production, arriving at Croydon after a sell-out success in Edinburgh, is of enormous fascination, even if ultimately it seems to be splashing about with the paints in the palette with rather too gay abandon.

Jane Edwardes

Frida and Diego (Croydon Warehouse)
City Limits, 7 September, 1989.

Blazing with colour and energy, this tempestuous celebration of the life, work and marriage of Mexican artists Frida Kahlo and Diego Rivera offers such a torrent of biography, politics and emotion that it threatens to burst at the seams under the weight of all the information and passion. Cullen's stimulating script handles the themes – art and life; the personal and the political – with a bold self-confidence which makes you long for a full-length version but he seems constrained by the need to offer audiences straightforward biography. Likewise, Jonathan Holloway's production gets all the hard bits right (the grand passion and pain of this love story about two people who were each other's artistic inspiration and emotional reef) but falters in the casting of some minor roles and some unusually clumsy staging (the confines of a playing area designed for touring are probably partly to blame). If offered the resources of one of the major subsidised companies (come on, Richard Eyre, how about it?) one wonders what this hugely talented company would be able to achieve, and as it is Anna Savva, looking uncannily like the fascinating Frida and Nicholas Jeune as the charismatic Diego turn in firework performances as brilliant as anything you're likely to see on the London stage this year. Hot stuff.

.Lyn Gardner

Frida and Diego (Croydon Warehouse)
What's On, 13 September, 1989.

This is a play of love, art and politics. Woven around the passionate and painful marriage of celebrated Mexican revolutionary artists, Diego Rivera and Frida Kahlo, it involves a stage of colour, music and a touch of carnival. Red Shift's production sweetens the modern and essential themes of the play.

An inventive use of dramatic tableaux brings the work of Frida and Diego to life as figures step out of pictures, comment on their predicament and provide the audience with an understanding of the political and social forces that drove the artists to paint.

Most powerfully expressed is Kahlo's relationship to her work, the quality of which dominates the design of the production. Skeletal figures loom from the exotic flowers and patterns in a dance of death evoking work increasingly bound up with the horror of a gruesome accident and miscarriage which left her in constant pain.

Anna Savva's wholly convincing Frida is sensuous, husky – a chain-smoking, painted figure in traditional Mexican dress.

Rivera's patrons were predominantly wealthy Americans and corporations who censored his images of the workers' struggle. I feel an interesting parallel can be drawn with the stranglehold of business sponsorship on the arts today.

His compromise is marked when Californian dream-girl and tennis champion Helen Wills Moody becomes the central figure in one particular mural. Frida asks why he does not paint the indigenous Indian population, not well-fed and glamorised by the capitalism he despises.

The battles of their polygamous marriage are fought against an international backdrop of political extremism. Caught up in the rise of Stalinism, Rivera's fellow revolutionaries ostracise him for his failure to renounce Trotsky.

The play's epic feel is a strength and a weakness: it provides a wealth of characters and events but occasionally clutters the narrative and leaves some moments oversimplified. However, this Fringe First winner is a fascinating journey through the life and work of Frida and Diego.

Emma Byrne

Frida and Diego (Croydon Warehouse)
The Listener, 14 September, 1989.

Years ago, I used to read unsolicited manuscripts for the National Theatre. I submitted a lengthy report on each text, and the NT handed over a crumpled fiver. (Or was it a tenner? Surely not . . .) Anyway, the vast majority of plays were pallid biographies, from which it was impossible to discern why the author was especially interested in his or her chosen subject.

Alarmingly, the same puzzle surrounds many of the bio-dramas I encountered in my present capacity. It's certainly the case with *Boswell for the Defence* (Playhouse), a dithering study of English literature's most notable parasite. By happy contrast, *Frida and Diego: A Love Story* (Croydon Warehouse) makes the source of the dramatist's enthusiasm abundantly clear. Greg Cullen's material brims with dramatic potential. *Frida and Diego* might have been a humdinger, in fact, and manages to be pretty exhilarating in places. Even so, you leave the Warehouse – a claustrophobic sweat-box, despite recent refurbishment – curiously unsatisfied.

Passions are high, and conflicts archetypal, in the marriage of the Mexican painters Diego Rivera and Frida Kahlo. Diego (Nicholas Jeune) persistently neglects Frida (Anna Savva) for his art, by which he is possessed, and for a succession of affairs, which he initiates casually but pursues with vigour. Frida's work is shamefully under-rated, meanwhile, and only made possible by ill health – polio, bone disease and further crippling infirmities sustained in a traffic smash. 'Without the accident', she announces blithely, 'I would never have sat down long enough to paint'.

Political contradictions are as thick on the ground as ex-spouses and discarded offspring. The pair are celebrated revolutionaries, but relish the indulgences of bourgeois life. Diego even conducts and unhappy flirtation with the patronage of Nelson A. Rockefeller. And as a helpmate of Trotsky, he finds himself shot at by both Nazis and Stalinists. He responds with barely a flicker of fear; like Frida, Diego is larger than life. Or, at least, he would have been, if the writing had more closely matched the scale of the events it plunders.

For this itinerant production by the much-praised Red Shift company, Charlotte Humpston has based her over-fussy design on Rivera's epic mural, *Dream of a Sunday Afternoon in the Central Alameda*. History provides a more vivid backdrop: the exiled Mr and Mrs Trotsky put in cameo appearances, hatchet-faced and at first bewildered by the Riveras' bohemianism. Natalia Trotsky (Kate Paul) discovers the bisexual Frida kissing André Breton's wife (Phoebe Burridge). Soon afterwards, Trotsky himself advises Frida sombrely: 'Women shouldn't smoke.' The two proceed to a little comradely adultery, though whether Frida lit up after bonking isn't reported.

These moments are, besides, small pleasures in an all-too-abbreviated venture. Cullen dispenses with the Spanish Civil War in about 60 seconds, for example. And his busily episodic script refers to, but rarely evokes, the compulsions of artistic endeavour and the principal couple's delirious sexuality. Like the text and setting, Jonathan Holloway's direction is more frenetic than enlightening. A small number of 'props' are incongruously and elaborately mimed. Helen Wills Moody, one of Diego's lovers, is preceded on stage by a tennis ball, though there's no sign of a racquet. The supporting cast wear body stockings with a 'skeleton' design, and provide unnecessary choric reactions. In short, Holloway crowds his production with the sort of would-be expressionism that constantly draws attention to itself. A few stirring bursts of Mexican dance (choreography: Petricio Quezada) hardly compensate. Surely there's more to the fabled Red Shift style than this?

Nicholas Jeune and Anna Savva look great – the major achievement of both performances. Jeune has exactly the right stubbled reprobacy, though he doesn't quite resemble the 'fat frog' Frida describes. Savva is a blazing-eyed beanpole, who occasionally – and not inappropriately – *sounds* like a frog. The rest of the cast betray a disturbing lack of technical proficiency. Any performer who can barely be heard at the tiny Warehouse is in serious trouble.

After Croydon, *Frida and Diego* will tour extensively, before settling at the Battersea Arts Centre for much of January. It may well elicit an indulgent response from radically minded audiences in need of acclaimable heroes.

Jim Hiley

Frida and Diego (The Gulbenkian Studio, Newcastle)
The Guardian, 19 October, 1989.

When the world finally goes up, how about saving a few things? Spotted Dick, say, or Greg Cullen's marvellous play from Red Shift Theatre about the Mexican artists Frida Kahlo and Diego Rivera. Jonathan Holloway's production tours after its sell-out Edinburgh Fringe dates, though (shame, shame) there were some empty seats at Newcastle's Gulbenkian studio.

It's that rare feeling at the end, rooted to your seat; who wants to amble into a bar, listen to chatter about water shares? I didn't even, fearing that analysis might dilute the experience, relish writing the review, more an instinct to climb on tables and shout 'See it!'.

What's art's answer to a spiritually bankrupt country, run by hucksters, self-publicists and cheap smoothies – predictable feeble polemics, jokey clever cynicism . . .? No, something like this. A different time, a different place, a sprawly play, odd weak acting spots, but fierce, passionate, beautiful. The heartbeat of a forge hammer; it's grabbing your mind, then your heart, then both, swirling colour, movement, soaring to occasional poetic power, then humour, a backdrop of great unfolding events; Stalin, Spain, wars, communism, yet somehow it's all there within the two of them, a hypnotic, at times intolerably painful love story spanning more than 20 years.

On Charlotte Humpston's cluttered set, visually celebrating Kahlo's paintings and her Mexico home, Holloway's production pulsates with an energy and conviction, mood and pace switching, rapid scenes followed by slow tableaux, breaking from political/artistic argument to sudden swirling dance, infectious folk music. Nicholas Jeune's Diego, the censored muralist, in a performance of compressed and dishevelled power, potently declaims that art (plus a touch of promiscuity) is everything as we whizz through the couple's tempestuous lives, infidelities, passions.

Yet this conviction is slowly surpassed with the growth of Anna Savva's Kahlo; crippled, beautiful, 21 miscarriages yet a fierce life force superseding art, ironically making her the better if more vulnerable artist. The huge passionate eyes, chiselled porcelain face, clothes ablaze with Mexican colour, reinforce a remarkable finely judged performance, the character slowly opening like a brilliant flower and proclaiming life even at the moment of death so that, ultimately the play's strength transcends our normal feeble expectations, intoxicates us.

André Breton's in it (fish in top pocket), Trotsky too, 22 characters, the remaining cast of four changing costume on set, revealing skeleton body stockings which take on increasing eminence. I've odd moans – the death scenes elongated, we shouldn't have filter tipped cigarettes – but it's theatre as intended, dangerous, exhilarating and irresistible, a play resonating long after it's finished, singing in your head; this is it, this is it.

Peter Mortimer

A CHRISTMAS CAROL

A Christmas Carol (Wyeside Arts Centre)
The Guardian, 15 December, 1989.

One of the more depressing aspects of Christmas is usually the lack of choice in entertainment: its panto or panto. In fact audiences in South Wales have a reasonable range of shows on offer and none, so far at least, is really a waste of time or money.

Theatre Powys's *A Christmas Carol* can be seen this year all over Wales, from Llanelli to Colwyn Bay, and a commendable production it is. This mid-Wales based company have the benefit of having as writer-in-residence Greg Cullen, whose Falkland play *Taken Out* and recent Red Shift *Frida and Diego* have revealed to wider audiences his talents as a politically acute playwright. His Dickens adaptation, unexpectedly, has far less political bite than we might have expected (after all, their *Robin Hood* and *Beauty and the Beast* of past years were disarmingly polemical) but is nevertheless a classy bit of work that never even has tints of the conventional condescension of so much Christmas theatre.

Directed by Cullen too, it managed to create clear characters and exploit the emotional as well as the social content of what is, after all, a rather soft reformist text. At its opening at the Wyeside in Builth Wells, the company was still getting used to the clever scene changing but the variety of little tricks employed by the four-strong cast was impressive – notably, perhaps, a lovely scene of a dog fight where we only see the animals through the expressions and demeanour of their owners. Good music from Steve Byrne, design Janis Hart. Catch it if you can.

David Adams

A Christmas Carol (Llanidloes Community Centre)
Mid Wales Journal, 1 February, 1990.

Llanidloes Community Centre was the venue for this year's production of *A Christmas Carol* by Charles Dickens and adapted by Greg Cullen, after nearly two months on the road.

On a cold winter's afternoon, with sleet and snow outside, the eerie set, depicting Victorian London, seemed to be an extension of the bleakness outside. Only the warmth and the comfort of the hall belied the ghost story that was about to unfold.

Children aged three to 73 came singly and in groups to be entertained, titillated, awed and amused by this tale of greed and selfishness which has altered little during the 143 years since Dickens wrote the tale.

A dog-fight held the audience's attention with a very entertaining sequence at the beginning of the play and, with slick scene-changing involving mobile sections and slow-motion movements accompanying nightmarish strobe-lighting, held it until the final monologue.

Costumes were imaginative and effective as was the dancing and London smog. Marley's face on the door handle was a shock but Jacob's 'ghost' brought the house down when it became the maid with a foot stuck in a bucket, a sheet over her head and a mop in her hand. Later, the real ghost burst upon the stage as a ghastly reincarnation.

The changes in pace and from serious to comic vein made this a fast-moving production that held the audience in its thrall.

JD

THE INFORMER'S DUTY

The Informer's Duty (Bute Theatre, Cardiff)
South Wales Echo, 24 March, 1992.

In a collaboration unique in Britain, students at the Welsh College of Music and Drama have joined forces for a new play based on a period in the life of Shostakovich.

The piece incorporates a complete performance of his Fifth Symphony. And the world premiere of this remarkable undertaking, *The Informer's Duty*, was staged at the Bute Theatre last night.

It emerged as a hard-hitting experience, riveting from start to finish, adding a completely new dimension and awareness of the reign of terror unleashed by Stalin in the 1930s.

For the Welsh College of Music and Drama, whose profile gains ground with everything they do these days, it was nothing less than a major achievement which would be the envy of many a professional company.

In Paul Clements' clever and perceptive production, Stalin – who boasts a Geordie accent – is played to perfection by Simeon Truby.

The way the orchestra all gather to listen to Shostakovich's famous speech to the Composers Union is another clever effect.

Dramatically, it could all have not been better-prepared and John Carlsen as Shostakovich is a convincing, superbly rounded character. Lynne Seymour is no less successful as Nina Shostakovich.

Stephen Broadbent conducted an account which created the right atmosphere from the start.

Miss this amazing experience at your peril.

A J Sicluna

RAGING ANGELS

Raging Angels (The Sherman Theatre, Cardiff)
The Guardian, 17 May, 1993.

The Made In Wales Stage Company's Write On! festival is 10 years old now, and still doesn't seem to know what it is or where it's going. Is it a public outing for fledgling playwrights? Then where's the public and why are so many of the writers hardly new? Is it a chance for would-be dramatists to see their scripts liberated from the page and given theatrical life? Then the script-in-hand process favoured this year hardly does that and can be obtrusive. But, for all its frustrating lack of identity, it's a fascinating fortnight at the Sherman Theatre.

This year one of the company's long-term favourite writers, Alan Osborne, has been given a retrospective with reading of his oeuvre from *Bull, Rock and Nut* . . .

Another established writer featured in the festival was Greg Cullen, whose play for Mid Powys Youth Theatre, *Raging Angels*, may have been the only full production in the festival but the young performers showed integrity and gutsiness. Cullen is one of the very best writers working in Wales and this attack on sexual hypocrisy and ignorance was startling in its honesty, his script (and direction) giving the non-professional cast something to be proud of.

David Adams

Raging Angels (The Sherman Theatre, Cardiff)
The County Times, 29 May, 1993.

The Mid Powys Youth Theatre has proved a big hit at this year's 'Write On!', the annual festival of new plays staged by the Made in Wales company at the Sherman Theatre in Cardiff.

The MPYT performed *Raging Angels* written and directed by Greg Cullen. Their passionate performance received an overwhelming response attracting praise in a national newspaper, as well as from Phil Clark, the Sherman's artistic director, and from Gilly Adams, the artistic director of Made in Wales who invited the company to appear at the festival.

LITTLE DEVILS

Little Devils (Wyeside Arts Centre)
Mid Wales Journal, 11 November, 1994.

The Mid Powys Youth Theatre performed their new play *Little Devils* at the Wyeside Arts Centre, Builth Wells, between Wednesday and Saturday of last week.

In the past year the company has been nominated for a BBC Wales Arts Award in the Company of the Year category, and up against professional companies came runners-up.

Earlier this year they performed at the Royal National Theatre, and look likely to return next year as part of a festival of six of the best youth theatre productions in Great Britain.

Last Thursday they appeared on the BBC Wales arts programme The Slate, this being the third time for the youth company on television, helping to put mid-Wales theatre in the picture for high class performances.

This brand new work was written by Greg Cullen, who is also the company director. The original idea of the storyline of the play came from a workshop. It was the collective desire of MPYT members to make a place which told the stories of people they knew – in other words of real lives.

The version of the play produced last week was devised during a three week period in the summer holidays.

Little Devils tells the story of four young people and a magistrate who, while mourning the loss of a friend, find themselves transported to Hell. They plead for the return of the soul of the dead local boy who has gone off the rails, with a visually spectacular Devil.

In a series of fast moving flashbacks initiated in the spirit of evil and his assistants, the lives of main characters are revealed.

The play moves quickly through comedy, tragedy, music, dancing, the relationships between members of families and different generations, the justification or otherwise of various moral and social issues including drink, drugs and theft.

The effect of no world wars, no work and divorce on today's younger generation are also examined in today's changed world which is defined as nothing truly black or white.

The burial ground-type set is impressive and becomes part of Hell and then back to earth near the end. The following were also first class, the timing, acting, lighting, costumes and visual effects, together with the fast moving storyline and production and top musical arrangement.

I was also fascinated as far as the general standard of acting was concerned with the ability of teenagers to play the parts of the older generation so visually, possibly because of the use of 'older' looking clothes.

I will reserve judgement on some of the contents of this very modern-type play but this is probably my age.

I only offer the opinion that probably the younger people in the audience, of which there were a good proportion on the night I attended, would identify with the issues more closely and be able to judge for themselves.

However, I would confirm the high standard of this MPYT production, and it is easy to see why they have achieved national recognition and will do in the future.

SILAS MARNER

Silas Marner (Theatr Clwyd)
Evening Leader, 18 September, 1996.

Adapting a wide-ranging classic 19th century novel for the confines of small stage and strict budget in a modern theatre is not a simple task.

But writer Greg Cullen and director Tim Baker can congratulate themselves on the success of their new production of George Eliot's *Silas Marner* which has just opened at the Emlyn Williams Theatre in Theatr Clwyd.

They have injected pace without losing the dramatic narrative, and tell a morality tale with humour to counter Eliot's sentimentality, which could otherwise seem mawkish to late 20th century tastes.

A cast of just seven provide all the characters, including some ingenious ones. Horses and babies have to be improvised, and are – brilliantly.

In addition to quick costume and character changes, the actors provide superb music on accordion, harp, whistle and with splendid singing, using Peter Knight's excellent score.

Silas Marner is the story of an epileptic, embittered and isolated weaver who is ill-used in one community, robbed in a second but finds that the golden heir of an orphan child is worth more than clinking sovereigns in a money bag.

Johnson Willis is the hunched old miser, washing his hands in the golden glow of his hidden hoard and discovering the theft with strange, animal cries echoed with discordant music.

But Marner is transformed by the arrival of Eppie, played with charm and delicacy by Nicola Reynolds.

Fergus McLarnon is Godfrey Cass, the squire's son who sows his wild oats and reaps a bitter harvest, while Jules Davison gives a moving performance as Nancy, his second wife – and has outstanding musical talents to match her acting.

Phyl Harries is custom built to play well-upholstered Squire Cass along with several other roles, while William Oxborrow tackles four contrasting parts, and Stephanie Jacob is the comfortable neighbour, Dolly Winthrop.

All seven are strong in their skills and provide the audience in such an intimate space as the Emlyn Williams Theatre with a powerful and enjoyable performance.

Congratulations too to designer Carys Tudor for her spare, economical and versatile set which complements the production.

Gail Cooper

Silas Marner (Theatr Clwyd)
Daily Post, 19 September, 1996.

You can almost smell the hay and meadow flowers in *Silas Marner*, having its stage premiere at Theatr Clwyd.

Adapted by Greg Cullen from George Eliot's novel, the saga of Silas is told in performance and occasional song, the characters mostly good country folk.

A single set with a number of porch entrances is all that is needed, the seven strong cast taking on a number of roles and attitudes.

In the studio setting of Theatr Clwyd's Emlyn Williams Theatre it all works a treat, director Tim Baker rightly concentrating on pure story-telling.

Silas is played by Johnson Willis, an actor who seems to age years with gesture and expression alone.

Falsely accused of theft, he settles in a distant village to become the miserable miser of popular myth. His life changes when a toddler wanders into his house after the death in the snow of her mother. Marner suddenly has a purpose in life and raises the girl as his daughter.

The child Eppie is played as both baby and teenager by Nicola Reynolds who in the former role offers authentic-sounding baby gurgling noises whilst sitting by an empty baby cloak.

It is a strange performance method but works superbly.

The play rattles along with a minimum of fuss over the changing scenes, the storyline always clear. There is some comedy, some melodrama and many solid performances, among them Fergus McLarnon as the tragi-comic Godfrey – Eppie's real father and Phyl Harries with a good bucolic squire.

Philip Key

Silas Marner (Theatr Clwyd)
Western Mail, 19 September, 1996.

Theatr Clwyd's opening production of what promises to be a highly exciting autumn season is an adaptation of George Eliot's pastoral tale, *Silas Marner*.

Greg Cullen's adaption follows the main thrust of the narrative without compromising Eliot's underlying social and philosophical message.

The production is further enhanced by the inclusion of songs and choruses in appropriate idioms composed by Peter Knight.

Silas Marner is generally regarded by critics as one of Eliot's minor masterpieces. However, it is, by any standards, a tightly integrated work of art and forms a vital link in her development as a novelist. It is, as this adaptation demonstrates, a cracking good story with strong fairytale elements, combined with powerful subversive components, earthy humour and tragic overtones.

It has a two-pronged plot in the sense that the destinies of Silas Marner, a young weaver, and Godfrey, a squire's son, interact dramatically.

Silas becomes an embittered eccentric workaholic as a result of being accused of a crime which he did not commit.

The arrival of a child is the catalyst that reveals to him the more profound aspects of human relationships.

Theatr Clwyd's production is a fine demonstration of disciplined ensemble acting.

The multi-talented actors inhabit a number of different characters adroitly and perceptively. The script enables some of the performers to probe deeper than others into the core of the individuals they represent. This applies notably to Johnson Willis as Silas Marner, Fergus McLarnon as Godfrey, Nicola Reynolds as Eppie and Jules Davison as Nancy. This truly versatile cast also includes Phil Harries, William Oxborrow and Stephanie Jacob.

Stage designer Carys Tudor provides a symmetrical group of arches sensitively lit by Kevin Heyes.

The director is Tim Baker whose reputation in Wales as a brilliant ensemble director is unchallenged.

Bob Roberts

Silas Marner (Theatr Clwyd)
North Wales Weekly News, 26 September, 1996.

Silas Marner is an outsider. A loner and a miser living in a small rural community, he is devastated when his money vanishes.

Then his life is transformed by an unexpected arrival at his cottage door.

Greg Cullen's adaptation of George Eliot's novel is an involving and enjoyable piece of theatrical story-telling in Tim Baker's imaginative production in the Emlyn Williams Theatre.

It's brought to life by a multi-talented cast of seven who also perform the atmospheric music on a variety of instruments.

Johnson Willis never plays Marner for superficial sympathy and his powerful performance is more moving because of it. Stephanie Jacob is delightful as a village woman whose simple goodness is her great strength.

The other actors play a kaleidoscope of parts creating a whole community out of seeming thin air.

There are wonderful moments of theatric magic which include a proud horse and rider, a hunt, a marriage, a birth and death, all created by the actors' movements.

Best of all is a small child conjured from a piece of cloth and an actress's voice.

Vic Hallett

CHRONOLOGY

GREG CULLEN – STAGE PLAYS

Title	Production	Year
The Flyboys	Unproduced	1979
The Bar	The East End Theatre Group	1980/81
Spiv	The East End Theatre Group	1981
Hansel and Gretel	Grove Theatre Hammersmith	1981
For the Benefit of . . . and Breakfast in America	Chats Palace, Hackney	1982
Order!	Chats Palace, Hackney	1982
Dozy Rosy and the Magic Samurai	The Grove Theatre	1982
A Piece of East	Chats Palace, Hackney	1982
Flaming Liberty!	Chats Palace Youth Theatre	1983
The Snow Queen	Theatr Powys	1983
rewrite	Queen's Theatre, Hornchurch	1986
	Old Bull Arts Centre	1995
The Bride of Baron Duprav	Theatr Powys	1984
Past Caring	Theatr Powys	1984
Aladdin	Theatr Powys	1984/5
Swashbucklers!	Theatr Powys	1985/6
Taken Out	Theatr Powys	1985
	Spark Theatre Company	1987
Sherlock Gnome and the Egg Snatchers	Theatr Powys	1985
	Masquerade Theatre Company	1985
	Spark Theatre Company	1987
Beauty and the Beast	Theatr Powys	1986
	Old Bull Arts Centre	1996
The Dragon of Bog Meadow	Theatr Powys	1987
The Balloonatics	Theatr Powys	1987
Mary Morgan	Mid Powys Youth Theatre	1987
	Red Shift Theatre Company and Mid Powys Youth Theatre, Riverside Studios, London	1988
	Armageddon Theatre Company	1995
Robin Hood	Theatr Powys	1987/8
Tarzanne	Mid Powys Youth Theatre	1988
rewrite	Theatr Powys and Footloose Dance Company	1990
rewrite	Mid Powys Youth Theatre	1995
The Children of Rebecca	Spectacle Theatre	1988
Frida and Diego – a Love Story	Red Shift Theatre Company	1989
	Stadsteatr, Stockholm, Stages Theatre,	1993
	Houston, City Theatre, San Francisco,	1993
	Mid Powys Youth Theatre	1993

	Mid Powys Youth Theatre at the Royal National Theatre, London	1994
Country Matters	Mid Powys Youth Theatre	1990
Raging Angels	Mid Powys Youth Theatre	1991/2
The Informer's Duty	Welsh College of Music and Drama	1992
Lysistrata	Mid Powys Youth Theatre	1992
The Ark	Ystradgynlais Youth Theatre	1992
Rhodri and the Bard	Mid Powys Youth Theatre	1993
The Walls (with Kelly Evans)	The Sherman Theatre, Cardiff	1994
rewrite	Armageddon Theatre Company	1995
Little Devils	Mid Powys Youth Theatre	1994
Cherubs	unproduced	1996
The Ring and the Piglet	Theatr Brycheiniog, Brecon	1997
The Wondering Town	(unproduced)	1996/7
Whispers in the Woods	Mid Powys Youth Theatre	1997

ADAPTATIONS

Hard Times	Theatr Powys	1986
A Christmas Carol	Theatr Powys	1989
	The Wilde Theatre, Bracknell	1995
Germinal	Wales Actors Company	1993
Silas Marner	Theatr Clwyd	1996

RADIO

Taken Out	BBC Radio Wales	1985
	BBC Radio 4	1986
Spoiled Papers	BBC Radio Wales	1986
A New World in the Mourning	BBC Radio 4	1988
Inside Me (co-devised)	BBC Radio 4	1990
Under Goliath Four part-dramatization of Peter Carter's novel	BBC Radio 5	1991
Landlocked (co-devised)	BBC Radio 4	1992
Mary Morgan	BBC Radio 4	1991/92
Rhodri Mawr and Welcome to the Feast	BBC Radio Wales	1993
The Informer's Duty	BBC Radio 3	1994
The Tower	BBC Radio 4	1994/95
The Whistleblower	BBC Radio 4	1996

FILM

Birdbrain	Winner of the Wales Film Council/BBC competition for a short film to celebrate fifty years of cinema	1996

PUBLICATIONS

Greg Cullen, *Taken Out* (translation) (Stuck Gut Press, 1987)
Mary Morgan, Frida and Diego and *Tarzanne* are due to be published by Seren Press during 1998

General Essays

STATE OF FLUX: Metaphors of Society and Nation in the Work of Charles Way, Dic Edwards and Edward Thomas.[1]

Roger Owen

What is a 'Welsh' playwright? The term has been applied, and undoubtedly will continue to be applied, to playwrights who are resident in Wales, whose work has been published or presented in Wales, and/or anyone who embraces a Welsh identity. This type of definition produces the broadest possible scope for the term 'Welsh', and reflects the variety of its use in the relevant media. But is such a broad definition of any real value, and what meaning does it actually carry?

Such speculations come into a particularly sharp focus when comparing the work of three, ostensibly 'Welsh', playwrights discussed in this essay. All three have lived in Wales for a number of years, and have also worked extensively in Wales, writing for a number of Welsh theatre companies. However, superficially at least, the Welsh connection may go no further. Charles Way, for example, does not regard himself as a Welsh dramatist. He is not a native Welshman (he was born and brought up in Devon) and, although resident in Wales, he does not ally himself with the culture. Dic Edwards, too, although born and brought up in Wales, does not see himself as a Welsh dramatist, rejecting the implicit and reductive nationalism of such a description. Only Edward Thomas regards himself as a Welsh dramatist, and he sees the task of redefining Wales's image and mythology as an essential part of his job as a writer.

Way's and Edwards's rejection of Welshness as a defining characteristic of their plays problematises this study considerably. Certainly, it would seem almost impossible to find any extant definition of 'Wales' or 'Welshness' that might unite the diverse cultural visions of these three playwrights. The challenge offered by their antipathy, therefore, is not to fit their work into a notion of Welshness, but to propose a notion of Welshness that can accommodate their work, or one which acknowledges the objections they raise.

In this essay I propose first of all to circumvent the question of Welshness, and to examine instead the general view of society posited by the work of these three playwrights; I will then readdress the question of Welshness in view of their social vision, and suggest a model of Welsh identity arising from their social critique and their use of theatrical form.

One of the primary functions of the theatre stage is to isolate a segment of lived experience, and define it as particularly significant. In so doing, a playwright creates a world on stage, a crystalisation of society which constitutes the minimum information necessary in order to construct an image of reality. The three playwrights under consideration here have chosen very different worlds for their plays, and have suggested different staging techniques as a means of perceiving these worlds. Each employs theatre as a basic paradigm for society, and, in the absence of a comprehensive view of Welshness, the values embodied in these paradigms must provide the evidence for the playwright's response to questions of national identity. For Charles Way, theatre is a communal gathering, a means of reintegrating people who are gradually being alienated from one another by the vicissitudes of contemporary life. Theatre acts, albeit temporarily, as a family; and, for fear of excluding some of its members, Way refuses to be labelled as being 'of Wales'. Dic Edwards's work is primarily concerned with democracy, and reflects this through a theatre which seeks to create and stimulate debate about the quality of people's participation in a just society. He regards nationalism as the antithesis of democracy, as a repository for dogmatic and insubstantial notions of 'belonging'. His theatre provides a forum wherein such a closing of the imagination may be countered. Edward Thomas seeks a theatre where Wales may be re-imagined and a new, radically changed culture asserted. In so doing he tacitly acknowledges the inadequacies of Wales as a nation, lacking real political power, unnoticed by much of the world, largely provincial in its outlook and habits, and definitely not sexy. His theatre acts as a transformational vehicle for Welsh identity, a sort of *Pair Dadeni*[2] for contemporary Wales.

In the work of Charles Way, we see two basic means of cementing relationships: for his characters, there is the family; for the actors and audience, there is community. The fusion of these two institutions is the essential element of his theatrical technique: his constant reference to family life in his plays indicates a fundamental belief in such an institution's capacity to bring people together in an environment of mutual respect and understanding. This type of trust also underlies his belief in the power of theatre to bring communities together, and alleviate the social alienation which has been a consequence of technological advancement and post-industrial decline.

Families feature prominently in his *Three Plays*. *Dead Man's Hat* concerns the encounter between the Watson/Averill family and a roving gunslinger, Clay, who is, in Way's own words, '. . . your run of the mill, voice in the head, all-American psychopath, intent on destroying the very thing he wants most, a family'[3]; and *In the Bleak Midwinter* parallels the Wakefield Mystery Plays in following a family of shepherds, Zac and Miriam and their baby, to Bethlehem at the time of the Nativity. However, it is *Paradise Drive* that is the most obviously family-orientated play. In four relatively brief acts, Way presents a study of an 'ordinary' family – a mother, father and two grown-up children – between 1979 and 1989, showing how the political and social upheaval of the Thatcher years changes their lives. All the scenes are set in the home, and the changing values of society may be perceived intermittently through snippets of chat. No characters outside the family unit are brought onstage. They are referred to obliquely, but with sufficient skill on the part of the dramatist to suggest an extra-marital affair between the (onstage) father, David, and the (offstage) work colleague, Anna Marie, and an unstable marriage between the (onstage) daughter, Sally, and an (offstage) advertising executive, Alan.

These veiled allusions to life outside the home indicate a crisis of communication within the family. Quite plausibly, the family do not spend hours locked in conversation about each others' problems. However, the tendency towards repression has a disastrous effect in the case of the son, John, whose aspiration to be an artist causes him to become dangerously isolated and culminates in his suicide. He manages to communicate his anxiety to Sally, but cannot assert his individuality before the family as a whole:

> Sally: I went to see him about five weeks ago. I didn't arrange it because I knew he'd put me off, so I just turned up. He didn't want to let me in at first . . . He said that he felt bad that he'd lied to you about going for job interviews
> . . . He hated lying – he said he didn't want to hurt you.[4]

However, in spite of the obvious role that repression and a lack of communication play in John's death, Way does not lose faith with the family as an institution. In fact, he apes the repressiveness of the family in his dramatic technique. He offers no alternatives to family life, and any disagreement or conflict between the characters is presented firmly within a single set of circumstances – private, intimate, and ultimately fulfilling:

> ['*Tenderness*']
> In the house and in the heart,
> Every communion is a giving and a receiving
> The taste of the food on the table,
> And the light, the light in the room,
> And the peace, the peace and wholeness
> Of the moment,
> In the house and in the heart,
> And in the love
> The taste of the food upon the table
> And the tenderness.[5]

This tight dramatic focus transforms the family into a kind of totem, conferring upon it the natural inevitability of myth.[6] The fact that this song is imbued with a deep sense of irony after John's death serves only to emphasise Way's refusal to present an alternative to the family, a refusal which becomes the central theatrical feature of *Dead Man's Hat* and *In the Bleak Midwinter*. In these two plays, the idea of the mythical family continues to inform the dramatic material, but it also becomes the basic model for the relationship between the actors and the audience, uniting family, community and theatre through the same set of values.

In *Dead Man's Hat*, a take on George Stevens's classic Western, *Shane*[7], the family unit is a somewhat tenuous one, consisting of Kate Watson, a prostitute-turned-sodbuster, Jim Averill, a labourer, gunned down by Clay on the day of their wedding, and Kate's daughter, Anne. However, the unusual nature of this unit is glossed over as Way focuses on the achievement of family status through marriage as the overriding ideal in people's lives. Jim is an archetypal family man – God-fearing, and a lousy shot; and Kate, although brusque, worldly and hammer-tongued ('. . . never get married to anyone, 'cos all men is bastards'), basically wants the same thing as Jim and, comically, proposes to him before he has plucked up sufficient courage to do so himself. Clay's half-mumbled proposal to Anne also occurs out of the blue, after they have been howling at the moon like wolves by their camp fire; but, even though it expresses the same familial aspirations, it does not represent the essential culmination of a way of life, as was the case with Jim and Kate. Its suddenness indicates Clay's essentially unhinged character.

An unusual adjunct to this play's familial preoccupation is its tendency towards violence. However, the theatrical impact of the violence is tempered by the knowledge that Way is quoting images from Hollywood westerns, and that the violent imagery is sometimes only a means of calling up the appropriate atmosphere. The hanging of Clay, for example, the first violent act in the play, is an *homage* to a similar sequence in Sergio Leone's *The Good, the Bad and the Ugly*[8]: through such quotation, Way sublimates the horror of the situation. The same might be said of the violence seen towards the end of *In the Bleak Midwinter* where, in spite of the epic scope of the source material for this adaptation of the Nativity, Way preserves his preferred, family-based approach. Zac and Miriam's child is spared during The Massacre of the Innocents when Mak, the sheep rustler-turned-soldier, is confronted by Gill, his former partner:

Gill: Mak. Mak?
[*He lowers the knife. Miriam rushes forward and takes the baby. Zac embraces her.*]
Gill: Mak?
Mak: I knew not oo it were. I knew not it were them. I swears it . . . Ee

> offered us 'alf his kingdom. All the wealth of the world. Don't look at me. Don't look at me. [*He slumps to his knees.*][9]

These violent incidents, though dramatically effective, do not violate the community's trust in the play, a trust which is crucial to Way's theatrical project: 'The act of theatre is an act of society,' he says, 'an act of hope'.[10] Good faith is the vital part of his hope that the collective engagement of an audience may lead directly to a realisation of commonly-held values and social interdependence; that a community may come to see itself not merely as a random assembly of individuals, but as a group which shares a common experience and a common humanity.

Dic Edwards prioritises theatre's function as a forum for debate, to be conducted on the nature of democracy. The value of democracy is paramount in his work, and he offers a scathing critique of those elements which he perceives to be contrary to the democratic ideal. His concern for democracy does not, however, yield a particularly liberal form of theatre: his plays are based on an interrogation and critique of society, and thus require a rigour which does not allow the kind of familial inclusiveness which typifies the work of Charles Way. Indeed, the family comes in for a particularly hard time in his *Three Plays*. The only one to feature a family is *Looking for the World*, set on a remote Greek island during the rule of the Colonels in the 1960s, in which a family of hoteliers is thrown into crisis by the return of their son from Athens after being trained as an army officer. Michalis Petrou has returned to the island to carry out its conversion into a prison camp, where communist enemies of the state will be imprisoned, tortured and executed. Family authority is seen here as an extension and a perpetuation of the oppressive rule of the Colonels; the family is effectively a totalitarian state, impenetrable and absolute in a way which presents the antithesis of Way's portrayal of family values in *Paradise Drive*. This view is expressed quite openly by the tramp, Nana Leros, at the beginning of the play:

> Nana: What does a family exist for? For security. The reasoning goes: if a brutal father were denounced before the world, the unity of the family would be threatened. . . . So the brutality is hidden and the security of the family is undisturbed.[11]

The family is the seat of brutality and brutalisation, where order is fixed and the destructive cycle perpetuated from generation to generation. This may be inferred from Michalis' experience of torturing fellow recruits as part of his military training:

> Michalis: One recruit didn't make it . . . He refused to take part in it . . . They beat him up more than they beat up anyone else. He just wouldn't do it back . . . I thought: 'I could never be like that boy because of my father.'[12]

Edwards rejects family values as a paradigm for theatre because they may be fixed, authoritarian and oppressive. They may resist interrogation, even by the members of the family itself. Instead, he insists on presenting reality as something to be challenged, criticised and negotiated by its members, with dire consequences for those who are content merely to inhabit it without question.

One such is the quintessential bourgeois, Casanova, whom we see playing out the sticky endgame of his great career in *Casanova Undone*. The play takes the form of a battle between the master, Casanova, and his servant, Costa/Sophie, who, during the course of the play, struggles to transcend the limits of Casanova's usage of him/her, and finds freedom at the former master's expense. This struggle manifests itself through a formal division of the stage into two conflicting worlds – the public, 'real' world where the characters normally interact, and the magical world-within-a-world of Casanova's bed, where reality is modified by erotic expectation and Casanova's reputation.

Ultimately, it is Casanova's occupation of one world only – his own – which causes his downfall. He is utterly preoccupied from the very beginning. We see him working on his memoirs, vainly attempting to preserve and promote the oppressive lie that his reputation has become in the face of the putrefaction of his own flesh. Even his hearing impedes him from participation, and reveals his inherent impotence:

> Casanova: I've discovered sublimity! I'm above ALL! I'm a god! Of a kind. [*Holds up papers*] My memoirs will ensure it! I have discovered my future!
> [*COSTA collapses. He gasps and speaks indistinctly*]
> Costa: Happiness is forsaken!
> Casanova: What? A penis has a foreskin?[13]

Unlike Way, Edwards does not exclude the enemy; he satirises them, and frequently delights in mocking the bourgeois, the nationalist, and the traditionalist for their predetermined notions of reality. In *Long to Rain Over Us*, set in a prisoner-of-war camp during the Second World War, Edwards uses satire to show how bigotry affects a particularly closed and contorted form of speech. He contrasts Lomax, a conscientious objector, with 'nationals' who have chosen to fight in the war, such as the prisoners Braun and Operarti. Operarti energetically asserts his unquestioning allegiance towards his national icons – 'I don't know what ideas are – I've never had any – . . . I love d'Annunzio even though I have never never read him!' – and Braun offers a faltering philosophical analysis of German identity:

> Braun: I will tell you how the German is in the head of Hitler. It all comes from the unconscience . . . [*Struggling*] . . . the unconSCIOUSNESS . . . this is where it all comes from and this . . . being German comes

> from influences that make unconscience. That influence is Adolf Hitler and we all live in his unconscience and he guides us in our soil and responsibility.[14]

The foremost example of satire in the play comes in the portrayal of Dangerfield, the camp commander, whose rhetoric never fails to lose touch with reality as soon as it gathers a momentum of its own – his inherent fascism is comically reflected as his wooden leg insists on presenting itself as in a Nazi goose-step during his exercises. Edwards does not allow such satirical comedy to dominate the play, however, and he is keen to point out the underlying danger of subjugating reason in service of a metaphor. Dangerfield's basic, poetic equation of the soil and the character of Englishness licenses acts of murder on a grand scale. His basic desire to see an end to the drought involves sowing 'the improper English' – conscientious objectors – in the soil of England to replenish the supply of 'good English' for the purposes of warfare:

> Kitty: . . . this mad, mad Englishman who's planted other Englishmen! Planted them like plants to have the English rain fall on them. To have them fertilized with Englishness. So that they will sing and fuck and fight and die in unison![15]

Neither is Edwards's deployment of satire confined absolutely to the enemies of democracy. In *Looking for the World*, his target is Paddy Millane, whose socialist and democratic 'mission' to use his holiday as a means of conducting an examination of the fascist regime is subsumed in wilful blindness, prompted by grief and self-loathing. Even Sylvia Millane, who becomes aware of the violence being perpetrated on the island, and seeks help, is revealed, implicitly, as a racist. Her frustration while attempting to telephone for help mirrors the kind of prejudice which has criminalised some of the islanders:

> Sylvia: I told you: I DON'T SPEAK GREEK! [*Spelling the words out*] Po..lice. And Am . . . bu . . . lance. . . . [*Suddenly beside herself*] Can't you get someone who speaks English! Can't you get someone civilised! God! . . .[16]

Edwards uses theatre as a means of demonstrating that the preservation of democracy and freedom requires an argument. However, rather than allowing the audience to 'make up their own minds', he challenges them to agree or disagree with the case that he makes through the play. The play – not the performance – is thus the primary vehicle for meaning in his theatre, and different stylistic interpretations of his work are unlikely to yield substantially different results in terms of the audience's perception of the argument. Edwards seems well aware of the fact that theatre itself, through an over-emphasis on direction and style, has the capacity to produce the kind of closed, reductive definitions of reality which he attacks in his plays, and he counters this in a warning to performers of his work: 'In my work what's important to understand is the argument . . . If actors were to have, say, a month of rehearsal time, I'd tell them to spend three weeks understanding the argument of the play, and then to spend one week blocking.'[17]

Edward Thomas's plays oppose such orthodoxy. His paradigm for theatre is the *Pair Dadeni*, the Cauldron of Rebirth, and the energy for such a rebirth may come from almost any direction. Reality is up for grabs in Thomas's world, and he who talks best, or just fastest, grabs most. This approach permits a continuous redefinition of reality by the characters in his plays, and a fundamental subversion of realism on his stage. The stage is a place to dream. But dreaming is not without its own consequences.

Language is the instrument of rebirth in Edwards's work, a fact most graphically demonstrated in *Flowers of the Dead Red Sea*. The play takes its shape from the verbal battle between the two slaughterman, Mock and Joe. As the fateful total of forty lambs a day looms ever closer (Mock insists on maintaining his father's practice of killing no more, lest his blade be blunted and the beasts die 'in a bloodbath of shame') the urgency of the struggle increases, until we arrive at the moment of Mock's inevitable and undignified defeat. The subsequent new order, to be instigated by Joe, shows no sign of charity; he is a hard-headed pragmatist who is happy to obey the call of a progress which bludgeons the redundant poeticism of tradition: 'I don't care about craftsmanship, sheep, people or beasts, I care about fuck all, I JUST FEEL LIKE KILLING, THAT'S ALL.'

The context of the play is sufficiently indistinct to allow throwaway remarks, wordplay, quotations and jokes to have a substantial effect on the relationship between the two characters. A good example of this is Mock's joke-dream in which he assumes the identity of 'a problem bucket' which Cragg, the slaughter-house manager, subsequently kicks, killing him. This manipulation of words provides Mock with a temporary victory in his struggle against the oppression of an authority which no longer values his principles. We are only too aware that this energetic wordplay provides a theatrical answer to Mock's problem, not a real one; but Thomas allows Mock his moment of glory, thus establishing the present condition of the dialogue as the only measure of reality.

This 'ever-present' reality has its price, however, and, like Estragon and Vladimir in Beckett's *Waiting for Godot*, Mock and Joe are in a world where coherence and memory are severely under threat:

> Mock: I don't remember a microwave.
> Joe: It fell a few days ago.
> Mock: I never saw it.
> Joe: I showed it to you, I said, "What do you think about this then?"
> Mock: You didn't say that about any microwave.

Joe: I did, I'm sure I did.
Mock: No, you've got it wrong there you said that to me when the chair came.
Joe: What chair?[18]

These falling objects provide a visual parallel to their imperfect possession of memory: the slaughter-house, like the mind, is only partially habitable. Likewise, Thomas seems regularly to exert only a partial control of his text, leaving it to its own devices, and allowing it to wander off on such extended detours to the beyond as Joe's description of the alley cat inside Mock's head, General Good, and Mock's taxi ride into the mountains in pursuit of his dicky bow. However, such passages are forcibly reintegrated into the play through the characters' persistence in attempting to animate them, and also by the characters' own dissatisfaction with arbitrary meanings. The ensuing friction challenges the audience to distinguish between the characters' conflict in the play and the actor's struggle in the theatre:

Joe: WE HAVE MADE ONLY A METAPHOR, A BAD METAPHOR.
Mock: IT HAS GIVEN US A START.
Joe: WHAT START?
Mock: THE START OF THE SOLUTION.
Joe: IT HAS GIVEN US NOTHING, WORDS, AVOIDANCE, EVASION, SHEER ORNAMENTATION.[19]

This technique of self-exposure obviously endangers Thomas's entire project. He risks reducing the attempt to find a new identity for his characters and theatre to a futile verbosity. His view, however, seems to be that the characters have to hit rock-bottom before the value of their persistence becomes appreciable. In Mock's case, his defiance transcends an obeisance to tradition only when he has been defeated and replaced by Joe. Hung by the slaughter-house chains, he still offers resistance to Joe's values:

Joe: Oh, don't worry, Mr Cragg, I'll kill as many as you need, I'm the main man now, Mr Cragg.
[*Pause*.]
Yes, goodbye, Mr Cragg, and thanks.
[*Joe puts down the phone. He sharpens a knife with a steel. He turns on some bland music on the radio. He moves over to Mock, who suddenly opens his eyes and stops Joe in his tracks*.]
Mock: I'm still here, Joe.[20]

The rootlessness implicit in *Flowers of the Dead Red Sea* is partially offset in Thomas's other plays by a yearning for home and family, which finds its most significant expression in the relationships between Bella, Ronnie and Trampas in *East from the Gantry*. However, family is only a temporary refuge from a palpably hostile world. Indeed, in *House of America*, the family is also the source of a disastrous illusion – it is Mam's lies about Clem's emigration to America which fuel Sid and Gwenny's incestuous game of Jack and Joyce. Thomas emphasises the insubstantiality of the family as a refuge from a nightmarish reality by deliberately confusing Boyo's dream, where he wanders lost in the hospital and is questioned by Mam in Welsh costume, with Mam's subsequent real-time reappearance in hospital wearing the same costume. There, Thomas again mocks the audience's willingness to suspend disbelief when Boyo decides to disabuse Mam of the idea that there is *cawl* in her bowl; but at the same time there is an awareness here that such belief in illusion is at the heart of theatre:

Boyo: There's nothing in the dish, mam

[*Pause. Mother looks into the bowl. Starts to laugh.*]

Mother: Isn't there?

[*She laughs a bit more. Suddenly throws it to the floor.*]

Mother: You're right, there's nothing there.

[*Pause.*]

You know what, I've been waiting for someone to say that to me all day.[21]

As suggested at the beginning of this essay, the nature of Welshness, if we are to perceive it at all in the combined visions of these playwrights, emerges as a dispute of the most fundamental order. Indeed, it would seem that these playwrights provide living proof of Gwyn A.Williams's memorable summation of the concept of nationhood: 'Wales is an artefact which the Welsh produce. If they want to. It requires an act of choice.'[22] That act of choice, it would seem, is far from being an automatic one.

But the conflict outlined here is not the rejection of Welsh identity that it may seem to be at first sight. Wales emerges from this study of three of its most distinctive modern playwrights as 'an essentially contested concept',[23] that is, an ostensibly singular form which has been appropriated in different ways 'in an atmosphere of "sophisticated disagreement" by participants who "do not expect to defeat or silence opposing positions, but rather through continuing dialogue to attain a sharper articulation of all positions . . ." '[24] This definition, quoted by Marvin Carlson in his book *Performance: a Critical Introduction*, lucidly articulates the condition of a form which is perpetually in the process of becoming. It provides an effective definition of both theatre and Welshness, and suggests, almost reassuringly, that dynamic disagreement is no impediment to growth. The dispute and division implicit in the work of these playwrights may thus be seen as *the* signifiers for Welsh identity in the contemporary age. By this token, Welsh identity is defined not as a prescription, and certainly not as a liturgy, but as a lively and ongoing debate, one which binds together virtually incompatible visions of the nation and the people.[25] Charles Way, Dic Edwards and Edward Thomas present us with a vision of a nation tenuously, but tenaciously, held together by conflict. For Wales, this conflict, in its instability and dynamism, provides the drama; and the theatre, in all its variety, provides the stage.

Notes

1 I have restricted this study to one volume by each playwright : Brian Mitchell (ed.), *Charles Way, Three Plays: Dead Man's Hat, Paradise Drive, In the Bleak Midwinter* (Bridgend: Seren, 1994) [hereafter cited as *Charles Way, Three Plays*]; Brian Mitchell (ed.), *Edward Thomas Three Plays: House of America, Flowers of the Dead Red Sea, East from the Gantry* (Bridgend: Seren, 1994) [hereafter cited as *Edward Thomas, Three Plays*]; and *Casanova Undone, Looking for the World, Long to Rain Over Us: Three Plays by Dic Edwards* (London: Oberon, 1992) [hereafter cited as *Three Plays by Dic Edwards*].

2 *Y Pair Dadeni* – the 'Cauldron of Rebirth', mentioned in the second branch of the Mabinogi, *Branwen Verch Lyr*.

3 *Charles Way, Three Plays*, p. vii.

4 Ibid., p. 128.

5 Ibid., p.129.

6 '. . . it transforms history into nature . . . everything happens as if the picture *naturally* conjured up the context . . .'. See Roland Barthes, *Mythologies*, translated by Annette Lavers (London: Paladin, 1973), pp. 140-1.

7 Paramount Pictures, 1953.

8 United Artists, 1966.

9 *Charles Way, Three Plays*, p. 200.

10 ibid. p.vii.

11 *Three Plays by Dic Edwards*, p. 68.

12 Ibid., pp. 125-6.

13 Ibid., pp. 12.

14 Ibid., p. 140

15 Ibid., p. 191

16 Ibid., p. 134.

17 Hazel Walford Davies, 'Theatre as Forum' [interview with Dic Edwards], *New Welsh Review*, 31 (Winter 1995-6), p. 79.

18 *Edward Thomas, Three Plays*, p. 120.

19 Ibid., p. 164.

20 Ibid., p. 166.

21 Ibid., pp. 81-2.

22 Gwyn A.Williams, *When Was Wales?* (Harmondsworth: Penguin Books, 1985) p. 304.

23 Taken from Marvin Carlson, *Performance: a Critical Introduction* (London: Routledge, 1996), p.1. Carlson attributes this phrase to W.B.Gallie in *Philosophy and Social Understanding*, (New York: Schocken Books, 1964) pp.187-8: 'Recognition of a concept as essentially contested implies recognition of rival uses of it (such as oneself repudiates) as not only logically possible and humanly "likely", but as of permanent potential critical value to one's own use or interpretation of the concept in question.' Gallie is quoted by Mary S. Strine, Beverly Whitaker Long and Mary Frances Hopkins, 'Research in Interpretation and Performance Studies: Trends, Issues, Priorities' in Gerald Phillips and Julia Wood (eds.), *Speech Communication: Essays to Commemorate the Seventy-Fifth Anniversary of the Speech Communication Association* (Carbondale: Southern Illinois University Press, 1990), p. 183.

24 Ibid., pp. 1,2.

25 See also M.Wynn Thomas, *Internal Difference* (Cardiff: University of Wales Press, 1992).

America and the Theatre of Small Nations

Gill Ogden

The images by which a nation chooses to project itself reveal a great deal about that nation, its people and its psyche. In examining the meaning and function of specific types of imagery in contemporary Welsh theatre, and that of the other small 'Celtic' nations I am adopting a number of assumptions regarding culture, representation, and literature which may be summarised by the statement that culture is a collectively agreed sign-system mediated by certain members of society.

'The history which becomes part of the fund of knowledge or the ideology of a nation state or movement is not what has been actually preserved in popular memory', writes Eric Hobsbawm, 'but what has been selected, written, pictured, popularised and institutionalised by those whose function it is to do so'.[1] In turn, A.P. Cohen has analysed what he sees as the 'symbolic construction of community'. He says that 'the quintessential referent of community is that its members make, or believe they make, a similar sense of things . . . The reality of the community in people's experience thus inheres in their attachment or commitment to a common body of symbols'.[2] It is the writers and intellectuals of a particular culture who fulfill this mediatory function, to meet the need for history, to establish the cultural signposts by which a society may rediscover, or reinvent, its identity. Social historians writing about the resurgence of national consciousness in the late nineteenth and early twentieth centuries note that a process of modernisation which involves the breakdown of traditional communities, the growth of the media and mass global communications, and the homogenisation of culture is, paradoxically, accompanied by a rise in national feeling. In the words of Patrick Wright, 'The nation works to re-enchant everyday life.'[3] The nation is seen as the conceptual space which replaces the former role of religion, face to face communication, traditional societal roles and the sense of belonging brought about by membership of such traditional communities.

'It is characteristic of minor literatures that everything in them is political', writes Robert Crawford, 'and that they have a particularly strong sense of collective cultural identity.'[4] Whilst only one of the writers studied in this volume, Edward Thomas, admits to an interest in national identity, nevertheless both Dic Edwards and Charles Way have reminded us of the politcal and cultural function of theatre: it is 'the only place left now where you can debate things publicly'[5]; 'It puts us in a situation where we can talk as a society about meaning'.[6] This essay examines the way a particular topos – that of the American Dream – in the theatre of Wales, Ireland and Scotland reminds us of 'the political and cultural function of theatre' and invites us to 'talk as a society about meaning'.

A topos has been defined as 'a recurring pattern of expression identified with motifs, images, symbols, keywords, and even genres and types of character'.[7] These images, like other texts, rely upon culturally determined codes. An interpretation of the topos requires an understanding of its ideological role in the contemporary world. What is the significance of America, in its various symbolic guises, to the audiences of contemporary Welsh performance? The plays of Arthur Miller and Sam Shepard, built around introspection, confession and revelation, reconstruct the guilt-ridden history of America. The theatre of recollection which is the immediate predecessor of the dramas under consideration here, was bound up with issues of belonging and identity. The recent theatre of the margins may be raising issues about a more reflective moment in the histories of the small nations around Britain, where the audience is invited to examine the process of representation itself rather than a specific ideological discourse.

Traditionally, the identity of small nations is concerned with myths of loss, dispossesion and oppression. Commonly held beliefs about the history and foundation of nations are embodied in stories, institutions and emblems invested with intense emotional meaning out of proportion to reality, thus creating myth. Such myths include the Welsh Not, Irish Talley Stick, the Treachery of the Blue Books, the Highland Clearances, the Irish Famine, Madoc, *Y Wladfa*, and what Gwyn Alf Williams describes as 'the rage to go to America' that took place during the middle of the last century.

In their study, *The Myths We Live By*, R. Samuel and P. Thompson discuss the function of myth in minority cultures;

> . . . for minorities, the less powerful, and most of all for the excluded collective, memory and myth are often more salient: constantly referred to both in reinforcing a sense of self and also as a source of strategies for survival. In this context it is often persecution and common grievance which define belonging. To call such stories myths is not to deny their roots in real incidents and real social conflicts. It is rather to indicate that, however we evaluate their literal meaning, the very fact that they recur so widely is real symbolic evidence of a collective sense of injustice.[8]

Sometimes the resonances of one myth implies the presence of another, for example; Irish playwright Tom Murphy's *Famine* is a lament about the combined effects of the Irish Potato Famine and a corrupt political regime; Bill Bryden's Dundee-based community play *The Ship* lamented the contemporary closure of shipyards and the death of a traditional way of life.

Neither of these plays directly concern emigration, but such is the strength of myth and the shared, selective history bound up with these moments, that the myth of mass emigration to America, emblematic of the loss and dispossession of the nation, is a powerful presence in the meaning of both plays, and of many others.

In the 1970-80s Irish drama began to abandon the old historic metaphors of loss, exile, and lament seen especially in the plays of Yeats and Synge – where Ireland is personified as woman; the nation emblematised through martyrdom, folk-tradition and bardic vision. A new concern with history and identity, half a century after the Anglo-Irish treaty, led to a preoccupation with memory and communication. Brian Friel's plays in particular reveal an almost obsessive concern with versions of history, and the self-delusion and loss of communication which arise from faulty recollection.

Post-colonial discourse would maintain that a preoccupation with histories and emblems of nationhood fuction partly to secure an identity which is perceived as oppositional; to place the small nation in opposition to its significant other, periphery versus core culture, oppressor versus the oppressed. However, recent plays and performances emerging from Wales, Scotland and, to a lesser extent, Ireland suggest that the margin has become a space for creative energy, that the core no longer functions as such, and that the redrawing of communal identity is taking place both within *and* without the nation's own psyche, not on an external, oppositional plane. America, in these dramas, has become an alternative 'other', by virtue of providing a frontier location similar to the marginality of small nationhood, rather than a hegemonic battlefield.

In Brian Friel's 1964 *Philadelphia, Here I Come!* we see the American Dream as a place to escape from narrow, small-town conformity, but Friel uses the device of double identity, a physicalisation of the private inner thoughts of the protagonist in order to scrutinise the experience of dispossession as private neurosis rather than external hegemony. The confessions of 'Public'Gar, egged on by his 'Private' alter ego, seen of course, only by the audience, form a piece of tragic meta-theatre, a story within a story which is juxtaposed by the bravado and naivety of his headlong rush for the great American Dream. At the beginning of the play the schizophrenic dialogue parodies itself, implying the adolescent excitement of escape and rebellion:

PRIVATE: You are fully conscious of all the consequences of your decision?
PUBLIC: Yessir.
PRIVATE: Of leaving the country of your birth, the land of the curlew and the snipe, the Aran sweater and the Irish Sweepstakes?
PUBLIC: (*with fitting hesitation*) I-I-I-I have considered all these, Sir.
PRIVATE: Of going to a profane, irreligious, pagan country of gross materialism?

PUBLIC: I am fully sensitive of this, Sir.
PRIVATE: Where the devil himself holds sway, and lust – abhorrent lust – is everywhere indulged in shamelessly?[9]

The final moments of the play reveal the sub-text of the internal dialogue. Gar is watching Madge, the housekeeper, his surrogate mother, preparing for bed for the last time. He describes the scene like a piece of silent movie which will constantly be rewound and replayed:

PRIVATE: Watch her carefully, every movement, every gesture, every little peculiarity: keep the camera whirring; for this is a film you'll run over and over again – Madge Going to Bed on My Last Night at Home . . . Madge . . . God, Boy, why do you have to leave? Why? Why?
PUBLIC: I don't know. I-I-I don't know.[10]

Philadelphia, Here I Come! is also a drama of recollection. Gar attempts to reconcile the profound lack of communication which has grown between himself and his father by reminding him of treasured memory from childhood; as is often the case in Friel's plays, the details of the two remembered histories are entirely different, the father/son relationship is never to be restored. Friel's drama has been condemned for perpetuating nationalist myths; for example writing of *Translations*, Edna Longley writes: 'The play does not so much examine myths of dispossession and oppression as repeat them.' Such charges of historical innacuracy and collusion with myth miscast Brian Friel as sociologist rather than *dramatist.* It is important to recognize that his plays function as dramatic interrogations of crises of identity and communication rather than as sociological tracts.

Liam de Paor has defined myth as 'a story which society tells itself about itself in order to describe itself – and to others'.[11] The theatres of recollection from Friel to Bill Bryden and Brith Gof seek to dramatise the stories of their peoples. 'The memory of a small nation is no shorter than that of a large one', wrote Kafka, 'it reworks the available material all the more thoroughly'.[12] In Wales, it was the experimental and community based theatre companies of the late 1970s and early 1980s that provided a platform for the theatre of recollection, reworking myths of defeat and defiance which culminated in Brith Gof's epic performance of the *Gododdin.* Memory, amnesia, and lie-telling as metaphors for identity continue to be present in the more recent plays under consideration here but performed as meta-theatre which uses a mythical America as an alternative location or frontier for contesting versions of identity. Joanne Tompkins has descibed meta-theatre in post-colonial drama as a 'strategy of resistance':

While theatre generally replays the present or the past to celebrate it, remember it or decipher it, meta-theatre in post-colonial plays is often a self

> conscious method of re-negotiating, re-working – not just re-playing – the past and the present . . . Increasingly, texts that are the subject of counter-discourse are less canonical and more 'popular'.[13]

In Edward Thomas's *House of America* Sid and Gwenny perform their fantasy play of the American dream in juxtaposition with a portrayal of family life in extremis. When the two stories collide, the results are catastrophic. Changes in rhythm and language mark the character of the fantasy, moving into a more lyrical, figurative style:

> SID: Nothing stays the same forever, get on the world's car and never get off, hitch a ride to the other side of the sun, c'mon, can't you smell the space of Iowa on the mountains, see Manhattan on TV and on our streets, play pool with a man who's seen the Chicago Bears. The world gets bigger as it gets smaller . . .[14]

By contrast, in the base-narrative the family embody one of the crucial hegemonic moments in Welsh history, the description of the Welsh by Gerald of Wales as a shiftless, cowardly, unstable and incestuous race. Looking out across the boundary, people construct what they see in terms of their own stereotypes.

The American meta-theatre within the play provides a location where a powerful myth is juxtaposed with a nation where, in Thomas's view, there are no heroes or a valid mythology. We see the play of Sid and Gwenny, not only through our own eyes, but also those of Boyo, their brother. This has the effect of both deepening the intensity of our scrutiny and of fracturing our perception, permitting a more critical interpretation. In an interview with Hazel Walford Davies, Edward Thomas analyses his own attachment to the American Dream:

> I envy America for its space and the fact that dramatists like Sam Shepard have inherited a culture which they can reject and attack . . . the American Dream contains within it numerous mythologies. America also has the immense advantage that the world hears about it, and that it is *the* land of the 'Go West' mythology. If you're Welsh you have no mythology.[15]

There are a number of American Dreams in the play – the Western, the Frontier, the Land of Plenty, and Kerouac's beat generation freedom of excess. But the version of the dream which is acted out by Sid and Gwenny is one which, in reality, posed a threat to established American values at the time. The novelist William Burroughs has described its impact:

> Once started, the beat movement had a momentum of its own and a world-wide impact. In fact, the intelligent conservatives in America saw this as a serious threat to their postion long before the Beat writers saw it themselves . . . Artists to my mind are the real architects of change, and not political legislators, who

> implement change after the fact. Art exerts a profound influence on the style of life, the mode, range and direction of perception. Art tells us what we know and don't know we know. Certainly *On the Road* performed that function in 1957 to an extraordinary extent. There's no doubt that we're living in a freer America as a result of the beat literary movement . . .[16]

Boyo's vision of America, however, matches neither this radical dream nor any of the more traditional versions; he is firmly rooted in his own world,

> BOYO: Who wants to be a film star anyway? . . . Pretending to be somebody else for a living, lies, all lies.[17]

He rejects Sid and Gwenny's repeated attempts to involve him in their play, the flat rationality of his refutations contrasting strongly with Sid's lyricism:

> SID: Plenty of work there too, Boyo, plenty of space, sun, sand, fancy riding across it chasing the sun on a Harley Davidson, money in your pocket, tiger in your tank, Hendrix on the Walkman – no helmet – just free and moving West.
> BOYO: You can do that in Pembroke, Sid . . .
> SID: That's what the old man did, I reckon.
> BOYO: What?
> SID: Chased his dreams.
> BOYO: Women he was after, Sid, not dreams.[18]

Sid and Gwenny have chosen the wrong dream. Like Arthur Miller's salesman, they 'had the wrong dreams. All, all wrong'.[19] We have the same observation on the disappointment of the Dream in Dic Edwards's *Utah Blue*. Gary Gilmore in the play 'never knew what he wanted! That's America, man! The AMER-ican fuckin Dream!'.[20]

Gary feels that he is playing a role, taking part in, or observing the film of his own life:

> GARY: Are you actors or killers? Am I just a member of the fucking audience? Am I just watching a film? [21]

Mother in *House of America* has her own nightmares to deal with; she also indulges in play acting, the 'Dream of the Remembered Wales'. When Boyo visits her in hospital, he finds her dressed in pointed hat and daffodil; she accuses him of forgetting St David's Day:

> MOTHER: Like my daffodil?
> BOYO: It's plastic.
> MOTHER: Didn't have real ones, and the plastic ones stay yellow forever.

But unlike Sid and Gwenny, she does not really believe in her dream:

> *She eats her cawl. Boyo watches. Then he walks over and looks in the bowl*
> BOYO: Cawl . . . ?
> MOTHER: Mmm . . . neck of lamb, I made a pot full of it. Are you hungry? You can have some if you want, it's still hot.
> BOYO: There's nothing in the dish, Mam . . .
> MOTHER: You're right, there's nothing there . . . You know what, I've been waiting for someone to say that to me all day.[22]

Edward Thomas sums up his own attitude to the fragility of Welshness: 'My desire to be Welsh is complicated by the insecurity of being a Welshman, and the fact that we can't be confident that Wales exists. Wales is only an idea, a desire, a sense of something'.[23] In saying this, Thomas is in accord with the prevalent concept of the nation in the West today as a matter of self-definition. This, of course, is not a modern notion: 'A nation is a soul, a spiritual principle', said Ernest Renan in a speech delivered to the Sorbonne in 1857.

Tony Conran has posed yet another alternative dream bound up with the symbolic relationship between Wales and America:

> The Valleys – the coalfield – provided Wales with its own America. The Great Valleys Dream – socialism, if you like – was no less potent than the Great American Dream . . . Like the American, the Welsh Dream belonged to a frontier, of villages suddenly upgraded into sprawling conurbations on the edge of a wilderness.[24]

House of America is located in just such a frontier village; Sid's American Dream takes place within Conran's Valleys' Dream; the ranch which Sid wants to build for Gwenny out West is imagined within the house on the frontier of a quarry which threatens to engulf them.

Charles Way locates his own American play on the frontier:

> The situation of *Dead Man's Hat* is indeed a reversal of the the film *Shane* where the lonely gunslinger who is trying to go straight – although that's a huge lie in itself – saves the homestead from the evil cattle barons. By turning it round I was trying to look at the image of the outsider and at the image of the family who trusted this man to save them. The outsider, Clay, in my play represents America but he is also the one bent on destroying it.[25]

In a study of the Western, Douglas Pye identifies the constituents of a paradigm of the 20th century Western:

> The Western is set on the frontier at a time when the forces of social order and anarchy are still in tension; the 'formula' . . . is an adventure story with its apotheosis of the hero who stands between the opposing forces in a symbolic [illegible]dscape; the plots generally involve some form of pursuit, almost invariably [illegible] in a moment of transcendent and heroic violence; the characters can be [illegible]nto three main groups: the townspeople or settlers; hero or heroes; [illegible]ains.[26]

Proceeding to attempt to explain the enduring fascination of the genre for cultural analysts and writers, Pye speculates that it could be 'partly due to their apparent visual coherence and to their amenability to analysis in terms of iconography'; to issues of gender, race and representation; and to the fact that writers were dealing with a genre in which 'as boys in the post-war period they had a substantial emotional investment'.

Charles Way admits to having been fascinated by Westerns as a boy and in *Dead Man's Hat* he exploits and subverts the genre as a 'plastic medium', capable of containing and transmitting a wide range of meanings with great economy. Structurally the play presents an unravelling of history; a layered story of deceit and duplicity which forms a reversal of the usual premise of the Western is placed within the narrative framework of a historical enquiry. A young man from The Historical Society of the American West turns up at the homestead:

> DICKSON: You see I'm trying to find out what happened to my Grandfather . . .
>
> ANNE: I'm sayin' I can only tell what I recall an' what I pieced together over the years an' that ain't the same as the truth.[27]

Way's ambivalence about the American dream is mirrored in our own uncertainty about the truths and lies of the history which is unravelled in the story within the play. Set against Dickson's demands for historical authenticity and the need to discover facts about his own identity, we see the flickering filmic metatheatre of contesting stories and assumed identities. The use of song affirms the performative nature of the story within the play, and we see the story not only through our own eyes, but also through those of Dickson, our fellow-audience. The images of this world carry astonishigly direct resonance for the late twentieth-century audience; their implications in the context within which they are placed are disturbing. Like the characters in Thomas's *House of America*, we are sent on a quest for truth and identity in a world where no real role models exist; where truth and goodness appear to be a chimera.

In his play describing the last days of the serial murderer, Gary Gilmore, Dic Edwards creates a house very like the frontier ranches of *Dead Man's Hat* and *House of America*. It is described in the dream of Gary's brother, Mikal:

> MIKAL: I've been having this dream. About the house where I grew up. In the dream it's always night. It's my father's house. On the outskirts of the town. A dead-end American town. A train whistle blows out in the night but no train ever comes . . .
>
> GARY: What is this shit? Writer!
>
> MIKAL: People go from the darkness outside the house to the darkness inside. Everybody's back from the dead.[28]

In *Place and Placelessness* the geographer Edward Relph develops the concept of existential insideness and outsideness. The most profound sense of place is 'experiential insideness', in which a place is experienced without deliberate and self-conscious reflection yet is full with significances.[29] This is the ideal of small nationhood as it was envisaged by the cultural elite at the end of the last century; it is a world portrayed with bitterness in Ibsen's stuffy drawing rooms and with the tongue firmly in the cheek in J.M. Synge's *The Playboy of the Western World*. It is so rare in a society increasingly mobile that it is representations of landscapes of placelessness, inhabited by existential outsiders, which have a more urgent resonance for us at the end of the 20th century.

The American West provides an archetypal landscape of placelessness:

> CHORUS: Oh the West, oh the West
> Where the wild winds blow
> Nobody knows, nobody knows
> Nobody knows
>
> Now the wind
> Is a howlin'
> 'Cross the prairie so old
> It whispers an' moans
> 'Bout the sad buffalo
> But the land
> Oh the land
> Is a killer so cold
> It can kill both the man
> With the gun or the hoe[30]

Like Shane or the High Plains Drifter, Way's Clay is the existential outsider who rides in from the wilderness but, rather than a restoration of order, his presence invokes a deeper chaos.

In *House of America* the echoing wilderness is contained within the house, which is not a home. 'Although there is a narrow sense of homelessness which can be alleviated simply by building a shelter', writes Heidegger, 'there is a much deeper crisis of homelessness to be found in the modern world; many people have lost their roots, their connection to homeland. Even those who physically stay in the same place may become homeless through the inroads of modern means of communication, such as radio or television . . . If we lose the capacity to dwell, then we lose our roots and find ourselves cut off from all sources of spiritual nourishment'.[31]

Sid and Gwenny both recognise their own homelessness, and project themselves as existential outsiders in an imaginary landscape derived from American novels and film:

SID: Yeah, fly to America, hire a car, and drive right across it, chasing the sun.[32]

Gwenny is seduced by Sid's fantasy and, Icarus-like, they fly too close to the sun to their destruction. So intense is the sense of homelessness that the fantasy alleviates, that Gwenny is unable to return; 'It's all lies, Gwenny, it's a dreamland'. Sid's caution cannot penetrate the dream.

The malaise of contemporary life was juxtaposed with direct references to American film iconography in a recent Irish play, *Stones in his Pockets* by Marie Jones. An American film crew arrive in a tiny community in the West of Ireland where once *The Quiet Man* was filmed. The new feature film is similarily saturated with stereotypical images of Irish peasantry provided by the local extras who have been sent by the Unemployment Office. The comic narrative is contained within a context of rural dereliction and by the tragic story of a young local boy who is an addict. At the close of the play the boy fills his pockets with stones and walks into the sea framed by the famous view for the opening of *The Quiet Man*. The play combines post-colonial opposition in the meta-theatre of self-conscious stereotypes with the tragic narrative of existential outsideness in a supposedly rooted community.

Writing from the context of a Scottish university, Greg Geisekam addresses the problem of how issues of identity and nationhood can be represented in a postmodern 'open' performance which is fragmentary, non-linear, dislocated, ambiguous and deconstructed. There is a concern that an emphasis on technique and technicality, instead of providing the audience with more interpretative options, turns in on itself to become a 'narcissistic exercise' on the part of actors and director; that the technicality of performance can be in advance of the audience's ability to interpret. He quotes Baudrillard on postmodern performance and technology:

> . . . we need to give more attention to those postmodern performances that do not let the multi-media apparatus represent itself to itself, but react against that mise en abyme by foregrounding and experimenting with the transformable theatricality of body and voice in real space-time – and thus addressing the actually changing conditions of representation for social subjects that we experience today . . . They [the changing conditions] can be engaged differently by collaborative artistic practices that are about the context-specific, social, and ethnic identities of the body and the subject of performance, and that even more anachronistically insist on an ethics of (re)productive choice.[33]

Geisekam cites Clanjamfrie's *At the World's Edge* as an example. Performed at Glasgow's Mayfest '92, the 'world's edge' of the title is linked to an anniversary of the arrival of Columbus in America. The performance consisted of a multi-media collage of personal and *found* texts: movement, video, and music to 'set aspects of American history against issues of identity and representation in a culture saturated with media images of America'. Like Irish theatre, Scotland's playwrights had been largely imprisoned in what John McGrath refers to as the 'lament syndrome'. Clanjamfrie decided to devise a performance consisting of American actors of different ethnic origins and Scots actors. They looked individually at memory and imagery of the past, using their own childhood memories of American iconography.

In *Once Upon a Time in the West*, Welsh performer and director Eddie Ladd revisited the Western movie *Shane* and juxtaposed the well known formula with a family history set in West Wales. Universal themes of land, identity and disposession are common to both narrative strands; the actor's body also 'became' the landscape, enacting the geological process of the landslip at the heart of the 'Welsh' narrative and placing itself within a meta-theatrical re-enactment of the film *Shane*. The use of simultaneous video transmission, stylised lighting, horse-riding, collages of music, soundtrack and projected sequences from the film provided a variety alternative texts. The 'Welsh' narrative was enacted in non-linear sequence using Welsh and English, recorded and live commentary and a variety of styles from documentary to soap opera.

These two examples of postmodern performance, and others such as Brith Gof's *Patagonia*, exploit the frontier myth in order to pose an alternative resistance to hegemonic discourse, not oppositional, but inclusive.

I have identified three functions of the topos of the American Dream in the theatre of small nations; as an invented emblem of nationhood, arising from traditional agreed myths of oppression and loss; as a site for discourse concerning identity in the form of meta-theatre; and as a symbol of existential outsideness. The functions overlap to some extent in the work of the writers studied in this volume, and elements of all three were found in the documented multi-media performances to which I have referred. The myth of the American West is, as Charles Way reminds us, an outstandingly 'plastic medium', capable of containing and transmitting a wide range of meanings; of fulfilling a number of related functions; and of participating in widely differing versions of the theatre event.

Notes

1 E. Hobsbawm and T. Ranger (eds.), *The Invention of Tradition* (Cambridge: Cambridge University Press, 1983), p. 13.

2 A.P.Cohen, *The Symbolic Construction of Community* (Chichester: Ellis Harwood, 1985), p.16.

3 Patrick White, *On Living In An Old Country: The National Past in Contemporary Britain* (London: Verso, 1985), p. 24.

4 Robert Crawford, *Devolving English Literature* (Oxford: Oxford University Press 1992), p. 6.
5 Hazel Walford Davies, 'Theatre as Forum' [interview with Dic Edwards], *New Welsh Review*, 31 (Winter 1995-96), p. 83.
6 Hazel Walford Davies, 'A Journey of Exploration' [interview with Charles Way], *New Welsh Review*, 33 (Summer 1996), p. 81.
7 Nina Witoszec, *The Theatre of Recollection: A Cultural Study of the Modern Dramatic Tradition in Ireland and Poland* (Stokholm: Stokholm Studies in English, 1988), p. 14.
8 Raphael Samuel and Paul Thompson (eds.), *The Myths We Live By* (London: Routledge, 1984), p. 29.
9 Brian Friel, *Selected Plays* (London: Faber and Faber, 1984), p. 32.
10 Ibid., p. 99
11 Liam de Paor, 'The People's of Ireland', Cited in *Transition: Narrative in Modern Irish Culture* , Richard Kearney (Manchester: Manchester Uuniversity Press, 1988), p. 270.
12 Max Brod (ed.), *Franz Kafka Diaries 1910-13*, translated by Joseph Kresh (London: Secker and Warburg, 1948), p. 193.
13 Joanne Tompkins, 'Spectacular Resistance: Metatheatre in Post-Colonial Drama', in *Modern Drama,* 38 (1998), p. 42.
14 *House of America* in, Brian Mitchell (ed), *Edward Thomas, Three Plays, House of America, Flowers of the Dead Red Sea, East From the Gantry* (Bridgend: Seren, 1994), p. 88. Hereafter cited as *Edward Thomas, Three Plays*.
15 Hazel Walford Davies, 'Wanted: a New Welsh Mythology' [interview with Edward Thomas] *New Welsh Review* 27 (1994), p. 56.
16 Ann Charters (ed.), *The Penguin Book of the Beats* (London: Penguin Books, 1992), p. xxxi.
17 *Edward Thomas, Three Plays*, pp. 36-7.
18 Ibid. pp. 44, 46.
19 Arthur Miller, *Death of a Salesman* (Penguin Books, 1982), p. 110.
20 Dic Edwards, *Utah Blue* (Cardiff: The Made in Wales Stage Company, 1995), p. 45.
21 Ibid., p. 32
22 *Edward Thomas, Three Plays*, pp. 81-2.
23 Hazel Walford Davies, 'Wanted : a New Welsh Mythology' [interview with Edward Thomas] *New Welsh Review* 27 (1994), p. 55.
24 Tony Conran, 'A Special Relationship', *New Welsh Review*, 32 (Spring 1996), p. 31.
25 Hazel Walford Davies, 'A Journey of Exploration' [interview with Charles Way], *New Welsh Review*, 33, (Summer 1996), p. 76.
26 Douglas Pye in Ian Cameron and Douglas Pye (eds.), *The Movie Book of the Western* (London: Studio Vista, 1996), pp. 10-15.
27 Brian Mitchell (ed.), *Charles Way, Three Plays, Dead Man's Hat, Paradise Drive, In the Bleak Midwinter* (Bridgend: Seren, 1994), p.14. Hereafter cited as *Charles Way, Three Plays*.
28 Dic Edwards, *Utah Blue*, pp. 43-4.
29 Edward Relph, *Place and Placelessness* (London: Pion, 1976), p. 55.
30 *Charles Way, Three Plays*, p. 60.
31 Martin Heidegger, 'Discourse On Thinking', cited in J.Bird et al. (eds.), *Mapping the Futures* (London: Routledge, 1993), p. 11.
32 *Edward Thomas, Three Plays,* p. 39.
33 Greg Giesekam, 'A View from the Edge', *Contemporary Theatre Review*, vol. 2, part 2, 1994, pp. 115-129.

COPYRIGHT ACKNOWLEDGEMENTS

Edward Bond:

Newspapers/ Periodicals:

Thanks are extended to the following newspapers and periodicals for permission to reproduce material copyrighted in their name. Within the review sections themselves the newspapers, periodicals and authors are acknowledged throughout.

Belfast Telegraph, Ballyclare Gazette, Cardiff Herald and Post, Carmarthen Times, Evening Standard, Evening Times, The Financial Times, Glasgow Herald, Golwg, The Guardian, The Independent, Irish News, The List, London Theatre Record, Liverpool Daily Post, New Welsh Review, North Wales Weekly News, The Observer, Opera Now, Planet, Plays and Players, Scotland on Sunday, The Scotsman, South Wales Argus, South Wales Echo, The Telegraph, Time Out, The Times, The Times Literary Supplement, Venue, Western Mail, What's On.

The following copyright lines have been requested by *The Guardian, The Observer* and *The Times*:

The Guardian:

The Observer:

The Times:

INDEX

3 Deaths of an Idiot (1995), Dic Edwards 55, 56, 58, 60, 110
views of Edward Bond on 53–4
606 Theatre 98, 100–01, 102, 110
1953, Craig Raine 95
Abigail's Party, Mike Leigh 86
Aces of Gaerlishe, Edward Thomas [*Gas Station Angel*] 123, 126, 127, 146, 149, 150, 151, 152, 153, 155, 158
see also *Gas Station Angel*
Action Pie 278
Adams, Gilly 90, 106, 107, 396
Adar Heb Adenydd (1989), Edward Thomas 147, 149, 150, 152, 153, 157, 190, 212, 213, 246
review by Claire Davidson 208
review by David Adams 207–08
review by Jan Fairley 208–09
review by Joy Hendry 210
After the Assassinations, Edward Bond 22
Aim, Pierre 205
Akhmatova, Anna 322, 338, 339, 341, 366
Aladdin (1984), Greg Cullen 351, 352, 354, 401
review by David Adams 373
Alexander, Janek 147, 222, 223, 225
Alheit, Peter 75
Allan, Larry 154
Allende, Isabel 209, 327
Allison, Steve 105
Allsopp, Dawn 306
Alma [*Wittgenstein's Daughter*]
views of Edward Bond 49–50
see also *Wittgenstein's Daughter*
Alma Theatre 75
American Dream 115–18, 121–2, 417–27
Anderson, Gordon 98, 100, 101
Angry Earth, The, Carl Francis 208
Arad Goch 154
Arcadia, Tom Stoppard 84
Ark, The (1992), Greg Cullen 402
Armageddon Theatre Company 401, 402
Arts Theatre, Belfast 203, 204
Ash on a Young Man's Sleeve (1991), Charles Way adapt. 314
review by David Adams 303–04
review by Jon Holliday 305
review by Nicole Sochor 303
review by Penny Simpson 304
Assembly Rooms, Edinburgh 386, 387, 388, 389, 390
Assumption [*Looking For The World*], Dic Edwards 20–1, 22, 24
see also *Looking For The World*
At The End Of The Bay (1982), Dic Edwards 5, 17, 18, 110
At the Inland Sea, Edward Bond 57
At the World's Edge, Clanjamfrie 425–6
Aylwin, Richard 229, 298, 300

Bailey, Matthew 297, 310, 311, 385
Baker, Tim 398, 399, 400
Bala, Iwan 124, 125, 148, 157, 216, 228
Bald Prima Donna, The, Ionesco 98
Balloonatics, The (1987), Greg Cullen 401
Baneswell Community Centre, Newport 293
Bar, The (1980/81), Greg Cullen 349, 401
Barclays New Stages Festival 237, 243
Barker, Howard 237
Batchelor, Helene 306
Battersea Arts Centre 195, 196, 197, 246
Baxter, Trevor 88
Beauty and the Beast (1986), Greg Cullen 351, 354, 394, 401
Beck, Ulrich 75
Beckett, Hilary 105, 107
Beckett, Samuel 35
Beer, Mike 241
Beggar's New Clothes (1993), Dic Edwards 110
review by Adam Goldstein 102

review by Alexander Waugh 99–100
review by Amanda Blinkhorn 101–02
review by Caroline Rees 101
review by Jeremy Kingston 100–01
review by Robert Maycock 98–9
Beggar's Opera, John Gay 98, 99, 100, 101, 102
Behind the Lines (1983), Charles Way 266, 272
Bellamy, Bill 305
Bellamy, Marcia 98
Belshaw, Warren 99, 101
Berry, Richard 297, 299, 300, 301, 308
Big Pitt mining museum 273, 290, 291
Bingo, Edward Bond 32, 49, 54
Birdbrain, film (1996), Greg Cullen 324, 402
Birth of Tragedy, The, Nietzshe 12
Black Parlour (1984), Charles Way 266
Blanchard, Christine 289, 290, 292
Bloody Chamber, The, Angela Carter 344
Bloomfield Centre, Narberth 194
Bond, Edward 5, 6, 15, 365
letters to Dic Edwards 17–64
Bordertown (1987), Charles Way 268, 314
Boswell for the Defence 392
Bound East for Cardiff, Eugene O'Neill 4
Boxer, Stephen 88
Boy Soldier, Karl Francis 192
Boyle, Danny 18
Bradford Peverall Village Hall 302
Bread and Roses (1983), Charles Way 266, 272–3, 313
review by Anne Hegerty 289–90
review by Brian Jarman 288
review by David Adams 289
Brecht, Bertolt 55
Brennan, Patrick 239, 240
Bride of Baron Duprav, The (1984), Greg Cullen 351, 354, 401
review by David Adams 371–2
review by Lawrence Garner 372–3
review in *The County Times* 372
Brith Gof 75, 128, 129, 141, 142, 154, 187, 188, 226, 242, 419
Broadbent, Stephen 396
Brogan, Michael 89
Broomhill, Tonbridge 96, 97, 98, 110
Brown, Dylan 100, 101, 102
Bryant, Beaux 306
Buchanan, Ian 156, 298, 301
Buffery, Bill 305
Bundy, Michael 229
Burridge, Phoebe 393
Burrows, Michael 13
Buster Young People's Theatre 264, 313
Buswell, John 241
Bute Theatre 395
Byrne, Steven 319, 322, 381, 384, 395

Cameron, Anne-Margaret 97
Canned Goods (1983), Dic Edwards 110
Cardiff East, Peter Gill 188
Cardiff Laboratory Theatre 154
Cardiff Marketing Ltd 199, 221
Cardiff Summer Festival 230
Carlsen, John 396
Carter, Angela 327
Casanova Undone (1992), Dic Edwards 5, 10–11, 34, 37, 110, 111, 410
review by John Fowler 93
review by Joseph Farrell [*Plays and Players*] 95–6
review by Joseph Farrell [*The Scotsman*] 94
review by Michael Coveney 94–5
review by Simon Reade 96
review in *Scotland on Sunday* 93–4
views of Edward Bond 26–8, 29
see also *Ecce Homo*
Cassidy, Neil 118
Castaway Theatre Company, Aberystwyth 77, 110
Castle Theatre, Aberystwyth 121
Cat in the Bag 266
Catatonia 190
Cats 58
Cefn Coed Community Centre 373
Centre for Performance Research 154
Chapter Arts Centre 15, 109, 110, 148, 156, 195, 196, 198, 199, 200, 213, 216, 217, 218, 228, 229, 230, 231, 232, 233, 235, 246

Chats Palace, Hackney 349, 353
Cherubs (1996), Greg Cullen 324, 343–4, 347, 357, 358–9, 360, 402
Children of Rebecca, The (1988), Greg Cullen 401
Chimes, The (1982), Charles Way adapt. 314
Christmas Carol, A (1989) Greg Cullen adapt. 354, 385, 402
review by David Adams 394–5
review by JD 395
Cillet, John 377
Citizens Theatre, Glasgow 78, 93, 94, 95, 102, 103, 110
City Theatre, San Fransisco 401
Clack, Boyd 220
Clanger & Boink 231
Clarence Hall, Crickhowell 92
Clark, Phil 303, 304, 305, 396
Clarke, Leonard 268
Clements, Paul 356, 396
Clwyd Youth Theatre 275
Cockpit, Lisson Grove 99, 100, 101, 102
Coffee, Edward Bond 56
Community House, Newport 288
community theatre 264, 265–6, 293
Company, The 123, 194, 208
see also *Y Cwmni*
Company of Men, Edward Bond 49, 57, 61
Constant, Vanya 154
Coslett, David 369, 370, 372, 373
Coult, Tony 17
Country Matters (1990), Greg Cullen 402
Cox, Diana 289, 291
Crown, Sheryl 293
Croydon Warehouse 391, 392
Crucible, The, Arthur Miller 254, 294
Cullen, Greg 154, 267
career 348–53
chronology 401–02
reviews 369–400
themes in his plays 327–46, 355–60, 362–8
youth theatre 353–5
Cwmni, Y 119, 122, 123, 128, 132, 146, 147, 148, 154, 155, 156, 186, 197, 198, 201, 202, 214, 215, 216, 217, 218, 219, 220, 221, 222, 224, 225, 231, 232, 234, 236, 237, 239, 240, 246
see also The Company

Daldry, Stephen 123, 128, 146
Dalier Sylw 147, 207, 208, 209, 212, 217, 226, 246
Dancing with Wolves 251
Dauncey, Terence 305
David (1996), Dic Edwards 15, 110, 111
Davies, Chris 382
Davies, Eirian 229
Davies, Idris 268
Davies, Jenny Spencer 124
Davies, Libby 382
Davies, W. H. 268
Davis, Steve 15
Davison, Jules 398, 399
de Mann, Paul 8
De Monarchia, Dante 24
Dead, The, Joyce 160
Dead Man's Hat (1992), Charles Way 251–62, 267–8, 269–70, 276, 277, 279–80, 284, 313, 406, 407, 408, 422, 423–4
review by Frank Kempe 305–06
Deal, The (1992), Dic Edwards 15, 110, 111
'Decline and Fall of the Roman Empire, The' 193
Derek, Edward Bond 22
Derrida 8
Design Stage 105
Dibbling, Jimmy 312
Dibling, Amber 384–5
Diversions Dance 264, 314
Doctor of the Americans (1998), Dic Edwards 110
Don't Just Sit There (1979), Charles Way 313
Don't She Look Funny (1980), Charles Way 313
Donmar Warehouse, London 148, 239, 246

Double Indemnity, Edward Thomas 125
Dove Maiden, The (1996), Charles Way 257, 261, 264, 266, 276, 277, 280, 284, 314
Dozy Rosy and the Magic Samurai (1982), Greg Cullen 401
Dragon of Bog Meadow, The (1987), Greg Cullen 401
Drama Centre, Abergavenny 292
Dream of a Sunday Afternoon in the Alameda Park, A, Greg Cullen 325, 336, 387, 388, 389, 393
Drescher, Hans-Jürgen 58
Drill Hall Theatre, London 377, 378
Dukes Playhouse, Lancaster 264, 293, 313
Dying For a Living (1982), Charles Way 313

Early Morning, Edward Bond 61
East End Theatre Group 349, 401
East from the Gantry (1992), Edward Thomas 119, 134, 139–41, 146, 147–8, 149–50, 151, 152, 153, 155, 158, 160, 165, 169, 177–8, 246, 247, 413
  review by Colin Donald 220
  review by Sara Villiers 220
  see also *New Wales Trilogy*
East from the Gantry, radio play (1997), Edward Thomas 247
Ecce Homo [*Casanova Undone*]
  views of Edward Bond 48–9
  see also *Casanova Undone*
Edinburgh Fringe First 356
Edwards, Dic 154, 267
  attitude to Wales and Welshness 3, 405–15
  chronology 110–11
  letters from Edward Bond 17–64
  reviews of his plays 88–109
  themes in his work 65–81
  views of himself as a Welsh dramatist 85–7
  views on Anglo-Welshness 4
  views on eviction 3–4
  views on language 7–13, 83
  views on stupidity 5–6
  views on theatre/television 13–16, 84–5
  views on working class/middle class 82–3
Eirian, Erica 299, 300, 305, 308
Elliot, Jack 89, 96
Elvery, John 304, 305
Elvis y Blew a Fi 192
Emperor of Ice Cream, The (1995), Dic Edwards 77
Enemy of the People, An (Ibsen) 342
Entertaining Mr Sloane 86
Envy (1993), Edward Thomas 147, 149, 151, 152, 159–60, 163, 164, 166, 246
  review by David Adams 230
Eos Chamber Orchestra 98, 100, 102
Epworth, Catrin 92, 93
Equus 86
Erhardt, Tom 52
Europeans, The, Howard Barker 77
Evans, Marc 125–6, 157, 165, 186, 202, 205
Evans, Samantha 382
Evans, Tudor 295
Eveling, Stanley 103
Eye of the Storm (1992), Charles Way 313
  review by Timothy Ramsden 306

Fall of the Roman Empire, The (1987), Charles Way 313
Fallen Sons (1994), Edward Thomas 230, 247
Famine, Tom Murphy 417
Farm Dance (1982), Charles Way 313
Feed the World (1978), Charles Way 313
Fiction Factory 119, 123, 132, 146, 148, 156, 158, 186, 188, 202, 203, 204, 205, 206, 207, 242, 244, 246
Figure of Eight, A (1996), Charles Way 314
Flaming Liberty! (1983), Greg Cullen 401
Flannery, Peter 346
Flood, The (1990), Charles Way 271, 285, 313

review by Francesca Turner 298
review by Sara O'Reilly 297
review in *The Independent* 297
Flood, The, radio play (1994), Charles Way 315
Flowers: opera, John Hardy
review by Mike Smith 229
review by Stephen Walsh 228–9
Flowers of the Dead Red Sea (1991), Edward Thomas 120–1, 125, 134, 137, 147, 148, 149, 151, 153, 155, 157, 158, 166–8, 170, 171, 176–85, 233, 246, 247, 412–13
review by Ben Francis 216–17
review by David Adams 217–18
review by John Linklater 214
review by Neil Wallace 215–16
review by Nicole Sochor 218–19
review by Penny Simpson 216
review by Sara Villiers 219
review by Simon Berry 214–15
Flowers of the Dead Red Sea, opera (1995), Edward Thomas 147
Flowers of the Dead Red Sea, radio play (1992), Edward Thomas 147, 247
see also *New Wales Trilogy*
Flyboys, The (1979), Greg Cullen 349, 350, 401
Folk-Lore of Herefordshire, Ella Mary Leather 307
Fool, The, Edward Bond 331
Footloose Dance Company 332, 362, 385
For the Benefit of... and Breakfast in America (1982), Greg Cullen 401
fourth world, the (1990), Dic Edwards 5, 13, 69, 70, 72, 110, 111
review by Guy Holland 91
review by Jeffery Wainwright 90–1
review in *North Wales Weekly News* 91
review in *The Evening Leader* 89–90
views of Edward Bond 39–42
Frankenstein (1991), Charles Way adapt. 314
Frida and Diego (1989), Greg Cullen 320, 322, 335–8, 347, 352, 353, 355, 356, 358, 359, 360, 401
review by Charles Spencer 390
review by Emma Byrne 391–2
review by Jane Edwardes 391
review by Jim Hiley 392–3
review by John Vidal 386–7
review by Joyce McMillan 387–8
review by Lyn Gardner 391
review by Michael Coveney 388–9
review by Peter Mortimer 393–4
review by Robert Gore-Langton 388
review in *Observer Scotland* 390
review in *Scotland on Sunday* 389
Friel, Brian 418
Fukayama 8
Funny Boys (1984), Charles Way 272, 313, 314
review by David Adams 292–3
Funny Boys, radio play (1985), Charles Way 314

Galvin, Anna 99, 100
Gardiner, Paula 298, 300, 301, 303, 305, 308
Garmon, Owen 210
Garven, Jamie 147, 198, 200, 201, 222, 224, 276, 294, 295, 308, 309, 310
Gas Station Angel (1998), Edward Thomas 123, 155, 246
British Tour Interview by Carolyn Hitt 240–1
review by Benedict Nightingale 242–3
review by David Adams 242
review by Dominic Cavendish 243–4
review by Michael Billington 244–5
review by Sarah Roberts 241–2
Gas Station Angel, film 146
see also *Aces of Gaerlishe*
Gascoigne, Andrea 305
Gaskell, Michelle 322
Gearing, Tessa 374
Germinal (1993), Greg Cullen adapt. 354, 402
Giddens, Anthony 75, 80
Gilmore, Gary 4, 65–7, 104, 105, 106, 107, 108
Glanville, Sue 320, 375, 377

Glass Shot, Duncan Bush 165
Gododdin (Brith Gof) 419
Gomer, Russell
 in *Ash on a Young Man's Sleeve* 305
 in *Envy* 147, 230
 in *Flowers of the Dead Red Sea* 215, 216, 217, 218, 219
 in *Gas Station Angel* 240
 in *House of America* 122, 147, 192, 194, 195, 196, 197, 200, 201
 in *Myth of Michael Roderick, The* 210
 in Royal Shakespeare Company 123, 156, 187
 in *Sleeping Beauty* 309
 in *Song from a Forgotten City* 148, 233, 235, 236, 238, 239
Good Person of Sezuan 36
Good, the Bad and the Ugly, The, Siergo Leone 408
Gorky's Zygotic Mynci 190
Gough, Lucy 154
Gough, Richard 154
Grace of Mary Traverse, The, Wertenbaker 71
Graham, Andy 306
Grand Pavilion, Llandrindod Wells 385
Gregor, Simon 241, 244
Griffin, Helen 204, 205, 207
Griffiths, Anne 290
Grove Theatre, Hammersmith 349, 353, 401
Guidi, Firenza 301
Guildhall, Brecon 369, 384
Gulbenkian Studio, Newcastle 393
Gwent Theatre 264, 265, 272, 278, 288–9, 290, 291, 292, 293, 313
Gwyn, Helen 90, 91, 299, 300, 301, 308

Hadley, Tom 100, 101, 102
Haearn 229
Hall, Peter 34, 58
Hamilton, Phil 231
Hamletmaschine, Heiner Muller 77
Hampton, Christopher 39
Hannaway, Patrick 103
Hansel and Gretel (1981), Greg Cullen 401
Hard Times (1986), Greg Cullen adapt. 354, 355, 402
 review by David Chapman 380
Hardy, John 125, 156, 228, 229, 235, 242, 311
Hariades, Nicholas 97
Harlow Playhouse Theatrevan 306, 349, 350, 351
Harries, Phyl 398, 399
Harries, Simon 123
Harrington, Richard
 in *Gas Station Angel* 241, 243, 245
 in *House of America* 203, 204, 205, 206
Harry Younger Hall, Edinburgh 198, 208, 210, 246
Hart, Janis 385, 395
Hatlades, Nick 98
Haymarket Studio, Leicester 88, 89
Hazlewood, Charles 97, 99, 295
Heal, Mark 100, 101
Hedd Wyn 229
Hemming, Keith 295
Henze, Hans-Werner 54
Hewetson, Nicholas 88
Heyes, Kevin 399
Heywood, Ian 374
High Noon 254
Hijinx Theatre 193, 257, 261, 263, 264, 269, 274, 276, 281, 282, 283, 296, 298, 299, 301, 302, 307, 308, 313, 314
Hill, Ian 156, 218, 230
Hill, Val 192
Hingorani, Dominic 90, 91
Hiraeth/Strangers in Conversation (1993), Edward Thomas 124, 139, 150, 151, 152, 153, 157, 165, 167, 246
 BBC Arts Award 148
 review by David Adams 228
 review by Rowan and Sara 227–8
Hitting Home (1986), Charles Way 266, 313
Holloway, Jonathan 356, 387, 388, 389, 390, 391, 393, 394
Holloway, Nina 304, 305
Homer, Jacqueline 98

Hooper, Dominie 311
House for Mr. Biswas, A, V.S. Naipaul 162
House of America (1988), Edward Thomas 115, 117–18, 119–20, 121–2, 125, 134–7, 149, 151, 152, 153, 155, 157, 158, 159, 160–5, 166, 167, 168, 169, 171, 188, 190, 233, 241, 246, 413–14, 420–2, 424–5
preview 192
review by Andy Lavender 197–8
review by Ann McFerran 197
review by Damien Murray 203–04
review by David Gow 205
review by Gareth J Ledbetter 200–01
review by Grania McFadden 203
review by Herbert Williams 199–200
review by Jane Bardon 204
review by Jayne Thomas 193–4
review by Jeremy Kingston 196–7
review by John Gower 206–07
review by John Linklater 200
review by John Williams 201–03
review by Judy Stenger 193
review by Mark Fisher 223
review by Martin Donovan 199
review by Penny Simpson 195–6
review by William Cook 198
review in *The Gem* 196
review in *The South Wales Echo* 198–9
review in *Western Telegraph* 194–5
Time Out/O1 For London award 147, 199, 209, 212, 237
House of America, film (1997), Edward Thomas 125–6, 146, 147,186, 190, 202, 205, 247
see also *New Wales Trilogy*
Howard, Andrew 105, 305
Hugh, Rhodri 200, 201, 304, 305
Hughes, Dusty 350
Hughes, Jason 123
Hughes-Jones, Liz 154
Human Cannon, Edward Bond 25, 54
Humbug (1980), Charles Way 264, 266, 272, 277
Humpston, Charlotte 388, 389, 391, 393, 394
Hurst, Deborah 89
Hutt, Rosamunde 274, 296, 298, 299, 300

Idiots, The (1996) Dic Edwards 5, 67–8, 69, 70, 71–2, 77, 110
Idiots! (1997), Dic Edwards 110
Ill Met By Moonlight (1994), Charles Way 268, 269, 275, 277, 280, 281, 314
review by David Adams 307
review by Jon Holliday 307–08
Illsley, Daniel 103
Importance of Being Earnest, Oscar Wilde 83
In Camera, Sartre 335
In Living Memory (1983), Charles Way 266, 272, 273, 313, 314
preview 292
review by Brian Jarman 290–1
review by David Adams 291–2
In Living Memory, radio play (1986), Charles Way 314
In the Bleak Midwinter (1990), Charles Way 266, 268, 270, 271, 274, 277, 280, 281, 282, 313, 406, 408
review by David Adams 298
review by M.C.301–02
review by Marian Cox 302
review by Nicole Sochor 300
review by Noel Lacey 300–01
review by Penny Simpson 299
review by Robin Thornber 299–300
Informer's Duty, The (1992), Greg Cullen 322, 338–9, 341, 353, 355, 356, 359, 360, 366, 402
review by A J Sicluna 395–6
Informer's Duty, The, radio play (1994), Greg Cullen 402
Inner City Limits (1980), Charles Way 266, 267, 272
Inside Me (1990), Greg Cullen 402
Invisible Woman, The, Claire Tomalin 307
Ionesco, Eugene 123
Irish drama 174, 176, 187, 417–19

Jackets, Edward Bond 17, 40, 61
Jackson, Terry 294, 295
Jacob, Stephanie 398, 399
James, Dafydd Lyr 312
James, Jack 239, 240
James, Richey 117, 234
Jameson, Martin 385
Jasper, Michael 311
Jellinek, Tristram 93, 94, 95
Jeune, Nicholas 389, 390, 392, 393, 394
Johnson, Joyce 161, 197, 200, 201, 206
Jones, Arbel 377, 378
Jones, Colin, boxer 206
Jones, Eluned 199, 200, 201
Jones, Joseph 310
Jones, Valmai 241, 244
Journey in Hell, A (1986), Charles Way 266, 314
Jumpers 29
Juniper Tree (1993), Dic Edwards 52, 110
  review by Andrew Porter 97
  review by Della Couling 97–8
  review by Meirion Bowen 96–7

Kahlo, Frida 322, 325, 336–7, 356, 366, 386–7
Kenny, Kim 295
Kerouac, Jack 118, 135, 149, 161, 190, 194, 196, 197, 199, 200, 201, 202, 203, 206, 420
Kerry, Ian 372
Kid (1997), Dic Edwards 15, 110
King, Mary 97
King, Trudy, 289
Knight, Mark 218
Knight, Peter 398, 399
Knives and Hens, David Harrower 243

Ladd, Eddie 297, 426
Lailey, James 305
Lancaster Theatre in Education 264
Landes, Brigitte 58
Landlocked (1992), Greg Cullen 402
Landsdowne, Harriet 372
Lane, Robert 308
Langridge, Stephen 97, 98
Language Machine, The, Dic Edwards 46
Late City Echo (1981), Dic Edwards 17, 18, 110
Lazo, Rina 387
Leadbitter, Bill 88
Leeds Theatre in Education 264, 265, 313
Leenane Trilogy, The, Martin McDonagh 243
Les Coup de Theatre, Montreal 314
Les Miserables 58
Leverton, Dek 154
Lewis, Gwyneth 327
Library Theatre Manchester 264, 278, 314
Light Shining in Buckinghamshire, Caryl Churchill 331
Linz-Roberts, Jane 156, 202, 205, 310
Little Devils (1994), Greg Cullen 335, 359, 402
  review in *Mid Wales Journal* 397
Little Yankee (1987), Dic Edwards 110
Llan Community Centre, Rhydyfelin 308
Llanelli Entertainment Centre 371
Llanidloes Community Centre 395
Llanover Hall Arts Centre 299, 300, 307
Lloyd, Gareth 229
Lloyd, Peter 106
Lockhead, Adrian 374
Lola Brecht (1995), Dic Edwards 5, 69, 72, 77, 80, 110
  views of Edward Bond 57
Loncraine, Rebecca 103
Lonergan, Kate 88
Long To Rain Over Us (1987), Dic Edwards 5, 42, 110, 111, 410–11
  review by Jeremy Kingston 88
Looking For The World (1986), Dic Edwards 5, 6, 68, 69, 70, 72, 75–7, 78, 80, 110, 111, 409, 411
  views of Edward Bond 19, 22, 24, 27–9
  see also *Assumption*
Looking Out To See (1994), Charles Way 314
Lorna Doone (1982), Charles Way adapt. 314

Lough, Dorian 105, 107
Lougher, Gaynor 297
Low People (1989), Dic Edwards 5, 11, 42, 69, 72, 110, 111
  review by Pat Ashworth 88–9
  review by Quentin Clark 89
  views of Edward Bond 35–8
Lulu, Wedekind 94, 95, 96
Lyn, Timothy 210
Lynch, Richard 148, 187, 188, 192, 194, 195, 196, 197, 216, 217, 218
  in East from the Gantry 220
  in Flowers of the Dead Red Sea 215
  in Gas Station Angel 243, 245
  in House of America 122, 147
  in Myth of Michael Roderick, The 211
  in Royal Shakespeare Company 123, 156
  in Song from a Forgotten City 233, 236, 238
Lynn, Bill 374
Lysistrata (1992), Greg Cullen 402

M6 Theatre Company 264, 298, 313
McCarthy, Michael 107, 108, 229
McCaw, Alison 374, 384
Macdonald, Robert David 93, 94, 96, 103
McDermott, Phil 100
McGough, Roger 118
McGoun, Susan 294
McGovern, Jimmy 128
McGuigan, Carol 374
Machen, Arthur 268
Mackie, James 369, 371
Mackintosh, Steven 186, 205
McLarnon, Fergus 398, 399
MacLiammoir, Neil 156
Macmillan, Joyce 350
Made in Wales Stage Company 19, 90, 91, 106, 107, 110, 128, 147, 208, 264, 268, 313, 343, 347, 396
Madoc, Philip 123
Magic Toyshop, The, Angela Carter 344
Man Who Gave His Foot For Love, The (1996), Dic Edwards 5, 13, 15, 110
  review by Mark Jenkins 109
Manic Street Preachers 190
Marat/Sade, Peter Weiss 77
Market Theatre, Johannesburg 314
Marquez, Gabriel Garcia 209, 327
Mary Morgan (1987), Greg Cullen 323, 331–2, 333, 355, 357, 366–7, 401
  review by Ian Kerry 380–1
  review by Siân Hawkins 381–2
  review in *Mid Wales Journal* 383
Mary Morgan, radio play (1991/92), Greg Cullen 402
Masquerade Theatre 352, 401
Mattison, Steve 322
Maycock, Hazel 311
Mayfest '92 425
Measure For Measure, Shakespeare 6–7
Mellor, David 149
Mercury Theatre 264
Meredith, Gary 289
Merlin (1989), Charles Way 315
Merton, Paul 228
Mestizo, Alan Osborne 379
Mid Powys Youth Theatre 322, 335, 348, 352, 354, 355, 356, 357, 362, 380, 382, 383, 397, 401, 402
  awards 327–8
Miles, Gareth 154
Miller, Kenny 93, 95
Miller, Les 307, 308
Miners' Welfare Hall, Ystradgynlais 221
Miraculous Engineering 241
Mitchell, Brian 133
Modernity at Large, Arjun Appadurai 74, 80
Mold Alun High School 299
Monk, Roger 104
Monkey and the Crocodile, The (1980), Charles Way 313
Moon River (1992), Dic Edwards 15, 110, 111
Moore, Geoff 146, 154
Moore, Robyn 104
Morgan, Geraint 305
Morgan, Goff 228
Morgan, Jonathon 370, 371
Morgan, Sharon 147, 192, 193, 194, 195, 196, 197, 210
Morgan, Siân 123

Morris, Richard 98
Morris, Siwan 243, 245
Morrison, Jim 117
Mourby, Adrian 363, 376, 378, 379
Moving Being 128, 146, 154, 187, 211, 226, 242
Mumford, Peter 242
Murray, David 301
Music Theatre Wales 125, 228, 229
Mwg Glas, Lleuad Waed [Blue Smoke, Blood Moon], Peter Edwards 208
Mystery Cycle, A (1989), Charles Way 314
Myth of Michael Roderick, The (1991), Edward Thomas 147, 149, 150, 151, 153, 157, 246
review by Ben Francis 217
review by Charmian C. Savill 211–13
review by David Adams 217–18
review by Penny Simpson 213–14, 222
review by Robin Williams 210–11

Nantybwch Senior Citizens Hall, Tredegar 289
Nathanson, Gill 305, 306
National Theatre 25, 57
National Theatre of Mannheim 313
Nativity, The (1996), Charles Way 271, 275, 276, 314
Neal, Tam 373
New Perspectives 264, 313, 314
New Wales Trilogy 134, 146, 148, 200, 220, 246
review by Joyce McMillan 225–6
review by Mark Fisher 222–3
review by Nicole Sochor 226–7
review by Penny Simpson 221–2, 224–5
review in *The Evening Times* 224
New World in the Mourning, A, radio play (1988), Greg Cullen 323, 333, 334–5, 352, 356, 363–4, 365, 402
Newcastle Playhouse Youth Persons Theatre 313
Newtown Youth and Community Centre 371
Nietzsche 12, 47
No Borders (1997), Charles Way 268–9, 279, 314
review by Nigel Jenkins 311–12
Noble, Adrian 54, 56
Noble, Roy 312
Nordon, Tom 260, 305
Nothing to Pay, Caradoc Evans 106
Numbers Plus (1993), Charles Way 314
Nunn, Trevor 57, 58

O'Brien, Bernadette 369, 370, 372
O'Reilly, Steve 204, 206
O'Shea, David 89
Octagon Theatre, Perth 206
Oedipus at Colonus 31
Oh Journeyman (1987), Charles Way 313
Old Bull Arts Centre 401
Old Country, The, radio play (1986), Charles Way 266, 314
Old Devils, Kingsley Amis 238
Olly's Prison, Edward Bond 42, 47, 49, 52, 55
On the Black Hill (1985/86), Charles Way adapt. 266, 268, 314, 343
review by David Adams 295
review by Robin Thornber 294–5
On the Black Hill, radio play (1988), Charles Way 314
On the Road, Jack Kerouac 134, 136, 161, 193, 195
Once Upon a Time in the West 426
Once Upon a Time in the West, Sergio Leone 257
One Giant Leap (1995), Charles Way 314
Orchard Theatre 264, 270, 313, 314
Order! (1982), Greg Cullen 401
Oriel Gallery, Cardiff 125, 148, 227, 246
Osborne, Alan 396
Osborne, Louis 354, 372, 373
Oscar, Gwyn Thomas 164–5
Our Friends in the North, Peter Flannery 333
Outlaw Josey Wales, The 252

Owen, Sion Tudor 294
Oxborrow, William 398, 399

Palace Theatre, Westcliff 306
Palfrey, Lisa 186, 199, 200, 205
Palitzsch, Peter 55
Paradise Drive (1989), Charles Way 263, 266, 313, 407, 409
  review by David Adams 295–6
  review by Erlend Cloustron 296–7
Parker, Mike 156
Past Caring (1984), Greg Cullen 351, 354, 355, 401
Patagonia, Brith Gof 426
Paul, Kate 393
Pauper's Carnival 154
Pax 229
Pearson, Mike 154
Peck, Bob 312
Peebles, Charles 98
Pen-y-graig, Rhondda 221
Penrhyn Summer, The, Alison Leonard 376
Perspectives Theatre 264, 314
Philadelphia, Here I Come!, Brian Friel 418–19
Philippou, Nick 37, 42, 47
Phillips, Sian 146, 186, 202, 205
Piece of East, A (1982), Greg Cullen 401
Pillars of the Community, Ibsen 342
Pinter, Harold 35, 40
Pioneers, The (1823), James Fenimore Cooper 251
Playboy of the Western World, The, J. M. Synge 424
Playing from the Heart, Charles Way 266, 314
Plimmer, David 305
Plough, The, Torrington 305
Point, The, Cardiff 79, 104, 105–06, 107
Polka Theatre 264, 314
Pope, Jon 94
Pope's Wedding, The, Edward Bond 22–3
Potter, Dennis 268, 323
Potter, Gareth 304, 305
Powys Young Farmers' Clubs 354
Price, Andy 312
Price, Wyndham 195, 197, 201, 219
Pritchard, Nicholas 90, 91
Public Parts 307
Pulley, Sarah 377

Queen's Theatre, Hornchurch 401
Quezada, Petricio 393
Quick and the Dead, The, Sharon Stone 254
Quinn, Linda 105, 107

Rabey, David Ian 133, 141, 213
Rach, Rudolph 57
Rafferty, Michael 229
Raging Angels (1991/92), Greg Cullen 320, 323, 335, 359, 402
  review by David Adams 396
  review in *The County Times* 396
Rancid Aliminium, James Hawes 146
Red Chair 297
Red Shift Theatre Company 331, 335, 356, 383, 387, 388, 389, 390, 391, 393, 394, 401
Rees, Ronald 104
Rees, Shelley 204, 206
Reeves, Bettina 308
Regan (1991), Dic Edwards 5, 6, 14–15, 48, 55, 70, 72, 77–8, 79, 80, 110, 111
  review by David Adams 92
  review by Marie Lewis 92–3
  views of Edward Bond 43–5
Rent a Role Theatre 264, 313
Restoration, Edward Bond 31, 32, 332
Reynolds, Nicola 398, 399
Rhodri and the Bard (1993), Greg Cullen 402
Rhodri Mawr and Welcome to the Feast (1993), Greg Cullen 402
Rhys, Matthew 186, 188
Richards, Ri 220
Riders of the Purple Sage (1912), Zane Grey 251
Ring and the Piglet, The (1997), Greg Cullen 402
Ritchie, Rob 18–19

Rivera, Diego 322, 324, 325, 336, 337, 356, 386–7, 392
Rivers, Andrew 290, 294, 295, 304, 305
Riverside Studios, London 383
Robin Hood (1987/88), Greg Cullen 354–5, 394, 401
review by Cynric Mytton-Davies 383–4
review by David Adams 384
Roderick, Guy 92, 381, 382
Rogers, Claire 382
Roses Theatre, Tewksbury 380
Rota, Nino 95
Rowlands, Ian 154
Royal Court Theatre 22, 23, 25, 123, 125, 126, 128, 146, 148, 186, 187, 191, 232, 235, 236, 238, 246
Royal Court Theatre Upstairs 242, 243, 244
Royal Lyceum, Edinburgh 239, 246
Royal Shakespeare Company 25, 30, 31, 32, 50, 54, 56, 57, 58
Rudkin, David 52, 65
Rumney, Peter 299, 300
Russell, Maggie 105, 106

S4C 127, 154
St Peter's Civic Hall, Carmarthen 192, 193
St Stephen's Theatre Space 147, 192, 210, 221, 246
Sapani, Danny 99, 100, 101, 102
Satellite City, Boyd and Jane Clack 146, 186
Saturn Tramp at the Bay's End, The, [*At The End Of The Bay*] Dic Edwards 18
see also *At The End Of The Bay*
Saunders, Alison 322
Saunders, Julie 94, 95
Saved, Edward Bond 22–3, 54, 56, 61, 355
Savva, Anna 388, 389, 390, 391, 392, 393, 394
Scam, The, Peter Lloyd 198, 208
Schofield, Alistair 306
Scott, Simon 290
Scott-Barrett, Jane 385
Sea, The, Edward Bond 49, 54
Sea Change, A (1988), Charles Way 314
Search for Odysseus, The (1993), Charles Way 267, 276, 285, 313
Second Shepherds Play, The 272, 274, 275
Seven Deadly Sins, The, Edward Thomas 147
Seymour, Lynne 310, 382, 396
Shakespeare Factory, The (1993), Dic Edwards 15, 110, 111
Shane, Jack Schaefer 251–3, 270, 408, 422, 426
Sharp, Janine 381
Shaw, Bernard 14, 15
She Scored for Wales (1981), Charles Way 266, 268, 272, 281, 313
review by David Adams 288
Sheen, Michael 123
Shepard, Sam 116, 237, 239
Sherlock Gnome and the Egg Snatchers (1985), Greg Cullen 352, 401
Sherman Arena 295, 298, 299
Sherman Theatre 110, 186, 201, 207, 241, 242, 269, 303, 304, 305, 308, 309, 310, 311, 314, 396, 402
Sherman Youth Theatre 264
Ship, The, Bill Bryden 417
Shostakovish, Dmitri 338, 339, 356, 357, 366, 395
Silas Marner (1996), Greg Cullen adapt. 354, 402
review by Bob Roberts 399
review by Gail Cooper 398
review by Philip Key 399
review by Vic Hallett 400
Silent Village, A Humphrey Jennings 149, 155
Silent Village, A/Pentre Mud (1993), Edward Thomas 247
Sleeping Beauty, Charles Way adapt. 267, 278, 285, 314
review by David Adams 310
review by Judith Davies 308–09
review by Richard Mackey 309
Smith, Vicci Jade 311
Snap Theatre 264, 306, 313
Snell, James 104

Snow Queen, The (1983), Greg Cullen 351, 354, 401
preview 369
review by Cynric Mytton-Davies 370–1
review by David Adams 371
review in *The Express* 369–70
Snow Spider, The 192
Soldier Blue 254
Soldier, Soldier 196
Somebody Loves You (1995/96), Charles Way 314
Song from a Forgotten City (1995), Edward Thomas 124, 125, 146, 148, 149, 150, 151, 152, 153, 155, 156, 158, 163, 164, 167, 168–9, 170–2, 242, 244, 246
review by Benedict Nightingale 239
review by Clare Bayley 233–5
review by Colin Dallibar 231–2
review by Jane Edwardes 236–8
review by Joyce McMillan 239–40
review by Lloyd Trott 235–6
review by Nerys Lloyd-Pierce 230–1, 235
review by Paul Taylor 238
review by Pauline McLean 233
Song of Streets, A (1985/86), Charles Way 267, 314
Songs of Experience, Blake 345
Southern, Clare 371, 373
Spark Theatre 328, 378, 401
Spectacle Theatre Company 15, 72, 110, 264, 272, 278, 313, 401
Spell of Cold Weather, A (1995), Charles Way 267, 269, 285, 314
review by Jon Holliday 311
review by Lauren O'Beirne 311
review by Sara O'Reilly 310
Spiv (1981), Greg Cullen 349, 401
Splott East Moors Community Centre 306
Spoiled Papers (1986), Greg Cullen 333–4, 339, 341, 352, 355, 360, 385
review by Duncan Bush 378–9
Spoiled Papers, radio play, Greg Cullen 376, 402
Stadsteatr, Stockholm 401
Stages Theatre, Houston 401
Stalin 338, 339, 356, 357, 366, 386, 395, 396
Standing Conference of Young People's Theatre 55, 351, 353, 356, 357
Stanley, Siobhan 93, 95
Starlight Express 58
Staunton, Caroline 369, 370
Stephenson, Denise 89
Sterrey, Andrew 382
Stevens, Grant 372, 373
Stewart, Reg 92
Stone Throwers, The (1989), Charles Way 313
Stones in his Pockets, Marie Jones 425
Stoppard, Tom 52
Stuart, Ian 42, 56
Stuffed Shirts and Marionettes 307
Summer: A European Play, Edward Bond 22, 47, 54
Sundance Playwrights Forum, Utah 314
Sunday Afternoon in The Alameda, Rivera 387
see also A Dream of a Sunday Afternoon in the Alameda Park
Super Furry Animals 190
Surrey, Meg 305
Sutherland, Donald 95
Swallows and Amazons (1990), Charles Way 315
Swansea Arts Workshop Gallery 228, 246
Swashbucklers! (1985/96), Greg Cullen 354, 401
review by David Adams 373–4
review by Lawrence Garner 374–5
review by Sue Glanville 375
Sweeney Todd (1993), Charles Way adapt. 266, 314

Taken Out (1985), Greg Cullen 320, 328, 329–31, 333, 339–40, 341, 342, 347, 351–2, 353, 354, 355, 356, 360, 363, 365, 366, 385, 387, 394, 401, 402
review by Jonathan Neale 377–8
review by Nicholas de Jongh 377
review by Paul Arnott 378

Taken Out, radio play (1985), Greg Cullen 402
review by David Ian Rabey 376
Tarzanne (1988), Greg Cullen 320, 332–3, 355, 362–3, 401
review by CB 385–6
review by David Adams 384–5
Taylor, Roberta 93, 95
Telling the Sea (1997), Charles Way 315
Theatr Brycheiniog 402
Theatr Clwyd 86, 87, 89, 90, 91, 110, 235, 264, 268, 294, 296, 314, 398, 399, 400, 401
Theatr Hafren 370, 373
Theatr Iolo 264, 313
Theatr Mwldan 211
Theatr Powys 77, 92, 93, 110, 264, 278, 328, 332, 348, 351, 352, 353, 354, 355, 356, 359, 360, 369, 370, 372, 373, 374, 375, 380, 383, 384, 385, 386
Theatr y Byd 154
Theatre Centre 264, 265, 269, 313
Theatre for Young Spectators, Novgorod 314
theatre in education 56, 57, 72, 264, 272–3, 354, 360
Theatre of the Young Generation, Dresden 313
Theatre Royal Stratford East 264
Thinkabout Science, Charles Way 314
Thomas, Dafydd Elis 351
Thomas, Dorien 148, 232, 236, 238
Thomas, Dylan 117
Thomas, Edward , 267
actor in Pobl y Cwm 125, 152, 192, 196
American Dream in his plays 115–18, 121–2
chronology 246–7
intertextuality 160–1
language in his work 153
mythology in his plays 119
naturalism in his plays126–7
on Wales Tour '94 221
popular culture in his plays151–3, 165–7
reviews of his plays 192–245
role of memory in his work 139–41
role of the female in his work 159, 162–3, 170, 171–2
role-playing in his work 134–7
views on Pobol y Cwm 127
views on television 128
theatre of invention 131–3, 141–2
visibility in his plays 137–9
Wales and Welshness 117, 126–7, 157–8, 164, 168–70, 186–91, 405–15, 422
Thomas, Eleanor 295
Thomas, Geraint 192–3
Thomas, Jams 204, 207
Thomas, Neil 382
Thomas, Philip 295, 296
Thornton, Neil 311
Three of Swords, Mike Dorrell 376
Three Plays, Dic Edwards 72
Threepenny Opera, The 99
Timoney, Anne Marie 103
Tomson, Bob 292, 370, 371
Toovey, Andrew 96, 97
Torch Theatre, Milford Haven 86, 110
Towards the Light, Alan Plater 339
Tower, The, radio play (1994/95), Greg Cullen 321, 324, 339–41, 352, 402
Trade Winds (1997), Charles Way 266, 315
Trainspotting, Irvine Welsh 202, 204, 239, 240
Tramway, The, Glasgow 120, 121, 148, 156, 200, 214, 215, 219, 220, 222, 224, 225, 246
Translations, Brian Friel 176, 177, 419
Tregear, Lucy 99, 101
Tregenna, Catherine 192, 194, 195, 196, 197, 211
Truby, Simeon 396
Tudor, Carys 398, 399
Tuesday, Edward Bond 50–1, 54
Turner, Jeremy 154
Twin Town 190
Tyne and Wear Theatre 264

Under Goliath (1991), Greg Cullen 402
Unicorn Theatre, London 264, 297, 313

Unity Too 154
Unsworth, Tony 7
Utah Blue (1995), Dic Edwards 4, 65–7, 68, 69, 72, 73, 79–80, 110, 111, 236, 421
  review by Graham Allen 107–08
  review by Hamish Nisbet 106–07
  review by Jeremy Johnson 104–05
  review by John Holliday 107
  review by Sarah Hemming 105–06
  views of Edward Bond 54

Velvet Underground 165, 166, 190, 196, 197
Verlag, Suhrkamp 57, 58
Vertigo (1997), Dic Edwards 15, 110
Vests 61
Volcano Theatre 75, 128, 154, 187, 188

Waiting at the Water's Edge, Lucinda Coxon 106
Wallace, Neil 156
Waller, Shaun 369, 370, 383
Walls, The (1994), Greg Cullen with Kelly Evans 402
Walters, Melanie 309
War Plays, Edward Bond 17, 25, 37, 38, 43, 47, 52, 54
Watermans Arts Centre, London 216, 246
Watershed Productions 313
Way, Charles 154, 364
  as theatre writer 278–9
  children's plays 267
  chronology 313–15
  reviews of his plays 288–312
  structure in his plays 280–1
  themes in his plays 263–77, 280
  views on a National Theatre for Wales 287
Wales and Welshness 405–15
writing for television 279
Way, Liz 265
Wells, Meri 92, 322
Welsh College of Music and Drama 338, 356, 395, 396, 402
Welsh National Opera 264
Welsh Playright's Group 87
What a Wonderful World, Boyd and Jane Clack 146
When You Were Sixteen (1979), Charles Way 313
Where we go when we drive a blue-tinted glass Marina 1800TC into the heart of a Saturday Night? [*Gas Station Angel*], Edward Thomas 123, 241
  see also *Gas Station Angel*
Whispers in the Woods (1996), Greg Cullen 320, 324, 343–4, 345, 352, 367–8, 402
Whistleblower, The, radio play (1996), Greg Cullen 321, 339, 341–3, 352, 402
White Bear Theatre, London 96, 104, 110
White-Jacket, Melville 47
Wilde Theatre, Reading 264, 314, 402
Williams, Clare 218
Williams, Raymond 268
Willie Rough 240
Willis, Johnson 398, 399, 400
Windhill Community Centre, Bridgend 295
Withernsea High School Drama Studio 301
Witness (1985), Charles Way 266, 313
review by Robin Thornber 293–4
Wittgenstein's Daughter (1993), Dic Edwards 5, 7–10, 11, 46, 48, 65, 67, 68–9, 70–1, 72, 78–9, 80, 82, 110, 111
  review by Joseph Farrell 102–03
  review by Louise Stafford Charles 104
  review by Mark Fisher 103–04
  views of Edward Bond 26, 29–30
  see also *Alma*
Woman, The, Edward Bond 47, 54
Women Beware Women, Howard Barker 213
Wondering Town, The (1996/97), Greg Cullen 402
Woolf, Ella 387
Wooster, Roger 372, 374
Wordplay '88 383

Wozzeck 46
Write On! festival 147, 396
Wyeside Arts Centre, Builth Wells 327, 372, 381, 384, 394, 397

York Theatre Royal Young People's Theatre 313
Young People's Theatre 285
Ystradgynlais Youth Theatre 402

ZAP Theatre Company 264, 313
Zen and the Art of Motorcycle Maintenance, Robert Pirsig 152, 156–7